The Tiddler Invasion

Other Books by Floyd M. Orr

Paradigm Shift: The Palin Matrix: *The Progressive Left Strikes Back!* (2011)

Ker-Splash 2: *The High Performance Powerboat Book* (2010)

Timeline of America: *Sound Bytes from the Consumer Culture* (2006)

The Last Horizon: *Feminine Sexuality & The Class System* (2002)

Ker-SPLASH! *Recreational Power Boaters Guide* (First Edition, 2002)

Plastic Ozone Daydream: *The Corvette Chronicles* (2000)

Also by Floyd M. Orr

"Stangworld" & "Magical Days", featured only in
Mustang Legends: *The Power, the Performance, the Passion*
(Voyageur Press, 2004)

"Vetteworld", reprinted from *Daydream* in
This Old Corvette: *The Ultimate Tribute to America's Sports Car*
(Voyageur Press, 2003)

The Tiddler Invasion

Small Motorcycles of the Sixties

Floyd M. Orr

NIAFS Press

Nonfiction in a Fictional Style
Horseshoe Bay, Texas

The Tiddler Invasion

Small Motorcycles of the Sixties

All Rights Reserved © 2013 by Floyd M. Orr

First Print Edition: 2013, NIAFS Press
Kindle & Smashwords First Editions, 2013, NIAFS Press

This book is a work of nonfiction. Any and all facts and figures presented herein are accurate to the best of our knowledge. The publisher and author disclaim responsibility for any misprints, math errors, or other inaccuracies presented. Any and all celebrity and trademark names are mentioned for identification purposes only. This is not an official publication sponsored or endorsed by any motorcycle manufacturer, either currently in operation or marketing motorcycles, scooters, or mopeds in the past, or any corporate entity mentioned in any capacity herein. The opinions stated throughout this book are solely those of the author.

The material in this publication is presented solely for historical research, nostalgic entertainment, and educational purposes only. Any trademarks appearing herein are the sole property of the registered owners. No endorsement by the trademark owners is to be construed, nor was any sought. The products, brand names, model names, advertising slogans and related materials are or may be claimed as trademarks of their respective owners. The use of such material falls under the Fair Use provisions of intellectual property laws.

Front cover photo: *1965 Honda CL-72 Scrambler* © Knut Hugo Hansen, owner and photographer, and President of the Classic Honda Club Norway.
Back cover photo, top: *1965 Bultaco Metralla 200* ©Michael Kiernan, Classic Motorcycle Company, St. Louis, MO.
Back cover photo, bottom: *1964 Yamaha YG-1T* ©Yamaha Motor Corporation.

ISBN 13: 978-0615841670
ISBN 10: 0615841678

Dedication

The Tiddler Invasion is dedicated to Miss Pamela, our herd of kitties, and the many progressive Americans who have steadfastly kept the faith throughout the Bullet Bike, Touring Queen Mary and Monster Hog onslaught of the past forty years. For at least a few of us, the relentless proliferation of these heavy, expensive machines has never extinguished our desire for a Honda CL-160, a Yamaha YG-1, a Bultaco Metralla, or a Ducati Diana.

Table of Contents Overview

Figure A4 - From most points of view, this is the machine that started it all, the 1958 Honda 50 Super Cub. Honda began exporting the model to the USA in 1959 and the motorcycle world has never been the same. This is a blue machine, the least common of the four colors offered. Image by Mj-bird under Creative Commons license.

Complete Table of Contents

xvi

Acknowledgements

The Tiddler Invasion is not only my biggest project to date, I have no intention of ever repeating the process on this grand a scale for any future book. I wanted to begin writing this book decades ago, but the massive project simply had to await its turn. The first thing that had to happen was for computers, the Internet, and publishing technologies to mature sufficiently to allow the project to be developed as I envisioned. The collection I have in print of motorcycle brochures and magazines began in 1962. The process of converting this material into a computerized format began with Windows 98. The limiting factors involved the necessary processing and handling of significant numbers of large photo files. The files I have been working with are comprised of several thousand photos sourced from more places than you can imagine and totaling more than 5 GB of file space.

The first people I want to thank for all their assistance with this project contributed words and information. Troyce Walls is the best expert on Allstate Motorcycles I have ever known. His treatise in its entirety on the subject of Allstate history is included in Chapter Two. His story also describes his personal experiences with the brand, especially the early Twingles. James Rozee is a collector of small Japanese machines. He has owned more rare and unusual Yamaguchis, Tohatsus, Hodakas, and Suzukis, among many brands of which I am personally more familiar, than I have even seen! His extended comments concerning certain subject machines will be invaluable to restorers of these brands and models. His nostalgic tales from the good old days will entertain you as well. Warren Paul Warner brought me a dose of material I was not expecting, many details on the production road racers sold by Yamaha in The Sixties. Bill Silver and Ed Moore added insight into the detailed production of the 1962-68 Honda Scramblers. I want to sincerely thank each of these for their contributions to my little project.

The second group contributed photos to the book and this is a much longer list. The complete details of these contributions are listed with the photos and in the Photo Credits in the Appendix. A brief copyright notation is listed within each photo caption, too. Let's begin with Lars Erikkson of the Classic Honda Club Norway. Without his help, I could not have featured the beautiful Honda Scrambler on the cover or some of the other rare Hondas featured in the book. Lars worked tirelessly to confirm ownership and attribute copyrights to some of the nicest early Hondas pictured. Warren Paul Warner took particular effort to take shots of his exquisite Yamaha road racers just for this book, as well as contributing other photos and information. Don Quayle of Costa Mesa, CA provided many beautiful shots from his eclectic collection. Many photos of machines from several countries of origin appear courtesy of Michael Kiernan of Michael's Classic Motorcycles in St. Louis MO. All of his pictured machines either are or were for sale from his business. Most are restorations of very desirable machines from the period. Chuck Schultz contributed many delightful photos of machines in the Barber Museum in Birmingham, AL through the Wikipedia Creative Commons files. Numerous others from the USA, Germany, the UK, Japan, and Australia contributed photos, both directly and through the Creative Commons licensing programs.

One of the earliest concepts I had for this book was to reprint photos and excerpts from period brochures and advertising. I have an extensive collection of materials from which to choose, but I had hoped that possibly the manufacturers still in business could supply me with more perfect materials. I soon found that this was not the case. Nothing was currently available from any of the major Japanese manufacturers. I would have to scan and repair the materials I had on hand if I wanted any such photos from the period included. For the record, I have European and American brochures, too, but from inception my goal was to feature the Japanese brands in this book. The Japanese have been the underdogs of classic motorcycles, particularly small ones, for fifty years and *The Tiddler Invasion* is their turn in the spotlight.

Farris Weinberg and Lisa McManus at Yamaha worked as liaisons between me and the legal department at the company to secure the rights to publish the Yamaha advertising and brochures included in the book. I know I must have exasperated them countless times, but they came through in the end like a pair of champs! I want to thank Sean Alexander at Freeman/McCue Public Relations for arranging permission for me to reprint the Kawasaki advertising and brochures used. Steve Turner and Tom Kingsbury at Bridgestone made the connections for me to obtain permission to reprint all the Bridgestone advertising materials in the book. Derek Schoeberle, Product Media Relations Manager, came through in a similar fashion for Suzuki. The official Media Pages of the manufacturers currently producing motorcycles have also been helpful, particularly with regard to the more modern machines covered in the last chapter. Unfortunately I must mention that Honda, Hodaka, and Tohatsu failed to adequately cooperate in the development of the project. Of course there are many additional brands that ceased producing motorcycles decades ago.

I want to thank many who went out of their way to contribute personal photos to the book. These include: Neil Geldof of Connecticut, Knut Hugo Hansen of Norway, Charles Hallam of Texas, Peter Abelmann of Germany, Paul Davies of England, Chris A. Harris of Australia, Peter Horton of the UK, Ken Ashbrook, David Struble, Dan Spanncraft, David Cassady, Dick Feightner, Jimmy Singer, Matt Hamilton, Douglas G. Sheldon, Steven Christmas, Terje Saethre, and John with his black Honda Dream.

Figure A5 (next page)- This is the brochure of the 1963 Yamaha step-through model similar to the Honda 50. ©1963 Yamaha Motor Corporation, U.S.A.

NEW YAMAHA 50

Model MF2
with ELECTRIC-STARTER
Model MF2-C
with KICK-STARTER

Upon request, we can supply 55cc Moped Model MJ2 with electric-starter and MJ2-C with kick-starter, the performance of which is same as Model MF2 and Model MF2-C, except the engine capacity and the maximum speed.

Introduction: *The Difference Between a Honda and a Harley-Davidson*

(Note: This story is reprinted from the author's political/economic book, *Paradigm Shift*.)

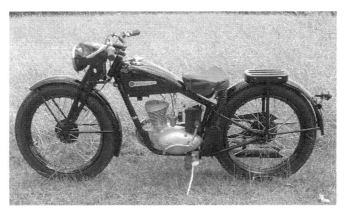

Figure A6 - 1948 Harley-Davidson Model 125-S. This is the first year of the small, American-made, two-stroke singles. Note the girder front fork, hardtail rear, and leather seat indigenous to the early models.
©Charles "Mutt" Hallam, Texas.

After World War II many American companies received the right to use the patents held by the defeated German corporations. One of these was the 125cc two-stroke motorcycle design created by DKW of Germany. BSA of England released their copycat version of the DKW 125 as the BSA Bantam, and in 1948, Harley-Davidson introduced their 125cc S-model. This was a very basic machine that was very cost-effective to produce. It had a three-horsepower, single-cylinder, piston-port, two-stroke engine powering a simple triangular frame on a 50-inch wheelbase. The S-model had no rear suspension and a very primitive, rubber-band-type front suspension. The wheels were 19" and the seat was of a spring-supported, bicycle type for one person. There was a battery for ignition and lights and a three-speed foot shift transmission. The 170-pound machine had a top speed of about 55 mph. The S-model was built by Harley-Davidson from 1948 until 1953 when the engine was enlarged to 165cc, which continued through the 1959 model year. From 1955-59 the 165cc was accompanied by the budget-model 125cc Hummer. These models had very little development or variation throughout all the model years between 1948 and 1959. They remained simple, straightforward machines with their technology firmly rooted back in World War II. There was very little competition in the small motorcycle market to force Harley-Davidson to significantly improve the bikes, so the company spent as little money on development as they could. They updated the colors annually, the horsepower was gradually increased, and a telescopic front suspension was introduced in 1951. Only a minimal amount of chrome plating was used and many models even had painted handlebars and wheel rims. The most interesting thing you can say about these little Harleys is that, like the $20,000 H-D behemoths of today, they had lots of style and charisma.

That was all about to change. Honda Motor Company brought its first motorcycles to the U.S. in late 1959. As soon as they did, it was all over but the crying, but nobody seemed to notice it yet. That is, no one except the Honda dealers with their businesses growing in leaps and bounds within months of the introduction of the first Honda motorcycles in America. Of course every kid whose parents bought him a Honda 50 Cub for half the price of a Harley-Davidson 165 or a Honda Benly Touring for about the same price as a Harley 165 knew instantly what was up. You know something is up, but you don't know what it is, do you, Mr. Davidson? Most new motorcycle buyers in 1960 met the nicest people on a Honda C-102 Cub 50. It had a three-speed foot shift like the H-D, but without a clutch to deal with when starting off. It had an electric starter. The C-102 had a kickstarter, too, but that electric starter was the big news of the day. It had a four-stroke, OHV engine, so you did not have to mix the gas with oil before pumping it into the tiny tank underneath the seat. The tank was only .8 gallon because the little tiddler got ridiculously high gas mileage. For only $300 you could hit that little starter button and putt-putt your way out the dealer's door to a 45-mph top speed. The quiet putt-putt-putt sound from the Honda 50's muffler was a lot more pleasant than the raspy, uneven pulse of the Harley-Davidson two-stroke. Not only did this put a smile on your face, but it brought one to the face of Aunt Matilda, too. You know the one. That old biddy who never liked motorcycles, never liked 'em at all. She knew a nice boy when she saw one, and he never rode a Harley-Davidson!

Figure A7 - This is one of those rare all-chrome Honda models you may have encountered or heard about back in the Sixties. This is a C-100 of unknown model year. On this example, the plastic parts, including the leg shields, side covers, rear shock covers, and headlamp trim, are red and the rest of the machine is chrome. Note the special chrome metal front fender and unusual black seat cover. ©Troyce Walls.

Harley updated the 125cc and 165cc models into one single 165cc model named the Super 10 in 1960. Optioned up to about $500-600 with chromed Buckhorn handlebars, dual Buddy Seat, crash bars, and leather saddlebags, the Super 10 was a real looker. Its large-diameter handgrips and 18-inch wheels made a teenager feel like he was riding a real motorcycle, and don't forget those added elements of style and charisma. Less than 2500 Super 10's were sold by Harley-Davidson in 1960. Surely there were two reasons for this sales limitation. The lesser reason was the Honda C110 Super Sports 50 and the greater reason was the Honda Benly Touring 150. Honda imported their more exotic 125's into the U.S. in very small numbers in 1960, but these rare, collectible models were designed for the racy, enthusiast crowd. The model Honda would shove out the doors of dealerships in unprecedented numbers would be the more mundane 150 Benly Touring. This was before Yamaha expanded the tiddler market with its 80cc YG-1 in 1963 and Honda cross-examined with its Super 90 in '64. In 1960 Honda sold their 50cc models for $270-$320 out the door and the 150 for $500-$550. You can see where this story is going already, but a detailed description of the Honda 50 line is significant here, too.

The Honda 50 was introduced into the U.S. as three models. A fourth, the C105T 55cc Trail model, introduced in 1962, would of course start a revolution of its own, but that's a later story. The basic Honda 50 was the C-100 with its step-through frame, white plastic leg shields, automatic clutch, and kick starter that sold for about $270. The C-102 was exactly the same as the C-100, but with the addition of an electric starter and a $30 price increase. The C110 Super Sports had the same 17-inch wheels, suspension, and OHV engine as its girly little sisters, but otherwise it was all boy. The gas tank was much larger and up front where it belonged. The handlebars were chrome and the transmission was a three-speed with a manual clutch, upped to four speeds in 1963. The engine had a higher-compression head, which added about half a horsepower. With the added power, the clutch, and the additional gear, the Super Sports was somewhat faster than the Cub 50. Its traditional motorcycle styling in a pint-sized package made it a lot more appealing to the budding motorcycle punk of the teenage persuasion. Since my cat could kick start any of the Honda 50's, no self-respecting teenage boy gave a rat's ass that the Super Sports had no electric starter. In fact, he probably considered that a plus. Both the C-102 and the C110 cost almost exactly $300 out the door. All the Honda 50 models had twin hydraulic shocks on the rear and leading-link front suspension, so they had a technological leg up on the Super 10 right off the bat. When you add a four-speed transmission and a standard dual seat for half the price, you begin to see the relevance of the Super Sports Cub to the slow sales of the H-D Super 10. It should also be obvious what Aunt Matilda thought of all this. She told her sister, the future motorcycle punk's mom, exactly how she should buy the kid a Honda 50 instead of that nasty old Harley-Davidson. You know what the kid did next. He said to his mom that if all he could have was that sissy Honda Cub, could he please have the Super Sports instead? It cost the same anyway, so you can imagine how many moms gave in to Junior's last request.

If Junior was light enough, the Super Sports Cub could hit 50 mph. The same lightweight might coax 60 mph out of a Super 10, but at twice the price. The only thing other than 10 mph the kid had to give up for his $200 change was the styling charisma of the Super 10. In exchange he got a machine that sounded better, did not need oil mixed with its fuel, sailed by the gas station, had a genuine four-speed, and was as reliable as a barn door. Did I mention that you could not kill a Honda 50 unless you threw it at a truck? For example, I personally bought a 1966 CA-100 Cub in 1967 from a dealership for the horrible price of $120. I rode that tiddler like a trail bike, crawling and duck-walking up steep, muddy hills while carrying a passenger. We did this a zillion times over the three years that I owned it. The Honda 50 used a small-diameter spark plug. I did not own a spark plug wrench of that size when I had the Honda 50, so I simply never even removed the spark plug to look at it. All I did was pump gas into that tiny little tank, get one of my trail-riding buddies, saddle up and head for the hills. When I traded it in for a new Kawasaki 90 Bushmaster that would climb those hills without the duck-walking operation, the dealer gave me $125 for it. Need I say more about the reliability of a Honda 50? Why did I buy a step-through in the first place, instead of a Super Sports? There was no Aunt Matilda in my story, but by the time I bought the Honda 50 I had already hit a bunch of stuff with my '63 Yamaha 80, which my parents had taken away from me years earlier. It had taken all the pleading I could muster, as well as a promise to ride the new machine only off-road, for my parents to give in to the CA-100. The look of the Super Sports would have brought back too many memories.

Figure A8 - 1967 Honda CA-160. This is the successor to the very similar 150cc CA-95, the Honda model sold in large numbers as serious competition to machines such as the Harley-Davidson Singles, the Triumph Tiger Cubs, and the Cushman Eagle. ©Michael Kiernan, Classic Motorcycle Company, St. Louis, MO.

The only detail that was left to bug me or any other future motorcycle punk was the small diameter of the Honda handgrips. The throttle handgrip of a Harley-Davidson was of a diameter larger than the handlebars, and it was not spring-loaded. The throttle grip on a Honda was spring-loaded and much smaller, adding to the impression of a smaller machine. Even the 150 Benly Touring had these smaller handgrips, but the machine was a 242-pound, 16.5 hp, SOHC (single overhead cam to you neophytes) four-stroke twin with 16-inch wheels and low angel wing handlebars that were almost as high and stylish as the Buckhorns on the Super 10. The claimed top speed of the Benly was 84, but we all found out quickly enough that that was the dropped-out-of-an-airplane speed. The real top speed was about 70-75 mph, but that was still at

Figure A9 - 1961 Harley-Davidson Sprint. This was the first year of the first model built by Aermacchi in Italy and imported by H-D. The Sprint was all alone in 1961, but it would be joined by the H Scrambler version in 1962. ©Michael Kiernan, Classic Motorcycle Company, St. Louis, MO.

least 10 mph more than the Super 10 could muster. Even with its little handgrips, the Benly felt and sounded like a real motorcycle. With its high-revving, twin-cylinder, twin-exhaust, four-stroke engine, the Benly sounded a lot better than the Super 10. When you can push the electric starter button and move a four-speed foot shift through the gears to reach that real highway cruising speed, you wonder what sort of Neanderthal Motorcycle

Punk would pay the same price for a Super 10? Even Aunt Matilda approved of its quiet purr, dual seat with a hold-on strap and rear foot-pegs, and its modern Sixties Jetsons styling.

Figure A10 - 1959 Ducati 200 SS. Small numbers of Ducati models were imported into the USA prior to the arrival of Honda. This B&W photo does not reveal the unusual red and gold paint combination, but the deeply sculpted tank and narrow seat are clearly visible. All three elements distinguished many early Ducatis. ©Michael Kiernan, Classic Motorcycle Company, St. Louis, MO.

The Super 10 had none of these attributes. A little over 1500 is the most Harley dealers could shove out the door in 1961. The last remaining 165cc Super 10 engines were used up in the Ranger trail model in '62, while the street-only 175cc Pacer was introduced with a street/trail companion, the 175cc Scat. Remember that trail-riding craze also started by Honda? After building less than 6000 Pacers and Scats through 1965, H-D tried one to sell one last American-built tiddler in 1966, the Bobcat trail model. These 1150 Bobcats became Harley's tiddler swansong, at least as far as U.S.-built models went. Harley-Davidson tried to stem the Honda tide by purchasing the Italian motorcycle manufacturer Aermacchi and putting their label on the firm's 50-350cc lineup, but this did not stop the Honda onslaught. While Harley-Davidson was dealing in production numbers in the thousands, the Honda 50 surpassed the million mark.

Harley-Davidson imported various Aermacchi models throughout the '60's and well into the '70's, beginning with the 250cc, single-cylinder, four-stroke OHV Sprint in late 1960. The original 250 Sprint and the later 350 Sprint created a fair amount of business for Harley, but the 65cc putt-putts, 100cc Baja off-road scrambler, 125cc Rapido, and many other Italian two-stroke models were less successful. During the same time period, Honda was growing like mad, and so were their leading competitors, which were all Japanese. Yamaha followed in the tire tracks of Honda, except they did it with two-strokes touting performance and handling above the civility and reliability of the Hondas. Suzuki entered the market as the me-too brand behind Yamaha. The shortest lived casualty of the Japanese tiddlers of the early Sixties would be the Pointer brand, which built some cleverly designed two-stroke models in 1961-62. Tohatsu played briefly in the U.S. market, but they soon gave up the two-wheelers in favor of outboard motors for American fishermen. Bridgestone decided to make something other than round, black, rubber doughnuts, but their models were a little too technically fancy with their rotary transmissions and chrome bores that could not be re-bored when they wore out. The rumor is also that the competing Japanese brands threatened to quit buying Bridgestone tires for their bikes if Bridgestone did not cease competing with them with the Bridgestone line of 50-350cc models. Whether that rumor was true or not, Bridgestone never really attacked the American market with the verve the earlier three had. You can see this pattern easily when you realize that Bridgestone never established their own distribution network outside Rockford Motors in Illinois. That, too, is another story.

Yamaguchi tried briefly to compete with Yamaha and Suzuki in the two-stroke tiddler market, but they never really got off the ground in U.S. sales. Fortunately for Yamaguchi, though, the trail bike craze in America was just getting cranked up by 1964, and the U.S. importers of the Yamaguchis had a good idea for a trail bike tiddler designed especially for the U.S. market. Rather than face direct and total extinction, Yamaguchi began to build engines for the new Hodaka brand, which would build its reputation in the same manner as the Volkswagen Beetle. The Hodaka Ace 90 was the brand's single model, built in any color you wanted as long as it was red. The whole gas tank and both fenders were chrome to give it a classy look. This red and chrome one-trick-pony was a good trail bike and it sold well. Hodaka would later update the Ace 90 to the 100 and then to the 100 B. The motocross Super Rat, and then the 125cc Wombat and its first cousin, the motocross Combat Wombat would be added later. Hodaka was always good at cute names for motorcycles.

After the original Honda/Yamaha/Suzuki juggernaut of 1960-62, the next big U.S. success for a Japanese motorcycle manufacturer would be the little-known Omega 125cc. Kawasaki dumped the Omega moniker soon after they sent the first few bikes to the U.S. Their Samurai 250 street model and the Samurai SS street scrambler would launch the company properly. The Avenger and Avenger SS swarmed the American market with the world's fastest 350's soon thereafter. Kawasaki was now king of the performance market in America with their lineup of two-stroke twins. Hold on to your handlebars! The Kawasaki Mach III, a two-stroke triple weighing in at 382 pounds and producing 60 horsepower, became the fastest production 500cc by a mile!

What were the Europeans doing while all this tire smoke was being produced? Mostly choking on it. Triumph, the most legendary and successful of the bunch, tried its best to ignore the Japanese stampede over America. They were never very successful at selling their smaller models over here, anyway. As long as they could peddle their beautiful but unreliable 500cc and 650cc models in America, they were complacent. Of course Triumph should have been acting a little more like the cows in the lineup at the slaughterhouse! The company should have been kicking and screaming its way to a dumping of the unreliable Lucas electrical systems, which were nicknamed The Prince of Darkness in the U.S., but instead, it just mooed its way through a slow and painful demise. By the end of the Sixties, the Bonneville was a beautiful machine that was cherished by those who could pay the asking price and deal with periodically getting stranded in Timbuktu, Texas, without a flashlight. The problem is that the 305cc Honda Super Hawk, although half the size of the Bonnie, looked and sounded almost as good, was not that much slower, was a lot cheaper, and most of all, was a lot more reliable. If you could deal with the smoke and ring-ding noise, many of the smaller and cheaper Yamahas, Suzukis, and Kawasakis could blow smoke in the Bonneville's face. The Mach III could run and hide from it, and the new Honda 750 four-cylinder could run and hide from it, and even sound like a baby Ferrari while doing it! BSA, which had already merged with Triumph, basically offered a twin-sister lineup to the Triumphs, much like Oldsmobile/Buick and Pontiac/Chevrolet. Norton offered only their antiquated 750cc Atlas models in the U.S. after a brief period of marketing their 400cc Electra model in the early Sixties. Hot-to-trot, scantily clad, young females in clever full-page, full-color magazine ads were unable to save Norton's later Commando models in the U.S., and expanding the lineup into street scrambler and off-road models didn't help much, either.

Figure A11 - 1966 BMW R-27 Single. Like all BMW's, this model was intended to be "black and white and rode all over". The R-27 would be the last small BMW model. ©Michael Kiernan, Classic Motorcycle Company, St. Louis, MO.

A few European brands from Germany and Italy fared somewhat better than the notoriously unreliable British. BMW became the darling of the I'm-holier-than-thou-because-I-have-more-money-than-thou set. The company has fared better in America mostly because they have never intruded directly into the Japanese competitive market. Ducati has also fared decently well in America by not hitting the Japanese market in the face. The company floundered a bit as the requisite adjustments to the Japanese onslaught settled in, but Ducati generally came out the other side with a cozy little two-wheeled-Ferrari reputation that has kept their big machines rolling across America in small, but steady numbers. As far as the laughable Austrian antiques sold by Sears as the Allstates go, you can guess that the Japanese sent them packing for a trip back to Austria. Sears tried importing a few Gilera models from Italy, but that didn't last long. Benelli tried to market models through the Montgomery Ward stores and catalog for a while in the Sixties, but they finally packed their bags for Italy. A little known sprout brand off the Benelli was the Motobi, but they, too, quickly retreated from the Japanese tidal wave. Parilla had also followed them back to Italy by the end of the Sixties. The trifecta from Spain, Bultaco, Montesa, and Ossa, fought off the tidal wave for quite a while mostly by appealing with lightweight, high-quality handling in an off-road environment.

The Japanese roared across America throughout the Sixties. The bikes grew bigger, faster, more technologically proficient, more diversified, and more expensive. Honda began marketing what would become known as the street scrambler in 1962. Taking much of the styling and a little of the off-road capability from the trail bikes, the '62 Honda CL-72 Scrambler 250 would take America by dust storm. American motorcycle enthusiasts loved the scramblers from the first moment they saw them. Of course the models proliferated like crazy. First the 250cc CL-72 grew into the 305cc CL-77 in 1965 and then all hell broke loose. Every brand built street scramblers in a multitude of sizes. All this time, the purely street models were also growing and proliferating, producing more performance and sportier styling with each new model generation. Yamaha introduced oil injection on its models in 1964, making the messy mixing of gas and oil that everyone despised a thing of the past for two-stroke lovers. All the competing brands adopted their own trade-name oil injection soon thereafter. Kawasaki built its large 650cc twins as big cruisers of moderate performance to compete directly with the Triumphs, BSA's, and Nortons, and many were sold to American police departments. Honda broke out of its SOHC 305cc maximum engines in 1965 with the introduction of its DOHC 450cc model with constant-velocity, vacuum-operated carburetors. Yamaha introduced a 650 twin to directly butt front wheels with the unreliable Triumphs and their Limey pals. Suzuki produced the first 750cc water-cooled two stroke that would forever be nicknamed the Water Buffalo. The company would even introduce a Wankel rotary model a few years later. Kawasaki forgot to spay its wildcat Mach III and it had kittens: a 350 Mach II that grew into a 400; a 250 Mach I that was a little too heavy to be really fast; and a 750 Mach IV that would peel the skin off an orange with the accelerating blast of wind.

Figure A12 - 1972 Kawasaki 750 H2 Triple. ©Michael Kiernan, Classic Motorcycle Company, St. Louis, MO.

As much technology as all that sounds like, another new world was born when Honda introduced the Ferrari scream of the 750 Four in 1969. It was only marginally faster than Kawasaki's 500 Mach III and the Mach IV would blast by the Ferrari shriek with a cloud of smoke and a Hi-yo, Silver! The difference was, of course, the technology that led to the riding experience. The Kawasaki Triples were wild and crazy beasts with tricky handling, mediocre brakes, an unusual sound, and vibration that would make you feel as if your hands were going to slip right off the ends of the handlebars! Like the Triumphs, Sportsters, and other antique hot-rods of the day, some part of your body went to sleep every time you went for a ride! On some models it was your feet, on some your hands, and others your posterior. The new, slick, smooth, and powerful Honda 750 Four left all of you awake to fully appreciate the experience. All of the competition that was not ready to develop and release a large four-cylinder four-stroke motorcycle may as well have packed their bags and gone back to where they came from right then and there. The company that best adapted to the challenge was Kawasaki. After the introduction of their 900cc DOHC Z-1 in 1973, the company ground out blazingly fast, smooth, good-handling, good-feeling Z-1's and their descendants like Led Zeppelin churned out albums. The Honda 750 Four was like Cream, the first power trio, and the big Z and its many Ninja descendants were like Led Zeppelin, a veritable juggernaut of the large motorcycle market in the U.S. Honda continued making the 750 Four in the early Seventies, but the company had another path to blaze. In 1975 they introduced the Gold Wing, an opposed, water-cooled, flat-four-cylinder, 1000cc touring model that made even BMW start to cry. By this time Harley-Davidson was blubbering like a little kid who just got a shot in the butt.

But things were about to change – for everybody. Back in '69, Harley-Davidson had been financially forced into a merger with AMF, American Machine & Foundry (yes, Martha, the bowling ball people). AMF wanted to buy H-D and increase the dickens out of its model lineup and production capacity to compete with the Japanese. Make no mistake: H-D was saved by AMF. Harley nuts try their best to forget the AMF H-D era. They know that the increases in production and models forced by AMF caused the quality of the machines to drop and a bit of tarnish to appear on the precious Harley-Davidson image. It was a marriage made out of necessity. AMF sought profitability and they got it. Harley got back on its feet well enough to do its own corporate buyback of the company in 1981. After regaining its footing, H-D dropped all the Aermacchis and all the tiddlers. From that point onward, Harley's smallest model would be the 457-pound, 883cc Sportster, which at the time of the buyback was actually 1000cc and a little heavier than that, but the company took itself back to its roots in every way it could. AMF went back to making pool tables and bowling balls, happy to be back out of the big, bellowing V-twin business.

Figure A13 - 1973 Kawasaki 900 Z-1. ©Michael Kiernan, Classic Motorcycle Company, St. Louis, MO.

In the meantime, Honda and the rest of what had become the big four Japanese motorcycle manufacturers continued to increase models, production, and technology, just like AMF wanted to do. The difference is that the Japanese are especially good at it. American companies are not. The Big Four continued not only increasing the aforementioned three elements, but they also were increasing the size and price of their motorcycles. This gradually put more and more pressure on the non-Japanese brands trying to sell large, touring-type motorcycles. Did I mention that Harleys as performance machines are the John Deeres and Massey Fergusons of the motorcycle world? The big Ninjas and other bullet bikes with more R's, S's, and X's in their names than are contained in a can of alphabet soup are not really Harley-Davidson competitors. The bullet bikes are market competitors to only a small degree, even to BMW, Ducati, and Triumph, who, believe it or not, has returned to the U.S. market with a small lineup of high-priced, large, snob-monsters. It's the big touring rigs, what I call the Queen Marys, who are the real threat to these brands. Back in the good old days of 1966, the largest and most expensive mass-produced (shut-up, Munch Mammoth fans) bike on the market was the Harley-Davidson ElectraGlide, which sold for $1850 with all the saddlebags, windshields, touring bags, luggage racks, and chrome doo-dads you could put on it! By the very early Eighties,

10

Honda's Gold Wing, its Japanese competitors, and its sport touring little brothers practically owned the motorcycle touring market. This was of course the high end of the motorcycle world as far as dollars and profits are concerned. These are the buyers who not only purchase the most expensive motorcycle in the store, but they buy most of the clothing and accessories, too.

What's the point of all this two-wheeled brouhaha? Harley-Davidson convinced the U.S. International Trade Commission to restrict the massive numbers of large motorcycles entering the U.S. by placing a sizable tariff on models larger than 699cc. Since the 750cc class has always been considered the entry point for the term *large* motorcycle, and since practically all motorcycles are of an actual displacement just a cc or two below the class name, this rule made sense as a 700cc dividing line. The tariff would be gradually reduced annually over the next few years, and any brand could choose to simply pay it if they wanted to continue importing 750 and larger motorcycles without interruption into this country. You can guess exactly what happened. BMW and Ducati, which were marketed as overpriced snot-brands in the first place, just pushed their prices up to meet the tariff. Many of the Japanese 750cc models the companies had been marketing either in past years, or currently in other national markets, were sent to the U.S. with smaller bores and pistons that made them 699cc. A few of the 900-and-up models were dropped from U.S. importation for a few years until the tariff amount receded. Guess what else happened? Just as had already been done with Japanese cars, the motorcycle companies began to build manufacturing plants in the U.S. especially to build their large-displacement models that were particularly popular in the land of the free to build your own factory country. They generally built these factories right where the Americans needed jobs, too. Big Kaws are now bred in Nebraska (where else?) and Gold Wings are born in Ohio. Yee-hahh!! Everybody wins!

Harley-Davidson successfully sold this plan to President Reagan by claiming that the Japanese companies were dumping their big high-tech monsters on the poor American consumer at less than cost or competitive prices. They may or may not have been right about the less than what they cost to build and ship part, but there is no question whatever in my mind that 1983 was the best year in history to purchase a Japanese motorcycle. Honda alone built an unfathomable array of different engine designs for the 1983 model year. A cycle enthusiast could choose from a single cylinder, a vertical twin, a longitudinal V-twin, a transverse V-twin, a longitudinal V-four, an inline four, and an opposed, flat four! Those were just the engine designs. The buyer could also select from many different styles and displacements. The only limited factors at Honda in '83 were the colors: most models offered only two choices. Many Japanese models had been increasingly overproduced in the years leading up to 1983. The market boom that had begun in 1959 had pretty much run its course. Everybody who had wanted to meet the nicest people by this time already had.

A sideshow to the main tent had been going on in the off-road market. As the trail riding hobby had increased in popularity, so had the power and adaptability of the trail models proliferating out of Japan. The Honda Trail 55 had introduced many people to the possibilities of off-the-pavement putt-putting back in '62. The off-road market grew slowly but steadily until Yamaha had the gall to develop a motorcycle intended particularly to appeal to the American off-road rider. The 250cc DT-1 was released in 1968 to instant success. Of course Yamaha forgot to neuter the little booger and he immediately started to produce offspring. Within a few years, there was a 90, 125, 175, 250, and 360 Trail model, and they each had to have a motocross brother; then Suzuki, Honda, and Kawasaki had to build their equivalent models. The competition brought higher and higher power outputs, and guess what happened to last year's motocrosser when it was retired from racing after only one season because it was no longer competitive with the latest racing models? Yep, all the old timers of trail riding, like me for instance, found those models to be the cat's meow for non-racing trail riding. For y'all who are unfamiliar with motorcycle specifics, motocross models of the period generally had knobbier tires, higher fenders, and noisier exhausts than their Enduro brothers with batteries and street-legal lighting. The motocross models' higher state of tune and lighter weight made them more fun to ride off-road than their Enduro brothers, but they also made more racket and tore up the ground more. How much racket? Imagine Flight of the Bumblebee on acid with 10,000 watts of power! Any fool could see that the number of motorcycles tearing up the dirt in Aunt Matilda's back yard was rapidly getting out of hand, and she started to squawk about it. Soon many of the off-road riding locations were closed off

Figure A14 - 1975 Yamaha MX-250B. The delicately slow, casual trail riding that had begun innocently enough with the Honda and Yamaha step-through trail tiddlers in 1961-62 gradually evolved into loud earth-rippers such as this by 1975. Although initially designed for offroad racetracks, countless numbers of exciting motocrossers spent time in Aunt Maybelle's corn field, leading to a slow squelching of the fun by the U.S. Forest Service, the EPA, and of course, the many anti-motorcycle Aunt Maybelles of America.
©1975 Yamaha Motor Corporation, U.S.A.

to motorcyclists and opportunities to enjoy the sport gradually diminished. The point of this dusty, dirty, muddy story is that the broad market for small Japanese motorcycles was shrinking in size in more ways than one. First there was the 50cc, you meet the nicest people, boom; then there was the increase the power and displacement to move the buyers up-market boom; then there was the trail riding boom; and finally, the large-displacement, ungodly speed boom. Every balloon must pop. Every product has a market cycle.

There were only three things the Japanese Big Four could do in 1984, and they did all three. They cut production, raised prices, and diversified their product lines. Many models were dropped from the '84 lineups and prices were distinctly higher. Honda had already been building cars for many years. (Yes, Maybelle, the first Honda 600 Convertible had been brought to California in 1965!) The Civic and Accord had already taught General Motors a lesson they would soon forget. Suzuki began importing their line of outboard motors to compete with the Tohatsus and Yamahas. The latter, of course, had been importing musical instruments and home audio equipment since the beginning. Kawasaki opened up the new jet ski market, and they still officially own the name *Jet Ski*. They did not invent the jet ski, but they were the ones who made it a successfully marketed product. Yamaha much later would market the most successful sit-down personal watercraft, the WaveRunners, and Honda even joined that market in 2002. In case you forgot, Suzuki even tried the personal watercraft market for a while. The now defunct Tiger Shark brand used Suzuki engines. Never again would new motorcycles be so deliciously cheap for the American consumer. New waterlogged buyers would come to know The Big Four for something we trail riders would never have dreamed in 1960. Whereas the Sixties motorcycles were built in Japan, the personal watercraft are built in America.

Do I really need to tell you about what became of Harley-Davidson? Believe me when I say I have been as shocked as you are that we now live in a world full of $20,000 motorcycles, and most of these are built by John Deere and Massey Ferguson. Just kidding, but you know what company I'm talking about. Harley-Davidson not only succeeded in buying themselves back from the bowling ball company, they have become the absolute darlings of the financial channel. The tariff was phased out as planned. H-D cut back their production, focused on their most popular models, and improved the quality and reliability of their product. The Big Four went on to bigger and better things. Maybe it has cost them a lot of money. It certainly has caused them to greatly trim their product lines, but would that not have happened anyway when the motorcycle market bubble popped? They may be importing a lot less product as counted strictly by the numbers, but look how much product they are now producing in U.S. factories. Consider, too, the enormous gain in retail prices for the current product that The Big Four has reaped. The game is almost over and everybody won.

There is one humorous footnote to this story. I cannot stop laughing at the gross absurdity of what has happened to the motorcycle market as it now stands in this new millennium. The out the door price of $20,000 for a new motorcycle is not a joke or a misprint. There are an incredible number of models that currently cost that much. What is really amusing to me is how many of those are JohnDeere/Massey-Ferguson/Harley-Davidsons! They are the most overpriced tractors in history! Their engines are so big we need something even more absurd to call them than Queen Mary! The cost of options on Porsches used to be laughable. Now, compared to the cost of a silly piece of chrome wahoo option on a Harley, Porsche's ridiculous prices bring only a smirk. The smallest tiddlers you can buy now from The Big Four are the 250cc twins. On a twisty road, even the Kawasaki Ninja 250 (that's the baby one, folks) can leave a $20,000 tractor behind! What's the matter with you people? Are those silly, red, Willie Nelson copycat, bandanas on your heads too tight? And y'all aren't the only motorcycle nuts out there, either. The Big Four makes so many Harley copycats that I have to pull right up beside one to read the name on the gas tank to even know what brand I'm looking at, and I've been a motorsickle nut for nearly fifty years! That ain't all, folks. Honda *finally* got their heads out of their exhaust pipes and realized that back in 1960, the H-D Super 10 had something after all: styling and charisma. They finally introduced a model for youngsters based on the same styling concept in 1985, the Honda 250 Rebel. Duh! Now every teenage motorcycle punk in America can have a bike that makes him feel like the Super 10 did to me back in 1960! Yamaha went even further than the Rebel with its Route 66 (now called the Virago 250) with a 250cc V-twin engine. What goes around comes around. Amen.

Figure A15 - 1987 Honda 250 Rebel. ©Michael Kiernan, Classic Motorcycle Company, St. Louis, MO.

Figure A16 - 1962 Harley-Davidson 175 Pacer. ©Charles "Mutt" Hallam

Chapter 1: *Tiddlywinkin' Through the Happy Days*

What is a Tiddler and Who Got Invaded?

Tiddler is the word that over time came to be the established designation for a small motorcycle. The word is technically slang in the English (American) lexicon, therefore few motorized two-wheeled enthusiasts actually agree on a final definition. Some might include mopeds and scooters in the definition, but others might not. Some might include small twin-cylinder machines while others might insist that only a single can be a real tiddler. A few might even insist that the invasion was purely a marketing boom emanating from Japan and that the definition applies only to machines arriving on our shores from that one origin. Probably the single issue that all motorcycle or scooter fans reading this book will agree upon is that the ubiquitous Honda 50 started it!

Figure B1 - Red Honda Cub with Gray & White Seat at the Toyota Automobile Museum in Japan. This is what many view as the original tiddler in one of its most common color combinations.

Image by D. Bellwood, photographer, under Creative Commons license (GNU).

Honda released the Honda 50 in Japan in 1958 and brought the first ones to the U.S. in the summer of 1959. As will be described profusely in this book, many brands of small machines were either built in the USA or exported here from Europe up to a decade or more prior to the arrival of the first Hondas, but most will agree that Honda lit the fuse leading to the explosion of sales numbers. So who got invaded? Certainly much of Europe and the rest of the world were affected, but this is a story told from the American perspective. This story is for sure long overdue to be published. I have dreamed of doing it literally for decades, and the time has finally arrived. As you will come to understand in great detail as you read through this book, I happened to have been born at precisely the right time to become enamored and downright obsessed with this story. I was drooling over the motorcycle pages of the Sears catalog from about the age of nine. At that point I lived in a very small town, far from the nearest city or motorcycle dealer. Mr. Roebuck was my only connection to motorized wheels. My best friend got a motorcycle when I was twelve. He not only took me for my first ride and later actually taught me to drive it, but he introduced me to trail riding practically from the beginning. Within only a few months, my favorite cousin got the first Honda I ever saw. As Sherlock Holmes might have said, "the game was now afoot" (except it rode two wheels with a motor).

The Tiddler Invasion is not my story; it's yours, especially if you are a baby boomer American. Many books covering some of this subject matter have been published in the past. Far too many of them have come from Europe and the American version of the story is long overdue. Every machine, every story, every article, every chart, and every detailed specification in this book is the *American* version. If any machine discussed in this book happens to be an Asian or European model only, it is simply because I was never able to prove any were officially imported into the USA. The point of the story is for each and every one of you to wallow in the nostalgia of one of the loveliest times in American history.

The focus of this story is the 1955-75 era with strong emphasis on the Sixties in the middle. There is a sort of warm up and cool down feeling to the story. It began in what we commonly refer to as the Postwar period when the factories throughout the world were recovering from WWII. The boom slowly morphed into something else as it waned throughout the mid-Seventies. As the country got back to civilian production after the war, we had Harley-Davidsons, Cushmans, Mustangs, and a few others emanating from our domestic factories. BSA's, Triumphs, and many other brands arrived from Europe. Here is a big hint concerning the birth of the next phase: Honda did not exist until much later than all these American and European brands. Honda started designing its modern machines more or less from scratch in the postwar period. Unlike all the producers whose machines were already here, Honda was starting with a new sheet of paper. What the company produced was truly modern when others were producing technical antiques, even if they were never labeled as such. Factor in the low retail price capability the Japanese brought to the table and the resulting boom seems inevitable as we look back on it now.

The definition of a tiddler is going to stick in the carburetor throats of many of you readers, so let's just dispense with the discussion right now. Believe it or not, this sticking point has been a major factor in why it has taken me so long to finally publish this story. What do I call it and what are my chosen parameters? I agree with all of you that we may never have thought up the name "tiddler" if Honda had not started an explosion of small motorcycles exported to the U.S. However you define the word, tiddlers started a revolution in America. We experienced the sheer open-hearted joy of an affordable market developed specifically for the burgeoning youth population of America. It may have begun with a three-cubic-inch step-through motorcycle design that looked like a girl's bicycle, but it ended with a two-stroke that could scorch the quarter mile in about twelve seconds, a 750 Four that would change the motorcycle world forever, a DOHC 903cc Four that would define the high-performance motorcycle world, and a big machine with a gas tank hidden underneath its seat that would redefine motorcycle touring. These machines signaled the finale of what I call The Tiddler Invasion. From that point forward motorcycles would continue to evolve into ever larger, faster, more powerful, more sophisticated, and most of all, more expensive machines. The larger machines would gradually pull the ladder up from the bottom of the market and the models designed for a very specific purpose would evolve further and further into whatever specific market had been chosen for them. The general-purpose machines would slowly fall into oblivion with the smaller motorcycles that had started the boom. Now those concepts are lost forever in the fog of our nostalgic memories.

Figure B2 - White 1959 Cushman Super Eagle at the Barber Museum in Birmingham, AL.

Image by Chuck Schultz, photographer, under Creative Commons license.

As you can quickly surmise, *The Tiddler Invasion* is not a picture book. There are photographs all over the internet. If that is what you are looking for, you will be sorely disappointed. This is not a history book, either, particularly not of the motorcycle factories or their racing histories. Like the photographs, there is plenty of that sort of information to be discovered all over the Internet and in many other books. Unfortunately much of that information derives from the Asian or European perspective since that is where most of the factories are located. The definitive technical details of each brand can be found in many brand or model specific books. That is not the purpose of this book.

The perspective of *The Tiddler Invasion* has never been published before, at least not in one source. This is what I call *The Big Picture*. It's my thing. It's what all my books are about. Fifty years ago I began reading *Cycle World* from the first year of its publication and I began collecting motorcycle brochures from the distributors and dealers. Not only have I read and stared at those publications over the decades, but also I spent countless hours researching through them for the information in this book. My bookshelves are covered in numerous books about specific brands and models, too, and although *Cycle World* has always been my favorite, it is not the only motorcycle monthly on my shelves. On top of this, I am an Internet junkie who retired over a decade ago just to sit at my computer all day most every day. The main reason you are just now reading *The Tiddler Invasion* is that it is my seventh book and it had to wait its turn in line. Most of the others took years to research and write, too.

Figure B3 - 1963 Bridgestone 7 Sportster Ad. ©1963 Bridgestone Corporation.

You might best understand my *big picture* if you examine it as a stupendous assemblage of relevant facts on a particular subject. In this case it happens to be the motorcycle boom in the U.S. that paralleled the youth market explosion of the baby boomers. Most of that explosion happened to come from Japan, so that is the focus of this book. The story began on our own shores, so that is where the book begins. The market boom culminated in the street scrambler concept that Honda greatly expanded for a hungry American market. That is aptly the climax of the book. Small Asian machines have not completely disappeared from American roads. They have just been shouted into obscurity by the boom in specialized V-twins and bullet bikes. The closing chapter describes some of the highlights of the tiddler market in the post-1975 era.

Pull up a chair and begin by reading *The Tiddler Invasion* cover to cover. You will have many opportunities to return to it for reference later. You may even want to refer to it as you surf the net for photos and details of your specific favorite marque or model. Here is a clue: the best parts of the book are the charts. The nostalgic stories about individual models are there for you to reminisce, but essentially you could do that without my help. If you are reading this book, you probably already know which machines are the great ones. What you may not know is the information I have collected into the charts. Although a few of the charts may seem obvious and superfluous, most of them represent countless hours of research to find information not readily available anywhere else. The goal was to put each model and brand into the perspective of its contemporary peers. To those of you who may have been born only thirty years ago, you will find the stated prices laughable, but I assure you they were very real. That is why this was such a golden era. When you look back and realize what a plethora of wonderful experiences was waiting for such a small donation from your bank account, you will realize what a special time The Sixties really were.

The charts can be considered something of an *ID guide* for whatever ancient machines you may discover in a dilapidated barn or on eBay. The only caveat is that I cannot claim perfection from my research. So much of this information has been lost forever to antiquity. Although I have tried my best, some of you experts on particular brands or models may uncover incorrect information. Let me just say right now that of course I know that Honda and many other manufacturers had very little respect for the American marketing tradition of hawking products by specific model year. This is precisely why I do not conclusively claim that *The Tiddler Invasion* should be considered the last word on anything! What this book is is the best American overview, so get over it now and you will enjoy the trip so much more than you would from a differing viewpoint.

Consider yourself hypnotized. I am going to take you back to what was for many of us the happiest time of our lives. We are going to walk the pathways of our adolescence. We are going to reminisce about just how special that time was to each of us. Most of this book is a focus on the Big Four Japanese brands as their products were applied to American culture. Many of the machines receiving the bulk of attention in this book were created and/or specifically modified for U.S. riders. These were the models that lit fires in our imaginations and under out butts. They took us on the rides of our lifetimes. Put on your helmet and stab that kickstarter. We're all going for a ride!

Concepts & Parameters to Consider

This first chapter is going to snap and pop all over the subject matter, just like a silly game of Tiddlywinks. We are going to start our long journey through the nostalgic history of small motorcycles in America by examining the many parameters involved. This is a story of emotions as well as technical achievements. We shall begin with a quick reference of the performance of the key models that resulted from the motorcycle boom of The Sixties. Although some of these performance figures may seem distinctly unimpressive today, I urge you to recall what it was like starting up a Cushman Eagle with its ratchet foot pedal or pedaling an Allstate Moped to life. Now those were primitive and slow to an excruciating degree. Now imagine pushing the starter button of a Z-1 and easing out the clutch. That was an amazing ride from 1963 to 1973, wasn't it?

Figure B4 - Black 1964 Suzuki 250 T-10. Note the squarish designs of the speedometer, tank and fenders that were indigenous to the era. ©Michael Kiernan, Classic Motorcycle Company, St. Louis, MO.

A lot of thought went into the order of things in this book. The final choices were made to make the storyline flow as smoothly as possible. There are no definitive rules concerning the order in which any machines or brands are presented, either by chapter, within a chapter, or within a chart. There are *general* patterns that have been applied throughout the book. In some cases how *long* the model remained in production was a factor. The brands and models usually progress from smallest to largest, from obscure to major, and by introduction date. Date of the founding of the factory is considered in some cases, but in others, the decision is based upon official arrival in the U.S. In the European chapter, marques from the same country of origin are grouped together. Honda is held until last simply because it is the elephant in the room. The order of the Yamaha, Suzuki, and Kawasaki chapters was a tough call. Suzuki comes first because it has usually been the #4 brand since Kawasaki fully launched its American beachhead in 1967. Kawasaki is next because Yamaha fully established itself here years before Kawasaki. The pattern throughout the book is to cover the lesser brands first and progress into the primary brands. I think you can see why the order of Suzuki-Kawasaki-Yamaha was such a difficult call. The many variations in content and structure among the charts were selected to best fit each situation. In cases where there are lots of NA's (Not Available) in a chart, it simply means either the information was unavailable or there was measurable uncertainty as to the correctness of the information I had. Yes, those charts with a lot of unknown entries could have been deleted, but if I left the chart as is, it was because I felt the same type of information as that omitted, but for other models for which the information could be substantiated, was important enough to include in the chart. Got that? I try not to confuse my readers, really I do!

The photos might be considered the weakest link in the book. Some of you may feel that my cursory knowledge of certain brands and models is the weaker issue, but I think many of you will first notice the photos. If you are reading *The Tiddler Invasion* in print, every interior photo is in black and white. The cost of color printing is simply prohibitive, and I wanted the price of this book to be affordable to everyone. Nearly all of the photos in the Kindle or other e-book versions are in full color. In spite of the color e-book versions, *The Tiddler Invasion* is distinctly *not* a book of pretty pictures. It has far more in common with the *Corvette Black Book* Series or the *Illustrated Buyer's Guide* Series. The photos came from whatever legal sources I had available, from museum snapshots taken by fans of individual models to personal photos. Kawasaki, Bridgestone, Yamaha, and Suzuki have allowed me permission to reprint any old brochure scans I might have available. Honda was initially cooperative, but then gave me the old runaround. After a couple of years of such nonsense, I gave up, As far as I am concerned, this will be Honda's loss, as well as yours. I have tons of classic brochure photos that you may never see. I honestly do not know what issues this corporate entity may have that the company does not want to see its classic products honored with dignity for all posterity. The details of every photo credit are listed with each picture and/or in the Photo Credits at the back of this book.

The real stars of this book are the charts! They required countless hours to compile from long rows of period motorcycle magazines, file folders stuffed with manufacturer's brochures, shelves of rare books on the subject, and of course Wikipedia and the rest of its Internet associates.

Unlike so many other books and research sources, *The Tiddler Invasion* does not elaborate on the special, ultra-rare machines such as the 1959 Honda Benly Super Sport CB-92, a very collectible and desirable tiddler. Yes, a few of them were imported into the U. S. in those heady days of the beginning of Honda's assault on the motorcycle market in 1959. As far as I know, Honda never imported the CA-92 because it was superseded by the CA-95, the ubiquitous Benly Touring 150. The CB-92 was sold as both Super Sport and Super Sport Racer models in the U. S., probably in 1959-61. The Racer had a special cam, megaphones, and a racing saddle. The weights, compression ratios, and eighteen-inch tire sizes were the same on both models. Apparently the cam and open exhaust added one horsepower to the fifteen of the standard Super Sport. My earliest Honda brochure, 1962, shows the various 125cc Hondas, but they have all been crossed out by the dealer, indicating that they were no longer being imported in '62.

Figure B5 - 1963 Red & Silver Honda 125 CB-92R. This machine is what most consider the crown jewel of collectible Hondas. In typical Honda fashion for the time, this rare machine was most likely built in 1962 and titled as a '63 model after it was originally sold. ©Michael Kiernan, Classic Motorcycle Company, St. Louis, MO.

The Tiddler Invasion is primarily about the commonplace machines of our youth. There are some rare models that have been included because they are so unusual and interesting. However you slice it, the time and place of the motorcycle boom of The Sixties was a complex event. Machines ranged from the heroic to the sublime and from the silly to the practical. You will be familiar with most of the product discussed. The majority of the models will be common Hondas, Yamahas, and Kawasakis, with a little less emphasis on Suzukis, and of course Bridgestone and Hodaka are included.

Cycle World published "The History of Japanese Motorcycles" in November 1967. Japan had produced over three-quarter of a million machines in 1959, and that figure had been slowly attained over the previous decade from a total production of only one thousand from a war-ravaged Japan in 1948. Japan exported only a little over 1000 machines worldwide in 1958, but this number topped 13,000 in 1959 and 52,000 in 1960. Due to the explosive success of the Honda 50, Japan's production reached 1.3 million in 1960, and as we all know, this was only the beginning. Welcome to The Tiddler Invasion! The two-million mark would be surpassed in 1964. According to the *Illustrated Encyclopedia*, Japan produced over 2.5 million motorcycles in 1969. The number had increased to over 4.5 million by 1974. The number decreased to only 3.8 million in 1975, indicating the coming end to the boom.

The Tiddler Timeline

1945 – 1949: Manufacturers around the world are recovering from WWII in their own ways. The design for the DKW 125cc, piston-port, two-stroke single is made available to other manufacturers by edict. The most notable of these offshoots are the Harley-Davidson Hummer and the first Yamaha. The first Hondas are sold in Japan.

1950 – 1954: The American motorcycle/scooter market becomes a hodge-podge of mostly American, British, and Italian brands, including Harley-Davidson, Cushman, Vespa, Allstate, Whizzer, Simplex, Triumph, and BSA, among many others.

1955 – 1959: Just about the time the Cushman Eagle, Harley Hummer, and various Allstates settle down to a nice, productive market, the first Hondas come to America.

1960 – 1964: The explosive technological and marketing success of The Big Three dominates the American landscape with a musical backdrop of surf music and the new English mop top invasion. A few Japanese brands, such as Yamaguchi, Tohatsu, Pointer, and Rabbit come and go rather quickly, leaving Honda, Yamaha, and Suzuki to parallel the longevity, popularity, and reputations of The Beatles, The Rolling Stones, and The Animals. H-D begins to expand its tiddler offerings, while Cushman buries its head in the sand, Sears markets its Allstates live at mall service centers, and BSA and Triumph concentrate on their 500's and 650's.

1965 – 1969: Honda dominates the market like no motorcycle brand in all of history and brings its first cars to the U. S. while Yamaha and Suzuki continue the popularity explosion. Bridgestone and Hodaka have already established themselves as the leading me-too brands and Kawasaki charges on the scene with a high-performance attitude that mimics that of Pontiac. By the end of the decade, they have all done their part to encourage enthusiasts to forget about tiddlers and move up to *real* motorcycles.

1970 – 1974: With the exception of a few stragglers such as the Kawasaki G3 and the unprecedented success of the three Honda 350 models, the tiddler invasion becomes obviously past its zenith by the middle of the decade. Triumph, BSA, and many others have either vanished from the U. S. market or they are on their way out the door.

1975 – 1979: The Gold Wing debuts, taking Honda deep into Electra Glide territory. Interest in tiddlers from The Big Four has waned considerably, leaving the few remaining models with highly reliable engineering, but boring styling and lackluster performance.

1980 – 1984: There is a new mini-boom in engine technology, cruiser styling, and what will later be called *bullet bikes*. Harley-Davidson will finally face and embrace its chopper heritage. Blazingly fast and/or heavily styled large machines from The Big Four will dominate the market with low prices for the last time.

23

1985 – 1989: Honda introduces the ubiquitous Rebel and I declare that Honda has *finally* decided that Harley-Davidson knew something they didn't back when they sold Hummers and Super 10's with Buckhorn handlebars, teardrop gas tanks and swayback Buddy Seats! Yamaha did them one better by offering the Route 66, and the later Virago 250, with a genuine V-twin engine.

1990 – 1994: Aprilia makes a name for itself with its beautifully designed and engineered Scarabeo scooter in 1993. Old scooter brands make a comeback and new ones from Asia join the market. Scooters ride higher in reputation than anytime before or since.

1995 – 1999: The high-priced Harley-Davidson Mania for doctors, dentists, and Wall Streeters is in full swing. Those guys wearing the silly *doo-rags* may have drilled out your cavities, but they never beat anyone up with a pool cue.

2000 – 2004: The boom in monster-sized bikes with monster price tags continues unabated. Even scooters cost $3000. You may as well buy a Honda Rebel with those prices.

2005 – 2009: Katrina and the Housing Bubble Pop was not the name of a girl group, but they effectively did a number on the many unsuspecting young males who dreamed of owning a pricey Gold Wing, Ninja, or Fat Boy.

2010 - 2013: Little seems to have changed in our world or anyone else's, either. We are all wallowing through the fog of a corporately-controlled, middle-class limbo. We may as well take off our helmets and kick back with a nostalgic book about our adolescent dreams.

Figure B6 - 1969 Kawasaki Full Line Brochure Front Page. ©1969 Kawasaki Motors Corporation, U.S.A.

Contemporary Performance Test Comparison Chart

Model	Wt.	HP	0 - 60	1/4	Top Speed
Benelli 200 Sprite (*CW* 5/65)	228	20	13.0	19.0	NA
Benelli Barracuda 250 (*CW* 9/68)	259	29	7.5	15.9	86 mph
Benelli Phantom 250 (*Cycle* 11/73)	309	NA	NA	16.8	85 mph
Benelli Mojave 360 (*CW* 8/68)	308	27	10.3	17.7	74 mph
BMW 250 R-27 (*CW* 5/64)	360	18	21.5	21.5	84 mph
Bridgestone Dual Twin 175 (*CW* 2/66)	282	20	NA	17.8	81 mph
Bridgestone 350 GTR (*Cycle* 8/67)	362	37	NA	14.3	104 mph
Bridgestone 350 GTR (*CW* 8/67)	355	37	NA	15.0	NA
Bridgestone 350 GTO (*CW* 10/70)	369	40	6.6	15.2	94 mph
BSA 250 Starfire (*Cycle* 9/69)	325	NA	7.8	17.3	79 mph
BSA SS-90 350 (*CW* 7/63)	328	NA	11.1	17.7	82 mph
BSA 750 Rocket Three (*CG* 9/71)	455	58	NA	13.5	118 mph
Bultaco 250 Metralla Mk. 2 (*CW* 9/67)	241	27.6	9.0	16.1	96 mph
Ducati 250 Scrambler (*CW* 8/62)	277	30	11.5	17.3	82 mph
Ducati Monza 250 (*CW* 5/63)	292	24	11.4	17.4	77 mph
Ducati Diana Mark III 250 (*CW* 12/63)	265	30	9.2	16.5	104 mph
H-D Sprint H 250 (*CW* 4/63)	280	21	15.0	19.2	76 mph
H-D Sprint CRTT 250 (*CW* 8/63)	245	28.5	7.6	17.5	116 mph
H-D Sprint CRS 250 (*CW* 1/66)	265	28	6.5	16.0	84 mph
H-D Sprint SS-350 (*CW* 11/68)	323	25	8.0	15.8	92 mph
Honda 90 (*Cycle* 6/64)	188	6.5	NA	NA	56 mph
Honda CB-160 (*CW* 5/65)	276	16.5	12.3	18.6	NA
Honda CL-175 (*CW* 10/68)	269	20	11.5	18.5	77 mph
Honda 250 Hawk (*CW* 6/63)	350	25	11.2	17.6	82 mph
Honda Super Hawk 305 (*CW* 5/62)	351	28	NA	16.8	105 mph
Honda 305 Scrambler (*CW* 12/65)	337	27.4	9.0	16.7	90 mph

Honda CB-350 (*Cycle* 5/68)	353	36	11.5	15.5	103 mph
Honda CL-350 (*Cycle* 5/68)	346	33	11.6	15.6	100 mph
Honda 350K2 Motosport (*CW* 12/70)	320	30	8.2	16.0	78 mph
Honda CL-450 (*CW* 5/68)	399	45	4.3	14.9	106 mph
Honda 550F Super Sport (*CW* 8/75)	441	NA	5.0	13.8	108 mph
Honda 750 Four (*CW* 8/69)	499	67	5.2	13.4	123 mph
Honda 750F Super Sport (*Cycle* 5/75)	538	58	5.0	12.9	NA
Honda 1000 Gold Wing (*Cycle* 4/75)	647	80	NA	12.9	NA
Honda 1000 Gold Wing (*CW* 4/75)	626	NA	4.0	13.1	129 mph
Kawasaki G3-TR 90 (*CG* 6/69)	180	NA	18.3	NA	62 mph
Kawasaki Samurai SS 250 (*Cycle* 6/67)	331	31	6.3	14.9	91 mph
Kawasaki 250 Samurai SS (*CW* 7/70)	352	31	7.2	15.6	92 mph
Kawasaki F5 Bighorn 350 (*CW* 1/70)	278	33	6.9	15.8	85 mph
Kawasaki 350 Avenger (*CG* 8/71)	360	42	NA	14.3	103 mph
Kawasaki Mach II 350 (*Cycle* 11/71)	352	45	5.4	14.9	95 mph
Kawasaki Mach III 500 (*Cycle* 4/69)	396	60	4.0	12.8	125 mph
Kawasaki 650 W1 (*CW* 8/66)	476	50	NA	15.6	101 mph
Kawasaki H2 750 (*Cycle* 12/71)	449	72	4.1	12.8	125 mph
Kawasaki 900 Z-1 (*CG* 10/72) - FT	539	82	NA	12.4	NA
Kawasaki 900 Z-1 (*CW* 3/73)	543	82	NA	12.6	120 mph
Marusho 500 ST (*CW* 12/64)	423	35.6	13.1	18.6	79 mph
Marusho 500 Magnum Electra (*CW* 5/67)	406	40	NA	15.7	96 mph
Montesa King Scorpion 250 (*CW* 9/70)	274	23	10.1	17.5	74 mph
Mustang Thoroughbred 320 (*CW* 9/63)	220	9.5	NA	20.1	71 mph
Ossa 230 Scrambler (*CW* 8/67)	221	25	8.6	17.7	68 mph
Puch 250 SG (*CW* 2/63)	340	14	22.0	22.0	66 mph
Sears SR-125 (*Cycle* 1/69)	198	12	NA	NA	64 mph
Sears SR 250 (*CW* 11/68)	315	16.5	16.6	18.8	78 mph
Suzuki Stinger 125 (*Cycle* 9/69)	227	15.1	NA	NA	70 mph
Suzuki X-5 Invader 200 (*CW* 5/67)	272	23	NA	17.4	88 mph

Suzuki 250 X-6 Hustler (*CW* 10/65)	305	29	6.0	15.3	92 mph
Suzuki 250 Savage (*CG* 12/69)	280	23	9.2	NA	82 mph
Suzuki 305 Raider (*CW* 10/68)	332	37	7.0	16.2	94 mph
Suzuki GT-380 Sebring (*CW* 6/72)	392	38	NA	14.6	98 mph
Suzuki T500-III (*CW* 10/70)	423	47	6.2	14.3	106 mph
Suzuki GT-550 Indy (*CW* 1/73)	472	50	NA	14.6	98 mph
Suzuki GT-750 LeMans (*CW* 12/71)	524	67	NA	13.9	107 mph
Suzuki GT-750 LeMans (*Cycle* 5/75)	556	57	4.8	13.3	NA
Suzuki RE-5 Rotary (*CW* 9/75)	617	62	NA	14.8	102 mph
Triumph 250 Trophy (*CW* 8/70)	348	22	9.6	17.7	83 mph
Yamaha 250 YDS-2 (*CW* 1/63)	338	25	7.9	16.9	90 mph
Yamaha 250 TD-1 (*CW* 1/63)	228	32	7.3	15.5	102 mph
Yamaha Ascot 250 (*CW* 11/63)	235	35	5.8	14.2	89 mph
Yamaha DT-1 250 (*CW* 2/68)	235	22	11.1	19.2	71 mph
Yamaha Cross Country 305 (*CW* 7/66)	343	29	NA	15.1	98 mph
Yamaha YR2 350 (*CW* 6/68)	361	36	6.5	15.6	103 mph
Yamaha YR2C 350 (*CW* 6/68)	361	36	7.7	16.2	96 mph
Yamaha 350 R3 (*CG* 8/69)	340	36	7.5	NA	99 mph
Yamaha R5 350 (*CW* 6/70)	326	36	6.4	15.5	95 mph
Yamaha RD-350 (*CW* 2/73)	344	28	NA	14.3	99 mph
Yamaha XS-500 (*CW* 6/75)	459	NA	6.3	14.3	103 mph
Yamaha XS-650 (*CW* 3/70)	428	53	5.4	14.2	105 mph
Yamaha TX-750 (*Cycle* 3/73)	518	NA	NA	13.7	110 mph
Zundapp KS-100 ISDT (*Cycle* 5/68)	186	9.3	NA	NA	56 mph

Notes: All weights are listed in pounds. The stated weight for the Z-1 is wet. The Benelli Barracuda as tested had an optional, dealer-installed hop-up kit. The *Cycle World* tests were with a half tank. *Cycle* used a half tank in 1971, but began reporting a full tank in 1973. *Cycle Guide* tested dry weights in 1969. *CG* was reporting a full tank in 1972. Basically, the *CW* tests were consistent with a half tank, but *Cycle* and *CG* started out reporting either dry weights or unstated details concerning the weight, sometimes reporting the manufacturer's claimed figure, but changed to reporting weights with full tanks beginning in 1972 or '73. The claimed dry weight of the Gold Wing was 584 pounds and the claimed top speed was 122 mph.

Figure B7 - Photo from 1969 Kawasaki Mach III Ad. ©1969 Kawasaki Motors Corporation, U.S.A.

Milestones

1947 - Piaggio Vespa
1948 - Harley-Davidson S-125 and Whizzer
1950 - Cushman Eagle
1951 - Allstate Cruisaire
1953 - Allstate 175 Twingle, Harley-Davidson ST-165, and Simplex Automatic
1954 - Allstate 250 Twingle & 125 Hardtail and Triumph Tiger Cub
1955 - Harley-Davidson Hummer and Yamaha 125 YA-1
1956 - Allstate Moped
1957 - Lambretta TV Series and Yamaha YD-1
1959 - H-D Topper, Honda 50, Benly 150 & Benly 125 SS, and Yamaha YDS-1
1960 - Honda Super Sports 50, CA-72 Dream 250 & CA-77 Dream 305
1961 - Honda Hawk & Super Hawk and Harley-Davidson Sprint
1962 - Ducati Diana 250, Honda CL-72 Scrambler, and Yamaha YDS-2 Sport
1963 - Honda 90 and Yamaha YG-1 Rotary Jet 80
1964 - Honda Super 90 & CB-160, Hodaka Ace 90, and Yamaha YG-1 Autolube
1965 - Honda CB-450 and Suzuki X-6 Hustler
1966 - Bultaco Metralla Mk. II, Honda CL-160, and Kawasaki W1 Commander
1967 - Kawasaki Samurai & Avenger
1968 - Bridgestone GTR, Honda CB/CL-350, Suzuki 500 Five, and Yamaha DT-1
1969 - Honda 750 Four & SL-350, Kawasaki Mach III, and Yamaha AT-1 & RT-1
1970 - Honda Trail 70 and Yamaha 650 XS-1
1972 - Kawasaki Mach II & Mach IV, and Suzuki GT-750 Water Buffalo
1973 - Kawasaki Z-1
1974 - Kawasaki KZ400 commuter
1975 - Honda Gold Wing and Suzuki RE-5
1984 - Yamaha RZ350
1985 - Honda Rebel
1986 - Kawasaki 250 Ninja
1987 - Yamaha YSR50
1988 - Yamaha Route 66 XV250
1993 - Aprilia Scarabeo

Figure B8 - Red 1967 Ducati Diana Mark III 250.
©Michael Kiernan, Classic Motorcycle Company, St. Louis, MO.

The Tiddler Hall of Fame (The Tiddlerosis Under 175cc Awards)

Allstate Moped - The Allstate Moped was the ubiquitous beginning, the bottom of the two-wheeled hierarchy in both power and price; however, it was readily available to any ambitious kid with a paper route and a Sears & Roebuck Catalog.

Vespa 125 / Allstate Cruisaire - The Vespa 125 probably sold a lot more editions in the USA as an Allstate Cruisaire, but I don't know that for a fact. What I do know is that there were many young punks out there in Small Town USA whose moms would not let them have a motorcycle, no matter how long and hard they begged. "Awwww.... please, Mom, it's just a scooter!"

Figure B9 - 1965 Allstate Cruisaire. This derivative of the Vespa 125 is red, like many of the Cruisaires produced. ©Michael Kiernan, Classic Motorcycle Company, St. Louis, MO.

Harley-Davidson Hummer - The Harley 125 was generally called the S model. The only genuine Hummer was a special economy version introduced in 1955, but whatever. The kid whose mom would let him have a real motorcycle, and lived near one of the big-city H-D dealers, wanted one of these. Before the Honda Revolution hit at least, the little Harley filled a kid's need for speed, up to about 50 mph, anyway.

Honda 50 Cub - What can I say? It's the Queen of the Tiddlers. It started the revolution all by its little electric-started, automatic-clutch self, with leg shields even!

Honda C110 Super Sports & Sports 50 - This was the *real motorcycle* version of the Cub. Not nearly as many were sold, but it was a lot more fun to look at and ride.

Honda CB-92R - This bike gets the award for being the most collectible of all the small Japanese machines. It was withdrawn from the U.S. market soon after it arrived. This was the race-kitted version of the standard CB-92, the second most collectible Honda.

Yamaha YG-1 Rotary Jet 80 - Yamaha went on the tiddler attack! For only about fifty bucks more than the Honda Sport 50, Yamaha offered a little machine with big-bike feel. It had a soft seat and man-sized handgrips (smaller than those of a Hummer, but distinctly larger than the common foo-foo grips of a Honda 50). The front forks were telescopic, the exhaust had a megaphone shape, and in contrast to the Hondas, there were few plastic parts. Best of all, a rotary valve made it go like stink! Within a year, the YG-1 would be used as a showcase to introduce oil injection.

Hodaka Ace 90 - The Ace 90 of 1964 was either long overdue or way ahead of its time, whichever way you want to look at it. It was a dual-purpose machine with a heavy emphasis in the dirt four years before Yamaha would bring out its DT-1. The Hodaka was built in Japan, but designed in Oregon. Its biggest claims to fame were a double-cradle tube frame and soft, long-travel suspension, things almost unheard of in the early years of Japanese tiddlers.

Honda Super 90 - Honda had to respond to Yamaha's YG-1 with something faster and sportier than its original Honda 90 and the S-90 filled the bill. How did it stack up against the YG-1? It had slower acceleration with a higher top speed. On looks and features, it was a tie. The S-90 sold more. After all, it was a Honda.

Honda Trail 90 - Speaking of selling, and selling, and selling, and... you get the picture.

Honda Benly Touring 150 - When a kid was able to move up above the single-cylinder putt-putt class, this was the most likely machine he graduated up to. The Benly was not particularly exciting. It wasn't even one of the sportier Honda models. It did have an SOHC twin with electric starter and could cruise at highway speeds and that seemed to be enough to make it a huge sales success.

Honda CL-160 - This model offered the most exciting Honda of the Sixties under the 175 class. It had a tube frame, twin carbs, crossbrace bars, crossover pipes, and those other Scrambler accoutrements. The CL-160's only blemishes were that horribly quiet single muffler, the fact that it came from the factory only in black, and its production was shorter than two years!

Kawasaki G3-SS/TR Bushmaster - This little Kaw was the Wal-Mart Superstore of tiddlers. It had everything you could want at an incredibly low price! Its features included a double cradle frame, 10.5-hp rotary valve 89cc engine with oil injection, speedo in a nacelle separate from the headlight, and big-bike feel and styling. Both the street and trail models were winners.

Yamaha AT-1 Enduro & Motocross - The DT-1 is too large for this list, so the award goes to its little brother. Like the G3 above, both models were excellent. Both were far better trail bikes than the G3, but at a much higher price.

Suzuki AS-50 Colt/Maverick - Was this the sportiest, sexiest-looking 50 ever built or what? No, of course it did not have the racing technology of the modern Aprilia RS 50, but for a 1968-70 machine, it was the cat's meow. The marketplace had left the 50cc class behind by the end of the Sixties, so it was never a common machine on the streets of America.

Photo B10 - This rare early brochure of the 1968 Suzuki Colt shows a lovely model posing with her petite helmet perched atop a very sporting 50cc motorcycle. ©1968 Suzuki Motor of America, Inc.

Chart Index Chart

This silly little exercise is to present you with a quick overview of the brands covered in this book. Every brand discussed herein is listed in five categories of vertical hierarchical order. Do not take these listings too seriously. Some of the categories were *very* difficult to arrange, such as the market size; i.e., then or now and compared to what? The first column simply lists the brands alphabetically. The second column represents how quickly the brand gave up in the U.S. market. The center column is the order in which the brands are presented in the book. The fourth, as mentioned, is by far the most subjective, and just an educated guess at this point. The last column indicates how much space has been given to each brand. However, even this category is not that precise since some brands have more photos and others have more charts affecting their allotted space.

Alphabetical	End Date	Book Order	Market Size	Page Count
Allstate	DKW	Whizzer	DKW	Miyata
Benelli	Whizzer	Simplex	Miyata	Silver Pigeon
BMW	Silver Pigeon	Mustang	Rex	Ossa
Bridgestone	Yamaguchi	Cushman	Pointer	DKW
BSA	Miyata	Allstate	Yamaguchi	Montesa
Bultaco	Pointer	H-D	Silver Pigeon	Cushman
Cushman	Rex	DKW	Tohatsu	BMW
DKW	Mustang	NSU	Simplex	Zundapp
Ducati	Simplex	BMW	Mustang	NSU
H-D	Tohatsu	Zundapp	Whizzer	Whizzer
Hodaka	Marusho	Rex	Jawa / CZ	Simplex
Honda	Rabbit	Jawa / CZ	Ossa	Rex
Jawa / CZ	Cushman	Triumph	Montesa	Lambretta
Kawasaki	Lambretta	BSA	Motobi	Marusho
Lambretta	BSA	Vespa	Marusho	Jawa / CZ
Marusho	Triumph	Lambretta	Pointer	Vespa
Miyata	Ossa	Ducati	Rabbit	Benelli
Montesa	Montesa	Benelli	Yamaguchi	Rabbit
Motobi	Zundapp	Motobi	Lambretta	Yamaguchi
Mustang	Jawa / CZ	Montesa	Benelli	Pointer
NSU	Motobi	Ossa	NSU	Tohatsu
Ossa	NSU	Bultaco	Bultaco	NSU
Pointer	Benelli	Silver Pigeon	BSA	Motobi
Rabbit	Bultaco	Miyata	Triumph	BSA

Rex	Allstate	Yamaguchi	Vespa	Bultaco
Silver Pigeon	Bridgestone	Pointer	Hodaka	Ducati
Simplex	Hodaka	Rabbit	BMW	Triumph
Suzuki	Vespa	Tohatsu	Bridgestone	Allstate
Tohatsu	Ducati	Marusho	Suzuki	Hodaka
Triumph	BMW	Hodaka	Ducati	H-D
Vespa	Suzuki	Bridgestone	Allstate	Bridgestone
Whizzer	Kawasaki	Suzuki	H-D	Suzuki
Yamaguchi	Yamaha	Kawasaki	Kawasaki	Kawasaki
Yamaha	Honda	Yamaha	Yamaha	Yamaha
Zundapp	H-D	Honda	Honda	Honda

Contemporary Publications

We take motorcycle dealerships and magazines for granted now, but these benefits we enjoy were only just beginning during the 1955-75 timeframe of this book. From the point immediately after the end of World War II until 1959 motorcycles were distributed in the U.S. through few sources. These included a small number of big-city dealerships for Harley-Davidson, Triumph, BSA, BMW, Norton, and a few others. Cushmans were sold by dealers, lawnmower shops, and in the Sears catalog. The Montgomery Ward catalog marketed Mitsubishi Silver Pigeons. Sears added the Vespa scooter to its catalog choices in 1951 and began adding Puch models in 1953. Whizzer and Simplex built motorbikes and Mustang made midget motorcycles. There was comparatively little out there to satisfy the growing demand for small, affordable, motorized two-wheelers.

There was an even greater dearth of published printed matter. You could pick up a brochure at a dealership if you lived in or near a major city. The rest of us had to make do with the catalogs before they made their dubious journeys to the outhouses and bathrooms of America. The history of motorcycle-specific magazines begins with Robert E. Petersen, the publisher of *Hot Rod* and *Motor Trend*, the same man who would later publish the *Motorcycle Sport Books* and other derivatives listed in the Bibliography of this book. Petersen founded *Cycle* magazine in 1950 and sold it to Floyd Clymer in 1953. You can track the changes to this magazine in the Bibliography by noting the magazine's title as Clymer's name is removed when it is sold again in 1966. From 1985 until 2011, *Cycle* would be owned by the same publishing company as *Cycle World*.

At this point you may be asking why I claimed above that we did not have motorcycle magazines in the Fifties? The magazines then were a far cry from the advanced level they would reach by the mid-Sixties. Early motorcycle magazines reflected a sort of *club* mentality. There was lots of racing coverage and personal stories by and of the enterprising men involved in the sport, but road tests as we know them were yet to materialize. There were a few black-and-white ads cheaply created for publication and the ads usually coincided with whatever machines were being discussed in that particular issue. You might say these magazines were just a personification of a certain specialized *good old boy network*. If you were not already a member of the club, you were not likely to learn a whole lot about the machines for sale by reading these publications.

Cycle World changed all that when it launched in January 1962. This was the first magazine born after Hondas, Yamahas, and Suzukis had arrived on our shores in significant numbers that could no longer be ignored. These upstarts had little apparent homage to pay to the old-guard European brands that had been trickling onto the East Coast for years. *Cycle World* would be the publication that readily compared any member of the old-guard to any member of the new, as long the two machines competed for the same customer. From this point forward a road test would mean something other than a reproduction of the manufacturer's specifications sheet. The *Cycle World* editors would tell truth to power in a manner new to the world of cycling in the USA. The advertising would grow exponentially until full-color, multi-page spreads from the major manufacturers would become common, not from just The Big Four, but from the European and American brands, too.

It didn't take *Cycle* long to figure out that competition had arrived. Readers could count on at least one or two road tests in every issue of both *Cycle World* and *Floyd Clymer's Motor Cycle*, as it was called back then. *Cycle* began publishing more articles and advertising from the Japanese brands to complement its extensive racing coverage. *Cycle World* never skimped on its racing coverage, either. From 1962-66 we had two formidable publications to look forward to each month. Then in 1967 we got a third.

Although the events did not occur at precisely the same time, *Cycle Guide* magazine was founded in 1967, the year that Kawasaki became really serious about its U.S. market penetration. Kawasaki had been exporting its big BSA copycat 650, its 125 Omega, and a few small models to the USA in limited numbers beforehand, but in 1967 the company launched its all-new Samurai 250 and the high-performance race was on! Latecomer *Cycle Guide* also took a somewhat different approach. Where *Cycle* and *Cycle World* seemed to be direct competitors like Suzuki and Yamaha, *Cycle Guide* appealed more to the future motorcycle buyer and less to the racer or hardcore hobbyist. There were plenty of road tests in *Cycle Guide*, quite often of the same machines you would see in the other two magazines, but the *Cycle Guide* tests usually offered a different opinion. The *CG* tests may have been less instrumented, but the content offered a pleasant alternative to their competitors.

Motorcyclist predated the publications referenced in the Bibliography by a decade or more, but that publication has little to offer to the specific subject matter of this book that the referenced publications have not covered thoroughly. I have a collection of the *Harley-Davidson Enthusiast* from the Sixties, too, but that publication has also not been referenced. Others not applicable to this book are *Rider, Road Rider, Motor Cycle World, Popular Cycling, Big Bike*, and the newspaper-styled *Cycle News*. This is now and that was then. Do you see why those few motorcycle pages in every new Sears catalog were so precious?

A Few Questions & Answers

Q. What tiddlers were available in the U.S. prior to the Japanese invasion of 1960?

A. *Harley-Davidson* built its line of 125cc and 165cc two-stroke singles. *Cushman* sold the Eagle, Highlander, and other scooter models. Sears sold the *Allstate* line of motorcycles and scooters. *Mustangs* were built as simple motorcycles with small diameter wheels. *Simplex* and *Whizzer* built motorbikes. *Vespa* sent its scooters from Italy, and a few *Lambrettas* may have been imported in the Fifties, too. Small numbers of 175cc-350cc *BSA's* and *Triumphs* were imported. A small, scattered number of models were imported from various other British and Italian brands.

Q. What Japanese brands came to the U.S. in the early Sixties?

A. *Honda* began shipping its models in the summer of 1959, with the aggressive plan of setting up many dealerships. *Suzuki* followed closely behind Honda, but the company kept its territory much more closely inside California, spreading very carefully and slowly to other parts of the country. *Yamaha* may have actually entered the U.S. market slightly before Suzuki. Yamaha was much more interested in racing and distribution expansion than was Suzuki. It is no coincidence that many early Yamahas were named after California racetracks such as Ascot and Catalina. Yamaha also already had a booming piano and guitar business, so they had a jump on the competition in the development of a U.S. dealer network. *Yamaguchi* arrived and left early to the U.S. market. The company hardly had time to develop a strong dealer network for their sporty 50cc models before the factory back in Japan was bleeding red ink. *Tohatsu* stayed a little longer than Yamaguchi, but not much. They later developed a substantial market in small to moderately sized outboards for U.S. fishermen. *Pointer* sent a small number of six models to the U.S. in approximately 1961-64, although some sources say it was only 1961-62. *Mitsubishi* imported a very small number of its Silver Pigeon scooters, probably no later than 1962. *Rabbit* imported a small line of technically advanced scooters from about 1962-67. *Bridgestone* entered the U.S. market in 1963 with their fan-cooled 50cc Super 7 and a companion step-through model. The company developed models with advanced features and commensurate higher prices than the competition. They quit building bikes in 1971 to concentrate on manufacturing tires, which was their primary business anyway. *Hodaka* was born from the ashes of Yamaguchi. Pabatco, the U.S. importer in Oregon, contracted with the Japanese engine builder for Yamaguchi, Hodaka, to build a 90cc two-stroke engine that the Pabatco people could install into a single trail model designed specifically for the U.S. market. The Ace 90 began to be marketed in 1964 in a manner similar to the VW Beetle as one model that receives constant developmental updates. *Kawasaki* was the last to enter the U.S. in 1966, but they didn't step gently into the market. They roared in with motorcycles designed for American riders. Their machines were slightly larger, heavier, and more performance oriented than the competition. You could sum it all up this way. Honda was interested in racing, reliability, and massive sales. Suzuki was interested in deluxe features and niche marketing. Yamaha was interested in racing, high performance, and technical development. Kawasaki was interested in street performance and sales. Their respective auto company images might be: Honda = Honda; Suzuki = Mazda; Yamaha = Ford; and Kawasaki = Pontiac. You did know that Yamaha developed the engines for the Toyota 2000 GT, the Ford Taurus SHO, and the Lotus Elise, didn't you?

Q. What colors were available for the Honda models?

A. From the time the Hondas began arriving in the U.S. in late 1959 until just prior to the introduction of the all-new 350's in 1968, practically all Honda models were offered in only four colors. Depending on the model, black or red was far the most common color. White was the third most common and blue was the least. Some models, such as the first generation CB-450 and the earliest CL-160's, came only in black. Some models were offered only in a choice of black or red. The sole common exception to this black-red-white-blue color selection seems to be the yellow that was offered as the only alternative to red on the ubiquitous Trail 55 and Trail 90 models. The CB/CL 350's ushered in a new era of styling heavily influenced by Triumph, leaving many of the previous Oriental distinctions behind.

Q. How can the colors be used to identify the various Yamaha Enduro models?

A. Yamaha introduced the DT-1 to an anxiously anticipatory American trail riding public in 1968. The instant success of the DT-1 led to increasing numbers of variants in the following years. From the beginning, Yamaha offered these models with black frames and silver fenders. Only the gas tanks and side covers carried the distinctive color patterns on the Motocross models. The headlight brackets and shells were also color-coordinated on the Enduro models. Each displacement of each model year displayed its own color that was unique to that model. The colors were traded back and forth among models throughout the years, but not within any given year; i.e., the '68 250's were white, then the '69 125's were white while the '69 250's were red. The first letter of the model number denotes the displacement: A (125cc) - C (175cc) - D (250cc) - J (90cc) - R (360cc), The third digit, after the T for Trail, denotes the series and the fourth letter denotes the consecutive year for that displacement. For instance, an AT-1C is a 1971 125cc, denoting the third production year of the 125cc displacement in the series. If you know the displacement and any appropriate trim details, you can properly identify the year and correct paint of any of these classic Yamaha Enduro and Motocross models.

Winners & Losers

Step-Throughs: The Honda 50 is the obvious winner in this category by a mile. Yamaha brought in its homely MF-1 and its more attractive MF-2 and MJ-2 in the early Sixties. Both the latter models looked much like the successful Honda, except with two-stroke engines, of course. The MF-1 had an electric starter and the other two Yamahas were offered with or without it, as was the Honda. All the Yamahas were quite rare, even in their heyday, as were the similar Bridgestone and Suzuki models. Honda continued to produce the only four-stroke step-through models, even up through the later 90cc versions. Rabbit, Pointer, Miyata, Benelli, Harley-Davidson, and even Ducati once offered step-through models, but none were very successful in the U.S. marketplace. Embarrassingly to all the hog fans, the sole exception was the H-D M-50 and M-65 that sold like hotcakes during the years they were offered, especially early on until the novelty wore off. Probably the most successful pre-Honda models were the Allstate Moped and Compact sold via the Sears & Roebuck catalog.

50 Sports: The Honda 50 Super Sport was the first to arrive here at the end of 1960, and its later iteration, the four-speed Honda Sport 50 continued to dominate the market up through its final production year in 1968. Suzuki and Bridgestone gave it the old college try with several quality models in this category through the mid-Sixties. The Suzuki Colt introduced in 1968 was the epitome of sportiness in a 50cc model. Strangely, Yamaha never entered this particular market niche until the mid-Sixties, and these Yamahas were little distinguishable from their larger, more legendary brothers. Ducati and Benelli, among a few other Europeans, tried hard to sell Americans sporty tiddlers with tube frames and other grownup accoutrements, but their market success was minimal.

The First Step Up: The first of those legendary brothers was the Yamaha YG-1 Rotary Jet 80. Although only 73cc, its lightweight, modern styling, and high performance (for such a mosquito) were ground-breaking enough to put Yamaha on the USA map! Honda's original CA-200 90 had been a snooze, but the release of the S-90 in late 1964 woke everybody up. Although Suzuki and Kawasaki offered numerous variations on the slightly up market bracket between 50cc and 100cc, few were particularly strong sellers. Both brands tried quite successfully to offer models with upscale and sporting features such as chrome fenders, luggage racks, upswept pipes, and trail versions, but none could surpass the sales of the YG-1 and S-90. Yamaha enjoyed enough success with its Twin Jet 100 to keep it in the line for several years. Ducati promoted this category, too, but the limited distribution and hand shifts held back their numbers.

Trail Tiddlers: The Honda and Yamaha step-through trail 50's began the trend respectively with four-stroke and two-stroke models in 1961 and '62. Ironically, the two-stroke Yamaha that any housecat could kickstart was the one with the electric starter! Cushman, Benelli, Ducati and others tried unsuccessfully to crack this market after Honda opened the door. Honda would up their displacement to 90cc and it would become one of the most ubiquitous motorcycles ever built. Yamaha moved their models up to 80cc. The step-through 80 would become a rare bird, but the direct companion to the YG-1 would build a reputation as a butt-kicker on the racetrack. Suzuki, Kawasaki, and Bridgestone built many models to compete with the Hondas and Yamahas, although few gained much notoriety despite their many innovative design features. The shining upstart of the era was most certainly Hodaka, a company that built *only* trail tiddlers and did it very well!

THE YAMAHA 80 TRAILMASTER BY YAMAHA COMES TO YOU FULLY EQUIPPED
INCLUDING STURDY ENGINE GUARD PLATE, FRONT FENDER, NEW TYPE CARBURETOR
WITH BUILT-IN QUICK START FEATURE, OVERSIZE REAR SPROCKET.
TRY IT AND YOU'LL BUY IT FOR TRAILING, HUNTING, FISHING WEEK-END FUN!!!

SPECIFICATIONS OF THE YAMAHA 80 MODEL YG-1T

DIMENSIONS		Ignition System	Battery Ignition
Overall Length	71 inches	TRANSMISSION	
Overall Width	25 "	Primary Reduction System	Gear
Overall Height	38 "	Second Reduction System	Chain
Wheelbase	45 "	Clutch	Wet-Type Multi-Plate
Net Weight	140 pounds	Transmission	Constant Mesh Forward
PERFORMANCE		Tire Front	2.50×16 4 ply
Max. Speed	41 MPH	Tire Rear	2.50×16 4 ply
Climbing Ability	30 degrees	Brakes Front	By Right Hand
Braking Distance	23 feet (22 MPH)	Brakes Rear	By Right Foot
ENGINE		Suspension Front	Telescopic
Model	YAMAHA (YG-1)	Suspension Rear	Swing Arm
Type	2-cycle Gasoline Engine	Cushion Front	Coil Spring, Oil Damper
Cooling System	Air-Cooled	Cushion Rear	Coil Spring, Oil Damper
Number of Cylinders	1	Tank Capacity	1.72 Galons
Max. Torque	0.47 lbs-ft/5,000 r.p.m.	Oil Mixing Ratio	20 : 1
Starting System	Kick Starter		

YAMAHA INTERNATIONAL CORPORATION

EASTERN BRANCH
YAMAHA INT'L CORP., U.S. Route 30 & Rell
Lane Downing Town, Penna. Phone 269 1611

Figure B11 - 1964 Red Yamaha YG-1T Trailmaster Brochure. ©1964 Yamaha Motor Corporation, U.S.A.

125's: The DKW design basically owned this class from WWII until the mid-Sixties when Suzuki and Kawasaki began to get creative. Far more Harley S models and Hummers were sold than BSA Bantams or Yamaha 125cc derivatives. Honda abandoned the 125 class in the U.S. market almost immediately after arrival, leaving the class open to Yamaha, who built a long succession of models. Kawasaki marketed a variety of models in this class, but none caught fire in the sales department. The same could be said for Suzuki with the additional comment that a few of the Suzis, such as the Stinger and Wolf, were particularly innovative in design.

150-200's: Honda's ubiquitous Benly Touring 150 and 160 covered the USA with its *Junior Dream* styling and performance. Ducati and Harley-Davidson fought gallantly to capitalize on this in-between class, but Honda was king, not only with the Benlys, but the CB and CL 161cc models are clearly treasured classics. Yamaha, Kawasaki, Bridgestone, and later Honda, produced a few very deluxe models in this size class, but none were ever sold in particularly large numbers.

Figure B12 - Black Honda CA-160. ©Troyce Walls

250's: Honda all but abandoned the 250 class after introducing the CL-72 Scrambler in 1962. This model would be produced in relatively small numbers until the CL-77 305cc version was put into production in 1965. Harley-Davidson hung tough until the end with its Aermacchi Sprint series until the only way to go was up market. In spite of the blistering performance of the Honda and Kawasaki twins, the most valuable and treasured 250's today surely are the Ducati Diana, Bultaco Metralla, and BMW R-27. Honda would soon abandon the class altogether, at least for the U.S. market. In contrast, the 250's continued to be the stars produced by Yamaha and Suzuki, particularly the YDS and X-6 models. Kawasaki would finally get serious about the American market with the release of its Samurai 250, but its fame was short-lived due to the larger models on the high-performance horizon. Bridgestone would skip the class altogether with its 350cc GTR and GTO.

305's: While 250cc machines had always set the class standard, mostly based on racing rules, Honda began its one-upmanship of building 305cc street machines in 1959. Yamaha and Suzuki countered with two-stroke competitors, but few of these dented the Honda juggernaut in this market segment. Many of their 250cc two-stroke sports models were already quicker than the Honda four-strokes anyway.

350's: The Triumphs and BSA's were here long before the arrivals from the Orient, but one look at the puddles on the floor after the Dreams and Super Hawks impressed buyers with electric starter buttons and it was soon all over but the whining about Lucas Electrics, Prince of Darkness. Kawasaki warmed up the market for its upcoming Mach III in 1967 with the introduction of its Avenger, the highest-performance twin of the time. The Avenger's only problem was that it was a bit *too* overstressed and quickly built an undesirable reputation. In contrast, Yamaha's RD-350 would become the darling of the racetrack, as well as road riders seeking a finely honed, high-performance handler for the street. Bridgestone produced a pair of high-quality 350's briefly toward the end of the company's motorcycle production. Although their reputations were good, high retail prices and few dealerships doomed them to relatively low production figures.

Enduros: Although many European factories, most notably Bultaco, Montesa, and Ducati, had been producing machines for serious off-road work for years, Yamaha set the mass-market loose on the fire roads of America with its DT-1 in 1968. Kawasaki responded with a line of Enduros that tended to be full-featured but overly heavy. The Suzuki models had much the same problem. Honda stuck with their four-stroke SL and XL models until late in the game when the company introduced its first two-strokes to the U.S. market. Although obviously lighter than the XL models still in the lineup, these new two-stroke competitors were mostly known for being somewhat slow and boring.

Motocrossers: The first serious dirt racer to enter the U.S. from Japan was the Yamaha Ascot. This super-rare, pioneering, 250 twin off-roader was more flat-tracker than motocrosser. Bridgestone would later test the market with 100cc and 175cc models in a similar vein, and these are of course also very rare. The Spanish brands produced many competitive models during the same period, and so did firms such as Maico and Penton. The first really successful factory motocrossers from Japan were the GYT-kitted Yamaha Enduros. Competition soon successfully sprang up from Honda with the Elsinores and later from Suzuki with its first TM, and later RM, models. Hodaka would compete in small numbers with its Super Rat and Combat Wombat models. Kawasaki brought up the rear in this class with several models produced, but few known for effectiveness on the track.

400's: Norton tried to market a twin in this class in the early Sixties, with an electric starter, no less, but the Electra was and is a rare sight on any American road. Kawasaki offered a double-barreled assault on the 400 class in the early '70's with its S3, the bigger, more tractable brother of the wild and crazy Mach II 350, and the KZ400 SOHC twin. The former was a fire-breathing drag strip demon and the latter was a mellow commuter, albeit a very successful model on the sales floor.

450's: When Honda unleashed its 450 *Humpback Black Bomber* in the '65 model year, it was the first Japanese model over 305cc, aside from the BSA-copycat Kawasaki W1. Although a bit cumbersome in both style and feel, the Honda CB-450 would eventually become one of the most ubiquitous Hondas. This displacement class has remained pretty much uncontested by the other three brands.

500's: Once upon a time the Triumph Daytona was considered the finest machine in this class; however, its antique heritage eventually caught up with it. Ditto the BSA models of similar type and heritage, even though BSA offered more competition variants. The BMW 500 class has always been the victim of Middle Child Syndrome, so these competent machines rarely affected anyone's blood pressure. The 1969 Mach III blazed a trail for Kawasaki that would establish the brand as the Kings of Speed on the street for decades to come. The first Honda 500 Four became famous as the smoothest of all motorcycle engine designs, and this reputation would continue all the way through the Nighthawk 550 of 1983. Yamaha introduced one of the earliest DOHC twins with its 500 in 1972, but its mediocre performance and high price doomed it to be a low production model.

Figure B13 - Green 1970 Yamaha 650 XS-1. ©Michael Kiernan, Classic Motorcycle Company, St. Louis, MO.

650's: The reigning king for decades was the Triumph Bonneville, still a treasured machine today. The other 650 Trumpets and Beezers followed in its tire tracks, at least until Yamaha showed buyers a more reliable, but similar machine. Kawasaki produced a copycat of the BSA big twin for a number of years without particularly strong sales numbers. With its vertically split engine cases, kickstarter, and separate transmission, the W-1 and its later derivatives truly were copies of the BSA twins of the early '60's. Yamaha produced an instant cult classic with the introduction of its XS-1 in 1970. The XS-1 sought to replicate the positive attributes of the BSA twin with updated Japanese technology such as reliable electrics, non-leaking, horizontally-split engine cases, five-speed transmissions, and SOHC engine designs. Honda would introduce a four-cylinder 650cc machine much later, but it would be overshadowed by Honda's own high-tech Nighthawk 650 in 1983.

750's: The Norton Atlas was tested as going from 0-30 mph in 1.1 second back about 1963, and its many Commando descendants are minor legends in the big-bike world. The Triumph and BSA Triples are probably very collectible by now, and the top British triple is certainly the Triumph Hurricane with its American styling job. Honda obviously defined the four-stroke Four class for all time in 1969. Yamaha's ill-fated TX-750 Twin never became much of a success. Kawasaki ruled the quarter-mile roost for a brief period with the H2 Mach IV Triple, at least until their own Z-1 changed everything the very next year in 1973. Suzuki was the first to offer a water-cooled two-stroke triple, but its sales paled in competition with the blazingly quick Kawasakis. Suzuki would effectively compete in the 750cc four-stroke marketplace much later, first with its GS750 and then later with the racetrack-ready GSX-R.

900-1000's: Two pioneers dominated this class for decades. The Kawasaki Z-1 would own the performance market, first as a 903cc, then as a full liter, and the Honda Gold Wing would raise the bar for big touring machines into the stratosphere of highways to oblivion. Honda, Suzuki, and Yamaha would all enter this market with many successful liter machines in later years after 1975. No matter how successful they were on the sales floor, the Japanese machines take a back seat to a few key Europeans and a couple of Americans in the collectible department. These include, in alphabetical order because I don't want to start a fight, the Benelli Sei, BMW R-90S and R-100S, Ducati 900SS, and the Harley-Davidson XLCR and XR-1000. The sole rice-grinder in this elite group is probably the 1979 Honda CBX.

Figure B14 - 1973 Kawasaki Z-1 First Year Brochure. ©1973 Kawasaki Motors Corporation, U.S.A.

The Emotions of Styling

Figure B15 - Black & Silver Bultaco Metralla Mk. II. Image by Jordi Carrasco under Creative Commons license.

Let me begin by saying that I have a *thing* for *skinny*, as opposed to *fat*, motorcycles. Of course I find machines such as the Harley-Davidson *Cowglide* and *Fat Boy* quite interesting style-wise, but I would never seriously lust after one. Longtime readers of my Tiddlerosis website from years back already know that I am obsessed with Honda Scramblers, certain Yamahas, the Ducati Diana, the Kaw H-1 Mach III, and of course, the Bultaco Metralla. In the latter case, I am not interested in just any Metralla, only the black and silver model from approximately 1970. I like the exact same look in red, but not nearly as well as the black one. I think this is mostly because the model has a red tank with the same black frame, headlamp, and fork covers as the black model, so the black one appears a little more *pure* to me in its styling, even though I usually prefer a red motorcycle over the black version of the same model.

Here is the unusual part about the Bultaco Metralla. Taken individually, I do not much care for a single component of this machine! I do not like the white area, for a European license number I presume, on the front fender. I don't like the rear support on the front fender not being matched by one in the front. I don't like that big, long blob of a headlamp shape. I prefer rubber gaiters to solid black front fork covers. I do not care for that flip-open gas cap, the lack of chrome on the machine, or the air filter that looks like an ashtray. I hate the fact that the shifter is on the right and the kickstarter is on the left. I am not crazy about the look of Akront rims and the shape of the exhaust pipe is boring. If I think of anything else to fuss about, I shall let you know.

Figure B16 - Black Honda CA-160. Note the thin wall tires. ©Troyce Walls

After the *skinny* concept, the next thing I look for in styling is how well a machine appeals to the eye in its overall look, and finally, I give large points to a machine that operates upon the KISS Principle, and the Metralla gets five stars in all three of these criteria. I may not think much of the styling of the individual components of the Metralla, but I love the total effect! There is not an unnecessary pound on this bike. It has little chrome because chrome parts are heavy. Every component is as simple and light as it can be. If the Metralla was a car, it most certainly would be a Lotus, a brand that rightfully prides itself on the ultimate development and utilization of lightness and simplicity to produce high performance from its delicate machines. I am sure that I shall never like the Metralla's right-side shifter or its magneto lighting and ignition, but I love the way its looks and function combine to make it one of my favorite tiddlers of all time.

Let's take a little detour into the larger world of motorcycles of the '60's, '70's, & '80's, examining and comparing some of the key Japanese machines with their American and European competition. The kind of scooters of importance here range from 50cc to 1000cc, but no larger. At the time I began riding motorcycles, a 250cc would have been almost too large for me and a 50cc was not necessarily too small. At my current age, a 250 is a good starting point and any 750 is plenty large. Any mega-tourer is a Queen Mary on wheels. My interest in motorcycles began at the beginning of the Japanese invasion. I learned to ride on a Harley Super 10 (a 1960 165cc two-stroke single, made in America, with optional handlebars, Buddy Seat, and saddlebags). My second ride was on a Honda 150 Benly Touring, followed by a Cushman Eagle, Allstate Cruisaire, Honda 50 Cub (3-speed Super Sport), and several regular Cubs. A guy down the street had a Triumph Tiger Cub (mostly for legendary atmospherics, since it rarely ran, but I can personally swear that I have seen it rattle down the block at least once). I feel very fortunate to have at least experienced the pre-Honda expression of two-wheeling. These are the stories of the motorcycles that run over me where I live. In this realm scooters are experiences, and size and value have little relevance.

The emotional desire for *high performance motorcycle satisfaction* was first quenched with the Harley-Davidson Sportster in 1957. The angelwing bars, sloping seat, bologna pipes, fat handgrips, and of course, the boogety-boogety sound all contributed to the Sportster's feel, and mystique. Essentially an American definition of macho, this two-wheeled Corvette was the first real Superbike of the modern U.S. era (never mind the Europeans). Before 1969, the advent year for Superbikes (Mach III, the Honda 750, and the British Triples), the Sportster held the field all to itself. Certainly the Norton Atlas could go from 0-30 mph in I.I second and outrun the Sportster to boot, but everybody knows the vibration of the Atlas twin shook the machine apart constantly, and what good is the fastest bike if it won't stay in one piece? The sounds of the pioneering superbikes are significant. The Mach Ill's "dub-dub-dub-dubbledy-bub" turned a lot of high performance enthusiasts off, but the Honda 750 had a sound similar to that of very expensive, high performance, OHC sports cars, which certainly helped its sales from the beginning. The most important aspect of a big-block Stingray and the Sportster is that in both you sit low in the saddle, while the engine bumps and grinds to the tune of "boogety-boogety".

Here is how little relevance I place on size when it comes to styling. I particularly like the Honda 50 Sport Cub of 1964-6, the CBX of 1979 in silver only, and the CBR 1000 in white only. After the whole pint-sized explosion was over, the littlest Sport 50 still seemed to be the best of the microscoots. It is the only one with (a) a zillion made for ridiculous reliability and parts availability, (b) a 4-stroke engine; (c) lasting styling (compared to its competition); and (d) full motorcycle appearance and operation. The 1979 CBX could be purchased in silver with a special Grand Prix kit attached (low bars and rear-sets, etc.), and oh, what a pig it was, but what a lesser pig it was in both operation and styling than anything else. There are only four Sixes: the slow Benelli Sei with weird styling, the super-pigs KZ 1300 tourer and Gold Wing, and this smooth, sleek, fast 1000cc Six, the CBX. The third one mentioned, the CBR 1000, has been offered in numerous guises, names and color schemes over the years, but the one in white, with gold pin-striping is the cat's meow of Japanese Superbike (faired) beauty.

From another part of the world comes the legendary Ducati Diana, a 250 cc four-stroke single of lightweight and simple construction, with a seat as hard as a board and handling for which it is famous. We get on it, we kick it over, and we scoot. There are no additional electronics or other complications. No concessions to comfort, just a simple sporting motorcycle. Motobi had 125cc and 175cc scooters of roughly the same type at the same time, but these are almost non-existent today, in this country anyway. Harley's Aermacchi Sprint series were relatives of the design, but the styling was spot on with certain years of the H series, which was a "dirt-type" style. The Dianas remain to this day a sort of benchmark for the 250 sportcycle.

Spain produced the Bultaco Metralla in the mid-Sixties and sent a certain model to the U.S. during this period that seems particularly appealing to me. All the later Metrallas and the related street Buls lacked a certain styling rightness attributed to the originally styled Metralla in black and silver. Although offered with a racing kit like the CBX and Diana, the appearance I like is the standard Metralla, without a fairing to obscure the lines of the machine. This is a characteristic of all my favorite motorcycles. The Metralla is a two-stroke 250cc single, obviously a pop-pop-popper, instead of a pow-pow-pow 4-stroke like the Diana.

The 1962 Yamaha YDS-2 had its own special smell because of the new-type two-stroke oil it burned. It was a lightly sweet aroma indigenous to Yamaha shops because the company was pioneering two-stroke development at the time, using a very high per-formance twin mixing their new Yamalube in lesser quantities than before. Want to know what really happened to the Metralla? The YDS-2 is the originator of the line of increasingly high-tech, high-performance two-stroke twins produced by Yamaha that dominated the market in 250 two-strokes from the YDS-2 -on. Formula: take one Metralla, double the cylinders and decrease the vibration, sweeten the sound, and most of all increase the flash and the marketing.

What does a motorcycle look like? A Triumph Tiger 500 Road/Sports. An 883 Sportster. A Nighthawk S. A Honda 250 Scrambler. Any Yamaha T-series Enduro. A Metralla. These are the purest of their respective designs and functions.

Fascinating details of the functions of several motorcycle designs have surfaced from the past. The Pointer Super Lassie most copies the Super Sport Cub in its styling, except it is a two-stroke with electric start and no kick starter! The Allstate 125/150 has no rear suspension and a 3-speed hand shift with clutch. The Allstate 250 was a "twingle": two pistons and one cylinder. The Rex KL-35 was a two-stroke 50cc single with twin carbs and twin exhausts! The H-D Pacer and Scat had a kick starter (non-folding) on the left side and the rear suspension was a big spring below the swingarm. The old Duo-Glides were offered with either a regular 4-speed or a 3-speed plus reverse gearbox. The Metralla has a unique oil tank with a manual pump to be utilized with every fill-up. Unlike the milder Dream engines, the Honda Super Hawk and Scrambler had a 180-degree crankshaft. The kick starter has a normal, but short arc on the Scrambler without an electric starter and one of the nicest exhaust sounds of all time. The Hawks had a kick and electric starter. The kick unit operated forward instead of backward, the high-rpm performance was beyond that of the Scrambler, and the sound was less enticing. The Cushman Eagle had a ratchet (non-spring-loaded) kick starter and a hand-operated 2-speed shift lever. The Metralla has a strip of suede sewn down the center of its seat to hold the rider in place. The CL-350 Honda

Scrambler (along with other Hondas) has a dual-tube exhaust system because the engines produce the most power with really skinny, less attractive, tube diameter systems and rusting was always a problem with the earlier ancestors of these models. All Triumphs looked great; they just did not sell that well due to vibration, which always affected their already delicate state of reliability.

The manufacturers have their engineering, inventions, and marketed developments that were successful. As noted above, Triumph had looks and handling down cold. Vertical twins with vertically split engine cases produced simple machines that were relatively easy to tinker with, but the vibration caused a need for lots of tinkering. Triumph invented the proper concept for a straight, versatile, simple and lightweight motorcycle. In a sense the Sportster is a Bonnie with an American attitude, a V-twin, and torque at the sacrifice of everything else. Honda was the first of the Japanese in the American market and their penetration has commanded the number one spot ever since. Engine technology and lasting styling are Honda's strong points on most all of their models and engine designs. Yamaha is far more concerned with individual accomplishments: oil injection, counter-balancers, eight-valve twins, Enduros, Monoshocks, etc. (and the list is long). The Kawasaki brand means designed for the American market more than usual, performance above all else, and solid reliable construction at a slight weight penalty. Suzuki is always the "me too" company with lots of features and value and sometimes flashes of fashion for the money with obviously less engineering clout than the competition.

The motorcycles I like the best have many characteristics in common. The footpegs are spring-loaded (except for all Honda 50's), rubber-covered, and positioned in the median range between full-tilt cruiser and hot-rod sportbike. The handlebars can be as low or high as the range stated above for footpegs and the styling must be perfect for its type. The engine must be fully exposed and the black/chrome styling of the engine must be correctly executed. With a few exceptions, all must have a downtube cradle type of frame and the color must be correctly chosen. All are air-cooled, and all are narrow (except the inline multis) -- if the engine is wide, the styling is still created to make the machine look sleek and narrow. The intent is usually street sprinting and small gas tanks are the norm purely for the sake of styling. The exhaust systems are considered a major component of the styling of all the machines and the system must be correctly styled, no matter what the configuration. With the exception of the 883, all the machines are high revvers with much less annoying vibrations in varying degrees and amplitudes. Blue color is usually preferred on most models, but black, white, silver, and red/silver are favorites also. I have no serious desire to own any motorcycle weighing over 500 pounds (official brochure weight) and the 416 pound Nighthawk 550 I recently owned for 28 years was simply the best compromise between high-speed road holding and low-speed garage handling. The bottom line why I like Japanese bikes is their low-maintenance qualities. It is obvious that the non-Japanese bikes mentioned are considered collector classics far more than the Japanese machines.

Harley-Davidson has my number in one certain way that if I did not value a lack of vibration and lots of go-power for the money so strongly, they would have already sold me an 883. The 1983 XLX-61 in black only at $3895 ($4295 list) was their first release and right move in the direction I sought. The 1986 883 got the same displacement as the original Sportster with lower insurance rates and the blue color for $3995. The nice price and color were still intact in 1988. The 1989's moved up to $4195 and the tank decals got uglied up! The '86-'88 in blue: that's the one, the real thing, the Stingray's pioneer pal, its soul-stirring torque defining its essence. Unfortunately, it vibrates with large amplitude and low frequency, from its front fender to its rear one... boogedy, boogedy, boogedy.

Back in the good old days we could make a lot more noise and feel a lot less immature about it than now, and noise was a key factor in the appeal of many of these machines. Each had their own signature, some pleasant and some not, but they all sound a lot better to me and a lot worse to a non-motorcyclist, no matter what the sound is like. To my ears any four or two stroke single sounds worse as it gets to a louder level and most any multi sounds better as the sound increases. Obviously I prefer the sound of multis. The best motorcycle noise I have personally experienced was a 1979 CBX with a six-into-one aftermarket exhaust being flogged up through the gears. The original Honda 750 of 1969 only was the first cheap production bike with that multi shriek so much like an exotic Ferrari or equivalent. The machine was quieted in 1970 and a zillion four-into's popped into the aftermarket to provide all sorts of howls and shrieks from fours of all sorts. Even one of the Suzis had a hot sound, the early sporting inline fours of the late '70's. The Mach III brought the world's first two-stroke triple air-powered, straight-cut-geared howl, with an out-of-time growling burble in low-speed idle mode. Then they had babies: the Mach I, II, and IV, with a distinctively similar, but higher or lower pitch level sound for each model. The pioneer howler was the Honda CL-72, the 250 Scrambler, a twin with a 180-degree crank and nicely curved sidepipes. The 883 Is the descendant of the boogedy, boogedy, boogedy. The Nighthawks represent the Sounds of the Eighties with a really nice high-rpm shriek while the overall dB level is kept low.

Defining the period of my interest in motorcycles as 1960-on are the following auto/motorcycle analogies. The H-D Hummer was the equivalent of the Bugeye Sprite. These were the original small, cheap pioneers for the U. S. market. The H-D Super 10 was like the later Sprites, modernized and improved versions meeting the Japanese. The Honda 50 was the VW Beetle, the first import mega-successes for the masses. The Yamaha 80 was the Fiat 850 Spider, representing high development for the U.S. market at very cheap rates. The Metralla was the Lotus Europa of motorcycles, the ultimate lightweight pioneer of great backroad handling. The Mach III was the Plymouth Road Runner of motorcycles, a cheaply mass produced hot rod, but also a born legend. The Sportster and the Corvette are the red, white, and blue legends that refuse to die! The original Triumph Bonneville was an unreliable English beauty like the Jaguar XK-E. The Eighties Nighthawks and the Nissan 300ZX offered the high performance with comfort the Yuppie masses demanded. The Nighthawk S, like the 1967 427 Sting Ray, presented inalienable greatness in its perfection. Ducatis and Maseratis have offered Italian snob appeal to those few who can afford them. The early Yamaha Enduros and various Jeep models brought off-road riding to the masses with low-priced reliability. When you talk about a Gold Wing or a Cadillac, how can you not think of a Queen Mary by another name?

This tale of nostalgia has reached a mature stage where speed and garage space are considered along with insurance costs and inspection trips. The definitive list above contains most of the cycles that know where I live. The interesting point here is that each one touches a nostalgic soft spot. The Super 10 was my first ride. The Yamaha 80 was my first motorcycle. The Honda 50's were the true origins of successful tiny motorcycles. The Metralla was that exotic but simple European representative of lightweight handling and style. The Bonneville is what the generic motorcycle should be and the Nighthawk S is what the modern motorcycle is. The Gold Wing, Hummer, Yamaha Enduros, and the sporting Ducatis defined what their own future markets would be. The remaining three beasties define the minimalist motor-and-two-wheels pinnacles.

Figure B17 - 1969 Kawasaki 500 Mach III. ©1969 Kawasaki Motors Corporation, U.S.A.

Kawasaki invented the superbike in the spring of '69 with a model specifically designed for the American market, the Mach III, in classic American racing colors, white with blue stripes. Long and lithe as a Bonnie, but quick as the upcoming porky, but successful Honda 750, the Mach III offered record-breaking performance and style at a bargain-basement price. In spite of the popularity, price, design, and sound differences, the bottom line on my preference of the Mach III over the Honda 750 and its zillions of descendants is weight. All 127 extra pounds on the 750 are carried up high, and you can feel every one of them.

The Nighthawk 550 is the only Nighthawk with pseudo-Sportster styling. From the rear quarter view, just like the '68-'72 Stingray, the 550 is the best-looking motorcycle of its type ever produced. For my body, it is also the most comfortable. For a socially quiet type it is the best sounding when brought up on its cams. Without discussing the details here, the cams on the 550 Nighthawk were designed for the model, not the 650. Vibration, weight, maintenance, and style are all uncompromised on the Nighthawk 550. The black 883 is the most minimalist motorcycle ever made. The blue 883 reminds me of the Super 10. The black 1200 Sportster is the direct equivalent of a black 1970 454 Stingray I owned for eighteen years. The macho cat's meow description of a Sportster may be the last thing you expected to read in this book, but you just did!

Figure B18 - 1983 Candy Presto Red Honda 572cc Nighthawk 550. ©2010 Floyd M. Orr

My First Motorcycle

My obsession began with the Sears & Roebuck catalogs of The Fifties. Immediately after perusing the bra and panty departments, the next place to go in the new Sears catalog was always the Allstate Motorcycle department. Back when the most common motorized two-wheelers were Cushmans, Whizzers, and Simplex Motorbikes, the Puch/Allstate lineup sold by Sears was pretty doggone excitin'! The next big event in my life was when my best friend got a new Harley-Davidson Super 10 in 1960. This was followed only months later by my favorite cousin's new acquisition, a black 1960 Honda 150cc Benly Touring. Not only were the Allstates beginning to look klunky in a hurry, but this turn of events put me in on the ground floor of what I would later name The Tiddler Invasion. The next Honda I had a close encounter with was a Super Sport Cub with its 3-speed transmission, manual clutch, and cream tank. Within a couple of years, America was covered up in small Hondas, Yamahas, and Suzukis. Kawasaki would not arrive until a few years later, beginning under the Omega nameplate. I was quite a Yamaha fanatic in those early days, at least partly because I have always enjoyed rooting for the underdog. This is a book dedicated to those wonderful little machines from the days of our youth. The gamut includes the ubiquitous Honda 50, the unknown Pointer Super Lassie, and all those in between these two extremes. Honorable homage should certainly be paid to the early Cushman scooters and the '40's DKW 125 that inspired the H-D Hummer, but the principal business of this book is to disseminate information about the Japanese invasion of The Sixties.

My first motorized two-wheeler was a 1957 Allstate Cruisaire. Other than the fact that I ran into the side of the house while circling my own back yard during my first day of ownership, my relationship with the scooter was uneventful. My dad traded the scooter in for a brand new, red and silver Yamaha Rotary Jet 80 YG-1 in the summer of 1963. That relationship was a bit tumultuous. I loved that tiddler with everything I had. I also hit a car, another motorcycle (a '62 Honda Super Sport 50), and a downed power line with it. The last incident occurred after a storm knocked a line across the street, and it caught under my neck and dragged me off the YG-1. I looked like a criminal who had escaped the hangman for a week! After this third trip to the emergency room, my dad took the Yamaha away from me and gave me a pool table as a consolation prize. Obviously, I never know when to quit while I'm ahead. However, the pool table did a fine job of turning my parents' basement into a gathering place for my gang. We were like the kids on *That 70s Show* with a pool table instead of *the circle*.

Three years later I managed to talk my parents into letting me cautiously back onto two wheels. The black and white '66 Honda 50 Cub looked so innocent to my loving parents, and I did at least manage to keep its tires on the ground. A few years later I graduated to a red Kawasaki G3-TR 90. I didn't keep this one long before visions of *Easy Rider* sent me up market for a trip to California (where else?). Since I had been quite enamored of trail riding from the very beginning of my motorcycle experience, only one machine would do both very well. Although I strongly considered a 1970 Kawasaki Mach III in red with white stripes on the tank for my long excursion, a friend talked me out of it, and he was absolutely right. The blue 1970 Honda CL-350 was a much better choice, and it offered me a passable trail ride, too. After two trips to San Francisco from Starkpatch MS, I finally bought a Mach III, one of the especially pretty blue ones with the laser decals on the tank. One of the strange parts of this story is that a friend had talked me out of the Mach III for my long journey, but two other motorsickle buddies of mine bought a matching pair of new '71 blue Mach III's and made a similar trip. These were the good old days, no doubt. There were young men of college age on Hondas and other brands crisscrossing the USA as if Captain America and Billy had rolled right off the big screen. I personally knew five other guys who drove across the country in 1970-71, mostly on what we would now call *tiddlers*. Those were the days....

Figure B19 - Purple & Silver Yamaha 80 YG-1 at the Yamaha Communication Plaza, Hamamatsu, Japan. Image by PekePON under Creative Commons license.

Figure B20 - Red & Silver YG-1 with Red Vinyl Saddlebags. This is a digital reproduction of a B&W photo taken by a kid with a Kodak 126 Instamatic. ©1963 Floyd M. Orr

Tiddlers on the Trail

The 1969-71 time frame was a fun time to be a trail rider. I had more college buddies who rode the trails near campus at that time than at any point before or since. This was that magical period immediately after Yamaha set the trails on fire with its 250 DT-1, but before most trail machines developed copious horsepower and put it to the ground through long-travel suspension and big knobby tires. As the boom rapidly accelerated in the early '70's, more and more non-riders got mad at us and more and more riding areas were closed to us. Of course some of us did ask for this sort of trouble by rutting up the muddy fire roads with our spinning knobbies or piercing unappreciative ears with expansion chambers. A few were even known to tear down private fences. Thankfully no rider I knew ever went that far to gain access to a trail, but most of us were guilty of the racket and the mud slinging.

Figure B21 - 1968 Yellow Honda CT-90. Image by Zul32 under Creative Commons license.

There were many trail tiddlers capable of waddling leisurely down a trail before 1968, but most were not quite what most of us really wanted. The Cushman Trailster was a primitive scooter. The step-through trail bikes from Japan were technologically far more advanced, but the pace of their capabilities was still quite slow. Then the small trail machines that actually looked like motorcycles began to flow into our wooded areas from Japan. These ranged from 50cc to 125cc and the choices were numerous, although most of them were at their core very much alike. Honda boosted its Trail 50/55 to a 90cc and offered the more street-oriented Scrambler 90 alongside it, and for years these would be the only four-stroke alternatives to the many two-strokes from the other major players. Of course Europe was sending us a cornucopia of serious off-road machines during the '60's. Most were larger and more expensive than the casual tiddler rider could afford. Reliability issues drooled from their electrical systems and dealers were few and far from the boonies. The 50-125cc Asian dual purpose tiddlers by far offered the best likelihood that we would enjoy the great outdoors on two wheels.

This step up from the step-throughs still left a lot to be desired, especially if we wanted to build up any significant speed over the bumps or climb any serious hills. Most of these bikes had pressed-steel frames and barely-adequate suspension for the dirt. Some had comfortable riding positions for the street, but not for the dirt, or vice versa. The Japanese had not yet learned to copy the Ceriani front suspension design or how to produce a riding

55

position that worked sitting down or standing on the pegs. The frames were strong, but heavy, and the engines produced between five and ten horsepower. Many of the fenders were too close to the tires for mud. Many of the tires were too knobby for the street. The gearing was usually a compromise: either two low for the street or too high for the dirt. Some models offered interchangeable rear sprockets with a job even messier than premixing the gas and oil. The only way to avoid the premix was to buy a Honda, which although was as reliable as an anvil and quiet as a church mouse, was also somewhat overweight. Some of the two-strokes could zip by the Hondas like a Road Runner in a gulch, but their sound effects were considerably more annoying than a *beep-beep!*

Yamaha took out a clean sheet of paper and developed its 1968 DT-1 and the whole world of trail riding changed for the better. The company took the design of the European exotic off-roaders and copied it into a reliable Japanese package. The ingredients included a double-cradle tube frame, a piston-port single cylinder with oil injection that had been designed for dirt riding, soft, long-travel suspension copied from Ceriani, a 3/4 seat and wide handlebars designed for sitting or standing, and an electrical system that worked reliably all the time. The following year Yamaha added a 125 Enduro and the competing companies began to climb on the bandwagon.

Figure B22 - Red 1962 Yamaha Omaha Trail Brochure Photo. ©1962 Yamaha Motor Corporation, U.S.A.

We are going back now to that wonderful, innocent time when we had a choice of many excellent dual purpose tiddlers. We are going to sample from each manufacturer one machine that was marketed very successfully, worked like a champ, and put a smile on our faces. Most of these represented the first trail tiddler from each brand that combined proper motorcycle styling, a tubular frame, at least a four-speed transmission, and adequate gearing, tires and suspension for both street and dirt riding. Of course the Honda is the only four-stroke. The rest are smokers, but at least they all have oil injection. You can see from the chart below how close they all are in size, weight, power and price. Their performance is probably closer than you might think since the Yamaha is slowed down by the weight of its electric starter and the Suzuki has only three speeds, although there are two sets of 'em.

The chart quotes factory brochure figures; however, some sources put the Bridgestone's horsepower as only 9.5 and I believe the Hodaka's price was actually about $30 higher. See how close these all are? The left-to-right order of the chart is roughly based on precisely when these models were released.

Honda	Bridgestone	Kawasaki	Suzuki	Yamaha	Hodaka
SL 90	100 TMX	G3-TR 90	Cat 120	AT-1 125	100/B
1969	1969-71	1969-71	1969-71	1969-71	1970
4-speed	4-speed	5-speed	2 x 3-speed	5-speed	5-speed
8 hp	11 hp	10.5 hp	12 hp	11.5 hp	9.8 hp
OHC	Oil Injection	Oil Injection	Oil Injection	Oil Injection	Premix
19" / 17"	17" / 17"	18" / 18"	18" / 18"	18" / 18"	19" / 18"
Trials Universal	Trials Universal	Trials Universal	Knobby	Trials Universal	Trials Universal
Dual Seat	3/4 Seat	Dual Seat	Dual Seat	3/4 Seat	3/4 Seat
Upswept	Upswept	Upswept	Upswept	Upswept	Upswept
None	Luggage Rack	None	None	Luggage Rack	Luggage Rack
Kick	Kick	Kick	Kick	Electric	Kick
216 lbs.	185 lbs.	175 lbs.	205 lbs.	218 lbs.	170 lbs.
$400	$399	$339	$464	$509	$395

Honda took the engine from its legendary street tiddler, the Super 90, and put it in a bike designed from the ground up to be a dirt machine. The CL-90 had the vaunted Scrambler styling and was a little more amendable to the dirt than its Super brother, but like all CL models, it was a street machine first and a dirt bike second. The SL-90 was Honda's first foray into approaching *dual purpose* from the dirty side. If the bike has any weakness, it is that small level of very reliable power. The seat and suspension were truly comfortable in off-road riding. The seat is listed as *dual* in the chart due to its length, but no passenger pegs were provided. The Candy Red or Blue paint contrasts nicely with the silver frame. You can stand comfortably on the rubber-covered pegs and putt-putt over or through most anything. The gearing is distinctly lower than that of the CL-90, so you will be buzzing along in top gear on the street. With the speedometer in the headlight nacelle and the lack of a tachometer, the SL looks a little dated, but with the mild anvil of an engine, you won't miss the tach. Honda's first Motosport never needs an electric starter, either. Those are for the foo-foo tiddlers.

Figure B23 - Gold 1970 Bridgestone TMX 100. ©Michael Kiernan, Classic Motorcycle Company, St. Louis, MO.

The Bridgestone TMX was the first model of its type from that short-lived builder. Even the company's first off-road racers had pressed-steel frames! The TMX lacks the sloping, shaped seat that would soon define this type of machine, but the biggest clue to its foo-foo heritage is its rotary four-speed shifter. The little 100 produced plenty of power from its modern rotary induction design, but you must keep in mind the presence of that other *rotary*, especially as you forget that the TMX is not a five-speeder! The first cosmetic item you notice is the crease through the middle of each side of the gas tank. The seat is comfortable, but the crossbrace bars may be a tad too high and narrow for standing on the pegs and wiggling between the trees. The upswept exhaust looks pretty, but it is not tucked in as well some other models. It won't catch on any branches, but its bulge could make standing on the pegs a little less pleasant. Like the Honda, its lonely speedo is mounted in the headlight, but also like the SL, the TMX's high fenders will never clog up with mud. Like all Bridgestones, the power is there if you keep it up on the pipe. The TMX is the only machine in this group that carries two rear sprockets. You can change the gearing anytime you don't mind getting your hands dirty.

Kawasaki introduced its bargain of the bunch in 1969. The G3-TR also has a street sister with downswept exhaust, different tires, and a little taller gearing. The TR comes in only one color, red, and its a nicely designed machine, particularly for the price. The seat padding is a little thin and its shape is of the standard street type. The crossbrace bars and upswept pipe are average in feel and appearance. The rear springs are too stiff and the front forks top out easily with an audible *clank* on rebound. I guess you can't have everything for $339. Like the Bridgestone, the G3 is a rotary valve, but the five gears are in a row, leaving neutral available only by going through first gear. The gearing is a little tall for tight dirt work and it is not the most comfortable machine for either standing or sitting. The speedometer at least has its own housing, giving the machine a more complete look. Did I forget something? Oh yeah, the little beastie goes like stink on a skunk for only $339. Whoopee!

Figure B24 - Red & White 1969 Kawasaki 90 G3-TR Brochure. ©1969 Kawasaki Motors Corporation, U.S.A.

The Suzuki Cat is an unusual trail machine, even for this wonderful space in time. The first thing your eye will spot on the little Suzi is the chrome *basket handle* protruding directly in front of the front fender. You can call it a handle for dragging the Cat out of a deep mud hole, a protruding fork brace, or a brush catcher. Whatever it is, the Bridgestone TMX has one just like it. In typical Suzuki fashion, the Cat is a flashy machine with a bright cab yellow paint job, a quilted seat, and lots of chrome. Like the Kawasaki G3, the Cat has a speedometer mounted in its own housing, the dual seat is straight, and the exhaust is a conventional straight line a few inches above the rear axle. Neither the Kaw nor the Suzi is that comfortable sitting or standing. The Cat's seat just *looks* softer than the

Kaw's. The piston port two stroke makes plenty of power, but unlike the G3, that power is geared lower for the dirt. The gearing is the big difference between these two similar machines. Where the G3 has a top speed of 62, the Cat can only reach 52, although they both reach their top speeds in about 18.5 seconds. You can change the Cat's pseudo-street gearing to the tree-climbing level with the flip of a lever. This dual three-speed personality is the Cat's claim to fame. Where the Kaw is a passable dirt machine, the Cat is a *serious* dirt motorcycle. Just look at the real knobby tires.

Figure B25 - 1969 Yellow Suzuki Cat 120 Brochure. ©1969 Suzuki Motor of America, Inc.

Yamaha had the gall to include an electric starter on their junior DT-1. Although my fourteen-year-old granddaughter could easily kickstart the AT-1 or any of these small trail machines, the marketing department felt that the pushbutton would attract more casual riders, including girls. I am not sure how that worked out for Yamaha, but I have owned an AT-1 for forty years now and it always sputters to life with a kick or two, even after holding down the garage floor for months at a time. Mine is an MX model without the electric starter, but I would not want the extra weight even if it had one. My understanding is that the little six-volt battery the AT-1 uses would rather you just kick the thing to life in the first place, especially when the engine and/or the weather is cold. The AT-1's big claim to fame is that it is exactly like its big brother in design, only at 4/5 scale. The wide crossbrace bars feel just right, the exhaust pipe is tucked in neatly out of the way, and the seat and gas tank offer a narrow little place for your knees whenever you need to stand on the pegs. The chrome, barrel-shaped speedo and tach and Ceriani-type front forks give the machine a big-bike look and the luggage rack adds practicality. The single most *impractical* part of the AT-1 is the low front fender. Unless you plan to ride where mud is nonexistent, you will want to replace it with a high fender attached to the triple clamp and put a fork brace in place of the low fender. The Yamaha Enduro engine is not the quietest kid on the block. Much of the racket emanates from the piston, in addition to the exhaust. The seat is wonderfully shaped for both sit-down comfort and standing on the pegs. You may object to the slope of the seat pushing you toward the tank a little more than you like, especially if you are tall, but that should end the complaint department. The AT-1's lovability emanates from its wide range of good manners. It will blast down the fire road, putt-putt through the trees, or escort you to class with the best of these dual-purpose tiddlers.

Figure B26 - 1970 Yellow Yamaha 125 AT-1B. ©1970 Yamaha Motor Corporation, U.S.A.

The best has been saved for last, especially from a standpoint of off-road comfort. Hodaka has refined its one-color-as-long-as-it's-red motorcycle over the years as if it thinks it's a VW Beetle! The seat and suspension are state of the art soft and comfortable. The seating and standing positions are superb! You sit down with a *squish* and go *aaah*. Where the Yamaha Enduro feels small and taut, the Hodaka feels tall and soft. Both are excellent off-road machines and somewhat less appropriate on the street, although the AT-1 is the superior street bike. Hodaka's emphasis has always been on the trail and the 100/B, and all its predecessors and descendants, shine like the sun in the rough stuff. The 100/B was selected for this fantasy because its longer suspension, crossbrace bars, larger wheels, and tucked-in exhaust are improvements over the '69 Ace 100. Like the Suzuki Cat and Kawasaki G3, the Hodaka has a speedo mounted in its own housing. Its tires are trials universals like all these machines except the Cat. Although the Hodaka may not be quite as versatile as the Yamaha, it is truly the most comfortable, and comforting, to bash around in the dirt. Designed primarily as a dirt machine, you still have to premix the 100/B, unlike the rest of this group, and a big demerit for Hodaka inconvenience at the gas pump. The Hodaka may be the most comfortable in the dirt, but the Yamaha kicks its butt as a street machine.

These six machines represent a time long gone by, a special period in our lives when we could step out of class with our buddies, kick these cheap little fun machines to life and ride straight into the nearest wooded area. We could putt, we could plonk, we could race down the winding dirt road or run the pipeline. We would be exhausted long before we could expend a dollar's worth of gas. Then our favorite little beastie could take us to class the next day and we could do it all over again.

Figure B27 - 1971 Yamaha AT-1CMX Covered in Mud After a Run Down the Pipeline and Around the Trail Loop. Notice the Preston Petty plastic front fender, aluminum fork brace, and Skyway silencer. This high-strung little motocrosser made a fine trail bike after a change in gearing dropped the top speed from 60 down to 45 mph. ©1978 Floyd M. Orr

The Honda Obsession

Figure B28 - Black 1965 Honda Super Hawk. Notice the flat handlebars. Although this particular example is on display at an outdoor show in the UK, early Hawks and Super Hawks exported to the U.S. had the flat bars, too.

Image by Mick in Northamptonshire, England, under Creative Commons license.

Honda first entered the U. S. market and the consciousness of its citizens in the summer of 1959. As I have pontificated lovingly and repeatedly, I used to drool over the Allstate models in the Sears & Roebuck catalog in the '50's, but it was not until my best friend got a Harley-Davidson Super 10 and my favorite cousin got a Honda Benly Touring 150 in 1960 that my personal in-the-saddle experiences began. My first Honda brochure came from Al's Cycle Shop in Memphis, the same dealership that sold Elvis his Hondas, in 1962. That small B&W brochure had certain recently discontinued models covered by a big X made by a ballpoint pen. These models included the C77 305 with pressed steel handlebars and the CB92 and CB92R, the highly collectible 125cc sport models.

Many patterns can be discerned from a study of the early Hondas. First of all, Honda cared very little for the model year tradition. That is one of the main reasons I have created the charts of these early models, to try to put them into a sort of American perspective. The next thing you might notice is that all the models prior to 1967 were painted in the same four colors. Some models were never offered in white or blue, but practically all were offered in black and most in red. The transition between the traditional paint of 1959 through 1966 occurred in '67. By 1968 all the models had made the change to candy colors and the variations would explode in number from that point forward. The next component you might notice is that most of the instruments were in the headlight nacelles until '68, too, and with the exception of a few CL's, all front and rear springs utilized body-colored covers. Gas tanks were either silver or body-colored with chrome sides. Frames could be either pressed steel or tubular, but the CL-72 was one of the few with a front downtube; i.e., a cradle frame. Seats were hard, suspensions were stiff, and engine vibration was always there to tingle. Until the humpback 450 of 1965, the most exotic engine specs consisted of SOHC twins with twin carburetors.

The new Honda 350's of '68 changed everything, or more accurately, the company set in motion product design changes that would soon permeate the entire lineup. Honda stylists had obviously been asking themselves exactly why Americans wanted to buy leaky, antiquey Triumph Bonnevilles? Style, Marvin, style! Do you see the similarity between a 1970 CL-350K2 and a Triumph Trophy? The slender, painted gas tank, the chrome fenders, and upswept pipes with bullet-shaped mufflers should provide a few clues. The new candy paint jobs displayed elegant depth. The suspensions were softened a bit and the engine vibes were brought under a little better control with rubber mounts. Most of all, the horizontally split engine cases kept the oil off the garage floor, the SOHC twin-carb engines revved up a storm, and the electrics were never named after George Lucas!

Honda lost the magic after 1970, when most models seemed to reach their pinnacle of styling and performance. Many of the traditional CA/CB/CL bloodlines would continue into the mid-Seventies, but the spirit was dying. Although the S600 Convertible had been brought to California in 1965, followed by the small coupe/sedan I call The Honda Roller Skate a few years later, the company obviously got serious about car production beginning with the introduction of the Civic in 1972. It is probably not a coincidence that the first homely styling attached itself to many Honda motorcycles that same year. Most of the '73-'75 models were more attractive, smoother, slower, and more expensive. The emphasis had already shifted to cars and large four-cylinder motorcycles years earlier. Who wants a tiddler when Mach III's, IV's, Z-1's and 750 Fours were flooding the U. S. market? The last great tiddler would be the legendary 400 Four with its gorgeous, swoopy, four-into-one exhaust system. It seemed even as if Honda couldn't wait to ruin this beauty with western bars in 1977! It was all over but the crying. Simple, reliable, visceral machines like the red 1968 CB-160 were gone forever. The tears for the glorious, excitingly affordable tiddlers have dampened the tire tracks of our memories.

That was Then and This is Now

Back then we had a ridiculous variety of exciting choices to make when we chose a small motorcycle or scooter, and compared to today, every one of them was ridiculously cheap! Now nothing is cheap and everything is more about money than emotion. Although this section will not put any actual dollar value, or even a dollar range, on any machine, I do have a lot to say about the financial issues of these tiddlers as they apply to modern buyers. Keep in mind as you read through this that I am not going to even list a 1-5-star rating for individual models, although I shall offer the next best thing, a detailed set of qualifications for certain models as you read through the book. I have never bought, restored, and resold a single vehicle. I have not even purchased a motorcycle since 1984! That is not my strong suit. I *have* literally *worshipped* many of these machines since 1960 and my entire career was in the financial field, so I have a *perspective* pertinent to precisely what you want to know. Can I tell you what a Honda S-90 sold for a decade ago or what it might sell for today? No. Can I tell you exactly how a 1965 S-90 might compare to a 1970 Suzuki Maverick today, within the issues of parts availability and resale value, yes.

What might or might not surprise you at this time is that the American brands hold a distinct advantage over the European and Asian ones in general. Any old antiquey Simplex or Cushman may bring a restored higher price than the best equivalent rice-grinder of the period, such as a Yamaha YG-1 or Honda Super 90. A finely restored, late-model Cushman Eagle with all the right options might bring a hefty price, whereas a CL-90 might not. The German Rex KL-35 has been included in this book in detail. This is a very rare, single-cylinder, 50cc motorcycle with twin carbs and twin exhausts. The whole idea is laughable. That's why it has been featured, however, its collector value is most likely minimal and finding replacement parts would be as laughable as its dual carbs and exhausts. The Maverick 50 mentioned above is probably the most technically sophisticated, fastest and best looking 50 ever made, yet its collectible value is questionable. The Cushman Highlander that I describe later is more valuable today! The Highlander is the most pathetic, disgusting, motorized two-wheeler I have ever ridden!

As a longtime trail rider, I have included some of the most popular trail machines in the scope of this book. Most of the more serious off-road racers, particularly the European brands, have not been included. From a *that was then, this is now* context, off-road machines rarely hold much interest for collectors or speculators, although possibly more so for many nostalgic hobbyists. There are certain models that have dedicated fans, the ubiquitous Honda Trail 90 being the most obvious such example. Numerous XL and SL Hondas are attention getters, as is the original Yamaha DT-1 and its derivatives. However, the interest in the equivalent lines from Kawasaki and Suzuki generally remains at a lower level. In any case, the earlier the better as far as collectible value is concerned. Many pre-1968 models from Kawasaki, Suzuki, Yamaha, and even Bridgestone have significant value even though parts sources may be quite scarce. The boom in trail bikes coincided quite precisely time wise with the tiddler invasion of 1955 to 1975. The small trail models were some of the earliest Japanese models exported to America. The release of the Yamaha DT-1 in 1968 signaled the final stage of the boom before the Honda 750 pushed everything over the *big multi* cliff. If you are weighing the future monetary value of a small trail model, keep in mind that the levels of value versus off-road operation and performance might be reversed. Most trail machines were perfected over time and later releases often were far superior to earlier ones; however, the best trail bikes in the world do not necessarily have great collector value. Americans of all types still seem to have a soft spot for the Honda Mini-Trail, Trail 70, and Trail 90, while you might struggle to find a buyer for a 250 Elsinore.

Some chapters have a Selected Models Ratings Chart at the end. These charts by no means cover all the models or brands in this book, only the major ones. You will find a chart for: Harley-Davidson, Allstate, the most popular European brands, Bridgestone, Hodaka, Suzuki, Yamaha, Kawasaki, and Honda. These charts are meant to offer a broad, generic viewpoint in line with the tone of the book. There are no dollar or star ratings and the grades of A-B-C-D are to be considered across the board, with little consideration of comparison within each chart. The charts are intended to provide the reader with an accurate "feel" for the products in today's marketplace. The intent is for the rating to apply in 1990 as well as in 2020. The point is to capture the concept for all time, not just point out the "hot" or "cold" models at whatever point you are studying the information. For example, Harleys will always have monetary value as restorations that Bridgestones do not. Wishing it otherwise will never change this concept. Generally the most reliable and user friendly machines are Japanese, yet they have always been the "poor stepchildren" of the motorcycle world, and this particularly applies to all the tiddlers.

Some of the charts are set up by brand and others by year. Whichever selection was appropriate for that group was chosen. The models included in each ranking category vary widely in appeal and value. Carefully consider the broad spectrum in this category wherever appropriate. Other more brand-specific books will break these categories down in more detail. Some compromises had to be made to brevity. Most other books and value sources concentrate heavily on the parameter of *Collectibility*. Yes, this is the column of each chart that attempts to place a monetary valuation of resale on each type of machine. Heed the warning above about differences between models that may have been clumped together just to keep the chart manageable in size. *Practicality* defines the ability of the machine to be ridden and enjoyed in the modern world. Such factors as parts scarcity, resale value, riding comfort, and noise figure into this rating. The *Desirability* rating is my favorite. I am attempting with this rating to offer something for the prospective buyer to ponder, a quality located directly between the first two parameters. We all have models in mind that kick our starters, that make us smile whenever we reminisce. We remember those machines that were designed *just right*. The color choices were perfect, the pipes had the sweet howl of a banshee, or the feel of the controls was perfect for the machine's intended purpose. Maybe it was just the model that we all wanted but few had as kids? Hint: this last point is a biggie! One final note is that no machine has been graded "F": all the models in the charts, and in this book in general, are ones that warm at least a few of our hearts.

There is good news and bad news when considering the restoring or collecting of particular brands. Let's start with the Americans. The little Harleys compete with all the attention from their big brothers. The same goes for the Sprints, plus the parts have to come from Italy. Of the American brands, only the Whizzer has been reinstated in a modern format. That can be both good and bad for the Whizzer restorer. Simplex probably gets less respect than either Whizzer or Mustang. Whatever the Mustang following, it is surely a small cult, particularly for an American brand. The Cushman cult has been consistent over the years, but mostly for the Eagle Series only. Allstate has a special place in the hearts of Americans, especially those who grew up in the heartland. Keep in mind that Allstate sold Cushmans built in the U.S., Vespas and Gileras from Italy, and Puchs from Austria. Although some of the regular Cushman models command steep prices, their Allstate counterparts are usually considered the stepchildren. Allstate probably scores best in the collector market with its early Puch models.

Figure B29 - Black 1966 BMW 250 R-27. This last year of the BMW Singles would be a relatively easy resale, even in the black color and if a few of the details are not original. ©Michael Kiernan, Classic Motorcycle Company, St. Louis, MO.

The collector market for the European models is as diverse as their reputations and nationalities. Ducati has Ferrari prices. Benelli gets no respect. Although marketed by Monkey Ward, the Benelli Riversides have never had the classic cache of the early Allstates. Motobi is little known and their machines have always been small in number in the USA. Vespas have retained a cult following that is much larger than that of Lambretta, even though the Lambrettas were the higher level scooters of their day. Of course any BMW 250 Single has a significant cult following and commands collector value, but the other Germans struggle for attention. The small German Rex machines are almost unheard of, making their collectibility suspect. DKW launched one of the seminal tiddlers, but the company's machines have never had much direct impact in the U.S. sales market. NSU and

Zundapp have equivalent collectible status in some ways, but you should never forget that the NSU models are four-strokes and the Zundapps are two-strokes. Yes, Maybelle, whether we like it or not, there is a social class system among motorcycles! Another example of the class effect can be observed when comparing BSA's and Triumphs. Even though BSA built a wider array of tiddlers and approximately the same lineup of larger bikes, Triumph has always been favored in the USA. Jawa is a brand that has marketed machines in the U.S. over a considerable period of time, but the company's market niche has always been small, with limited appeal. The street Jawas could be viewed as similar to the classic Allstates without the ubiquitous Sears catalog connection held by Allstate. The three Spanish brands each have their own little niche. Bultaco has always been far the most successful in the American market, although it is not the oldest firm. Street machines generally carry a lot more weight as collectibles. Since the forte of the Spanish companies has always been serious off-road machines, the American collectibility of most Spanish models is somewhat suspect. The emphasis of this book is on the street machines for this reason, and the Spanish brands are no exception. The Metralla is the legend in this department with the Mercurio, Impala, and Wildfire following behind. All three brands have produced some fine off-road machines, but it will be difficult to assess any particular model's collector appeal.

Now for the mass producers of the tiddler phenomenon. No matter how vehemently their numerous fans try to deny it, Suzuki will always be the *me too* brand. Suzuki is simply the Chrysler of The Big Four. Although the company has produced many nice, pretty, reliable motorcycles through the years, there have been few collectible legends, at least from the perspective of the parameters of this book. The X-6 Hustler is the one that immediately comes to everyone's mind, followed by the GT-750. Suzuki would later go on to excite the motorcycle world with its GSX-R and Intruder series, but that's another story. Kawasaki has produced more than its share of legends, although most are above the official tiddler category. Yamaha has been there practically since the beginning of The Tiddler Invasion and has produced numerous impressive small machines. The catch in the modern world is the acquisition of parts, particularly cosmetic ones. Honda is King of the USA as far as total production and marketing on our shores. If your desire is an old Japanese tiddler without the agonizing parts scavenger hunt, Honda is the way to go, no matter which model you select. Yamaguchis offer their connection with the Hodakas as their only hope of surpassing Rabbits, Pointers, or Tohatsus in the scavenger hunt. Bridgestones will be somewhat easier than all the extinct brands except the Hodakas. At least the company still markets tires in the U.S.! Locating parts for a Miyata or Silver Pigeon will most likely be quite challenging, and then if you manage to rebuild the scooter, it will be quite a primitive machine.

There are several rules of thumb to consider whenever you are thinking of purchasing a classic tiddler. Some of these points are obvious and some are not. Take these issues to heart when you crunch a few numbers. (a) It is usually more financially rational to purchase a restored machine than it is to restore a junker yourself. If you enjoy the process, then by all means take on a project, but if you are simply comparing the final costs, this rule usually applies. (b) In the USA at least, American machines usually can be resold at the highest prices the most conveniently and Japanese machinery remains at the other end of that spectrum with most European machines holding the middle ground. (c) The "real"

Japanese tiddlers of less than 250cc will always suffer the most in the resale value department. (d) The Honda 750 Four unleashed a monster that has never been put back in his cage. Any old Ducati 900 SS or BMW R-90S will always fetch more cash a lot faster than any of the smaller machines discussed in this book. (e) Parts availability for any Japanese machines, especially for any older and/or smaller models, other than Hondas will be a challenge. Resale after the restoration could be difficult, too. (f) Cosmetic detail parts always take on a new prominence with old machines. Correct badges, emblems, exhaust systems, and colors can become the bones of contention for a restoration project. (g) If you are reading this book, you probably already have an interest in small Japanese motorcycles. Don't let these rules stop you from fulfilling your dreams!

Figure B30 - 1966 Yamaha Twin Jet 100 Brochure Cover. We believed we were all going to be flying our personal spaceships around by 2013. Who needs boots and helmets? Certainly not us cool people of 1966.

©1966 Yamaha Motor Corporation, U.S.A.

Figure B31 - 1962 Yamaha 50 MF-1 Brochure Cover. This photo was an obvious ploy to interest liberated young women in the latest electric-start, step-through tiddlers. Check out those sexy hairdos and skirt lengths, boys. Woohoo!

©1962 Yamaha Motor Corporation, U.S.A.

Chapter 2: *The Home Front*

Whizzer Motorbike

Figure C1 - 1947 Whizzer 150 Museum Display from Yesterdays Antique Motorcycles in the Classic Motorcycle Archive, The Netherlands. Image under Creative Commons license (GNU).

Produced from 1948 through 1965, the Whizzer was a true motorbike competing with the Simplex, among others. The Whizzer phenomenon was just a little before my time. I am not even sure if I have ever seen one, recently or during those production years. I clearly remember its Simplex competitor, but that may have been because the Simplex was built not that far from me in New Orleans. The Whizzer company began producing its engine kit for bicycles in 1939 before actually building and selling complete motorbikes. Whizzer introduced the Pacemaker model in 1948 and the Sportsman model a little later, followed by the Special, the WZ Series, and the Ambassador. However, the original engine kits were sold in far higher numbers than were the complete bikes, leaving a wide array of function and styling issues unique to the choice of the pedal-powered machine employed. Many of these were originally built by Schwinn, J. C. Higgins, and Cleveland Welding.

Whizzer motorbikes were resurrected in 1997 with a new operation in Carrollton TX. Current models include the $1795 NE-R Classic and the $1995 Ambassador. Both models are powered by a 138cc four-stroke. The base engine produces two horsepower and the Ambassador has an upgraded 3.25-hp version. The Ambassador also features an electric starter, larger seat and ape-hanger bars. Earlier models you might encounter on the used market include the 24-inch Blue Sportsman, the 24-inch Black Knight, and Pacemaker II built in both 24 and 26-inch versions. Most Whizzers of both the original and replica types utilized 26-inch wheels. The latest NE-R weighs 115 pounds and the Ambassador weighs 151 pounds. Both models are belt-driven with mechanical disc brakes and modern suspension systems.

Wikipedia states that competition from other motorbike brands caused the demise of the original Whizzer. If they mean the Simplex and others, that statement would be hard to swallow. If they are calling the 140-pound, 4.5-hp Honda 50 a motorbike, the truth has been revealed!

Figure C2 - 1952 Whizzer Pacemaker 700 Series.

Image by Russ Davis under Creative Commons license (GNU).

Simplex

Figure C3 - Red Simplex Servi-Cycle at the Barber Museum.

Image by Chuck Schultz under Creative Commons license.

The Simplex brand was founded by a Harley-Davidson dealer in Baton Rouge LA in the early '30's. Paul Treen released the first model of what he called the Simplex Servi-cycle from his advanced new factory in New Orleans in 1935. Produced from that year up through 1960, the Servi-cycle was a primitive, but cost-effective beast with spindly wheels and a low-horsepower, four-cycle engine. When I think of the term *motorbike*, I think of the Simplex. Of course this may be only because I knew a pair of identical twins who owned a pair of identical, used Simplex Automatics in about 1963. They rode these to high school only for about a year or less before trading up to a matched pair of Honda C-102's. When you trade *up* to a Honda 50 step-through, maybe now you will see the appropriateness of the term *motorbike*!

The 1935 model used a direct belt drive with no additional starting mechanism other than your *duck-walking* feet! There wasn't even a clutch mechanism to take the rolling beast out of gear until 1941, and the automatic drive was not available until 1953! The H models of 1945-47 finally had a foot brake and right twistgrip throttle. Suspension was minimal on the Servi-cycles and later Automatics with a primitive spring suspension at the front and a hardtail rear. The front suspension was a leading link type with two small diameter springs at the top, visible between the headlamp and the top of the front fender. This was essentially a pint-sized facsimile of the Harley-Davidson suspension of Peter Fonda's chopper in *The Wild Angels* or the more modern Springer Softail. Simplex built the Automatic model from 1953-60 with its own 125cc two-stroke engine with belt drive. After the demise of the big-wheel Simplex Automatic in 1960, the company continued to build small motorcycles with proprietary engines such as the Villiers through 1975.

The Servi-cycle was replaced by an entirely different machine in 1960, the final year of big-wheeled Simplex production. The *Compact* series was much closer to the Mustang brand than anything else. Riding on fat, six-or-twelve-inch wheels, the new Sportsman series was composed of two separate chassis. The Sportsman Compact was more of an overgrown minibike than a real motorcycle, and the Sportsman Senior Series was the direct Mustang competitor. Both models had less than zero design details in common with the Servi-cycle other than the brand name. Production of the Sportsman Compact began in 1960 with a 175cc, 4.9 horsepower engine built by Continental. With its solo seat and six-inch wheels, it didn't intimidate anyone riding anything larger than a Doodle-bug or a Big Wheel. The 1958 Senior Sportsman 150cc was the larger model with the rare Buckhorn-shaped bars made famous by Harley-Davidson and was close to the final development of the model series. *Cycle*'s June 1964 road test of the Simplex Senior described the 200cc machine as weighing 200 pounds with a four speed foot shift for a retail price of $440.

After several iterations built for a minimal level of trail riding, Simplex released the much bigger and better Sportsman Senior in 1965. The Senior had a longer wheelbase, twelve-inch wheels that were much less of a bad joke, and a traditional, real suspension system at both ends. A kick starter and front brake were even offered at extra cost, and the Continental seven-horsepower engine at least made the Simplex a viable Mustang competitor. The final development of 1965 was the top-dog V model with a 200cc, 11 hp, Villiers engine hooked to a four-speed transmission. With its magneto lighting, dual seat, and Buckhorn bars, it almost looked like a real motorcycle. Unfortunately, the company would turn south and head down the drain before 1965 had even ended. We all know why. Remember that *trade up* comment?

Mustang

When the Simplex company totally changed the design of the machines it built in New Orleans in 1960, they were obviously adopting a style of small motorcycle created by Mustang in Glendale, California, in 1945. The original Mustang was designed as a compact, cost-effective alternative to the limited selection of small bikes available immediately after World War II. Simplex was building tall, skinny motorbikes, Cushman was building scooters, and the Hummer was still several years away.

The original Mustang design employed a 125cc British Villiers two-stroke, but this was replaced in 1947 with a 320cc, single-cylinder, side-valve engine in a triangular, hardtail frame with twelve-inch wheels. All Mustangs used a British-built gearbox and the footshift was on the right side. A sprung, solo seat and painted handlebars were standard. There was very little chrome on any Mustang. The entry level Mustang was the 9.5 horsepower Pony with disc wheels, three-speed transmission, and only a rear brake. The Bronco model added another horsepower, wire wheels and a front brake, and the Stallion added a four-speed and a little more deluxe trim to a 12.5-horsepower engine. All of these solo hardtails changed very little up through the cease of production in 1963. The company also built a three-wheeled utility model and a trail model with a tractor-tread rear tire design!

Figure C4 - 1960 Black Mustang Stallion. The Stallion model looked very similar to its little brother the Pony. You can identify this example as a Stallion by the shape of its four-speed gearbox. All Mustangs shifted on the right and the Pony had only a three-speed.

©Michael Kiernan, Classic Motorcycle Company, St. Louis, MO.

The October '64 issue of *Cycle* displayed a Mustang Trail Machine with a tractor-type rear tire, albeit small in diameter. The little beastie weighed in at 170 pounds with its four-speed, six-horsepower Briggs & Stratton OHV four-stroke. According to Wikipedia, Mustang ended production after the 1965 model year. This would make the trail model the final Mustang introduced. With its blocky foam-pad seat and primitive rear suspension, The Trail Machine was either a minibike on steroids or a pint-sized Cushman Trailster, whichever way you want to look at it.

The 1964 Thoroughbred was the top of the Mustang line. All Mustang production halted in 1963, but the inventory was continued until sold out in 1965, not coincidentally the same year the *You Meet the Nicest People* company first sold more motorcycles than all other brands combined! The Thoroughbred had originated in 1960 with an all-new frame featuring a dual seat and conventional rear shocks. The 350cc engine and four-speed transmission with foot shift were the same as on the Stallion. Thoroughbreds could be outfitted with optional passenger footpegs, chrome crash bars, and leather saddlebags. *Cycle* tested one in December 1960, but *road tests* were very rudimentary back in those days prior to the advent of *Cycle World*. All the factory specifications, including the 220-pound dry weight, were listed, but no performance testing was actually done. Horsepower was mentioned only in the context that a special five-horsepower model was available for youngsters.

Cycle World tested the 320cc Thoroughbred in September 1963. No horsepower figure had been provided to the magazine by Mustang, but the more basic Pony model was rated at 9.5 horsepower and the testers expected the Thoroughbred's horsepower to be about the same. The new machine felt faster than the Pony, of course, because it had the new four-speed gearbox while the Pony had only a three-speed. The Thoroughbred had a top speed of 71 mph and ran the quarter in 20.1 seconds. The shifter and kickstarter were on the right side and the price was $539. A comment was made about the painted handlebars being welded to the front forks and the obvious low center of gravity on the fat little twelve-inch, laced wheels.

Mustang represents one of those last gasps from an American brand in the tiddler market. The Cushman Eagle would be gone in another couple of years. So would all the little American-built Harley singles. The Mustang may have been primitive and clunky, but at least it is interesting in retrospect for its American entrepreneurship.

Cushman

Figure C5 - Red Cushman Super Silver Eagle at the Barber Museum. This is a model between 1962 and 1965. This is the deluxe big boy from Cushman. The Super designation can be distinguished by the luggage rack assembly over the rear tire. The Silver part designates the aluminum alloy engine. Note the modern motorcycle kickstarter, optional black leather saddlebags, chrome seat rail, and chrome crash bars on this late model. Image by Chuck Schultz under Creative Commons license.

I have been pondering what I would say about Cushman for some time. I have collected a number of photos, but I am still somewhat unsure how to identify certain models or model years. The company had been established long before beginning production of scooters in Lincoln, Nebraska, in 1936. The first postwar models were the Pacemaker and Road King in 1946, and the first model badged as an Allstate and sold by Sears Roebuck appeared two years later. The Road King with its large, deluxe, styled body panels looked sort of like an early, economy version of the Harley-Davidson Topper.

The legendary Eagle, easily the company's trademark model, was released in 1950 with a Husky cast-iron engine for $282.50. Outboard Marine Corporation bought Cushman in 1957 and continued to develop the Eagle. The Super Eagle, introduced in 1959, featured body panels that covered the scooter's rear section. The Silver Eagle became the top-dog Cushman with a 9-hp aluminum engine designed by OMC in 1961. This model even had an optional electric starter.

Cushman became the official U. S. distributor for Vespa at the beginning of '61, and the 1963 brochure I have includes three Vespa models, the Silver Eagle, the still very primitive Highlander, and the Trailster, a little yellow beastie with the old 8 hp Husky engine and a tractor-tread rear tire. You might look at the Trailster as a very primitive ancestor of the Honda Ruckus. That's certainly what it looks like! There is no mention of the Super Eagle with its smooth bodywork or the standard Eagle with the cast-iron engine, so I assume they had been discontinued from the line by '63; however, I have never been able to definitively ascertain if the Super Eagle bodywork continued as an option or not. Final Cushman Eagle and all other scooter production had ceased by 1966. The company was soon sold off from OMC and continued to build golf carts and variations of its Truckster for police departments until earlier in this decade.

Figure C6 - Blue 1958 Cushman Eagle. Image by Chuck Schultz under Creative Commons license.

Here is a broad outline of the Cushmans and their rightful place in *The Tiddler Invasion*. Like Mustang and Simplex, Cushman was an American brand that sold its primitive, but pervasive, machines to high school kids in the Fifties and Sixties. At least where I was in Mississippi during this period, Cushmans were far more prevalent than these other two pioneers. The Sears connection of the Vespas and Highlander added to the brand's availability, but the Eagles were by far the most common of the American-built Cushman models. The Eagles I have seen and ridden were mostly from the 1955-64 range, and most of these were of the manual start, cast-iron 8-hp variety. As we all know, Honda owned the whole market by 1965, so the last years of the Eagles were always a bit rare. My personal acquaintance with Cushman/Vespa was probably quite typical.

I got my first motorized transportation in the early spring of '63, a 1957 Allstate Cruisaire. In the summer of that same year, my dad bought an old Cushman Highlander from I don't remember who or where. It may have even been an Allstate version. The funny part of the story is that I had that primitive toad only one day! I rode it around the back yard once to discover how truly minimalized transport felt compared to my zippy three-speed Vespa. The big surprise to me was that Dad had already planned to trade in both scooters for a new Yamaha YG-1, which thrilled me silly, so by July I was no longer a scooter owner. Zippy-de-doo-dah! The Highlander was little more than two little wheels, a crude, painted handlebar, and a big vibrator with an automatic clutch. My last memorable encounter with a Cushman would be when my Rotary Jet 80 blew a fancy Super Eagle into the weeds in a drag race. No, I cannot recall if it was a 9 hp Silver Eagle or not, but I believe it had the Super's sheet metal panels and it was probably about a '62 or '63 model.

Let's flash back a year or two so I can describe my first drive of a Cushman Eagle. Two neighbor boys, one a year older than me and one a year younger, owned at least two Eagles. Due to the ages of all of us at the time, I think I am about to describe the earlier Eagle owned by the older boy, the only one who would have been old enough for a license in 1961 or '62. I wanted a motorcycle or scooter so badly at that time that I could chew an old rubber tire, so one afternoon the owner and our respective parents let me drive that Eagle in a circle around their back yard. Of course I left a white track hours later. Although I had ridden several machines, including this one, as a passenger and had learned to drive a Harley-Davidson Super 10, this was my first solo effort on a Cushman.

The first thing anyone notices about a Cushman Eagle is that it has little wheels like a scooter, but tubular handlebars and a top-mounted tank like a motorcycle. The next thing you notice is the left-hand gearshift knob beside the gas tank and sprouting up from the engine, like certain ancient Harleys of the big hog variety. The two-speed gearshift is accompanied by an equally unexpected foot clutch. Back then the only thing that had an electric starter was a Honda, but even the kickstarter on an Eagle was unique to the brand. There was a pedal sticking out of the front of the engine. The pedal lay flat on the floorboard most of the time, until you reached down and lifted it up into its *cocked* position. Standing beside the machine, on the *right* side, you then held the scooter upright off its left-side stand, stood up on the pedal with your right foot, and threw all your weight down onto the pedal. If the Eagle didn't chirp on the first try, you then reached down and lifted up the ratcheted kick pedal and started over. Once the big four-stroke single pop-pop-popped into life, you swung your leg over from the wrong side of the beast, sat down and mashed in the heavy clutch with your left foot. The rear brake pedal was on the right, facing back at you up off the floorboard, sort of like that on a car, and the front brake was controlled by a lever on the *left* handlebar. Push the gearshift into first gear (I think it was forward) and ease out the clutch. Once you are going a decent speed, push in the long-travel clutch and pull the gear lever all the way back, through neutral in the middle, and you are cruising for a bruising from any Yamaha 80 or Super 90 that you haplessly may encounter!

Figure C7 - 1962 Cushman Super Silver Eagle. This example is not as perfect as the museum piece shown above. This view shows a slightly different variation on the rear panel arrangement with a large passenger pillion. Don't ask me what that trapezoidal shape in front of the engine is because I don't have a clue. It is a cover of some sort because you can see it is not in the next photo. The color of this machine is an off-white. ©Michael Kiernan, Classic Motorcycle Company, St. Louis, MO.

Figure C8 - This close-up shot of the same machine shows the left-hand gearshift knob and the speedometer with the key switch to the right of it in the flat panel in front of the driver. Notice the black kneepad placed over the large tank seam. I am not sure if this was a factory option or just a homemade idea the owner had. I have never seen this before. ©Michael Kiernan, Classic Motorcycle Company, St. Louis, MO.

Allstate / Sears

One brand name stands out in its own unique way, and that is all it is, a brand name called Allstate, the house brand of Sears, Roebuck & Company in The Fifties. Unlike all the European brands, Allstate did not compete for small numbers of buyers scattered throughout pockets of big cities. For most of the wide expanse of America throughout the '50s, Allstate was the most accessible brand of motorcycles, scooters, and mopeds, both foreign and domestic. Sears began by slapping their brand on a few Cushman and Vespa scooter models. The concept was so successful they quickly branched out into mopeds and full-size motorcycles built by Puch of Austria. All these models were little more than basic transportation for hordes of war-torn Europeans. For millions of American teenagers raised in the outback regions of the broad USA, the fact that an Allstate could be mail-ordered from a catalog was a dream come true! Beginning in 1951, any teen dreaming of exchanging his pedals for a two-stroke engine with only a few horsepower could do so, just as soon as he saved up enough cash mowing lawns. We all knew the wild, fascinating tales of adults and rich city kids who rode Sportsters, Bonnevilles, and BSA's, but Sears brought motorized two wheels to the masses. Each of us knew at least one lucky kid who had an Allstate Moped, Cruisaire, or Twingle. Allstate smacked us upside the head right where we all lived, in our aspirations.

Sears first began selling a few of the Cushman scooter models built in the U.S. These were shown in the Sears catalogs through 1960 with the Allstate Jetsweep, a variation on the Cushman Road King, being the last Cushman marketed as an Allstate. Cushman would continue producing its popular Eagle series well into the '60's, but these were never offered by Sears. The later machines sold by the catalog company were badged as Sears models instead of as Allstates. Probably many more were sold directly from the mall stores and less from the mail-order catalog business during the later years. The Cushman models were deleted from the lineup after 1960, but Sears continued to market Vespas until about 1969. Cushman and Vespa were linked as companies back then, so it is no surprise that Sears sold some of the lower-priced models from each brand as Allstates. In the latter years, after the Cushmans were gone, Sears began importing a pair of Italian Gileras, the 106SS and 124. You can spot these a mile away if you have a general idea what all Italian motorcycles looked like back then. The much homelier Puchs received updated styling about the same time, along with a few model changes in the lineup. This made for two basic series of Sears machines that we could call "early" and "late", those from 1948-63 and those last machines badged as Sears models in 1964-69. As you can see from the chart at the end of the Allstate section, this was a gradual transition over time instead of a one-step change on a particular date. The later models were sold from mall stores that competed with numerous brands of motorcycle dealerships. The early models competed quite successfully with Benellis sold from Monkey Ward catalogs and Bridgestones sold from Alden's and/or Spiegel. (Note that this statement concerning Bridgestone has been hotly contested in recent years, but research and my personal memory indicate that small numbers of Bridgestones were marketed through at least one catalog.)

Allstate Moped

Back in my childhood days of The Fifties, I would grab up every new Sears & Roebuck catalog that arrived in my family's mailbox moments after the postman drove away. Of course this was the era in which the Sears catalog was every young man's visual access to bras and panties, so of course I had to peruse those first, even if they were in stunning black and white. As soon as I left the B's and the P's in the index, the M's offered my next fantasy, the Allstate motorcycle pages. I am not sure how many years the Allstate Moped and its derivatives were produced by Puch and sold by Sears, but it could have been as wide an era as 1954-69. Moped production covered at least the '56-'66 period, and probably a wider span than that. For a boy living out in the sticks, in my case, the town of North Carrollton, Mississippi, where McQueen went to appear in the movie *The Reivers*, the Allstate motorcycle catalog pages were the only contact with motorized two-wheelers available in those innocent years before Honda woke us all up and set the world on fire.

The Allstate Moped was produced by Puch and sold by Sears with few changes for more than a decade. All models had a pressed steel frame in a U-shape like a girl's bicycle, with an underslung 49cc two-stroke engine started with pedals and accompanied by a two-speed hand shift. Horsepower ranged from 1.8 to 2.3 and the top speed was about 30 mph. A single molded rubber seat, and on most models, a luggage rack were the only accommodations. The rack was chrome wire on some models and painted flat sheet metal on others. Some Mopeds had chrome wheel rims and others were painted. The front and rear suspension, handlebars, and headlight rim were the only additional chrome parts. The headlight nacelle, front forks, and gas tank were one color and the rest of the machine was painted in the base color. Most were red with cream components as described, but the last years of production were blue with white trim instead. The rubber seats and handgrips varied from cream to shades of gray to black, usually but not always matching on each machine. These color schemes would be replaced by the all-red Campus 50, which with its three-speed foot shift was not technically a moped, although it certainly looked like one when it became the entry-level Allstate in 1967.

The lowest priced Moped Sears offered was a special economy 1961 model without a speedometer, rear shocks or luggage rack for $155.50. This was something of a pivotal period for Allstate, less than two full years after Honda's arrival in the U. S. The Honda 50 would provide a young man with a 4.5 horsepower four-stroke engine, a real foot shift, battery-powered lighting, and a dual seat. Selling for about $245 list, the Honda C100 was a whopper of a deal. Sears wanted to advertise a price that was nearly $100 cheaper. This was a moped, a slick derivative of a motorized bicycle, but the Honda 50 was a real *motorcycle*! The introduction of the Honda 50 would herald the swansong of the previous king of the entry-level, motorized two-wheelers for ambitious little boys. The Sport Moped and Campus 50 would carry the torch deeply into The Sixties, but the original Moped's master of the outback domain would never be repeated.

For all the kids who wanted to stop the uphill pedaling before they passed out in the heat, the Allstate Moped was a twinkle in our eyes. How many lawns would we have to mow to pay for it? How could we convince our parents to let us have it? Exactly how much would shipping be to Bumfuzzle, Alabama, and could you please translate that amount into lawns?

Allstate Compact

Figure C9 - 1965 Allstate Compact. Note the horizontal white tank and tail lamp cover. This example could use new foam and a cover for the seat. ©Ken Ashbrook, owner and photographer

The Allstate Compact was one of the Puch models badged as an Allstate in the '60's. The Compact was produced and sold with the earlier group of Allstates. It was sold in two color combinations, red and cream and all-white and it was not updated like the 250 or the Sport 60 when the newer generation of Puch/Allstates were produced. Although the Compact was easily available and low-priced, it was never a popular model, as either an Allstate or a tiddler, since a Honda Sport 50 could blow it into the weeds in both style and performance. A good description of the Compact would be a Sport 60 on scooter steroids. The two models share the same engine, but the Sport 60 is tall and lanky while the Compact is short and stocky. If you view a Honda 50, as I do, as an official motorcycle with scooter attributes, you could say the Compact is a scooter with motorcycle attributes.

There were two variations on the Compact and only the latter one was available in white. The earlier version was distinguished by its chrome-topped gas tank mounted in about a 45-degree downward slope, following the contour of the step-through frame. The handlebars were pressed steel painted red and raised a few inches above the top of the headlamp nacelle, giving them a sort of funky appearance. The headlamp itself was fixed to the frame and surrounded by a large cream molding. In other words, the headlamp did not turn with the handlebars. The headlight molding, bottom section of the gas tank, and the side panels of the seat cover were cream. The rest of the machine was red. The newer version of the Compact had rounded pressed steel bars with the headlight assembly mounted in the center that turned with the bars. This look was very similar to that of the far more common (and modern) Vespa. The gas tank had a rounded, bulbous shape, was painted cream, and mounted in a straight line back from the scooter's frame. This deaccentuated the step-through look a little at the expense of sleek lines and chrome flash. Some of these later models were painted all-white, updating the Compact's frumpy appearance a little further.

The Compact holds a place in the world of tiddlers that is unique to itself. There are a number of machines with a similar style described in this book, but none of them have ever sold more than tiny numbers in the USA. When I compare these to the Compact, what I mean is that they are sort of motorcycles, sort of scooters, and all of a step-through design of some variety. None had four-stroke engines, the nameplate, the dealer network or the consistent motorcycle qualities of the ubiquitous Honda 50. The Yamaha MF-1 was a pudgy little Honda 50 copycat with smooth, yet somehow funky, bodywork and a putt-putt personality. The Rabbit S-90 had the requisite larger diameter wheels of a motorcycle, but the floorboards of a scooter. The Rex Como Deluxe had a pressed steel frame, a sort-of step-through design, and a three-speed hand shift. The Compact's claim to fame is that none of these had the Sears availability connection. They all remain super rare and mostly unnoticed while someone is always scouring a barn to unearth a strange little scooter/motorcycle called the Allstate Compact.

Figure C10 (left) - Red 1952 1-hp Allstate Scooter. I have no knowledge of the details of this primitive little machine. I assume that it was in the Sears catalog in 1952, but I am not even certain if this was a Sears/Allstate product. If it is a Sears product, I am not sure where it fits within the chart shown later within this chapter. Was it built by Cushman or someone else? That's a good question. ©Michael Kiernan, Classic Motorcycle Company, St. Louis, MO.

Figure C11 (right) - 1956 Red Cushman Allstate at the Barber Museum, Birmingham, AL. This is a much more familiar machine to me. I do not know the exact model number, but this is either the same or a very similar scooter to the Allstate Cushman I owned for one day described elsewhere in this book. Image by Chuck Schultz under Creative Commons license.

Allstate Cruisaire

Figure C12 - 1964 Red Allstate Cruisaire. ©Michael Kiernan, Classic Motorcycle Company, St. Louis, MO.

The Cruisaire may actually be the most ubiquitous true scooter in U.S. market history. Let's eliminate the Honda 50 because it has seventeen-inch wheels and the Cushman Eagle because it has an up-front gas tank. Although Vespas have been in the U.S. market for decades, it was the Cruisaire version that had access to the hinterlands through the catalog sales market. Although Sears sold white Cruisaires, 90cc Cruisaires and 150cc Cruisaires in small numbers during certain model years, the great majority of Cruisaires sold here were all the same. The early ones were a pale green and had chrome handlebars and the later ones were red with molded pressed steel bars. All were 125cc two-strokes with about five horsepower and hand shifts. Most had three speeds, but later models had four. There was a small storage compartment in one side of the bulbous body panels and a small gas tank for premix underneath the seat. The top speed was about 45 mph.

My first (and last) scooter, if you don't count the Cushman Highlander I owned for one day, was a 1957 Cruisaire. I rode it to school and around town for less than two years from early 1962 to mid-1963, when I replaced it with a new Yamaha YG-1. The model I had was obviously five years old at the time. It was originally a dull Pea Soup Green, but a kind and enterprising uncle of mine had repainted it a lustrous red. He had also reupholstered the worn single saddle with a shiny black Naugahyde cover. It had the usual three-speed hand shift and chrome handlebars.

I spent the first day of my fourteen-year-old ownership circling our big back yard. I had made about a dozen laps, improving my confidence, daring, or stupidity, whichever you choose, when I revved up a little too much speed to turn as I rapidly approached the backside of our house. Rather than risk spilling the machine, I blasted right into the wall at about twenty miles per hour. It seemed faster, but it was probably less. The only damage was a front fender mashed against the tire. I pried it outward, leaving a slightly misshapen fender that would never be repaired. All I can say is that the Cruisaire was trying to send me a message that would be soundly and somewhat dangerously delivered later by its replacement, the YG-1!

Starting the magneto-fired Cruisaire was always easy. A moderate poke at the right-side kickstarter would usually do the trick. The sound of the puttering two-stroke was never anything to write home about. Compared to the YG-1, the *fun* of riding the Cruisaire was muted, just like the exhaust note. It was a big reach to the clutch for a little guy like me and the hand shift was not very taut. I missed the *snick-snick* of a tight foot shift. You curled your left wrist backward about as far as it would comfortably go to reach first gear. Once you were underway, neutral and the higher two gears fell to hand more readily. There was a fair amount of front dive from the soft suspension when you firmly squeezed the right hand lever controlling the front brake. I never got used to the brightening and dimming of the headlamp as the revs rose and fell, and the horn made a sad little sound at idle. The most amazing part of ownership to me was that I never did a horrible endo going through a deep pothole with those fat little tires!

Figure C13 - 1964 Red Allstate Cruisaire. This second example of a 1964 Cruisaire has an optional spare tire attached. ©Ken Ashbrook, owner and photographer

Allstate Cheyenne

Back about 2005 I needed to clear some stuff out of my garage prior to a move, so my wife and I staged a garage sale. Probably the best deal I offered to the browsers was my 1960 Allstate Sport 60. I had purchased this machine back about 1967-68 from a dealer for $60. At the time I bought it, the little bike was running, but it severely needed a complete tune-up, polishing, and a lot of TLC. I removed the headlight because I thought it was ugly and fastened the speedo, wrapped in foam rubber, to the bare fork assembly with a homemade bracket. Although the machine only had about 3000 miles on it, the seat cover had already been replaced with a dark brown one that always looked just a bit funky. The front fender had a dent in it and was mounted too close to the tire to suit me, so I removed it and sold it to a friend to mount on another machine. Like the rest of that rolling technological anachronism, I could never understand why the rear fender was high enough to navigate a swamp without clogging, yet the low-mounted front would lock up at the mere sight of mud. The red paint was a little faded, but otherwise my Sport 60 looked clean enough. Oh yeah, one last slab of funk was a Honda 50 (C100/102) exhaust pipe welded onto the mid-rise header pipe. Who knows why the original pipe had already been discarded so callously, but we all know these little Sears Rowbutt bikes got little respect back in those days! Some teenage punk (me) ran the little beastie without oil in the clutch a few decades ago and trashed it. Instead of fixing it, I just parked it in one garage after another until some lucky soul stuffed it into the back of his station wagon for the princely sum of only $10!

I owned a C-100 in the mid-Sixties, but I always lusted after a better trail bike. One of the leading contenders was the Allstate Cheyenne. I was fully aware of its Sport 60 heritage, but the black paint and knobby tires looked immeasurably better than the red Sport 60 with its sky-high rear fender over the skinniest rear tire with street tread this side of a Schwinn. I studied the Cheyenne in the Sears catalog and I even have a brochure of it. When Sears began unloading the last of their Cheyennes from the Sears Auto Centers for a measly $199.95, I went bananas for one, but that didn't make me a chimp with a dirt bike. Since I usually carried about 85 cents around in my pocket at the time, even that pitiful sum was beyond my budget. All I could do was to periodically visit the Sears Auto Center and stare longingly at what I would one day discover was a *lousy* trail bike!

The Sport 60 was marketed from 1960-65 and its much improved Cheyenne brother was sold from 1966-68. According to the brochures I have, the Sport 60 was offered in black at one time, too, but I have never seen one, only red and cream like mine. The Cheyenne may have been geared lower because its top speed is listed as only 37 mph, whereas the Sport 60 was claimed to scream up to 47! Interestingly, the machines are listed at almost the same weight of 140 and 141, with the Sport as the heavier! To my eyes, the spindly Sport 60 has always *looked* lighter. The biggest difference between the two models are the tires and wheels. The Sport 60 used the Moped's 2.25 x 23's and the Cheyenne had much more appropriate 2.50 x 19-inch knobbies. Both models were powered by 4.5 mice desperately peddling in the engine room protected by a skid plate. The archaic leather strap that held down the gas tank of both models was a nice touch. Hand-painted gold pin striping on the black fenders of the Cheyenne (and some Sport 60's) added a delicate European flair and unlike many much more modern Japanese tiddlers of the day, at least these bikes had proper front and rear suspension components. Enough of the faint praise, let's hit the dirt!

Figure C14 - 1965 Red & Cream Allstate Sport 60. ©David Struble, owner and photographer

Since I have not actually ridden a Cheyenne, I shall have to extrapolate the experience from my Sport 60. The first thing you noticed was that unless you had the legs of a giraffe (as I do), the 31-inch seat height was a bit much. Of course later motocrossers would be built for giraffes, too, but at least those would be competent, exciting machines. These two clowns were worse than tiddlers; they were *piddlers*. You could adjust the footpeg height and position in a 360-degree arc. I'm not sure exactly who would want to do this, but you could, nonetheless. The crossbrace handlebars were a bit too high and way too narrow. The seat on the Cheyenne was a little sportier in style than that of the Sport 60, but they both were way too narrow, with too much leg reach down to the adjustable footpegs. Don't ask me why the Cheyenne received a road-racing style seat design to go with its crossbrace bars and knobby tires, but like many of its other features, this is precisely why a Cheyenne is interesting today. You might call it The Edsel Factor. The skinny tires, tall seat, and narrow bars made you feel like Miss Priss on her girl's bicycle, but worst of all, with a couple of well-toned legs, she could probably outrun you on her Schwinn! The three-speed footshift was on the left like the Japanese machines and the clutch was very light. The shift throw was so long that the engineers probably thought the rider needed to tailor that footpeg position to perfection to avoid injured ankles! Once you got balanced upon the tall, skinny machine, your next job was to try to keep those mice peddling at their maximum levels just to keep up with the Honda 50 accompanying you on your pleasure cruise through the dirt and mean streets of small town America. Since I owned a Honda 50 at the same time, I can tell you which one was always ahead, and it didn't come from Sears & Rowbutt!

Sears SR 125

The SR 125 was sold in 1967-69 from the Sears catalog and stores. I don't think I have ever seen one of these except in the catalog. I may have seen an SR 125 in a Sears store back when they were being sold, but if so, I do not recall it. I certainly have never seen one on the street! As I remember it, this model was sold in only one color combination, red and silver with 17-inch wheels. The 125cc single used a chrome bore and a distinctive radial head. *Cycle* tested one in January 1969 and listed the price as approximately $350. Note that this model is listed as costing $435 in the Sears chart. I am not certain which figure is more correct. The weight was listed as 198 pounds and the tested machine topped out at 64 mph. The magazine's leading criticism was for the lack of a battery for the machine's lighting that drifted to a pitifully dim level at idle and a potentially dangerous blackness if the engine stalled in traffic. The tested model was red and silver as stated, but it is possible that other colors were offered. As I said, I have never seen one. *Cycle* indicated that a trail kit or a trail version from Puch might have been in the works, but as we know now, the Sears motorcycle brand was reaching the end of the line in 1969.

You could see from the styling, particularly the gas tank, that this was a contemporary of the later Puch 250 Twingle. I do not recall exactly how this marketing plan fit in with the Gilera 106 and 124. The 106 was sold alongside the SR 125, at least for a time. My best guess is that the Gilera 124 was not. The short version of a short story is that the SR 125 would always remain a rare Sears model, although one little sought by collectors. Its later, more modern styling has not been as popular with modern day enthusiasts as the earlier Puch Allstates. When the SR 125 was a contemporary choice, it was overshadowed by the two popular Sears Gileras. If a modern Sears enthusiast is looking for one of the later Puch models, he is usually seeking either the Twingle or the Sabre for nostalgic reasons, since both of these far outsold the SR 125. If you are looking for a rare Allstate without the early Puch price, the SR 125 might be your Holy Grail after all!

Figure C15 - This close view of the rare Allstate Scrambler shows that the Sport 60 was not the only Allstate with a gas tank tied down with brown leather belt straps. ©Troyce Walls

Allstate 175 & 250 Twingles

Figure C16 - Maroon Allstate 250 SGS - ©Troyce Walls, owner and photographer

Sears sold Puch motorcycles from 1953 until 1968. These included the Allstate 175 in both Standard and Deluxe trim, the 250 in deluxe trim only, the Scrambler, the hardtail 125/150 single with three-speed hand shift, and a number of others, mostly in the later years. The 175 and 250 deserve special mention because these were the standard road models with pressed steel frames, full-coverage fenders, and "twingle" engines that were sold in large numbers over a number of years. With the exception of the *genuine tiddlers*, the Moped, Sport 60, Cheyenne, Compact, etc., more of the Allstate 175 and 250 were probably sold through the catalogs than the other machines offered. As the 1960's progressed, fewer and fewer Allstates were sold through the catalogs as more and more were sold at Sears Auto Centers that accompanied the mall anchor stores in big cities across America. As the malls proliferated in suburbia, more and more Americans lived in these areas instead of the small towns and farming communities of the Forties and Fifties. Particularly in the late '50's and early 60's, before The Big Four came to dominate the small motorcycle market, the Allstate 175 and 250 were the fantasies of every teenage bicyclist in America. Of course many of them settled for a Compact, Vespa, or Moped, but that's another story.

The earlier Allstate 175 is easily identified by its blue color and solo seat. The later ones were black or maroon with dual seats and looked just like their big brother. Before the end of Sears sales, the 175 would be discontinued and the 250 would get a styling facelift and continue as the Sears SR-250. The Twingle nickname was derived from the two pistons that moved up and down together in a single combustion chamber. All the Puch Allstates were piston-port two-strokes and all except the Scrambler had single carburetors.

The 175 and 250 had an early version of oil injection. The gas tank had a filler cap on each side, one for gas and one for two-stroke oil in a one-quart compartment. The Twingles, including the Scrambler, were the only Allstates with this feature.

Figure C17 - Maroon Allstate 250 SGS ©Troyce Walls, owner and photographer

Allstate Scrambler (ISDT)

Figure C18 - Black Allstate ISDT Scrambler. ©Troyce Walls, owner and photographer

The rarest Allstate tiddler is certainly the 250 Scrambler. This model was imported by Sears in very small numbers in the very early '60's. I don't even know the exact years. I lost my catalog photos of this model decades ago, but I have one ad from my very first issue of *Cycle Magazine* of August '63. That ad indicates that Sears was running a summer sale price on the Scrambler for $488. The original price was $699, as stated in the 1959 catalog. The Scrambler was called the ISDT by Puch, and it was equipped for that sort of competition, what we now call an enduro, a motocrosser with lights for night racing through the boonies. It was a souped up Twingle with twin carbs, upswept pipes, tubular frame, trim chrome fenders, a 2.7-gallon teardrop tank, knobby tires and crossbrace bars. The gearing could be set up for whatever type of riding or racing the owner had in mind. The 1959 model was offered with lights, extra sprockets, and even a sprocket puller! The 1963 $488 special ad does not mention the extra sprockets, but the lighting kit (battery not included) was a $25 option. Interestingly, both ads list the weight of the Scrambler as 298 pounds; is that with or without the lighting kit? Only The Shadow knows.

Figure C19 - The Smiths speedo on this Allstate Scrambler shows only 1554 miles on the odometer. Notice that the needle sweeps backwards from right to left. ©Troyce Walls, owner and photographer

Figure C20 - The left-side kickstarter and gearshift are clearly visible in this view of the Allstate Scrambler. ©Troyce Walls, owner and photographer

Figure C21 (next page) - A close view of the gas tank and engine area of the Allstate Scrambler.
©Troyce Walls, owner and photographer

Allstate 250 by Troyce Walls

Editor's Note: I first discovered Troyce Walls while researching Allstates for my Tiddlerosis blog several years ago. If you read the photo credits in this book, you will see his name on a few beautiful photos of certain very rare Allstate models. This article was published online at Tiddlerosis and elsewhere by Troyce some years ago. I have edited it to fit the purpose and subject matter and reprinted it here. Troyce Walls is truly one of the most knowledgeable experts on these rare machines in the USA!

Figure C22 - Maroon Allstate SGS. ©Troyce Walls, owner and photographer

The motorized two-wheelers sold by Sears, Roebuck & Co. (hereafter: Sears) during the Fifties and Sixties in the U.S. were actually produced by three major manufacturers. These were Cushman of the USA, Piaggio (Vespa) of Italy, and Steyr-Daimler-Puch of Austria. All these Sears units were essentially re-badged versions of the parent manufacturers' wares. The motorcycle I am about to describe in detail is from Steyr-Daimler-Puch, and was sold by Sears as the Allstate 250. This motorcycle was first offered by Sears in the mid-1950s for the princely sum of almost $500, and complimented a previously offered 175cc Standard and Deluxe version, and a rudimentary 125cc, fan-cooled single with a twist-grip three-speed shift. All four were sold in addition to the Allstate/Cushman and Allstate Cruisaire/Vespa line. A Puch Moped was added to the catalog a couple of years after the introduction of the 250. Apparently the 250cc was never offered in a "Standard" version (the equivalent of a Sears "Better" as opposed to "Best") in the manner of the 175cc, and was always sold with chrome wheels, generator electrics, and other deluxe features. The "Standard" 175 sometimes had body-color wheels and always a magneto system. The earlier 250 was painted "Rich" or "Lustrous Maroon," according to the catalog description. The most abundant models found today were produced later and were finished in a shiny deep black. The 175 was "Rich Medium Blue" for the standard and "Lustrous Maroon" for the Deluxe. By the end of the run, the 175 had been dropped from the catalog and the 250 had lost a bit of its previous charm with the introduction of the "Italian" models that used CEV switchgear and lights, with the body color in either black or red, with silver painted tank and headlight case. The tank on these models had lost the chrome panels and romantic teardrop shape in favor of a blocky, more modern, racer style.

Figure C23 - Black & Silver-Gray 1967 Sears SR 250. ©Dan Spanncraft, owner and photographer

As an aside, the fact that so many of the bikes keep appearing out of barns and fields can mostly be attributed to the very attractive "$50 down and $42 a month" purchase alternatives and home delivery advertised in the Sears catalogs. You could order one and within a couple of weeks, the truck would arrive at your door with your cycle in a crate, whether you were in the Pacific Northwest, the Midwest Plains, The Florida Keys, Manhattan or Maine. Some Assembly Required.

A twin-carb scrambler version of the 250 was sold for a couple of years alongside the toaster-tank models. This bike used a tube frame, lightweight off-road fenders, dual ignition system, and a high-mounted exhaust running up either side. The catalog praise for this model was really very convincing in that, "Professional riders tell us that the Allstate Scrambler handles so well that it seems to correct for the errors in the rider's judgment." Now that's what I need, because I make my share of judgment errors. This statement was accompanied by a drawing of a very silly-looking and grinning fellow wearing goggles and a soup bowl helmet. This model was listed for a whopping $700. That's a lot of early Sixties groceries. However, although I have never actually seen one of these models for sale, I would imagine that the acquisition of one today could set a body back a whole lot of mid-Nineties groceries. Certainly, this enthusiast finds the machine highly desirable.

Figure C24 - Another close-up of the Allstate Scrambler engine. ©Troyce Walls, owner and photographer

Both the 175 and the 250 had the unique two-piston/common combustion chamber engine design. This configuration is often referred to as the "Twingle", although I've seen that designation applied to other types of engines. That's what I call them for now, at least until a better and more accurate handle comes along. According to my meager historical resources, this layout was used by at least one other manufacturer, also of European origin, DKW, in their Gran Prix racer in the 1930s. Interestingly, the DKW folks also experimented with a third dummy cylinder lying horizontally forward at 90 degrees (similar to a Ducati L-twin forward cylinder) to the twin cylinders that was used as a crankcase supercharger. It has been written that the exhaust racket from this machine could be heard up to three miles from the track. Never let it be said that my stodgy old Allstates have no heritage! Besides that, as an 11 to 12 year old youngster I used to fall asleep with the Sears catalog open on my face to the motorcycle pages and that's enough heritage for me. What a wonderful, mystical beast was that huge black 250.

Quickly here, I shall recount my experiences with an Allstate 250, as it happened back in the halcyon '60's. Most of us had some sort of small bike, mine happened to be an Allstate/Puch MoPed, but most of the guys had the bulletproof little Honda singles or small displacement twins. One day that summer one of the older fellows that hung around the gym and played basketball with us had unearthed this big black greasy thing that no one but me could identify. I knew it from the pages of the Sears catalog, and the showroom way over in Huntsville. Somehow I talked this guy into letting me ride his machine while he took my place on the court for a quick game. We agreed that I would be back in ten or fifteen minutes which sounded like plenty of time, as if I wouldn't have agreed to any amount. Forty-five minutes later he tracked me down at the local gas station, and found me attempting to gas up both cavities in the fuel tank as I, realizing how late I would be, knew I would have to be very apologetic as well as offer some compensation when I finally returned. When he had finished hollerin' at me and had finally decided, with a lot of fast talking on my part, not to beat my ass, I was able to walk back to the gym thinking of how great it had been. So much power, so big, so mean, and so stinky, smelly, and neat. And even now, although I can remember having trouble then with shifting into second, I wondered why the folks who knew of them seemed to speak disparagingly of the Sears motorcycles. Later of course, as being cool with a succession of Hondas, Triumphs, etc., came to mean much more than objectivity and open-mindedness, I began to use the Allstates and their ilk as an object of derision as well. Smoky East-European dinosaurs, they became.

The advantages of the subject engine design in the days before widespread use of the rotary valve in two-strokes lay basically in the enhanced ability to time the fuel air charge and in better combustion chamber scavenging. Disadvantages are increased weight and complexity, of course. In the Puch/Sears engine one cylinder is situated directly behind the other; the front contained the exhaust ports and the rear the intake ports. The carburetor is mounted oddly on the left side of the front cylinder and is oriented rearward on the early bikes, directly to port side outboard on later models. The pistons arrive at TDC a couple of degrees apart in order to provide the aforementioned advantageous charge/scavenge timing. The engine is tuned in the Puch/Sears version to be very tractable at low RPM and to be reliable, as the bike was built for post-WW2 Southern Europe. The idea was to give the automobile and income starved populace affordable transport that would be effective in the Alpine geography. The fact that Sears decided to import and sell this bike in the U.S. had no bearing on its initial design and arrangement of parts.

That's a very brief history as I know it, and I realize that there will be hecklers and detail mongers pointing out discrepancies, but I believe I got it fairly close. At least close enough to proceed with my evaluation of this beautiful old machine with my admittedly baby-boomer, out of focus, but present day jaundiced, eye and posterior.

The unit used for this road test is model 810.94180 and was sold by Sears in the late Fifties to early-mid Sixties. Color for the particular model tested was "Lustrous Maroon" when new. Tank panels, wheels, shocks, and various other trim pieces were chromium plated and were mixed in with scattered polished alloy pieces. A sprung solo seat was supplied with this model, with a similar one offered for pillion as an option. Windshields, saddlebags, etc., were also available.

Starting a properly kept Allstate 250 from cold is relatively simple if one is accustomed to a variety of vintage bikes. Here's how I would tell the reader to do it. Do not get on the bike first. Turn on the fuel supply at the petcock, tickle the carb with the plunger on top of the float bowl until fuel leaks down the side, and turn the simple but effective choke disk so that the carb intake is closed off. Push the BMW-style (Hella, I think) plunger type Ignition key down into position in the top of the headlight. If the red generator and green neutral lights come on you're ready to kick. If they don't they're probably not working, but in that case it's still a good idea to check manually that you're in neutral. Now, if you got on the bike to do all this in the beginning, it's best now, in my experience, to get off again and put it on the center stand because the kick lever is on the left. Upon hearing me complain about this arrangement once in the infield at Daytona, an old Allstate aficionado asked me, "Why would ye want to git on the damn thang if it ain't runnin'?" Two healthy strokes on the kick lever with the throttle just slightly open is usually all it takes to get the relaxed two-stroke burbling away. If it doesn't crank this easily something is amiss. Once running, immediately open the choke windows a bit to preclude fouling. It's possible to hop on now and ride away, but in a few seconds reach down and open the choke windows completely. This last step requires the operator to look down at the choke disk since there is no positive indication of rotational position that can be felt. Or you could stand there beside the bike until it warms a bit before riding away, I suppose, if you aren't anxious to sample the subtle joys of riding this wonderful, torquey old machine.

First is one down with the left side shift lever (unlike the classics from that foggy island off the French coast). Engagement into first and pulling away using the clutch lever on the left bar is a smooth operation, but shifting into second on all the examples of this bike that I've ridden isn't. First is an extremely low ratio (probably for starting with a passenger aboard and the bike pointed up an Alpine incline) and optimum power/torque rpm are reached quickly. Second is up on the other side of neutral and engagement can require two distinct shifts to clear neutral. Second ratio is quite a bit higher than first. Maybe others can do it better than me, but I've never been able to get the set of gears that make up the second ratio to meet agreeably. If I shift from first at low revs where things aren't spinning so quickly the engagement to second is better but the ratio is so high that the engine bogs. If I allow the revs and forward motion to build to a proper velocity before shifting, there's a lot of unhappy gnashing of (gear and my own dental) teeth. But after that the power, what there is of it, and torque build smoothly and shifts into third and fourth are much more gratifying. I've found that even moderately high engine speeds do nothing to increase acceleration and that short shifting between the upper three ratios is not only more agreeable, but more effective. The practical, utilitarian design of the engine really comes through here.

Very few two-strokes of this capacity that I've ridden pull so well from low in the rev range. The Suzuki TS250, a Seventies vintage one-lung two-stroke enduro I rode recently, pulled fairly well from down low but had a definite "on the pipe" area up the rpm range. I know for a fact that the Yamaha Big Bear Scrambler (YDS3-C) that I drag out of its cave occasionally truly demands that a lot of noise and rpm be present to move on down the road. But then the YDS would kick the doo-doo out of the Allstate in a sprint. It's amusing to note here that the stump-pulling Puch engine is in a street bike, and that the peaky oriental unit is in an alleged scrambler. But then we all know about early Japanese so-called scramblers. The point is, the Allstate pulls well from down low, and excessive engine speed is a waste of time and motor.

Through the corners, the pressed steel frame performs adequately. Things start touching down fairly early, even for yours truly, a fellow not known specifically for his curve slicing skills. Little bar effort is required to change direction, and the old Puch is willing to do so even after taking a set through a rounder. Never having had the delectation of using one of these machines with fresh suspension damping, it's difficult to say how much that would help. The dampers are rebuildable, but the parts are scarce and I'm never sure that I've done it as well as our Austrian buddies did originally. With the large mufflers and silencers intact, and good main bearings, the machine is acceptably quiet, even to today's more socially critical ear. The aforementioned Yam Big Bear is much noisier.

Figure C25 - Black 1965 Allstate 250 with Classic Styling at the 2009 Seattle International Motorcycle Show. Image by Dennis Bratland, photographer, under Creative Commons license.

Seating position for my portly 6' 2" and 235 lbs. is a bit cramped, but not too bad. The pegs are a bit forward for me in relation to the European-bend bars. But that's OK because the sprung solo saddle is so close to the front of the machine that that's where I have to be anyway. Me and the Allstate look pretty ridiculous together, sort of like John Wayne on a burro, only in this case the Allstate is prettier than me. Note, however, that the ergonomics start to feel very natural as time and miles pass. Later versions of the bike with the dual saddle, and eventually - with the "Italian" versions - a western handlebar height and bend, allow for more freedom of butt placement but don't look or feel nearly as cool and Continental.

Stopping the Allstate is covered more than adequately by the large drums front and rear. Probably another symptom of the Alpine heritage. If it's possible to go quickly and enthusiastically enough to cause fade in a well tended example I've never done it, but then I've never actually used one of these bikes in anger. By and large, the brakes are up to their intended task.

Maintenance on one of these old classics is fairly straightforward if parts can be found. More on that later. The points/condenser ignition, oil bath primary chain and clutch, and enclosed rear drive chain will provide years of service if looked after with a conscience. The 250 utilizes an oil pump in the engine case to provide a throttle related oil/gasoline mix. The fuel tank incorporates about a quart-sized oil tank in the left side, ergo the two caps on the tank. The oil pump should be kept operational, as opposed to disengaging it and using pre-mix, since the oil is also injected onto the main bearings by the pump. The primary weak point in the otherwise very robust unit has to do with the engine top end. According to my sources, the front pistons seem to burn up within five to eight thousand miles. It is unusual to see a machine with more miles than that still retaining enough compression to run properly. This probably usually has something to do with overly casual maintenance. However, the exhaust piston is separate from the cooling incoming charge and is located directly behind the frame downtube and out of laminar air flow; not a really optimal design. Occasionally, one will come across an engine that just seems plain noisy, i.e., not piston slap or rod knock or whatever, and that overall noise is symptomatic of a main bearing having become rough and worn. Altogether though, the motor and frame are very strongly built.

Overall, the shift from first to second not withstanding, riding the Allstate/Puch 250 motorcycle can be a Zen-like event. It's completely obliging and easy to get along with, as long as one doesn't require a blistering pace that day (that's where the Zen comes in). As a similar life-lesson, I've found that in my small city when I go out shopping for building materials or hardware or whatever, I might as well set myself to the slow and rambling pace of my town, otherwise I end up just being aggravated and it all takes the same amount of time anyway. Over the past several years, since my return to the motorcycling fold after a fifteen-year hiatus, I've come from thinking the Allstate ugly and silly, to viewing the visual and visceral elements of this motorcycle as ones of beauty, with form and function blended into a surprisingly beckoning whole. There's literally more character than a dozen of other certain cycles could ever muster; maybe even a hundred of them. Realizing that there are those of us, myself included, who find this same magic on our Harleys, IN our Gold Wing Interstates, or aboard our long-legged Beemer Boxers, I have to say that very few machines fall to my eye and heart as easily as the Twingle. But that's me, all others must judge for themselves. Give one a try.

Parts availability is quite limited, although Motor West seems able to eventually supply critical items, either from stock or upon request. DomiRacer/Accessory also have a quantity of parts as they bought the remainder left in the States from Sears in the early '80's. Cosmetic and accessory items, as with all vintage bikes, are the most difficult, i.e., chrome and other shiny bits, tool kits, tail lights, tire pumps, pillion seats, and so forth. Additionally, it's always a good rule with classic bikes to purchase more than one example at a time if possible as a parts source. Some seals and bearings can be purchased through specialized retail outlets.

Motor West, Inc., 3211 West Senator Avenue, Milwaukee, WI 53216, (414) 875-8787. Matthew Quirk at Motor West has lots of parts and access to even more, and knowledge of what fits what. DomiRacer Distributors, Inc., P. O. Box 30439, Cincinnati, OH 45230, (877) 451-0354.

Figure C26 - 1968 Sears 124. ©Michael Kiernan, Classic Motorcycle Company, St. Louis, MO.

Figure C27 - 1968 Sears 124. ©Michael Kiernan, Classic Motorcycle Company, St. Louis, MO.

Figure C28 (next page) - A final top view of the Maroon Allstate SGS. You can clearly see the gas and oil caps on the tank, the chrome rear shocks, and the tiny tail lamp in this photo.
©Troyce Walls, owner and photographer

The Allstate Cushman / Vespa / Gilera Chart

Model	Years	Colors.	HP	Gears	Price
Allstate 711.30	1951	Red	3	One	$180
Standard 811.30	1948-54	Red	3	One	$235-255
Deluxe 811.40	1951-57	Red	4	One	$220-295
Allstate Standard	1959	Red & White	NA	One	NA
721 Tubular	1958	Red	NA	One	NA
Jetsweep	1957-60	Blue & White	8	One	NA
Cruisaire 90	1968-69	Red or White	NA	Three	NA
Cruisaire 125	1951-68	Sea Green / Red / White	5	3 / 4	$299-440
Cruisaire Sprint 150	1966	Silver	NA	Four	NA
106 Super Sports	1966-68	Red & Silver Blue & Silver	9	Four	$385-399
124 Sport	1967-68	Red & Silver	12	Five	$479

Cushman / Vespa / Gilera Notes: Earlier colors are listed first. The Cushmans were built in the USA and the Vespas and Gileras in Italy. All the Cushman and Vespa scooters had small wheels and metal bodies. All the Cushmans were OHV four-strokes with Husky engines. All the Vespas were two-strokes. The early Cruisaires, all 125cc, had chrome tubular handlebars and three-speed hand shifts. The handlebars were changed to the painted scooter type in approximately 1960. The hand shift was changed to a four-speed on the later 125cc models, probably in about 1966. The two Gilera models were OHV four-strokes. Unlike all other Allstates, the Gileras had right-side foot shifters. Wikipedia lists 1969 as the final year of the Sears (Gilera) 106 and 124. The 1962 Cushman Trailster was the last Cushman model introduced aside from the Eagle. It is possible, but not likely, that a few Trailsters were sold as Allstates. *Cycle World* tested a Trailster in August 1962 with a claimed horsepower rating of 7 1/2 and a price of $382.

The Allstate Puch Chart

Model	Years	Colors & Details	HP	Wheels	Price
Moped	1956-66	Red & Cream Blue & White	2.3	23-inch	$159-199
DeLuxe / Special Moped	1958	DeLuxe - Bronze Special - Maroon	2.3	23-inch	$190
Economy Moped	1961	Red & Cream No Rear Suspension	2.3	23-inch	$155
Campus 50	1966-68	Vibrant Red 3-speed Foot Shift	3.2	23-inch	NA
Compact	1960-66	Red & Cream / White 3-speed Hand Shift	4	12-inch	$329
Sport 60	1960-65	Red & Cream 3-speed Foot Shift	4.5	23-inch	$269
Cheyenne	1966-68	Black 3-speed Foot Shift	4.5	19-inch	$199-330
Allstate 125	1954-61	Red 3-speed Hand Shift	5	16-inch	$295-349
Allstate 150	1961-66	Red 3-speed Hand Shift	5	16-inch	NA
Scrambler ISDT	1959-65	Black with Chrome Fenders	16.2	19-inch	$488-699
Standard SR 175	1953-60	Blue with Fully Painted Tank	10	16-inch	$370-475
Deluxe SR 175	1953-67	Lustrous Maroon or Black w/Chrome Panels	10	16-inch	$370-475
Allstate SR 250	1954-67	Lustrous Maroon / Black	16.5	16-inch	$500-639
Sabre 50	1964-67	Red & Silver Four Solid Colors	5	17-inch	$275-285
Sears SR 125	1967-69	Red & Silver	12	17-inch	$350-$435
Sears SR 250	1967-68	Black, Red, or Blue & Silver	16.5	16-inch	$579

Allstate Puch Notes: Earlier colors are listed first. The Puchs were built in Austria. The DeLuxe & Special Mopeds had leg shields, fender skirts, tiny metal saddlebags, and chrome tank panels. The Economy Moped did not have a luggage rack and a speedometer was $5.95 extra. The late-model Moped for $199 was Blue & White. The $199 Moped price and all the other models and prices above are from the same catalog, but we do not know from what year. The Campus 50 looked like a moped, but it had a dual seat and three-speed foot shift. The Sport 60 weighed 141 pounds. The prices listed for the Sport 60 and Compact indicate an early figure for the Sport 60 and a late quote for the Compact. The last Cheyennes were sold at the closeout price of $199. There were two series of Compacts. The earlier models were available in red and cream only and they were distinguished by their gas tanks that had chrome tops and sloped downward at the rear, following the contour of the frame. The handlebars were raised pressed steel painted red. The headlight was fixed to the chassis with a large, squarish, cream nacelle. The later Compacts were mostly red and white, but some solid white models were sold. The gas tanks were painted all over and fitted horizontally straight in the chassis. The headlamp was in a smaller, rounder nacelle that was molded into and turned with the handlebars, which were flat and formed of white, rounded pressed steel. A red or white housing covered the tail lamp mounting bracket on the later models, too. I am uncertain in which model year this change took place, but the 1965-66 models definitely had the later styling.

The 1960 price of the 125 may have been $294.50. The early 125 had funky, two-piece handlebars and a solo saddle. The later 150 had conventional handlebars and a 3/4-length foam seat. All Standard 175's and early Deluxe 175's had solo seats. All the 175's with dual seats may have been black. Later DeLuxe 175's had dual seats. The Standard 175 had magneto ignition without a battery. The Scrambler weighed 298 pounds and came with many spare parts for racing. Early advertising claimed 20 hp for the Scrambler, but this was reduced to 16.2 @ 5200 rpm. A $25 lighting kit was optional on the later 250 Scrambler. The 1964 SGS 250 sold for $500. The all-black, early style 250 Twingle was still sold as late as 1966. The later style debuted in 1967. Early Sabre 50's may have been also available in Black & Silver. The later Sabre 50's came in Icy White, Spicy Red, Brilliant Blue, or British Racing Green. *Cycle World* tested a 1963 250 SG: the specs were 14 hp, 340 pounds, 66 mph top speed, 0-60 in 22 seconds, $560.

Figure C29 - Allstate Scrambler ISDT. ©Troyce Walls, owner and photographer

Allstate/Puch Production Figures

I found an online source that quotes the production/sales figures of a few Puch models; however, I have never been able to verify the actual origin of these figures. I also have not been able to firmly ascertain if these figures refer only to Allstate-branded machines or if they include all the Puch production of these models worldwide. Sometimes I look at these and think they refer to Allstates only. Other times, I am not so sure. You can find a breakdown by serial number at Sheldon's EMU website.

Year	125 Single	150 Single	175 Twingle	250 Twingle	Totals
1953			6033	57	6090
1954	1610		15,549	9535	26,694
1955	2		12,773	3487	16,262
1956	600		9804	1260	11,664
1957	802		9097	667	10,566
1958	605		7087	540	8232
1959	1004		5682	531	7217
1960	1314		3916	519	5749
1961	199	241	1876	700	3016
1962		900	1152	824	2876
1963		782	716	1677	3175
1964		2001	415	2248	4664
1965		1001	2520	3478	6999
1966			4361	6673	11,034
1967			24	3884	3908
1968				2211	2211
1969				154	154
1970				139	139
Totals	6136	4925	81,005	38,584	130,650

Harley-Davidson

Harley-Davidson Super 10 & Scat

Figure C30 - 1960 Red Harley-Davidson Super 10. ©Charles "Mutt" Hallam, photographer

I had my first motorcycle ride on the rear half of a gray Buddy Seat with white side panels. It was attached to a 1960 Hi-Fi Blue Super 10 with Buckhorn handlebars, crash bars, and black leather saddlebags. This was also the machine on which I learned to drive a motorcycle down a residential back alley in North Greenwood, Mississippi. It was the Spring of '60 when I took that first passenger ride. I was twelve and it scared the dickens out of me when the pilot took that viciously fast machine through the backyard shrubbery at 20 mph! Hooooeeee! It was all over but the crying from that moment onward. Sure, I had been carefully drooling over the Allstate models in the Sears & Roebuck catalog since about 1955, but that was mostly because I so vividly despised pedaling! I lived in North Carrollton MS back then, a town located in hilly terrain. I had wheezed and panted up those hills in ninety-degree heat and humidity quite enough, thank you. My 26" J C Higgins felt like a boat anchor at my feet. I wanted to be motorized - I just did not really know what that would feel like. Besides, I was just a big chicken nerd anyway.

My best friend's older brother, who was away at college in France in 1960, had had a Harley-Davidson Hummer when he was back home in high school, so little brother went on a crusade to his parents for his own Hummer. The 165cc ST model was officially replaced in 1960 with the Super 10. I am uncertain of exactly all the detailed differences between a 1959 165cc and a 1960 Super 10, but I am sure there must be at least a few or the company would not have changed the name. The description that follows probably applies in practically all detail to all of the U.S.-built H-D tiddlers.

Unlike practically all other motorcycles, the kickstarter is on the left side of the machine. You approach from the left, hold the bike upright by the handlebars, and kick with your right foot while standing on your left. Of course you don't have to start it this way, but it never felt right to me to approach from the right. The side-stand is on the left and kicking with your left foot just feels weird. The next thing you notice is the large handgrips with a cross-hatch pattern. They feel as if they are made for big American hands, unlike the tiny grips on Hondas of the Sixties. This feature, along with the large seat and wheels, make even the scrawniest teenager feel like he is riding a real motorcycle. The '61 Super 10 and all of its descendants lost a little something when the company changed to 16-inch wheels. After the engine starts, you swing your leg over and feel the comfortable seating position. Pull in the large, straight, heavy clutch lever and push the left toe shifter down to the first of its measly three gears. You're about to notice the lack of a throttle return spring as you putt-putt away. If you are on relatively smooth streets you may not notice the lack of a rear suspension due to the comfort of the seat. The short-travel, Tele-Glide front suspension was relatively soft, too. Back then most Japanese bikes had short-travel rear shocks that were too stiff at the rear, in concert with leading-link front forks with limited travel, too. The difference in riding comfort between Japanese tiddlers of the period and the Super 10 was far less than you would expect, although many of the Hondas certainly were superior in the high-speed handling department. The speedometer has a big-bike look to it, too, and you know the gas tank was taken from this machine to the XLCH!

The second motorcycle I had a close encounter with was the Super 10's nemesis, the Honda 150 Benly Touring. Everything the Super 10 was, the Benly was not, and vice-versa. They both cost about $500 out the door and they were probably a high school kid's first graduation from a Schwinn. They were within 15cc of each other, but otherwise they were mortal enemies. The Super 10 had 18-inch wheels; the Benly had 16-inch ones. The Super 10 was started from the left and the Benly from the right, not to mention the starter button. The Super 10 had 1948 DKW single-cylinder, piston-port, mix-it-before-you-pour-it technology while the Benly was a SOHC twin. Honda probably fudged the advertised weight of 242 pounds like a fat lady, but that was still about 25 pounds porkier than the Harley-Davidson. The 16.5 hp rating of the Benly was probably a stretch, but so was anything approaching 10 hp for the Super 10. Although the Honda would reach its 84-mph claimed top speed only if you pushed it out the back of a cargo plane, it would go 70-75 mph readily. The Super 10 lost its spunk at about 50-60 mph, depending on the weight of the rider. The Honda Benly Touring represented the future and the Super 10 the past; or did it? Honda did later prove the Benly to be quite a basic toad with its single carburetor, basic cam, and leading-link front suspension. The CB-160 of five years later would join its brothers in the almost total takeover of the motorcycle market. What the Super 10 had tons of was style, image, and visceral appeal. Honda would finally figure this out twenty-five years later when it introduced one of its longest-running models, the 250 Rebel. And what exactly does a Rebel look like? A Super 10. And what does a Harley-Davidson Hugger of this millennium look like? A Super 10.

Almost as soon as I began my motorcycling career back in 1960, I began riding off-road. The Scat was the trail variant of the direct descendant of the short-lived Super 10, a model made only in 1960 and '61. The 165cc Super 10 became the 175cc Pacer in 1962, and a trail model with upswept exhaust, high, bobbed fenders, and knobbier tires was also added to the line of small, U.S.-built Harleys. (Yes, Martha, Harley-Davidson used to make motorcycles in the US of A that cost three figures instead of five and weighed somewhat less than a boxcar full of elephants!) The handlebars were a little higher than the flat ones of the Pacer in '62, but the Pacer received the Scat's handlebars in 1963, along with the same new rear suspension. The Scat finally got an actual rear suspension system in 1963 consisting of a large spring mounted underneath the frame at the swingarm pivot point. Although the spring worked as a solo artist, this was not exactly what Yamaha would later call a Monoshock. In five-figure elephant lingo, this is now called a Softtail. The Harley-Davidson Scat is a rare little beastie. I have encountered only a few of these personally in my lifetime.

The Harley-Davidson Hummer Charts

Harley-Davidson built a series of small two-stroke singles in their U.S. factory from 1948 to 1966. These models were marketed in three displacements under various model names. We are using the name *Hummer* here to loosely define the entire model group. All of these were piston-port two-strokes with three-speed, left-side foot shifts. The kick-starters were on the left side and were not foldable. Most of the mufflers were black with chrome header pipes, but chrome mufflers may have been an option on some models. The wheel rims and handlebars were also painted black on some models, with chrome components offered as options. The handgrips were larger in diameter than the handlebars and the throttles did not have return springs, making them feel quite different to the hand than those on small Japanese machines. A popular low-priced option was a choice of several colors of handgrips, from white to colors approximately matching the paint. A chart of the color codes shown immediately follows The Hummer Charts.

Figure C31 - Black 1948 Harley-Davidson S-125. ©Charles "Mutt" Hallam, photographer

110

Harley-Davidson 125cc S-model Single Chart

Year	Colors	Production	Suspension	Tank	Price
1948	A1	10,117	Girder	Solid Color	$325
1949	A1 - B - R	7291	Girder	Solid Color	$325
1950	A1 - B - B1 - R - Y	4708	Girder	Solid Color	$325
1951	B2 - B3 - G - G1 - R1 - Y	5101	Tele-Glide	Solid Color	$365
1952	B2 - B4 - G2 - R1	4576	Tele-Glide	Solid Color	$385

Harley-Davidson 125 S Notes: The original S-model had 1.7-3 hp, battery ignition and lighting, a 50-inch wheelbase, 19-inch wheels, a top speed of about 55 mph, weighed about 170 pounds, and had a 3-speed foot shift. The bore and stroke were 2.06" x 2.28". The 1948-50 models had fishtail-shaped muffler ends. The 1951-52 models were round. Some listed colors were optional at extra cost. Early models had a body-colored shroud over the top of the black headlight case. This may have been optional at extra cost.

Harley-Davidson 165cc ST-model Single Chart

Year	Colors	Production	Tank	Wheels	Price
1953	B5 - G3 - G4 - R2	4225	Solid Color	19-inch	$405
1954	B5 - G3 - I - I/A1 - R2 - Y1	2835	Solid Color	19-inch	$405
1955	A - B6 - G5 - R2 - Y1 - Z	2263	Solid Color	19-inch	$405
1956	B6 - G6 - J - R2 - X - Y2	2219	Solid Color	18-inch	$405
1957	B7 - F - R2 - W	2401	Round H-D Decal	18-inch	$445
1958	B7 - B8 - C - G7 - R3 - W/A	2445	Large 165 Logo	18-inch	$465
1959	B7 - C1 - R3 - R4 - T	2311	H-D Arrow Logo	18-inch	$475

Harley-Davidson 165 ST Notes: All of the 165cc ST's had Tele-Glide front suspension, no rear suspension, color-coordinated upper fork cover plates, 5.5 horsepower, a bore and stroke of 2.37" x 2.28", and battery ignition and lighting. Some listed colors were optional at extra cost. The 1958 model can be identified by its large white tank panel with a decal that states "Harley - 165 - Davidson".

111

Figure C32 - Red 1951 Harley-Davidson S-125. Note the Tele-Glide front fork that was new that year.
©Charles "Mutt" Hallam, photographer

Harley-Davidson Hummer 125cc Chart

Year	Colors	Production	Tank	Wheels	Brake	Price
1955	B6 - R2	1040	Solid Color	19-inch	None	$320
1956	B6 - G6 - J - R2	1384	Solid Color	18-inch	None	$320
1957	B7 - F - R2 - W	1350	Round H-D Decal	18-inch	Drum	$356
1958	B7 - B8 - C - G7 - R3 - W/A	1677	Hummer Decal	18-inch	Drum	$375
1959	B7 - C1 - R3 - R4 - T	1285	Large White Logo	18-inch	Drum	$385

Harley-Davidson Hummer 125 Notes: The 125cc was brought back into the lineup as a 3.5-hp economy model in 1955. The economizing was clearly visible in the black handlebars and wheel rims, you-squeeze-it bulb horn, and the deletion of the battery ignition and lighting. The weight had crept up to 178 pounds. This is the only model that was officially named *Hummer*. Note: The 1955-56 models had no front brake! The change from 19" to 18" wheels in 1956 may not be correct for this model. Some listed colors were optional at extra cost. The 1958 model can be identified by its large white tank panel with a decal that states "Harley - HUMMER - Davidson".

Figure C33 - Black Harley-Davidson Hummer of unknown vintage. This shot was taken by the author at the annual motorcycle races held between what was then called Town Lake and Riverside Drive in the heart of Austin, TX in the early Eighties. ©1980 Floyd M. Orr

Figure C34 - 1959 Red Harley-Davidson 165 STU with Accessories. This five-horsepower U model has been loaded up with options. Note the windshield with bag attached, black leather saddlebags, and mudflaps. It is not evident in this black and white picture, but the machine also has matching red handgrips and red cables, such as the clearly visible front brake cable. ©Charles "Mutt" Hallam, photographer

Harley-Davidson Super 10 165cc Chart

Year	Colors	Production	Tank	Wheels	Price
1960	B7 - B8 - G7 - R4 - W/R4	2488	Single Stripe thru White Panel	18-inch	$465
1961	B8 - G7 - H - P - R2 - R4	1527	Curved Parallel White Stripes	16-inch	$465

Harley-Davidson Super 10 Notes: The Super 10 had a 9-hp (actually closer to 5.5 hp) version of the B (Hummer) engine. A version restricted to 5 hp was also offered. This transition model between the ST and Pacer was offered with options such as Buckhorn handlebars and Buddy Seats in white or gray. All Super 10's had magneto ignition instead of a battery. Harley Hummer.com lists the 1961 production total as 1587. Some listed colors were optional at extra cost.

Figure C35 - Red 1961 Harley-Davidson Super 10. Note the optional passenger pillion and the smaller sixteen-inch wheels that were new that year. ©Charles "Mutt" Hallam, photographer

Harley-Davidson Ranger 165cc Chart

Year	Colors	Production	Tank	Wheels	Price
1962	B7 - P - R4 - R5	186	White Top Panel	18-inch	$440

Harley-Davidson Ranger Notes: The Ranger was produced until the factory ran out of 165cc engines. The Ranger was basically a stripped Scat without lights or a front fender. The gearing was very low for off-road work, and the same gearing was offered as an option on the Scat. This Trail option on the Scat included very radical gearing with a 12-tooth countershaft and 84-tooth rear sprockets!

114

Harley-Davidson Pacer 175cc Chart

Year	Colors	Production	Suspension	Tank	Price
1962	B7 - P - R4 - R5	807	rigid	White Top Panel	$465
1963	A - R4 - R5 - T	625	spring	Birch White Lower Panel	$485
1964	A - B8 - R6	650	spring	Large White Side Panel	$495
1965	A - B8 - B9 - R4 - R7	550	spring	White Lower Panel & Stripe	$505

Harley-Davidson Pacer Notes: The Pacer and Scat both had six horsepower, a bore and stroke of 2.37" x 2.41", a 52-inch wheelbase, and a 1.9 gallon tank painted in the same colors and patterns for each year. All Pacers had 16-inch wheels. The listed weight of the Pacer was 205 pounds. Some listed colors were optional at extra cost. The 1962 Pacer had the flat handlebars of its predecessors. The 1963-65 Pacers had the Scat's higher bars.

Figure C36 - Black 1964 Harley-Davidson Pacer 175. ©Charles "Mutt" Hallam

Harley-Davidson Scat 175cc Chart

Year	Colors	Production	Tank	Suspension	Price
1962	B7 - P - R4 - R5	993	White Top Panel	Rigid	$475
1963	A - R4 - R5 - T	1125	Birch White Lower Panel	Spring	$495
1964	A - B8 - R6	800	Large White Side Panel	Spring	$505
1965	A - B8 - B9 - R4 - R7	700	White Lower Panel with Stripe	Spring	$515

Harley-Davidson Scat Notes: The listed weight of the Scat was 220 pounds. All Scats had high-mounted fenders, 18-inch wheels, and semi-knobby tires. The most interesting component of the Pacer and Scat of 1963 was the new rear suspension spring mounted underneath the engine, predating the Softtail by about twenty years! Some listed colors were optional at extra cost.

Figure C37 - 1962 Red Harley-Davidson Scat. This is the only year the 175cc Scat did not have rear suspension. The 1963 model would get the new rear suspension comprised of a big spring hidden underneath the swingarm, the progenitor to the Softtail designs of the Eighties. ©Charles "Mutt" Hallam

Harley-Davidson Bobcat 175cc Chart

Year	Colors	Production	Exhaust	Wheels	Price
1966	R7 - S - U	1150	Chrome	18-inch	$515

Harley-Davidson Bobcat Notes: The main distinction of the Bobcat was its one-piece, fiberglass tank cover, seat base, and rear fender, much like the one that would later appear on the original Super Glide. The standard muffler was painted black, but I believe nearly all Bobcats were sold with the optional chrome muffler. The Sparkling Burgundy paint color was optional at extra cost.

Hummer Color Code Chart

Solely for the purpose of easily fitting all of the color names into the charts above, each color has been assigned a letter designation. These are as follows:

A - Black	G - Metallic Green	R2 - Pepper Red
A1- Brilliant Black	G1 - Spring Green	R3 - Calypso Red
B - Azure Blue	G2 - Tropical Green	R4 - Hi-Fi Red
B1 - Riviera Blue	G3 - Forest Green	R5 - Tango Red
B2 - Rio Blue	G4 - Glamour Green	R6 - Fiesta Red
B3 - Metallic Blue	G5 - Hollywood Green	R7 - Holiday Red
B4 - Marine Blue Metallic	G6 - Tampico Green	S - Sparkling Burgundy
B5 - Glacier Blue	G7 - Hi-Fi Green	T - Hi-Fi Turquoise
B6 - Atomic Blue	H - Hi-Fi Flamingo	U - Indigo Metallic
B7 - Skyline Blue	I - Daytona Ivory	W - Birch White
B8 - Hi-Fi Blue	J - Sun Gold	X - Tangerine
B9 - Pacific Blue	P - Hi-Fi Purple	Y - Sportsman Yellow
C - Tropical Coral	R - Flight Red	Y1 - Anniversary Yellow
C1 - H-Fi Coral	R1 - Persian Red	Y2 - Champion Yellow
F - High Fire		Z - Aztec Brown

Harley-Davidson Topper

HolySchmoly, Batman, talk about an ugly stepchild! No tiddler has ever been so embarrassingly locked in the stinky back closet of the garage as has the 1959-65 Harley-Davidson Topper. Whether it was named after Hopalong Cassidy's horse or a giant bunny rabbit, nobody knows. What we do know is that H-D decided to challenge Cushman to a duel and found itself blasted back to the hog farm where it belonged. Even the Allstate Cruisaire landed a few punches from the Sears Roebuck catalog. At least the Cruisaire had a fan-cooled engine and a plump (but sexy in a strange way) Italian body. Although the product developers at Harley probably thought it was time to go after a piece of the scooter market, their more likely nemesis came from the unexpected arrival of Honda. The Topper was launched in May 1959, only a couple of months before Honda began its siege. With a base price of $430, the Topper was nearly double the opening price for a Honda Cub, especially when you added the traditional Harley accessories, which always raised the price a little. My guess would be that it was all over but the crying soon after Honda launched its Benly Touring 150 on 9/1/59. For about fifty dollars more, the Benly brought a twin-cylinder four-stroke with a four-speed transmission, electric starter, 16.5 (although exaggerated) horsepower, battery-powered electrics, and a heapin' helpin' more styling, handling, speed and pizzazz!

The Topper story began in a place you would never expect. The Tomahawk Boat Manufacturing Company was founded in Tomahawk, Wisconsin, in 1945 to build small wooden recreational boats. At some point in time approximating the beginning of the 1950's, Tomahawk began to shift its emphasis to fiberglass boats. When the boat market fell into a temporary slump a few years later, the company branched out into the manufacturing of miscellaneous other fiberglass products. These included saddlebags, sidecars, and golf carts for Harley-Davidson. At some point between 1960 and February 1962, depending on the source, H-D purchased portions of the Tomahawk manufacturing operation. Harley owned 51%, then 60%, and eventually the whole company. You can see where this is going, can't you? Not only have there been many Harley-Davidson golf carts swarming the fairways, but there were even Harley-Davidson Tomahawk boats built and marketed in 1962! Sources do not agree as to exactly how many H-D boats were built or for how long, but the Tomahawk Division still builds fiberglass components for Harley-Davidson today. Just imagine the board meeting that surely occurred at some point back in the foggy reaches of time. "If we are going to buy all this fiberglass stuff from Tomahawk, we might as well have them build us a whole damn scooter!"

All Toppers had two-tone paint jobs featuring Birch White engine covers and headlamp nacelles. Additionally, the early models had a white panel running down the center of the front side of the leg shields and continuing onto the front fender. The frame, floorboards, and front fender were made of steel and the rest of the bodywork on the crudely-styled Topper was fiberglass. This included the engine cover and the panel behind the leg shields. The front fender was riveted to the leg shields, leaving the front tire to swing side to side underneath the broad fender. The Topper shared a 9.5-hp, 165cc two-stroke engine with the Super 10. The speedometer was the elegantly readable 60-mph model from the Super 10, too. The Topper used a centrifugal clutch with pulleys that created an *automatic transmission*. There was no battery; starting and lighting were powered by magneto. One of the most plebeian details of the Topper was its lawnmower-style rope starter! The 1960 colors included Pepper Red, Granada Green, and Strato Blue. The 1960 Strato Blue model had matching wheels. We do not know about the other two colors, but most photos (of all years) show white wheels. Like the early Mustangs, technically there were no 1959 models. You can see from the production figures in the chart below that 1960 was a long production year.

New colors for 1961 included Hi-Fi Red, Granada Green, and Strato Blue, and this seems to be the only change from the 1960 models. Prices were increased slightly and you can see where the sales slump begins. The 1962 model introduced the white pressed steel handlebars. There was no longer a standard white front panel, however, this trim piece may have become optional at extra cost. The '62 colors included Birch White, Tango Red, and Granada Green. The key slot was in the center of the handlebar. I have not been able to ascertain if the ignition switch was located elsewhere on the earlier models with chrome tube handlebars. Many H-D books cover the first model in detail and I have an original '63 brochure on hand, but locating firm details of the '61-62 models has been difficult.

The 1963 model had a *Harley-Davidson* decal on the side of the white panel on the engine cover, instead of a *Topper* emblem. The handlebars continued as white-painted pressed steel. The seat was a new for '63 all-black lump with a tiny ridge along the rear edge. Its covering was plain without pleats and the foam was slightly thicker. There was no white panel in front. Optional was an ungainly, sharp-cornered, white *utility box* attached behind the leg shields, crowding the rider's knee room. Other options included a windshield, chrome luggage rack, folding passenger pegs, and a rearview mirror attached low on the left front side of the leg shields. The dry weight was 227 pounds. The wheels were 4 x 12. The '63 colors were Black, Birch White, and Tango Red.

The '64 and '65 models soldiered on practically identical to the '63's. The 1964 colors were Black and Fiesta Red. The colors in 1965 were Pacific Blue and Holiday Red. Either a sidecar or a giant white utility box in place of a sidecar was offered as an option, at least from 1963-onward. These may have been available on the earlier models, too. It is very difficult to define a precise model year in some cases, but Toppers can generally be divided between the early and late models. If you squint, you can see where Harley-Davidson deftly cut a few costs on the trim of the later models. The elegant, two-tone seat, standard white front panel, and attached ID emblem disappeared. You can also see in the chart that the price increased another ten dollars and the sales continued to plummet. If you review in your mind the array of Hondas, Yamahas, and Suzukis that rolled onto American soil during the tiddler boom of these years, the quick and permanent demise of Harley-Davidson's lonely, homely scooter will be clearly defined. It was bulky, plain, crude, and slow, with all the cache of the fat boy you knew in the Eighth Grade.

Harley-Davidson Topper Chart

Year	Production	Front Panel	Bars	Seat	Emblem	Price
1959	(see 1960)	White	Chrome	Two-tone	Topper	$430
1960	3801	White	Chrome	Two-tone	Topper	$430
1961	1341	White	Chrome	Two-tone	Topper	$445
1962	NA	Body Color	White	Two-tone	H-D decal	$445
1963	978	Body Color	White	Black	H-D decal	$460
1964	825	Body Color	White	Black	H-D decal	$470
1965	500	Body Color	White	Black	H-D decal	$470

Harley-Davidson Topper Notes: All Toppers had 165cc, 9.5-hp two-stroke engines, CVT *Scootaway* transmissions, drum brakes, leading link front suspension, white headlamp nacelles, and white handgrips. The optional passenger pegs were usually black, but some were equipped with white ones. Oddities such as red handgrips and unusual colors have been seen. These could have been non-stock restorations or legitimate, original options. With Harley-Davidson, sometimes it is difficult to tell.

The May 1964 issue of *Cycle World* devoted its Report from Italy feature column to the Harley-Davidson Brezza, a 150cc scooter built by Aermacchi. The fan-cooled, six-horsepower two-stroke had a three-speed hand shift and twelve-inch wheels. Its modern styling for the day looked very much like a Lambretta with its two-tone paint, wide, flat, dual saddle, and removable side panels for drive train servicing. Like the Topper, its unstressed body panels were made of fiberglass. The Brezza made the Topper look like a big square toad. Harley-Davidson imported five of these to test the machine for possible importation into the U.S. market. You can see from the Topper's sliding sales figures above that the company had probably absorbed a good dose of scooter market paranoia by 1964, but it is interesting now to ponder what might have been a much better Harley-Davidson scooter than the Topper!

Harley-Davidson Sprint

Figure C38 - Red 1961 Harley-Davidson Sprint. ©Michael Kiernan, Classic Motorcycle Company, St. Louis, MO.

I have had an approach/avoidance conflict with the Sprint H since 1963, my favorite model year of this lovable/cantankerous beast. We all know the storyline. H-D was having its V-twin lunch eaten by a horde of little Japanese minisquirts, and the company just had to do something about the onslaught. They thought that Americans had respect for Italian motorcycles, and the troubled Aermacchi factory was for sale, so they bought it and began to put their logo on the gas tanks of a bunch of 50-350cc models imported throughout The Sixties.

My feelings toward the Sprint are no better or worse than they are toward most '60's Italian bikes. I simply do not care for OHV thumpers, hard, narrow seats, right side shifters and left side kickstarters, or machines that feel compelled to make just starting up a fussing, cussing affair to remember. The '63 H-D brochure showing the Sprint H climbing a hill is one of my fondest marketing memories. I love the off-road styling with its exposed rear springs, rubber gaiters, high, abbreviated fenders, and high exhaust pipe, but you can still take that buckboard seat and shove it. I would guess that the 1963, and to a slightly lesser degree, the '64, Sprint H is my favorite classic Italian tiddler after the Ducati Diana.

The 1961 Sprint C was brought in much as the Italians had originally designed it, with a large tank and fenders, seventeen-inch wheels, eighteen horsepower, and a somewhat crouched riding position. Did I mention that the Sprint had a one-up, three down shift pattern exquisitely designed to be an accident ready to happen? The sportier, off-road oriented H became the companion to the basic C in 1962. The first H can be distinguished by its eighteen-inch wheels, high exhaust, white tank panels, chrome covered rear shocks, and low front fender. The '63 model had a red tank with a wide white stripe, exposed chrome rear springs, and a high-clearance front fender. The white tank panels returned in '64, and this was the last dirt-oriented 250cc Sprint H. The 1965 model H had chrome covers on the upper rear springs and the new low pipe and front fender. Other photos I have show an exhaust pipe more like that of the earlier H's, with a bullet-shaped muffler bulging from a smaller diameter pipe.

Although the Sprint continued in the Harley-Davidson lineup for several more years, the party was quietening down rapidly as the CL-160 showed the Sprint H its tailpipe for a much lower price. Even my extensive collection of H-D books offers little confirmation of the model year details as the Sprint continued into the later '60's. Harley added the SS model and the option of a black paint job, but even a shorter-stroke engine design was not enough to launch the Sprint rapidly off the showroom floor. The Sprint grew to 350cc in 1969. Just imagine the ease with which the CL-350, SL-350, DT-1, and RT-1 would run and hide from a 350 Sprint while its rider was still back at the ranch trying to start it!

Figure C39 - 1961 Red Harley-Davidson Sprint. Note the left-side kickstarter and the somewhat unusual rear shock mounts. The first-year Sprint model probably was imported from Aermacchi only in red. There may have been a few Sprints with European-style low bars sent here in the early years, but I am not sure about that point. There certainly were European-style models imported under the Aermacchi brand, instead of Harley-Davidson, though. ©Michael Kiernan, Classic Motorcycle Company, St. Louis, MO.

Harley-Davidson Sprint Chart

Year	Model	Color	Tank Panels	Exhaust	Wt.	Price
1961	C	Red	White Front Portion	Down	261	$650
1962	C	Red	Front Portion Curve	Down	261	$695
1962	H	Red	Front Portion Curve	Upswept	271	NA
1962	R	Red	Front Portion Curve	Down	NA	NA
1963	C	Tango Red	White Top Panel	Down	261	NA
1963	H	Tango Red	White Top Panel	Upswept	271	$720
1964	C	Tango Red	White Side Panel	Down	261	NA
1964	H	Tango Red	White Side Panel	Upswept	271	NA
1965	C	Tango Red	White Bottom Portion	Down	NA	NA
1965	H	Tango Red	White Bottom Portion	Down	NA	NA
1965	CR	Tango Red	White Bottom Portion	Down	265	$855
1966	C	Black	White Side Panel	Down	NA	NA
1966	H	Black	White Side Panel	Down	NA	NA
1966	CRTT	Red	White Side Panel	Down	215	NA
1967	H	Black	Wide White Stripe on Top	Down	273	$720
1967	SS	Black	Wide White Stripe on Top	Down	281	$750
1967	CRS	Orange	NA	Down	NA	NA
1968	H	Blue / Black	Pebble Grain on Top	Down	273	$720
1968	SS	Blue / Black	Pebble Grain on Top	Down	281	$750
1968	CRS	Orange	Black Stripe on Top	Down	256	NA
1969	SS-350	Bl/Blk/Or	White Pinstripe	2 Down	323	$770
1969	ERS	Orange	Black Trim	Down	259	$975
1970	SS-350	Blue	White Pinstripe	Down	311	$793

1970	ERS	Orange	Black Trim	Down	259	$995
1971	SS-350	Green	*Sprint* in Big Letters	Down	311	$825
1971	SX-350	Red / Green	*Sprint* in Big Letters	Upswept	298	$870
1971	ERS	Orange	Black Trim	Down	259	$995
1972	SS-350	Red / Green	Orange Swirl Decal / HD	Down	298	$795
1972	SX-350	Yellow	Orange Swirl Decal / HD	Upswept	298	NA
1972	ERS	Orange	Black Trim	Down	259	NA
1973	SS-350	Red	White Band Across Tank	Down	311	$879
1973	SX-350	Black	White Band Across Tank	Upswept	298	$879
1974	SS-350	Blue	Yellow/Red H-D Decal	Down	311	$995
1974	SX-350	Dark Blue	Red/Blue H-D Decal	Upswept	298	$995

Harley-Davidson Sprint Notes: All 250 Sprints had single-cylinder, horizontal, OHV engines, four-speed, right side foot shifters, kickstarters, and backbone tube frames. Early C models had 17-inch wheels and H models had 18-inch ones. The '62 H has a small front fender mounted low to the tire. The front fender was raised several inches above the tire in 1963, and lowered again in 1965. At least one source has stated that the original Sprints were available in Red & Silver and Gray & Black color combinations, but I have never seen anything except red with white trim on these early models, even in photographs. The 1965 Sprint H may have been available with either a high or low exhaust pipe: I have seen photos of both. The 1961-66 250 C-models were rated at 18 horsepower, the H's at 21, and the Competition models at 25. The 1961-66 250 Sprints had an undersquare OHV engine. New dimensions changed this to an oversquare engine in '67 with a claimed 18% power increase. A longer stroke brought the displacement up to 346cc in 1969. The 1969 SS-350 came in Radiant Blue, Midnight Black, or Orange. The weight listed for this 1969 model is with a half tank of fuel, as published by *Cycle World*. The '73 and '74 SS and SX models had cradle frames, Ceriani-style front forks, electric starters, turn signals, and left-side, five-speed shifters. Harley-Davidson sold about 2000 Sprints a year in the early Sixties and about 5000 annually later in the decade. There were probably about 40,000 Sprints sold in the USA throughout the entire production run.

An unknown number of CRTT road racers and CRS short trackers were produced in 1961-65 at a rate of no more than fifty per year. The production numbers of the Sprint 350 ERS were: 250 (1969) - 102 (1970) - 50 (1971) - 50 (1972). Sources indicate that 120 were built in 1968, but it is unclear whether those were 250's or 350's. The total ERS production has been reported as 572. All claimed dry weights are in pounds. The 1963 CRTT road racer had 28.5 horsepower, weighed 245 pounds, and cost $900. The 1966 five-speed CRTT model had 35 horsepower.

Figure C40 - Red Harley-Davidson SS-350 Sprint. ©Troyce Walls, photographer

Figure C41 - Red 1968 Harley-Davidson Sprint CRS. ©Warren P. Warner, owner and photographer

Harley-Davidson/Aermacchi Two-Stroke Chart

Year	Model	Type	Colors	Tank	Price
1965	M-50	Step-Thru	Red	White Panels	$225
1966	M-50	Step-Thru	Red	White Panels	NA
1966	M-50 Sport	Street	Red	White Panels	$275
1967	M-65	Step-Thru	Bronze Red	White Stripes	$230
1967	M-65 Sport	Street	Bronze Red	White Stripes	$275
1968	M-65	Step-Thru	Blue	White Panels	NA
1968	M-65 Sport	Street	Red	Pinstripes	$275
1968	Rapido	Street	Black	Pinstripe	$395
1969	M-65	Step-Thru	Gold	H-D Emblem	$215
1969	M-65 Sport	Street	Gold	H-D Emblem	$230
1969	Rapido	Street	Black	Silver Panel	$400
1969	Rapido Trail	Scrambler	Orange	Silver Panel	$425
1970	M-65	Step-Thru	NA	NA	NA
1970	Leggero	Street	Sandy Gold	Black Band	$240
1970	Baja 100	Off-road	Black	Pinstripe	$670
1970	Rapido	Scrambler	Red	Silver panel	$450
1971	M-65	Step-Thru	NA	NA	NA
1971	Leggero	Street	Red	White Stripe	$295
1971	Baja 100	Off-road	Black	Checkered Decal	$670
1971	Rapido	Scrambler	Orange / Green	Silver Panel	$495
1972	Shortster	Mini-bike	Yellow	Orange Swirl	NA
1972	Leggero	Scrambler	Dark red	Orange Swirl	$295
1972	Baja 100	Off-road	Black	Orange Swirl	$670
1972	Rapido	Enduro	Orange	Silver Panel	$495
1973	X-90	Mini-bike	Brown	H-D Emblem	$325
1973	Z-90	Scrambler	Blue	White Band	$375

1973	SR-100	Off-road	Black	White Band	$690
1973	TX-125	Enduro	NA	White Band	$565
1974	X-90	Mini-bike	Brown	H-D Stripes	$375
1974	Z-90	Scrambler	Blue	H-D Stripes	$425
1974	SR-100	Off-road	Black	H-D Stripes	$690
1974	SX-125	Enduro	Blue	H-D Stripes	$635
1974	SX-175	Enduro	Blue	H-D Stripes	$795
1975	X-90	Mini-bike	Blue	Swoopy Stripes	$495
1975	Z-90	Street	Brown	Swoopy Stripes	$565
1975	SX-125	Enduro	Blue	Swoopy Stripes	$749
1975	SX-175	Enduro	Blue	Swoopy Stripes	$930
1975	SX-250	Enduro	Brown	Swoopy Stripes	$1130
1976	SS-125	Street	Orange	AMF H-D Decal	$799
1976	SXT-125	Enduro	Orange	AMF H-D Decal	$799
1976	SS-175	Street	Brown	AMF H-D Decal	$999
1976	SX-175	Enduro	Blue	AMF H-D Decal	$971
1976	SS-250	Street	Black / Orange	AMF H-D Decal	$1215
1976	SX-250	Enduro	Black	AMF H-D Decal	$1168
1977	SS-125	Street	NA	*125* Decal	NA
1977	SXT-125	Enduro	Black	*125* Decal	NA
1977	SS-175	Street	Red	*175* Decal	NA
1977	SS-250	Street	NA	*250* Decal	NA
1977	SX-250	Enduro	Red	*250* Decal	$1142
1977	MX-250	Motocross	Orange	*250* Decal	$1695
1978	SX-250	Enduro	Black	*250* Decal	NA
1978	MX-250	Motocross	Orange	*250* Decal	$1695

127

Figure C42 - I think this photo of a Harley-Davidson tiddler in the Barber Museum is a 1966 M-50 Sport, but it could be an M-65 Sport from a later year. Charting this particular tiddler that few care about today was really tough. Image by Chuck Schultz under Creative Commons license.

Harley-Davidson/Aermacchi Notes: All M models had three-speed transmissions with left-hand shifters. Harley sold about 9000 M-50's in 1965, but the sales of the M-series models dwindled downward through the production years. The 1969 brochure states that the Rapido and Rapido Trail were available in Midnight Black, Jet Fire Orange, and Radiant Blue, but there is no other evidence of blue ones being produced. I have never even seen a photo of a street Rapido in any color other than black or a trail model in anything other than orange. The Baja came with lights in 1972-onward. The 1965-72 models were premix with right-side shifters; the 1973-78 models were oil injected with left-side shifters. The 90cc models were four-speeds. The SS models had downswept pipes and low fenders and the SX models had upswept pipes and high fenders. The 1973 TX-125 and the SS & SX 124cc, 174cc, and 242cc models of 1974-78 had oil injection and five-speed transmissions with left-side shifters. *Cycle Guide* had an ad for the SX-175 in dark blue with a blue decal and in black with a yellow decal in its October 1975 issue. Did the SX-175 also come in a black, very similar to the blue, or was that a 125 pictured also? Note that the decal type shown in this ad is a 1976. The MX-250 motocrosser may be the rare bird of the bunch today since only 87 were imported before Harley-Davidson called a halt to the whole two-stroke Aermacchi fiasco.

Figure C43 - Red 1962 Harley-Davidson 175 Pacer with Buckhorn Handlebars. This is one of my favorite photos in this book because it closely captures my first motorcycle riding experience. Like the Super 10, the first-year Pacer is a hardtail. Like the 1961 Super 10, the Pacer has sixteen-inch wheels. This particular example has the optional fender trim and chrome crash bars. The fantasy machine that I need to take me back to 1960 would be a Hi-Fi Blue 1960 Super 10 with Buckhorns, Buddy Seat with a gray top and white side panels, chrome passenger rail behind the seat, chrome crash bars, and black leather saddle bags. ©Charles "Mutt" Hallam

129

Selected Allstate Models Ratings Chart

Years	Models	Collectibility	Practicality	Desirability
1956-66	Mopeds & Compact	C	D	C
1951-69	Cruisaire	B	B	C
1960-68	Sport 60 & Cheyenne	D	D	C
1954-66	125 & 150 Hardtail	C	D	C
1953-67	175 Twingle	B	C	B
1954-67	250 Twingle	B	C	B
1967-68	SR 250	C	B	C
1959-65	ISDT Scrambler	A	C	A
1966-68	106 & 124 Sport	C	B	C
1964-69	Sabre 50 & SR 125	C	C	D

Selected Harley-Davidson Models Ratings Chart

Years	Models	Collectibility	Practicality	Desirability
1948-59	125 & 165 S-models	A	D	A
1960-61	Super 10	A	D	A
1962-66	Pacer, Scat, Ranger, Bobcat	A	D	A
1959-65	Topper Scooter	C	D	B
1961-68	250 Sprint	A	D	B
1969-74	350 Sprint	C	C	C
1965-72	M-models & Leggero	D	C	D
1968-74	Rapido 125 & Baja 100	C	C	C
1973-78	SS & SX Two-strokes	D	B	D

Models Ratings Chart Definitions:

Years: Some early model years within a series may be considerably more desirable than later years. All grade ratings are based on evaluations of all the machines covered in this book, not just as a comparative rating within each marque.

Models: In some cases many variations are included in this category and in others the models included are very homogeneous.

Collectibility: This is what most of you want to know, the bottom line on how likely the model or series is likely to climb in value over the coming years.

Practicality: This is an indicator of how adaptable the machine can be to ride for transportation or pleasure in the modern world, considering parts availability, fuel quality, comfort, performance and miscellaneous other obvious factors.

Desirability: This defines the nostalgic, emotional wow factor, without regard for collector values or everyday usage.

General: No machine is given a failing grade. If it made it into a rating chart, at least a few hobbyists find that model interesting.

Figure C44 - Cushman Super Eagle. You can clearly see the Husky cast iron engine, hand shift lever, and primitive ratchet kickstarter lever in this photo. This model is probably more common and less expensive to restore than the Silver Eagle with its aluminum engine. Image by Chuck Schultz, photographer, under Creative Commons license.

The Home Front

Chapter 3: *The Europeans Were Here First*

The story of motorcycles in World War II and the immediate postwar period has been published numerous times in great detail. If you are a fan of motorcycle history, you know all about the participation of Harley-Davidson in the war, followed by the early formation of the biker gangs comprised of bored ex-WWII riders wanting to continue their exciting lifestyles. BMW participated with the same opposing team that bombed the motorcycle factories of Britain. Several other motorcycle-producing European countries were affected, too. Strangely enough, the most avidly sought machines in postwar Japan were big Harleys, BSA's, and Triumphs! Of course you remember that the Kawasaki W1 650 was a direct copy of a BSA. It would be a decade before the Japanese tiddler industry really got going. So what was happening in the U.S. motorcycle market between World War II and Honda's arrival in 1959?

Relatively small numbers of machines from many European brands were scattered across the USA. Keep in mind that most of these arrived on the East Coast, not the West, and the suburban sprawl that would come to dominate the West, South, and Midwest had only just begun. The most prevalent brands and models will be covered briefly later in this chapter, generally in the order in which they became relatively common in the American market. For the purpose of this book, they are presented by origin. The Germans are listed first, followed by the English, then the Italians, and finally the Spanish. The focus of *The Tiddler Invasion* is 1955-75. By the end of that boom period in U.S. motorcycle sales, all but BMW, Ducati, and Vespa would be gone from the U.S. market. Most of these barely established a beachhead before Honda with its relentless market dominance slapped them back to Europe. Each of these key brands shipped significant numbers of small machines to the U.S. during the boom. Each deserves mention to set the stage for the Japanese Tiddler Invasion; however, far more brands were actually here in tiny pockets of this great nation, albeit in very small numbers. This book hits only the highlights, or in some cases, the lowlights.

Numerous European brands may have been here in the 1955-75 period, but are not included in this book because (a) they were not here very long, (b) they did not sell many machines in the USA, (c) most or all of their sales were of machines larger than 450cc, and/or (d) most of the company's products were off-road machines. The decision to include each brand or not usually involved a combination of two or more of these four factors. The list of brands not included is a long one: AJS, Ariel, Batavus, Bianchi, Broncco, Capriolo, Cimatti, Cooper, Garelli, Gilera, Giulietta, Greeves, Hercules, Husqvarna, Indian, Italjet, Maico, Mobylette, Mondial, Motobecane, Moto-Beta, Motobic, Moto Guzzi, Moto Morini, MV Agusta, Norton, Ocelot, Pannonia, Panther, Parilla, Penton, Royal Enfield, Sachs, Tempo, Velocette, Vincent, White, and at least a few I have forgotten to mention.

DKW RT 125

Although the focus of *The Tiddler Invasion* is on models ranging from 1955 through 1975, the little DKW 125 of the Thirties deserves special mention. Dampf Kraft Wagen was founded in Germany in 1916 and began building small, two-stroke motorcycles in the 1920's. DKW was the world's largest motorcycle manufacturer in the '30's. After several mergers with Audi, Auto Union, and Benz, DKW joined VW in '64 and the brand name was finally phased out at the end of 1966.

Why do we give a Super Rat's ass about this ancient tiddler? The design of the DKW 125cc two-stroke engine became a significant part of war reparations paid to Allied countries after WWII. All the U. S.-built Harley two-strokes, from the first 1948 Model S to the last 1966 Bobcat owe their heritage to the DKW RT 125. Would there ever have been a line of Yamaha motorcycles without the RT 125? We shall never know if the inspiration could have come from elsewhere anyway, but we do know that the DKW 125 was the direct predecessor of the first Yamaha, just as with the Harley-Davidson tiddlers. Although never sold in high numbers in America, the BSA Bantam was yet another model founded upon the DKW tiddler. Yes, I know that Japan was not exactly in on the reparations deal, but Yamaha's 125cc YA-1 was a direct copy of the DKW design.

With their large wheels, triangulated, hardtail frames, teardrop gas tanks, low handlebars, and sprung, solo saddles, there is no mistaking the similarities of the models by DKW, BSA, Yamaha, and Harley-Davidson described here. There was even a Russian version, the name of which I cannot even pronounce, and MZ continued production of the design later than the other brands. I cannot be sure of the model year of the black RT 125 pictured here. It has been designated as a 1950 model by one source and a 1952-58 model by another. You might accurately call the DKW RT 125 the true founding father of The Tiddler Invasion!

Figure D1 - 1950 Black DKW RT 125 at the Audi Museum in Ingolstadt. This is the machine that started it all. Image by Lothar Spurzem under Creative Commons license.

NSU Max & Maxi

Figure D2 - Sea Green 1955 NSU Superlux. Image by Lothar Spurzxem under Creative Commons license.

Techno-motorheads, listen up! NSU tiddlers were imported into the U. S. in very small numbers from the postwar era until the Japanese took over the market in the early '60's. On the surface, you may be saying, *So?* These machines were so stinking interesting from an historical, mechanical standpoint that I hope I can remember all the technological points I want to mention in this brief synopsis!

NSU first built the 100cc Fox in 1949, followed by the 250cc Max in '53. Over the next few years, these would be joined in the lineup by the 175cc Maxi, a 300cc, a moped, and the Prima scooter. The ones you are most likely to have encountered are the Max and Maxi, and maybe the Fox and Prima. We're going to concentrate on the Max and Maxi in our techie discussion here, but many of the same details also apply to the other models.

NSU sent these machines to the U. S. up through 1963, at least. I don't know if there were any '64's imported or not, but the 1963 brochure I have is definitely from the last year of the Max. According to Sheldon's EMU, Maxis were built through 1964, and they far outnumbered the quantity of Max 250's throughout most production years. Were more

Maxis brought to the U. S. than Maxes? I don't know. I highly recommend the EMU site for far more detailed information about all NSU models. Wikipedia covers the car line in more detail. The brand is merely on the fringe of the subject range of this book. One of the most fascinating things about NSU is that the company produced the first rotary-engined car with the Wankel Spider in 1964. Mass production of that technology would later make Mazda a household name. NSU continued to innovate and produce cars, becoming a part of Audi in 1969.

According to European Motorcycle Universe, NSU built 31,471 Maxis from 1957 to 1964 and 15,473 SuperMaxes from 1956 to 1963. The production figures quite obviously appear as if the Japanese were pushing NSU into the dustbin of tiddler history in the early Sixties, since only 851 250's were built in 1962 and '63 combined. Although there were more than 13,000 Maxis built in '63-'64, I strongly suspect that these stayed home in Europe. Until I carefully examined Sheldon's numbers, I would have guessed that the Super Max was the biggest seller in the USA, and it may very well have been. Note that the model actually imported was the 18-hp Super Max. The last year of the regular, 17-hp Max was 1956.

What's all the brouhaha about technology? The 175cc Maxi had strange-looking

pressed steel handlebars similar to the ones on the early Honda Dreams sent to the U. S. in very small numbers. The engine is an OHC single with a patented system of rods called ULTRAMAX operating the cam. Ducati Desmo, anyone? The engine is a wet-sump type. The front suspension is leading-link type. Look at how the headlamp is attached! The standard seat was a solo model attached at the front. A passenger seat, perched high above the driver's saddle, or luggage rack was optional on some models, and some had conventional dual seats, similar to the Allstate Twingles. The frame is pressed steel and the chain is fully enclosed. All models had the distinctive little metal tool boxes straddling the rear wheel like tiny saddlebags. Notice the swoopy fenders and delicate pin striping. The four-speed footshift was on the left, and so was the kickstarter. The exhaust pipe is on the left on the Super Max and on the right on the Maxi. You can see many styling and design parallels with the Puch two-stroke 250 and 175. The more expensive and exotic NSU's will always be rare collectibles. How different would things have been if Sears & Roebuck had chosen to market the OHC version instead?

Figure D3 - Sky Blue 1957 NSU Supermax. Image by Huhu Uet under Creative Commons license.

BMW R-27

Figure D4 - Black 1964 BMW R-27 250 Single.

Image by Jeff Dean, photographer, under Creative Commons license in the Public Domain.

The legendary German snot brand BMW built a single tiddler model consistently from prior to World War II until 1967. The company sold the R-23 250cc single prior to WWII, but Germany was forbidden from manufacturing motorcycles immediately thereafter. The ban was lifted a few years later and BMW released its R-24 model in 1948. The hardtail R-24 was replaced by the R-25 with plunger-type rear suspension in 1950. The 1956 R-26 brought a real swingarm rear suspension, the Earles-type front fork, a foot shift, and a fully enclosed driveshaft.

Figure D5 - 1957 White BMW R-26. ©Michael Kiernan, Classic Motorcycle Company, St. Louis, MO.

The 1963 brochure is an example taken from the center of the production life of BMW's last traditional, shaft-drive single. The R-27 was introduced in 1960 and continued through the 1966 model year. Changes from the R-26 were minimal. Its eighteen horsepower numbered three more than the previous model, but it was still offered only in *black and white and rode all over.* You may recognize that clever phrase from the magazine advertising of the '60's. The black paintjobs with white pinstriping were by far the more common, so the rare few painted in white with black pinstriping are highly sought collectibles. The R-27 was the smoothest of the BMW singles due to rubber mounting of the engine. Remember that snot I mentioned? The base price of the 18-horsepower, 345-pound single was $792 in 1963. The R-27 at $849 with the dual seat option was considered the Cadillac, uh, Beamer of the tiddlers of The Sixties. Although any Hawk or YDS-2 could blow it into the weeds, there's no price like a BMW price. Even Peter Fonda purchased a new R-27 back in his shorthair days before he decided to reach out for the apehangers.

Zundapp

Zundapp was a lesser German brand that developed a small presence in the U.S. market in the '50's and '60's. Although the company built everything from small mopeds to midsize four-strokes for sale in Europe, a few particular models were somewhat familiar on these shores, although never common here. All were two-stroke singles divided into three distinct categories: the Bella scooters, the Super Sabre 250 street bike, and the later ISDT 100 and whatever variations made their way to our shores. Zundapp was absent from the U.S. market from

about 1963 until 1968, when a new distributor for the brand brought in the zippy little ISDT off-road machine. Zundapp trickled along from the early Seventies until finally filing bankruptcy in 1984. The brand and all its product line was sold to a Chinese company that markets modern Honda copycat machines.

Zundapp sold its Bella scooters from 1953 through 1964. The first Bella model was the 150 model built from 1953 to '58, the 200 was sold from 1955 through 1962, and a 175 was sold in 1961-64. As far as I can tell, nearly all Bellas were sold in Europe and very few in the U.S. The 200cc model got an electric starter in 1955 and a model called the Suburbanette was released in the USA only that same year, but only 370 were sold. The Suburbanette had eight horsepower and sold for $397 at the time of its release. It was distinguished by its cutaway side panels exposing the engine and rear suspension. All the Bellas, including the Suburbanette, had a left-side, four-speed foot shift. The Bella 200 had ten horsepower and a full-coverage steel body, selling for $499 in '55. All the Bellas were large, serious scooters with real suspension and 12-inch wheels. Restored examples bring a high price in America today.

The earliest Sabre brought to the U.S. had thirteen horsepower and cost $519 in 1955. The August 1963 issue of *Cycle* had a Zundapp ad for the Super Sabre with 18 hp, 80-mph top speed, and electric starter and turn signals. The 1963 model was available in Jet Black or Royal Blue. At this point, Zundapp would soon give up on the U.S. market. The Super Sabre was very much equivalent to the Allstate 250, although the Allstate was an oil injected twin, or the NSU Super Max, although the Max was an OHC single. The Jawa of the period is another similar machine; i. e., conservatively styled, primitively reliable, somewhat dated for the era, and about as exciting as a box of generic brand corn flakes. The main thing the Super

Sabre had going for it was its Germanic engineering quality. The foot shift and kick starter were both on the left, but at least the late-model Super Sabre had an electric starter and turn signals.

Zundapp found a new distributor in the U.S. in 1968 to release the ISDT 100 Replica and two other versions of the 100cc two-stroke. Zundapp built three modern, 10-hp 100cc models in 1968: Classic Street KS, Scrambler, and ISDT Scrambler at $419, $449, and $629 respectively. All were four-speeds weighing about 195 pounds. *Cycle* tested the ISDT in the May '68 issue, listing the specs as 9.3 hp and 186 pounds with a 56-mph top speed. The testers loved the handling, build quality, toughness, and all-around competent performance, but $629 was a steep price for a 100cc piston-port dirt bike. The brand-new Honda CB-350 tested in the same issue cost only $665. An even better comparison would be the Hodaka 100/B discussed in Chapter 1. The *Cycle* writers mentioned in the ISDT test that the Hodaka had previously been their favorite off-road 100cc bike, and that was before the Hodaka got a five-speed transmission and other improvements. The five-speed 100/B would cost *$200 less* than the ISDT *two model years later*! The 1974 ISDT 100 was probably the last hurrah in the U.S. for Zundapp, which should be no big surprise.

Figure D6 (previous page) - 1961-64 Blue & White Zundapp Bella Scooter. Image by ChiemseeMan under Creative Commons license in the Public Domain.

Figure D7 (previous page) - Black 1962 Zundapp 250 S. Image by Piero under Creative Commons license (GNU).

Figure D8 - Sea Green Zundapp Bella R-154. Image by Lothar Spurzem under Creative Commons license.

Rex KL-35 & Como Deluxe

Rex is one of the rarest, strangest of the tiddler brands. The German company built five 50cc models in the late '50's and early '60's. The small company was formally in business from 1948 through 1964, but I suspect that only a few machines were imported into the USA during a narrow time frame. There were several other European brands named Rex, but this one may be the most obscure. These 50cc tiddlers were built in Munich and distributed out of Salt Lake City. How's that for strange? If I had not seen an ad for the top-of-the-line KL-35 in the August '62 issue of *Cycle World*, I might never have discovered this unusual tiddler. I wrote the distributor for a full-line, 1962 brochure, an 8.5 x 5.5-inch affair printed in glorious black and white. Other than this brochure and a few ads and photos, I have never seen a Rex.

The Rex brand in general, and the top two models in particular, are interesting in their unusual design. These were referred to as *Economy Motorcycles* in the brochure. They were built in Munich, West Germany, and the importer was located in Salt Lake City, of all places, not exactly an East Coast checkpoint! Of course my brochure may have come from the western distributor and there was actually a P.O.E. for Rex on the Eastern Seaboard, but my brochure calls the SLC office the U.S. and Canadian distributor. Rex offered five 50cc models, and nothing larger, as far as I know. Note, however, that this Rex is not to be confused with several other makers of larger motorcycles under the same brand name, but different companies.

A Motorbike Kit for $99.95 was the entry-level machine. Shown in the brochure was an English-style touring bicycle with a gas tank attached to the top frame bar and an engine nestled in the V of the frame, just above the pedals. I don't know if this machine retained its original three-speed hand shift or not. It is not clear from the brochure if the bicycle was included in the price, but I would guess not. Next up the scale was the Piccolo Moped for $199, sort of a heavy-duty bicycle frame with the engine mounted in front of the pedals. The Piccolo made the Allstate Moped look like a roguish escapee from *The Wild One*. In other words, it, too, was little more than a glorified bicycle. The middle of the line was the Monaco Moped, a machine roughly equivalent to the much more common Allstate Moped. The Como Deluxe and KL-35 were the only actual motorcycles in the Rex lineup.

The Como Deluxe was one of those tiddlers that you don't know quite what to call it. I have photos of 1959 and 1961 models with pedals, but the '62 version in the brochure had a conventional set of footpegs and kickstarter. The photos of the early ones are blue and the '62 is white. The Como was shaped like a motorcycle, but there was a shallow step-through area behind the conventional gas tank. The tire diameter was larger than that of the Allstate Compact, but less than that of the Honda Cub. The Como was like a primitive, German version of the cycle/scooter hybrids that would come much later. The engine was fan-cooled and the left side kickstarter tilted forward like that on a Super Hawk. The three-speed hand shift was on pressed-steel handlebars in front of a conventional dual seat. The Como was basically a toned-down version of the KL-35 in a semi-scooter suit.

The top of the line was the KL-35 for $349 sporting twin carbs and twin exhausts on a single-cylinder 50. Now Rex had my attention! The KL-35 screamed out 4.4 horsepower with its silly dual accoutrements on a single cylinder two-stroke, but the Como makes do with 3.6. With its 155-pound curb weight, I wouldn't challenge any Honda Sport 50's to a drag race, and you may want to avoid a girl driving a Cub, too. The three-speed hand shift is not exactly sporting, either, but you can lift your nose in the air when you tell them your Como has an Earles front suspension design, just like you-know-who. The white paint job also sports hand pinstriping just like the famous snotbrand, too. The handlebars and frame are pressed steel on the Como, just like on a Honda Cub, and the chain is fully enclosed, but the tank is up front, even though there is a downward dip in the frame. It is puzzling why this one holds only 1.5 gallons when the one on the KL-35 holds 2.9. Leaving space between the tank and seat seems totally unnecessary. The engines on the KL-35 and Como are fan-cooled. Both models were obviously trying to offer German quality and detail in a smaller machine. $309 for the Como in 1962 pushed its price above even the Honda Sport 50. Is it any wonder that this is a very rare tiddler?

The KL-35 offered numerous weight-adding features. Its fan-cooled 50cc engine pumped 4.4 horsepower through *dual* carbs and *twin* upswept exhausts. Yes, you read it right. This was a little more power than the 3.6 hp of the Como, but it still drove through a three-speed hand shift. Rex touted the Earls (sic) front fork for the bike's comfortable ride and the electrics were via magneto. The 21-inch wheels gave it a distinctly *motorcycle* look, but its pressed-steel frame, fully enclosed chain, and narrow handlebars brought the sissy look back. In its favor, there was the classic German pinstriping on the fenders, and I'm sure any fourteen-year-old could be impressed by its dual input and output! Hey, that's the ticket. *I* happened to have been fourteen in 1962!

Figure D9 - Black NSU Super Max. Note the unusual rear shock mounts, leading link front suspension, storage box attached to the rear fender, and the nice gold pinstriping.

Image by Rikita under Creative Commons license.

Figure D10 (next page) - Maroon Jawa 250 Type 353. Notice the smooth styling of the pressed steel frame, the long forks attached to a sixteen-inch wheel, and the single shift/kickstart lever.
Image by Lukfa under Creative Commons license (GNU).

Figure D11 (second page down) - Red 1968 Jawa Cross 90. Note the more modern look of this tiddler with its slender chrome fenders and large tail lamp.
©Michael Kiernan, Classic Motorcycle Company, St. Louis, MO.

Jawa / CZ

This rare Czechoslovakian tiddler brand has been familiar to many of us from the many ads the company ran in U.S. motorcycle magazines during The Sixties. Many were printed

during those heady days of the early tiddler invasion and indeed, for many of us, these ads represent the full extent of our direct experience with Jawa or its sister brand CZ. Jawa began producing motorcycles in 1929 and they still continue production in the Czech Republic today; however, I think they were imported here only during the '60's boom market. The Wikipedia page provides a brief overview of the brand. Jawa and CZ merged in 1948 and the CZ brand continued in Europe until it was bought by Cagiva, who unsuccessfully marketed CZ until its final demise in 1997.

Although the first Jawa was a 500cc four-stroke, most of the models sent to the U. S. were 175cc, 250cc, and 350cc two-strokes. You may remember that the Jawas were generally marketed here as high-quality machines with pedestrian looks and performance. There is an unmistakable similarity to a few of the Allstates of the era. Jawas were even sold through Sears in Canada for a time! CZ had already built a name for itself in off-road competition in Europe, so the CZ name was mostly applied to the motocross line in the U. S. The distinctive exception to this was the Jawa 500cc Speedway model. Probably the most memorable street model was the Jawa Californian, a last ditch effort to sell a 250cc twin in the land of the free, the brave, and The Big Four. With its trim fenders and low, but upswept pipes (think Norton Commando), the Californian was an heroic effort, but by this time the need for speed was rampant and the competition horrendous.

The Czech Republic, or Czechoslovakia, as it was called when these classic machines were marketed in the USA, is right next door to Austria and Germany. Surely you could see, even at the time of the contemporary ads when you were just a kid, that the Jawas appeared very similar to certain NSU and Zundapp models from Germany and the Puch Allstates from Austria? You cannot miss their small-diameter, fat tires, bulky, yet rounded, pressed-steel frames and other distinctive details. These machines were made to *transport*, not play. They were built to last, but not for speed. Of course we are talking about the 175-250-350 street machines here. CZ has built numerous competitive off-road racers through the decades and the Jawa Speedway 500 single is a legend in its own circular track of time.

If Sears & Roebuck had decided to make a contract with Jawa instead of Puch, maybe Jawas would be scattered all over the USA now. There are several similarities in the machines. Jawa built a 50cc Scooterette that was the same sort of homely little beastie as the Allstate Compact. The Jawa 175 and 250 road toads looked pretty much like the Allstate Twingles. The low performance, low-stress powertrains were designed from similar viewpoints. The rounded teardrop gas tanks with chrome panels were attached to rounded, heavy pressed-steel frames. The wheels and tires were of a somewhat small

diameter, usually sixteen inches, and the fenders were close and full coverage. One of the more primitive qualities of the Jawas was that, unlike the Allstate 175 and 250, they did not get oil injection until 1971!

The 1971 Jawa CZ lineup included the 90cc Cross/Roadster (trail), CZ 125 & 175 Sport, 350 Californian IV, and the CZ Motocross 250 & 360. The '72 Jawa CZ lineup included the 175 CZ Sport, Jawa Californian 250 III, and the Jawa Californian 350 IV. *Cycle Guide* tested a CZ 175 Trail in April 1972. The testers reported a $525 list price for a 13-hp, oil injected, four-speed trail bike with a top speed of 72 mph. The 251-pound machine had a left-side foot shift.

A few distinguishing characteristics set the Jawa street models apart. The Road Cruiser models had handlebars of painted pressed steel and shaped as a pair of flat, straight lines aimed outward from the triple clamp, back toward the rider. The Roadster models had conventional chrome bars with a crossbrace like those on street scramblers and off-road machines. The Roadsters also had larger diameter wheels and slightly skimpier fenders. The dual seat had a distinctively narrow center section with wider, rounded seating areas for the driver and passenger. The transmission was advertised as requiring the clutch only to start from rest, not for shifting between gears. There was no separate kick starter: the toe shift lever did double duty as the kick starter. Unlike their British, Spanish, and Italian competitors of the day, Jawas had left side shifters. All the Jawas and CZ's were two-strokes: the 350's were twins and all the smaller models were singles.

It is difficult to say exactly how successful either Jawa or CZ was in the showroom wars. Certainly a number of CZ off-road machines competed in U.S. events, and their look or reputation was not quite as strange as that of their Jawa street brothers. The Californian was probably the leading street model Jawa emphasized in its U.S. advertising. The Californian was marketed in both 250 Single and 350 Twin configurations, all with four-speed transmissions. Both models were somewhat more contemporary in styling than the earlier, *more European*, Jawa street models, but you can see where this story is going. By 1970 Jawa had updated most of its styling issues, but like so many other European brands, the company never really offered much widespread competition to the modern Japanese machines that had invaded our shores so completely by that date. While electric starters,

OHC engines, snappy rotary-valve engines, and five-speed transmissions had become old news for the Asian brands, new Jawa owners could finally put away their premix cans!

JAVCO MOTORCYCLE CORP.

EXCLUSIVE · JAWA · IMPORTERS

555-557 GRAHAM AVENUE
BROOKLYN 22. N. Y.

SUGGESTED 1963 RETAIL LIST PRICES - JAWA & CZ MOTORCYCLES

```
125cc CZ Roadster - Model 453.............................$359.00
175cc CZ Roadster - Model 450.............................$409.00
250cc CZ Roadster - Model 455.............................$499.00

250cc JAWA Roadster - Model 559/02........................$489.00
250cc JAWA Super Sport Roadster - Model 559/03............$589.00
350cc JAWA Roadster - Model 354/06........................$599.00

125cc CZ Trials/Scrambler - Model 461....................$399.00
175cc CZ Trials/Scrambler - Model 460....................$479.00

250cc JAWA Trials/Scrambler - Model 553/04...............$569.00
350cc JAWA Trials/Scrambler - Model 554/03...............$658.00
250cc JAWA Motocross/Scrambler - Model 557/03............$640.00
350cc JAWA Motocross/Scrambler - Model 558/03............$714.00

50cc JAWETTA Moped - Model 551............................$139.00
50cc JAWETTA Moped Sport - Model 551......................$169.00
50cc JAWA Scooterette - Model 05..........................$199.00
50cc STADION Moped - Model S23............................$179.00

100cc MANET Scooter With Electric Starter - Model S100....$349.00
175cc CEZETA Scooter With Kick Starter - 502/01...........$439.00
175cc CEZETA Scooter With Electric Starter - Model 502/00..$469.00

175cc CZ Three-Wheel Pick Up - Model 505..................$800.00
```

Prices are FOB New York or Los Angeles. State and local taxes, freight and set-up charges if any, are extra. Prices and specifications subject to change without notice.

Figure D12 - 1963 Price List for the Jawa Lineup. ©1963 Javco Motorcycle Corporation

Triumph

A Triumph of Style

Figure D13 - 1967 Triumph Mountain Cub. The gas tank on this machine is blue. According to the chart below, the Mountain Cub should have a red tank. I have never been able to verify one way or the other if more colors should have been listed in the chart or if the tank or paint job is incorrect on this example. According to the chart, the Mountain Cub was the only Tiger Cub imported in 1967. ©Michael Kiernan, Classic Motorcycle Company, St. Louis, MO.

This legendary English brand had been around years before most of us were born. Many of its biggest fans consider the early models to be the more collectible classics, and practically all of its fans feel that the 650 or 500 is more desirable than the lesser tiddler models. Even the author of this book would choose a mid-Sixties 500cc over any other Triumph model, but this page is about Triumph tiddlers.

Triumph built, and exported to the U.S. in limited numbers, a range of 200cc-250cc single-cylinder models from 1954 through 1971. There was also a little-known 350cc model called the Twenty-one sent here up through 1962. My first encounter with the brand was with a friend's brochure in the very early Sixties. I cannot remember the exact year, but it definitely was 1960, '61, or '62, and the 350cc model was included in the lineup. The earliest brochure I currently own is 1963, and the 350 was no longer present in the U.S. lineup at that time. That brochure included only 200cc, 500cc, and 650cc models. Since *Cycle World* began publishing in 1962, and I do not own any pre-1963 issues of *Cycle*, I do not have even a single photo of an early Sixties 350cc Triumph. The photos I have in print are all of the 200cc Cubs of the early Sixties, and some of the later 250cc models. As we all know too well, Honda reliability triumphed over English style. Triumph tiddlers rolled quietly out of the U.S. market at the beginning of the Seventies.

Beyond all else you want to say about vertically-split engine cases and the Prince of Darkness being in control of the light show, Triumphs had style. A Triumph always looked the way a motorcycle was supposed to look. The gas tank was smooth, trim, and always painted. Black rubber knee pads were allowed, but chrome sides were not. Slender fenders would never allow a Triumph to be mistaken for a Dream. Seats were wide and flat, with pleats and a passenger strap, but no two-tier shapes were allowed. The handlebars were a nondescript Western shape and the headlamp was in a compact nacelle. Rubber boots covered the front forks and square rear shock covers were left in Japan. The bullet-shaped mufflers were particularly lovely to view and hear. The sportiest models had tachometers, but the lesser models had only speedos. When you watch the chase scene in *Coogan's Bluff*, you know that Clint Eastwood was riding a Bonneville because he had a tach. The punk he was chasing had only a speedometer. I guess that second carburetor allowed Clint to catch his man! There were no turn signals or electric starters on the classic Triumphs. You get to see Coogan kickstart his Bonnie like a real man should. Clint wasn't the only celebrity to increase the Triumph legend, either. Look at Bob Dylan's t-shirt on the cover of *Highway 61 Revisited*. We all know how the future of rock and roll was altered forever when Bob later fell off his 1964 T100 Tiger and left the nasal wheeze and melodic rock of *Blonde On Blonde* back at the studio in Nashville while he rediscovered God and his acoustic roots.

Figure D14 - Maroon & Silver 1964 Triumph Tiger Cub on Display in Europe. I am not sure if this shade of red is the same as the Scarlet listed in 1964 in the chart or not.

Image by Alan, photographer, under Creative Commons license.

Figure D15 - 1967 Triumph Mountain Cub - ©Michael Kiernan, Classic Motorcycle Company, St. Louis, MO.

Triumph Singles Chart

Year	Model	Name	Colors	Exhaust	Price
1960	TW2	Tigress Scooter	Blue	Down	NA
1960	T20	Tiger Cub	Aztec Red	Down	NA
1961	T20	Tiger Cub	NA	Down	NA
1961	T20R/S	Road Sports T C	Red & White	Down	NA
1961	T20/T	Trials & Woods Cub	Red & White	Upswept	NA
1961	T20/S	Scrambler Cub	Red & White	Upswept	NA
1962	T20	Tiger Cub	Burgundy & White	Down	NA
1962	T20S/S	Sports Cub	Burgundy & White	Down	NA
1962	T20S/C	Competition Cub	NA	Upswept	NA

1963	Tina	Tina Scooter	Lilac	Down	$332
1963	T20/J	Junior Cub	Ruby Red & Silver	Down	$598
1963	T20	Tiger Cub	Ruby Red & Silver	Down	$598
1963	T20S/R	Road Sports	Flame & Silver	Down	$675
1963	T20S/C	Competition Sports	Flame & Silver	Upswept	$670
1963	T20/R	Trials Cub	NA	Upswept	NA
1964	Tina	Tina Scooter	NA	Down	NA
1964	T20	Tiger Cub	Scarlet & Silver	Down	NA
1964	T20S/R	Road Sports T C	Kingfisher Blue & Silver	Down	NA
1964	T20S/C	Competition Sports	NA	Upswept	NA
1965	T20	Tiger Cub	Scarlet & Silver	Down	NA
1965	T20S/R	Road Sports Cub	Pacific Blue & Silver	Down	NA
1965	T20S/C	Competition Sports	Gold w/Polished Fenders	Upswept	NA
1966	T20/M	Mountain Cub	Grenadier Red & Alaskan White	Upswept	$650
1967	T20/M	Mountain Cub	Red & White	Upswept	NA
1968	TR25W	Trophy 250	Hi-Fi Scarlet	Upswept	$695
1969	TR25W	Trophy 250	Trophy Red	Upswept	NA
1970	TR25W	Trophy 250	Trophy Red	Upswept	$715
1971	T-25SS	Blazer 250 SS	Red	Upswept	NA
1971	T-25T	Trail Blazer 250	Red	Upswept	NA

Triumph 200/250 Single Notes: All 200/250 Triumphs had single-cylinder, OHV engines, four-speed transmissions, right-side shifters, kick starters, and single-downtube cradle frames. The original Tiger Cub was launched in 1954 with a ten-horsepower engine and plunger rear suspension. Conventional rear shocks appeared after about three years of production, but the power may not have increased much above the original ten horsepower over the Cub's lifespan. The basic road models can be identified by their "stylish rear

149

enclosure panels" (as stated in the brochures). The most visible Triumph on American roads with these panels was probably the 650 Thunderbird.

Available information on the 1954-59 models is sporadic, so the chart is beginning with the 1960 models. The Tiger Cub got traditional swingarm rear suspension in 1957. Some models prior to 1960 were probably painted in solid colors. The 1960 Tigress Scooter had a 250cc OHV engine with a four-speed hand shift. The 1962 T20S/S was available with Western or low Sports handlebars. The 1964 model weighed 220 pounds. The 1960 Tigress Scooter had a 250cc, fan-cooled, OHV engine with a four-speed transmission. The 1963-64 Tina Scooter had a 100cc, fan-cooled two-stroke engine with a centrifugal clutch-type transmission and a belt drive. The 1963 T20/R Trials Cub was a limited production model with trials-type handlebars, a solo seat, a large rear sprocket, a different gearbox, and only ten horsepower, detuned from the other 16-hp Tiger Cubs. The 1968 Trophy had 22 horsepower.

Figure D16 - 1967 Triumph Mountain Cub - ©Michael Kiernan, Classic Motorcycle Company, St. Louis, MO.

BSA Singles

Figure D17 - Red BSA 441 Shooting Star. Image by TR001 under Creative Commons license.

You might think of BSA as the Austin-Healey of the motorcycle world, a legendary brand that for whatever reason, never properly brought itself into The Sixties, and therefore signed its own death warrant. Much has already been written on this subject by far more detailed researchers than I can count, so I shall just hit the high points of the story as they apply here. The engineering of both A-H's sports cars and the motorcycles built by Birmingham Small Arms was a product of an earlier time. The Austin-Healey 3000 was phased out after 1967 due to the more stringent safety and emission requirements placed on cars beginning in the '68 model year. Although the Austin-Healey Sprite would continue into production through 1971, I believe the last ones imported into the U. S. were 1970 models. British Leyland controlled MG and Austin-Healey at the time, and the Healey name would be phased out, although it would make one last appearance as the short-lived Jensen-Healey. The whole story was roughly parallel to that of BSA and Triumph. The two brands would become more and more alike under the same corporate ownership as the model years continued. The only fluke in this story is that, although BSA had originally bought Triumph, the BSA brand was never as popular in the U. S. as Triumph. This is the reason the little Triumphs have been charted here but the little BSA bikes have not. Although BSA was decently successful in marketing its 650cc and 500cc machines here, the company's numerous tiddlers were famous in the USA mostly as cantankerous to start and unreliable over the long haul.

This story could be told from several different viewpoints, but I have chosen the last hurrah of the BSA tiddlers in the U. S. as the focal point. The official, original BSA tiddler was the 175cc two-stroke Bantam, built from 1958 to 1969, and based on the even earlier 125cc and 150cc, low-production models. The Bantam was sold alongside the heavier, more expensive 250cc and 350cc four-stroke singles during the same general time period. The original Bantam had a triangular, hardtail frame, a teardrop gas tank and a sprung solo saddle. It looked much like a Harley Hummer, Yamaha YA-1, or DKW 125. Now imagine that! The Bantam later evolved into a plain, but semi-modern machine with conventional suspension at both ends and a straight, dual seat in the middle. It remained a very low-budget, low expectations machine until the end. The company even tried to market a trail version with knobby tires, minimal muffling and no lights or front fender in 1965, but as we all know it was too little too late for most of the small English antiques in this country by that point.

BSA began its line of what is known as *unit construction* singles in 1958. These were modern machines at the time with the engine and gearbox within the same enclosure. Displacements included 250cc and 350cc, and like the two-stroke Bantams, these OHV tiddlers would soldier onward to the end, albeit with relatively few sales in the U.S. As you reminisce over these English antiquities, remember that for the Japanese brands, a 250 was as big as some of them produced at the time and a 350 was beyond the pale. The same displacements in the BSA and Triumph stables were the little stepchildren who would soon be ill-equipped to face the twin-cylinder, overhead cam engines and electric starters of Dreams and Hawks.

In all fairness, the little Beezers did offer the accoutrements of *real motorcycles*. All had black tube frames, painted or chrome fenders, proper suspensions that offered at least decent handling, and American adult-sized dimensions. BSA offered several versions of these machines in most model years. A basic road model offered full-coverage fenders, a large gas tank with chrome side panels, and a chrome, downswept exhaust pipe with a tastefully designed muffler, usually of a bullet shape. Next up would be a *Road Sports* machine with trim fenders, a warmed up engine, and possibly a slimmer gas tank. A third variation could be a trials, desert racer, scrambler or pseudo-motocross model with knobby or semi-knobby tires, lower gearing, and a sexy upswept exhaust that made a big racket. Many of these machines were marketed without lights or a battery. They looked great and sounded great... if you could get them started. The electrical systems often left something important on the cutting room floor. Nevertheless, where do you think Honda got some of the famous styling cues for its CL-72 Scrambler? The witches threw a few things into a cauldron and stirred it up. Take the crossover sidepipes from a BSA 650 scrambler and attach them to a twin-cylinder the size of the smallest BSA four-stroke, add an overhead cam and modern, reliable electrics and voila!

The most successful BSA singles happened to be the last and largest of the breed. The claim to fame of the final Victor Special and Shooting Star models is that these were exceptionally big sellers for BSA in the U. S. The 441cc Victor was marketed as BSA's final enduro model in the trail-crazed U.S. market. The BSA brand would not survive to be included in the final Triumph attack on the American tiddler market with its Trail Blazer in

1972. The smaller 250cc Starfire was somewhat less successful, although it looked almost exactly like the Shooting Star, and it, too, would disappear after 1970. Americans seemed to generally favor the Triumph styling cues of the Trophy 250, as they did with most of the larger models competing with BSA equivalents.

There are two more sides to this story and they are both true, although they may seem to be diametrically opposed. I clearly remember drooling over a 441 Victor Special, alongside a Yamaha Big Bear, in the Columbus MS K-mart; not in the parking lot, on a pedestal in the showroom. I was in awe of its clean styling, compact design, and relative light weight. The Big Bear looked positively *bulky* in comparison. I loved the idea of that big, thirty-horsepower engine in such a small chassis, unhampered by something as sissified as an electric starter. But we all know there is a downside to all this fawning over styling, don't we? A long-stroke, 441cc single would shake a python's grip loose from a rat. It took the powerful kick of a kangaroo to start that beast, too, and that was when it was in a good mood! I'll take that Big Bear instead, thank you, and so did everybody else. Go back to making guns, you limey bloke, and don't let the stiff kickstarter hit you on the way out! In the backs of our adolescent minds, we all knew it was true, even back then. The Big Bear actually did not have an electric starter, but with its two-stroke twin and Japanese (read modern and effective) electrics, it didn't need one.

Figure D18 - Yellow 1970 BSA 441 Victor Special.

©Michael Kiernan, Classic Motorcycle Company, St. Louis, MO.

Vespa

Piaggio began to conquer the U.S. scooter market when a Vespa was given a starring role in the 1952 Gregory Peck / Audrey Hepburn movie, *Roman Holiday*. Following on the heels of an agreement with Sears Roebuck & Company to import the Vespa scooter under the company's house brand Allstate, the movie was released at the perfect time to introduce the slick Italian product to American buyers. I suspect that Piaggio soon found the primitive Cushmans sold alongside their sophisticated machines to be little competition. As we know now, the Cruisaire continued to be one of Sears' best sellers and the Vespas have dominated the worldwide traditional scooter market ever since, although Vespas were not officially sold in the U.S. for two decades, from 1981 to 2001. The company bought out their elitist competitor Aprilia in 2006.

The 1963 Cushman-Vespa brochure shows a 125, 150, and Grand Sport. The 125, essentially the same as the Allstate Cruisaire, had a three-speed handshift, 46-mph claimed top speed, and weighed 192 pounds. The 150 had a four-speed, went 53 mph, and weighed 204. Both scooters rolled on eight-inch wheels. The GS was a high-performance 150 with a 62-mph top speed and 244 pounds on ten-inch wheels. The Light Gray 125 had 4.5 horsepower, the Metallic Blue 150 had 5.5, and the Metallic Silver Grand Sport had 8. The GS came with a dual saddle while the two lesser models had a solo seat and body-colored luggage rack. A square foam pillion that attached to the rack was optional.

The December 1964 issue of *Cycle World* featured an ad for the new Vespa 50 at $244. The ad mentioned two Western distributors, but there was no mention of Sears. Vespa marketed 90, 125, 150, and 180 models in the U.S. in 1971. By 1978, long after Cushman was gone and Vespas were imported by Vespa of America Corp. in Brisbane CA, the three U.S. models were the 50 Special, P125X, and P200E. All had ten-inch wheels, rotary valves, dual seats, and four-speed hand shifts. The dry weights were 160, 218, and 225 pounds. The claimed top speeds were 30, 50, and 62 mph. The two more powerful models with a two-inch longer wheelbase and fatter tires would come to be referred to as the "large body" Vespas, and they had oil injection and twelve-volt electrical systems, too. The "small body" 50 made do with six volts and premix.

Figure D19 (previous page, top) - 1962 Vespa GL 150. Image by Christian Scheja under Creative Commons license.
Figure D20 (previous page, bottom) - 1963 Vespa 150. Image by Paulgoo under Creative Commons license in the Public Domain.

Figure D21 - Red 1977 Vespa P200E. Image by Jay Cross, photographer, under Creative Commons license.

Lambretta

Lambretta made a fearless attempt at becoming the premiere Italian scooter brand in the '50's and '60's. These scooters built in Milan were longer and sleeker than their more common, chubbier cousins wearing the Vespa and Allstate nameplates. Unlike other scooters, the Lambrettas used steel body panels attached to tubular frames. All models were piston-port two strokes of 50-200cc, and most of those imported here were either 125cc or 175cc. The Innocenti company built Lambrettas from 1947 to 1972, but most of the imported U. S. volume arrived in the early Sixties.

Jayne Mansfield posed with a Lambretta on the cover of the 1963 brochure. During the Fifties and early Sixties, Jayne Mansfield was sort of the number two blonde bombshell celebrity in America. Following in the footsteps of Marilyn, she was featured in *Playboy* and a number of movies, but she also was the poster girl for Lambretta scooters. You could see her posing sexily on a Lambretta in numerous magazine ads and shop posters. Like Marilyn, Jayne's life came to a premature, tragic end. She was killed instantly in a car accident between Biloxi MS and New Orleans in 1967, with daughter Mariska Hargitay (of *Law & Order SVU*) and two sons in the rear seat. The three adults in the front never left the Electra 225 alive, but all three kids in the rear did.

Vespas began production with their monocoque bodies a year prior to the Lambrettas, setting the scooter marketing stage for all time. Although Vespa has always had the production volume and name recognition, the Lambrettas appealed to buyers who wanted something a little less common. Most Lambrettas can be identified by their sleek, angular styling, and many had distinctive two-tone paint jobs, usually red and white, blue and white, or yellow and white. All had handshifts and manual clutches on the left handlebar with three or four forward gears, just like the Vespas.

Figure D22 - 1967 Blue & White Lambretta 150. Image by Piero Tasso under Creative Commons license (GNU).

Innocenti, the parent company of Lambretta, sent three Series 3 models to the U.S. in 1962 and 1963. The 125/LI claimed a 50 mph top speed with a retail price of $373 with a solo seat. A second, separate, rear seat was a $12 option, as was a speedometer. The 150/LI claimed a top speed of 55 at a base price of $425. A speedo was standard equipment, while the second seat was $12 extra and a spare wheel and tire combo was $21. The 175/TV with a top speed of 65 mph came with a speedo and dual, motorcycle-type saddle as standard equipment for $499. A spare wheel and chrome luggage rack was a $30 option. All models had the innovative Lambretta front disc brake, predating the Honda 750 Four by seven years!

I have not been able to verify if any models after 1964 had oil injection, as did practically all street model Japanese tiddlers at the time. Since Lambrettas were rapidly shrinking in number in the U. S. as the '60's progressed, I suspect that oil injection was never developed for the models imported. How could any scooter compete with the zillions of successful tiddlers from The Big Four? I suspect that Vespa's contract with Sears did

wonders for their sales success in this country.

Cycle World tested the Lambretta 150/LI in May 1962. The claimed horsepower was 6.5 and the top speed 50 mph. The claimed dry weight was 231 pounds, but it was worded as "unladen" weight so that figure may have been with fluids. The magneto electrics were six-volt without a battery. There was surprisingly no mention of price. The testers commented on the convenient storage area for tools and such under the front seat. Like the 175/TV tested later by *Cycle World*, both machines had four-speed hand shifts. Unlike the later machine, the 150 had separate, spring-mounted seats in the old style. Some fans now lament the *move up* to motorcycle-style dual saddles.

When I wax nostalgic for the Lambrettas of the Sixties, I am reminded of the Aprilias of today. The Lambretta 175 TV was sort of the Scarabeo of the '60's, the top dog of style and class. *Cycle World* tested one in October 1962. Horsepower was rated at 8.75, up from 7.8 in 1961. The colors offered in '62 were red, gray, or yellow, all with light gray trim, or all-white. The claimed top speed was 65 mph, and the testers did not question it, although the test machine was not run at the strip. The price was $500 plus $30 for a chrome luggage rack and spare wheel option. What a deal!

Figure D23 (this page) - Red & White 1967 Lambretta SX200.
Image by Mick in Northamptonshire, England, under Creative Commons license.

Ducati

With the Ferrari of Motorcycles image a Ducati enjoys now, it is difficult to believe that back in the '60's, Ducati more or less unsuccessfully marketed in the U.S. a line of 50-450cc two-stroke and four-stroke singles, at reasonable prices, no less! There were several 50-80cc two-strokes that simply got their exhaust pipes kicked back to Italy by Honda and Yamaha, with very few sales to even show they were here. Ducati's four-strokes fared much better and several are now legends from their own time. The Monza, Diana, 250 Scrambler, Mach 1, and numerous larger Desmo models were quality handlers while the Japanese were still trying to sort that suspension thing out. Nevertheless, few buyers were willing to pay even a little more for the Italian stallions when the Yamahas had reliable Japanese electrics and literally went like stink! The Hondas were somewhat mellower of sound and exhaust smoke, and they were as reliable as washing machines. You might say that these sweet-handling little Ducks were ahead of their own time. The snob factor hadn't kicked in yet. Even BMW's were closer to reasonable prices back then. Like Daffy, they held their little bills high and swore, *I shall return!*... and they did. Most of the Ducati singles were painted black, red, or blue. A few had an unusual color such as bronze. Practically all colors were in combination with silver trim on tanks, fenders, and side covers.

Ducati 1962 Chart

Model	Type	Engine	Gears	Seat	Wt.	Price
Sport 48	Street	48cc 2S	3	Dual	108	$229
Bronco	Street	124cc OHV	4	Dual	201	$359
Monza	Street	248cc OHC	4	Dual	275	$579
Diana	Road Sport	248cc OHC	4	Dual	265	$679
Scrambler	Off-road	248cc OHC	4	3/4	277	$669

Ducati 1962 Notes: The two-stroke Sport 48 had a hand shift. All Ducati OHC singles had right-side foot shifters, most of a rocking type. All four-strokes except the Bronco used single overhead cams. All claimed dry weights are listed in pounds.

Ducati 1963 Chart

Model	Type	Engine	Gears	Seat	Wt.	Price
Falcon 50	Street	49cc 2S	3	Solo	108	$229
Super Falcon	Street	80cc 2S	3	Solo	110	$289
Bronco	Street	124cc OHV	4	Dual	201	$359
Monza	Street	248cc OHC	4	Dual	275	$579
Diana Mk. III	Road Sport	248cc OHC	4	Dual	265	$679
Scrambler	Street	248cc OHC	4	3/4	277	$669

Ducati 1963 Notes: The 1963 horsepower ratings were 4.2 for the Falcon 50, 22 for the Monza, and 24 for the Diana. The Falcon 50 & Super Falcon had hand shifts. All Ducati OHC singles had right-side foot shifters, most of a rocking type. All four-strokes except the Bronco used single overhead cams.

Figure D24 - Blue & Silver Ducati Sport 48. Image by Alf van Beem under Creative Commons license in the Public Domain.

Ducati 1964 Chart

Model	Type	Engine	Gears	Seat	Wt.	Price
Falcon 50	Street	49cc 2S	3	Solo	108	$229
Falcon 80	Street	80cc 2S	3	Solo	NA	NA
Cadet 90	Street	90cc 2S	3	Dual	NA	$309
Mountaineer 90	Trail	90cc 2S	3	Solo	NA	$329
Bronco	Street	124cc OHV	4	Dual	201	$379
Monza	Street	248cc OHC	5	Dual	275	$579
Diana Mk. III	Road Sport	248cc OHC	5	Dual	265	$679
Scrambler	Scrambler	248cc OHC	5	3/4	277	$669

Ducati 1964 Notes: All the 1964 two-stroke models had hand shifts. All Ducati OHC singles had right-side foot shifters, most of a rocking type. All four-strokes except the Bronco used single overhead cams.

Figure D25 - 1964 Black & Silver Ducati Bronco 125 at the 2009 *Cycle World* **International Motorcycle Show, Seattle, Richard Smith, owner.** Image by Dennis Bratland under Creative Commons license.

Ducati Falcon 50 & 80

Ducati marketed several tiddlers in the USA in the 1962-65 period. The regular Falcon was a fan-cooled 50cc and was definitely advertised in the U.S. in 1963. The Ducati Super Falcon 80 Sport was the top banana of these little two-stroke Ducks. The photo is of its 50cc little brother, called simply the Sport 48 in Europe. I am not sure what years the Super Falcon was imported; however a brochure appears to be from 1964. There probably was a regular, less sporty Falcon, too, but I am not sure if it was imported, and if it was, I have never seen one. The photo is technically of the European Sport 48, the first cousin of the Falcon 50 with racy European bars.

The little Ducati Super Falcon was one of the last of its type that the company tried, generally unsuccessfully, to market here in the early Sixties. The little beastie was thrown to the wolves who had names such as Super 90, Rotary Jet 80, and many others. The Honda offered four-stroke technology and sound surrounded by reliability you couldn't kill with a stick. The little Yamaha went like stink off the line with sleek bodywork and big-bike feel. By the time Yamalube was introduced in '64 and Suzuki, Kawasaki, Bridgestone, and Hodaka were hammering the Super Falcon with speed, modern styling, and exotic features, the Little Duck had little choice but to waddle back to Italy and stay there.

The Super Falcon offered traditional big-bike styling with its 18-inch wheels, tube frame, and grown-up suspension system. It is a shame that it had to be saddled with a left-hand, three-speed shifter on the handlebar like an Allstate Cruisaire! I guess the company figured that at least this way it did not have to meet the usual American resistance to a right-side foot shifter. The horsepower is not stated in the brochure, but its Falcon 50cc little brother was claimed to have 4.2 horsepower. The top speed was listed as 50-55, putting it closer to the YG-1 than the S-90 in this respect. The weight is listed as 125, twenty pounds less than a Honda Sport 50! I am sure part of that is due to the magneto ignition and primitive lighting. There was no oil injection on this model. I do not know if the Super Falcon was ever continued into production with oil injection, but I doubt it, at least not in the USA. By 1967 there would be a 100cc Mountaineer trail version that looked very similar to the 80 Sport. The solo saddle, luggage rack, tank, and fenders were practically the same. My best guess is that the four-stroke Bronco 125 would soon be the littlest Duck sold here.

Ducati wasn't the only Italian company building a plethora of two-stroke tiddlers in the Sixties, but the name turned out to be the one that would carry its glory into the present day. The story might have been very different if the Italians had been competing only with Allstate, BSA, and Harley-Davidson for a share of the novice motorcycle market. We are all too familiar with the invasion that signed their death warrant, and as these things go, it is probably just as well. You cannot stop technological progress. Old-world style usually gets trampled in such a situation. In this case, it was run over by a horde of buzzing speed bunnies outfitted in candy colors and chrome accompanied by a stampede of purring Cubs as reliable as toasters. Now we can all amaze our grandchildren with stories of the Ducatis we owned as kids that cost only a few hundred American dollars, brand new! Nah... they will never believe us.

161

Figure D26 - Red & Silver Ducati Monza 250. ©David Cassady, owner and photographer

Ducati 1965 Chart

Model	Type	Engine	Gears	Seat	Wt.	Price
Brio 100	Scooter	94cc 2S	3	Dual	177	NA
Cadet 90	Street	90cc 2S	3	Dual	NA	$309
Bronco	Street	124cc OHV	4	Dual	201	$379
Monza	Street	248cc OHC	5	Dual	275	NA
Diana	Road Sport	248cc OHC	5	Dual	242	NA
Scrambler	Scrambler	248cc OHC	5	3/4	240	NA

Ducati 1965 Notes: The Brio Scooter and Cadet 90 had hand shifts. All Ducati OHC singles had right-side foot shifters, most of a rocking type. All four-strokes except the Bronco used single overhead cams.

Ducati 1966 Chart

Model	Type	Engine	Gears	Seat	Wt.
Mountaineer	Trail	97cc 2S	3	Solo	150
Cadet	Street	97cc 2S	4	Dual	145
Bronco	Street	124cc OHV	4	Dual	200
Monza Junior	Street	156cc OHC	4	Dual	238
Monza	Street	248cc OHC	5	Dual	275
Diana Mk. III	Road Sport	248cc OHC	5	Dual	242
Scrambler	Scrambler	248cc OHC	5	3/4	240

Ducati 1966 Notes: No 1966 prices are available. The Mountaineer had a hand shift. The Cadet 100, new for '66, had a four-speed foot shift. Certain later two-stroke models were listed as having four-speeds in the *Motorcycle Sport Books*, but that may have been an error. All Ducati OHC singles had right-side foot shifters, most of a rocking type. All four-strokes except the Bronco used single overhead cams.

Ducati 1967 Chart

Model	Type	Engine	Gears	Seat	Wt.	Price
Falcon 50	Street	49cc 2S	3	NA	108	NA
Brio Scooter	Scooter	97cc 2S	3	Dual	177	NA
Cadet	Street	93cc 2S	3	Dual	145	$319
Mountaineer	Trail	97cc 2S	3	Solo	141	NA
Bronco	Street	124cc OHV	4	Dual	201	NA
Monza Junior	Street	156cc OHC	4	Dual	238	$529
Monza	Street	248cc OHC	5	Dual	275	$625
Diana	Road Sport	248cc OHC	5	Dual	247	$719
Scrambler	Scrambler	248cc OHC	5	3/4	240	$729
Sebring	Street	340cc OHC	5	Dual	271	$729

Ducati 1967 Notes: All Ducati OHC singles had right-side foot shifters, most of a rocking type. All four-strokes except the Bronco used single overhead cams.

Ducati 1968 Chart

Model	Type	Engine	Gears	Seat	Wt.	Price
Brio Scooter	Scooter	97cc 2S	3	Dual	177	NA
Cadet	Street	93cc 2S	4	Dual	145	$340
Cadet Sport	Street	97cc 2S	4	Dual	144	$350
Mountaineer	Trail	97cc 2S	4	Solo	NA	NA
Monza Junior	Street	156cc OHC	4	Dual	238	$550
Monza	Street	248cc OHC	5	Dual	275	$750
Diana Mk. III	Road Sport	248cc OHC	5	Dual	246	$710
250 Scrambler	Scrambler	248cc OHC	5	Dual	220	$799
350 Scrambler	Scrambler	340cc OHC	5	Dual	270	$849
Sebring	Street	340cc OHC	5	Dual	271	$750

Ducati 1968 Notes: All Ducati OHC singles had right-side foot shifters, most of a rocking type. All four-strokes used single overhead cams. The Cadet 90 was a fan-cooled two-stroke.

Ducati 250 Scrambler

The Ducati 250 Scrambler was tested in my very first issue of *Cycle World*, August, 1962. The 250 lost a little emphasis in the U. S. market when the company introduced its 350 and 450 Desmo models in the mid-Sixties, although none of the later Scrambler engines were Desmos.

There are many similarities and a few differences between various Scrambler models I have seen pictured and the 1962 model in the road test. The tank is slimmer and sleeker on the later model. The seat has a chrome strip at the base on each side instead of a row of rivets. The front shocks changed to rubber gaiters from body-colored covers and the rear fender extends a little further at the rear underneath a larger tail lamp. A small, slim muffler has been added to the exhaust, although thankfully not adding any length to the short, sporty, downswept pipe, and the tires are more of a road tread than the Trials Universals on the 1962 model. The main styling element that seems to have made a step backwards is the elongated headlamp on the later model. The '62 has a pleasantly abbreviated design. All of these changes except the headlamp shape would have been typical styling and functionality updates a manufacturer might have made during the early '60's time period.

The 250 Scrambler was an interesting machine from many angles. The simple tube frame had a large backbone and a single downtube enclosing the engine, with thinner tubes comprising the rear subframe. The engine was a SOHC, gear-driven design producing thirty horsepower. Standard gearing offered a top speed of 82 mph, a zero to sixty time of 11.5 seconds, with the quarter in 17.3. A full selection of alternate sprockets was also offered, allowing a top speed up to 100 mph or much shorter gearing for cow-trailing with quicker acceleration. There was no speedometer fitted, but a tach was optional. The price for this little Duck in '62 was $669 and it weighed 277 pounds. Compare these figures to the high-volume Honda CL-72 introduced that same year in a similar price range. The CL-72 was a SOHC twin producing 25 horsepower with twin carbs. Its performance was almost identical to that of the Ducati with standard gearing. The obvious differences were that the Honda was much more of a street machine with instruments, battery, full passenger accommodations, and a claimed weight of 315 pounds. What's not to like in a bike that was essentially an off-road Diana?

Ducati 1969 Chart

Model	Type	Engine	Gears	Seat	Wt.	Price
Cadet Sport	Street	97cc 2S	4	Dual	144	$350
Monza Junior	Street	156cc OHC	4	Dual	238	$550
Monza	Street	248cc OHC	5	Dual	275	$750
Diana Mk. III	Sport	248cc OHC	5	Dual	246	NA
250 Scrambler	Scrambler	248cc OHC	5	Dual	220	$810
350 SSS	Scrambler	340cc OHC	5	Dual	270	$860
Sebring	Street	340cc OHC	5	Dual	271	$750
350 Mark 3D	Street	340cc OHC-D	5	Dual	NA	$860
Jupiter	Scrambler	436cc OHC	5	Dual	320	$899
450 Desmo	Street	436cc OHC-D	5	Dual	NA	$939

Ducati 1969 Notes: All Ducati OHC singles had right-side foot shifters, most of a rocking type. All four-strokes used single overhead cams. Two OHC street models employed the Desmodromic valve actuation system without springs created by Ducati. These are denoted OHC-D in the chart.

Ducati 1970 Chart

Model	Type	Engine	Gears	Seat	Wt.	Price
Cadet Sport	Street	97cc 2S	4	Dual	144	$339
Monza Junior	Street	156cc OHC	4	Dual	238	$449
Monza	Street	248cc OHC	5	Dual	275	$589
Diana Mk. III	Street	248cc OHC	5	Dual	246	$689
Scrambler	Off-road	248cc OHC	5	Dual	220	$789
250 Desmo	Street	248cc OHC-D	5	Dual	NA	$789
350 Sebring	Street	340cc OHC	5	Dual	271	$689
Scrambler	Scrambler	340cc OHC	5	Dual	270	$839
Mark III	Street	340cc OHC-D	5	Dual	NA	$839
Jupiter	Scrambler	436cc OHC	5	Dual	320	$899
450 Desmo	Street	436cc OHC-D	5	Dual	NA	$939

Ducati 1970 Notes: All four-strokes used single overhead cams. Three OHC street models employed the Desmodromic valve actuation system without springs created by Ducati. These are denoted OHC-D in the chart.

Ducati 1971 Chart

Model	Type	Engine	Gears	Seat	Wt.	Price
450 R/T	Off-road	436cc OHC-D	5	Dual	285	$1199

Ducati 1971 Notes: Note that the U.S. distributor was overstocked in 1971 so the 450 R/T

was the only model imported for two model years. The 450 R/T had a 38-hp Desmo engine with magneto ignition and no battery or lighting equipment. The machine had Ceriani-type front suspension, uncovered black rear springs, silver single-downtube frame, yellow fiberglass tank, fenders, and side covers, no muffler, and knobby tires.

Figure D27 - 1969 Silver 350 Desmo. This is a very clever cafe racer with rearsets and a racing seat.
©Michael Kiernan, Classic Motorcycle Company, St. Louis, MO.

Ducati 1972 Chart

Model	Type	Engine	Gears	Seat	Wt.	Price
450 R/T	Off-road	436cc OHC-D	5	Dual	285	$1199

Ducati 1972 Notes: Note that the U.S. distributor was overstocked in 1971 so the 450 R/T was the only model imported for two model years.

Ducati 1973 Chart

Model	Type	Engine	Gears	Seat	Wt.	Price
250 Road	Street	248cc OHC	5	Dual	NA	$869
350 Road	Street	350cc OHC-D	5	Dual	NA	$939
450 R/T	Off-road	436cc OHC-D	5	Dual	285	$1199
750 Road	Street	748cc OHC-D	5	Dual	440	$1964

Ducati 1973 Notes: All Ducati OHC singles had right-side foot shifters, most of a rocking type. All four-strokes used single overhead cams. The 250 was the last OHC single sold in the U.S. without Desmodromic valve actuation. The last Ducati singles delivered to the U.S. were the 1973 models. All U.S. Ducatis would be big twins from 1974 onward. All claimed dry weights listed are in pounds.

Figure D28 - Orange 1972 Ducati 350 Scrambler. Image by The Javelina under Creative Commons license.

Figure D29 - Red & Gold Ducati 200 SS. Image by Ronald Saunders, photographer, Warrington, UK, under Creative Commons license.

Figure D30 - 1970 Ducati Mach I. This is a beautiful Euro-spec machine in black with a red frame. Image by Spath Chr. under Creative Commons license.

Figure D31 - 1966 Ducati 160 Monza Jr. This model was not much of a success for Ducati. It replaced the 125cc OHV Bronco in the lineup, but failed to compete with the Honda CB-160 and the comparable two-stroke Japanese machines. Notice the unusually sculpted shape of the headlamp housing.

©Michael Kiernan, Classic Motorcycle Company, St. Louis, MO.

Figure D32 - 1962 Blue Ducati Diana Mark III. ©Michael Kiernan, Classic Motorcycle Company, St. Louis, MO.

Ducati Diana

Figure D33 - Red & Silver 1964 Ducati 250 Mach I. The Diana was called the Mach I outside the U.S.
Image by El Caganer, photographer, under Creative Commons license.

My favorite Duck doesn't quack. It goes thump, thump, thump, vrooooom! I have always been a sucker for small, skinny, sporty, street motorcycles. It's all about the feel of the machine. I don't like riding in winter because I want to ride without gloves. When I stop I want to see the imprint of the handgrip on the palm of my hand. I want to feel as if the motorcycle turns just because I blink. I want to feel as if I am riding it, not as if it is riding me. This explains it all when you see the big picture. The Honda 450 has always felt too piggish to me. It feels top-heavy. Do not misunderstand. I came very close back in 1970 to buying a new CL-450. It was certainly one of my favorite choices, as was the Kawasaki Mach III, which I also did not buy. I chose a Honda CL-350 for my cross-country trip, and my only regret is that I sold it after I bought a '71 Mach III eight years later. I should have kept them both. Now my only street bike is a 550 Nighthawk, which happens not only to be the largest and heaviest motorcycle I have ever owned, but it is the biggest one that I even desire. Now don't bring up that Sportster issue you may have read about in my first book, *Plastic Ozone Daydream*. Yes, I have always wanted a Sportster. It's lean; it's mean; it only weighs 457 pounds; and yes, it's the real thing, baby; but, I just cannot see myself squandering that kind of cash on a two-wheeler that is about as technically sophisticated as a John Deere tractor! The 550 Nighthawk is the most attractive, most comfortable, and best compromise of a large-but-skinny motorcycle for me personally. I don't do European bikes mostly because I don't do wrenches. I am a dreamer and a writer. I am a lousy mechanic.

Figure D34 - Candy Presto Red 1983 Honda Nighthawk 550. ©2010 Floyd M. Orr

The subject at hand is one of the most legendary tiddlers of all time. It comes from the Ferrari of motorcycles, Ducati, generally the most famous and successful of many Italian motorcycle brands. Don't tell me about Europe. We're talkin' about the US of A here. I don't know nuttin' about speakin' no Eye-tallion! In the U.S., Ducati is revered as the Ferrari of two-wheelers, and the Diana was the first model in the U.S. to bring the company that reputation. When you read the Bultaco Metralla story later in this chapter, you will learn of one of the Diana's leading competitors. Take into account that I am a sucker for blue as much as I am for skinny motorcycles. What color do you think both my CL-350 and Mach III were? Yes, I know the 550 Nighthawk came only in red or black, but the red is the prettiest shade I have ever seen.

Ducks were even more rarely seen on American streets back in The Sixties than they are today, so I cannot be certain of much of the Diana's production details, but here is what I think is true. The Diana was imported into the USA in 1960-64 as a sportier version of the much more common Monza. The original 1960 version was painted medium-light blue and silver. The shock covers both front and rear were the body color. There was a small windscreen attached to the headlight. The gas tank had a very distinctive shape indigenous

171

to the model. Even the gas cap was a special racing type. The handlebars were flat. The seat had "buttons" along the lower edge. There was a separately-mounted tachometer and no speedometer. The headlight had a shallow shell, half the size of the one on the Monza. There was no battery. The frame was a single-downtube-type with the downtube attached to the engine casing, as opposed to being a cradle type. The fenders were appropriately thin and sporty. The standard muffler was a linear, round, chrome tube. The transmission was a four-speed with a right-side, rocking-type shift lever. Now here is where the plot thickens. I am unsure of the model year changes from this point forward. Later models had a battery, the rear springs were uncovered, and a black megaphone exhaust was included as standard equipment (in addition to the standard chrome muffler). The later seat might have had red piping and no buttons, however, this may have been just a detail I saw on a non-stock machine. Was the black megaphone always standard, or was it an extra-cost option in some years? Some rear springs were chrome plated and others had blue covers. Were there colors other than blue and silver for the model? Red was probably an alternate color: I have seen photos of red examples, but factory photos only of blue and silver ones. Dianas are so rare that even finding good photos of them is difficult.

The Diana was replaced by the Mach 1 with a five-speed transmission in 1965. (This model is not to be confused with the 250cc Kawasaki two-stroke triple called the Mach I released five years later.) Most, maybe all, of the Mach 1's were red. The Mach 1 can be distinguished by its lack of a small windscreen, chrome, exposed rear springs, Monza-type, deep headlamp with included speedometer, and small, silver side covers that still left the battery exposed. Later models had a racing-type lip at the rear of the dual seat. Arriving during the U.S. motorcycle boom of the later '60's as it did, the Mach 1 is probably far more common than the Diana. The Mach 1 may have been an improvement, but the Diana was a legend.

Figures D35 & D36 - Red & Silver 1967 Ducati Diana Mk. III.

©Michael Kiernan, Classic Motorcycle Company, St. Louis, MO.

Benelli

Figure D37 - 1965 Red Benelli 125 Cobra. Image by K. Ivoulin, photographer, under Creative Commons license.

The Benelli Phantom street 250 did not get oil injection until 1975! In a way, that says it all, doesn't it? Benelli is a very old Italian motorcycle company. They produced countless machines in Italy for the European market and tried to sell some of them in the U.S. under the Riverside brand name through the Montgomery Ward catalog and stores. The 50cc Fireball Scrambler and the Mojave 360 were two common models at Monkey Ward. So were the Sprite street models, which were actually Motobi designs manufactured as Benellis and then marketed as Riversides. The company marketed its big 650 OHV Tornado twin through a few motorcycle dealers, but this was never a big seller, either, although it was a decent machine.

The reason there is not a Benelli chart in this section is the lack of consistent information on the yearly lineups, particularly regarding Monkey Ward. A Motobi brochure I have was printed in Italy for Cycle Products of Boston, but the particular copy I have came from the California distributor. This brochure may have been originally printed as a 1962 model, but I received it in 1963. Benelli bought out Motobi at some point in 1962. I bet my brochure was printed prior to the change in marketing strategy, but maybe not. All the magazine advertising for Benelli was done by Cosmopolitan Motors in Philadelphia. It seems that Benellis were simultaneously marketed in the U.S. as both Benellis and Riversides. Most likely the most common Motobis in the USA are probably Benelli Sprites, etc., designed as Motobis, but sold as Riversides.

Figures D38 & D39 - 1968 Red Benelli Riverside Nuovo Luincino 125. ©Michael Kiernan, Classic Motorcycle Company, St. Louis, MO.

A good example of the inconsistencies was shown in the May 1965 issue of *Cycle World*. An ad for the 200cc Sprite, an obvious Motobi design, claims a dry weight of 211 pounds, a top speed of 90 mph and a list price of $589 ($599 in the West), The road test of this machine in the same issue lists the weight as 228. Well, that is hardly a case for court. However, the price is listed as $479 and the testers said the Sprite could barely top 70 mph. A comparison with the prices of the '67 models noted below indicates that the higher price listed in the ad is correct and *CW* misprinted the test price, but 20 mph difference in the top speed? Maybe they put a little Italian guy on a finely tuned Sprite with low bars and shoved him downhill with a stiff tailwind! These test results are shown in the chart in Chapter 1, which also displays the results from the test of the CB-160 in the same issue. The Honda test resulted in a little higher performance from 3.5 less horsepower and fifty more pounds. Did *CW* confuse the Benelli 200 Sprite with the 125 Sprite? Only The Shadow knows....

A typical Benelli lineup was offered in 1967, as advertised by Cosmopolitan Motors. The Fireball Trail, sometimes called the Fireball Scrambler, was a well-developed 50cc two-stroke motorcycle with a double downtube frame, four speed foot shift, high fenders, uncovered springs front and rear, solo seat, luggage rack, and upswept pipe. Weighing in at a claimed 130 pounds dry, the Fireball Trail was a good deal for $309. The 125cc and 200cc Sprites at $489 and $599 were a pair of Motobi-derived models. The Sprites can easily be identified by their pressed steel backbone frames and horizontal round-head OHV engines directly off the Motobi design board. Both were available in the same Black,

174

Metallic Red, or Metallic Blue paint jobs with Silver trim and both weighed 211 pounds. The claimed top speeds were 78 mph and 90 mph. Benelli offered yet another pair of 125's that same year. These were two-strokes built by Benelli as the Cobra and Cobra Scrambler. The standard road Cobra had a dual seat and low fenders and exhaust for $409. A street scrambler called the Cobra California had upswept exhaust for $419. The Scrambler offered the same engine in a much altered chassis for $449 with a teardrop tank, high fenders, fat tires, solo seat, and luggage rack. At 230 pounds, the Cobra Scrambler outweighed the four-stroke 200 Sprite, or even the 250 Barracuda! (Maybe it was the cradle frame or fat tires?) The Motobi-derived Barracuda was produced as a standard with big tank and downswept exhaust for $639 and a California model with teardrop tank and upswept pipe for $10 more. Not mentioned in this particular ad was a 250cc OHV that was *not* a Motobi design. This machine was sold that same year by Montgomery Ward as a Riverside 250. This $569 machine had a double downtube frame housing an upright four-stroke single. Have you figured out that Benelli seemed to use a shotgun approach in its U.S. marketing, offering numerous machines of different configurations, but within the same price and displacement classes? My best guess is that the weakest link in the Benelli lineup was the prevalence of magneto-based electrical systems. Nothing says *modern* like a battery-powered ignition system with reliable, consistently bright lighting and quick starting.

Figure D40 - Red Benelli Riverside 250. Image by El Caganer under Creative Commons license.

The 1968 Benelli 250's came in several flavors. The Metisse was the pure road version and the California was the Scrambler with upswept exhaust. Both were derivatives of the Barracuda model and each were available with either four or five speed transmissions, in black, silver, or candy apple colors. The Metisse Super Sport 250 was Benelli's prominent street scrambler in 1968. A test of the Benelli Barracuda Super Sport Metisse showed a 14.9-second quarter-mile and a 108-mph top speed; not bad for a 250 single. The Metisse was marketed alongside the Mojave 360 with the latter being the dirt/street dual purpose model. The 125cc Cobra Scrambler had a four-speed with dual sprockets, upswept pipe, high front fender, luggage rack, and single seat. The 125 Sprite road model came with either four or five speeds. The Fireball (road) and Fireball Scrambler had four-speed foot shifts. The Scrambler had small, high fenders, upswept exhaust, single seat, and a luggage rack. The *Cycle* November 1973 test of the Benelli Phantom had plenty of negative things to say. Although they praised the looks and handling, the lighting was weak, there was no oil injection, the price was high at $939, and it was slow with a 16.8 quarter and 85 mph top speed. The weight with a full tank was 308. This was beyond the Monkey Ward era and De Tomaso had purchased the brand. An ad for the Benelli lineup in *Cycle* in the April 1967 issue mentions only dealers, not Monkey Ward.

Figure D41 - 1972 Red Benelli 650S Tornado. Image by El Caganer under Creative Commons license.

Benelli will probably be most remembered for bringing the six-cylinder 750 Benelli Sei to market several years before the larger Honda CBX. The Sei reached our shores in 1974. The company had added the four-cylinder 500 Quattro to the lineup by '75, but that svelte machine never stirred up the same excitement level as the Sei. Both machines were quite attractive with typical Italian emphasis on both style and handling, although the engines were heavily based on the Honda 500 Four. The two four-pipers had five-speed transmissions and the 750 Six surprisingly weighed only 22 pounds more than the 500 Four. The Sei retailed for $3995 and the Quattro for $2875 in 1975, the final parameter of this book. The Sei was enlarged to a 900 and updated with a bikini fairing and six-into-two exhaust in 1979 with no increase in price over the 1975 750 model.

Motobi

Figure D42 - Red Motobi on Display at the Barber Museum in Birmingham, AL. Image by Chuck Schultz, photographer, under Creative Commons license.

The Motobi name began as a sprout off the Benelli brand in 1951. My personal fascination with Motobi began with a 1963 brochure I have in my collection. I know very little about Motobis, other than they were one of several Italian brands imported into the U.S. in the late '50's and early '60's. The company built OHV four-stroke singles, and even a few two-strokes. The thumpers may have been the only Motobis imported, and certainly only in very small numbers.

The 1963 brochure displayed only four models for the U.S. market. The 75cc Scooterino had sixteen-inch wire wheels and a slimline scooter body with a two-piece dual seat. The 3.5-hp four-stroke was teamed with a three-speed hand shift. The front suspension was leading link and the rear shocks were partially covered by the scooter body. Claimed top speed was 44 mph. Benelli would offer this exact same scooter in 1965 as the 125cc Monaco with a fan-cooled two-stroke engine for $319. The claimed top speed of the Monaco was 60 mph.

The remaining three models were sporting street tiddlers, all with OHV single-cylinder engines and four-speed foot shifts on the right side. The 175cc Catria came in standard and Sport models. The base unit had the prerequisite Western bars, straight-as-a-board twin saddle, and full coverage fenders. The Sport model had flat bars, trim fenders, a road racing style seat with the little lip at the rear, and a longer gas tank. The two Catrias weighed the same at 220 pounds and they utilized the same nineteen-inch wheels. The standard had 15 horsepower and the Sport 18 with claimed top speeds of 80 and 90 miles per hour respectively. The Imperial Sport 125 looked very similar to the Catria Sport except with Western bars, 18-inch wheels and a slightly rounder gas tank. The Imperial

Sport claimed a top speed of 80 from its 15 horsepower. Its claimed dry weight was only 190 pounds. Both Sport models also had exposed chrome rear springs. All the '63 Motobis had pressed steel frames and magneto ignition.

Figure D43 - Red 1960 Motobi 125. ©Michael Kiernan, Classic Motorcycle Company, St. Louis, MO.

The Motobi thumpers were built in sizes up to 250cc, all with distinctive, horizontal, egg-shaped cylinders. If you spot a machine that looks sort of like an early Harley-Davidson Sprint with a rounded, rather than sharply squared, cylinder head, it is probably a Motobi. The motorcycles were quite generically Italian, sporting narrow seats that were probably as stiff as boards. Since I have never actually seen a Motobi, I cannot swear to this in court, but other Italian motorcycles seem to be better suited for hanging onto, rather than comfortably lounging. The suspension is probably equally stiff, too. The headlamp nacelles appear long and clunky, but the gas tanks are long and elegant. The four-speed foot shifters were on the right side, but the kickstarters were on the left. Light weight was of course one of their claims to fame. You can see on the brochure that the Catria Sport 175 weighed only 220 pounds. Would anyone else like to own a pint-sized Ducati Diana?

Figure D44 - 1960 Red Motobi 125. ©Michael Kiernan, Classic Motorcycle Company, St. Louis, MO.

Figure D45 - 1960 Red Motobi 125. ©Michael Kiernan, Classic Motorcycle Company, St. Louis, MO.

Figure D46 - Red 1970 Motobi 125 Sport Special. Image by Huhu under Creative Commons license.

Montesa

Figure D47 - Red 1963 Montesa Impala 175 at the Museum de la Moto, Barcelona (Catalonia). Image by Peprovira under Creative Commons License (GNU).

Montesa was the oldest of the three big Spanish motorcycle manufacturers that sent machines to the U. S. during the tiddler invasion of the '60's. Only four years after Montesa was founded in 1944, an economic downturn in Spain caused the racing division to sprout off to form Bultaco as Montesa continued selling production bikes. Practically all Montesas were 125cc, 175cc, or 250cc two-strokes. Although a few smaller models were built, I am not sure if any were ever exported to this country. Practically all the Montesas were 125's until the introduction of the Impala 175 in 1962.

The Impala 175 Sport is typical of the breed. All Impalas were 175's in '62-'64, and the 250 was produced from 1965 through '69. Although the 175 continued all the way through 1971, I bet that most of the Impalas sent to the U. S. were 250's. With obvious similarities to the Bultaco Metralla and Mercurio, its obvious rivals both in the showroom and on the track, the Impala is distinguished visually by its elongated red and white tank, black covers over the front and rear suspension springs, and distinctive silver cover behind the air cleaner. Like the Buls, the Impala is the company's sole, consistent, pure-street model offered among a cadre of off-roaders. The design of all Montesas is very simple and straightforward, leaving the weight and complication to the Japanese. Nothing to see here, folks: no oil injection, electric starters, turn signals, or heavy batteries.

Three Montesa 250's were advertised in the July 1967 issue of *Cycle*: Impala Sport, Scorpion, and La Cross. The 1968 250 Montesas included the Scorpion 230-pound enduro for $745, the 240-pound Sport model for the road at $665, and the La Cross motocrosser at 225 pounds and $815. All were four-speeds with 21, 26, and 30 hp respectively. The street models from Montesa and Ossa were apparently imported in very small numbers, limiting these brands' appeal in this book.

Figure D48 - Black & Silver Montesa Impala Sport 250. Note the paint detailing on the fenders of this machine. ©Michael Kiernan, Classic Motorcycle Company, St. Louis, MO.

Figure D49 - Black & Silver Montesa Impala Sport 250.

©Michael Kiernan, Classic Motorcycle Company, St. Louis, MO.

The Impala did not make the Montesa brand famous. That honor probably goes to the Cota trials, Cappra motocross, and King Scorpion enduro models. I only featured the Impala here in the spirit of Tiddlerosis. We all know that rare street models, especially sporting types such as the Impala, are usually the ones lusted after by collectors and lovingly restored by enthusiasts. I would expect that most Cappras and Scorpions have long ago met their grimy, muddy ends leaned up against a pole in a cold garage somewhere. After all, that scenario describes my lovable little 1971 Yamaha AT-1 MX the first time I saw it. Although it now lives in a warmer garage, you might still find a bit of dirt on its original paint job. The Cota Trials line has probably made the biggest impression on Americans, particularly those who have seen the exquisite cop chase scene in the 1974 James Caan movie, *Freebie & The Bean*. Who can forget Caan riding a Cota 247 over the top of a string of parked cars or waltzing on one wheel through a city park in San Francisco? It was clear that Caan (actually an experienced trials rider stunt double) nearly lost it that time he came down a little sideways on the front wheel! Remember that?

Figure D50 - Red Montesa Impala 250 Sport. Image by Peprovira under Creative Commons license.

Ossa

The Ossa brand barely made the cut to be included in *The Tiddler Invasion*. Unlike many of the smaller brands included here because of their eccentricities, the Ossa machines were styled quite nicely, as opposed to strangely. The Barcelona factory tried very earnestly to gain a foothold in the American market with a number of nicely finished, adequately performing motorcycles. The company focused very strongly on off-road machines, and that is one reason Ossa barely made the cut. Another is that they were always the #3 Spanish brand. Montesa had the long-established company name in Europe and Bultaco had the strong presence in the U.S. market. Ossa really did try harder, though. The contemporary magazines of the day were full of tests of Ossa machines. The company just could never seem to coordinate an extensive, successful dealer network with its competent promotional department. *Cycle Guide* claimed this was because early Ossa ignition systems caused too many problems for otherwise successful Ossa riders in motocross competition. Although the problem had been solved by the end of The Sixties, possibly it was just too late. Ossa merged with Bultaco in 1979, but the Ossa factory finally closed anyway in 1982. A new Spanish consortium purchased the rights to the name in 2010 and is now producing small numbers of off-road machines for European competition.

Although the company began with another typical DKW 125 copycat in 1944, the Ossa lineup imported throughout most of the '60's included the Pioneer enduro, Stiletto motocrosser, Plonker trials, and Wildfire road machine. Although the company did produce a few smaller models for the European market, practically all the U.S. models were 175cc, 230cc, or 250cc. The 250 replaced the 230 in 1969 with a greatly improved product, including the problematic ignition system. In the early '70's, an enterprising American distributor produced 760 Yankee Z enduros in the USA. These 500cc twins utilized a pair of Ossa 250 cylinders set into a single crankcase. Ossa released its up-to-date Phantom 250 motocrosser in 1974, and *Cycle World* tested the model in October, but overall Ossa sales remained slow as the '70's waned. There were many distribution problems in Ossa's USA operations throughout the years. The company never seemed to reconcile its issues with the American marketplace. For example, according to the U.S. distributor at the time, only about twenty-five Wildfire SS 230 street scramblers, a model tested by *Cycle* in November 1968, were imported.

Cycle Guide tested the OSSA 175 in January 1970. The testers reported a $785 retail price for the machine with sixteen horsepower and a four-speed foot shift and weighing in at 225 pounds. The Ossa Pioneer got a five-speed in 1971. Ossa never built up its dealer network to a substantial level. Ossa produced a lot of machines, though most stayed in Europe. *Cycle World* tested the Super Pioneer in October 1975, calling it a good beginner's woods bike for competition. The Super Pioneer produced 21 horsepower, weighed 226 pounds with a half tank of fuel, and retailed for $1595.

Figure D51 - 1958 Blue Ossa 150 on display at the II Show *Toda una Vida en Moto* of the Asociacion Motociclista Zamorana, Zamora, Spain, February 2012. Image by Antramir under Creative Commons license.

Figure D52 - Green & White 1972 Ossa Plonker 250 Trials.

©Michael Kiernan, Classic Motorcycle Company, St. Louis, MO.

Bultaco

CEMOTO EAST IMPORTING CO., INC.

1967 BULTACO MOTORCYCLE PRICE SHEET
(ALL PRICES RETAIL, FOB SCHENECTADY, LESS SET-UP)

ROAD MODELS

175cc Mercurio - 18 HP (red & silver, blue & silver)	$515.00
200cc Mercurio - 20 HP (red & silver)	560.00
250cc Metralla - 25 HP (black & silver, red & silver)	660.00

ROAD/TRAIL MODELS

100cc Lobito - 10 HP (blue & black)	$449.00
175cc Campera - 16 HP (maroon & silver)	585.00
*200cc Matador - 16.5 HP (red & silver) *(Special order)	775.00
250cc Matador - 20 HP (red & black)	775.00

COMPETITION MODELS

100cc Lobito S - 14 1/2 HP (blue & black)	$475.00
125cc Sherpa S - 20 HP (red & silver)	669.00
175cc Sherpa S - 28 HP (red & silver)	684.00
200cc Sherpa S - 29 HP (red & silver)	704.00
250cc Pursang - 36 HP (red)	860.00

ENGINES

125, 175, 200cc engines	$350.00
250cc engines	428.75

NOTE: All models now have 12V lighting system.

Figure D53 - 1967 Bultaco Price List from Author Collection. ©1967 Cemoto East Importing Company, Inc.

Bultaco Lobito

Figure D54 - Yellow 1969 Bultaco Lobito Mark III 125.

Image by Peprovira under Creative Commons license (GNU).

The Lobito was the smallest Bul imported into the USA in the company's heyday of the late '60's. Sold here from '66-'70, the 100cc, two-stroke single was placed into a tubular frame that emphasized a sporty, off-road look for a tiddler. The 1966 model was typical of the breed. The fenders were trim, mounted unusually low in the front combined with extra high in the rear. The little Bultaco had Ceriani-type front suspension two years before Yamaha made the look commonplace with its DT-1. The end of the exhaust pipe was high, but the tank was large and bulbous and the handlebars were somewhat low and without a cross brace. The '67 model sold for $449 (plus setup and taxes) and it had an 18-inch rear wheel and (I think) a 19-incher on the front. The Lobito was not exactly marketed as an off-road machine, but the brand was already more famous for its off-road motorcycles than its road bikes by the time the Lobito was released, so a bit of dual purpose styling shines through. The official nomenclature used by Bultaco was *Street/Trail*. The 1969 model received a five-speed transmission and the price increased to $595 in 1970.

There were actually three Lobito Trail models offered in 1970. The ten-horsepower 100cc model weighed 180 pounds and had 21 and 18-inch wheels. The 125 model propelled its 220 pounds with 18.4 horsepower on the same wheel sizes. The Lobito Trail 175 for some reason was equipped with only a 19-inch front wheel, but its 22 horsepower

186

had to push only 225 pounds. For a little perspective, the 1970 Metralla 250 weighed only 230 with 28 horsepower.

The Lobito had the typical right-side shifter, simple ashcan shaped air filter, and long, black headlamp of larger Bultacos of the period. It should come as no surprise that this smallest Bul is as light, simple, and efficient as the brand's larger models. The 180-pound Lobito produced ten horsepower from its slightly undersquare engine. There is not a turn signal, an electric starter, battery, or extra pound in sight!

Figure D55 - Silver 1967 Bultaco Metralla. ©Michael Kiernan, Classic Motorcycle Company, St. Louis, MO.

Figure D56 (next page) - 1970 Bultaco Price List from Author Collection.
©1970 Cemote East Importing Company, Inc.

CEMOTO EAST IMPORTING CO., INC.

SUGGESTED RESALE PRICE

EFFECTIVE AUGUST 15, 1970

*STREET

200cc Mercurio	$ 498.00
250cc Metralla Mk II	626.00

*STREET SCRAMBLERS

250cc El Tigre	686.00
200cc El Tigre	546.00
200cc Mercurio SS	525.00

*TRAIL

100cc Lobito 5 speed	595.00
125cc Lobito 5 speed	696.00
175cc Campera Mk II	776.00
250cc Matador Mk III	895.00
250cc Sherpa T	895.00
360cc Montadero	1096.00

SCRAMBLERS

100cc Sherpa S	654.00
125cc Sherpa S	749.00
175cc Sherpa S	787.00
200cc Sherpa S	797.00
250cc Pursang America (TT)	996.00
250cc Pursang Europa (MX)	996.00
360cc El Bandido America (TT)	1135.00
360cc El Bandido Europa (MX)	1135.00

ROAD RACERS

TSS 125cc Water-cooled	1421.00
TSS 250cc Water-cooled	1541.00
TSS 360cc Air-cooled	1583.00

*Prices include warranty and 2 service checks with no labor charge.

All prices FOB Schenectady, New York and subject to change without notice.

BULTACO SPECIFICATIONS

Effective August 15, 1970

MODEL	DISPL CC	BORE & STROKE	WT.	MTR. NO.	BRAKE HP AT RPM	F & R WHEEL SIZE	NO. OF CYL.
SCRAMBLERS							
Sherpa S	100	49.5 x 51.5mm	170	M30	16.3@9500	21"-18"	1
Sherpa s	125	51.5 x 60mm	210	M63	22 @ 9000	21"-18"	1
Sherpa S	175	60.9 x 60mm	210	M66	28 @ 8000	19"-18"	1
Snerpa S	200	64.5 x 60mm	210	M67	29.5@8000	19"-18"	1
Pursang A	250	72 x 60mm	220	M68	37 @ 8500	19"-18"	1
Pursang E	250	72 x 60mm	220	M68	35 @ 8000	21"-18"	1
El Bandido A	360	85 x 64mm	250	M61	45 @ 7500	19"-18"	1
El Bandido E	360	85 x 64mm	250	M61	43 @ 7000	21"-18"	1
ROAD							
Mercurio	200	64.5 x 60mm	210	M35	20.2@7000	18"-18"	1
Metralla	250	72 x 60mm	230	M23	28 @ 8700	18"-18"	1
El Tigre	200	64.5 x 60mm	215	M35-T	20 @ 7000	18"-18"	1
El Tigre	250	72 x 60mm	225	M23-T	27.6@8700	18"-18"	1
TRAIL							
Lobito Trail	100	49.5 x 51.5 mm	180	M54	10 @ 8000	21"-18"	1
Lobito Trail	125	51.5 x 60mm	220	M74	18.4@8500	21"-18"	1
Lobito Trail	175	60.9 x 60mm	225	M76	22 @ 8000	19"-18"	1
Matador MkIII	250	72 x 60mm	247	M26	23 @ 5500	21"-18"	1
Sherpa T	250	72 x 60mm	203	M49	20 @ 5500	21"-18"	1
Montadero	360	85 x 64mm	251	M70	32.6@6000	21"-18"	1

Figure D57 - 1970 Bultaco Lineup Specifications Sheet from Author Collection.

©1970 Cemoto East Importing Company, Inc.

Bultaco Metralla

Figure D58 - Black & Silver 1966 Bultaco Metralla Mk. II 250 at the Moto Barcelona Museum in Catalonia, Spain. Image by Peprovira under Creative Commons license (GNU).

The year was 1970. I remember it correctly because I was visiting the local Kawasaki dealer in Memphis to drool over the current Kawasaki Mach III. The early 1970 Mach III's were Metallic Charcoal with black stripes on the tank. The later '70's were red with white tank stripes. I did not have the cash for a 1969 model in white with blue stripes, just like the '66 Ford GT-40 or the '65 Shelby Mustang that I also could not afford. I thought the charcoal Mach III's were a bit bland in color, although they were certainly unusual then and rare today. I felt that the fire engine red of the later '70's was a more appropriate color for such a fire-breathing motorcycle. When the metallic blue '71's came out, I absolutely had to have one! Instead I bought a new, blue Honda CL-350, of which my biggest mistake was selling it eight years later, after I bought a used, blue, '71 Mach III. Although I liked the Mach III enough to keep it until 1996, the simple little motorcycle I saw on that Memphis dealer's showroom has never left my memory. It was a black Bultaco Metralla, one of the very few European bikes I have ever truly desired. This particular Kaw dealer was also a Bultaco dealer, and every time I went to look at the Mach III's, I felt compelled to examine the Metrallas, too. If, like me, you like skinny, minimalist motorcycles and the KISS principle, then you must stare really hard at a Metralla. There was not a piece or a pound on it that was unnecessary. Swing your leg over this motorcycle. Feel this motorcycle.

The Metralla was built throughout most of The Sixties, and an updated model with less elegant styling was built in small numbers in The Seventies. The Metralla Mark II debuted

190

in 1967 with a five-speed transmission. *Cycle Guide* tested one of the new Metrallas in its September issue. The machine weighed in at 231 pounds, produced 27.5 horsepower, and cost $699. The model came in one of two colors: black with silver or red with silver. The long, semicircular gas tank was the Metralla's most distinguishing feature from its little 200cc brother, the Mercurio, which had a rounder, more conventionally-shaped tank and a four-speed transmission. Most Mercurios of all years were red and silver, while some versions of the Metralla were silver and the later types were even offered in blue.

The Metralla was an incredibly simple machine. Its dry weight was a measly 225 pounds. The 250cc single-cylinder, piston-port two-stroke made 27.5 horsepower. There was a minimal electrical system without a battery. The air cleaner assembly was a simple tin-can shape. The single-downtube frame was crude in finish, yet efficiently simple in design. The seat had more shape than can be noted from a side view. The driver's portion is much wider than the passenger's, and the top surface has a suede strip sewn down its center length for traction. The single glaring exception to this ultimate simplicity is the manually-operated oil pump behind the side cover. No, you do not mix the gas and oil the old-fashioned way, but you do not have modern oil injection, either. You pump straight gas into the tank; then refer to an included chart to determine how many squirts of the manual pump you need apply to match the amount of gasoline you just pumped!

The Metralla was very famous for its speed and handling. Like its four-stroke rival of the era, the Ducati Diana, a racing kit for the Metralla was offered by the factory. The kit consisted of a flat-black expansion chamber, high-compression head and piston, larger carb, close-ratio gearset, Femsatronic ignition, rear-set footpegs, racing gas tank, racing seat, a small fairing, and many smaller parts. In contrast, some Diana models were sold with megaphone exhaust, clip-on bars, and other racing accoutrements included in the standard package, in addition to the equivalent road components. To contrast the two competitors, you might say the Metralla was sold as a road machine with superb handling and spunky performance, but if the owner also purchased the racing kit, metamorphosis into a competitive racer would be extensive. The Diana offered the racing goodies as a bonus with the road equipment, but with the exception of rattling the neighbors' attitudes with the open megaphone exhaust, you can easily imagine that many Dianas were probably driven on the street, even with the racing parts attached. The neighbors probably would not have felt as accommodating to a crackling expansion chamber....

Figures D59, D60, & D61 (next page) - Three Metralla Views: a 1965 Mark I in left side and close up views and a Mark II in right side view. In simplified terms, Bultaco built the Mark I 200cc Metralla with a four-speed transmission through the 1966 model year. In 1967 the company came out with a 250cc Mark II version with a five-speed transmission. The Mercurio model was created as a less expensive alternative with the 200cc engine and four-speed. You can spot a Mercurio by its more bulbous tank shape. Only the gas tanks were painted red on the Metrallas; the rest of the machine was the same color as the black model. All of these machines had silver painted fenders with striping and other delicate details to show off the craftsmanship put into these machines.

All three photos ©Michael Kiernan, Classic Motorcycle Company, St. Louis, MO.

Figure D59 - 1965 Red Bultaco Metralla 200.

Figure D60 - 1965 Red Bultaco Metralla 200.

Figure D61 - Silver 1967 Bultaco Metralla 250.

Selected European Models Ratings Chart

Brand	Model	Collectibility	Practicality	Desirability
BSA	Bantam 175	C	D	D
BSA	Early 250 / 350 Singles	B	D	C
BSA	Starfire 250	C	C	D
BSA	Shooting Star 441	C	C	C
BSA	Victor Special 441	B	C	B
BMW	250 R-25, R-26, & R-27	A	C	A
Bultaco	Lobito	D	C	C
Bultaco	Mercurio 200	B	C	B
Bultaco	Metralla 250	A	C	A
Bultaco	Matador 250	C	B	B
Bultaco	Alpina 250	C	B	B
Ducati	Falcon 80	D	C	D
Ducati	Bronco 125	C	C	C
Ducati	Monza 250	B	C	B
Ducati	Diana 250	A	C	A
Ducati	Scrambler 250	C	B	B
Triumph	Road & RS Tiger Cubs	A	D	A
Triumph	Off-road Tiger Cubs	B	D	A
Triumph	Trophy 250	B	D	C
Triumph	Blazer 250	A	D	A

Models Ratings Chart Definitions:

Brand: Only a few of the models more common in the U.S. are listed. Some early model years within a series may be considerably more desirable than later years. All grade ratings are based on evaluations of all the machines covered in this book, not just as a comparative rating within each marque.

Models: In some cases many variations are included in this category and in others the models included are very homogeneous.

Collectibility: This is what most of you want to know, the bottom line on how likely the model or series is likely to climb in value over the coming years.

Practicality: This is an indicator of how adaptable the machine can be to ride for transportation or pleasure in the modern world, considering parts availability, fuel quality, comfort, performance and miscellaneous other obvious factors.

Desirability: This defines the nostalgic, emotional wow factor, without regard for collector values or everyday usage.

General: No machine is given a failing grade. If it made it into a rating chart, at least a few hobbyists find that model interesting.

Figure D62 - 1962 Blue Ducati 125 TS. ©Michael Kiernan, Classic Motorcycle Company, St. Louis, MO.

Figure D63 - 1965 Red Tiger Cub. Image by Mick in Northamptonshire, England, under Creative Commons license.

Chapter 4: *Early Asian Birds from Whom the Worms Escaped*

Silver Pigeon

The Silver Pigeon was a motor scooter produced by Mitsubishi Heavy Industries for the domestic market from approximately 1946-64, however, none were likely officially imported here until 1957. The earliest models were very primitive in nature and copies of early Cushman models. They had four-stroke engines of a few horsepower enclosed in slab-sided bodywork and rolling on small wheels. The array of models developed by the company expanded and gradually improved technologically, but even at the end of production, the Pigeons represent some of the most boring road toads covered in this book! The main rival of the Pigeons in Japan were the Fuji Rabbits, although the numerous models built by the future Subaru automaker continued to evolve way beyond the limited scope of the Pigeons, at least those models Mitsubishi sent to the USA. There was a rather sophisticated Pigeon developed for the Japanese market with a nine-horsepower twin-cylinder engine and a sleek body that looked similar to a Rabbit Superflow. This 150cc, three-speed two-stroke was the last model designed for 1964, but if it was ever imported here, surely the number was small.

There were only a small number of Silver Pigeons sold in the USA. No one seems to know really how many. The scooters were originally imported by Rockford Scooter Company in Rockford IL. Yes, this is the same Rockford that would later import the Bridgestone brand of motorcycles before the name became synonymous with tires. These models sported a Rockford badge instead of the Mitsubishi name. The importation of Pigeons and Bridgestones overlapped briefly in 1963, and there is yet another significant issue to be discussed.

The leading retailer of Silver Pigeons was Montgomery Ward through catalog sales. Just as with the Puchs, Vespas, Cushmans, and Gileras marketed in the U.S. through the Sears & Roebuck Catalog, Monkey Ward sold Pigeons through other names. The official Pigeon model numbers were the 74, 75, 80, and 90, but the monkeys at Ward's changed these to Miami, Waikiki, Nassau, and Commuter, respectively, from the entry level to the top of the line. As on the later Benellis, Montgomery Ward marketed the Pigeons as Riversides. There was never any question that most of the Pigeons sold in the U.S. were marketed through the catalogs, but there has been heated debate as to whether or not Bridgestone motorcycles were ever sold by Montgomery Ward or Spiegel through their catalogs. The Bridgestone connection with Silver Pigeon and Rockford dregs that question back up, doesn't it?

Figure E1 (previous page) - Early Mitsubishi Silver Pigeon. The later Pigeons were considerably more sophisticated than this primitive little scooter, but this was the only photo available at the time of publication. Image by Mitsucarman under Creative Commons license.

Miyata

Model	Name	Type	HP	Seat	Starter	Shift
1961-63	Miyapet	50cc 2S Single	4.3	Dual	Electric	3S - Foot

Miyata Notes: The Miyapet was the only motorcycle or scooter imported into the USA from this bicycle manufacturer, although many of the brand's bicycles were shipped here in the '70's and '80's. Strangely enough, Miyata had produced the very first Japanese motorcycle, a 3.5-hp two-stroke, way back in 1913. That machine was sold under the Asahi brand. The word means Sunshine in English. The Sunshine was loosely based on a Triumph model of the day and no more than forty were produced over a four-year period. Like several others, the Miyapet could be called either a motorcycle or a scooter, depending upon your attitude about such things. It had a step-through frame with leg shields, but the transmission shifted through a conventional motorcycle left-side, three-speed, rocking footshift with a hand clutch. At least one source indicates that the Miyapet had 22-inch wheels, although photos appear to show approximately 17-inch wheels with the same general proportions as those on a Honda Cub. From photos the Miyapet looks a little more like a scooter than a Yamaha MF-2, but less so than an MF-1. It had a kick starter, conventional tube shocks, and leading link front suspension. Some versions had a solo seat with luggage rack in place of the dual seat. The Miyapet was distributed by Ferndale Motorcycle Sales, Route 3, Ferndale WA. Ferndale is eight miles north of Bellingham. The tiny Miyapet ad ran in *Cycle World* January-May 1963.

Yamaguchi

Yamaguchi Chart

Year	Model	Type	HP	Seat	Exhaust	Price
1962	SPB Scrambler	50cc Single	4.8	Solo	Upswept	$295
1963	SPB Scrambler	50cc Single	4.8	Solo	Upswept	$295
1963	Ace 80	80cc Single	NA	Dual	Down	$345

Yamaguchi Notes: All Yamaguchis had kick starters. Pabatco imported 5000 Yamaguchis in 1961-63. Pabatco declared bankruptcy in April 1963. The first Hodakas arrived in the U.S. in June 1964.

Yamaguchi Autopet Sports

The 1962 Yamaguchi Autopet Sports SPB was a tiny blue bomber. It was probably the most common Yamaguchi model imported into the U. S., but the word *common* is a misnomer. After Honda broke American ground in 1959 with its ubiquitous 50, a flood of little Japanese squirts began to roll off the boat in L A. Yamaha and Suzuki would quickly establish themselves as the #2 and #3 brands respectively, but they were far from alone. One of the pioneers was Yamaguchi, but unlike most of their competitors, Yamaguchis were imported by Pabatco in Athena, Oregon. According to the Hodaka story, Pabatco imported 5000 Yamaguchis throughout 1962 and early '63 before Yamaguchi declared bankruptcy.

Some of you may already know that the 1964 Hodaka Ace 90 was a phoenix from the Yamaguchi ashes. Just before the Hodaka introduction, Pabatco was advertising the Yamaguchi Ace 80 alongside the Sports 50. The September 1963 issue of *Cycle World* showed an ad for these new 1964 models. The road-only Ace 80 was not exactly a fire-breathing sportster, with its enclosed chain, full, low fenders, and three-speed transmission. The only Yamaguchi models that I am aware of are the SPB, a very similar, sporty 50 called the LR, and the rather clunky Ace 80. I have heard about Yamaguchis for more than forty-five years, but I have never seen a single one.

James Rozee Speaks: "The pressed frame Yamaguchis are rare. Most of the bikes they sold here in the Northwest U.S. were the SPA and SPB Sport 50 models with hanger-type tube frames. They sold only about 5000 of these. plus a handful of their other models. That is why they are hard to find now. Honda would build more than that in an afternoon! Hodaka made only 10,000 Ace 90's from 1964-67, so that is also a very low number. Anyone who finds an old Yamaguchi and thinks parts are going to be easy to find, like old Honda parts, will be in for a shock!

I sold my collection to the Barber Museum in Leeds, Alabama, all of my stuff, 35 years of bikes, parts, and literature. Yamaguchi did not produce very much literature: only a couple of parts books, some owners manuals. a few ads. and some road tests in a few motorcycle magazines. You might see a few Yamaguchis show up in Athena OR each year for *Hodaka Happy Days* in June. Yamaguchi used the Hodaka motors in the SPB Sports 50 & 55, the S-2 street 55, and the Ace 80. All other models utilized Fuji power plants.

I knew Joe Dobbins and his son Jerry, too. I worked for them in the parts department back in the '70's after going to West Coast training to be a motorcycle wrench. Jerry Dobbins gave me my first break. I loved working there. I still keep in touch with others who worked there to this day! We would go back to the old building to put battery acid into a new Kawasaki's battery and would be wading through piles of old Tohatsu, Yamaguchi and early Kawasaki parts thrown all over the floor. It was called *the shed* then. I wish I had all those parts now! I remember when I was a kid it was the main shop. They later built the new one in front to handle all the new Kawasaki models. My dad test rode many bikes there in the early 1960's, such as Tohatsu and Yamaguchi Sports 50's and even a 250 Yamaguchi twin, a model I had two of in my collection that went to the Barber Museum. I really had fun working for and talking to Joe who was about 80 at that time, and Jerry, who always had great old stories to tell! Great memories!

The price is whatever a collector will spend. I have seen SPB Scramblers go for $250 to $2000. Anyone below the age of 45 won't even know what a Yamaguchi is!

Most all Yamaguchis had the red seat with white piping. Only the 50-55's had the Yamaguchi reflective sticker on the back. Other models had painted-on lettering. Frame colors were all red or all white and a weird combo of metallic greenish blue frame with a royal blue and white tank. All had the white swoosh down the top of the tank. except the all-white one. of course. Other models were the S2 55cc, an all-black full-cradle-framed street bike that evolved into the Ace 80. Both had the red seats that I have owned. There may have been a black seat but all the ones I have ever seen were re-done. and covering a red seat. All had white piping around them, too. The pressed frame 50-55s were named BPs and a few more letters, too. All were mostly the same machine. One had a chrome plated gas tank. All the pressed frame Yamaguchis engines were made by Fuji. The SPB, S-2 and Ace 80 used Hodaka engines, and none were interchangeable with the Fuji engines. The Ace 80 was the progenitor of the Ace 90, but with a three-speed transmission. The few odd Yamaguchi models imported into the USA in very small numbers were the step-through 50, a 125 twin, and their last model, the YMB 250 twin. The YMB was heavy but cool. I had two and they were one frame number off one another. The Ace 80 was reworked by P.A.B.A.T.C.O. (Pacific Basin Treading Company) and left over 50-55 motors sold off. Yamaguchi went bankrupt in 1963 and the Hodaka Ace 90 was born out of that. Many early 1964 Hodakas have Yamaguchi Ace 80 parts on them! I love them all. I am in the Hodaka Owners Registry and the Hodaka Underground.

I sold my Yamaguchi collection to the Barber Vintage Motorsport Museum in Birmingham Alabama, a really nice place with hundreds of bikes on display. I sold my Tohatsu collection some years back and it all went back to Japan, never to be seen again."

Pointer

Pointer 1961 Chart

Name	Type	HP	Exhaust	Wt.	Top Speed	Price
Lassie	89cc Single	6.5	Down	198	53 mph	$290
Senior	123cc Single	9	Down	253	NA	$439
Comet	155cc Single	NA	Down	264	69 mph	$467
Ace	250cc Twin	NA	Down/Up	NA	NA	NA

1961 Pointer Notes: The Lassie was a step-through with a tank and leg shields up front and a three-speed foot shift. All 1961 Pointers had two-stroke engines, pressed-steel frames, leading link front suspension, rotary shifts, 12-volt batteries, electric starters, and turn signals. The 1961, and maybe the early '62, Super Lassie had a solo seat with a cream tank and luggage rack. On these models, the headlight nacelle was longer and a "90" was on the gas tank instead of the later "P" Pointer emblem. All claimed dry weights are listed in pounds.

Pointer 1962 Chart

Name	Type	HP	Exhaust	Wt.	Top Speed	Price
Lassie	89cc Single	6.5	Down	198	53 mph	$318
Deluxe Lassie	89cc Single	6.5	Down	206	53 mph	$387
Super Lassie	89cc Single	7	Upswept	176	60 mph	$377
Senior	123cc Single	9	Down	253	NA	$439
Comet	155cc Single	11	Down	264	69 mph	$467
Ace Scrambler	123cc Single	12	NA	NA	65 mph	NA

1962 Pointer Notes: All street Pointer models have dual seats and electric starters. Some models may not have kick starters. The Comet does; the Super Lassie does not. The Ace Scrambler had a pressed-steel frame, full-coverage fenders, and a solo seat with luggage rack. It did not have turn signals and strangely enough, the Scrambler had a 17-inch front wheel and an 18-inch rear wheel. All the other Pointers had 17-inch wheels, except the base Lassie rolled on 20-inchers! The 1962 brochure states the following prices: Lassie $358, Senior $496, and Comet $529. No price is listed in that brochure for the Super

Lassie. An article in the second issue of *Cycle World* (February 1962) lists the prices as $290 for the Lassie, $377 for the Super Lassie, and $390 for the Senior. All claimed dry weights are listed in pounds.

"POINTER" SALES OF AMERICA

NATIONAL DISTRIBUTORS OF MOTORCYCLES & AUTO-SCOOTERS

A Division of Parma Motors, Inc.
5 4 6 1 R I D G E R O A D
P A R M A 2 9 , O H I O
Telephone: TUxedo 4-3100
Cable Address:
POINTMOTOR CLEVELAND

"POINTER" MOTORCYCLES & AUTO-SCOOTERS
RETAIL PRICES AND SPECIFICATIONS

1963 MODEL	ACE SCRAMBLER	COMET	LASSIE	DELUXE LASSIE	SUPER LASSIE
DIMENSION & WEIGHT	125 cc	155 cc	90 cc	90 cc	90 cc
Length (inches)	74.8	76.3	71	71.7	71.7
Width (inches)	31.5	26	20.9	23.6	23.6
Height (inches)	N.A.	36.6	36.6	36	36
Wheel Base (inches)	50.0	49.8	47.3	47.3	47.3
Min. Road Clearance (inches)	8.27	5.9	5.1	5.1	5.1
Tire Size (inches) Front	2.75-17, 4 p	2.75-17, 2 p	2.5-20, 2 p	2.25-17, 2 p	2.25-17, 2 p
Rear	3.00-18, 4 p	2.75-17, 4 p	2.5-20, 4 p	2.25-17, 4 p	2.25-17, 4 p
Unloaded Weight (lbs.)	N.A.	264	198	206	176
Max. Speed (miles per hour)	65	69	52.8	52.8	59.4
Stopping Distance (from 22 m.p.h.) (ft.)	N.A.	18	24.5	N.A.	N.A.
Minimum Fuel Consumption (miles per gallon)	N.A.	136	188	176	176
Fuel Tank Capacity (U.S. gallon)	2.4	2.6	2.2	2.4	2.4
Cubic Inch Displacement	N.A.	N.A.	N.A.	N.A.	N.A.
Maximum ft. lbs. Torque at 4,500 r.p.m.	N.A.	N.A.	N.A.	N.A.	N.A.
Maximum Power @ 6,000 r.p.m.	12 HP	11 HP	7 HP	7 HP	7 HP
Dir. Signals - Standard Equip.	No	Yes	Yes	Yes	Yes
12 V. Electrical System	Yes	Yes	Yes	Yes	Yes
Rear View Mirror	Yes	Yes	Yes	Yes	Yes
Availability	N.A.	Yes	Yes	Yes	Yes
RETAIL PRICES		$499.70	$357.82	$386.45	$388.90

Add:
Dealer Set-up Charge = $7.50
Local Freight = $20.00
Warranty (Optional) = $20.00
(4,000 miles or 90 days)

Accessories:
Leg Shields
Windshields
Luggage Carrier

Figure E2 - Pointer Specifications. ©1963 Pointer Sales of America

Pointer 1963 Chart

Name	Type	HP	Exhaust	Wt.	Top Speed	Price
Lassie	89cc Single	6.5	Down	198	53 mph	$318
Deluxe Lassie	89cc Single	6.5	Down	206	53 mph	$387
Super Lassie	89cc Single	7	Upswept	176	60 mph	$402
Senior	123cc Single	9	Down	253	NA	$439
Comet	155cc Single	11	Down	264	69 mph	$547
Ace Scrambler	123cc Single	12	NA	NA	65 mph	NA

1963 Pointer Notes: All street Pointer models have dual seats and electric starters. Some models may not have kick starters. The Comet does; the Super Lassie does not. Prices were riding a roller coaster during these final months of the brand. The 1963 Specifications Sheet from the Ohio distributor lists the Lassie at $358, the Deluxe Lassie at $387, the Super Lassie at $389 and the Comet at $500. All of these prices were plus $47.50 prep. The Senior 125 was not mentioned on that price list. The 1963 prices listed in the chart were from the Ohio distributor, but advertised elsewhere. The advertised El Paso prices were usually a little lower. Jay's Cycles in El Paso was still advertising for dealers (without a mention of the latest closeout prices) in the November 1963 *Cycle World*. Pointer Sales of America in Cleveland OH published a small ad in the May 1964 issue of *Cycle World* for the closeout prices on the Comet and Super Lassie, calling it a "Mid-Season Sale". All claimed dry weights are listed in pounds.

Pointer Super Lassie

Remember that girl back in junior high that you were secretly in love with? You didn't dare tell anyone because she was that tall, gangly nerd with glasses. You had no choice but to secretly glance in her direction whenever no one was looking. Not only do I remember that girl very well, but there was also a two-wheeled equivalent to her called the Super Lassie. I have never been able to figure out exactly what it is that so enamors me of the Super Lassie. The girl, I understand: I am a nerd myself, I still love smart girls, and much later, of course, I married one. Pointer would be out of business less than two years after I first saw the Super Lassie, but something about this tiddler still draws my attention. I find the remaining models of the small Pointer lineup to be rather clunky in the styling department, but the Super Lassie has my number!

The styling was obviously copied from that of the Honda Super Sport 50. You can see the same or very similar shapes in the leading link front suspension, plastic front fender, stamped steel rear fender, rubber mudflap on the front fender, headlamp nacelle, low bars, seat, and slim tank. They both roll on 2.25 x 17 tires. The two models are technically very different, though. This is a 90cc two-stroke instead of a 50cc OHV. Although they share an upswept exhaust and a three-speed footshift, the one on the Super Lassie is a rotary style. One can easily see today the lopsided stupidity of such an arrangement, and the gas tank molded into the frame was obviously cut from the same shortsighted mode of stupid engineering. Notice that the rear brake lever is missing from the photo.

The photo is a 1962 Super Lassie, displaying two colors and views in its official brochure. No, I have never seen one, but I have every photograph, brochure, and article I have been able to locate on this very rare tiddler. Pointer sent a small number of Super Lassies to the U.S. in 1960-63. I am not even certain if they were actually imported in 1960 or 1963. I have a brochure photo in my files showing a '61 model with a solo seat and slightly different coloring. I also have ads showing the closeout sale of this model in 1963. Were these all unsold '62's? I am unsure.

The other models in the small Pointer lineup included the regular Lassie with a step-through style, the Deluxe Lassie with the same step-through styling and more features, the 155cc Comet and a very similar 125cc little brother. All were single-cylinder two-strokes of somewhat conventional nature for Japanese tiddlers of the time. Electric starters and rotary gearshifts were featured. Two very unusual points about the Super Lassie were its gas tank integrated into the frame (look at the picture again) and an electric starter only on a 90cc two-stroke that my cat Tabitha could kickstart! Aside from the obvious styling copy of the early Honda Super Sport 50 of the same era, the rest of the story of this rare tiddler is unremarkable. As mentioned earlier, I wisely chose the new Yamaha Rotary Jet 80 YG-1 instead for my first motorcycle. A four-speed with a kickstarter is always sportier than a rotary three-speed with an electric starter - even on a tiddler.

James Rozee Speaks: "In good condition, a Pointer could bring around $3000 at least, but on Ebay just about anything is possible, depending on the bidder. As with any other machine, everything is *condition, condition, condition*. There are no parts sources so everything missing would have to be made. The Pointers have a lot of weird parts that just cannot be found. Even the Japanese can't find parts!

I love this stuff! I have owned so many of these weird bikes. I had a Super Lassie just like your photo. they were cool! Not only did they have rubber front fork action but the motor was rubber mounted, the gas tank was part of the frame and under the seat was a neat little stash area. You have to keep it together when riding a rotary shift; you always keep count. I had an early B-8 Kawasaki and a Tohatsu. Both had their gearboxes in a bucket all because someone did not count very well. My B-8 Kaw was great once you got used to it. You could race up to a corner, then click it into low and blast off with out changing down! I miss my Lassie. I traded it for a couple of Hodakas. One was a Rickman I sold later. I'm kicking myself for that one, too! I restored the seat and re-lettered it *Pointer*, then all I was missing were the amber turn signal lenses. I found cut down pill bottles worked great and looked good, not the same as stock but where are you going to find a Pointer dealer? Mine went to a collector in Eastern Washington who has lots of Pointers of all sizes. Most of the photos I have seen with solo seats were domestic models. Many Japanese bikes that were sent here had double seats and a buddy strap. Some have higher Western-style bars. You can always tell domestic Japanese bikes by the speedos: they will be in kilometers, and some will have more Japanese writing on them than usual.

The Super Lassie also featured rubber front fork springing and a rubber mounted motor! It was a well made bike and I loved riding it! The gas tank was as you said part of the frame and made the bike much stronger. It was well done, too. All domestic models had the short solo seat. The one I had was the longer U.S. one. it was titled as a 1964, the last year they made them. Most Super Lassies were an almond color with maroon tank.

Shin Meiwa Industry Co., Ltd., of Japan built Pointer motorcycles, including many models we did not get in the U.S. Before the Lassie and Super Lassie, they offered the 90cc Junior, Senior 125, and Comet 175 two-stroke singles, along with the Ace 250cc. twin cylinder two stroke. All had pressed steel frames except for the early 90 that was replaced with the Lassie, and a revamped 125 twin with tube frame produced in 1962. They even made a 125 road racer called the RJ1. I have only seen the Lassie 90 and Comet 155cc models in the flesh or should I say steel? Most models stayed in Japan unless a serviceman brought one back to the States with him after being stationed over there. I love the weird Japanese stuff best, don't you?"

"POINTER" SUPER LASSIE 90c.c.

for sports lovers! King of the lightweights — the style leader — with trim-line design. Can't be matched for luxury!
It's excitingly new!
It's fun to ride — with "POINTER" finger-tip handling ease and built in cornering control.

"POINTER" gives you a run for your money — no other 90 cc can match!
0 — 60 m. p. h. in 25 seconds.
"POINTER" puts plenty of miles between gas pumps too!
Nobody beats "POINTER" for value!

Figure E3 - 1963 Pointer Super Lassie Brochure. This is a composite overlay of two photos in the Pointer brochure to show both sides and colors of the Super Lassie. The gas tank was integral with the frame. The tank and surrounding area are a mellow brownish red on the top machine and charcoal gray on the lower one. The remainder of both machines is cream. Note that there is no kick starter or brake pedal on the lower machine. Why this is, I do not have a clue! ©1963 Pointer Sales of America

Figure E4 (next page) - This letter from the distributor makes no mention of the fact that the Pointer machines were going nowhere fast in the USA. ©1963 Pointer Sales of America

~"POINTER" SALES OF AMERICA
NATIONAL DISTRIBUTORS OF MOTORCYCLES

A Division of Parma Motors, Inc.
5 2 1 9 R I D G E   R O A D
CLEVELAND 29, OHIO
Telephone: TUxedo 4-3100
Cable Address:
POINTMOTOR CLEVELAND

Mr. Floyd Orr, Jr.
516 McCord Street
West Point, Mississippi

Subject: Annual Year-End Inventory Clearance Sale on "Pointer" Motorcycles

Dear Mr. Orr:

We have "Pointer Motorcycles available which are warehoused in Miami, Florida and Cleveland, Ohio, and are offering them at special inventory year-end clearance prices. These vehicles are 1964 models and are packed two per crate of the same model. In the Miami, Florida warehouse there is an inventory of 28 Super Lassie Motorcycles and 6 Comet Motorcycles; In the Cleveland, Ohio warehouse there is an inventory of approximately 18 Comet Motorcycles and 20 Super Lassie Motorcycles.

The above quantity of vehicles only are being offered at dealer cost, f.o.b. Cleveland and Miami, for the remainder of this year only. The prices are as follows:

"Pointer"Comet 155 cc Motorcycle   — $364.78

"Pointer"Super Lassie 90 cc Motorcycle — $283.87

These prices are tremendous savings, as the Comet 155 cc Motorcycle retails at $499.70 plus freight, warranty and set-up charges of $47.50, or a total of $547.20; and the Super Lassie 90 cc Motorcycle retails at $388.90 plus freight, warranty and set-up charges of $47.50, or a total of $436.40. Should you desire an 1800-mile, 90-day parts warranty, please add $20.00 to the cost of the vehicle. We are prepared to ship any of the above quantities at the above prices only as long as our supply lasts. These are being sold on a first come, first served basis. Your certified check, bank draft, or money order will be accepted as payment. Shipment will be made within five days after receipt of order. Parts are available in our Cleveland Parts Store.

"Pointer" vehicles include a 12-Volt electrical system, electric starter, front and rear directional lights, side view mirrors, and tool kit assembly at the above prices. We are enclosing literature and brochures.

We shall await your early reply.

Very truly yours,
"POINTER" SALES OF AMERICA

Ernest Gerzeny
President

EG:mlp
Enclosures

Rabbit

Fuji Rabbit 1962 Chart

Model	Name	Type	HP	Seat	Starter	Price
S201-C	Minor	88cc Single	5	Solo	Electric	$299
S-202A	Rabbit 90	88cc Single	5.5	Solo	Electric	$299
S-85	Junior	148cc Single	7.5	Twin	Electric	NA
S601-B	Superflow	199cc Single	11	Twin	Electric	$495

Rabbit 1962 Notes: The S-202A had a claimed dry weight of 184 pounds. A *Cycle World* test of an 11-hp Superflow in August 1962 listed the price as $495, but a Rabbit ad in the same issue stated $559.

Fuji Rabbit 1963 Chart

Model	Name	Type	HP	Seat	Wt.	Price
S-202A	Rabbit 90	88cc Single	5.5	Twin	184	$299
S-402-A	Junior	148cc Single	7.5	Twin	260	$410
S-402-AT	Jr. Touring	148cc Single	7.5	Dual	260	$449
S601-B	Superflow	199cc Single	11	Twin	337	$559

Rabbit 1963 Notes: All 1963 Rabbits had electric starter, gas gauges, and turn signals. There is some question of exactly when the newer S601-C with 18 horsepower was received in the U.S. A December 1963 ad in *Cycle World* states 18-hp for the model without mention of a B or C suffix. The 150 Junior and Junior Touring models have four-speed, left hand shifts. All claimed dry weights are listed in pounds.

Fuji Rabbit 1964-67 Chart

Model	Name	Type	HP	Seat	Wt.	Price
S-202A	Rabbit 90	88cc Single	5.5	Solo	184	$310
S-402BT	Touring	148cc Single	7.5	Dual	260	$449

S-601C	Superflow	199cc Single	18	Twin	337	$559

Rabbit 1964-67 Notes: All 1964-67 Rabbit scooters had electric starters, gas gauges, and turn signals. Sources quote that 4648 S-402's were built from 1961-68 and many of these probably came to the USA. A much larger number (26,924) S-202A's were produced from 1962-67, apparently mostly for the home market. The prices stated above are the same as the earlier years. There may have been price increases throughout this period. All claimed dry weights are listed in pounds.

Fuji Rabbit 1968 Chart

Model	Name	Type	HP	Seat	Starter
S-402BT	Touring	148cc Single	7.5	Dual	Electric
S-601	Superflow	199cc Single	18	Twin	Electric

Rabbit 1968 Notes: According to the *Illustrated Encyclopedia*, Rabbits continued in production through 1968, but they certainly became extremely rare in the U.S. before that. There were 74,694 Superflows built from 1961-68, mostly for the Japanese market. Few details are available on whatever 1968 models were sold here. No 1968 prices are available.

Rabbit Superflow

Fuji Heavy Industries, the maker of Subaru automobiles, built and imported a small line of luxury scooters to the U. S. in the early '60's. I don't know how many years the Rabbits were imported, but it certainly wasn't many. I have a set of brochures for a year or two, and my best guess is that they represent three 1963 or '64 models. Rabbit built the 200cc flagship called the Superflow, a 150cc Junior, and a 90cc model. American Rabbit Corporation in San Diego imported these premix two-strokes, and I would guess that they are very rare today. Malcolm Bricklin was even involved in their importation in the early '60's, sandwiched between the time he was the importer of Lambretta scooters and the development of his Bricklin sports car.

The Superflow was intended as a top-drawer model, featuring electric starting (which was very rare for a scooter back then), a trunk underneath the rear seat, whitewall tires, automatic transmission, and an elegant, two-tone gold paint job. The scooter's eleven horsepower produced a top speed of 60 mph, and if I recall the *Cycle World* test correctly, the claimed top speed was not overly optimistic. The tested machine was in the August 1962 issue before the horsepower rating was increased to eighteen. Did the power actually increase by more than 50% only a couple of years later? I don't know. Regardless, the

Superflow was a very advanced scooter for its day. Specifications also included an air-compression rear suspension, turn signals, and a fuel gauge. The entire rear body section simply lifted up without tools, like the front bonnet of an XK-E Jaguar, to expose the engine, transmission, and rear suspension for servicing. Unlike most scooters, final drive was via a fully enclosed chain running in its own oil bath. The only flies in this modern ointment of scooter technology were the Superflow's little eight-inch wheels. You can see from the chart in Chapter 10 that many of the modern, and cheap, scooters made in China today have wheels of 12-16-inch diameter!

The Junior was a less deluxe, less powerful version of the Superflow. Its 150cc engine produced 7.5 horsepower and a claimed top speed of 58 mph. The Junior used a three-speed manual transmission with an automatic clutch. There was a hand clutch lever accompanying the handshift on the left handlebar, allowing some manual control over the clutch mechanism. I'm not sure how well this system worked, since I have never seen a Junior. With its slab sides and colors only a hospital attendant could love, the Junior was distinctly the Superflow's ugly cousin.

The Rabbit 90 was a pretty innovative, elegant little scooter. Its fifteen-inch spoked wheels made it look like a Honda 50 Cub's scooterized cousin. You could call it the ancestor of the Aprilia Scarabeo or Kymco People. An electric start, 5.5 horsepower engine propelled the 90 to a claimed 52 mph, using a clutch and three-speed handshift similar to that of the Junior 150.

Figure E5 - Rabbit 150 Touring. Image by Eric, photographer, under Creative Commons license.

James Rozee Speaks: "A question I get asked a lot is: Is this Fuji the same company that worked with Hodaka and Yamaguchi? The answer is No. There were many companies named after the highest mountain in Japan, and many others with Fuji in their names. Fuji Heavy Industries, who made the Rabbit scooters and the Subarus, and Fuji Motors Corporation, who made the engines for Yamaguchis and Hodakas, were different companies. Hodaka and Fuji had worked together since the early Fifties."

Tohatsu

Tohatsu 1962-63 Chart

Year	Name	Type	HP	Exhaust	Wt.	Price
1962	Runpet Sport	49cc Single	6.8	Down	135	$299
1963	Runpet Sport	49cc Single	6.8	Down	135	$299
1963	Trailmaster	49cc Single	5	Upswept	140	$318
1963	Scrambler	49cc Single	6.8	Upswept	NA	$318
1963	Sport LE 125	124cc Twin	15	Down	NA	NA

Tohatsu 1962-63 Notes: The Sport LE 125 had a dual seat. The remaining models had solo seats. All claimed dry weights are in pounds.

Tohatsu 1964 Chart

Model	Name	Type	HP	Exhaust	Wt.	Price
CA-S	Runpet	49cc Single	4.7	Down	132	$249
CA-2	Runpet Sport	49cc Single	6.8	Down	135	$299
CA	Trailmaster	49cc Single	5	Upswept	140	$318
CA-2UP	Scrambler	49cc Single	5	Upswept	140	$318
LA-2B	Arrow	123cc Single	10.3	Down	253	$433
LA-3	Twin Arrow	124cc Twin	12	Down	253	$498
LE	Sport LE 125	125cc Twin	15	Down	NA	NA
LD-3A	Sport 125	124cc Twin	17	Down	253	NA

Tohatsu 1964 Notes: The Runpet Sport and Trailmaster had solo seats. All the remaining models had dual seats. The Scrambler was similar to the Trailmaster, but with a little higher gearing. Both dual purpose models had skid plates. The Trailmaster had knobby tires and a luggage rack. The model year breakdown of the Tohatsus is not exactly clear. The Sport LE model is shown in *Cycle World* ads, but the other variants are in the brochure. All the 50's had kick starters and all the 125's had electric starters, apparently without kick starters. The Newbirdy 90 was an unusual model. It had a pressed steel frame, solo seat, and an unusually angular side cover shape in contrasting silver. I have no idea where to put this street tiddler in the chart. According to the *Classic Japanese Motorcycles*

Illustrated Buyer's Guide, Tohatsu declared bankruptcy in February 1964. Other sources back this up; however, it is not clear if the last of the production was sold in the USA as 1964 models or not. In *Cycle World*'s Report from Japan in the November 1963 issue, a new Tohatsu 90 (not the Newbirdy) was announced, but it obviously never came to the U.S. There was a full-page ad for the Runpet in the same issue. The same ad was repeated in the December 1963 issue, too. There were no ads for Tohatsu in the next *Cycle World* issue I have, May 1964. All claimed dry weights are in pounds.

Tohatsu Arrows & Runpets

The company began building small motorcycles in Japan in 1950, but of course none were sent to this country until The Sixties. Although Tohatsu first sent its tiddlers here, the brand has become synonymous with small to medium displacement outboard motors from Japan. Tohatsu began building outboards for the home market in 1956. Now they not only export them to the U. S., they build them for other companies who stick their own labels on them. You may be surprised to know that all current Mercurys of thirty horsepower or less are built by Tohatsu, and all Nissan outboards are built by Tohatsu and marketed in the U. S. under the familiar automobile brand.

As far as I know, Tohatsu tiddlers were imported by Hap Jones Distributing Company in San Francisco only in 1963 and '64, and all were two-strokes without oil injection. There were only eight models that I have ever seen in brochures or advertised in cycle magazines, three 50cc Runpets, the Newbirdy 90, and four 125cc Arrows.

Probably the most successful Tohatsu in the U. S. was the Runpet 50 Sport. The 1964 blue beauty seems to be typical of the brand. It is by far the most common Tohatsu in the USA without a propeller! The Runpet was a basic small motorcycle with 4.7 hp, downswept exhaust, dual seat, full front fender, and covered shock springs. The Runpet Sport featured abbreviated fenders and seat and a 15:1 compression that boosted the power to 6.8. There was a Trailmaster model with the base engine, higher bars, large luggage rack and a humongous rear sprocket. All the Tohatsu 50's used three-speed transmissions.

There were four 125cc models, the fourth of which was a derivative of the other three that I'm not sure if and when it was actually imported. The 125's were called Arrows and all had electric starters. The basic model was a single-cylinder, four-speed with full fenders and covered shocks. Next up was the Twin Arrow, strangely enough, the same motorcycle in a twin-cylinder configuration. The top of the line was the Sport 125, featuring uncovered rear springs, abbreviated fenders, low bars, 18/17-inch tires instead of the 16's of the lesser Arrows, and 17 hp aided by a five-speed tranny. These three 125's are shown, along with the Runpets, in what I am generally certain is a 1963 full-line brochure.

Advertised in the July 1963 issue of *Cycle World* is a somewhat different 125cc Sport. This one is referred to as an LE-type, whereas the aforementioned Sport is called an LD-3A type. This model is noted as having 15 hp, instead of the ten of the Arrow Single, the twelve of the Twin Arrow, or the seventeen of the other 125 Sport. In appearance this model has the long seat, covered rear springs, and Western bars of the slower models. with the tank, fenders, and uncovered chain of the, shall I say, *sportier* Sport. Who knows where that last two horsepower went, but the ad touts this as being the brand-new model designed for the U. S. market. My best guess is that my brochure is an earlier release than the ad.

The company must have thought that what Americans wanted at the time was a bike that looked a little more like a Honda Benly Touring 150 than a Ducati Diana. They may have been right at that brief moment in time, but we grew up fast and Tohatsu motorcycles quickly disappeared from the market.

James Rozee Speaks: "One of the Tohatsus I had was a road racer I built out of an extra parts bike to ride around the racetrack in Portland. It was a pretty stock Runpet Sport motor but had the racing seat, chrome chamber and rearsets. I made a fairing out of a full shell helmet and put a blue Plexiglas bug screen on it like Tohatsu did on the stock model. I had a Yamaha 80 long gas tank with filled in tank badge holes. I even made a vent for the front brake shoes with a scoop. It went pretty good. The only problem was it only had a three-speed gear box and in third with the tiny rear sprocket, it didn't have the guts to go over 50, and that was with me tucked in and bent over and no headwind. One time we were running a club parade lap and two friends of mine decided to race each other on the back straightaway at P.I.R. They both went around me as I was flat out at 50 m.p.h., one on a Suzuki 500 twin with two smoking chambers on one side of me, and the other friend on a H-D Aermacchi 350 road racer on the other side of me at about 80+ mph! The wind gust alone off of them almost blew me off the track. They were both so loud I could not hear my little Tohatsu Runpet 50, even with it's open chamber! I almost stepped off thinking I had stopped!

Any of the Blue Runpet Sports with upswept exhaust pipes will be 1963-64 models. This and the high handlebars and bigger tail light were on all models sent to the U.S.A. with the turn signals removed. The black street model and orange trail model were sold right up to the end in 1964 when they went under. All trail and street models had the covered rear shocks; only the Sport had exposed chrome plated rear springs on its shocks. All frames were the same on the 50cc. except the center stand mount on the non-sport models. The Sport had a side stand only and chrome plated fenders that were much different than the other two models. For some reason Tohatsu removed the front fender on their trail model. It was the black street model with orange paint, knobbies and a huge rear sprocket, single seat, and big rear carrier rack for deer hunting. Tohatsu copied Honda's 1962 55cc that had removed their front fenders, too. It made them look like cool bikes! Many people seized their motors when they overheated the little engines because of being caked in mud! I had a few Tohatsus that would seize up now and then. It happened to new rebuilds, mostly because the person who bored it out to fit the piston made the bore too tight. At other times it was an aftermarket piston that expanded too much. Both problems were fixed with a light honing of the cylinder wall. You have to watch your oil mixture, too. I found that good old outboard motor oil works better than all these new oils. It may smoke a bit more, but it will run forever. You do have to de- carbonize it now and then, as with most old two strokes, but you should not need to do it that often unless you are running too rich or too much oil. The down pipe on the black street model was not the tuned expansion chamber pipe of the Runpet Sport. The sports pipe had a long center bolt that could be undone and out came the whole outside of the muffler, exposing a cute little chrome chamber, loud but way cool! That way, after the race you could bolt it back on and ride home. The Sports model had not only a different high-compression cylinder head but a bigger carb, too. The weak link of a Tohatsu wasn't the motor, but the top engine mount and rear hub. The tiny handlebar clutch and brake levers are very thin and can snap off if you brush by the bike in the garage! Keep them loose on the bars like you would a dirt bike. These bikes are so rare now. and parts are really getting so hard to find. Many of the Tohatsus I have found in the past were stockers or completely modified for dirt racing or riding. I had heads that were milled down for racing and lots of aftermarket and well-made home shop parts and mods. Knowing the right parts was a long, hard learning curve for me that took forty years!

You can identify the Runpet Sport of 1963-64 by the 'Lucas' tail light and black tail light bracket. Earlier models had a much smaller bracket that was painted silver with a tiny tail light with 'Fuse' type bulbs. The lens was held in place by two pan head standard screws. Standard straight head screws were correct on all Tohatsus. I have had many stock unrestored Tohatsus, so I know for a fact that anyone who has Phillips head fender bolts and side cover screws will be incorrect. Cracking of the top cylinder head bolt frame bracket is very common on these machines. Have a professional match the blue color if you are repainting. It is an especially difficult shade to match correctly. All Sport chain guards were silver, as were the engine side covers. and most other parts that were cadmium plated on other Japanese bikes. The black seat with white piping should have *Tohatsu* lettered in silver on the back.

There were many differences in the 50cc Tohatsu tube models. The blue Runpet Sport was the coolest and most popular one sold in the States. I had many of them and it's the one that is in such demand now. The Trail Master was all orange and was in fact the black street model with the front fender removed and a huge chrome rack like a Honda Trail 90 bolted to it's little painted rear rack. The black street model has the same rack on its rear fender, but the long red seat sits right on top of it. All models had center stands, and the Runpet Sport had a side stand, too. Both the black street model and the orange trail model shared the same high exhaust pipe. The trail model had its own single black seat. with no writing on the back. The Sport had low bars and the rest had Western bars.

The Runpet Sport had many parts indigenous to that model: the headlight bucket with its blue plastic bug screen on it with a larger faced speedo, the cool key that looked like a switch when inserted into the headlight bucket, and the small leather bags that looked like racing number plates with a zipper on top could hold a pair of gloves and goggles. The rear exposed spring shocks and the rear rack were chrome plated. The heads on the Sport model had much larger, square fins and were of course of a higher compression.

The street and trail models got the teardrop-shaped head. All models shared gas tanks and forks and the plastic horn covers, the air cleaner and cool side covers. Under one side sat the battery and on the other a tin tool bag tray that is missing on a lot of bikes because they were held on with a rubber strap that can come loose or break. They were held to the bottom of the seats with only two slotted push-in brackets. Once the rubber band gave out, they would just drop off! All models could get stress cracks in the head mount on the frame. Another common problem was in the rear brake hub. The shoe casting was so thin they would break in half and take out all the lugs in the hub bracing webs, popping big holes in the hub. You can tell this when looking at one: you see holes in the rear hub between the spokes!

I worked for and knew many old Tohatsu dealers. I asked a Japanese friend how come they always use the name *Pet* on machines in Japan? Toyopet, Runpet, Autopet? He said it's because they are *pets*. That makes sense, I guess. I thought it meant something different. Cool stuff!"

Marusho

Figure E6 - Black Marusho ST-500 at the Barber Museum. You can see the Marusho's distinguishing, deeply scalloped gas tank on this example.

Image by Chuck Schultz, photographer, under Creative Commons license.

The Marusho Chart

Year	Model	Type	HP	Starter	Price	Production
1964	ST-500	493cc Flat Twin	35.6	Kick	$995	NA
1965	ST-500	493cc Flat Twin	35.6	Kick	NA	600
1966	Magnum	493cc Flat Twin	40	Kick	NA	180
1967	Electra	493cc Flat Twin	40	Electric	$1195	123

Marusho Notes: All Marushos had dual seats and downswept dual exhausts and were painted either Black or Candy Apple Red. The kick starter had to be pushed outward from the left side of the machine, an unpleasant type of starting mechanism due to its copycat BMW design. All Marushos had left-side, four-speed shifts. A small, unidentified number of ST-500's were sold in the U.S. as 1964 models. Marushos were marketed under the Lilac brand in all countries outside the U.S. According to the *Classic Japanese Motorcycles Illustrated Buyer's Guide*, Marushos were sold in the U.S. for three years. All three models had serious engine problems, leading to their early demise. The claimed dry weight of the 1964 ST-500 was 406 pounds. According to the December 1964 *Cycle World* test, the ST weighed 423 pounds, and its performance was leisurely: 0-60 in 13.1 and the quarter in 18.6, with a top speed of 79.

Figure E7 - Candy Apple Red Marusho ST-500. ©Troyce Walls

Hodaka

Figure E8 - A Row of Hodakas at the 2006 AMA Vintage Motorcycle Days, Lexington, OH. The distinctive, all-chrome gas tanks are clearly visible on these machines.

Image by Jamie Aaron under Creative Commons license in the Public Domain.

Hodakability

The dirt riding boom across the U. S. was just getting wound up to launch when Yamaguchi went up in two-stroke smoke in 1963. Although I had been personally clued in to the joys of off-road riding practically from the time of my first ride on any motorcycle in 1960, the earliest Japanese imports of the day were not yet on that wavelength. The Yamaha Omaha Trail of 1962, followed by the ubiquitous Honda Trail opened up the pathway for a cyclist to get dirty in a manner that did not involve bugs in the teeth or leaky British machinery. Pacific Basin Trading Company (PABATCO) was a small firm operating out of a small town in the hills of Oregon that happened to be the U. S. importer of Yamaguchis. When the Japanese company gave up on motorcycle production, the enterprising folks at PABATCO decided to design their own small, dual-purpose chassis and power it with the Japanese company's engine.

The first Hodaka was the 1964 Ace 90. Like the original Model T, it came in only one color, and like the Volkswagen Beetle, it was designed from the ground up to be a single, long-running model with constant engineering tweaks and updates. Even the Hodaka ads were similar to those memorable ones made in the '60's for the Beetle. *Hodakability* is probably the brand's most famous ad concept. The Hodaka brand began with the Ace 90, progressed to the Ace 100, and then the 100-B. The B model I rode once was absolutely the most comfortable off-road machine I have ever ridden. Just as a comparison to my '71 Yamaha AT-1CMX, the sloped seat on my bike makes me slide a little too close to the tank, and the seat is not particularly soft. The one on the Hodaka shared the perfection of its riding position, and the Hodaka was one of the first Japanese off-road machines to have wonderfully squishy, long-travel suspension. Why, then, don't I have an Ace 100? Comfort isn't everything.

Hodaka expanded their line a bit as the years passed, but the later iterations were somewhat rare then, as well as now. First there was the 100cc Super Rat motocrosser, then the Wombat 125cc, the Combat Wombat 125cc motocrosser, and finally, the 250cc Thunderdog. The company gets an obvious *A* in cute names for cute motorcycles. In my estimation, there were probably less built of each of these succeeding models. There are still a number of Hodaka enthusiasts around.

Figure E9 - Yellow Hodaka Combat Wombat 125 at the Barber Museum, Birmingham, AL.

Image by Chuck Schultz, photographer, under Creative Commons license.

James Rozee Speaks: "I think Hodaka should have stuck to building the best trail bike in the world. They were selling more under-100cc dirt bikes than anyone at the time! The original Hodaka was a far better product than anyone else had, and for 350 bucks out the door! They were winning all kinds of races too, and these bikes are still being ridden in Vintage MX, Trials and enduros, and trail rides today! My pal has a 1966 Ace 90 motor that we both have abused for years and it is still going strong. The Combat Wombat was a great bike but by the time it was built, The Big Four were spending millions on R&D and had lighter and faster bikes by then. It is a great bike, but the old Ace 90 based motor with heavy flywheels was already showing its limitations.

I have the Enduro model, a 1973 Wombat that has 800 miles on the speedo. Like all of my motorcycles it has been displayed at many shows in Oregon. I have lots of friends that have Wombats and Combat Wombats in the Hodaka Owners Registry, so I have ridden many. I ride mine near the same mountains that the 125 Wombat had won the Trask Mountain two day trial at in 1972-73. Hodaka always had a laid-back funny sense of humor with their bikes, much like the men themselves that made Hodakas.

I admit as before that Hodaka did not have the R&D money to dump into their machines as The Big Four did, so comparing them is really dumb. Some parts for The Big Four are as rare as Yamaguchi stuff! Honda is not reproducing parts because The Big Four changed bikes and parts like we change our underwear! Many were just stupid changes not improvements, making their bikes hard to find the correct year parts for now, if you can find any at all. I still ride one on trails today and it handles pretty good for a 40 year old machine. and I can get all the parts I need to keep it going forever! Hodakas were designed in Oregon and built in Japan to P.A.B.A.T.C.O. specs. That's why they last.

Hodakas were like VW Beetles in that they had running changes casual observers would never notice. The 1968 Ace 100 was indeed the first Hodaka 100cc and was made for only two years. It had wider wheel rims and rear fender, a different exhaust and five speeds, a plastic battery cover, and miscellaneous other changes. The only change in 1969 was the addition of reflectors on the sides of the headlight and rear luggage rack. The model that took its place was the pretty Ace 100 B model in 1970. The B shared many parts with the Super Rat. I bought a new 1968 Ace 100 and rode it hard as a kid. It taught me how to really ride and wheelie a bike. It handled really well compared to the pressed frame bikes of the day. I still have Hodakas and I think my 1972 Wombat 125 still handles pretty good today on trails. These bikes were well made and I know many of the people involved in making them. They were Oregon trail riders and motocross racers, etc., so they knew what worked and what didn't."

The Hodaka Chart

Year	Model	Type	HP	Exhaust	Wt.	Price
1964	Ace 90	90cc Single	8.2	Upswept	135	$379
1965	Ace 90	90cc Single	8.2	Upswept	135	NA
1966	Ace 90	90cc Single	8.2	Upswept	135	NA
1967	Ace 100	98cc Single	9.8	Upswept	170	NA
1968	Ace 100	98cc Single	9.8	Upswept	170	$425
1969	Ace 100	98cc Single	9.8	Upswept	170	$425
1970	100/B	98cc Single	9.8	Upswept	170	$395
1970	Super Rat	98cc Single	NA	Upswept	NA	$495
1971	100/B+	98cc Single	10.5	Upswept	183	$495
1971	Super Rat	98cc Single	NA	Upswept	173	$535
1972	100/B+	98cc Single	10.5	Upswept	183	$495
1972	Super Rat	98cc Single	NA	Upswept	173	$535
1972	Wombat	123cc Single	NA	Upswept	225	$660
1973	100/B+	98cc Single	10.5	Upswept	188	567
1973	Super Rat	98cc Single	NA	Upswept	173	$612
1973	Wombat	123cc Single	NA	Upswept	225	$660
1973	Combat Wombat	123cc Single	NA	Down Up	NA	NA
1974	Dirt Squirt	98c Single	10.5	Upswept	188	$545
1974	Wombat	123cc Single	NA	Upswept	208	$795
1974	Combat Wombat	123cc Single	NA	Upswept	192	$795
1974	Super Combat	123cc Single	NA	Down Up	NA	NA
1975	Dirt Squirt	98cc Single	NA	Upswept	188	$499
1975	Road Toad	98cc Single	NA	Upswept	228	$529

1975	Super Rat	98cc Single	NA	Down	173	$695
1975	Wombat	123cc Single	NA	Upswept	208	$795
1975	Combat	123cc Single	NA	Upswept	192	$549
1975	Super Combat	123cc Single	NA	Down	192	$745
1975	Thunderdog	250cc Single	NA	NA	NA	NA

Hodaka Notes: All Hodakas had kick starters and 3/4-length seats. Ten-thousand Ace 90's were built from 1964-66. All claimed dry weights are listed in pounds, except that shown for the 1973 Wombat is wet. All the quoted 1975 prices were taken from 1976, as the 1975 prices were unavailable at the time of publication.

Hodaka Combat Wombat

You might call Hodaka the Mazda of the Japanese motorcycle companies, a little niche-market giant killer. After the demise of Yamaguchi in 1963, Hodaka rose from its charred tiddler ashes in '64 with its single model, the Ace 90. Unlike the Big Four, Hodaka concentrated all its energy into the small recreational dirt bike market. That first Ace 90 came only in one color, red, with what would become a Hodaka signature, an all-chrome tank. Changes to the Ace in succeeding years would be as carefully controlled as those to the legendary Beetle, and its advertising scheme would follow a similar pattern. The company was somewhat ahead of its time with its soft, long-travel suspension systems for off-road motorcycles. All Hodakas except the Ace used Ceriani-style front fork legs with uncovered rear springs. Models prior to the 100B had painted front spring covers or rubber gaiters. Hodaka owns some of the best model names in tiddler history: Road Toad, Dirt Squirt, Thunderdog, Super Rat, and of course Combat Wombat.

Let's examine the perspective of the motorcycle market during the Hodaka's approximate lifetime of 1964-79. Some people credit Hodaka with launching the off-road motorcycle boom, but I'm not one of them. Was the brand a booster rocket for a trend already begun, yes, but certainly not the pioneer of the genre. I took my own first off-road excursions in 1960, so you could say that *I was there*. Those first trips to the dirt were on a Harley-Davidson Super 10, and the trail models of that same machine, the Scat and Ranger, would be released in 1962. Honda and Yamaha were both producing several trail tiddlers prior to the release of the Ace 90. Hodaka's big distinctive difference was that the Ace 90 was never just a trail version of a street-only model, and many design features were incorporated from the beginning, such as the double downtube frame, long-travel suspension, upswept exhaust, and high, skinny fenders. In the early Hodaka days of 1964-67, the company did have a nice jump on the market while most of the competitors were still utilizing pressed steel frames and stiff suspension. The engines were pretty much comparable to those produced by Yamaha, Suzuki, and Kawasaki. Since this was prior to the launch of the Elsinores, all the Hondas were four-strokes at this time. The main differences among the bevy of two-strokes were the choices of regular or rotary shifters, automatic or manual clutches, and single or dual rear-sprocket arrangements.

We all know that Yamaha took charge of the party with the release of its DT-1 in 1968, and I think this is most likely what finished off Hodaka. All the new Yamaha Enduro and Motocross models had the same off-road attributes as the Hodakas with the piano-builder powerhouse operation behind them. Of course the whole trail riding fad was beginning to wane, too, but all Yamaha had to do was to go in the opposite direction and start building big four-stroke twins such as the XS-1. Hodaka never had that level of corporate diversity to back them up. The tiddler that I have now owned for more than 35 years has obviously always been my favorite, the AT-1 Motocross. This little bike had already been produced in very large numbers and even starred in a movie by the time mine was built in '71. The mood struck me a few days ago and I dragged out my copy of *Little Fauss and Big Halsey* and watched it for the umpteenth time, and it's still good!

This brings us to the subject of this story. Hodaka released its first 125, the Wombat, in 1972 and followed up with the motocross version in '73. This model was lovingly named the Combat Wombat, and it was a direct competitor in every way to the Yamaha motocrossers. Although Hodaka's first competition machine had been the 100cc Super Rat, the company really released the hounds with the Combat Wombat into the highly competitive 125cc racing class and marketplace. The technological design changes for small motocrossers were developing furiously. Yamaha released its second generation AT-2 in '72 and the first Elsinore blasted onto the market in 1973. The original 250 Elsinore was joined by its 125cc little brother in '74. The Combat Wombat ran against the Yamahas in 1973, but its souped up Super Combat successor was surrounded by Yamahas and the new 125 Minisnore on starting lines all across America in 1974. This was a very competitive market in which Hodaka was trying to survive!

Bridgestone

Figure E10 - 1963 Bridgestone B-50. Note the two-piece seat and square headlight nacelle on the tire company's first shot at the Honda 50 with its step-through two-stroke model. ©1963 Bridgestone Corporation

Bridgestone 1963 Chart

Model	Name	Type	HP	Seat	Exhaust	Wt.	Top Speed
B-50	Step-Thru	50cc Single	4.2	Dual	Down	153	45 mph
B-7	Sportster	50cc Single	4.1	Dual	Down	150	45 mph

Bridgestone 1963 Notes: The B-7 is kickstart with an electric starter optional. Production in Japan began in 1958, but no Bridgestones were exported to America until 1963. Bridgestones were imported by Rockford Scooter Company, the same importers of the Silver Pigeon. Some sources say that the Bridgestone 7, and possibly other early models, were sold through Aldens and Spiegel catalogs. As far as I know, this was true in 1963, but I am not sure how long the practice continued. No prices are available for the 1963 models. All claimed dry weights are in pounds.

... NEW NEW NEW NEW NEW NEW!

*BRIDGESTONE 7 Sportster

Figure E11 - 1963 Bridgestone 7. Note the pressed steel handlebars, painted tank, and non-black seat cover. I am not sure what color the seat actually is because I have never seen a color photo of this very early Bridgestone. You can see from the next photo that this model received chrome handlebars and tank panels in 1964. The fan-cooled engine distinguished the Model 7 from many of its close rivals. ©1963 Bridgestone Corporation

Bridgestone 1964 Chart

Model	Type	HP	Seat	Exhaust	Wt.	Speed
B-50 Step-Thru	50cc Single	4.2	Dual	Down	153	45 mph
B-7 Sportster	50cc Single	4.1	Dual	Down	155	45 mph
B-7 Deluxe	50cc Single	4.1	Dual	Down	159	45 mph
Bridgestone 90	88cc Single	7.8	Dual	Down	174	60 mph

Bridgestone 1964 Notes: No prices are available for the 1964 models. The B-7 Deluxe had an electric starter. All other models are kickstart. No prices are available for the 1964 models. All claimed dry weights are listed in pounds. The B-50 had a three-speed with automatic clutch. The B-7 had a rotary three-speed and the 90 had a rotary four-speed. All models had pressed steel frames.

Figure E12 - 1964 Bridgestone 7. ©1964 Bridgestone Corporation

THE QUALITY SPORTSTER WITH
EXCLUSIVE FEATURES FOUND ON NO OTHER 50CC MACHINE

- **Fan-cooled engine**
- **Rotary-type transmission — 3-speed foot shift**
- **Lowest center of gravity**
- **Largest capacity fuel tank**
- **Rugged all-steel unitized frame**
- **Shock-mounted engine, handle bars, & fuel tank**

THE NEW STANDARD OF EXCELLENCE

MODEL C206—STANDARD with kick starter
MODEL C207—DELUXE with electric starter

BRIDGESTONE 7 by Rockford

UNEQUALLED PERFORMANCE...WITH YEARS AHEAD STYLING

BRIDGESTONE 90 by Rockford

✳ 4-SPEED   ✳ ROTARY VALVE   ✳ ROTARY TRANSMISSION

CHECK THEM ALL BEFORE YOU BUY!

	Bridgestone "90"	Brand "A"	Brand "B"	Brand "C"
PISTON DISPL.	88cc	86cc	73cc	79cc
ROTARY VALVE STROKE	Yes	No	Yes	No
MAXIMUM SPEED	60.0 mph	55.2 mph	53.1 mph	53.1 mph
ACCELERATION 200 METER	13.0 Sec.	13.9 Sec.	13.0 Sec.	14.7 Sec.
MAXIMUM H.P.	7.8 HP @ 7000 rpm	6.5 HP @ 8000 rpm	6.5 HP @ 7000 rpm	6.5 HP @ 7000 rpm
MAXIMUM TORQUE	850 KG-M @ 5000 rpm	654 KG-M @ 6000 rpm	700 KG-M @ 6000 rpm	810 KG-M @ 5000 rpm
BRAKE DIAMETER	5.12 inches	4.33 inches	4.33 inches	4.33 inches

Looking for real performance? Here's the ultimate in 90cc engineering achievement — BRIDGESTONE 90 by Rockford. This is the lightweight built to lead in every performance category . . . plus – – – BRIDGESTONE'S built-in reputation for reliability! Also available in a trail model.

- **Greatest Torque**
- **Largest Brakes**
- **Highest Horsepower**
- **Best Acceleration**

ROCKFORD SCOOTER CO., INC. ROCKFORD, ILLINOIS

Figure E13 - 1964 Bridgestone 7 & 90 Ad. This ad displays a lighter color Bridgestone 7 and introduces the new Bridgestone 90. The 90 lacked much of the now-endearing funky styling of the earlier 7 model.
©1964 Bridgestone Corporation

Bridgestone 1965 Chart

Model	Type	HP	Seat	Exhaust	Wt.	Speed	Price
Step-Thru	50cc Single	NA	Dual	Down	153	45	$240
7	50cc Single	NA	Dual	Down	155	45	NA
50 Sport	50cc Single	5	Dual	Down	NA	53	$300
60 Sport	58cc Single	5.8	Dual	Upswept	NA	55	$330
90	88cc Single	7.8	Dual	Down	174	60	$380
90 Deluxe	88cc Single	7.8	Dual	Down	174	60	$405
90 Trail	88cc Single	7.8	Dual	Down	NA	60	$425
Mountain	88cc Single	7.8	Solo	Upswept	174	60	$400
90 Sport	88cc Single	8.8	Dual	Down	NA	65	$425
Dual Twin	177cc Twin	20	Dual	Down	271	85	$600

Figure E14 - This rare 1965 Bridgestone 50 Sport is owned by Neil Geldof of Connecticut, who took this photograph of his black beauty. It has optional chrome crash bars, a popular accessory of the day for many brands of machines, particularly small Japanese and American models. ©Neil Geldof

Bridgestone 1965 Notes: The 90 Deluxe, 90 Trail, 90 Sport, and the Dual Twin had oil injection standard and it was optional on the Mountain 90 for an additional $25. The 90 Deluxe also had a chrome front fender. All models had kick starters and the 7 was available as a Deluxe model with electric starter. All claimed dry weights are listed in pounds. All top speeds are listed in MPH. The Step-Through 50 had a three-speed with automatic clutch. The 7 had a rotary three-speed and most other models had rotary four-speeds. The Sport, Trail, and Mountain models had luggage racks and the Trail and Mountain models had dual rear sprockets.

PRINCIPLE FEATURES

- **Fan-Cooled Engine**—*Eliminates overheating during low speed operation or long periods at idle.*
- **Fully Automatic Clutch**—*Anyone can ride. No levers to squeeze.*
- **Silent Operation**—*Practically noiseless, a "neighbors dream."*
- **Lowest Center of Gravity**—*Easy to balance. An ideal "beginners" cycle.*
- **Strongest Frame in its Class**—*Tubular Steel for extra long life.*
- **Shock Mounted Engine**—*Rubber pads take out vibration virtually no "rider fatigue."*
- **Highest Torque Engine in its Class**—*More "pulling power" for longer engine life.*
- **Two Cycle Engine**—*No valves to replace. Far lower maintenance cost.*

SUGGESTED LIST PRICES*

C204	Bridgestone 50	$239.95*
C300	Bridgestone 50 Sport	299.95*
C301	Bridgestone 60 Sport	329.95*
C208	Bridgestone 90 Standard	379.95*
C308	Bridgestone 90 Deluxe (Oil Inj.)	405.00*
C309	Bridgestone 90 Trail (Oil Inj.)	425.00*
C210	Bridgestone 90 Mountain	399.95*
C310	Bridgestone 90 Mountain (Oil Inj.)	425.00*
C312	Bridgestone 90 Sport (Oil Inj.)	425.00*
C305	Bridgestone 175 Dual Twin (Oil Inj.)	599.95*

*Plus modest destination and set up charge. All prices subject to change without notice. Rockford Motors, Inc. reserves the right to make changes in specifications and equipment at any time without liability of any kind to provide same on models previously sold.

Printed in U.S.A.

BRIDGESTONE 90 STANDARD
BRIDGESTONE 90 DELUXE (Oil Injection)
IMPORTANT FEATURES

- **Oil Injection**—*(90 Deluxe)—No fuel mixing*
- **4 Speed Rotary Shift**—*Smooth and Positive*
- **Chrome Front Fender** *(90 Deluxe)*
- **Primary Kick Starting**—*Start in any gear*
- **Telescopic Front Fork**—*Smoother ride, better control*
- **Rotary Valve Fuel Induction**—*More "Go"*

COMPARE WITH ANYTHING IN ITS CLASS

	BRIDGESTONE 90	HONDA CA-200	SUZUKI K-10	YAMAHA YG-1K
Displacement	88cc	90cc	79cc	75cc
Engine Type	Rotary Valve 2-cycle	OHV 4-cycle	conventional 2-cycle	Rotary Valve 2-stroke
Max. H.P.	9 H.P. @7000 rpm	6.5 H.P. @8000 rpm	7 H.P. @6000 rpm	7 H.P. @7000 rpm
H.P. to Weight Ratio	1 H.P. to ea. 21.7 lb.	1 H.P. to ea. 28.9 lb.	1 H.P. to ea. 22 lb.	1 H.P. to ea.
Max. Speed	60 mph	56 mph	51 mph	55 mph

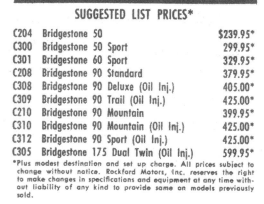

Figure E15 - 1965 Bridgestone Lineup Price List. This was the first year oil injection was offered by Bridgestone. Note the small photo of the C-204 50. The most noticeable difference between this model and the earlier B-50 is the one-piece dual seat. ©1965 Bridgestone Corporation

Figure E16 - Sometimes the clever Bridgestone ads appeared to be more about people and personalities than tiddlers! ©1965 Bridgestone Corporation

Bridgestone 1966 Chart

Model	Type	HP	Seat	Exhaust	Wt.	Speed	Price
Step-Thru	50cc Single	4.2	Dual	Down	132	45	$240
60 Sport	60cc Single	5.8	Dual	Upswept	152	55	$330
Mountain	88cc Single	7.8	Solo	Upswept	174	60	$400
90 Trail	88cc Single	7.8	Solo	Upswept	178	60	$425
90 Sport	88cc Single	8.8	Dual	Down	158	65	$425
100 Sport	99cc Single	9.5	Dual	Down	174	70	$400
100 Racer	99cc Single	15	3/4	Upswept	155	NA	NA
Dual Twin	177cc Twin	20	Dual	Down	271	85	$600
Hurricane	177cc Twin	20	Dual	Upswept	271	85	$625

Bridgestone 1966 Notes: All claimed dry weights are listed in pounds. All top speeds are listed in MPH. All models had kick starters and pressed steel frames. The 50 had an automatic clutch and three-speed. The 175's had switchable four-speed rotary or five-speed return shifts. All other models had four-speed rotary shifts.

Figure E17 - This page of a small 1967 brochure shows three models that were sold in both 1966 and 1967. ©1967 Bridgestone Corporation

Bridgestone 1967 Chart

Model	Type	HP	Seat	Exhaust	Wt.	Speed	Price
Step-Thru	50cc Single	4.2	Dual	Down	132	45	$240
50 Sport	50cc Single	5.2	Dual	Down	151	50	$300
60 Sport	60cc Single	5.8	Dual	Upswept	152	55	$330
90 Deluxe	90cc Single	7.8	Dual	Down	175	60	$405
90 Trail	90cc Single	7.8	Dual	Down	178	60	$425
Mountain	90cc Single	7.8	Solo	Upswept	174	60	$400
90 Sport	90cc Single	8.8	Dual	Down	158	65	$425
100 Sport	99cc Single	9.5	Dual	Down	174	70	$400
100 Racer	99cc Single	15	Solo	Upswept	171	NA	NA
175 Racer	177cc Twin	18	Solo	Upswept	239	NA	NA
Dual Twin	177cc Twin	20	Dual	Down	271	85	$600
Hurricane	177cc Twin	20	Dual	Upswept	271	85	$625
GTR	350cc Twin	37	Dual	Down	355	104	$850

Bridgestone 1967 Notes: All top speeds are listed in MPH. The 175 Hurricane Scrambler had an unusual shifter mechanism. You could push or pull a lever on top of the transmission that would switch it from a rotary four-speed to a standard five-speed return shift. The 175 Racer had a claimed quarter-mile e.t. of 15.3. The stated weight for the GTR is wet. This figure comes from the August 1967 *Cycle World* Road Test. The horsepower figure is claimed in the ad in the same issue. Note that the '68 model shows a claimed 40 horsepower. All claimed dry weights are listed in pounds.

Bridgestone 1968 Chart

Model	Type	HP	Seat	Exhaust	Wt.	Speed	Price
50 Sport	50cc Single	5.2	Dual	Down	151	50	$300
100 Sport	99cc Single	9.5	Dual	Down	174	70	$400
100 Racer	99cc Single	15	Solo	Upswept	155	NA	NA
175 Racer	174cc Twin	28	Solo	Upswept	234	NA	NA
Dual Twin	177cc Twin	20	Dual	Down	271	85	$600
Hurricane	177cc Twin	20	3/4	Upswept	271	85	$625
GTR	344cc Twin	40	Dual	Down	363	104	$850

Bridgestone 1968 Notes: All claimed dry weights are listed in pounds. All top speeds are listed in MPH. All 1968 models had rotary valve engines.

Figure E18 - Just how sexy was that 1968 Dual Twin, anyway? ©1968 Bridgestone Corporation

Bridgestone 1969 Chart

Model	Type	HP	Seat	Exhaust	Wt.	Speed	Price
50 Sport	50cc Single	5.2	Dual	Down	151	50	$300
100 GP	99cc Single	9.5	Dual	Down	174	72	$400
100 Sport	98cc Single	11	Dual	Down	174	70	$400
100 TMX	99cc Single	11	Dual	Upswept	174	60	$425
Dual Twin	177cc Twin	20	Dual	Down	271	85	$600
Hurricane	177cc Twin	20	Dual	Upswept	271	80	$625
175 SR	177cc Twin	NA	3/4	Upswept	234	NA	NA
Mark II RS	198cc Twin	21	Dual	Down	271	85	$600
Mark II SS	198cc Twin	21	Dual	Upswept	271	85	$625
350 GTR	344cc Twin	40	Dual	Down	363	105	$850

Bridgestone 1969 Notes: All claimed dry weights are listed in pounds. All top speeds are listed in MPH.

Bridgestone 1970 Chart

Model	Type	HP	Seat	Exhaust	Wt.	Speed	Price
100 GP	99cc Single	10.5	Dual	Down	174	72	$399
100 Sport	98cc Single	11	Dual	Down	174	NA	$399
100 TMX	99cc Single	11	3/4	Upswept	174	60	$399
Dual Twin	177cc Twin	20	Dual	Down	271	85	$425
Hurricane	177cc Twin	20	Dual	Upswept	271	80	$499
Mark II RS	198cc Twin	22	Dual	Down	271	85	$574
Mark II SS	198cc Twin	21	Dual	Upswept	271	85	$599
350 GTR	344cc Twin	40	Dual	Down	363	105	$699
350 GTO	344cc Twin	40	Dual	Upswept	363	100	$799

Bridgestone 1970 Notes: All top speeds are listed in MPH. All 1970 models were rotary valve two-strokes with oil injection and primary kick starting. All models had tubular cradle frames, telescopic front suspension and traditional rear shocks. The 100cc models had 17-inch wheels, the 175cc and 200cc models had 18-inch wheels, and the 350cc models had 19-inch wheels. The 175's and the GTR were Candy Red. The remaining models came in a choice of Imperial Gold or Sequoia Green. The 100 GP and TMX were also available in 5-hp versions. All claimed dry weights are listed in pounds. Note that the slight discrepancies in claimed dry weights between the 1970 and '71 models is probably simply the result of different sources, not actual differences in the machines. As with the prices, the 1970 weights were sourced from the *Motorcycle Sport Books*. The 1971 weights are from the '71 full-line brochure.

Bridgestone 1971 Chart

Model	Type	HP	Seat	Exhaust	Wt.	Price
Chibi (mini)	60cc Single	5.8	Solo	Upswept	120	$239
100 GP	99cc Single	10.5	Dual	Down	180	$400
100 TMX	99cc Single	11	3/4	Upswept	185	$400
MCB Enduro	125cc Single	18	3/4	Upswept	250	$840
Mark II RS	198cc Twin	22	Dual	Down	266	$575
Mark II SS	198cc Twin	21	Dual	Upswept	274	$594
350 GTR	344cc Twin	40	Dual	Down	355	$750
350 GTO	344cc Twin	40	Dual	Upswept	355	$800

Bridgestone 1971 Notes: No top speed data is available for the 1971 models. All claimed dry weights are listed in pounds, as stated in the full-line brochure. The prices are from the *Motorcycle Sport Books*.

Figure E19 - Bridgestone built four 90cc models in 1967: the Mountain, Deluxe, Sport, & Trail. ©1967
Bridgestone Corporation

Figure E20 - 1967 Bridgestone 350 GTR Ad. ©1967 Bridgestone Corporation

Bridgestone GTR & GTO

Figure E21 - Gold 1970 Bridgestone 350 GTO. This was the cover photo on the full-line brochure in 1970. ©1970 Bridgestone Corporation

It seems to be difficult to find information you would think would be more available, if for no reason other than that the company has remained in business all these years producing tires. There seems to be a lot of disagreement among the fans as to the exact details of the marque's history. For example, everyone agrees that this pair of two-stroke, rotary valve 350's were the last hurrah of the company, but I cannot be absolutely sure what years they were built. The best consensus seems to be that the GTR was introduced to America in late 1967 and the GTO arrived in 1970. Most sources agree that '71 was the last year for both

233

models, yet I cannot help but wonder if many stragglers were not sold as holdovers in 1972 or even '73 by U. S. dealers. The GTO is far and away less common than the purely road-going GTR, but I have not found a source that provides any actual production figures.

Bridgestone began its foray into the U. S. market with its fan-cooled 50cc Super 7 model and its step-through companion in 1963. There is a lot of controversy surrounding the fact (or not) that a few early Bridgestones were sold through Monkey Ward, either as catalog sales or in the giant anchor mall stores with their separate automotive service centers. I am of the opinion that some Bridgestones were sold in this manner; however, I cannot clearly remember if I saw these machines in a catalog or a store. During this time period, the Sears & Roebuck catalog was always sent to my parents' home, but I do not recall us ever receiving a Monkey Ward catalog. Therefore, I strongly suspect that I saw Bridgestones on sale at a Montgomery Ward mall store in Memphis, since I left my teenaged drool all over any machines I could find to examine in an up close and personal manner in any store during those days when I was obsessed with any motorcycle I didn't own. I certainly do not claim to have ever seen a 350 GTO or any other later Bridgestone in a mall store, but there were never many Bridgestone independent motorcycle shop dealers, and I don't think I have ever seen one.

Bridgestones tried to be the brand that offered a little higher quality for a little higher price. Magazine road tests of the day always mentioned Bridgestone's chrome cylinder bores, and how they would last the longest, but could never be rebored. The company loved to drape exquisitely mod young women over their motorcycles, especially in the later advertising programs. Norton and BSA would also become known for this blatantly sexist tactic, but I suspect it worked quite well for all of them.

Figure E22 - Red 1968 Bridgestone 350 GTR. Notice the light-colored seat cover insert for traction on its top surface. Although the roughly textured insert was standard equipment on this model, I am unsure if the contrasting light color on this machine is original.

©Michael Kiernan, Classic Motorcycle Company, St. Louis, MO.

There were a *lot* of distinguishing features of these rare beauties. They had twin-rotary-valve engines producing either 37 or 40 horsepower, depending on which source you believe. The six-speed transmissions were ahead of their time. The foot shifter and rear brake pedal were interchangeable so that either Nippon or Limey riders could be happy. The six-speed was a rotary shift, a style that has come under fire for its obvious downside of shifting inadvertently from sixth to first gear! Magazines of the time thought the chrome cylinder liners were innovative and long-lasting, but they questioned the appropriateness of a design that could never be rebored. The front *and* rear wheels were nineteen-inch, making for good handling with a tall seat height. The seat itself sported a non-slip suede-like top surface ala Bultaco Metralla. (The Kawasaki Mach III desperately needed one of these, and soon after my '71 model sent me sliding to the back of the bus a few times, I recovered the seat with corduroy!)

The styling of the GTO and GTR was quite elegant. Of course I preferred the GTO since I am an addicted street scrambler maniac, even though something about the GTO's crossbrace handlebar bend looks just a little bit too tall. I like the usual upswept pipes and abbreviated front fender, though. I could do without the left-side kickstarter and the chrome upper and lower rear shock covers on both models, but the slim tank and seat add a bit of elegance. The GTO had a skid plate to distinguish its *off-road* capability, but I have not been able to ascertain if any part of the gearing was lower than that of the GTR. Again, sources do not agree: I have read top speed quotes of both 95 and 105 from books and magazines, never mind whatever the official brochure said. All sources agreed that the quarter-mile was in the upper 13's or lower 14's, though, quite enough to embarrass a few British 650's, especially the slower single-carb models.

If you ask me to define exactly how I feel about the Bridgestone GTR and GTO, I shall have to remind you how analogous that would be to asking me my opinion of a certain rock band or two in 1973. You see, I think 1973 was the absolute, ultimate epitome of rock music. There was so much omigawd good stuff coming out of Britain, West Germany, and other European outposts in '73 that it was difficult to adequately pay heed to it all. This is how it was at the end of The Sixties for motorsickles, too. The GTR was launched amid the last of the Super Hawks and CL-77's and the first of the CB/CL-350's. The latter would set the motorcycle world afire with sales in the '68-'71 period, right when the GTR and GTO were just trying to get noticed. Yamaha was a storm of raging Big Bears and Catalinas working their way up to the BSA death knell they called the XS-1. Suzuki was developing classy, stylish, reliable twins and triples. Kawasaki was redefining performance with Avengers and enough triple-Machs to stomp any upstart brand into the ground! I think Can's *Future Days* is still today one of the greatest albums ever recorded, but have you heard it? It competed with *Goodbye Yellow Brick Road, Quadrophenia, Aerosmith, Sabbath Bloody Sabbath, Tubular Bells, Brain Salad Surgery, and Dark (F***ing) Side of the Moon* that year, for heaven's sake! In my humble opinion, the Bridgestone 350 GTR/GTO faced a similar uphill battle just to get noticed, and as with Can's magnum opus, the world is the worse for it.

Selected Rare Japanese Models Ratings Chart

Brand	Models	Collectibility	Practicality	Desirability
Yamaguchi	SPB Scrambler	B	D	C
Pointer	Lassie & Deluxe Lassie	C	D	D
Pointer	Super Lassie	B	D	B
Pointer	Comet & Senior	B	C	C
Rabbit	90cc Step-Through	C	C	D
Rabbit	150cc Scooter	C	C	C
Rabbit	200cc Superflow	C	C	B
Tohatsu	50cc Runpets	C	D	B
Tohatsu	125cc Models	B	D	B
Marusho	All 500cc Models	A	C	B

Selected Hodaka & Bridgestone Models Ratings Chart

Brand	Models	Collectibility	Practicality	Desirability
Hodaka	Ace & B Models	B	B	B
Hodaka	Super Rat	A	B	A
Hodaka	Wombats & Combats	B	B	A
Hodaka	Later 100cc Models	D	C	D
Bridgestone	Step-Through 50	C	D	D
Bridgestone	50-90cc Sport & Trail	B	C	B
Bridgestone	100 & 175 Racers	B	D	A
Bridgestone	177 & 200 Twins	C	C	C
Bridgestone	GTR & GTO 350	A	C	A

Models Ratings Chart Definitions:

Brand: Some early model years within a series may be considerably more desirable than later years. All grade ratings are based on evaluations of all the machines covered in this book, not just as a comparative rating within each marque.

Models: In some cases many variations are included in this category and in others the models included are very homogeneous.

Collectibility: This is what most of you want to know, the bottom line on how likely the model or series is likely to climb in value over the coming years.

Practicality: This is an indicator of how adaptable the machine can be to ride for transportation or pleasure in the modern world, considering parts availability, fuel quality, comfort, performance and miscellaneous other obvious factors.

Desirability: This defines the nostalgic, emotional wow factor, without regard for collector values or everyday usage.

General: No machine is given a failing grade. If it made it into a rating chart, at least a few hobbyists find that model interesting.

Figure E23 - This 1967 Dual Twin is finished in bright red paint with lots of chrome. The Dual Twin name referred to either its dual rotary valves or two-way shift mechanism that could be a four-speed rotary or five-speed return type. I am not certain which special feature was referenced with the name, but both were unusual at the time. This was the first model to employ dual rotary valves because they increased the width of the engine cases. The Hurricane Scrambler was practically identical to the Dual Twin except for its crossbrace bars and high pipes, one on each side. ©1967 Bridgestone Corporation

Figure E24 - Front Page of the 1969 Bridgestone Full Line Brochure. ©1969 Bridgestone Corporation

Chapter 5: *Suzuki: Express Yourself.*

This chapter should begin with a few statements concerning Suzuki's position and image in the U.S. marketplace and its preconceived positioning in *The Tiddler Invasion*. I have never claimed a very extensive knowledge of Suzukis. I am not even certain if I have ever ridden one or not. If so, I cannot recall the experience. The early Suzukis were imported by the Ken Kay Distributing Company. I am not sure how long the machines were officially imported before U.S. Suzuki was fully operational. All these events occurred nearly a decade prior to my first visit to California. I cannot even remember when I saw the first Suzuki dealer in the Southeast where I resided during the period. The first purely motorcycle magazine I saw as a kid was the arrival of *Cycle World* in 1962, which contained ads for Suzukis imported by Ken Kay. There were also ads for Yamahas, but it is a difficult call to say which company's machines were here first. This is mostly because *first* can be defined in many ways. We know about the first Yamaha entering a race held on Catalina Island, off the coast of California, in 1958. There does not seem to be a comparative event that defines exactly when Suzuki arrived on our shores. One thing I do know for certain is that Yamaha had a dealership near my little backwater town in Mississippi in 1962. The nearest Suzuki dealer at that time would have been in Jackson MS, Memphis TN, or Birmingham AL, and I was too young at that time to drive to those distant cities. Suzuki dealerships had reached those places by the middle of the decade, but I cannot tell you in which years they arrived.

Figure F1 - This shot of a black Suzuki T20 and a white Honda 90 was taken at an unknown location with a Kodak 126 Instamatic. Note the background scenery of a 1965 Oldsmobile, 1965 Pontiac, 1959 Buick, and a '66 GTO. ©1967 Floyd M. Orr.

This book has been designed not to present The Big Four in the tired old alphabetical order or in strict chronological order, either. We all know that Honda *owned* the market. There is no need to let the first half of the book be about Honda before you reach the material about many lesser-known machines. One of the most difficult decisions I had to make was whether or not to place Yamaha before Kawasaki in the book. Yamaha is the #2 brand, but Kawasaki was distinctly the latecomer to the party. Suzuki got pushed into the earlier chapter regardless.

What exactly is Suzuki's image, their marketing plan, their perceptive history? These questions are all tricky to answer, whereas the remaining Big Three represent memorable concepts. Honda is the big shot, four-stroke brand that builds machines that are as reliable as washing machines and dominate the market. Yamaha is the innovative racing brand, and when you are familiar with the company's history, you know this statement says a lot more than is obvious from the simplicity of it. Kawasaki develops high-performance street machines for American-sized Americans. Suzuki offers a lot of flash and content for the money. They are the me-too, we-try-harder brand. They innovate a little less than the other two. They fill market niches. In later years, outside the realm of this book, the company produced the innovative and successful GSX-R and Intruder Series. Earlier experiences with technical innovations such as the RE-5 Rotary have not encouraged the company to lead in that direction. One UK source stated that only 400 of the rotary motorcycles were sold there. I have no idea how many left U.S. dealerships, but it certainly wasn't many. Other brands have produced marketing campaigns we all remember. *Solo Suzuki. Express Yourself.* What exactly do these mean?

Figure F2 - Red 1968 Suzuki TC-250 Scrambler. This derivative of the legendary X-6 Hustler features upswept exhaust pipes on each side and crossbrace handlebars. Unlike the four-stroke Hondas that popularized this style, there were few, if any, additional changes from the basic street X-6. ©1968 Suzuki Motor of America, Inc.

Suzuki Model Charts, 1962-75

Suzuki built a number of motorcycle models from 1954 through 1961 that were not exported to the USA. The company manufactured a moped and a four-horsepower 90cc motorcycle with a hardtail frame in 1954. The lineup quickly expanded to include the 16-hp, 250cc twin called the Colleda that would be a mainstay for years to come. There were also 100cc and 125cc singles. The 1960 lineup brought an electric-start 50cc step-through and a 10-hp, 150cc Sport model with upswept exhaust. The 1961 Colleda 250 had reached twenty horsepower, but its flat bars, whitewall tires and white leg shields gave it that Asian-market-only look. Many of the same machines with funky styling were continued in Japanese and other markets in '62. The 1962 chart below represents the U.S. models from the latter part of the model year.

The first Suzukis arrived in California in 1962. The early models were imported by Ken Kay in North Hollywood CA. The official U. S. distributor, called U. S. Suzuki Motor Corporation, was founded in Santa Ana CA in 1963. The 1963-65 models were all mix-it-yourself two-strokes with pressed-steel frames. The Sport models were distinguished by lower handlebars, upswept exhausts, and trimmer gas tanks and fenders. Some of the road models had white sidewall tires. Every Suzuki in the charts below, with the sole exception of the RE-5 Rotary, is a two-stroke, as the company held out until 1977 for the release of its first OHC model.

James Rozee Speaks: "Suzuki made some really nice bikes. I have owned a lot and have a real soft spot for them. I grew up riding them in the dirt. I thought they lost their unique edge when they changed their headlight to a round one in the late '70's. Do you know how the Suzuki flat-bottom headlight came to be? The early Suzuki 250 had a rectangular running light under the headlight, so a flat bottom was needed. Then they dropped the running light and kept the flat bottom lights as a trademark look. The very early Kawasaki B-8 of 1962 had a flat top to its headlight! I really like Suzukis.

The early Suzuki ads were so Japanese, then McCormick took over their ads. He did the *You Meet the Nicest People* ads for Honda before they fired him. He started the *Solo Suzuki* ads and Suzuki took off. He later did his own thing and re-badged other bikes as American Eagles. You may have heard of them? The U. S. Department of Transportation required larger taillights on all motorcycles beginning in 1964. You can divide early and later models from most brands by examining their taillights.

I rode Suzukis for many years growing up, starting with a 1971 TS 125, then I went to a 1972 TS 185, but as a crazy 18-year-old I decided I wanted more power and went straight to a brand new 1973 TM 400. Yes, I loved it even though it did throw me on the ground every once in a while. It would do a wheelie in any gear! It climbed any mountain I pointed it at, with or without me on its back! Since then I have owned a TC-125, two 120 Cats, a Hillbilly 80, and even a few 90's and a 1964 50 that was given away by a local radio station. I still show that one. I never owned a TS 250 Savage. but I rode with many guys who did, and I have ridden many. They were as good as any Yamaha 250. and if you wanted to go fast you bought a TM-250! I rode my Suzukis hard in tight woods and never had a problem with any of them that wasn't self-inflicted.

For 40 years I have collected all kinds of weird bikes and models. but love the 50cc stuff the best. Always try to find complete bikes, if you can. Even free bikes need to be complete, if possible. Suzukis are just as hard to find parts for as Yamaguchis and many other odd Japanese bikes. Trust me, I am still looking for parts for many of my projects. Also anything that is not stock or complete can be made into a *Vintage Period Racer* and sometimes that is much easier to do because aftermarket parts can be discovered at many swap meets. E-Bay has both helped and hindered the hobby, but good old car and motorcycle swap meets are still what works best for me. You would be amazed at all the bike stuff I have found at *auto* swap meets. When you collect weird stuff you need to put yourself out there more, and look everywhere. Having a booth at a swap meet is great: you can sell some extra parts and find and meet others in the hobby. Joining a club or registry is another good idea. Good luck, and happy hunting. That's the fun part, anyway!"

Reason enough to make The Suzuki Hill-Billy the best buy in trail machines? Definitely. But if you're still skeptical, here are 10 more great features you won't find on any trail bike sold in America — unless it's Suzuki.

(1) Dual drive sprockets – never a change necessary. (2) Extra large saddle with non-slip cover. (3) 275 x 17 knobby tires — front and rear. (4) High clearance, heavy-duty, chrome front fender. (5) Heavy-duty engine guard. (6) Folding foot rests. (7) Chain guard with chain guide. (8) Easy-action toe shift lever. (9) Detachable rear fender section. (10) Ball end control levers for extra ease of handling.

Congratulations! if you held out for the superior Suzuki Hill-Billy.

U. S. SUZUKI MOTOR CORPORATION,
200 WEST CENTRAL AVENUE, SANTA ANA, CALIF.

	other well-known nationally advertised trail bikes	Suzuki Hill-Billy
horsepower	3-6½ hp	8 hp with high torque, lower rpm.
gear ratio	40-72 to 1	40-1. Suzuki's high torque, full hp engine gives low speed power and 38 mph cruising speed without changing to touring sprocket.
gas consumption	up to 200 mpg	up to 150 mpg
speed	12½ to 25 mph (45 w/touring sprocket)	38 mph (55 w/touring sprocket)
climbing ability	45° or more	50° or more
load capacity	250 lbs. plus rider	350 lbs. plus rider
weight	up to 400 lbs.	150 lbs.
transmission	2 to 3 speed w/centrifugal or automatic multi-plate clutch	4-speed synchromesh with heavy duty wet multi-plate clutch
engine	flat head, overhead valve or 2-stroke	Suzuki championship high torque 2-stroke
brakes	front and rear, or rear only	full width cam type heavy-duty 4½" water proof brakes, front and rear
suspension	rigid to hydraulic, front and rear	telescopic hydraulically dampened front forks. Swing arm rear suspension with hydraulically dampened shocks and progressively wound heavy duty springs.
lights	from none to head and tail light	fully approved headlights with both high and low beams. Tail and brake light combination. (Legal for highway use in all 50 states.)

Figure F3 - 1964 Suzuki Hill-Billy 80 Ad. ©1964 Suzuki Motor of America, Inc.

Suzuki 1962 Chart

Model	Name	Type	HP	Seat	Exhaust	Wt.	Price
M15D	Classic	49cc Single	4.2	Dual	Down	133	$295
K10	Trojan	79cc Single	6.5	Dual	Down	155	NA
S30	Standard	124cc Twin	11	Dual	Down	265	NA
S31	SS	124cc Twin	12	Dual	Upswept	265	NA
S250	Colleda	248cc Twin	20	Solo	Down	308	NA
T10	Street	248cc Twin	21	Dual	Down	309	NA
TB250	Street	248cc Twin	18	Dual	Down	NA	NA
TC250	El Camino	248cc Twin	20	Dual	Down	315	$589

Suzuki 1962 Notes: The Trojan and Colleda models have only kickstarters. The El Camino had electric start. The El Camino may be just a fancy name for the T10 in the U.S. market. The TB250 was very similar to the El Camino. There seemed to be only a few differences. The TB had low bars, body-colored rear shock covers, whitewall tires, and a white headlamp housing. The upper half of the gas tank was also painted white. The TB had twin carbs, as did the El Camino. It is difficult to say in hindsight if all three of these 250 twins were sold simultaneously or not. The Colleda was obviously the Japanese touring model that would soon be discontinued from the U.S. lineup. All claimed dry weights are listed in pounds.

Suzuki 1963 Chart

Model	Name	Type	HP	Seat	Exhaust	Wt.	Price
M30	Step-Thru	49cc Single	4	Dual	Down	123	NA
M15	Standard	49cc Single	4.2	Dual	Down	128	$265
M15D	Classic	49cc Single	4.2	Dual	Down	133	$295
K10	Trojan	79cc Single	6.5	Dual	Down	155	$350
K11	Sport 80	79cc Single	7.3	3/4	Upswept	155	NA
S30	Standard	124cc Twin	11	Dual	Down	265	NA
S31	SS	124cc Twin	12	Dual	Upswept	265	NA
T10	Street	248cc Twin	21	Dual	Down	309	NA
TC250	El Camino	248cc Twin	20	Dual	Down	315	$589

Suzuki 1963 Notes: The Trojan had only a kickstarter. All other '63 models have electric and kick starters. All claimed dry weights are listed in pounds. The 1963 Trojan was offered with a choice of a three-quarter-length or dual seat and low, medium, or high bars.

These options may have been offered in other model years, too. It is possible that the El Camino is the same bike as the T10. Ads for the El Camino in 1962 state 20 hp and the machine pictured has black upper shock covers and blackwall tires. The T10 in the 1963 brochure states 21 hp, the shock covers are chrome and the bike is shown with whitewall tires.

Figure F4 - Black 1964 Suzuki T10. Note the bright side panels, silver rear shocks, bulbous tank, and painted fenders. The reverse-cone megaphone-shaped exhaust pipes on this example may not be original.
©Michael Kiernan, Classic Motorcycle Company, St. Louis, MO.

SUZUKI Classic "50"

Tops in its class. Fully equipped with Electric Starter. 180 m.p.g., 4-speed gear box, 50 m.p.h. Low price is **$295⁰⁰**

F.O.B. Los Angeles

SUZUKI El Camino "250"

Looking for Silky-Smooth twin cylinder performance? . . . Then the El Camino is the model for you! A great value at **$589⁰⁰**

F.O.B. Los Angeles

at Your Authorized Suzuki Dealer Coast to Coast
These Models Now Available

Sherman Way, North Hollywood, Calif. Phone POplar 4-7000

Figure F5 (previous page) - Compare the previous T10 to the one pictured in this excerpt from an ad published in *Cycle World* in November 1963. The El Camino has a chrome front fender and chrome luggage rack with the same tank and side covers. The rear shocks are clearly chrome plated on the El Camino. The earlier shocks may have been chromed or painted silver. Current materials available are unclear on this point. This model would not get oil injection until 1965 when it was renamed Model T20. ©1963 Suzuki Motor of America, Inc.

Figure F6 - Here is a left-side view of the same early T-10. You can see in this shot that the left exhaust pipe lacks the indentation for the side stand that is clearly visible in the ad of the later model. My best guess, but this is unconfirmed, is that this is more evidence of an aftermarket exhaust on this particular machine. ©Michael Kiernan, Classic Motorcycle Company, St. Louis, MO.

Suzuki 1964 Chart

Model	Name	Type	HP	Seat	Exhaust	Wt.	Price
M30	Step-Thr.	49cc Single	4	Dual	Down	123	$245
M15	Standard	49cc Single	4.2	Dual	Down	138	$267
M15D	Electric	49cc Single	4.2	Dual	Down	133	$297
M12	Cavalier	49cc Single	5	Dual	Upswept	132	$292
K10	Sport	79cc Single	6.5	Dual	Down	155	$334
K11	SS	79cc Single	8	3/4	Upswept	155	$353
K15	Trail	79cc Single	6.5	3/4	Upswept	154	$350
K10T/S	Trail	79cc Single	NA	Solo	Upswept	NA	NA
S31	SS	125cc Twin	15.6	Dual	Upswept	265	NA
S32	Touring	149cc Twin	16	Dual	Down	NA	NA
S33	SS	149cc Twin	17	Dual	Upswept	NA	NA
T10	Touring	246cc Twin	24	Dual	Down	309	$603

Suzuki 1964 Notes: All single-cylinder models are kickstart only, except the M15D has both kick and electric start. All twin-cylinder models had electric starters. All claimed dry weights are listed in pounds. The M30 Step-Through had white leg shields with a red, black, or white body. The K10T/S came in red, black, or yellow. All other models were red, black, white, or blue, just like Hondas of the period. The M30 had leading link front suspension and a three-speed foot shift with automatic clutch. All other models were manual four-speeds with telescopic front suspension. Most or all of the four-speeds were rotary shifts.

Figure F7 - 1964 M31 50. This beautiful white Suzuki step-through is owned by Dick Feightner.

©Dick Feightner

U.S. SUZUKI MOTOR CORPORATION

200 West Central Avenue, Santa Ana, California

SUZUKI—The line of lightweight champions

1964 RETAIL PRICE LIST

RETAIL PRICE
P.O.E. Jacksonville, Florida

M30 — Standard: 5 HP single cylinder w/automatic clutch and 3 speed transmission. K/S only. Colors: red & white, black & white, white.

Available approximately April. Price to be announced.

M15 — Sports Standard: 5 HP single cylinder 50cc w/manual clutch. 4 speed transmission. K/S only. Colors: red, black, white, blue.

$267.00

M15D — Sports Electric: 5 HP single cylinder 50cc. Manual clutch, 4 speed transmission, electric starter. Colors: red, black, white, blue.

297.00

M12 — Super Sport: 5 HP single cylinder 50cc w/ manual clutch, 4 speed transmission. Sport exhaust, folding pegs, K/S only. Colors: red, black, white, blue.

292.00

K10 — Sport Standard: 7 HP single cylinder w/ manual clutch, 4 speed transmission. K/S only. Colors: red, black, white, blue.

334.00

K11 — Super Sport: 8 HP single cylinder w/manual clutch, 4 speed transmission. Sport exhaust. Folding pegs. K/S only. Colors: red, black, white, blue.

353.00

K10T/S — Trail & Scrambles: High torque single cylinder w/road & trail gearing, special suspension, 4 speed transmission, folding pegs, skidplate and many other extras. Colors: red, black, yellow.

Available late March. Price to be announced.

Equipment

American style handle bars are standard equipment on all models (except where specified) includes: dual seat (except K10T/S), passenger foot rests, folding kick starter and/or electric starter, security lock, passenger hand hold strap (except K10T/S), sidestand, center stand (except K10T/S), telescopic forks (except M15 & M15D) and automatic spark control.

All prices and specifications subject to change without notice.

U.S. SUZUKI 〜 MOTOR CORPORATION

200 West Central Avenue, Santa Ana, California

SUZUKI Twin Cylinder Models

1964 RETAIL PRICE LIST

RETAIL PRICE
P.O.E. Jacksonville, Florida

S31 — Super Sport: 125cc, 15.6 HP. Sport exhaust dual carburetors, 4 speed transmission, electric starter. Colors: To be announced.

Available April.
Price to be announced.

S32 — Touring: 150cc, 16 HP. Telescopic forks. Electric starter. 4 speed transmission. Colors: To be announced.

Available April.
Price to be announced.

S33 — Super Sport: 150cc, 17 HP. Sport exhaust, dual carburetors, 4 speed transmission, electric starter Colors: To be announced.

Available April.
Price to be announced.

T10 — Touring: 250cc, 24 HP. Telescopic forks, hydraulic rear brake, dual carburetors, electric starter. Colors: red, blue, black, white.

$603.00

Equipment

American style handle bars are standard equipment on all models. Other standard equipment on all models (except where specified) includes: dual seat, passenger foot rests, folding kick starter and/or electric starter, security lock, passenger hand hold strap, sidestand, center stand, telescopic forks and automatic spark control.

All prices and specifications subject to change without notice.

Figures F8 (previous page) and F9 - Suzuki was only just beginning to develop an extensive lineup of U.S. models by the end of 1963. You can see from Figures F8 and F9 that the 1964 lineup was not yet finalized, with some models due in the spring and prices not yet announced. ©Suzuki Motor of America, Inc.

Figure F10 - The Cavalier ad shown in Figure F10 is somewhat different from what was listed in the lineup. The M12 Super Sport had flat bars, turn signals and a front downtube support to the engine case.
©Suzuki Motor of America, Inc.

Suzuki 1965 Chart

Model	Name	Type	HP	Seat	Exhaust	Wt.	Price
M31	Suzi	55cc Single	5	Dual	Down	122	$245
M15	Collegian	49cc Single	5	Dual	Down	128	$260
M12	Cavalier	49cc Single	5	3/4	Upswept	146	$285
K10	Sport	79cc Single	6.5	Dual	Down	155	NA
K10D	Deluxe	79cc Single	6.5	Dual	Down	155	NA
K11	Challenger	79cc Single	7.3	Dual	Upswept	154	$345
K15P	Hillbilly	79cc Single	7.3	3/4	Upswept	176	$350
B100	Sport	118cc Single	9	Dual	Down	NA	NA
S10	Standard	124cc Single	10.5	Solo	Down	257	NA
S32	Standard	149cc Twin	16	Dual	Down	253	NA
T20	Crusader	250cc Twin	29	Dual	Down	316	$589

Suzuki 1965 Notes: The K10 Sport and Hillbilly have kickstarters. The Hillbilly, written

as Hill-Billy in some advertising of the day, had a piston-port engine and a black suede seat cover. The K10D with electric starter, whitewall tires, and a few additional chrome bits may or may not have been imported into the U.S. Many of these listings and prices came from a January 1965 *Cycle World* ad. All claimed dry weights are listed in pounds. The S10 single had twin exhausts. The X-6 was introduced in the latter part of 1965 as a '66 model replacing the Crusader.

Figures F11, F12, & F13 (this page and next two pages) - Red 1966 Suzuki X-6 Scrambler.

©Michael Kiernan, Classic Motorcycle Company, St. Louis, MO.

Suzuki 1966 Chart

Model	Name	Type	HP	Seat	Exhaust	Wt.	Starter
M15	Collegian	49cc Single	5	Dual	Down	128	Kick
M12	Cavalier	49cc Single	5	3/4	Upswept	146	Kick
K11	Challenger	79cc Single	7.3	Dual	Upswept	154	Kick
K15P	Hillbilly	79cc Single	7.3	3/4	Upswept	176	Kick
A100	Sport	98cc Single	9.5	Dual	Down	NA	Kick
B120	Sport	118cc Single	9	Dual	Down	NA	Kick
S32	Standard	149cc Twin	16	Dual	Down	252	Electric
T20	X-6 Hustler	247cc Twin	29	Dual	Down	316	Kick

Suzuki 1966 Notes: All claimed dry weights are listed in pounds. Most (or all) of the '66 models received oil injection. The X-6 was the first Suzuki model with either a six-speed transmission or a tube frame. No prices are available for 1966 models, but the price of the Hustler was about $650.

Suzuki X-6 Hustler

When I set up a poll question on my Tiddlerosis website several years ago asking what your favorite classic 250 is, the Suzi X-6 came in second. My old favorite, the CL-72, came in first by one vote. I was quite surprised that the Harley-Davidson Sprint received no votes, but I featured it anyway, since it was a distinctive model in its day, although some might say that it was distinctive in an unfortunately negative manner. It was certainly no CL-72, or Diana, or Metralla!

The model was officially sold in the U. S. as the X-6 Hustler from late 1965 through 1968. The Hustler name came from the U. S. publicity department. The model was called Super Six in European markets. The Hustler name continued in the U. S. on later Suzuki 250 twins at least through 1970, and maybe even later. The model was called a GT 250 in '73, but I am not sure about 1971-2. Note that it has been listed as Hustler in the charts for those years.

Suzuki marketed a 250cc two-stroke twin in the U. S. from virtually the beginning of the brand's entrance into America. The 1963-65 models were relatively klunky with pressed-steel frames, full-coverage fenders, enclosed shocks, four-speed transmissions, premix fuel systems, 21 hp, 17-inch wheels, and the trademark flat-bottomed headlamp housing. The sporty, five-speed YDS-2's and '3's were giving them a hard time.

Suzuki made their first indelible mark on the American psyche with the introduction of the world's first six-speed motorcycle. The X-6 featured a double-downtube frame, 29 horsepower, chrome fenders, uncovered springs, oil injection, and a 14-second quarter-mile. The chrome fenders were changed to silver with a single stripe down the center that matched the gas tank color in 1967.

Figure F14 - 1966 Red Suzuki X-6 at the Salon de la Moto, Paris, 2011. This styling displays the look of the original X-6 released in late 1965 with downswept exhaust, chrome tank panels, silver painted fenders, and exposed chrome front fork springs. Image by The Supermat, photographer, under Creative Commons license.

There are a number of styling details of which I am not sure at this time, mostly because I have never been that much of a Suzi fan, so I don't have as many Sixties brochures as I do of some of the other Japanese brands. I am sure that the 1965-67 models had chrome fenders, as did the later '69-'70 versions, but I am unsure of the 1968. My best guess is that it had the silver fenders. Even the 1964 T-10 sports model had a slim, chrome front fender, but I don't have any photos to verify if there was a smooth styling transition between this model and the '66 X-6. The later Hustlers of 1969 and '70 produced 32 horsepower, yet the brochure quotes only a 15.3 1/4-mile. I think all the Hustlers had 18-inch wheels, but the T-10 had 17's. The changes to create the scrambler models were held to a minimum with crossbrace bars and upswept pipes, one on each side.

The X-6 brought real pizzazz to the Suzuki name. The machines were flashy, stylish, and fast, and the battle with Yamaha for 250 two-stroke domination had only just begun. Generally speaking, Yamaha usually won on the racetrack, if not the showroom. With 20/20 hindsight, my best guess is that the earliest Yamahas were more common than the early Suzis, then the X-6 brought some serious sales to Suzuki for a few years, only to be eclipsed again by the legendary RD-350. At the peak of production, Suzuki was making 5000 of this model a month. Approximately 35,000 were sold worldwide in the first three years.

I also bet that the early X-6's are more desirable to collectors than the '69-'70 models. The Morro Green and Mesa Orange shades of the later models offset whatever styling gains they had made with separate instruments and chrome fenders. Most of the tiddlers have always looked best in bright, primary colors, even with single instrument nacelles, chrome-sided gas tanks, and silver fenders. Some of the juiciest nostalgia seems to have rubbed off of many or our favorite tiddlers as they entered the styling trends of the Seventies. I think this is particularly true of the Suzuki X-6 Hustler. Its time was fading fast.

Suzuki 1967 Chart

Model	Name	Type	HP	Seat	Exhaust	Wt.	Starter
M31	Suzi	55c Single	5	Dual	Down	123	NA
K10P	Corsair	79cc Single	7.5	Dual	Down	167	NA
K11P	Challenger	79cc Single	7.5	Dual	Upswept	154	Kick
K15P	Hillbilly	79cc Single	7.5	Solo	Upswept	176	Kick
A90	Sport	86cc Single	8.4	Dual	Down	176	NA
A100	Charger	98cc Single	9.3	Dual	Down	176	Kick
AS100	Sierra	98cc Single	9.3	Dual	Upswept	176	Kick
B100P	Magnum	118cc Single	10	Dual	Down	198	Kick
B105P	Bearcat	118cc Single	11	3/4	Upswept	194	Kick
B120	Standard	118cc Single	9	Dual	Down	NA	Kick
TC120	Cat	118cc Single	8	Dual	Upswept	222	Kick
T125	Standard	124cc Twin	NA	Dual	Down	280	NA
X-5	Invader	196cc Twin	23	Dual	Down	290	Kick
TC200	Stingray	196cc Twin	23	Dual	Upswept	276	Kick
T20	X-6 Hustler	247cc Twin	29	Dual	Down	316	Kick
T21	Super	247cc Twin	33	Dual	Down	319	Kick
TC250	X-6 Hustler	247cc Twin	29	Dual	Upswept	297	Kick

Suzuki 1967 Notes: Posi-Force Lubrication, Suzuki's version of oil injection, was officially introduced in 1967 for all models. The gimmick was that the bearings were injected with oil, in addition to that going into the cylinders. According to advertising of the day, the 1967 Charger and Sierra were the first street Suzukis with rotary valves, although the A100 Sport had actually been introduced in 1966; only the name and the street scrambler model were new. The T125 and 200cc models had five-speed transmissions. A test of the five-speed, rotary-valve TC200 Stingray produced a quarter-mile time of 16.0. All claimed dry weights are listed in pounds. Few prices are available for the '67 models at this time. According to contemporary road tests, the K15 Hillbilly was $365, the B105P Bearcat was $430, and the X-5 Invader was $575.

Figure F15 - Black 1967 Suzuki B-105P Bearcat 120. ©Don Quayle

Suzuki 1968 Chart

Model	Name	Type	HP	Seat	Exhaust	Wt.	Price
AS-50	Colt	49cc Single	4.9	Racing	Upswept	165	NA
AC-90	Scrambler	86cc Single	8.4	Dual	Upswept	NA	NA
A-100	Charger	98cc Single	9.5	Dual	Down	176	$345
AS-100	Sierra	98cc Single	9.5	Dual	Upswept	176	$380
T200	X-5 Invader	196cc Twin	23	Dual	Down	269	$575
TC200	Stingray	196cc Twin	23	Dual	Upswept	276	$599
T-20	X-6 Hustler	247cc Twin	29	Dual	Down	301	$649
TC-250	Scrambler	247cc Twin	29	Dual	Upswept	308	$680
TM-250	Motocross	249cc Single	32	3/4	Upswept	220	$975
T-305	Raider	305cc Twin	37	Dual	Down	317	$701
TC-305	Laredo	305cc Twin	37	Dual	Upswept	310	$722
T-500	Five	492cc Twin	46	Dual	Down	383	$1039

Suzuki 1968 Notes: All 1968 models were kickstart only. All claimed dry weights are listed in pounds. All models had Suzuki's Posi-Force Lubrication. Suzuki entered two new markets in 1968. Factory motocross models built by the Japanese companies for public consumption were just entering the market and Suzuki got in on the ground floor, although the company's TM 250 was not the most competitive against its familiar rivals. It had taken nearly three years for Suzuki to respond to Honda's CB-450 of late 1965, but the company's T-500 would be a long-lasting success.

1968-70 Suzuki AS-50 Colt & Maverick

Figure F16 - Late 1968 or early 1969 Candy Red Suzuki Maverick 50. ©Suzuki Motor of America, Inc.

I'm just a sucker for exquisitely designed and styled little tiddlers. In the 50cc class, there are three standout models that I rate somewhat above the rest. Now don't get me wrong: the Honda Sport Cub and several of the little Yamahas are some of my favorites among the more garden variety tiddlers, but I'm talking *special* machines here. You could include the 1990 two-stroke Honda NS-50 in this group, too, but I won't simply because the turquoise and pink on white colors with too much black engine and exhaust just didn't make it in my styling department. I never did like punk rock very much, either, for many of the same reasons: long, natural hair on Leon Russell and Mark Farner, fine, but pink and green spiked hair, no thank you. You can spot my age bracket now, but you already knew that if you have read very much of this book. Although technically speaking the NS-50 belongs in this elite group, but I'm sending him back home to change his clothes first if he wants to join my elitist club!

The point of this story is that among the *common* tiddlers, the later Honda Sport 50 with the higher bars is the most successfully styled 50cc tiddler, with several others following closely in its 2.25 x 17 tire tracks. The NS-50 is a very sporty Honda tiddler, but the company had nearly thirty years to design it. The most exotic, and expensive, of all the 50cc Hondas is the Dream 50. The most exotic, and expensive, currently produced 50cc tiddler is the Aprilia RS 50.

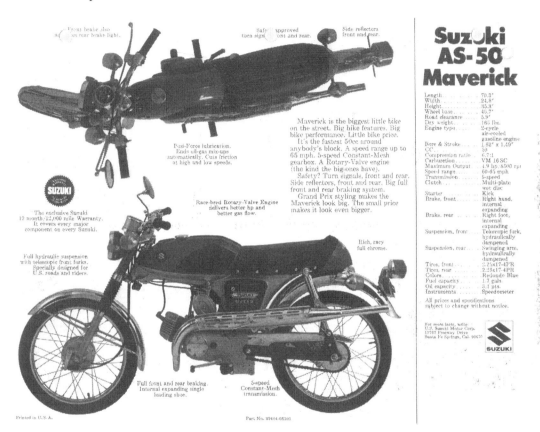

Figure F17 - Redondo Blue 1969 Suzuki Maverick 50. Compare this to the earlier Maverick brochure photos. Apparently the earliest Mavericks were not painted in candy colors, but the later ones were. This change was made in either 1968 or early 1969. The candy red paint on the earlier model was applied to some of the metallic silver parts of the later version. My best guess is that there were three versions of this racy little 50cc machine built. The early 1968 models were called Colts and had red, non-candy paint. The later 1968 version was renamed Maverick and painted candy red. The painted components were reversed in 1969 in Candy Redondo Blue. The racy styling was replaced with street scrambler styling in 1970, as shown in the next photo. ©1969 Suzuki Motor of America, Inc.

The Suzuki AS-50 was an under appreciated tiddler produced in 1968-70. The little Suzi's claim to fame was that it was such a highly sporting machine for its day, with all the correct styling cues and lots of flashy chrome. Unlike the Aprilia, it had neither a full-race fairing nor high-tech suspension, and the price was quite ordinary for the day. You spell that *ridiculously cheap* compared to now, for either an RS 50 or an AS-50! Although not as exotic or special as the Dream 50 produced decades later, the AS-50 was sort of a properly dressed NS-50 that was twenty years ahead of its time. Yes, you could say that certain Bridgestones, Yamahas, and even the Yamaguchi SPB offered much the same package, but the styling and technical details of the AS-50 conspired to create racy tiddler perfection for the street.

Figure F18 - Lime Green 1970 Suzuki AC-50 Maverick. Suzuki kept the Maverick name, but changed the model from AS-50 to AC-50 when the model evolved from a racy 50 into a small street scrambler.
©Dick Feightner

The name carried on into 1971, but the racy look was exchanged for a pseudo-trail one. The 1968 model was referred to as the AS-50 Colt. The frame, swing arm, and side covers on this model were red, the rear exhaust support was chrome, and there were no turn signals. The Colt name was not mentioned in the '69 brochure, the exhaust support was red, and the model now had turn signals. The name was changed to Maverick in 1970 and the color was blue, but the color pattern was changed. The '68-69 AS-50 had a silver tank and seat tail with a body-colored frame. The 1970 Maverick had a body-colored (blue) tank on a silver frame. The other blue parts were the seat tail, side covers, headlight shell, and upper fork covers. The swing arm was black and the exhaust support was changed back to chrome. It's a toss-up which year is the most perfect. I like the silver tank and body-colored frame of the earlier models, but since I am a sucker for blue, anyway, I give them all an A+ in styling.

The AS-50 offered technical proficiency to back up its sporty looks. The engine was a rotary valve two-stroke producing 4.9 horsepower through a five-speed transmission. The brochure claimed a top speed of 65 with a tiny Japanese teenager driving off a cliff, but 55 was more like the truth for normal people and terrain. Since the most I could ever coax out of my '63 Yamaha Rotary Jet 80 was 53 mph, 55 was quite respectable for a 50cc machine. There was no tach, but at least the speedo was a separate unit outside the headlight nacelle. The skinny chrome fenders, chain guard, and expansion-chamber type exhaust added to the tiny machine's racy flavor. Of course all the Japanese two-strokes had oil injection by 1968, and the AS-50 was no exception. The long, skinny gas tank had a stylishly angular shape, but the racing-type seat was a bit controversial, although its visual appeal was outstanding. The AS-50 was a solo affair with no rear pegs present at the party!

James Rozee Speaks: "I love Suzuki 50's. I own one of the first ones shipped here, a 1964. but there were a few before mine but not many as 1964 was when Suzuki really took off in the States. The AS-50 was a cool looking bike and it only lasted through 1970, taken over by the cute TS-50 Gaucho. Unlike my Suzuki, these models were all rotary valve 50's from the AS on. A much different bike than early efforts, the Gaucho gained a different squared off cylinder head and a low exhaust pipe, just like the big bikes. It was the first Suzuki 50 to not have gas tank knee rubbers. The Suzuki "S" tank badge was replaced with an alloy plate with *Suzuki* lettering on it in black."

Figure F19 - Aspen Yellow 1975 Suzuki TM-100 Contender. Suzuki pursued motocross wins from the very beginning. By 1975 the company was producing many competitive machines, including this little screaming yellow zonker. © 1975 Suzuki Motor of America, Inc.

It changes your attitude about altitude.

For fact-filled reading on the Sting Ray Scrambler (shown) and other models, write: U. S. Suzuki Motor Corp., P. O. Box 2967, Dept. 159 , Santa Fe Springs, California 90670

Aim high! The new Suzuki Sting Ray Scrambler gets to the top without gasping for air. It's the first bike ever with compensating carburetion that adjusts for altitude change automatically.

For power, the 200cc rotary-valve Dual-Stroke engine teamed (for the first time in its class) with a 5-speed transmission puts 23 horses under you, the ¼-mile behind you in 16 seconds. And the Posi-Force lube system ends oil-gas mix-ups for good.

For hill-hugging, the deep-tread tires are where the traction is.

For smooth-sailing, the deep-flexing hydraulic suspension reigns over any terrain.

For sure-footedness, the water-tight, cam-type brakes make stops sudden, not sodden.

For long-life, ask your nearby Suzuki dealer about the exclusive 12 month/12,000 mile Warranty. It leaves the leading competition at sea-level.

While you're there, solo Suzuki. The ones that go where others dread to veer.

solo SUZUKI

STING RAY SCRAMBLER

Figure F20 - 1967 Suzuki Stingray ad. ©1967 Suzuki Motor of America, Inc.

Suzuki 1969 Chart

Model	Name	Type	HP	Seat	Exhaust	Wt.	Price
AS50	Maverick	49cc Single	4.9	Racing	Upswept	165	$244
AC100	Wolf	98cc Single	10	Dual	Upswept	184	$374
TC120	Cat	118cc Single	12	Dual	Upswept	205	$460
T125	Stinger	124cc Twin	15	Dual	Upswept	206	$471
T-200	Invader	196cc Twin	23	Dual	Down	270	$565
TS250	Savage	246cc Single	23	Dual	Upswept	271	$782
T250	Hustler	247cc Twin	32	Dual	Down	310	$692
TC250	Scrambler	247cc Twin	32	Dual	Upswept	311	$672
T-305	Raider	305cc Twin	37	Dual	Down	315	$710
TC-305	Laredo	305cc Twin	37	Dual	Upswept	320	$722
TC350	Rebel	315cc Twin	39	Dual	Down	321	$749
T500 II	Titan	492cc Twin	47	Dual	Down	407	$980

Suzuki 1969 Notes: All 1969 models were kickstart only. All claimed dry weights are listed in pounds. The Cat had a dual-three-speed transmission. According to the road test in the September 1969 issue of *Cycle*, the Stinger weighed in at 227 pounds with a top speed of 70 mph.

Suzuki 1970 Chart

Model	Name	Type	HP	Seat	Exhaust	Wt.	Price
F-50	Cutlass	49cc Single	4.5	Dual	Down	150	$224
AC-50	Maverick	49cc Single	4.9	Dual	Upswept	165	$264
TC-90	Blazer	89cc Single	11	Dual	Upswept	200	$374
TS-90	Honcho	89cc Single	11	Dual	Upswept	200	$379
TC-120	Cat	118cc Single	12	Dual	Upswept	205	$464
TC-125	Stinger	124cc Twin	15.1	Dual	Upswept	209	$474
T-250	Hustler	247cc Twin	33	Dual	Upswept	316	$699
TS-250	Savage	246cc Single	23	Dual	Upswept	271	$789
T-350	Rebel	315cc Twin	40	Dual	Down	321	$759
T-500	Titan	492cc Twin	47	Dual	Down	407	$899

Suzuki 1970 Notes: All 1970 models were kickstart only. All claimed dry weights are listed in pounds. The Cat had a dual-three-speed transmission.

Suzuki 125 Stinger

Front brake also activates rear brake light.

Tri-Form frame.

Grand Prix-styled seat. Flip-top for easy maintenance.

Power-pipe exhausts with new competition design.

Speedo/tach panel cushioned for exact readings. Only bike in its class with it.

Slimline, lightweight competition headlamp.

Safety approved turn signals and side reflectors front and rear.

125cc's of fast moving excitement. That's the new spunky city-street bike from Suzuki.

15.1 hp at an easy 8500 rpm. A slick 11.3 in the SS¼. And a quick 75 mph top speed range.

More, too: 5-speed Constant-Mesh transmission. A Grand Prix flip-top seat for easy maintenance. A Tri-Form frame design for smoother ride. Power-pipe exhausts. A speedo/tach module to check out Stinger's performance. At a glance.

The only thing small about the Stinger is the price.

For expressing yourself in urban affairs, Stinger can't be beat.

Wide-bridge handle bars for added strength.

SUZUKI

The exclusive Suzuki 12 month/12,000 mile Warranty. It covers every major component on every Suzuki.

Posi-Force lubrication. Ends oil-gas mix-ups automatically. Cuts friction at high and low speeds.

Twin down-draft carbs.

Full hydraulic suspension.

Competition styling. Suzuki's unique, new design concept.

Full front and rear braking. Internal expanding single leading shoe.

Printed in U.S.A.

Part No. 99404-20106

Suzuki T-125 Stinger

Length	72.2"
Width	31.3"
Height	39.3"
Wheel base	45.9"
Road clearance	6.7"
Dry weight	206 lbs.
Engine type	2-stroke air-cooled parallel-twin cylinder
Bore & Stroke	1.69" x 1.69"
CC	124.8
Compression ratio	7.3:1
Carburetion	Two-MD18
Acceleration	11.3 SS¼ mi.
Maximum Output	15.1 hp/8,500 rp
Speed range	70-75 mph
Transmission	5-speed
Clutch	Multi-plate wet disc
Starter	Kick
Brake, front	Right hand, internal expanding
Brake, rear	Right foot, internal expanding
Suspension, front	Telescopic, oil dampened
Suspension, rear	Swinging arm, oil dampened
Tires, front	2.50x18-4PR
Tires, rear	2.75x18-4PR
Colors	Roman Red
Fuel capacity	1.9 gals.
Oil capacity	3.0 pts.
Instruments	Speedometer Tachometer

All prices and specifications subject to change without notice.

For more facts, write: U.S. Suzuki Motor Corp. 13767 Freeway Drive Santa Fe Springs, Cal. 90670

SUZUKI

Figure F21 - Roman Red 1969 Suzuki Stinger. ©1969 Suzuki Motor of America, Inc.

The Suzuki Stinger was one of the company's flashier, and more unusual, models. I picked this model to feature here more or less at random. I know very little about the Stinger, and I am not even sure that I have ever seen one on the street. The one at the dealership where I picked up a brochure in 1970 may be the only one I have actually seen, but I simply cannot remember for sure. I can tell you that I obtained this particular brochure from a dealership, one of the first Suzuki dealerships to which I had access at the time. All of my earlier Suzi brochures were ordered by mail directly from the U. S. distributor. The Stinger was a very impressive machine, compared to its competition, and I have always been surprised at how rare it has always been. The styling is nearly perfect, with its separate instruments, upswept pipes, crossbrace bars, simple, triangular frame, long, racy tank, trim headlamp and fenders, and boatloads of chrome! The claimed top speed of 75 mph was somewhat high for a 125. I wonder if it would really do that with a full-sized American on board? There were several Suzukis back then that caught my eye, and the Stinger was certainly one of them.

James Rozee Remembers the Stinger: "I rode the Suzuki Stinger at my local Suzuki dealer here in Portland when they were new. It was cool, very light and nimble, but not very powerful. It reminded me of my Twin Jet 100 Yamaha. I loved the cylinders sticking straight out the front and it had a great sound. It felt light, like you were on an 80cc single. I liked the neat little tube frame, too."

Figure F22 - Green 1971 Suzuki Stinger 125. ©Michael Kiernan, Classic Motorcycle Company, St. Louis, MO.

Suzuki 1971 Chart

Model	Name	Type	HP	Seat	Exhaust	Wt.	Price
MT-50R	Trailhopper	49cc Single	3	Solo	Upswept	132	$259
F-50R	Cutlass	49cc Single	4.5	Dual	Down	152	$239
TS-50R	Gaucho	49cc Single	4.9	Dual	Down Up	156	$294
TC-90R	Blazer	89cc Single	11	Dual	Upswept	199	$389
TS-90R	Honcho	89cc Single	11	Dual	Upswept	197	$384
TC-120R	Cat	118cc S.	12	Dual	Upswept	205	$460
T-125R	Stinger	124cc Twin	15	Dual	Upswept	207	$470
TS-125R	Duster	123cc S.	13	Dual	Down Up	198	$499
TS-185R	Sierra	183cc S.	17.5	Dual	Upswept	218	$599
TS-250R	Savage	249cc S.	23	Dual	Upswept	300	$799
T-250R	Hustler	247cc Twin	33	Dual	Down	315	$699
T-350R	Rebel	315cc Twin	40	Dual	Down	323	$759
TM-400R	Cyclone	400cc S.	40	3/4	Down Up	236	$999
T-500R	Titan	492cc Twin	47	Dual	Down	420	$899

Suzuki 1971 Notes: All 1971 models were kickstart only. All claimed dry weights are listed in pounds. The weights stated for the Savage and Titan are wet. The rest are claimed dry weights. Suzuki began tacking a letter onto the end of each model to designate the year; in this case, R = 1971. The Cat had a dual-three-speed transmission. This would be the last year of this type of Suzuki trail machine. The Cat would be replaced by the Yamaha Enduro copycat-style Duster and Prospector.

Figure F23 - Blue 1972 Suzuki 500 Titan. ©Michael Kiernan, Classic Motorcycle Company, St. Louis, MO.

Suzuki 1972 Chart

Model	Name	Type	HP	Exhaust	Wt.	Price
TS-50J	Gaucho	49cc Single	4.9	Down Up	156	$327
RV-90J	Rover	88cc Single	8	Upswept	185	$435
TC-90J	Blazer	89cc Single	11	Upswept	199	$435
TS-90J	Honcho	89cc Single	11	Upswept	197	$429
TC-125J	Prospector	123cc Single	13	Down Up	209	$569
TS-125J	Duster	123cc Single	13	Down Up	198	$547
TS-185J	Sierra	183cc Single	17.5	Upswept	218	$742
TS-250J	Savage	246cc Single	23	Upswept	245	$849
TM-250J	MX	246cc Single	30	Down Up	220	$1070
TC-250J	Hustler	247cc Twin	33	Down	315	$759
T-350J	Rebel	315cc Twin	40	Down	323	$799
GT-380J	Sebring	371cc Triple	38	Down	366	$925
TS-400J	Apache	386cc Single	34	Down Up	277	$949
T-500J	Titan	492cc Twin	47	Down	408	$949
GT-550J	Indy	543cc Triple	NA	Down	412	$1199
GT-750J	Lemans	738cc Triple	NA	Down	472	$1575

Suzuki 1972 Notes: All models had dual seats except the Gaucho 50 and 250 MX, which had 3/4-length seats. All 1972 models were kickstart only, except the Indy and LeMans had electric and kick starters. All claimed dry weights are listed in pounds. The Rover 90 was an unusual, mildly-tuned trail machine with big fat tires. The GT-380 had a drum front brake this year only. The forty horsepower of the Rebel may be a bit optimistic. It is difficult to imagine that the Rebel made two *more* horsepower than the new, larger displacement Sebring triple. The water-cooled Lemans was considered technologically advanced in its day. Nicknamed the Water Buffalo, it would successfully carry the top banana flag at Suzuki until two significant new machines could be developed, the RE-5 rotary sales flop of 1975 and the DOHC GS-750 screaming success of 1977.

Suzuki RV-90J Rover

Length	71.1"
Width	32.3"
Height	39.0"
Wheel Base	46.5"
Ground Clearance	7.7"
Dry Weight	185 lbs.
Engine Type	2 stroke, air-cooled aluminum, single cylinder, reed valve
Bore & Stroke	1.97" x 1.77"
C.C.	88
Compression Ratio	6.2:1
Carburetor	VM17SC
Maximum Output	8 hp/6000 rpm
Maximum Torque	7.23 ft.-lbs./4000 rpm
Speed Range	45-50 mph
Transmission	4 speed, constant mesh
Clutch	Multi-plate, wet disc
Starter	Primary kick
Brakes: Front	Right hand, internal expanding
Rear	Right foot, internal expanding
Suspension: Front	Telescopic
Rear	Swinging arm, oil-dampened
Tires: Front	6.70-10 4PR
Rear	6.70-10 4PR
Color	Daytona Blue
Fuel Tank Capacity	0.9 gal.
Oil Tank Capacity	1.7 pts.
Instruments	Speedometer
Climbing Ability	30°

Famous 12 month/12,000 miles warranty*

Deep cushioned, dual passenger seat

Take 30° hills

High clearance polyeurethene fenders

Tire pump

Primary kick starter

10" wide all terrain tires

All prices and specifications subject to change without notice.

Part No. 99404-23000

Suzuki: built to take on the country.
U.S. Suzuki Motor Corporation, Santa Fe Springs, California 90670

Litho in USA

Figure F24 - Daytona Blue 1972 Suzuki Rover RV-90J. Suzuki responded to the explosive success of the Honda Trail 70 with the Rover in 1972. The chubby little eight-horsepower two-stroke would be joined by a 125cc Tracker big brother with two more horsepower in '73. There are no records available to indicate exactly how successful the company was in this gambit, but certainly Rovers and Trackers did not completely take over the RV parks the way Trail 70's did! ©1972 Suzuki Motor of America, Inc.

Figure F25 - This dark blue 1967 Suzuki B-120 is another rarity. ©1967 Suzuki Motor of America, Inc.

Suzuki Savage

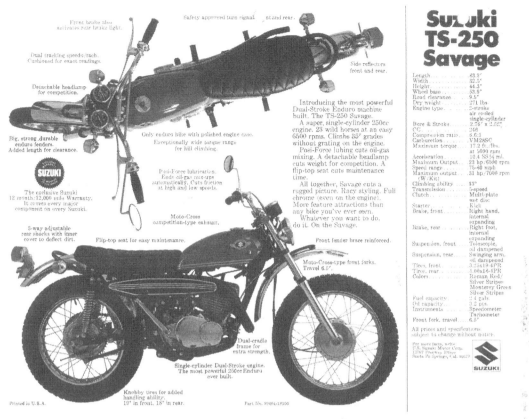

Figure F26 - Roman Red 1969 Suzuki Savage 250. This is the first-year brochure of Suzuki's answer to Yamaha's DT-1. The Savage was also available in Monterey Green that year. ©1969 Suzuki Motor of America, Inc.

The Suzuki Savage was a dual-purpose machine of a different nature from the previously discussed Allstate Cheyenne. Although the Savage was a much later and better designed dirt bike, it was far from the best of its day. Whereas the Cheyenne was far too spindly and weak to be effective in the dirt, the Savage was a deluxe porker of the opposite persuasion. What did you expect me to compare the Savage to, a DT-1?

When Yamaha set the trail riding world on fire with the introduction of its DT-1 in 1968, all the competing brands scrambled to copy it. Suzuki joined the trail revolution with the Savage in 1969. The Savage came in two colors, red and green, and only the tank was painted either color. The TS-250 would continue in the Suzi lineup for over a decade, but the Savage name was applied only to the early models. Suzuki sought to chase the high-sales models of Honda and Yamaha with additional features, flashy styling and finishes, and more than acceptable prices. The Savage was no exception to this marketing ploy, showing off polished engine cases, chrome fenders, and turn signals. The enduro model had 23 horsepower, but a kit was a available to up that to 31 hp. Residing in a muddy area in those heady days, I always liked the really high front fender and wished a lot more brands would raise the front fenders on all their enduro models. The 3.25 x 19 front tire gives the bike a chunky look.

A Savage of early vintage has always been relatively rare. I have seen only a few in my lifetime. Yamaha pretty much owned the two-stroke market in enduro-type machines in those days. Of course Honda sold a zillion of its early, heavy, and slow, but very quiet and very reliable, Motosports and XL singles. However, the wide array of enduro models designed and sold by Kawasaki and Suzuki produced only moderate fires out the showroom doors. Many motocrossers from Suzuki became exceedingly popular in wild spurts of dirt-throwing competition, but the Kaws were rarely able to meet the Suzis head to head on the track or the showroom floor. The word on the trail was that the trim and agile Yamaha Enduros generally left the heavier Kaws and Suzis in their dust. Kawasaki was destined to be more successful with its high performance street bikes. Suzuki would put a lot of effort into the development of their TM, and later RM, motocrossers, eliminating trail-hugging weight and improving suspensions. Just looking at a photo of one of these early Savage models takes me back to an era of trail riding innocence. The Savage will always be overlooked in the motorcycle history books, sandwiched between the exquisitely designed Yamaha Enduros that unleashed the explosion and the ponderous, but likable, Honda Motosports.

Figure F27 - Pine Green 1973 Suzuki 125 Prospector. ©1973 Suzuki Motor of America, Inc.

Suzuki 1973 Chart

Model	Name	Type	HP	Seat	Exhaust	Wt.	Price
MT-50K	Trailhopper	49cc Single	3	Solo	Upswept	132	$299
TS-50K	Gaucho	49cc Single	4.9	Dual	Down Up	156	$349
RV-90K	Rover	88cc Single	8	Dual	Upswept	185	$459
TC-100K	Blazer	97cc Single	11	Dual	Down Up	205	$464
TS-100K	Honcho	97cc Single	11	Dual	Down Up	202	$459
RV-125K	Tracker	123cc S.	10	Dual	Upswept	244	$595
TC-125K	Prospector	123cc S.	13	Dual	Down Up	209	$595
TS-125K	Duster	123cc S.	13	Dual	Down Up	198	$579
TM-125K	Challenger	123cc Sincle	18	3/4	Down Up	189	$605
TS-185K	Sierra	183cc S.	17.5	Dual	Upswept	218	$679
GT-185K	Adventurer	184cc Twin	21	Dual	Down	253	$695
GT-250K	Hustler	247cc Twin	31	Dual	Down	322	$810
TS-250K	Savage	246cc S.	23	Dual	Upswept	245	$859
TM-250K	Champion	246cc Single	28	3/4	Down Up	220	$910
GT-380K	Sebring	371cc Triple	38	Dual	Down	408	$985
TS-400K	Apache	396cc Single	34	Dual	Down Up	277	$975
TM-400K	Cyclone	396cc Single	36	3/4	Down Up	235	$1020
T-500K	Titan	492cc Twin	47	Dual	Down	409	$969
GT-550K	Indy	543cc Triple	50	Dual	Down	480	$1265
GT-750K	LeMans	738cc Triple	67	Dual	Down	551	$1665

Suzuki 1973 Notes: The Adventurer, Indy, and LeMans models have electric and kick starters. All the rest have kick starters only. All claimed dry weights are listed in pounds. The stated weights for the Sebring, Indy, and LeMans are wet.

Suzuki 1974 Chart

Model	Name	Type	HP	Seat	Exhaust	Wt.	Price
TS-50	Gaucho	49cc Single	4.8	3/4	Down Up	156	$395
TM-75	MiniCross	72cc Single	5	3/4	Down Up	165	$395
RV-90	Rover	88cc Single	7.8	Dual	Upswept	185	$545
TC-100	Blazer	97cc Single	10.8	Dual	Down Up	205	$555
TS-100	Honcho	97cc Single	10.8	Dual	Down Up	202	$545
TM-100	Contender	98cc Single	14	3/4	Down Up	187	$645
RV-125	Tracker	123cc Single	9.8	Dual	Upswept	244	$695
TC-125	Prospector	123cc Single	12.7	Dual	Down Up	209	$685
TS-125	Duster	123cc Single	12.7	Dual	Down Up	198	$670
TM-125	Challenger	123cc Single	17.5	3/4	Down Up	189	$720
TC-185	Ranger	183cc Single	16	Dual	Upswept	271	$855
TS-185	Sierra	183cc Single	17	Dual	Upswept	218	$795
GT-185	Adventurer	184cc Twin	20	Dual	Down	253	$795
RL-250	Exacta	246cc Single	18	Solo	Upswept	199	$1045
TS-250	Savage	246cc Single	22	Dual	Upswept	245	$995
TM-250	Champion	246cc Single	27	3/4	Down Up	220	$1080
GT-250	Hustler	247cc Twin	30	Dual	Down	322	$895
GT-380	Sebring	371cc Triple	37	Dual	Down	377	$1165
TS-400	Apache	396cc Single	33	Dual	Down Up	277	$1145
TM-400	Cyclone	396cc Single	35	3/4	Down Up	235	$1205
T-500	Titan	492cc Twin	44	Dual	Down	412	$1045
GT-550	Indy	543cc Triple	48.5	Dual	Down	441	$1445
GT-750	LeMans	738cc Triple	65	Dual	Down	507	$1899

Suzuki 1974 Notes: The Ranger, Adventurer, Indy, and LeMans models have electric and kick starters. All the rest have kick starters only. The Rover 90 got a fat-tired big brother called the Tracker 125 in 1974. The new Exacta trials model was not yet shown in the *Sport Book* from which the stated prices were sourced. Its specifications came directly from the Suzuki brochure. All claimed dry weights are listed in pounds.

Figure F28 - 1974 Suzuki RL-250 Exacta. Suzuki enters the trials game. ©Don Quayle

Figure F29 - 1975 Suzuki GT-380 Sebring Triple. A cursory look at the 1975 chart below displays Suzuki's marketing outlook in the '70's. The company's lineup was split between one emphasis on the trail, enduro, trials, and motocross tiddlers and another on big two-stroke road burners. Suzuki would finally join the high-performance four-stroke world in 1977. Image by Reg McKenna under Creative Commons license.

Suzuki 1975 Chart

Model	Name	Type	HP	Seat	Exhaust	Wt.	Price
TS-75	Colt	72cc Single	4.9	3/4	Down Up	172	$485
TM-75	MiniCross	72cc Single	5	3/4	Down Up	132	$475
RV-90	Rover	88cc Single	7.8	Dual	Upswept	185	$615
TC-100	Blazer	97cc Single	10.8	Dual	Down Up	205	$640
TS-100	Honcho	97cc Single	10.8	Dual	Down Up	202	$620
TM-100	Contender	98cc Single	16.5	3/4	Down Up	187	$815
RV-125	Tracker	123cc Single	9.8	Dual	Upswept	244	$765
TC-125	Prospector	123cc Single	12.7	Dual	Down Up	209	$770
TS-125	Duster	123cc Single	12.7	Dual	Down Up	198	$750
TM-125	Challenger	123cc Single	17.5	3/4	Down Up	189	$815
TC-185	Ranger	183cc Single	16	Dual	Upswept	260	$930
TS-185	Sierra	183cc Single	17	Dual	Upswept	218	$875
GT-185	Adventurer	184cc Twin	21	Dual	Down	253	$925
RL-250	Exacta	246cc Single	18	Solo	Upswept	199	$1145
TS-250	Savage	246cc Single	22	Dual	Upswept	245	$1085
TM-250	Champion	246cc Single	27	3/4	Down Up	220	$1175
GT-250	Hustler	247cc Twin	30	Dual	Down	322	$995
GT-380	Sebring	371cc Triple	37	Dual	Down	377	$1295
TS-400	Apache	396cc Single	33	Dual	Down Up	277	$1230
TM-400	Cyclone	396cc Single	35	3/4	Down Up	235	$1295
T-500	Titan	492cc Twin	44	Dual	Down	412	$1175
GT-550	Indy	543cc Triple	48.5	Dual	Down	441	$1635
GT-750	LeMans	738cc Triple	70	Dual	Down	556	$2145
RE-5	Rotary	497cc Rotary	62	Dual	Down	507	$2475

Suzuki 1975 Notes: For the first time since the first Suzukis came to the U.S., there was no 50cc machine in the lineup. The Ranger, Adventurer, Indy, and LeMans models have electric and kick starters. All the rest have kick starters only. All claimed dry weights are listed in pounds. The stated weight for the GT-750 LeMans is wet, per the May 1975 *Cycle* Road Test. The horsepower was rated on the dyno as 57.3 in the same test. The stated figure is the claimed gross figure. Suzuki ended its long era of building only two-strokes with the introduction of the RE-5 Rotary model that would be built only in 1975 and '76.

Figure F30 - Here it is, folks, the first Wankel-engined motorcycle planned for mass production. Hercules beat Suzuki to the two-wheeled Wankel street by one model year, but that company's numbers were tiny. Suzuki hoped to expand that production level considerably. The problem was mostly that the rotary motorcycle was a question few prospective buyers asked. When Suzuki supplied an answer, the 1975 RE-5 was a technological marvel, but a styling boo-boo. You can begin by removing that silly looking cylinder containing the RE-5's instruments! The RE-5 was intended as a touring, as opposed to sporting, machine, but the long wheelbase, considerable weight, and questionable servicing issues failed to impress coast-to-coast riders. It certainly did not help matters that the RE-5 was launched the same year as the Honda Gold Wing. Image by Gtregs75 under Creative Commons license.

Figure F31 - This silly instrument barrel-pod was replaced with conventional styling on the 1976 RE-5, but the sales damage had already been done. ©Michael Kiernan, Classic Motorcycle Company, St. Louis, MO.

The Big Suzis

Figure F32 - 1968 Suzuki T-500 Titan. ©1968 Suzuki Motor of America, Inc.

The Kawasaki Mach III was not the first 500cc two-stroke. The Kaw 500 Triple was preceded by the Suzuki 500 Five by a year. The 1968 Suzi was the largest two-stroke yet at that time, but it was otherwise conventional in every way. The T500 was a piston-port 492cc twin with oil injection and air cooling in an ordinary tube cradle frame. The machine was never quite a *tourer* or a hotrod, but something between. If you squint at one just right, you might see how the T-500 was marketed as a two-stroke predecessor to Yamaha's XS-1 650. Both companies were trying to produce a long-running *standard* model and they were completely successful. Like the XS-1, a lot of Suzuki 500 two-strokes were sold over the years and neither model ever became infamous for some particular quirk or other. When Kawasaki began to hog the big two-stroke spotlight in '69, Suzuki was more than happy to trail along in the Number Two position. If that was all that had occurred, I might not have bothered with this story. Suzuki did anything but rest on their chain guards after the release of their 500 twin. The company continued to develop and refine the Titan, as it would later be christened. The styling and comfort of the Titan continued to improve while the price barely moved.

Figure F33 - 1972 Suzuki GT-380 Sebring. ©1972 Suzuki Motor of America, Inc.

After four years of proving that a big two-stroke could be effectively civilized and reliable, Suzuki pulled out their really big guns in '72. While the Kawasaki 500 Triple had been rearing up on its rear wheel and racing from stoplight to stoplight for three model years, Suzuki prepared three triples for release. Each was somewhat different from the other two. The GT-380 Sebring was a middleweight with a conventional front drum brake in its first year. The GT-550 Indy sported the same Ram Air Induction cooling as the 380, but with a disc brake up front. Unlike the Ram Air Pontiac Firebirds of the period, the Ram Air systems on the Suzukis cooled the fins instead of feeding the carburetors cool, condensed air. The Ram Air system was actually little more than a shroud over the cooling fins of the three-cylinder engine, but Suzuki used it to pull a lot of mileage out of the magazine press with ads and road tests. The big gun GT-750 LeMans was the first water-cooled mass-produced street two-stroke, and boy, did the press have a lot to say about *that*. The press wasted no time in nicknaming the machine The Water Buffalo. The name has stuck, even after forty years!

Suzuki was hell-bent on being the final holdout against switching to four-stroke engines just because the U.S. EPA said so. The three GT triples would be the last hurrah for the smokin' street bikes with horny bumble bees up their exhaust pipes. Suzuki and Kawasaki would both continue to market their triples in the U.S. through 1976, but anybody could read the writing on the wall. Yamaha would even ship a few street RZ350's to our shores in the mid-Eighties, but basically 1976 could be considered the end of two-strokes on the streets of America. The next year Suzuki would release their first GS-series DOHC machines to tumultuous acclaim.

Figure F34 - Pearl Red & Tan 1973 Suzuki GT-750. Image by Edward A. Zunz III, photographer, under Creative Commons license.

Figure F35 - 1975 Suzuki GT-550 Indy in Jet Black. This air-cooled triple also came in Candy Orange.
©1975 Suzuki Motor of America, Inc.

Figure F36 - 1975 Suzuki GT-750 in Jewel Gray. The 1975 model also came in Gypsy Red.

Figure F37 - Black Suzuki 250 T-10 at the Salon de la Moto, Paris, 2011. Isn't this where we came in? The T-10 was Suzuki's first twin sent to the USA back in 1962. The T-10 was Suzuki's top of the line in the U.S. market for the first few years and the Water Buffalo was the company's big two-stroke finale. The last word on the big Suzis: you know a model has fans when it remains in the lineup for years with its own personal nickname. The last word in Suzuki tiddler collectibility is probably the X-6, the legend born from the T-10. Image by The Supermat, photographer, under Creative Commons license.

Selected Suzuki Models Ratings Chart

Years	Model	Collectibility	Practicality	Desirability
1962 - 66	Street 50's	A	D	C
1968 - 70	Colt & Maverick	B	B	A
1962 - 67	80 & 100 Singles	B	D	C
1968 - 75	90 & 100 Singles	C	C	D
1967 - 71	Cat 120 Trail	B	C	B
1969 - 71	Stinger Twin 120	B	C	B
1971 - 75	125 & 185 Enduros	D	C	C
1967 - 69	Invader & Stingray 200	B	C	B
1962 - 64	Four-speed 250 Twins	B	D	C
1965 - 75	X-6 Hustler 250	A	B	A
1969 - 75	Savage Enduro 250	D	C	C
1968 - 69	Raider & Laredo 305	C	C	C
1969 - 72	Rebel 350 Twin	C	C	C
1972 - 75	GT-380 Sebring	C	C	C
1968 - 75	500 Five Titan	C	C	C
1972 - 75	GT-550 Indy	C	C	C
1972 - 75	GT-750 LeMans	B	C	B
1975	RE-5 Rotary	A	D	B

Models Ratings Chart Definitions:

Years: These are the total production years for a particular model series. Some early model years within a series may be considerably more desirable than later years.

Models: In some cases many variations are included in this category and in others the models included are very homogeneous.

Collectibility: This is what most of you want to know, the bottom line on how likely the model or series is likely to climb in value over the coming years.

Practicality: This is an indicator of how adaptable the machine can be to ride for transportation or pleasure in the modern world, considering parts availability, fuel quality, comfort, performance and miscellaneous other obvious factors.

Desirability: This defines the nostalgic, emotional wow factor, without regard for collector values or everyday usage.

General: No machine is given a failing grade. If it made it into a rating chart, at least a few hobbyists find that model interesting.

Chapter 6: *Kawasaki: Let the Good Times Roll*

1964 Omega Sports Special 125

Figure G1 - 1964 Omega Sports Special 125. This photo excerpt from an ad represents one of Kawasaki's earliest forays into the U.S. market. ©1964 Kawasaki Motors Corporation, U.S.A.

Consider this the mystery machine of the day. A two-page B&W ad paid for by Ken Kay Distributing Company of North Hollywood CA appeared in the August 1964 issue of *Cycle World*. Ken Kay had been the western distributor of Suzukis since 1962, but this particular ad seemed to have been unique unto itself. The ad featured two machines, the obviously Italian 1964 Trojan Magnum Super Sport, seemingly named after a legendary condom, and the earliest Kawasaki imported into the USA, the Omega. The 125cc Omega did not carry the Kawasaki badge, and it was the predecessor to the 1966 Kawasaki F1 model, a bored out B-8 125.

The following statements are quoted directly from the ad, as I have never found another speck of information on the Trojan. The brand name is not even listed at Sheldon's EMU site, which offers quite extensive coverage of European machines. The ad states that the Trojan was the lowest priced 175cc sold in the U. S. in '64 at $465. It produced 15 horsepower with a four-speed foot shift, and it weighed 175 pounds featuring its sport tank and fenders and magneto ignition. However, it looks to me like a small battery was strapped to the frame just behind the air cleaner. Maybe it used the battery only to power the lights. The claimed top speed was 70 mph.

Here is what I have been able to ascertain outside the ad copy. I assume this is an Italian machine just because of all the obvious styling and design cues, but I do not have a clue what company actually built it. Was there a short-lived Trojan company? This little bike has an awfully long name. Did they tack on the Super Sport to distract the snickering little boys to whom all the Sixties tiddlers were marketed? Was there a regular Magnum with a larger tank and fenders? The main reason I don't have a clue who built it are the presence of the straightforward, vertical, two-stroke cylinder and the large single downtube frame. The cylinder and air filter container look very Spanish, like those of a Metralla, but the frame design looks Italian. Could it be Austrian? Notice that the gearshift is on the right and the kickstarter on the left, in typical English/Italian fashion. The tank and seat look very typically Italian to me. The strangest component seems to be a black vertical bar in front of the downtube. Is that a tire pump, or maybe some sort of steering damper? I think there is a screw-down knob for a conventional steering damper just behind the handlebar mount. There were many more Italian builders of tiddlers back in those days than we saw commonly imported into the U. S. Maybe this is one of those.

Ken Kay claimed the Omega was the lowest priced 125cc with electric starter sold in the USA in 1964 at $435. The specifications included a rotary four-speed foot shift on the left side, turn signals, sealed beam headlight, and an electric gear position indicator. A luggage rack and whitewall tires were optional above the $435 price. The front fender was chrome and the rear was molded from the pressed steel frame. An unusual chrome downtube was bolted to the front of the engine case.

The big story is that, as far as I know, this was actually the first Kawasaki imported into the U. S.! The Kawasaki moniker was not used on this machine. It was as if the company was testing the market. I have in my files a photo of a 1964 Kawasaki 125 imported into Canada. Of course I have no proof that that stated year is correct, but that machine is almost identical to this one. The tires are blackwall, there is no mudguard on the rear fender, the trim on the engine case and side covers are different, and the rubber knee pads are different, but otherwise it is the same. A photo of a 1966 Kawasaki 125 shows the same machine yet again, except the suspension styling has been updated with rubber gaiters in the front and exposed chrome springs in the rear. Brochures of other Kawasaki models in 1966 show machines with Superlube oil injection, so I assume that the 1966 125 has it, too, but this Omega does not. The other Japanese brands had obviously had time to copy Yamaha's Autolube for the release of their 1966 models.

James Rozee Speaks: "Ken Kay was an importer of the early Kawasaki 125 B-8. I had a few of them. He also sold them as Omegas. I had one and like you said the tank badge was the only change I could see. The main reason he changed the name is because no one had ever heard of Kawasaki here in the States. but they were a household name in Japan. They wanted to establish that household name thing in the U.S. I worked for a huge Kawasaki distributor here in Portland. I always liked the flat-top headlight of the first Kawasaki B-8. It looked like an early Suzuki light turned upside down. They also had rotary trannies but not rotary valves. The B-8 only lasted until 1965, then Kawasaki went to the rotary valve motors for all their small bore bikes."

Kawasaki Model Charts, 1963-75

Figure G2 - 1970 Kawasaki 90 G3-SS. ©1970 Kawasaki Motors Corporation, U.S.A.

Kawasaki entered the motorcycle market in Japan with four-stroke models originally designed by Meguro. The company next began building single-cylinder two-stroke engines and soon followed up with machines wholly designed and built by the Kawasaki factory. The Meguro SG 250 and the BSA copycat W1 650 would remain the company's only four-stroke models until the release of the Z-1 900 in late 1972. The history of the company's model nomenclature is quite difficult to follow. Letter prefixes followed by numerical digits, and in some cases additional letters, seem to have been erratically assigned. Even the established haphazard pattern began to shift in 1973, adding to the confusion, although if one looks simply at the later models within their own context, it actually makes sense.

The focus of this book is on the earlier models, and these can be sorted out in the following manner. Why Kawasaki began with a model called B8, I do not know, but the development of the line launched from that point, just as Yamaha had earlier with its YA-1 of the same general type and displacement. As the lineup expanded, the suffix *D* denoted an electric starter and *L* oil injection. My guess is that these designations stood for *Dynamo* and *Lube*. The *T* for Touring is more difficult to understand. These were generally more deluxe models with dual seats, luggage racks, whitewall tires, and/or upswept exhausts. The confusing part is that most enthusiasts would call these the *Sport* models instead. They usually did not have enclosed chains or full-coverage fenders and were confined to the 85cc and 125cc models. A 150cc upgrade was added to the B8 line and this was called the *S*. Although it is called a Sport in the chart, maybe the *S* stands for Super? It is the same klunky machine as the original B8 with a larger bore. Apparently, the *T* actually meant Sport and the *S* meant Super or big-bore.

My best guess is that very few examples of the many early models listed in the charts were actually sent to the USA, especially the ones lacking Superlube. The October 1963 issue of *Cycle World* reported that Kawasaki sent twenty-seven machines to a dealer established in Hawaii. These bikes were a combination of Kawasaki 50 and 125 two-strokes and a few four-stroke models built by Meguro. The article stated that many more were awaiting shipment from a warehouse, in Japan, I suppose. In the U.S. market at least, electric starters and rotary shifts on small two-strokes were rapidly giving way to an accent on high performance. You could say that Kawasaki did not really establish a significant U.S. beachhead until the arrival of the hot-rod rotary valve twins with return-shift five-speeds in 1967.

Kawasaki 1963

Kawasaki introduces its first models, the B8 and B8T (Touring). Both models are 123cc two-stroke singles with eight horsepower. It is not clear how many were officially imported into the U.S., if any at all. The Omega model would be advertised a few months later as a model to be imported by Ken Kay, the early distributor of Suzukis. The original plan was to export whatever Kawasakis to the USA under the Omega brand name. Kawasaki would not really get serious about establishing a brand in the U.S. until the introduction of the Samurai in 1967.

Figure G3 - 1964 Kawasaki SG 250. ©1964 Kawasaki Motors Corporation, U.S.A.

Kawasaki 1964 Chart

Model	Name	Type	HP	Seat	Exhaust	Starter
B8	Standard	123cc Single	11	Solo	Down	Kick
B8T	Touring	123cc Single	11	Dual	Down	Kick
SG	Standard	250cc Single	18	Solo	Down	Electric
NA	Omega	123cc Single	NA	Dual	Down	Kick

Kawasaki 1964 Notes: All models had rotary four-speed transmissions. The three 125's were piston-port two-strokes with pressed steel frames, chrome tank panels, and 16-inch wheels. The SG was a basic, electric-start, OHV commuter, painted in plain black, with a tube frame and eighteen-inch wheels, actually built by Meguro. If the SG was exported to America, I am sure the numbers were very small. The Omega was advertised in the August 1964 *Cycle World* as the lowest priced 125cc with electric start. The Omega was basically a B8 tarted up for the American market with a chrome front fender, dual seat, chrome luggage rack, and whitewall tires. These last two items were optional at extra cost over the $435 advertised price. The Omega would not be tested by *Cycle World* until September 1965.

Kawasaki 1965 Chart

Model	Name	Type	HP	Seat	Exhaust	Starter
J1	Street	85cc Single	7.5	Solo	Down	Kick
J1D	Street	85cc Single	7.5	Solo	Down	Electric
J1L	Deluxe	85cc Single	7.5	Dual	Upswept	Kick
J1T	Touring	85cc Single	7.8	Dual	Upswept	Kick
J1TL	Touring	85cc Single	7.8	Dual	Upswept	Kick
B8	Standard	125cc Single	11	Solo	Down	Kick
B8T	Touring	125cc Single	11	Dual	Down	Kick
B8S	Sport	150cc Single	12	Dual	Down	Kick
SG	Standard	250cc Single	18	Solo	Down	Electric

Figure G4 - 1965 Kawasaki B8S 125. ©1965 Kawasaki Motors Corporation, U.S.A.

Kawasaki 1965 Notes: Kawasaki expanded its lineup in 1965 past its initial 125cc B8 Series and the four-stroke built by Meguro with the Kawasaki brand name attached. Although only two new displacements were added, a precedent was set. Once Yamaha had set the market standard with oil injection, Kawasaki promptly followed up with its Superlube version. All models had rotary four-speed transmissions.

The 85cc models had pressed steel frames, 17-inch wheels, and rotary valves. The J1 & J1D were premix. I have two photos in my collection that each claim to be a 1965 B8. One states that the machine is a B8T. This machine has whitewall tires, a chrome luggage rack, and a standard-type chain guard. The engine support brace is painted silver. The second machine has an emblem on the side cover that says *Sport Special 125* instead of *Kawasaki*. This machine has turn signals, but no luggage rack. The chain is enclosed and the support brace is painted red. Both machines are red, but the Sport Special seems to be a bright red and the B8T is a more maroonish red. Both kickstands are painted black on the B8T and red on the SS. All other details of the two machines appear to be identical.

Figure G5 - Kawasaki G31M Centurion. Kawasaki would enter offroad racing categories soon after seriously entering the U.S. market in 1967. The company began with a pair of models in the 100cc and 250cc classes prior to the explosion of the popularity of motocross. You can see the high fenders and black upswept expansion chamber that would define most later motocrossers from many competing brands. Note, however, the universal tread design of the tires more suited to flat-track racing. ©Kawasaki Motors Corporation, U.S.A.

Kawasaki 1966 Chart

Model	Name	Type	HP	Seat	Exhaust	Starter
M10	Street	51cc Single	4.5	Dual	Down	Kick
M11	Street	52cc Single	4.5	Solo	Down	Kick
J1	Street	85cc Single	7.5	Solo	Down	Kick
J1D	Street	85cc Single	7.5	Solo	Down	Electric
J1L	Deluxe	85cc Single	7.5	Dual	Upswept	Kick
J1T	Touring	85cc Single	7.8	Dual	Upswept	Kick
J1TL	Touring	85cc Single	7.8	Dual	Upswept	Kick
J1TR	Trail	85cc Single	8	3/4	Upswept	Kick
J1TRL	Trail	85cc Single	8	3/4	Upswept	Kick
D1	Street	99cc Single	10	Dual	Upswept	Kick
C1	Street	115cc Single	10	Dual	Down	Kick
C1D	Street	115cc Single	10	Dual	Down	Electric
C1L	Street	115cc Single	10	Dual	Down	Kick
C1DL	Street	115cc Single	10	Dual	Down	Electric
B8	Standard	125cc Single	11	Solo	Down	Kick
B8T	Touring	125cc Single	11	Dual	Down	Kick
B1	Street	125cc Single	12	Dual	Down	Kick
B1L	Street	125cc Single	12	Dual	Down	Kick
B1T	Touring	125cc Single	12	Dual	Upswept	Kick
B1TL	Touring	125cc Single	12	Dual	Upswept	Kick
B8S	Touring	150cc Single	12	Dual	Down	Kick
F1	Street	169cc Single	17	Dual	Down	Electric
F1TR	Trail	169cc Single	17	Solo	Upswept	Electric
F2	Street	169cc Single	18	Dual	Down	Kick
F2TR	Trail	169cc Single	18	Solo	Upswept	Electric
SG	Standard	250cc Single	18	Solo	Down	Electric
W1	Commander	624cc Twin	50	Dual	Down	Kick

Kawasaki 1966 Notes: The OHV W1 shifted on the right with a return shift. All other models had left-side rotary shifters. All models had four speeds, except the two 50cc models had three speeds. The 175 F1 of early '66 did not have Superlube; the later F2 did. The F2 may have had an electric starter, but that is unconfirmed. The F1TR 175 trail model would be the first machine tested by *Cycle World* with a Kawasaki nameplate in March 1966. A test of the W1 would be published in August. The M and J models had pressed steel frames, 17-inch wheels, and rotary shifts. The M models came only in Rocket Red or Black. The D1 was distinguished by its thinline whitewall tires (in all three production years). The new F1 was a piston-port, premix street model with 18-inch wheels, pressed steel frame, and a stainless steel front fender. The claimed dry weight of the D1 was 174 pounds and that of the W1 Commander was 398 pounds. One source quotes the wet weight of the W1 as 471 pounds.

KAWASAKI 650

MODEL W1

*DESIGNED FOR FREEWAY SPEEDS
*SAFEST BIG MOTORCYCLE SOLD
*SPORTY LOOKING, EASY TO RIDE

THE BIGGEST, FASTEST, MOST POWERFUL JAPANESE MOTORCYCLE

Here's the magnificent motorcycle you've been waiting for. It's the biggest, fastest, most powerful motorcycle made in Japan. Yet it's the safest, easiest to control big machine on the market. Perfect for 250cc riders ready for a real motorcycle.

Unsurpassed acceleration; an amazing 13.8-second standing start quarter mile. A full 50 horsepower from the vertical twin OHV 4-stroke engine; 115 mph top speed. Plenty of horses left at highway cruising speed of 80 mph. Needle bearings in con rod big ends. Engineered with Kawasaki's superb standards of craftsmanship — the highest in the industry. And what a beautiful piece of machinery it is! Chrome front fork, rear fender, mufflers, tank, chaincover; stainless steel front fender; metallic paint; buffed engine and hubs.

Figure G6 - 1966 Red Kawasaki 650 Commander W1. This is an early U.S. brochure for the Kaw 650. You can clearly distinguish the separate gearbox and right-side shift lever on this BSA copycat. Also in typical BSA fashion, the kickstarter is on the right and the machine is covered in chrome, including the fenders, tank panels, headlight ears, fork legs, and rear shock covers. ©1966 Kawasaki Motors Corporation, U.S.A.

Kawasaki 100 D1 & 175 Trail

One of my oldest Kawasaki brochures is a 1966 100cc D1. Note the three holes punched in the top, something that must easily score among the top ten stoopidest things I have ever done in my life! You don't see the holes in the F2TR brochure because I was able to crop them out of the photo. It is quite unfortunate that all my readers must suffer the consequences of what some crazy teenager did to my precious brochure collection so many years ago, but at least you get to see these rare photos, though flawed they may be. The Omega was advertised in *Cycle World* in 1964 and the Samurai was introduced in '67. The 1965 lineup was minimal and it mostly originated from an earlier design era in Japan. This 1966 model year would introduce several all-new, all-Kawasaki, rotary valve designs, and all have Superlube and the same general style, both the brochures and the motorcycles. Another model from the same brochure group was the 650cc BSA copycat W1. The strangest quirk is that the 175 Trail is the only one of the three models with an electric starter! Maybe the designers' thinking was that if you killed the engine on the side of a rough, steep hill, a pushbutton starter would come in handy on a trail machine. After all, even my smallest cat, who is as feisty as her namesake, Jackie Burkhart, can kick start a Japanese 100cc two-stroke, and only *real men* rode British 650's or a copy of one!

You can easily see the pressed steel frame that was used only on some of the earliest Kawasakis, and the *Superlube* decal on the right side cover of both the D1 and F2TR. You can see from the 1965 chart that Superlube was introduced on the 85cc model and spread among many more models in 1966. On the older designs, you will see the *L* designation, but that was not added to the newer models, such as the F2 with Superlube and its F1 predecessor without it.

Figure G7 - 1966 Red Kawasaki 100 D1. The D1 was one of the first tiddlers seriously marketed in the USA by Kawasaki. You can see from the charts that there were several versions of the D1, but I strongly suspect the sportier models with oil injection were far the better selling models here. ©1966 Kawasaki Motors Corporation, U.S.A.

The F2TR is a particularly interesting machine. Note the solo seat, luggage rack, high chrome front fender, and bulky gas tank that were indigenous to some pre-1967 Kawasakis. The rotary-valve two-stroke had a claimed 18 hp and a top speed of 77 mph using its smaller sprocket. As with many small trail models of the day, the 175 Trail came with two rear sprockets installed. The company claimed that a rider could switch sprockets in just three minutes using the tool kit included with the bike. Notice how the skid plate is attached to the engine in front, and the chrome downtube goes directly from the frame at the gas tank mount to the front of the engine just behind the skid plate. Is this some sort of brush bar, or did the engine require a little extra bracing or vibration dampening? The claimed weight is 273 pounds and the eighteen-inch tires are called Knobby, but they look more like the very common Trials Universals mounted as standard equipment on many Japanese trail bikes in the '60's and '70's. The transmission was a four-speed rotary type. To you youngsters, that means 0-1-2-3-4-0-1-2-3-4, etc. I cannot tell you if that is going down or going up. I seem to remember at least one Japanese tiddler from the period that shifted all down and at least one that shifted all up, but I cannot remember which applies to the 175 Trail.

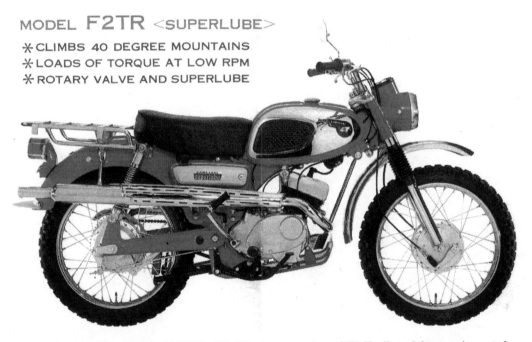

MODEL F2TR <SUPERLUBE>

* CLIMBS 40 DEGREE MOUNTAINS
* LOADS OF TORQUE AT LOW RPM
* ROTARY VALVE AND SUPERLUBE

Figure G8 - 1966 Red Kawasaki F2TR 175. Whatever number of F1 Trail models were imported was surely very small, making the F2TR Kawasaki's first well-known U.S. trail machine. Note the high chrome front fender, large chrome luggage rack, and knobby tires. Kawasaki would soon stop shipping machines to the U.S. with pressed steel frames. ©1966 Kawasaki Motors Corporation, U.S.A.

The company improved its U.S. model line in a big hurry after 1966. The 120cc C2-TR that would appear soon thereafter with a stylishly slimmer tank and what would become the Kaw trademark, among the early Japanese brands, double downtube frame, weighed 85 pounds less than the 175 Trail. I am sure that dropping the silly electric starter shed a few pounds, too. The stylish and quick Samurai would arrive in '67, too, quickly followed by the even faster Avenger, and then the legendary Blue Streak aka Mach III would wheelie onto the scene in 1969.

James Rozee Speaks: "One of the first restorations I did was a 1962 Kawasaki B-8 125, and it was hard to find parts for, even thirty-five years ago! This was Kawasaki's first complete bike. They built motors for other bikes like Meihatsu in Japan in the '50's before that. I worked for a large local Kawasaki dealer here in Portland and they sold lots of dirt bikes in Oregon. I liked the Big Horn 350 single. We called them 'Pig Horns' as they were a bit heavy. I always remember the whine of the straight-cut gears in those engines. They had a lot of low-end grunt! The Green Streak 125 and 250 did very well in motocross in the late '60's. They were the first Kawasakis to have the now-common lime green paint colors for which Kawasaki is known. Kawasaki bought out Meguro in the mid-Sixties so they would have a great big 650 four-stroke to compete with Honda, but Meguro had copied the BSA, so it had a right-hand shift."

Figure G9 - 1968 Red Kawasaki W2SS. ©Michael Kiernan, Classic Motorcycle Company, St. Louis, MO.

Figure G10 - 1968 Red Kawasaki W2SS. The later versions of the Kawasaki 650 were updated to suit the trends of the time. Note the trimmer front fender, uncovered chrome rear springs, pleated seat, twin carbs with chrome air filters, and shorty mufflers. These rear shocks may not be original equipment for this model. There was even a W2TT model with upswept pipes on one side built for one year only in 1969. ©Michael Kiernan, Classic Motorcycle Company, St. Louis, MO.

Figure G11 - This is one of Kawasaki's earliest full-page color ads released to U.S. magazines. This particular example comes from the August 1967 issue of *Cycle World*. Although the company imported a number of smaller models, you can see the big-bike performance coming from this brand a mile away just from this one ad. ©1967 Kawasaki Motors Corporation, U.S.A.

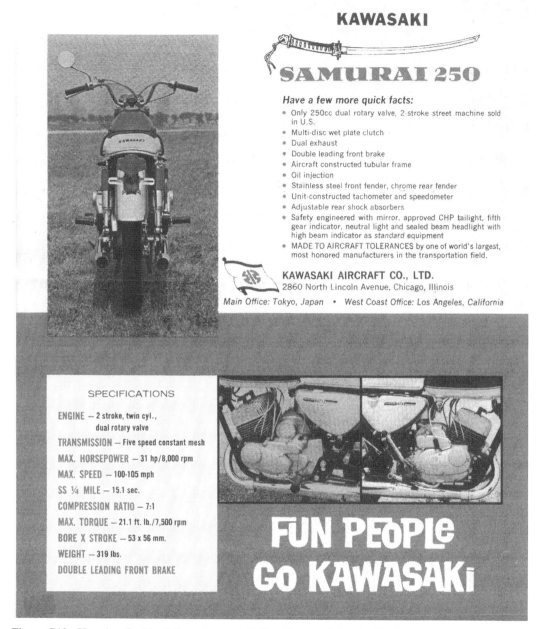

KAWASAKI

SAMURAI 250

Have a few more quick facts:

* Only 250cc dual rotary valve, 2-stroke street machine sold in U.S.
* Multi-disc wet plate clutch
* Dual exhaust
* Double leading front brake
* Aircraft constructed tubular frame
* Oil injection
* Stainless steel front fender, chrome rear fender
* Unit-constructed tachometer and speedometer
* Adjustable rear shock absorbers
* Safety engineered with mirror, approved CHP taillight, fifth gear indicator, neutral light and sealed beam headlight with high beam indicator as *standard* equipment
* MADE TO AIRCRAFT TOLERANCES by one of world's largest, most honored manufacturers in the transportation field.

KAWASAKI AIRCRAFT CO., LTD.
2860 North Lincoln Avenue, Chicago, Illinois

Main Office: Tokyo, Japan • West Coast Office: Los Angeles, California

SPECIFICATIONS

ENGINE — 2 stroke, twin cyl.,
dual rotary valve

TRANSMISSION — Five speed constant mesh

MAX. HORSEPOWER — 31 hp/8,000 rpm

MAX. SPEED — 100-105 mph

SS ¼ MILE — 15.1 sec.

COMPRESSION RATIO — 7:1

MAX. TORQUE — 21.1 ft. lb./7,500 rpm

BORE X STROKE — 53 x 56 mm.

WEIGHT — 319 lbs.

DOUBLE LEADING FRONT BRAKE

FUN PEOPLE Go KAWASAKi

Figure G12 - Here is a flashback from the past. Before Kawasaki *Let the Good Times Roll*, the slogan was *Fun People Go Kawasaki*. This is the back page of the first Samurai 250 brochure released in 1967.

Kawasaki 1967 Chart

Model	Name	Type	HP	Seat	Exhaust	Wt.	Starter
M10	Road	51cc Single	4.5	Dual	Down	NA	Kick
M11	Road	52cc Single	4.5	Solo	Down	NA	Kick
J1	Road	85cc Single	7.5	Solo	Down	NA	Kick
J1D	Road	85cc Single	7.5	Solo	Down	NA	Electric
J1L	Deluxe	85cc Single	7.5	Dual	Upswept	NA	Kick
J1T	Touring	85cc Single	7.8	Dual	Upswept	NA	Kick
J1TL	Touring	85cc Single	7.8	Dual	Upswept	NA	Kick
J1TR	Trail	85cc Single	8	3/4	Upswept	NA	Kick
J1TRL	Trail	85cc Single	8	3/4	Upswept	NA	Kick
G1	Street	90cc Single	8.2	Dual	Down	NA	Kick
G1L	Street	90cc Single	8.2	Dual	Down	NA	Kick
G1DL	Street	90cc Single	8.2	Dual	Down	NA	Electric
G1TRL	Street	90cc Single	8.2	Dual	Down	NA	Kick
G1M	Motocross	90cc Single	16	3/4	Upswept	NA	Kick
D1	Street	99cc Single	10	Dual	Upswept	174	Kick
C1	Street	115cc S.	10	Dual	Down	NA	Kick
C1D	Street	115cc S.	10	Dual	Down	NA	Electric
C1L	Street	115cc S.	10	Dual	Down	NA	Kick
C1DL	Street	115cc S.	10	Dual	Down	NA	Electric
C2SS	Road Runner	115cc S.	11.5	Dual	Upswept	179	Kick
C2TR	Road Runner	115cc S.	11.5	3/4	Upswept	187	Kick
B1T	Touring	125cc S.	12	Dual	Upswept	NA	NA
B1TL	Touring	125cc S.	12	Dual	Upswept	NA	NA
F2	Street	169cc S.	18	Dual	Down	NA	Kick
F2TR	175 Trail	169cc S.	18	Solo	Upswept	273	Electric
F21M	Scrambler	238cc S.	28	3/4	Upswept	218	Kick
SG	Street	250cc S.	18	Solo	Down	NA	Electric
A1	Samurai	247cc Twin	31	Dual	Down	319	Kick
A1SS	Samurai SS	247cc Twin	31	Dual	Upswept	331	Kick
A1-R	Road Racer	247cc Twin	43	Racing	Down	255	Push
A7	Avenger	338cc Twin	42	Dual	Down	329	Kick
A7SS	Avenger SS	338cc Twin	42	Dual	Upswept	329	Kick
W1	Commander	624cc Twin	50	Dual	Down	398	Kick

Kawasaki 1967 Notes: This was the first banner year for Kawasaki. The company would introduce several advancements on its newest models, from twin cylinders to five-speed, return-shift transmissions and tubular frames. Ultimate performance was in and electric starters, rotary shifters, and pressed steel frames, while not yet gone, were clearly on their way out. Even the extensive June 1967 test in *Cycle* does not state if the A1-R has a kick starter or not, but it appears in photos to be push-start only. All weights are listed in pounds. Prices for the 1967 models included $695 for the Samurai, $725 for the Samurai SS, $750 for the F21M Scrambler, and a whopping $1300 for the A1-R Road Racer. All claimed dry weights are listed in pounds. S = Single.

Figure G13 - Blue 1967 Kawasaki Avenger. The Avenger was top banana at the drag strip for the 350 class when it was introduced in 1967. The rotary valve two-stroke was a wee bit overstressed in the pursuit of ultimate performance. Finding one today in excellent condition is a rare happenstance. Good 250 Samurai models are probably more numerous and a little more reliable. Both rotary models would be overshadowed in two years by a piston-port triple. ©1967 Kawasaki Motors Corporation, U.S.A.

Kawasaki 1968 Chart

Model	Name	Type	HP	Seat	Exhaust	Wt.	Price
M10	Road	50cc S.	4.5	Dual	Down	NA	NA
M11	Road	52cc S.	4.5	Solo	Down	NA	NA
J1	Road	85cc S.	7.5	Solo	Down	NA	NA

J1D	Road Electric	85cc S.	7.5	Solo	Down	NA	NA
J1L	Road	85cc S.	7.5	Solo	Down	NA	NA
J1TR	Trail	85cc S.	8	Solo	Upswept	NA	NA
G1	Street	90cc S.	8.2	Dual	Down	NA	NA
G1L	Street	90cc S.	8.2	Dual	Down	NA	Kick
G1DL	Street	90cc S.	8.2	Dual	Down	NA	Electric
G1TRL	Street	90cc S.	8.2	Dual	Down	NA	Kick
G1M	Motocross	90cc S.	16	3/4	Upswept	NA	NA
G31M	Centurion	99cc S.	18.5	3/4	Upswept	178	NA
D1	Street	99cc S.	10	Dual	Upswept	174	NA
C2SS	Road Runner	115cc S.	11.5	Dual	Upswept	179	$419
C2TR	Road Runner	115cc S.	11.5	3/4	Upswept	187	$419
B1T	Touring	125cc S.	12	Dual	Upswept	NA	NA
B1TL	Touring	125cc S.	12	Dual	Upswept	NA	NA
F2	Street	169cc S.	18	Dual	Down	250	$453
F2TR	Trail	169cc S.	18	Solo	Upswept	274	$517
F3	Bushwhacker	169cc S.	20	Dual	Upswept	247	$565
F21M	Scrambler	238cc S.	28	3/4	Upswept	230	$870
F81M	Green Streak	246cc S.	34	3/4	Upswept	238	NA
SG	Street	250cc S.	18	Solo	Down	NA	NA
A1	Samurai	247cc T.	31	Dual	Down	319	$695
A1SS	Samurai SS	247cc T.	31	Dual	Upswept	319	$725
A1-R	Road Racer	247cc T.	43	Racing	Down	240	$1300
A7	Avenger	338cc T.	42	Dual	Down	329	$785
A7SS	Avenger SS	338cc T.	42	Dual	Upswept	319	$845
W1	Commander	624cc T.	50	Dual	Down	398	$1195
W1SS	Commander	624cc T.	50	Dual	Down	396	$1193
W2SS	Commander	624cc T.	53	Dual	Down	430	$1295

Kawasaki 1968 Notes: The J1D & SG had electric and kick starters. All other models were kick start only, with the exception of the push-start A1-R. All claimed dry weights are listed in pounds. S = Single / T = Twin.

Figure G14 - Here is yet another W2SS, this one of uncertain model year and shown at the Barber Museum in Alabama. You can clearly see the shorter front fender and double downtube frame from this angle. Note the chrome covers on the rear shocks and the addition of turn signals on this example. Image by Chuck Schultz, photographer, under Creative Commons license.

Figure G15 - 1968 Kawasaki C2 SS Road Runner. ©1968 Kawasaki Motors Corporation, U.S.A.

Kawasaki G3-TR Bushmaster

90 MODEL **G3TR**

ONLY TRAILSTER IN 90cc WITH BIGGER-BIKE FEEL

The peppy 90 G3 in trail trim takes the backwoods country like a bigger trail bike. Unrivalled in maneuverability because of its greedy stamina, sports-design double cradle tube frame, and five-speed gearbox with return shift. High-rise muffler with spark arrestor for rough off-the-road riding. Sprocket kit optional for converting gearing to climbing steep 32 degree inclines in wild terrain — a feat never possible with other machines of the same displacement. All parts aircraft-engineered for precision power.

Both G3TR and G3SS incorporate these bigger-bike super-sports features made possible by fine aircraft engineering.

- Amazing performance turned out by two-stroke rotary valve single
- Dashing acceleration SS 1/8 in 11.5 sec.
- Superbly maneuverable five-speed gearbox with return shift
- Easy-to-start primary kick requiring only a light depression
- Extra sturdy construction yet only 170 lbs in weight

Figure G16 - 1969 Kawasaki G3-TR Bushmaster 90. ©1969 Kawasaki Motors Corporation, U.S.A.

The company that built some of the Japanese ships and planes of World War II entered the motorcycle market a few years later than the rest of the Big Four brands. Everything about their machines can be traced back to this fact. Since Kawasaki entered the U.S. market more than five years later than Honda, the company arrived on these shores long after the 50cc tiddler boom had begun to mature. Their first motorcycle was sold in the U.S. as an Omega, not a Kawasaki, and it was a 125. Although Kawasaki has built a number of machines in the 50-85cc range, most of the product exported to America has been of the 90cc and up variety.

Most Kaws have tube frames and all have telescopic forks. They rolled right past the era of leading link front suspension, and only a few of the smaller models brought to the U.S. in 1966 had pressed-steel frames. After the Omega 125, the company sent over a series of smaller machines for a brief period, and then a 120cc range, but the 250cc Samurai of 1967 was the first model the company really promoted. It's big brother, the 350cc Avenger, was the fastest street 350 in motorcycle history at that time. Certainly most of you know that Kawasaki built a Japanese copy of the 650 BSA and imported it almost from the very beginning into the U.S., but this was a design purchased, not created, by the company. Kawasaki did participate in the trail riding boom, producing a number of models and displacements of enduro and motocross persuasion, with the 350 Big Horn being the largest. The motocross Kaws were rarely particularly competitive and the enduro models were generally a bit heavy and full-featured. The engines produced a lot of power and some of the suspension systems were very adjustable to the rider's preferences. Although the current Ninja 250 is probably the closest thing to a Bultaco Metralla or Ducati Diana being manufactured today and this model is covered in the final chapter of this book. I personally loved the Mach III from the first time I saw one in a magazine. I owned a 1971 model (the blue one) for 17 years, so I must have liked it. It was the last model before the company prescribed a muscle relaxer. In case you didn't know, the 1972 versions (the orange ones that came with either a disc front brake or CDI) were slightly detuned from the highly strung level of the '69-71's.

Some years prior to my purchase of the Kawasaki legend, I had a 1969 G3-TR Bushmaster for a trail bike. This machine compared quite favorably with other small trail machines of its era, as described in the story in Chapter 1. For the abominably horrific out-the-door price of $340, it included a cradle tube frame, aluminum alloy fenders, telescopic forks, a speedometer separate from the headlamp, chrome rear shocks, and many other little details that made it the bargain of the day. Yes, the front shocks should have been dampened in both directions and the rear springs were too stiff, but what do you expect for $340? That was one sweet little tiddler! I owned the Bushmaster only nine months before I sold it and bought a blue 1970 Honda CL-350. My little '69 G3 was red, and I've never been a *red* kind of guy. The only reason the tiddler I've owned for thirty-five years is red is because that specific model of that particular year came only in red. The Yamaha AT-1 is described in that same article with the G3-TR earlier in the book.

James Rozee Speaks: "My first bike I restored was a 1962 Kawasaki B-8. They were piston-port singles and were sold as Omegas and Kawasakis. I worked for Joe Dobbins Kawasaki in Portland OR back in the 70's and we would get these weird bikes in trade all the time. Kawasaki made motors for motorcycles in Japan before making their own whole bike. The 650 BSA copy was really a Meguro. Kawasaki bought them out so they could have a large four-stroke to compete with the other companies. Many early Fifties Japanese bikes copied the Brits and the Germans. Kawasakis were always fast. When I worked for them I got to ride many models. The Z-1R scared me to death, and then they put a turbo on it! I have owned a 500 and 750 triple and they were just too crazy for me. I like the small stuff best. Our shop sponsored MX racers aboard the 238 Green Streaks, the first Kawasaki to be panted green."

Kawasaki 1969 Chart

Model	Name	Type	HP	Seat	Exhaust	Wt.	Price
M10	Street	50cc Single	4.5	Dual	Down	NA	NA
M11	Street	52cc Single	4.5	Solo	Down	NA	NA
G1	Street	90cc Single	8.2	Dual	Down	NA	NA
G1L	Street	90cc Single	8.2	Dual	Down	NA	Kick
G1DL	Street	90cc Single	8.2	Dual	Down	NA	NA
G1TRL	Street	90cc Single	8.2	Dual	Down	NA	NA

GA1	Street	90cc Single	10.5	Dual	Down	NA	NA
GA2	Street	90cc Single	10.5	Dual	Down	NA	NA
G3SS	Bushmaster	89cc Single	10.5	Dual	Down	170	$305
G3TR	Bushmaster	89cc Single	10.5	Dual	Upswept	175	$345
C2SS	Roadrunner	115cc Single	11.5	Dual	Upswept	185	$405
C2TR	Trail	115cc Single	11.5	Solo	Upswept	193	$445
B1T	Touring	125cc Single	12	Dual	Upswept	NA	NA
B1TL	Touring	125cc Single	12	Dual	Upswept	NA	NA
F2	Street	169cc Single	18	Dual	Down	250	$453
F3	Bushwhacker	169cc Single	20	Dual	Upswept	245	$595
F4	Sidewinder	238cc Single	23	Dual	Upswept	248	$705
F21M	Green Streak	238cc Single	30	Solo	Upswept	215	$877
SG	Street	250cc Single	18	Solo	Down	NA	NA
A1	Samurai	247cc Twin	31	Dual	Down	319	$708
A1SS	Samurai SS	247cc Twin	31	Dual	Upswept	317	NA
A7	Avenger	338cc Twin	42	Dual	Down	330	$804
A7SS	Avenger SS	338cc Twin	42	Dual	Upswept	329	$825
H1	Mach III	498cc Triple	60	Dual	Down	395	$999
H1R	Road Racer	498cc Triple	80	Racing	Down	NA	NA
W1SS	Commander	624cc Twin	50	Dual	Down	398	$1213
W2SS	Commander	624cc Twin	53	Dual	Down	398	$1295
W2TT	Commander	624cc Twin	53	Dual	Upswept	398	$1325

Kawasaki 1969 Notes: All 1969 models except the electric-start G1DL & SG were kickstart only. All claimed dry weights are listed in pounds. The Mach III and Avenger had Injectolube oil injection; all other models with oil injection had Superlube.

Figure G17 - 1968 Kawasaki C2 TR. ©1968 Kawasaki Motors Corporation, U.S.A.

Kawasaki 1970 Chart

Model	Name	Type	HP	Seat	Exhaust	Wt.	Price
GA1	Street	90cc S.	10.5	Dual	Down	NA	NA
GA2	Street	90cc S.	10.5	Dual	Down	NA	NA
G3SS	Bushmaster	89cc S.	10.5	Dual	Down	170	$299
G3TR	Bushmaster	89cc S.	10.5	Dual	Upswept	175	$339
G4TR	Trail Boss	99cc S.	11.5	3/4	Upswept	185	$470
G31M	Centurion	99cc S.	18.5	3/4	Upswept	178	$499
F3	Bushwhacker	169cc S.	20	3/4	Upswept	245	$585
F4	Sidewinder	238cc S.	23	Dual	Upswept	248	$695
F21M	Green Streak	238cc S.	30	3/4	Upswept	215	$845
F5	Big Horn	346cc S.	33	3/4	Upswept	265	$873
A1A	Samurai	247cc T.	31	Dual	Down	319	$696
A1SSA	Samurai SS	247cc T.	31	Dual	Upswept	319	$713
A7A	Avenger	338cc T.	42	Dual	Down	329	$792
A7SSA	Avenger SS	338cc T.	42	Dual	Upswept	329	$814
H1	Mach III	498cc TR.	60	Dual	Down	395	$995
H1R	Road Racer	498cc TR.	80	Racing	Down	NA	NA
W1SS	Commander	624cc T.	50	Dual	Down	398	$1213
W2SS	Commander	624cc T.	53	Dual	Down	398	$1295

Kawasaki 1970 Notes: All 1970 models were kickstart only. The F3 Bushwhacker apparently got a 3/4 seat and return shifter in 1970. Mach III sales for the year were approximately 24,000, according to the *Sport Book*. All claimed dry weights are listed in pounds. S = Single / T = Twin / TR = Triple.

Figure G18 - Early 1967 Kawasaki Commander W1 650. ©1967 Kawasaki Motors Corporation, U.S.A.

Figure G19 - 1967 Kawasaki Samurai first year brochure. ©1967 Kawasaki Motors Corporation, U.S.A.

Kawasaki 1971 Chart

Model	Name	Type	HP	Seat	Exhaust	Wt.	Price
MT1	Dynamite	73cc Single	4.2	Solo	Upswept	121	$299
MB1A	Coyote	132cc Single	5	Solo	Upswept	93	$189
GA1/2A	Street	90cc Single	10.5	Dual	Down	NA	NA
G3SS	Bushmaster	89cc Single	10.5	Dual	Down	170	$335
G3TRA	Bushmaster	99cc Single	11.5	Dual	Upswept	182	$376
G4TRA	Trail Boss	99cc Single	11.5	3/4	Upswept	185	$475
G31M	Centurion	99cc Single	18.5	3/4	Upswept	178	$495
125E	Enduro	125cc Single	17.5	3/4	Upswept	231	$535
175E	Enduro	174cc Single	21.5	3/4	Upswept	233	$635
F8	Bison	247cc Single	23.5	3/4	Upswept	271	$785
F81M	Competition	247cc Single	34	3/4	Upswept	NA	NA
F5A	Big Horn	346 Single	33	3/4	Upswept	265	$885
A1B	Samurai	247cc Twin	31	Dual	Down	319	$695
A1SSB	Samurai SS	247cc Twin	31	Dual	Upswept	319	$715
A7B	Avenger	338cc Twin	42	Dual	Down	329	$795
A7SSB	Avenger SS	338cc Twin	42	Dual	Upswept	329	$815
H1A	Mach III	498cc Triple	60	Dual	Down	382	$1025
H1R	Road Racer	498cc Triple	80	Racing	Down	NA	NA
W1SS	Commander	624cc Twin	50	Dual	Down	398	$1213

Kawasaki 1971 Notes: All 1971 models were kickstart only. The Dynamite and Coyote are mini-bikes. The Dynamite was a Lime Green copycat of the Honda Mini-Trail with a three-speed transmission, automatic clutch, and eight-inch wheels. All claimed dry weights are listed in pounds. The wet weight of the Mach III was 417 pounds. The Trail Boss had a dual five-speed transmission with a high and low range.

Kawasaki 1972 Chart

Model	Name	Type	HP	Seat	Exhaust	Wt.	Price
MT1A	Dynamite	73cc Single	4.2	Solo	Upswept	121	$299
GA1/2A	Street	90cc Single	10.5	Dual	Down	NA	NA
G3SS	Bushmaster	90cc Single	10.5	Dual	Down	170	$377
GA5A	Enduro	100cc S.	11.5	3/4	Upswept	195	$399
G4TRB	Trail Boss	100cc S.	11.5	3/4	Upswept	185	$541
G5	Enduro	100cc S.	11.5	3/4	Upswept	191	$476
F6A	Enduro	124cc S.	17.5	3/4	Upswept	231	$596
F7A	Enduro	174cc S.	21.5	3/4	Upswept	233	$701
F8A	Bison	247cc S.	24.5	3/4	Upswept	270	$865
F81M	Motocross	247cc S.	34	3/4	Upswept	NA	NA
F9	Big Horn	346cc S.	28	3/4	Upswept	265	$984
S1	Mach I	250cc TR.	28	Dual	Down	326	NA
S2	Mach II	346cc TR.	44	Dual	Down	320	$893
H1B	Mach III	498cc TR.	60	Dual	Down	382	$1147
H2	Mach IV	748cc TR.	72	Dual	Down	422	$1406

Kawasaki 1972 Notes: All 1972 models were kickstart only. All claimed dry weights are listed in pounds. The 1972 H1B was unique in that it was offered in two versions: one with a chrome front fender, CDI, and drum brake as the previous year model, and a second version with a disc front brake, painted front fender, and traditional ignition system. S = Single / TR = Triple.

Figure G20 - 1971 Kawasaki F81M 250 Motocross. ©1971 Kawasaki Motors Corporation, U.S.A.

Kawasaki 1973 Chart

Model	Name	Type	HP	Seat	Exhaust	Wt.	Price
MT-1A	Trail	73cc Single	4.2	Solo	Upswept	121	$299
MC-1	Enduro	89cc Single	6.6	3/4	Upswept	165	$385
GA1/2A	Street	90cc Single	10.5	Dual	Down	NA	NA
G3SS	Bushmaster	89cc Single	10.5	Dual	Down	178	$345
G7T	Street	99cc Single	11.5	Dual	Down	NA	NA
GA5A	Enduro	99cc Single	11.5	3/4	Upswept	195	$399
G4TRC	Trail Boss	99cc Single	11.5	Dual	Upswept	198	$499
F6B	Enduro	124cc S.	14.3	Dual	Upswept	231	$560
F7B	Enduro	174cc S.	16.5	Dual	Upswept	233	$663
F11	Enduro	247cc S.	22	Dual	Upswept	264	$855
F11M	Motocross	247cc S.	30	3/4	Upswept	207	NA
F9A	Big Horn	346cc S.	28	Dual	Upswept	279	$975
S1A	Mach I	249cc TR.	28	Dual	Down	330	$815
S2A	Mach II	346cc TR.	44	Dual	Down	335	$885
F12MX	Motocross	441cc S.	38	3/4	Down Up	215	NA
H1D	Mach III	498cc TR.	59	Dual	Down	407	$1135
H2A	Mach IV	748cc TR.	71	Dual	Down	422	$1395
Z1	Street	903cc Four	82	Dual	Down	542	$1895

350S-350T AVENGER

(Models A7 and A7SS)

- SS quarter mile in 13.8 sec
- Unique twin-cylinder rotary disc valve engine
- 42 horsepower with 28.9 ft-lbs of torque
- 5-speed transmission
- CDI (capacitor discharge ignition)
- Hi pipe on 350T, low pipe on 350S
- WARRANTY: 12 months/12,000 miles

Figure G21 - 1971 Kawasaki Avenger A7SS. This is the later styling of the Avenger, as well as that of the Samurai of the same period. The most noticeable differences are the slim white tank with laser decals and the flat black upswept exhaust pipes. The downswept pipes on the 1971 A1 and A7 were still chrome, as on the earlier models. ©1971 Kawasaki Motors Corporation, U.S.A.

Kawasaki 1973 Notes: The Z1 four-stroke inline four-cylinder had electric and kick starters. All other models were kick start only. The MT-1 Trail is a mini-bike. The F11M had a Lime Green plastic tank, black-painted chrome molybdenum frame and black fenders. The Z-1 was the first Kaw in several years to have an electric starter. It was also the first all-new four-stroke Kawasaki engine design in the company's history. (Remember that the SG and W1 were originally designed by Meguro.) All claimed dry weights are listed in pounds. The stated weight for the Z-1 is wet. S = Single / TR = Triple.

Kawasaki 1974 Chart

Model	Name	Type	HP	Seat	Exhaust	Wt.	Price
MT-1B	Trail	73cc S.	4.2	Solo	Upswept	121	$325
MC-1A	Enduro	89cc S.	6.6	3/4	Upswept	165	$385
MC-1M	Motocross	89cc S.	6.6	3/4	Upswept	150	$299
GA1/2A	Street	90cc S.	10.5	Dual	Down	NA	NA
G2S/T	Street	90cc S.	10	Dual	Down	NA	NA
G3SS	Bushmaster	89cc S.	10.5	Dual	Down	178	$395
G7T	Street	100cc S.	11.5	Dual	Down	NA	NA
G-5 100	Trail	99cc S.	11.5	3/4	Upswept	195	$479
G4TRD	Trail Boss	99cc S.	11.5	3/4	Upswept	198	$540
KS125	Enduro	124cc S.	15	3/4	Upswept	230	$669
KX125	Motocross	124cc S.	22	3/4	Upswept	201	$840
F7C	Enduro	174cc S.	16.5	3/4	Upswept	233	$729
F11A	Enduro	247cc S.	22	3/4	Upswept	264	$939
KX250	Motocross	250cc S.	34	3/4	Down	207	$1150
S1B	Mach I	250 TR.	28	Dual	Down	330	$890
F9B	Big Horn	346cc S.	28	3/4	Upswept	279	$1030
S3	Mach II	400 TR.	44	Dual	Down	335	$975
KZ400D	Street	398cc T.	35	Dual	Down	393	$995
KX450	Motocross	441cc S.	38	3/4	Down Up	215	$1350
H1E	Mach III	498 TR.	59	Dual	Down	407	$1349
H2B	Mach IV	748 TR.	71	Dual	Down	422	$1625
Z1A	Street	903cc Four	82	Dual	Down	542	$2075

Kawasaki 1974 Notes: The MT-1, MC-1A, and MC-1M are mini-bikes. The F11 had body-colored fenders. The Lime Green KX-250 had Ivory fenders, 21/18-inch aluminum rims, CDI, and a molybdenum frame. The KZ-400 & Z-1 had electric starters. All claimed dry weights are listed in pounds. S = Single / T = Twin / TR = Triple.

100E TRAIL BOSS (Model G4TR)

- 10-speed transmission
- Rotary disc valve engine
- 40-degree climbing ability
- 66 mph top speed
- 5-way adjustable rear suspension
- WARRANTY: 12 months/12,000 miles

Figure G22 - 1971 Kawasaki Trail Boss 100. Note the dual five-speed transmission and knobby tires that were hallmarks of the Trail Boss. ©1971 Kawasaki Motors Corporation, U.S.A.

Figure G23 - 1974 Kawasaki 175 Enduro. The F7 was the company's conventional mid-size enduro model and one of its better sellers in the enduro market. ©1974 Kawasaki Motors Corporation, U.S.A.

Figure G24 - 1973 Kawasaki 900 Z1. The first-year brown and orange Z1 was released in late 1972. You could say that The Tiddler Invasion ended with the release of the 1965 Honda 450 or the Kawasaki Mach III or Honda 750 Four in 1969, but this DOHC hot-rod that handled a lot better than its wet weight would indicate certainly buried the small Japanese motorcycle market once and for all. ©1972 Kawasaki Motors Corporation, U.S.A.

Figure G25 - Kawasaki has always had a sense of humor, as this 1972 F7 brochure attests. ©1972 Kawasaki Motors Corporation, U.S.A.

Kawasaki 1975 Chart

Model	Name	Type	HP	Seat	Exhaust	Wt.	Price
MT-1C	Mini	73cc Single	4.2	Solo	Upswept	121	$407
MC-1	Enduro	90cc Single	6.6	3/4	Upswept	168	$499
MC-1MA	Motocross	90cc Single	6.6	3/4	Upswept	150	$459
G2T	Street	90cc Single	10	Dual	Down	NA	NA
G3SSE	Street	99cc Single	10.5	Dual	Down	183	$539
G4TRE	Trail	99cc Single	11	3/4	Upswept	209	$663
G5C	Enduro	99cc Single	11	3/4	Upswept	195	$549
KS125A	Enduro	124cc Single	13	3/4	Upswept	214	$749
KX125A	Motocross	124cc Single	22	3/4	Down Up	178	$890
KD175A1	Enduro	174cc Single	18	3/4	Upswept	239	$849
KH250B1	Mach I	249cc Triple	28	Dual	Down	339	$1018
250 F-11	Enduro	247cc Single	22	3/4	Upswept	264	$1089
KT250	Trials	250cc Single	17	Solo	Upswept	198	$1185
KX250A3	Motocross	250cc Single	34	3/4	Down	212	$1216
350 F-9C	Enduro	346cc Single	28	3/4	Upswept	279	$1164
KX-400	Motocross	401cc Single	42	3/4	Down Up	234	NA
KH400A3	Mach II	400cc Triple	42	Dual	Down	353	$1197
KZ400S	Street	398cc Twin	35	Dual	Down	380	$995
KZ400D	Street	398cc Twin	35	Dual	Down	385	$1219
KH500A	Mach III	498cc Triple	59	Dual	Down	407	$1519
750 H-2C	Mach IV	748cc Triple	71	Dual	Down	422	$1700
Z-1B	Street	903cc Four	82	Dual	Down	542	$2475

Kawasaki 1975 Notes: The MT-1 is a mini-bike. The MC-1 and MC-1M are mini machines. The KD175 came in Candytone Green or Brown with silver painted fenders. The F11 had silver fenders. The KZ400D and Z1B have electric starters. The KZ400S was a new economy model with a drum front brake and kick starter. All claimed dry weights are listed in pounds.

I've always wanted to just take off and keep going.

But for most of my life I resisted the temptation. Instead I settled into a nice groove that finally became a rut. Then one day I went out and bought a motor-cycle. Just went out and bought it. Rather than work my way up I started at the top with a Kawasaki Z-1 900. I'd heard so much about it. I couldn't see buying anything else.

One night a couple of weeks ago, I hopped on the Z-1 to run into town for some cigarettes. Between the feeling of the warm night air rushing by and that four stroke engine quietly throbbing, I just didn't want to stop. So I didn't. It was morning before I stopped for those cigarettes. And I was in St. Louis before I called back to New Jersey to let them know I was taken some vacation time. Now, me and the Z are here in California. It's a beautiful state. So were Wyoming and Oregon. I guess that one of these days I'll have to send home for some clean clothes.

Figure G26 - 1975 Kawasaki Z1 brochure. ©1975 Kawasaki Motors Corporation, U.S.A.

Figure G27 - This small 1971 brochure photo of the blue Mach III shows off the line's new laser decals.
©1971 Kawasaki Motors Corporation, U.S.A.

Kawasaki Triples Charts

Kawasaki Mach I 250 (249cc) Chart

Year	Model	Color	Trim	Wt.	Price
1972	S1	Pearl Ivory Pearl Candytone Red	Curved Stripes	330	$815
1973	S1A	Candytone Orange, Blue or Gold	Straight Stripes	330	$815
1974	S1B	Candytone Green	Rounded Decal	330	$890
1975	S1C	Halibut Blue	Pointed Decal	339	$1018

Kawasaki 250 Notes: All Mach I's had 28 horsepower, five-speed transmissions and drum brakes. All claimed dry weights are listed in pounds. The 250 is the only displacement of the Kawasaki Triples that was not at the top of its class in overall performance. My best guess is that the law of diminishing returns kicked in as the company decreased displacement without decreasing complexity or significant weight. The natural low-end torque of a competitive twin was probably a factor, too. The Mach I was competing with very experienced models in the art of performance, mainly the Yamahas. This lack of a performance edge is most likely the reason the Mach I has never been as popular in the collector marketplace as its larger brothers.

Figure G28 - 1973 Kawasaki S-1 250 Triple in Candytone Orange.

©1973 Kawasaki Motors Corporation, U.S.A.

309

Kawasaki Mach II 350 (346cc) Chart

Year	Model	Color	Trim	Brake	HP	Wt.	Price
1972	S2	Pearl Candytone Red Pearl Ivory	Curved Stripes	Drum	45	320	$893
1973	S2A	Candytone Blue, Orange or Gold	Straight Stripes	Disc	44	335	$885

Kawasaki 350 Notes: All Mach II's had five-speed transmissions. The earliest 350 Triples were wildly fast, and somewhat uncontrollable with their chassis shorter than that of the 500 models. The '73 models were mellowed somewhat before the model was replaced by the 400 in 1974. All claimed dry weights are listed in pounds.

Kawasaki 350 S2 Mach II

Figure G29 - 1973 Kawasaki S-2 350 Mach II in Candytone Blue. Note the front disc brake that easily distinguishes the S-2 from its little brother 250. Although similar in size, the 350 was a lot faster than the 250 S-1. ©1973 Kawasaki Motors Corporation, U.S.A.

This may be the fastest super-tiddler (by modern standards) of all time, at least in a straight line. Here is a brief history to refresh your memory of the good old days of two-stroke screamers with drum front brakes. Kawasaki was late to the party in the USA in the mid-

'60's, but the company did not waste much time trying to lasso the ultimate high performance crown and keep it away from its competitors. Honda built wonderfully reliable, but heavy, four-strokes, Suzuki built models with a lot of style and flash for the money, and Yamaha built the best handlers. This left Kaw in control of the whole corral of straight-line acceleration kings.

The performance image began with the 250 Samurai and 350 Avenger twins, accelerated like a banshee with the H-1/Blue Streak/Mach III in '69, and blew everybody in the weeds with its H-2 in 1972, before double-overhead-camming Honda into the pavement with its Z-1 the following year. The first Mach III's were supposed to have been called Blue Streaks, but I think the name was changed to the more aggressive moniker for the U. S. market at the last minute. We all know how the white-with-blue-stripes model morphed into the unusual metallic charcoal color before becoming red with white stripes. The last Mach III of the original specifications was sold in '71 in blue with laser stripes on the tank and side covers.

Nineteen-seventy-two brought a number of changes to the Kaw corral. The big news, of course, was the 750 H-2 with its blisteringly blue speed. The company began to monkey with the H-1, giving it a yucky orange color and a choice of CDI and drum front brake or points and a new disc front stopper, either offered at the same price. Kawasaki introduced the new little brother S2 that same year. Except for the overly complex, heavy, and pokey (for a Kaw Triple) S1 250, the 350 S2 is and was probably the most ignored of all the legendary Triples. The S2 was built only a couple of years before being updated and replaced with the smoother (and more boring) KH400, which surprisingly stayed in the line for several years and sold quite well.

I have always been a fan of the Kaw Triples, and I owned a '71 H-1 for nearly twenty years. This friend of mine who I was associated with in the early Seventies could tell you some good stories about the 1972 S2. This guy was a hobby racer and employed as a mechanic at a Honda/Kawasaki dealership back in '72. He bought the first S2 as soon as it hit the dealership, and he claimed it was actually faster than the H-1, which I always doubted just a bit. He was particularly impressed with the ridiculous degree of wheelie-bility the S2 had. I suspect that was due to its 52-inch wheelbase in relation to the H-1's 55. He did not own that S2 for very long. He tended to crash it repeatedly in a very short space of time. In case you are wondering why I never met him on a drag strip, either officially or unofficially, it was because I did not purchase my H-1 until several years later as a used model. I was still in love with my CL-350 at the time, but that's another story. Anyway, my buddy eventually gave up the straight-line speed demon for the better handling qualities of a Yamaha RD-350. He went on to race Yamaha 350's in endurance competition for many years after that. The very last time I saw him was when he came to Texas to uphold his title as the #1 national 350-class endurance racer.

Kawasaki S3 400 (398cc) Chart

Year	Model	Color	Trim	Brake	HP	Wt.	Price
1974	S3	Candy Red Candy Blue	Rounded Decal	Disc	44	335	$975
1975	S3A	Candy Green Candy Super Red	Pointed Decal	Disc	42	353	$1197

Kawasaki 400 Notes: All S3 400's had five-speed transmissions. All claimed dry weights are listed in pounds, however the stated weight for the 1975 model may be wet.

Figure G30 - 1974 Kawasaki S3 400 Triple in Candy Blue. The S-3 400 replaced the short-lived S-2 350 in the lineup and continued as the KH400. After the explosive debuts of the Mach III in 1969 and the 350 and 750 in 1972, Kawasaki carefully developed the 1974 400 as a more refined and sophisticated mount, albeit at the expense of the ultimate performance of the earlier Triples. The 400 was dimensionally similar to the 500 and larger than the 250 and 350. A longer wheelbase and somewhat mellower engine helped keep the front wheel on the ground. The S-3 and KH400 were very successful models on the sales floor up until the inevitable demise of two-stroke street bikes in the U.S.

©1974 Kawasaki Motors Corporation, U.S.A.

Kawasaki Mach III 500 (498cc) Chart

Figure G31 - Late 1970 Candy Red Kawasaki Mach III. ©1970 Kawasaki Motors Corporation, U.S.A.

Year	Model	Color	Trim	Brake	HP	Wt.	Price
1969	H1	Midnight White	Blue Stripe	Drum	60	395	$999
1970	H1	Peacock Gray	Black Stripe	Drum	60	395	$995
1970	H1	Candy Red	White Stripe	Drum	60	395	$995
1971	H1A	Candy Blue	Laser Decals	Drum	60	382	$1025
1972	H1B	Pearl Candy Orange	Curved Stripes	Disc	60	382	$1147
1972	H1C	Pearl Candy Orange	Curved Stripes	Drum	60	382	$1147
1973	H1D	Candy Lime	Black Letters	Disc	59	407	$1135
1974	H1E	Candy Green Candy Red	Rounded Decal	Disc	59	407	$1349
1975	H1F	Sky Blue Green Candy Yellow	Pointed Decal	Disc	59	407	$1519

Kawasaki 500 Notes: All Mach III's had five-speed transmissions. The *Kawasaki ID Guide* lists the late-69/early-70 Charcoal Mach III officially as a 1969 model. The official 1969 colors are listed as Midnight White and Peacock Gray. The 1969-71 models all had the new Capacitive Discharge Ignition and chrome front fenders. Buyers were offered a choice in 1972 only of the same CDI and drum front brake or a model in the same color with a disc brake, a traditional ignition system, and a body-colored (orange) front fender. The reason was that some earlier owners experienced fouling problems with the new-type surface gap spark plugs designed to be used with the new CDI. The price was the same for either model. All later models had a redesigned CDI system, an improved version built for the H2, and a very trim front chrome fender without side braces. All claimed dry weights are listed in pounds.

Figure G32 - Early 1970 Peacock Gray Kawasaki Mach III. ©1970 Kawasaki Motors Corporation, U.S.A.

314

Figure G33 - Late 1970 Candy Red Mach III in European trim. ©1970 Kawasaki Motors Corporation, U.S.A.

- the fastest 500 in the galaxy: 60 hp/382 pounds
- lift-off acceleration: 12.4 sec. ss 1/4 mile
- retrorocket disc brake

The machine you always knew you'd own someday.
Now better than ever.
The classic motorcycle that showed riders the outer limits of the possible.
The unsurpassed, brought to an even higher level of perfection for 1972.

Figure G34 - 1972 Kawasaki Mach III in Pearl Candy Orange. ©1972 Kawasaki Motors Corporation, U.S.A.

Kawasaki Mach IV 750 (748cc) Chart

Year	Model	Color	Trim	Front Fender	Price
1972	H2	Pearl Candytone Blue	Curved Stripes	Blue	$1406
1973	H2A	Candytone Gold or Candytone Purple	Straight Stripes	Chrome	$1395
1974	H2B	Candytone Gold or Candytone Lime	Rounded Decal	Chrome	$1625
1975	H2C	Candytone Purple or Candytone Super Red	Pointed Decal	Chrome	$1700

Kawasaki 750 Notes: All Mach IV's had 72 (or slightly less) horsepower, five-speed transmissions, disc front brakes, CDI ignition systems, and a claimed dry weight of 422 pounds. At least one online source states that the 1975 model was produced in Candytone Green instead of Candytone Purple. The colors listed in the charts are from the official *Kawasaki ID Guide*.

Figure G35 - 1972 Kawasaki 750 Mach IV in Pearl Candytone Blue. This first-year brochure shows off the distinctive stripe pattern for that year and the turn signals that would be on all the Kaw Triples beginning with the 1972 models. ©1972 Kawasaki Motors Corporation, U.S.A.

Figure G36 - 1972 Kawasaki H2 Left Side. ©Michael Kiernan, Classic Motorcycle Company, St. Louis, MO.

Figure G37 - A grasshopper's eye view of a beautiful blue 1972 Kawasaki H2. ©Michael Kiernan, Classic Motorcycle Company, St. Louis, MO.

Justifying the Mach III

Figure G38 - 1971 Candy Blue Mach III. This is the author's machine purchased for less than $700 in 1978. As you can see, it is not quite stock. The chrome pseudo-chambers are by Bill Wirges. The pipes and K&N air filters were on it when I bought it. The main effect they had was to raise the powerband upward a bit. You felt as if you had to lift your weight off the seat as you let out the clutch to get it moving, and it seemed to idle down the street at about 30 mph. It did not much like going between 0 and 30 mph. The open air filters made an overpowering racket when you whacked open the throttle. I don't think I ever actually heard the pipes in acceleration mode during the eighteen years I owned the machine. I forgot what brand the rear shocks with black exposed springs were, but I ditched the stock shocks soon after I rode the bike the first time. The handlebars were from a BMW R-90S. I never liked the lines of the stock Western bars with the upswept chambers. I even mounted the bars upside down briefly for a really low cafe racer feel, but then I returned them upright. This seemed to be a good compromise between upright comfort and the wind blast. There were two things I learned about the Mach III after long-term ownership. My bike always vibrated more than I liked and numerous searches for improvement failed. The relatively new 1971 Mach III I had ridden briefly in that year vibrated far less. I always assumed that wear on the engine and certain rubber parts caused this, or else my example just happened to think it was Long Dong Silver with three big batteries. The other thing I learned was that the tires were very sensitive to pavement irregularities. Original tires were Japanese Dunlops of a specific design. My machine had already had these replaced with Michelins when I got it. After years of wondering why the front wheel seemed to be so sensitive to ridges and bumps in the road, I replaced the Michelins with Kendas recommended by the BMW shop and the squiggly tire action ceased. By the way, the same BMW shop had years earlier installed a pair of Fiamm horns that would blast a Honda 50 clean off the road! ©1979 Floyd M. Orr

Nothing else sounds like it. Nothing else looks like it. Very little else goes like it, and those that did in 1969 were of much larger displacement. Its handling is infamous. Its noise is all its own. When it comes on the pipe, it yanks forward as if Bluto had just kicked you in the butt. You're so busy changing gears, watching your immediate environment, and just generally hanging on that you cannot even accurately observe that outrageous RPM you just touched or that correspondingly nerve shattering e.t. you just registered. You're on a 1971 Mach III which is mostly stock, except for the Bill Wirges chambers, the three exposed, K & N air filters, the Michelin tires, and the corduroy seat cover (to keep you at the front of the bus). The acceleration is nothing less than phenomenal. The power is astounding. The weight (according to Kawasaki) is 382 pounds. My name is Orr. I'm a professional driver. I spend most of my life in a 1979 Buick Regal with a super-quality stereo, 120 albums on tape at any given time, and a pitiful excuse for a motor. (Update; My 1980, '81, and '82 Regals have been blessed with that new darling of the GM Corporate Bullshitters, THE BUICK SIX, and I don't mean that pavement-ripper that Bob Dylan sang about back when cars were honest and used-car salesmen were not.) The Mach III retains my sanity.

Remember when the original Shelby Mustang was white with blue stripes? The original Trans-Ams were also white with blue stripes. And so were the original 1969 Mach III's. The 1971 blue Mach III's give away very little in appeal to the original, white, pedigreed ones. The tank is no longer sculpted, the stripes have morphed into the blue "laser" decals, and an early defect in the crankshaft has supposedly been displaced in the later models. The weight is still listed as 382, the horsepower is still listed as 60, and the 0-60 time is still road-tested at that downright exciting 4.0 seconds!

Getting down to the real erotica of the matter, and covering a few specifics of the machine in the process, we have a no-nonsense, stark, rabid, stand-up-and-git motorcycle. The shape is long and lanky like a thoroughbred, with a three-cylinder,
two-stroke quarter horse for power. The seat is entirely too slippery, especially If you polish it--as I did-- to bring the natural beauty out of... (that's another story). The seat is now covered in ribbed, black corduroy, which keeps the rider on the front seat without affecting the classic look of the machine. The bars are now the shorter, narrower ones from a BMW R-90S, cosmetically necessitated by the change to chrome Bill Wirges chambers, which are kicked up in the rear very handsomely, but destroyed the machine's coherent lines with the western bars. The new bars are mounted upside-down for that serious cafe look, which the machine adapts to very well. The low bars also cause a forward weight shift, which doesn't hurt a bit. The unsuspecting outside air is now crammed into the carbs through three separate, highly direct, K & N air filters. Aside from these points and the addition of Fiamm (read loud) horns, the bike is completely stock and original. The stock factory horn is a pathetic little squeaker that no one can hear past the intake roar.

When it is cold you might expect a thirty-kick affair to start the beast, which is not as bad as it sounds, when you consider you're just starting three little old 165cc motocrossers. The routine is: starting lever on, no throttle, take a deep breath, and run 'em through. When it's warm, just a kick or two will do it. When this cold-blooded engine fires up, you don't know what it is. It sounds like a four-stroke six-cylinder with a super-hot cam and a cold. Somehow I am at a loss for words to adequately describe it. You are also about to discover that, in addition to being extremely cold-blooded and having a high, 1800 RPM, idle, that the motorcycle has almost no torque at that idle speed. The beast has three speeds: "I don't want to", "Well maybe", and "OK, we're here!" Simultaneously, ease out the clutch and dial on the throttle until you see 3000 RPM on the tach, at which time the pipes with their light silencers will briefly growl at you and the scooter will move out abruptly. The 3000-

6000 RPM range can be used for all semi-respectable driving in the 40-70 mph speed range. The motorcycle is not at all happy with any speed below 40 mph -- it becomes a chore for both of you. I doubt that there are any more than a few cars on the streets these days that could catch you even below 6000 rpm.

At 6000 rpm it is time for an all new paragraph. If everything serviceable is in proper shape, particularly the air filters, as soon as you hit 6000 rpm the tach leaps somewhere past 9000! This is when you learn what the word concentration really means. All within a fraction of a second, you hear many voices: "Drop that tach needle!" "I hope I haven't damaged the engine." "Grab the brakes?" "Scoot forward." and "Hang on!" (All are spoken with new meaning). The 40-80 mph passing speed is astonishing. Just pull up beside a grandma holding up traffic, drop two gears and gas it. The miscellaneous thrashing noises of the engine turn into a combination of the loudest air cleaner snort you have ever heard and the shriek of some very strange exhaust pipes. Road tested at 0-60 in 4.0 seconds, a time shared with Fonebone's Roller coaster down the first hill, the Mach III's acceleration below 90-mph is in very exotic territory. You can go this fast on several other machines and in a few cars, but the cost in both dollars and general engineering exotica is enormous. *High-tech* and *vintage* bring big bucks these days, especially if the machine is particularly fast.

The old rat would not be so endearing if I were not so painfully aware how motorcycles have become so boringly similar in recent years. Probably the current average weight superbike is 525 pounds, and the displacement 1000cc. There is something to be said for a nimble, truly reasonably-priced and sized motorcycle. It isn't black. It does not have pull-back bars, stepped seat, disc brakes, multiple or any cams, or mag wheels. Other than being the first motorcycle with electronic ignition, it has no electronics or other gadgetry on it. No electric starter. No turn signals. But it is Japanese, and it does stay together. Could the Mach III be the ultimate reliable, cheap, classic?

Author's Note: Believe it or not, the story you have just read was the official beginning of *The Tiddler Invasion*. Back about 1984 or 1985, years before computers and my knowledge of them were developed even remotely enough to produce this book, I imagined a book that I would like to publish under that title one day. I began by composing a story on my 1959 IBM typewriter describing my experience with my Mach III. The plan was to write more stories and compile the information that is in this book. After nearly three decades you are finally getting to read it!

Figure G39 - Yvon Duhamel's Racing Triple. Image by Chuck Schultz under Creative Commons license.

Figure G40 - 1974 Kawasaki KX-125. ©1974 Kawasaki Motors Corporation, U.S.A.

Figure G41 - 1970 Kawasaki F5 Big Horn. ©1970 Kawasaki Motors Corporation, U.S.A.

Figure G42 - Yellow 1969 Kawasaki A7SS Avenger Scrambler. ©1969 Kawasaki Motors Corporation, U.S.A.

Figure G43 - Kawasaki H1-R 500 Road Racer. Image by Andrew Basterfield, 2011, under Creative Commons license.

Figure G44 - Blue 1969 Kawasaki G3SS 90 brochure. ©1969 Kawasaki Motors Corporation, U.S.A.

Selected Kawasaki Models Ratings Chart

Years	Model	Collectibility	Practicality	Desirability
1965 - 68	85cc Singles	B	D	C
1969 - 75	90 & 100 Singles	C	C	B
1964 - 69	115 & 125 Singles	B	C	B
1966 - 75	125/175/250 Enduros	C	C	C
1967 - 73	M-series Scramblers	B	D	B
1967 - 71	Samurai & SS 250	B	B	C
1972 - 75	Mach I 250 Triple	D	C	C
1967 - 71	Avenger & SS 350	B	C	C
1971 - 75	350 Big Horn Enduro	D	C	C
1972 - 73	Mach II 350	B	C	B
1974 - 75	S3/KH 400 Triple	C	C	C
1974 - 75	KZ 400 Twin	D	B	D
1969 - 75	Mach III 500	A	C	B
1966 - 69	650 Commander Twin	B	C	B
1972 - 75	750 Mach IV	A	C	B
1973 - 75	Z-1 900 Four	A	A	A

Models Ratings Chart Definitions:

Years: These are the total production years for a particular model series. Some early model years within a series may be considerably more desirable than later years.

Models: In some cases many variations are included in this category and in others the models included are very homogeneous.

Collectibility: This is what most of you want to know, the bottom line on how likely the model or series is likely to climb in value over the coming years.

Practicality: This is an indicator of how adaptable the machine can be to ride for transportation or pleasure in the modern world, considering parts availability, fuel quality, comfort, performance and miscellaneous other obvious factors.

Desirability: This defines the nostalgic, emotional wow factor, without regard for collector values or everyday usage.

General: No machine is given a failing grade. If it made it into a rating chart, at least a few hobbyists find that model interesting.

Chapter 7: *Yamaha: Meet the Exciters!*

Yamaha Model Charts, 1955-75

Every Yamaha motorcycle built from 1955 through 1969 was a two-stroke. The first four-cycle would be the SOHC 650 XS-1 of 1970. Yamaha employed both piston port and rotary valve designs during this period. Most of the small street singles had rotary valves and the remaining models were piston-port. All Yamahas had return foot shifts on the left side. As far as I know, all models had Mikuni carburetors.

Yamaha 1955 - 1957

After the establishment of Yamaha Motor Company on July1, 1955, the brand began producing about 200 machines a month for the domestic market. The first production Yamaha motorcycle, the YA-1 of 1955, had a tube frame, plunger rear suspension, primitively sprung front suspension, a rubber solo seat suspended from the front, and a painted luggage rack over the rear fender.

The similarly engineered and styled 175cc YC-1 was added to the YA-1 in 1956. The YA-1 and YC-1 had the same general style as the DKW 125 from which they were derived, as well as the familiar Harley-Davidson 125cc and 165cc Singles of the same period. The elegant triangular frame and smooth, slender tank style would be dumped by Yamaha in search of a more modern look over the next couple of model years.

In the 1957 model year, the YC-1 continued as it was before, but the original YA-1 was updated with a totally new chassis design. This new YA-2 was powered by the same 125cc two-stroke engine suspended from a new pressed steel frame. The suspension was updated to modern tube shocks at the rear and a leading link system at the front. The seat was now either a more modern foam pad, still with a painted steel luggage rack over the rear fender, or a new dual seat. The tank was a strangely shaped affair with a downward curve at the bottom rear edge and rubber knee pads reflecting the contour of the tank. The gas tank was more bulbous than before and it had chrome side panels. The fenders were of the full coverage type and turn signals and a fully enclosed chain completed the package. A new 250cc twin was introduced in 1957. The YD-1 was a modern, conventional machine, quite visibly the direct ancestor of the later YD-3 of the '60's. The YD-1 featured a twin-cylinder, two-stroke engine suspended from a pressed steel frame. The front suspension consisted of standard telescopic forks with covered springs and the rear shocks had matching, body-colored covers over the springs. The fenders were a full coverage design, the tank was bulbous, rounded, and fully painted, without chrome side panels. The seat was a conventional dual type with a hand strap across the center. It also featured turn indicators and a fully enclosed chain. All three 1957 models utilized kick starters and had low-rise, chrome handlebars.

Figure H1 - 1957-58 Yamaha YD-1 250. This maroon and beige YD-1 is either a '57 or '58 and seems to be in an unidentified museum. Note the full-coverage fenders, flat bars, solo seat, painted tank with kneepads, and small turn indicators mounted close together. These were generally distinguishing marks of the earliest Yamahas, as well as other Japanese brands of the time. Image by Rikita under Creative Commons license.

Yamaha 1958 Chart

Model	Name	Type	HP	Seat	Starter	Wt.
MF-1	Step-Thru	50cc Single	3.5	Solo	Electric	143
YA-2	Touring	125cc Single	NA	Solo	Electric	NA
YD-1	Touring	250cc Twin	NA	Dual	Kick	NA
YD-2	Touring	250cc Twin	NA	Dual	Electric	NA

Yamaha 1958 Notes: Since the YC-1 was discontinued, all 1958 models had pressed steel frames. The MF-1 was a new step-through model with full coverage fenders. The YD-2 had a chrome tank. Catalina Island is 22 miles from Long Beach via toll ferry. The Catalina Grand Prix of 1958 was probably held the first weekend in May. After making a splash at the Catalina GP in the spring, small numbers of the MF-1 and YD-1 were brought into the U.S. via the gray market by Cooper Motors. The YA-2 was also sold with a dual saddle. The sportier styled YD-2 with trimmer fenders and tank, an updated dual seat, an electric starter, and a single front downtube support for the engine, replaced the stodgy YD-1 late in the model year. No official prices are available for 1958 models.

Yamaha 1959 Chart

Model	Name	Type	HP	Seat	Starter	Wt.
MF-1	Step-Thru	50cc Single	3.5	Solo	Electric	143
YA-3	Touring	125cc Single	NA	Solo	Electric	234
YD-2	Touring	250cc Twin	NA	Dual	Electric	NA
YDS-1	Sports	250cc Twin	NA	Dual	Kick	NA
YDS-1S	Scrambler	250cc Twin	NA	3/4	Kick	NA
YDS-1R	Racing	250cc Twin	NA	Racing	Kick	NA
YES-1R	Racing	255cc Twin	NA	Racing	Kick	NA

Yamaha 1959 Notes: The YDS-1 had a tube frame; the rest were pressed steel. The MF-1 Step-Through was still the entry machine, the YD-2 still featured a chrome tank, and the YA-3 was distinguished by its passenger grab bar if the machine had a separate passenger seat. Some YA-3's may have been imported with dual seats. The YDS-1 had a four-speed transmission. The 1959 Scrambler was a unique machine, similar to, yet quite different from the later Ascot. With chrome, upswept expansion chambers, knobby tires and high fenders, the Scrambler was a motocross version of the Ascot flat-tracker. No information is available to discern if this model continued in later years or if it was ever imported into the U.S. No official prices are available for 1959 models. Dealers in 1959 offered two racing kits for the YDS-1 that included 197 parts. The E model was a special 255cc kit that allowed the machine to race in the 350 class. No prices or horsepower ratings are available for these rare kitted machines. All claimed dry weights are listed in pounds.

Figure H2 - 1959 Gold & White Yamaha YDS-1 in Germany. Yes, that white chain guard angled upward at the rear is correct, as is the white paint on the lower fork legs. See the next photo of a different YDS-1. Notice the tiny windshield attached to the headlamp on this example. I do not know why the chrome rear fender of the YDS-2 looks like peeling paint in this shot. It appears this way in some brochure photos of the period, too! ©Peter Abelmann, owner and photographer

Yamaha 1960 Chart

Model	Name	Type	HP	Seat	Starter	Wt.
MF-1	Step-Thru	50cc Single	3.5	Solo	Electric	143
YA-3	Touring	125cc Single	NA	Dual	Electric	234
YD-2	Touring	250cc Twin	NA	Dual	Electric	309
YDS-1	Sports	250cc Twin	NA	Dual	Kick	332

Yamaha 1960 Notes: The four-speed YDS-1 had a tube frame. The other models had pressed steel frames and both electric and kick starters. The YA-3 now had a red dual seat and a high front fender. Some YD-2's were imported into the USA. The SC-1 scooter may or may not have been imported in very small numbers. The SC-1 was a 175cc two-stroke weighing 265 pounds with a top speed of 56 mph. No official prices are available for 1960 models. All claimed dry weights are listed in pounds.

Figure H3 - 1959 Yamaha YDS-1. Here is another example of a pristine gold and white YDS-1. The color was very distinctive, a rich, dark, metallic orange/gold. Image by Rikita under Creative Commons license.

Yamaha 1961 Chart

Model	Name	Type	HP	Seat	Starter	Wt.
MF-1	Step-Thru	50cc Single	3.5	Solo	Electric	143
MF-2	Step-Thru	50cc Single	4.5	Solo	Electric	165
YA-3	Street	125cc Single	NA	Dual	Electric	234
YA-5	Street	125cc Single	10.5	Dual	Electric	242
YD-2	Street	250cc Twin	NA	Dual	Electric	309
YDS-1	Sport	250cc Twin	NA	Dual	Kick	332

Yamaha 1961 Notes: The YA-5 was distinguished by its higher handlebars and other cosmetic details. All models except the YDS-1 still used pressed steel frames. The 50cc models had three speeds and the larger models had four. The MF-1 was also available with a dual seat. The SC-1 scooter was again shown in at least one 1961 brochure, but there is no other evidence that any were imported. All claimed dry weights are listed in pounds. No official prices are available. Yamaha produced a small number (ten or less) factory racers under the model name RR250 in 1961. The engines were kitted versions of the upcoming street YDS-2 placed in a custom-built road race chassis.

Yamaha 1962 Chart

Model	Name	Type	HP	Seat	Starter	Wt.
MF-1	Lightning	50cc Single	4.4	Solo	Electric	143
MF2-C	Step-Thru	50cc Single	4.5	Solo	Kick	NA
MF2	Step-Thru	50cc Single	4.5	Solo	Electric	165
MJ2-C	Step-Thru	55cc Single	5	Solo	Kick	NA
MJ2	Step-Thru	55cc Single	5	Solo	Electric	165
MJ2-TH	Omaha Trail	55cc Single	5	Solo	Electric	165
YA-5	Street	123cc Single	10.5	Dual	Electric	242
YD-3	Street	250cc Twin	20	Dual	Electric	320
YDS-2	Sports	250cc Twin	25	Dual	Kick	338
YDS-2M	Ascot	250cc Twin	30	3/4	Kick	NA
YDS-2R	Road Racer	250cc Twin	NA	Racing	Kick	NA
TD-1	Road Racer	250cc Twin	32	Racing	Kick	228

Yamaha 1962 Notes: The MF-1, YA-5, and YD-3 had pressed steel frames. The YDS-2 Sports and Ascot Scrambler had tube frames and five-speeds. The YA-5 and YD-3 had four-speeds and all the step-through models had three-speeds. Most of the step-through M models had automatic clutches, but the MJ2 was also offered with a manual clutch. The YA-5 was distinguished by its low bars and red seat. The MF-1 was also available with a dual seat. At least one ad referred to the 1962 MF-1 step-through as the Lightning! The new YDS-2 differed from the YDS-1 with its new five-speed transmission. All claimed dry weights are listed in pounds. Advertised prices for 1962 included $285 for the MJ-2 with electric start or Omaha Trail, $449 for the YA-5, $549 for the YD-3, and $599 for the YDS-2. East Coast prices were $15 higher. No other official prices for 1962 are available. Yamaha released a production racer called the YDS-2R in 1962 and replaced this model mid-year with the legendary TD-1.

Figure H4 - 1962 Yamaha YDS-2 first-year brochure. ©1962 Yamaha Motor Corporation, U.S.A.

Yamaha YDS-2

This is another very special story that is close to my nostalgic heart. Back in the good old days, we used to have these dirty, dingy little motorcycle shops lit by bare light bulbs and inevitably owned or managed by local, low-budget racers just trying to fund their expensive hobbies. These were places that I am sure Tim the Tool Man loved and boys like me, not yet quite old enough to drive, loved to visit. My mom used to actually drive me over there. Yeah, I know that's embarrassing to admit, but the shop was twenty miles from my home. What did you expect me to do, ride my bicycle? Honda had just recently established a beachhead and Yamaha was the next Japanese brand I discovered. I would graduate from my Allstate Cruisaire in a year or two with one of the first YG-1's to arrive at this dealership in the spring of '63.

This shop had not only a YDS-2, but an Ascot Scrambler and a TD-1! They probably all left the dealership with my drool on them! Although I was a dirt rider from the beginning, when all you have for wheels is a three-speed bicycle built in Japan or a '57 Cruisaire, the YDS-2 with its five-speed transmission and blistering acceleration that would leave a Super Hawk in its blue smoke was a real dream machine. Soon thereafter my next door neighbor got a YD-3, but there was an unmistakable excitement quotient missing from its blue, full-coverage fenders, electric starter, and four-speed transmission. There was a homely little baby-blue MF-1 in town, too, that all the Honda Cub riders looked upon with disdain. I met another local racer who probably went up against an Ascot Scrambler or two. His machine was a Hawk with wide bars, knobby tires, a C110 tank, and wonderfully loud exhausts. I am reminded of a quote from Robert Redford in *Little Fauss & Big Halsey* when he says *sickles is a dangerous toy*. The Hawk racer would forfeit his life on that machine in competition a few years later.

As far as I know, the leading difference between the YDS-1 and the YDS-2 is that the former had only a four-speed transmission. The main improvement in the YDS-3 was, of course, Autolube. I'm sure there were many additional, detail differences, but these were the big two. Facts are hard to come by on these rare models today. The YDS-1 was sold from 1959 through 1961. The YDS-2 premiered in 1962 and the YDS-3 Catalina received oil injection in '64, along with all the Yamahas except the racers. The Big Bear Scrambler was added to the line in 1965 and the YDS-5 Catalina Electra came along in 1967. This model added electric starting and I think the 5 refers to the introduction of a new five-port engine that had one or two additional horsepower. There does not seem to have ever been a YDS-4. The standard road series YD-1-2-3 ended in late '65 or early '66. New, sleeker styling and a general evolution of the breed arrived in 1969.

In my mind, I divide Yamahas at the 1968 model year, much as I do Hondas. The introduction of the Honda 350's brought styling borrowed from Triumph, with painted black frames and slender, painted gas tanks, as well as new model nomenclature. Hondas became CB/CL 350, 450, 175, etc., with K1, K2, etc., added to denote year and detail changes. Yamaha introduced the DT-1 in 1968 and the whole Enduro/MX series exploded into DT-1-2-3, AT-1-2-3, etc., with B-C-D suffixes to denote model year detail changes. By 1970 the company even began building four-strokes! Don't for a minute think Yamaha didn't already know how. The engine in the legendary Toyota 2000 GT was designed by Yamaha. James Bond's girlfriend drove one in *You Only Live Twice*. The YDS-2's excitement had a lot of competition by 1968 from the Suzuki X-6, the Kawasaki Samurai, and even from up market with the Bridgestone GTR. Those mean, ugly old CL-77's and Super Hawks continued to dominate the YDS-2 in the showroom sweepstakes, even while they were being coated in two-stroke smoke from the few YDS models that roared out the doors of dealerships. Ah, those were the days.

James Rozee Speaks: "One of my first real motorcycle collections I owned was the YDS-1&2 250 Yamahas. I had a beautiful all-stock turquoise and white 1962, black and silver 1959 and '60 YDS-1's, and a YD-1 pressed-frame 250. I think they are cool. I showed the turquoise and white one for years all around Oregon. Yamaha, like Honda, made many changes. By the time the 305 showed up nothing would interchange as usual. They are rare birds today. I sold all of mine to a Japanese collector who took them back to Japan with him. They are really into motorcycles over there. They ride everything they own and have all kinds of great events, too, but the USA and Canada still have the most old parts to be found around the world. I have been in contact with many Japanese friends over the years and they cannot find any of the parts that I have needed in the past. Everything was shipped out of Japan. Now they are buying it all back, like the British are with their bikes.

I enjoyed my old YDS 250 Yamahas but did not ride them much. By the early 80's they were rare. Many others who I knew who did race them told me all kinds of tricks they did to keep them going. A book called *Yamaha Two Stroke Twins* by Colin MacKellar through Osprey Collectors Books is great. I got to meet many of the guys who helped out with the book when I was at Donnington Raceway in England for a vintage race. They had some great TD-250's and were telling me all the tricks you could do to them. The Yamaha twins were always getting better and better each year. With racing they learned more and more, and by the time the RD-250's hit the streets no one could touch them except a few other Japanese two-strokes. They could all make a Honda 350 look like an anvil. I do admit a Honda 350 was a great road bike, dependable as a good dog, but Honda should have never told anyone to take it off-road! What a beast! The Yamahas did not stay together as long as a Honda but were much more of a thrill to ride and own!"

Figure H5 - Black 1962 Yamaha 125 YA-5. Notice the distinctive seat with deep foam on the front portion and shallow on the rear, the enclosed chain guard, and the tiny windscreen. ©1962 Yamaha Motor Corporation, U.S.A.

New YAMAHA *model* MJ2 55cc Moped *with* ELECTRIC STARTER

The famous Yamaha rotary valve engine which has won a world-wide reputation for its power and reliability is used. The Yamaha engine has a capacity of 55cc making it the most powerful engine in its class.

The new type engine always keeps the RPM steady when going up hills or at the slowest speed; balance is perfect all the times even on bad roads or sharp curves.

400 meters in 25 seconds: faster pick up than any competitive moped in its size. The same pick up as a 125cc motorcycle.

THE SPECIFICATIONS OF NEW MOPED MJ2

Name	YAMAHA MJ2	Fuel Consumption, on level, paved road	Clutch	Automatic Centrifugal system
Overall Length	67.6" (1,715mm)	211.3 mile/U.S. gal. (90km/l)		or hand clutch system
Overall Height	37.6" (955mm)	Climbing Capacity ⅕	Transmission	Foot-operated 3 Speed
Overall Width	29.5" (640mm)	Cylinder Single Cylinder		Gear-Box and Chain
Wheelbase	44.9" (1,140mm)	Cylinder Capacity (55cc)	Front Brake Operation	Hand-operated, Cable
Weight	4.9" (75kg)	Starter System Starter-dynamo & Kick starter	Rear Brake Operation	Foot Pedal

Figure H6 - 1963 Red Yamaha 55 MJ2 with Electric Start. Yamaha built several step-through variations in 1963. Compare this machine to the MF-2 shown in the Introduction. ©1963 Yamaha Motor Corporation, U.S.A.

334

Yamaha 1963 Chart

Model	Name	Type	HP	Seat	Starter	Wt.	Price
MJ2S	Step-Thru	55cc Single	5	Dual	Electric	165	NA
MJ2-T	Omaha Trail	55cc Single	5	Solo	Electric	165	$275
YG-1	Rotary Jet	80cc Single	7.7	Dual	Kick	140	$340
YG-1T	Trailmaster	80cc Single	7.7	Solo	Kick	140	NA
YA-5	Street	123cc Single	10.5	Dual	Electric	242	NA
YD-3	Street	247cc Twin	19	Dual	Electric	320	NA
YDT-1	Electra Sport	250cc Twin	20	Dual	Electric	NA	$595
YDS-2	Sports	246cc Twin	25	Dual	Kick	340	$615
YDS-2M	Ascot	246cc Twin	35	3/4	Kick	235	NA
TD-1	Road racer	246cc Twin	35	Racing	Kick	NA	NA

Yamaha 1963 Notes: The single-cylinder models and the YD-3 had pressed steel frames. The 250cc sports models had tube frames. All except the 250cc sports models had four-speed transmissions; those two still had five-speeds. The MF2 could be equipped with either a manual or automatic clutch. The YA-5 could be had with either low or western bars. All models were two-strokes running on premixed fuel. The YDT-1 & YG-1 were advertised as 63 1/2 models in the April 1963 *Cycle World*. The YG-1 was supposedly also sold in small numbers with a solo seat. The YDT-1 was a new hybrid: it had the YD-3 standard engine, four-speed gearbox, and electric starter in the YDS-2's chassis. It had turn signals and a chrome-sided tank. All claimed dry weights are listed in pounds.

Figure H7 - Blue 1964 Yamaha 250 YD-3A. ©Warren P. Warner, owner & photographer

Yamaha 1964 Chart

Model	Name	Type	HP	Seat	Starter	Wt.	Price
YJ-1	Riverside	55cc Single	NA	Solo	Kick	140	$255
MJ-2TH	Omaha Trail	55cc Single	5	Solo	Electric	165	$285
MG-1T	Omaha	73cc Single	7.7	Solo	Kick	135	$315
YG-1S	Rotary Jet	73cc Single	7.7	Dual	Kick	140	$340
YG-1T	Trailmaster	73cc Single	7.7	Solo	Kick	140	$355
YA-6	Santa Barbara	73cc Single	11	Dual	Electric	242	$454
YD-3	Electra	250cc Twin	19	Dual	Electric	320	$549
YDT-1	Electra Sport	250cc Twin	20	Dual	Electric	NA	$595
YDS-3	Catalina	250cc Twin	27	Dual	Kick	340	$630
YDS-3M	Ascot	250cc Twin	35	Racing	Kick	235	$800
TD-1A	Daytona RR	250cc Twin	35	Racing	Kick	NA	$1130

Yamaha 1964 Notes: All the singles and the YD-3 had pressed steel frames; the rest had tubes. The Omaha Trail 55 had a three-speed, the Catalina, Ascot, and TD-1 had five-speeds, and the rest were four-speeds. Autolube appeared on the YG-1S and a few other models for the first time. All models had downswept exhaust systems. The YD-3 had a claimed top speed of 78 mph. A full-race fairing was optional at extra cost on the TD-1. All claimed dry weights are listed in pounds. The Catalina, Santa Barbara, and Riverside were announced as 1965 models with oil injection in the August 1964 issue of *Cycle*. The YJ-1 was advertised in *Cycle* at $285 in July. The YDS-3 had Autolube, a single air filter instead of two, adjustable rear shocks, and a new front fender as changes from the YDS-2.

Figure H8 - 1963 Yamaha YG-1 in Unusual Solid Red Color. ©1963 Yamaha Motor Corporation, U.S.A.

Winner of Auto & Motor Sport Magazine's Safety & Engineering Award

YAMAHA INTERNATIONAL CORPORATION

1124 SOUTH 14TH PEDRO STREET, LOS ANGELES, CALIFORNIA ■ UNITED STATES ROUTE 30, BELL LANE, DOWNINGTOWN, PENNSYLVANIA

1964 - 1965 MODEL INFORMATION

1964 YAMAHA YDS3 CATALINA 250cc TWIN

The pride of Yamaha represents engineering refinements years ahead of the competition. Similar to the YDS-2 in appearance but with identifying features such as the separate oil reservoir on the right side and the combination speedometer-tachometer. This machine is rated at 27hp at 7500rpm with power going to the wheels through a 5-speed gearbox. Model YDS3, $630, fully equipped. Set-up Charges $20.00

1964 YAMAHA YA6 SANTA BARBARA 125cc SINGLE

Engineering-wise this 125cc single has the greatest features of any lightweight in this displacement category. It has the rotary valve, electric starter, and the Yamaha Injection System. A high performing 2-stroke single that will surprise many people by its performance. Model YA6, $454, fully equipped. Set-up Charges $20.00

1964 YAMAHA YDT-1 ELECTRA SPORT 250cc TWIN

This 20hp, 250cc street model has a 4-speed gearbox and an Electric Starter. With its tube frame, and smart chrome features and a ripper YD3 engine. Model YDT-1, $595, fully equipped. Set-up Charges $20.00

1964 YAMAHA YG-1T TRAILMASTER 80cc

This 80cc never quits — road or no road. A rugged backwoods beauty. Knobby tires, oversize sprocket, 4-speed gearbox. Cruises at an easy 45mph, can give over 150mph. Engine guard plate, carrier rack. Model YG-1T "Town and Country Eighty," $365, fully equipped. Set-up Charges $20.00

1964 YAMAHA YD3 ELECTRA 250cc TWIN

At home on highways, this 2-cylinder 250cc model gives out a lively 19hp. Cruises at 70 mph. Sleek. Swift. Smooth. A motorcycle built for two, for one hard-to-beat price. Electric Starter, 4-speed gearbox. Model YD3, $549, fully equipped. Set-up Charges $20.00

1964 YAMAHA YG-1S ROTARY JET 80cc

Sweet and saucy, the 80cc street model goes to town with a motor that lets you hum along at 50-60mph, gives up to 160mph. Smooth, 4-speed gearbox. Model YG-1S "Eighty," $350, fully equipped. Set-up Charges $20.00

SUGGESTED SELLING PRICE ... $
SET-UP CHARGES ... $
SALES TAX ... $
DEPARTMENT OF MOTOR VEHICLE FEES ... $
INSURANCE CHARGE ... $
DESTINATION (FREIGHT) CHARGES ... $
TOTAL ... $
DOWN PAYMENT (%) ... $
BALANCE ... $
12 Monthly Payments $ 24 Monthly Payments $

1964 YAMAHA MG1T OMAHA TRAILMASTER 80cc

By popular demand—the best selling Omaha 55 is used as the basis for this model with the 80cc engine replacing the 55 with a 50% increase in usable horsepower and 4-speed gearbox. This is one of the finest Trail type machines on the American market today. Model MG1-T "Omaha Trailmaster 80," $315, fully equipped. Set-up Charges $15.00

1964 YAMAHA YJ-1 RIVERSIDE 55cc

This is a completely redesigned 55cc single rotary valve engine with big bike styling. It is equipped with a 4-speed gearbox and is a price leader. Model YJ-1 "Riverside 55," $285, fully equipped. Set-up Charges $15.00

1964 YAMAHA ASCOT SCRAMBLER 250CC

YAMAHA ASCOT SCRAMBLER 1st in all types of racing. YAMAHA 35 hp., 10,500 rpm outstanding performance engine. YAMAHA'S new design scrambler faster than ever — 115 mph, close ratio trans. Hi-Compression heads improved port timing large 24 mm carbs. Price of this fabulous machine only $800.

1964 YAMAHA MJ2TH MOPED OMAHA TRAILMASTER 55cc

Blaze your own trail with this 55cc model. Oversize sprocket, knobby tires, rotary valve engine, and 3-speed transmission go all out for you. Includes luggage rack, Electric Starter, engine guard plate. Model MJ2TH, $285, fully equipped. Set-up Charges $15.00

1964 YAMAHA TD1 DAYTONA ROAD RACER 250CC

YAMAHA'S TD1 ROAD RACER, sleek, fast, champion of the road racing circuits. YAMAHA TD1 production 250 cc road racer 35 hp at 10,500 Carburetors are Amal. Remote float bowl type, with dyno tuned exhaust system. Price of this Streamlined machine $1130. (Fairing not included, but available.)

ALL PRICES F.O.B. LOS ANGELES. ADD $10.00 FREIGHT CHARGES FOR ALL MODELS SHIPPED FROM PHILADELPHIA AND SAVANNAH.

Figure H9 (previous page) - 1964-65 Yamaha Model Lineup. ©1964 Yamaha Motor Corporation, U.S.A.

Yamaha 1965 Chart

Model	Name	Type	HP	Seat	Starter	Wt.
YJ-1	Riverside	55cc Single	5	Dual	Kick	135
MG-1T	Omaha TM 80	73cc Single	7.7	Solo	Kick	155
YG-1S	Rotary Jet	73cc Single	7.7	Dual	Kick	160
YG-1T	Trailmaster	73cc Single	7.7	Solo	Kick	160
YA-6	Santa Barbara	123cc Single	11	Dual	Electric	242
YD-3	Electra	247cc Twin	19	Dual	Electric	320
YDT-1	Electra Sport	246cc Twin	20	Dual	Electric	NA
YDS-3	Catalina	246cc Twin	27	Dual	Kick	340
YDS-3C	Big Bear	246cc Twin	27	Dual	Kick	340
YDS-3M	Ascot	246cc Twin	35	Racing	Kick	235
TD-1B	Daytona RR	246cc Twin	35	Racing	Kick	245

Yamaha 1965 Notes: All singles and the YD-3 had pressed steel frames. The remaining 250's had tubular frames. No official prices are available for the 1965 models. All claimed dry weights are listed in pounds.

The Big Bear would be the first of many two-stroke street scrambler competitors or copycats of the Honda CL-72. The 250 and 305 Big Bears probably sold more than any other two-stroke street scramblers. However, the whole street scrambler concept worked much better for Honda's four-strokes, and there were probably several reasons for this other than simply Honda's market dominance at the time. Although Kawasaki emulated the crossover pipes of the Hondas, their styling was less than perfect, and there was no contest which machines had the better sound! The upswept pipes on either side of the Yamaha, Bridgestone, and Suzuki models were a bit nonsensical from an offroad standpoint, since they made the machines appear wider and less adaptable to a standing position. The Honda four-strokes offered more low-end torque and Honda subtly modified their Scrambler engines to produce more low-speed power. Gearing was altered a little, too, and the ergonomics were at least a bit accommodating to standing on the pegs. Larger diameter wheels were even added to some Honda Scramblers. Most of the scramblers built by the other four brands had few changes from their pure-street brothers other than the obvious high pipes and crossover bars. Aside from Honda's relentless lead in the market, the Yamaha Big Bears are still probably the second most popular street scramblers today.

Figure H10 - 1963 Yamaha YG-1 Rotary Jet 80 in Purple & Silver on a Light Blue Background.

©1963 Yamaha Motor Corporation, U.S.A.

Yamaha 1966 Chart

Model	Name	Type	HP	Seat	Starter	Wt.
U-5	Newport	50cc Single	4.4	Dual	Kick	141
YJ-2	Campus 60	58cc Single	5	Dual	Kick	161
MG-1T	Omaha TM	73cc Single	7.7	Solo	Kick	155
YG-1K	Rotary Jet	73cc Single	7.7	Dual	Kick	158
YG-1T	Trailmaster	73cc Single	7.7	Solo	Kick	160
YL-1	Twin Jet 100	97cc Twin	9.3	Dual	Kick	180
YA-6	Santa Barbara	123cc Single	11	Dual	Electric	242
YDS-3	Catalina	246cc Twin	27	Dual	Kick	340
YDS-3C	Big Bear	246cc Twin	27	Dual	Kick	340
YDS-3M	Ascot	246cc Twin	35	Racing	Kick	235
TD-1B	Daytona RR	246cc Twin	35	Racing	Kick	245
YM-1	Cross Country	305cc Twin	29	Dual	Kick	340

Yamaha 1966 Notes: All the 250's and the new 305 had tubular frames and all the smaller models used pressed steel. The step-through Newport had a three-speed and the remaining small models were four-speeds, including the new 100cc twin. The big twins all had five-speeds. The Newport was also offered with an optional electric starter. The Campus 60 and Big Bear had upswept exhausts. All claimed dry weights are listed in pounds. No official prices are available for the 1966 models.

This is also the year Yamaha developed the engine for the rare and exotic *baby-XK-E-styled* Toyota 2000 GT. The joint venture between Toyota and Yamaha would produce 337 Coupes and two Spyders in 1967-70. Approximately sixty of the coupes were imported into the U.S. One of the Spyders was featured in the 1967 James Bond movie, partly filmed in Japan, *You Only Live Twice*. Yamaha would reprise its influence upon the enthusiast automotive world again in late 1988 with the debut of the Ford Taurus SHO with its hot-rod V-6 engine designed by Yamaha.

Figure H11 - Red 1966 Yamaha Twin Jet 100 on Red. This tiny twin-cylinder offered a new idea in tiddler one-upmanship. It's a tiny twin! ©1966 Yamaha Motor Corporation, U.S.A.

YAM[ ]A 250

BIG BEAR SCRAMBLER

MODEL YDS3C 5-SPEED WITH
YAMAHA INJECTION SYSTEM

SINCE 1887

[ ]SITION
[ ]STABLE
[ ]CUSHION

[ ]ACHABLE
[ ]NCER

[ ]DING
[ ]T PEG

5-SPEED
GEAR BOX

STRONG
ENGINE GUARD
PLATE

SPEEDOMETER
&
TACHOMETER

TELESCOPIC
FRONT FORK

POWERFUL
BRAKE DRUM

Figure H12 - 1966 Yamaha Big Bear Scrambler. ©1966 Yamaha Motor Corporation, U.S.A.

YAMAHA'S REVOLUTIONARY INJECTION SYSTEM

SPECIAL FEATURES OF YAMAHA 60

Rotary Valve Engine

Yamaha's rotary valve engine gives more power & greater efficiency.

OIL INJECTION SYSTEM

No troublesome mixing required & no more plug failures.

250 WORLD CHAMPIONS

Yamaha's world grand prix racer proves the value of advanced engineering.

SPECIFICATION OF YJ2

PERFORMANCE

Speed Range .... 50~55mph
Fuel consumption on paved flat road ....
.... 200mi/gal. 85km/ℓ(30km/h)
Climbing ability .... 18 degree
Min. turning radius .... 5'8" 1,780mm
Brake distance ...... 7m(35m/h) 23feet(22 mph)

ENGINE

Lubricating System ... Separate oil supplying system
Displacement 60cc
Bore & Stroke .... 1.7×1.7inch(42×42mm)
Compression ratio 7.1:1
Max. horsepower 5.0/7000rpm

Max. torque .... 0.55/6000(kgm/rpm)
Starting method .... Kick starter
Ignition system .... Flywheel Magneto

FUEL TANK CAPACITY 5.2ℓ 1.33gal
OIL TANK CAPACITY .... 1.1ℓ 1.16qt.

DIMENSIONS

Overall length 72.4in. (1,810mm)
Overall width 25.4in. (635mm)
Overall height 38.4in. (960mm)
Wheelbase 45.8in. (1,145mm)
Min. road clearance 6.0in. (140mm)

WEIGHT .... 161 pounds 72kg

Figure H13 (previous page) - 1967 Red Yamaha Riverside 60 Brochure Touting Yamaha's Oil Injection System and Rotary Valve Induction. ©1967 Yamaha Motor Corporation, U.S.A.

Yamaha 1967 Chart

Model	Name	Type	HP	Seat	Starter	Wt.
U-5	Newport	50cc Single	4.4	Dual	Kick	141
U-5E	Newport Electra	50cc Single	4.4	Dual	Electric	NA
YJ-2	Campus 60	58cc Single	5	Dual	Kick	161
YG-1	Rotary Jet	73cc Single	7.7	Dual	Kick	140
YGS1	Rotary Jet Sport	73cc Single	7.7	Dual	Kick	140
YG1-TK	Trailmaster	73cc Single	7.7	Solo	Kick	158
YGS1-T	Trailmaster	73cc Single	7.7	Dual	Kick	160
YL-1	Twin Jet 100	98cc Twin	9.3	Dual	Kick	180
YL-1E	Twin Jet Electra	98cc Twin	9.3	Dual	Electric	NA
YL-2	Rotary Jet 100	97cc Single	9.5	Dual	Kick	NA
YL-2C	Trailmaster	97cc Single	9.5	Solo	Electric	205
YA-6	Santa Barbara	125cc Single	15	Dual	Electric	242
YCS-1	Bonanza	180cc Twin	21	Dual	Electric	262
YDS-3	Catalina	246cc Twin	27	Dual	Kick	340
YDS-5	Catalina Electra	246cc Twin	29	Dual	Electric	NA
TD-1C	Daytona RR	246cc Twin	35	Racing	Kick	245
YM-1	Cross Country	305cc Twin	29.5	Dual	Kick	340
YM-2C	Big Bear 305	305cc Twin	29.5	Dual	Kick	NA
YR-1	Grand Prix	348cc Twin	36	Dual	Electric	345

Yamaha 1967 Notes: The Newport through the Santa Barbara had pressed steel frames and the larger models had tubular frames. The Newport models utilized three-speed transmissions and the Bonanza 180 through the Grand Prix 350 had five speeds. The YJ-2, YGS-1, YG-1TK, YGS-1T, and the YM-2C had upswept exhausts. The YG-1TK also had a luggage rack. No official prices are available for the 1967 models, but one source listed the price of the YL-2C Trailmaster as $430 including set-up charges. All claimed dry weights are listed in pounds. All the early 250 and 305 twins had kick starters on the left side. Later twins such as the Santa Barbara, Bonanza, and Grand Prix had right-side starters, as most of the tiddler singles had had since the beginning.

Figures H14 & H15 (next page) - 1967 Yamaha Trailmaster 100 & 1967 Yamaha Santa Barbara 125. You can see that the Trailmaster was a single-cylinder 100, a separate design from its Twin Jet sister. Note the huge rear sprocket on this yellow machine. The Santa Barbara was the direct descendant of the first Yamaha, a story detailed in the next article in this chapter. ©1967 Yamaha Motor Corporation, U.S.A.

YAMAHA TRAILMASTER 100

THE MOST POWERFUL, BEST HANDLING BIKE
IN ITS CLASS—ON OR OFF THE ROAD.

SINCE 1887

SANTA BARBARA 125

YA 6 125CC ROTARY VALVE WITH ELECTRIC STARTER
YAMAHA INJECTION SYSTEM

SINCE 1887

344

CATALINA 250 MODEL YDS-3
5-SPEED YAMAHA INJECTION SYSTEM

Figure H16 (above) & H17 (below) - 1967 Yamaha Catalina 250 & 1967 Yamaha Bonanza 180.

©1967 Yamaha Motor Corporation, U.S.A.

YAMAHA BONANZA 180
PATENTED ALUMINUM TWIN CYLINDER
5-SPEED GEARBOX & ELECTRIC STARTER

SINCE 1887

Lighting equipment may differ from country to country.

Figures H18 & H19 (previous page) - Compare these two similar machines. The black 1964 YDT-1 (top) was a hybrid model made from parts of the YD-3 and YDS-3. The blue and white 1965 YDS-3 (bottom) is a USA-spec machine that was imported into Australia, where this photo was taken. H18 ©Warren P. Warner, USA. H19 ©Chris A. Harris, Australia.

Yamaha 1968 Chart

Model	Name	Type	HP	Seat	Starter	Wt.	Price
U-5	Newport	50cc S.	4.4	Dual	Kick	154	$219
U-5E	Newport Electra	50cc S.	4.4	Dual	Electric	NA	NA
YJ-2	Campus 60	58cc S.	5	Dual	Kick	161	$285
YG5-T	Trailmaster 80	73cc S.	6.5	Solo	Electric	175	$340
YL-2	Rotary Jet 100	97cc S.	9.5	Dual	Kick	200	$341
YL-2C	Mountain Goat	97cc S.	9.7	Solo	Electric	230	$390
YL-1	Twin Jet 100	98cc T.	9.5	Dual	Kick	185	$385
YL-1E	Twin Jet Electric	98cc T.	9.5	Dual	Electric	184	$393
YA-6	Santa Barbara	125cc S.	13.5	Dual	Electric	264	$454
YAS1-C	Scrambler	124cc T.	15.2	Dual	Kick	219	$475
YCS-1	Bonanza	181cc T.	21	Dual	Electric	262	$565
YCS-1C	Bonanza SCR	181cc T.	21	Dual	Electric	265	$595
DT-1	Enduro	246cc S.	21	3/4	Kick	264	$755
YDS-3	Catalina	246cc T.	28	Dual	Kick	325	$613
YDS-3C	Big Bear	246cc T.	27	Dual	Kick	349	$645
YDS-5	Catalina Electra	246cc T.	29.5	Dual	Electric	324	$660
YDS-2R	Road Racer	246cc T.	36	Racing	Kick	228	$1150
TD-1C	Daytona RR	246cc T.	35	Racing	Kick	245	NA
YM-1	Cross Country	305cc T.	29.5	Dual	Kick	331	$670
YR-2	Grand Prix	348cc T.	36	Dual	Kick	345	$810
YR-2C	GP Scrambler	348cc T.	36	Dual	Kick	342	$840

Yamaha 1968 Notes: The Newport through Santa Barbara models had pressed steel frames and the rest had tubular frames. The Newports were the only three-speeds. All claimed dry weights are listed in pounds. The similar weights listed for the Twin Jet 100 with or without electric starter are suspect. This probably means that one, but not both weighed about 180 pounds and this applies to all other years of these models, too. Judging from the listed weight of the YL-1 in 1969, the kickstart model was most likely the one that weighed about 180 pounds. The stated weight of the DT-1 is wet. (*Cycle World* claimed 235 wet in its February '68 test.) The $150 optional GYT Kit brought the DT-1 up to 30 hp. The Campus 60, Trailmaster 80, Mountain Goat, YAS1-C Scrambler, Bonanza

Scrambler, DT-1 Enduro, Big Bear, and the Grand Prix Scrambler had upswept exhausts. All the rest had downswept pipes. Except for the later years of multiple Enduro models, 1968 may be the peak year for the application of upswept exhausts on Yamahas.

Yamaha claimed a 14.9-second quarter for the Cross Country 305. The claimed top speed of the YDS-3 Catalina 250 was 90 mph. Since the same top speed was claimed for the Big Bear, maybe we can assume the gearing was identical. The YDS-5 Electra had a claimed top speed of 100 mph, which may have been a bit optimistic, but the claimed top speed of the Road Racer probably was a realistic 130 mph. An ad for the 125 and 180 Scramblers touted the release of the movie *Rosemary's Baby* for its inclusion of one or more Yamaha motorcycles. No details of the model or models featured in the movie were mentioned. S = Single / T = Twin.

Grand Prix Scrambler 350 (YR2-C)
You are looking at a new street scrambler that combines high performance with all the features most enthusiasts demand. Such as: twin-cylinder 5-port power, constant mesh 5-speed gearbox and upswept exhaust pipes. Its 348.2 cc engine will clock the Grand Prix in at 90-100 mph.

Grand Prix 350 (YR-2)
This is Yamaha's new masterpiece—the sleekest, most exciting 350 cc street bike ever built. In traffic, she's as docile as a kitten. But when you want her to, she'll lay the needle on the century mark with almost an air of insolence. The Grand Prix's impressive list of advantages includes: twin-cylinder 5-port power, 36 BHP at 7000 rpm, top speed of 100-110 mph and a constant mesh 5-speed gearbox.

Figure H20 - 1968 Yamaha Grand Prix 350 & GP Scrambler. ©1968 Yamaha Motor Corporation, U.S.A.

Figure H21 - 1968 Yamaha YAS1-C 125 Street Scrambler. Compare this red and white machine to the blue 1969 equivalent below. The later model has the gas tank shape from the Enduro Series and the turn signals on the '68 are probably representative of a European-spec machine. ©Peter Abelmann, Germany.

MODEL AS2-C

AVAILABLE COLORS: Hawaiian Blue
Candy Orange

The new Yamaha 125cc twin cylinder street scrambler boasts highest performance and all desirable safety features.

Figure H22 - 1969 Yamaha AS2-C in Hawaiian Blue. ©1969 Yamaha Motor Corporation, U.S.A.

Yamaha 1969 Chart

Model	Name	Type	HP	Seat	Starter	Wt.	Price
YJ-2	Campus 60	58cc Single	5	Dual	Kick	192	$250
G5-S	Street	73cc Single	5	3/4	Kick	168	$290
YG-5T	Trailmaster	73cc Single	6.5	Solo	Electric	173	$342
YL-2	Rotary Jet	97cc Single	9.5	Dual	Kick	199	$320
L5-T	Trailmaster	97cc Single	8	Solo	Electric	200	$399
YL-1	Twin Jet	98cc Twin	9.5	Dual	Kick	208	$330
YA-6	Santa Barbara	123cc Single	13.5	Dual	Electric	248	$430
AT-1	Enduro	124cc Single	11.5	3/4	Electric	218	$509
AT-1 MX	Motocross	124cc Single	18	3/4	Kick	202	$540
AS-2C	Scrambler	124cc Twin	15	Dual	Kick	219	$494
CT-1	Enduro	171cc Single	15.6	3/4	Kick	211	$599
CS-1	Bonanza	181cc Twin	21	Dual	Kick	263	$515
CS-1C	Scrambler	181cc Twin	21	Dual	Kick	263	$572
DT-1B	Enduro	246cc Single	21	3/4	Kick	232	$779
DT-1BMX	Motocross	246cc Single	30	3/4	Kick	215	NA
DS-3	Catalina	246cc Twin	28	Dual	Kick	342	$580
DS-6C	Scrambler	246cc Twin	30	Dual	Kick	304	$665
TD-2	Road Racer	246cc Twin	NA	Racing	Kick	NA	NA
M-1	Cross Country	305cc Twin	29.5	Dual	Kick	338	$624
YR-2	Grand Prix	348cc Twin	36	Dual	Kick	345	$810
YR-2C	GP Scrambler	348cc Twin	36	Dual	Kick	342	$840
R3	Grand Prix	348cc Twin	36	Dual	Kick	340	$779
TR-2	Road Racer	348cc Twin	NA	Racing	Kick	NA	NA

Yamaha 1969 Notes: All claimed dry weights are listed in pounds. All Enduros had upswept pipes and tube frames. Yamaha marketed only single and twin-cylinder two-strokes from 1955 through 1969. The Enduro craze really kicked in with the introduction of the AT-1 and CT-1, the 250's little brothers, identical in every way except actual dimensions and engine displacement. Since the 175 was rarely a racing class, that displacement would usually remain a single enduro model, while its brothers were GYT-kitted directly from the factory, launching the mass-produced motocross concept that is still prevalent today.

Figure H23 - Black & White Yamaha YM2-C Big Bear 305. ©Peter Abelmann, Germany

MODEL DT-1B

Available color: Candy gold only

Figure H24 - 1969 Yamaha Candy Gold DT-1B. Compare the two photos on this page. The first one defined where Yamaha had been and the second one pointed to where they were going. ©1969 Yamaha Motor Corporation, U.S.A.

Yamaha 125 YA-5

Here is the story. I became a Yamaha fan as soon as I learned of the brand. I think it was in early 1962. I remember going down to the local Yamaha shop and drooling over the YDS-2 and Ascot Scrambler. I cannot recall for certain if I have ever seen a YA-5, but if I have, it was in that primitive, dimly-lit dealership on a back street in the less glamorous part of town. I have a number of brochure sheets of the early Yamaha 125's and the black one with the red dual seat that is twice as thick for the rider as the passenger shown in this book is the first such brochure I acquired. I have always assumed that this is a 1962 model, but it could be a '61, and maybe even a '63. I know for certain that Yamaha built this model in those three years only, but the brochures I have are quite confusing. None lists a model year, but I have attempted to match the style and design of the brochures with those of other Yamaha models of the period. Let's just assume that the YA-5 pictured is a 1962 brochure.

What makes this model so important is that the very first Yamaha motorcycle was the YA-1 released in 1955. Derived from the DKW 125 as part of World War II reparations, the YA-1 looked quite a bit different from its direct descendant. The YA-1 had a triangular tube frame similar to the early American Harley tiddlers of the same period, also derived from the DKW. The YA-1 featured simple spring suspension on the front and plunger shocks on the rear. Yamaha also distinguished its model from the DKW and the Harleys with a four-speed transmission. Like the Harleys, the footshift *and* the kickstarter were on the left. This pattern would continue until the YA-6 Santa Barbara was introduced in 1964. The YA-1 also featured long, skinny fenders, a bulbous headlamp nacelle, a teardrop tank, a solo, tractor-style seat, a painted luggage rack, and a conventional carburetor. In other words, the first Yamaha appeared similar to the H-D Hummer and Allstate 125 of the same period. The YA-1 continued into 1956 in either black or maroon (like several Allstate models).

Yamaha broke out of the copycat styling mode in 1957 with the YA-2 looking like some weird Japanese perception of what an ultra-modern motorcycle should look like. The YA-2 had a pressed steel frame and a swoopy-odd gas tank shape that was curved into a slightly upside down U-shape along its bottom edge. The tires and fenders were now much fatter and the chrome handlebars were as flat as those of pressed steel on some early Hondas. The luggage rack and seat took on a more modern shape, and a fully enclosed chain guard and turn signals were added. The YA-2 continued through 1958 and became the YA-3 for 1959-60. The only change I have been able to ascertain from the few photos available is that the YA-3 received a passenger grab bar behind the solo seat and in front of the luggage rack. Maybe it was there to aid putting the bike on the center stand? Maybe a pillion attached to the rack was optional? I also have a photo of a YA-3 with a conventional dual seat and a high-mounted front fender. After extensive research, I have never found any evidence of the existence of a YA-4, at least not in this country.

Specifications

Yamaha
125

Model	YA-5
Overall length	1,870 mm (73.6″)
Overall height	955 mm (37.6″)
Overall width	680 mm (26.7″)
Wheelbase	1,250 mm (49.1″)
Net weight	110 kg (242 lbs)
Maximum speed	105 km/h (70 m.p.h.)
Climbing ability	⅓
Brake efficiency	12 m/50 km/h (47′/30 m.p.h.)
Brakes	Front : Drum Type Hand Brake
	Rear : Drum Type Foot Brake
Tires	Front : 3.00″ × 16″, 2 ply
	Rear : 3.00″ × 16″, 4 ply
Suspension system	Front : Telescopic Oil-Damper
	Rear : Swing Arm Oil-Damper
Fuel tank capacity	8.5 litre (2.3 gallon)
Starting system	Starter Dynamo & Kick-starter

Engine	YA-5, 2 stroke Engine
Cooling	Air-cooling
Cylinder	Single Cylinder System
Bore and Stroke	56mm × 50mm (2.2″ × 1.9″)
Cylinder Capacity	123 cc
Compression Ratio	1 : 6.75
Ignition System	Battery Ignition
Carburetor	Model AMAL M21S1
Clutch	Multi-plate clutch
Transmission	Foot-Operated 4 Speed Gear-Box and Chain
Transmission Ratio	Low 1 : 22.57
	2nd 1 : 13.60
	3rd 1 : 9.80
	Top 1 : 7.60
Fuel consumption	142 mile/gallon
Motor Oil Mixing Ratio	20 : 1
Maximum power	10.5 HP/6,500 r.p.m.

N. B. These specifications are subject to change with or without notice.

Model YA-5

This brings us to the vaunted YA-5. The main reason so much of this information is questionable and difficult to find is that this time period is precisely when the company was establishing a national beachhead in the U.S. I understand that Yamaha entered its first American race on Catalina Island in 1958 before setting up its first dealer network in California. This was about a year before the first Honda dealers were set up in California and Yamaha was at least a few months, maybe longer, behind Honda's schedule. What we know is that you could buy a Yamaha from a dealership in obscure little Columbus MS by 1962. My YG-1 was one of the first Rotary Jet 80's to arrive at that same dealership about a year later. What we don't know is exactly when the first Yamaha dealerships were set up in California, and then in big cities outside the state. I found at least one source that stated a few YA-3's were imported here, but I have certainly never seen one. To be safe, let's say the YA-5 was one of the first Yamaha models brought to the U.S., along with the lowly 50cc MF-1, and possibly a few 250cc YD-2 road models and the beginnings of the 250 Sports, the YDS-1. I can speak from experience when I say that small Mississippi dealer sold YD-3's and MF-1's, but I do not think the YDS-1, YD-2, or YA-3 ever reached national U.S. distribution.

The YA-5 captures that magical time in tiddler history when the Japanese invasion was exciting and new. Electric starters were all the rage, and the new YA-5 had one, although as I have said many times before, my cat can kickstart most any two-stroke tiddler. The YA-5 had the tiny turn signals of some of the earliest machines sent here from Japan. Remember that the popular early Hondas with which we are all familiar did not have them. That is because the early tiddlers from 1960-63 had small turn signal lamps that the U.S. authorities said were too small and too close together. During the boom years of 64-67, none of those Hondas had them. The company just deleted them from their export versions, but one of the big changes of the 1968 period brought the turn signals back to Hondas, though this time they were larger, brighter, and mounted on stalks that spread them further apart, and some were located higher off the ground than on previous versions. The '64 Santa Barbara would not have turn signals, but the earlier YA-5's still had the small ones. One distinguishing feature of all the YA-5's is the unusual seat shape, with the front section being much deeper than the passenger section. Some YA-5's, such as the one in the photo in this book, had low bars, but later ones had the more common Western bars similar to those of the Santa Barbara, but a little lower. I have one brochure showing high bars with low bars as an option. Some of the early YDS-2's and Super Hawks were offered with both, too. Was this a choice with *all* YA-5's? I don't know. Unlike its predecessors, the YA-5 had a rotary valve, but the kickstarter was still distinctively mounted on the left. The pictured model shows off its red seat on a black bike, but most of the photos I have seen show a more conventional red bike with a black seat and Western bars. The tank shape is now stylish and conventional, and the trademark Yamaha tall, as opposed to long, headlamp nacelle with the speedo in the raised portion has been established. A tiny tail lamp, the distinctive, early-60's tiny windscreen, and the lack of emblems on the tank panels are distinguishing marks of the YA-5. This last detail is one of the elements that have been driving me crazy for months. All the other YA-5 photos I have show either a round tuning fork emblem or a *YAMAHA* badge on the tank. I do not know why the one in the photo appears to feature a blank chrome panel. Maybe this tank was never actually imported?

Model year 1964 would introduce the much more common, at least in the U.S., Santa Barbara model with high bars, the new Autolube oil injection system, and finally, a kickstarter on the right side of the machine for any of my cats needing a little exercise. Of course the YA-6 still had an electric starter, too. It has always been about the marketing, y'all. I may never have seen a YA-5, but I have always known in my gut that it was a key model in Yamaha history.

Figure H25 (first photo in this article) - Maroon & Cream 1955 Yamaha 125 YA-1. This museum display shows an example of the first production Yamaha, the 125cc YA-1. Very few, if any, Yamaha 125's were officially imported into the U.S. prior to the YA-5. Image by Rikita under Creative Commons license (GNU).

Figure H26 (middle photo in this article) - 1962 Yamaha 125 YA-5. This first-year brochure shows the YA-5 with only minimal concessions to the U.S. market. Note the low bars, small windscreen, and left-side kickstarter. ©1962 Yamaha Motor Corporation, U.S.A.

Figure H27 (this page) - 1963 Yamaha 125 YA-5 Brochure. Notice the new standard high bars with the low ones still offered as an option. The windscreen is gone, but the starter is still on the left. The Santa Barbara would debut in late '64 with oil injection and a right-side kickstarter. ©1963 Yamaha Motor Corporation, U.S.A.

The epoch-making new characteristics of Yamaha 125, YA5

1) Jet-like acceleration and remarkable high horsepower by adapting the disk type rotary valve.
2) Easy starting by newly adopted starter carburetor.
3) Superior brake efficiency by enlarged waterproof brake drum.
4) Simple and refined design.

Bar Handle model is also available upon your request

YAMAHA MOTOR CO., LTD.

Hamamatsu, Japan

Specifications

Model	YA-5	Engine	YA-5, 2 stroke Engine
Overall length	1,870 mm (73.6")	Cooling	Air-cooling
Overall height	955 mm (37.6")	Cylinder	Single Cylinder System
Overall width	680 mm (26.7")	Bore and Stroke	56 mm × 50 mm (2.2" × 1.9")
Wheelbase	1,250 mm (49.1")	Cylinder Capacity	123 cc
Net weight	110 kg (242 lbs)	Compression Ratio	1 : 6.75
Maximum speed	105 km/h (70 m.p.h.)	Ignition System	Battery Ignition
Climbing ability	⅓	Clutch	Multi-plate clutch
Brake efficiency	12 m/50 km/h (47/30 m.p.h.)	Transmission	Foot-Operated 4 Speed Gear-Box and Chain
Suspension system	Front: Telescopic Oil-Damper	Fuel consumption	142 mile/gallon
	Rear: Swing Arm Oil-Damper	Motor Oil Mixing Ratio	20 : 1
Fuel tank capacity	8.5 litre (2.3 gallon)	Maximum power	10.5 HP/6,500 r.p.m.
Starting system, Starter Dynamo & Kick-starter			

Yamaha Racers

From the beginning of its U.S. operations, Yamaha supported privateer racing by offering very competitive models for sale to the public. The company offered a YDS-1 Scrambler in 1959 to accompany its first YDS street-sport model. There is no publishable photo available, but I shall describe that machine from a tiny file photo I have. The Scrambler preceded the Ascot, pictured below, and was somewhat similar. Whereas the Ascot was an obvious, and very successful, flat-tracker, the Scrambler was intended for a little less specialized off-road racing. Keep in mind that motocross was in its infancy and the sky-high jumps of Supercross were still decades away. The Scrambler had upswept chrome expansion chambers, one on each side, high chrome fenders, and knobby tires. The gearing was lowered from the street YDS-1 and the footpegs were raised. The center stand was removed and their was no lighting equipment. The gas tank shape and gold and white paint were familiar to early YDS viewers. The seat was changed to a three-quarter style with its rear section tilted upward, predating the DT-1 style by nearly a decade.

Photo H28 - 1965 TD-1 & Ascot. This small B&W brochure photo advertised Yamaha's two racing models of that year. Notice the similar racing-style solo seats and twin, downswept expansion chambers, but the similarities ended there. Each machine was a truly specialized racer. ©1965 Yamaha Motor Corporation, U.S.A.

Photo H29 (next page) - 1966 Ascot & Daytona. This more detailed brochure from the following year includes a few specifications. Both machines were rated at 35 horsepower, with the Ascot at 500 rpm higher. The Ascot came with a tachometer like its Scrambler predecessor, but you can see its abbreviated rear fender and uncovered front tire in this brochure. The fenders of the Scrambler were high, but full-sized. The TD-1B sports a common fairing style for the day. ©1966 Yamaha Motor Corporation, U.S.A.

YAMAHA ASCOT SCRAMBLER YDS-3M Winningest dirt-track 250 in America. Amazing acceleration and reliability. Buy it and make a shelf to hold your trophies.

Cylinders	2	Clutch	Multi-disc, wet plate
Displacement	246cc		
Lubrication System	Oil & Gas	Gear Box	Constant mesh 5-speed
Maximum Horsepower	35 @ 10,500 rpm		
Speed Range	105-115 mph	Wheelbase	51"
Carburetion	Vm 24mm	Electrical System	Mag.

Tachometer, tuned exhaust, alloy rims and knobby tires are standard equipment.

YAMAHA

YAMAHA DAYTONA ROAD RACER TD-1B Only bike ever to take 1-2-3-4, 7-8-9-10 at Daytona. Finely tuned...rarin' to win. Suit up...fire up...hop on...get on it and GO. Strictly for racing.

Cylinders	2	Clutch	Multi-disc, wet plate
Displacement	246cc		
Lubrication System	Oil & Gas	Gear Box	Constant mesh 5-speed
Maximum Horsepower	35 @10,500 rpm	Net Weight	245 lbs.
Speed Range	120-125 mph	Wheelbase	51"
2 carburetors	1-1/32" Amal type	Electrical System	Mag.
		Road Clearance	4½"

Photo H30 - 1964 Yamaha TD-1B. This particular machine was last ridden by John Buckner at Daytona in 1966. Buckner came in second on this machine in the 100-mile, 250-class race. This bike has been stored for 43 years. The paint is not stock: the machine was left just as it was raced except the racing plate number was changed from 155 to 53. ©Warren P. Warner.

Photo H31 - 1967 Yamaha TD-1C. You can see the powertrain on this unfaired model. Note the exposed countershaft sprocket for weight reduction as well as quick gearing changes. The large tachometer has a nice mounting arrangement for driver visibility in a racing crouch. ©Warren P. Warner.

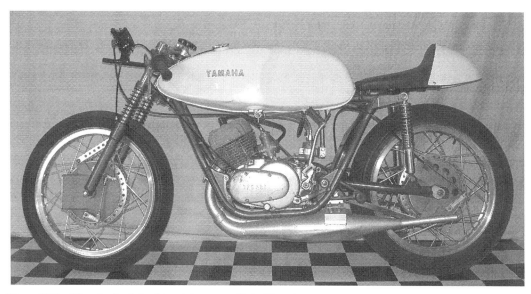

Photo H32 - Here is the left side of the same 1967 TD-1C. Note the humongous brakes with large scoop and ventilation holes. This example still has its kick starter. Most were removed and discarded by the weight-conscious owner/racers. ©Warren P. Warner.

Photo H33 - 1969 White & Red Yamaha TD-2. Get a load of that smooth fairing style! The drum front brake and conventional rear shocks would not be replaced on the Yamaha road racers until about 1974. Image by Ytak171 under Creative Commons license (GNU).

Yamaha 1970 Chart

Model	Name	Type	HP	Seat	Starter	Wt.	Price
G-6S	Street	73cc Single	4.9	3/4	Kick	170	$299
HS-1	Street	89cc Twin	4.9	Dual	Kick	196	$409
HT-1	90 Enduro	89cc Single	8.5	3/4	Kick	187	$409
L5-TA	Trail	97cc Single	8	Solo	Electric	200	$399
AT-1B	125 Enduro	123cc S.	11.5	3/4	Electric	218	$509
AT-1BMX	Motocross	123cc S.	18	3/4	Kick	202	$539
AS-2C	Scrambler	124cc Twin	15.2	Dual	Kick	221	$489
CT-1B	175 Enduro	171cc S.	15.6	3/4	Kick	211	$599
CS-3C	Scrambler	200cc Twin	22	Dual	Electric	262	$599
DT-1C	250 Enduro	246cc S.	23	3/4	Kick	232	$799
DT-1CMX	Motocross	246cc S.	30	3/4	Kick	227	$814
DS-6B	Street	246cc Twin	30	Dual	Kick	304	$659
TD-2	Road Racer	246cc Twin	44	Racing	Kick	NA	$1400
R5	Street	347cc Twin	36	Dual	Kick	340	$739
TR-2	Road Racer	348cc Twin	54	Racing	Kick	NA	$1500
RT-1	360 Enduro	351cc S.	30	3/4	Kick	252	$869
RT-1M	Motocross	351cc S.	36	3/4	Kick	243	$904
XS-1	Street	653cc Twin	53	Dual	Kick	390	$1245

Yamaha 1970 Notes: All claimed dry weights are listed in pounds. The 90cc HS-1 replaced the 100cc YL-1 as the small twin in the lineup. The 4.9 horsepower rating probably represents Yamaha's restricted five-horsepower model rating, and the HS-1 most likely produced about 9 hp. The color of this model was California Orange.

Yamaha made an unusual choice in 1970 that seemed puzzling at the time, but in retrospect, the company knew exactly what it was doing. Instead of copying the Honda 750 Four, Yamaha chose to update the BSA/Triumph antique twin. The XS-1 became a legendary cult favorite as soon as it hit our shores. Many American riders had been asking for nothing more than a 650 twin that always started, didn't shake your teeth loose or leak oil, and offered easy maintenance and long life. Apparently not everyone was seeking the power of a Cobra or the shriek of a Ferrari. Some just wanted to return to the simple time of *Happy Days* where Fonzi's Triumph always started on the first kick and all the girls in town loved him. The XS-1 offered a direct solution. Design the machine with horizontally split engine cases to stop the drip. Utilize modern Japanese electrics so the beast always starts and lights the way at night. Add a modern overhead camshaft for higher rpm performance. Rubber-mount specific components to lessen the quake, or at least minimize the effects, and move the shifter over to the left side where Americans feel it belongs. NOW we are getting somewhere! S = Single.

Figure H34 - 1970 Blue & White G6S 80. Compare this model to its direct ancestor, the YG-1. The most noticeable changes are the slim tank, racing-style seat, upswept exhaust, and sportier fenders. Otherwise its pretty much the same little 73cc Rotary Jet Fun Machine! ©1970 Yamaha Motor Corporation, U.S.A.

Figure H35 - 1970 & '72 Yamaha 350 DS-7's. These 250cc Twins are a beautiful pair. The purple and white 1970 is in the background and the black and gold 1972 is in the foreground. Note that the kick starters are now on the right. ©Peter Abelmann, Germany.

Yamaha 1971 Chart

Model	Name	Type	HP	Seat	Starter	Wt.	Price
JT-1	Enduro	58cc Single	4.5	3/4	Kick	121	$300
G6S-B	Street	73cc Single	4.9	Racing	Kick	173	$319
HS-1B	Street	89cc Twin	4.9	Dual	Kick	199	$419
HT-1B	Enduro	89cc Single	8.5	3/4	Kick	190	$409
AT-1C	Enduro	123cc Single	11.5	3/4	Electric	221	$525
AT-1CMX	Motocross	123cc Single	18	3/4	Kick	202	$560
CT-1C	Enduro	171cc Single	15.6	3/4	Kick	214	$625
CS-3B	Street	195cc Twin	22	Dual	Electric	258	$619
DT-1E	Enduro	246cc Single	23	3/4	Kick	264	$795
DT-1CMX	Motocross	246cc Single	30	3/4	Kick	232	$870
TD-2B	Road Racer	246cc Twin	44	Racing	Kick	NA	$1400
R-5B	Street	347cc Twin	36	Dual	Kick	311	$779
TR-2B	Road Racer	347cc Twin	54	Racing	Kick	245	$1450
RT-1B	Enduro	351cc Single	30	3/4	Kick	258	$925
RT-1BMX	Motocross	351cc Single	36	3/4	Kick	238	$970
XS-1B	Street	653cc Twin	53	Dual	Kick	433	$1295

Yamaha 1971 Notes: The JT-1 Enduro is a mini-bike. The HS-1B came in Competition Yellow, had turn signals, and like its 1970 version, probably produced far more than 4.9 horsepower. All claimed dry weights are listed in pounds. The weight stated for the DT-1E Enduro and the XS-1B are wet. The AT-1C prices with setup were $580 for the Enduro and $650 for the MX.

Yamaha 1972 Chart

Model	Type	Type	HP	Seat	Starter	Wt.	Price
RD60	Street	55cc Single	NA	3/4	Kick	163	$359
JT-1	Enduro	58cc Single	4.5	3/4	Kick	121	$300
JT-2L	Enduro	58cc Single	4.5	3/4	Kick	121	$300
JT-2MX	MX	58c Single	NA	3/4	Kick	NA	$314
GTI-80	Enduro	73cc Single	NA	3/4	Kick	141	$356
GT-80MX	MX	73cc Single	NA	3/4	Kick	130	$319
U7E	Step-Thru	73cc Single	NA	Dual	Electric	170	NA
G-6SB	Street	73cc Single	4.9	3/4	Kick	173	$319
G7S	Street	73cc Single	NA	3/4	Kick	NA	NA
HS-1B	Street	89cc Twin	4.9	Dual	Kick	199	$419
HT-1B	Enduro	89cc Single	8.5	3/4	Kick	190	$409
LS-2	Street	98cc Twin	10.5	Dual	Kick	NA	NA
LT3-100	Enduro	97cc Single	10	Solo	NA	187	$489
LT-100MX	MX	97cc Single	NA	Solo	Kick	185	$514
LT-2	Enduro	97cc Single	10	3/4	Kick	187	$459
AT-2	Enduro	123cc S.	13	3/4	Electric	221	$525
AT-2MX	MX	123cc S.	18	3/4	Kick	202	$560
CT-2	Enduro	171cc S.	15.6	3/4	Kick	214	$625
CS-5	Street	195cc Twin	22	Dual	Electric	258	$619
DS-7	Street	247cc Twin	30	Dual	Kick	304	$739
DT-2	Enduro	246cc S.	24	3/4	Kick	258	$795
DT-2MX	MX	246cc S.	30	3/4	Kick	232	$870
RD250	Street	247cc Twin	NA	Dual	Kick	309	$759
TD-3	RR	247cc Twin	NA	Racing	Push	231	NA
R-5C	Street	347cc Twin	36	Dual	Kick	311	$779
TR-3	RR	347cc Twin	54	Racing	Push	245	$1450
RD350	Street	347cc Twin	NA	Dual	Kick	349	$839
TZ350	RR	347cc Twin	NA	Racing	Push	254	NA
RT-2	Enduro	351cc S.	32	3/4	Kick	262	$999
RT-2 MX	MX	351cc S.	36	3/4	Kick	234	$1125
SC500 MX	MX	496cc S.	NA	3/4	Kick	236	$1225
TX500	Street	498cc Twin	NA	Dual	Electric	456	$1369
XS-2	Street	653cc Twin	53	Dual	Electric	427	$1399
TX750	Street	743cc Twin	63	Dual	Electric	518	$1554

Yamaha 1972 Notes: All claimed dry weights are listed in pounds. The listed weight of the TX500 is wet. Yamaha expanded its big four-stroke line for the first time, but the move was not particularly successful. The DOHC Twin TX models were slower than their multi-cylinder competitors, and they were generally slow sellers, too, while the cult status of the 650 continued to climb. Both models were hurt by high prices for the displacement and performance levels while the 650 soldiered onward, viewed as a good value by buyers. The TX 500 and 750 were competing with smoother, faster four-cylinders on one side and traditionally designed, lower priced models on the other. Perceived value won and technology lost. MX = Motocross / RR = Road Racer / S = Single.

Figure H36 - 1972 Red Yamaha XS-650B. ©Michael Kiernan, Classic Motorcycle Company, St. Louis, MO.

Figure H37 - Purple & White 1972 Yamaha RD-200. ©1972 Yamaha Motor Corporation, U.S.A.

Yamaha 1973 Chart

Model	Name	Type	Seat	Starter	Wt.	Price
RD60	Street	55cc Single	Racing	Kick	163	$359
GTI-80	Enduro	73cc Single	3/4	Kick	141	$356
GT-80MX	Motocross	73cc Single	3/4	Kick	130	$319
LT3-100	Enduro	97cc Single	Solo	NA	187	$489
LT-100 MX	Motocross	97cc Single	Solo	Kick	185	$514
AT3-125	Enduro	123cc Single	3/4	Electric	221	$589
AT-125 MX	Motocross	123cc Single	3/4	Kick	202	$638
CT3-175	Enduro	175cc Single	3/4	Kick	214	$699
DT3-250	Enduro	246cc Single	3/4	Kick	262	$859
MX250	Motocross	246cc Single	3/4	Kick	227	$1025
RD250	Street	247cc Twin	Dual	Kick	309	$759
TA250	Road Racer	247cc Twin	Racing	Push	231	NA
TZ250-A	Road Racer	247cc Twin	Racing	Kick	NA	NA
RD350	Street	347cc Twin	Dual	Kick	349	$839
TZ350	Road Racer	347cc Twin	Racing	Push	254	NA
TZ350-A	Road Racer	347cc Twin	Racing	Push	NA	NA
RT3-360	Enduro	351cc Single	3/4	Kick	262	$999
MX360	Motocross	351cc Single	3/4	Kick	234	$1125
SC500 MX	Motocross	496cc Single	3/4	Kick	236	$1225
TX500	Street	498cc Twin	Dual	Electric	456	$1369
TX650	Street	653cc Twin	Dual	Electric	439	$1419
TX750	Street	743cc Twin	Dual	Electric	518	$1554

Yamaha 1973 Notes: The TA250 Road Racer offered only early in the 1973 production year had the old air-cooled engine installed in the new TZ chassis. The TZ250-A and TZ350-A were liquid cooled, but still used twin rear shocks and drum front brakes. All claimed dry weights are listed in pounds. The RD350, TX500 and TX750 listed weights are wet. Yamaha did not officially publish horsepower figures in 1973, but one source listed the TX750 as having 63 horsepower.

Figure H38 - 1973 Blue & Gold Yamaha TX-650. ©Michael Kiernan, Classic Motorcycle Company, St. Louis, MO.

Figure H39 - Blue 1973 RD-60. ©Jimmy Singer, owner and photographer

Yamaha 1974 Chart

Model	Name	Type	Seat	Starter	Wt.	Price
RD60	Street	55cc Single	Racing	Kick	163	$475
GT-80	Enduro	73cc Single	3/4	Kick	141	$442
GT-MX	Motocross	73cc Single	3/4	Kick	130	$400
TY80	Trials	73cc Single	Solo	Kick	130	$442
DT-100	Enduro	97cc Single	3/4	Kick	187	$603
MX-100	Motocross	97cc Single	3/4	Kick	185	$702
DT-125	Enduro	123cc Single	3/4	Electric	221	$728
MX-125	Motocross	123cc Single	3/4	Kick	202	$835
YZ125	Motocross	123cc Single	3/4	Kick	192	$967
DT-175	Enduro	171cc Single	3/4	Kick	214	$832
MX-175	Motocross	171cc Single	3/4	Kick	220	$1071
RD250	Street	247cc Twin	Dual	Kick	309	$963
DT-250	Enduro	246cc Single	3/4	Kick	262	$1087
MX-250	Motocross	246cc Single	3/4	Kick	227	$1199
YZ250	Motocross	246cc Single	3/4	Kick	209	$1700
TY250	Trials	246cc Single	Solo	Kick	224	$1123
TZ250-A	Road Racer	247cc Twin	Racing	Push	NA	NA
RD350	Street	347cc Twin	Dual	Kick	349	$1071
TZ350-A	Road Racer	347cc Twin	Racing	Push	NA	NA
DT-360	Enduro	351cc Single	3/4	Kick	262	$1212
MX-360	Motocross	351cc Single	3/4	Kick	234	$1246
SC500	Motocross	496cc Single	3/4	Kick	236	$1407
TX500	Street	498cc Twin	Dual	Electric	456	$1688
TX650	Street	653cc Twin	Dual	Electric	439	$1804

Yamaha 1974 Notes: Yamaha did not officially publish horsepower figures in 1974. All claimed dry weights are listed in pounds. The listed weight of the TX500 is wet. The TX750 was dropped from the lineup after only two model years while the 500 and 650 carried on. There was some discussion in the magazines of the period that the TX750 was essentially Yamaha's one big white elephant. The model never developed much of a market niche and there were some mentions of long-term reliability issues. Basically, the Omni-Phase Balancer system caused crankshaft bearing failures on early models. Yamaha responded to the problem promptly, but the damage to the TX750's reputation was already done.

Figure H40 - 1970 California Orange Yamaha HS-1. ©Don Quayle, Costa Mesa, CA

Figure H41 - 1971 Competition Yellow Yamaha HS-1B 90 Twin. ©Peter Abelmann, Germany

Yamaha 1975 Chart

Model	Name	Type	HP	Seat	Starter	Wt.	Price
RD-60B	Street	55cc Single	NA	Racing	Kick	163	$499
GT-80B	Enduro	73cc Single	NA	Solo	Kick	141	$499
GT-MXB	Motocross	73cc Single	NA	Solo	Kick	130	$454
YZ-80B	Motocross	73cc Single	NA	Solo	Kick	138	$499
TY-80B	Trials	73cc Single	NA	Solo	Kick	131	$499
RS-100B	Street	97cc Single	10.5	Dual	Kick	212	$599
DT-100B	Enduro	97cc Single	10	3/4	Kick	187	$684
MX-100B	Motocross	97cc Single	16	3/4	Kick	200	$796
RD-125B	Street	124cc Twin	16	Dual	Kick	255	$699
DT-125B	Enduro	123cc S.	13	3/4	Electric	221	$799
MX-125B	Motocross	123cc S.	20	3/4	Kick	202	$896
YZ-C 125	Motocross	123cc S.	23	3/4	Kick	185	$995
DT-175B	Enduro	171cc S.	16	3/4	Kick	214	$942
MX-175B	Motocross	171cc S.	18	3/4	Kick	220	$1095
TY-175B	Trials	171cc S.	12	Solo	Kick	192	$965
RD-200B	Street	195cc Twin	22	Dual	Electric	275	$995
DT-250B	Enduro	246cc S.	21	3/4	Kick	262	$1229
TY-250B	Trials	246cc S.	17	Solo	Kick	205	$1123
MX-250B	Motocross	246cc S.	28	3/4	Kick	227	$1288
YZ-250M	Motocross	246cc S.	34	3/4	Kick	209	$1850
RD-250B	Street	247cc Twin	30	Dual	Kick	309	$1099
TZ250-B	Road Racer	247cc Twin	NA	Racing	Push	NA	NA
RD-350B	Street	347cc Twin	39	Dual	Kick	349	$1211
TZ350-B	Road Racer	347cc Twin	NA	Racing	Push	NA	NA
YZ-360B	Motocross	351cc S.	42	3/4	Kick	209	NA
DT-400B	Enduro	397cc S.	27	3/4	Kick	268	$1371
MX-400B	Motocross	397cc S.	42	3/4	Kick	240	$1486
TT-500C	Motocross	499cc OHC	NA	3/4	Kick	282	NA
XS-500B	Street	498cc Twin	48	Dual	Electric	452	$1749
XS-650B	Street	653cc Twin	53	Dual	Electric	440	$1889

Yamaha 1975 Notes: All four 72cc dirt models are mini machines. The stated weight for the RS-100B is the wet weight of the '76 model, as tested by *Cycle* in November 1975. The stated weight of the RD-125B is wet, as stated in the April 1975 *Cycle* Road Test. All claimed dry weights are listed in pounds. The latest 1975 road racing TZ-model 250 and 350 still had twin rear shocks and front drum brakes! They would finally get monoshocks and front disc brakes the next year in 1976. S = Single.

Figure H42 - Red & White Yamaha RD-350. Image by John Goetzinger under Creative Commons license.

1968 Yamaha DT-1

I was twelve in 1960 when my best friend got a Harley-Davidson Super 10, and before the year was out, he had introduced me ever so briefly to what would later become known as *trail riding*. We rode down to the levee next to the Yazoo River in Greenwood MS, where the kids had created a small maze of trails they named The Bicycle Chute. It was a simple little area down near the river where the trees grew tall and thick enough to create challenging trails for bicycles and small motorcycles. The Chute itself got its name from a group of little up-and-down, roller coaster hills and jumps that the kids rode, surrounded by dense forest. This obviously was a pioneering event not only for motorized tiddlers, but what would later be developed and called BMX and Mountain Bikes. Yes, George, I said 1960, and I have generally been ahead of my time in most of my endeavors ever since.

I loved trail riding right from the beginning. Boys in Mississippi have always been of the outdoorsy type. After all, it's not exactly an area famous for its big cities. Not only was it fun to explore the countryside, but you could learn new riding skills and enjoy new challenges in an environment that was safer than the street in front of your own house. My off-road riding was as limited as my street time for the next three years, until I got a Yamaha Rotary Jet 80 in the summer of '63. In 1967 I bought a Honda CA-100, removed the leg shields and front fender, changed the rear tire to a full knobby, the handlebars to a low-rise chrome set, and lowered the gearing, and off through the mud and trees I went, albeit slowly.

I put all the standard equipment back on the little Honda 50 and traded it in on a Kawasaki G3-TR at the end of '69, getting $5 more in trade on the little step-through than I had paid for it! The little Kaw was the first bike I had that was actually designed for trail riding, so it was naturally a huge improvement. I had this habit of befriending young men a couple of years older than me who had better toys, and in 1969, my best riding buddy was a true-blue Honda fan. Are you ready for the funny part? I met him out on the trails where he was riding a Super Hawk, with tall, apehanger bars, no less! I soon got to know him as a particularly strong fan of the CL-160, of which he owned several immediately after the Super Hawk. No trail riding memory will ever replace the one when he showed me what a CL-160 could really do. He took a CL-160 of the type that had been shipped to the dealer as a CB, removed the electric starter, changed the gearing and carburetor jets, and replaced the ugly, stifling muffler with a pair of upswept megaphones that howled like a banshee! Man, was that one mean trail-riding machine!

At about the same time that I bought the G3-TR, he bought one of the early SL-350's with the heavy, single-downtube frame and the fat front tire. Together we made a huge system of trails in a wooded area just off campus at Mississippi State University. He made the big whomping, climbing dips that he so loved with the enormous torque of his 350-pound beast, and I made the little *cheater trails* that went around them. Together, it was a delight to riders of everything from tiddlers to Honda 350's for many years to come. I actually owned the G3-TR for only nine months before I traded it for a new CL-350 K2, which believe it or not, I wound up riding through our little trail maze far more times than I had the G3. He didn't keep the SL-350 that long, either, before he discovered the machine that was really the hot ticket for our little maze of tight turns, dips, and hills full of trees and mud: a 1971 AT-1CMX with lowered gearing, high front fender, and a 21-inch front wheel. A little later mine would have the lowered gearing, a high, plastic Preston Petty front fender, and a Skyway silencer that made it just quiet enough to stop the splitting of my own ears. They were both red. They were both 1971 125cc Yamaha motocrossers slightly modified for tight, muddy trail riding. Mine is still in my garage. It still runs and looks just like it did thirty-five years ago. That's how much I like the Yamaha DT-1 and what it did for the sport of trail riding.

There were many American and European trail models long before the DT-1 reached America in early '68. Greeves, Bultaco, BSA, Ducati, Harley-Davidson, Triumph, Allstate, and many others built scrambler models in the late '50's and early '60's. They ranged from the seriously off-road competitive models of Bultaco and Greeves to the much less serious H-D Scat, Sprint H, and Ranger. Cushman made the putt-putt Trailster. Rokon stole a couple of tires from a Massey-Ferguson (or John Deere, if you prefer your fantasies green) and created the Trail-Breaker. Honda and Yamaha brought their tiddliest little Trail 50's to the USA in the very early Sixties. Trail riding in America was a rapidly growing hobby.

After Honda shook up the motorcycle world with the underwater-howl of its CL-72 in 1962, most of the Japanese brands jumped onto the Scrambler bandwagon as fast as their upswept pipes and crossbrace handlebars could carry them. Although I personally rode the trails with the CL-72's greatly improved descendant, the CL-350 K2, it was of course a compromise (some would say *compromised*) street machine. This is why Honda had to develop the Motosport models. Of course Yamaha *forced* Honda to do this with the extreme success of its own Enduro line. The DT-1 launched itself right off the showroom floor onto the trails of 1968 better than any machine ever had. What about the Bultacos? You mean those finicky, expensive, not so durable things for which spare parts were hard to come by? What about the BSA's and Triumphs? Did they not look and sound wonderful? Yes, they did, between the electrical outages, starting difficulties, and drips on the floor.

The DT-1 was released in Japan in 1967. The first one I actually encountered had been brought back to MSU by an ex-serviceman stationed you-know-where. Of course I knew exactly what it was the first time I saw it because *Cycle World* had been my favorite reading material since 1962. Yamaha extended its Enduro lineup in '69 with the 125cc AT-1. As most of you know, the company chose to do something weird. The AT-1 featured an electric starter to try to interest girls and other foo-foo riders in the *new* trail riding hobby. The original DT-1 was officially sold only as the Enduro. An optional, aftermarket GYT Kit turned the Enduro into a motocrosser. I am not sure in exactly which model year it happened, but by 1971, the AT-1CMX like my friend and I bought was a separate model. The *C* stands for third year or third generation. The '69 was simply called the AT-1; the '70 was the AT-1B; and the '71 was the AT-1C. The 1972 models began the first major changes that brought the AT-2 designation instead of an AT-1DMX. The machine I have is the last year of the original design. That's part of why I'm so attached to it.

As the years progressed after the 1968 DT-1, Yamaha expanded the line into other displacements. The RT-1 was the 360cc model; the CT-1 was the 175cc model; and the HT-1 was the 90cc model. I have never personally ridden an HT-1, but I have ridden the other two. Surprisingly, I have never ridden any of the 250cc models, either! One has never seemed to come my way. I really liked the torque of the RT-1, and I might have bought one if friends had not talked me out of it. They always said that starting the beast could be a real pain in the leg or shin, and with lowered gearing and well developed riding skills, the 125cc-250cc models were more satisfying. Since I never rode an RT-l except briefly, I am going to assume that my friends were right. Obviously if the little 125 sweetheart had not been so lovable, I would never have kept it all these years.

Figure H43 - 1968 Yamaha 250 DT-1 Enduro. Image by Rikita under Creative Commons license (GNU).

Figure H44 - 1968 Yamaha 250 DT-1 Enduro. ©Don Quayle, Costa Mesa, CA

Figures H45 & H46 (next two pages) - First Brochure of the 1968 Yamaha DT-1. This first brochure for the U.S. market was a single sheet printed on two sides in black and white.

©1968 Yamaha Motor Corporation, U.S.A.

The most exciting motorcycle for 1968. Designed for action in desert, mountain, trail or street.

The new Yamaha 250 single incorporates functional styling and rugged design, and is engineered for performance plus. This new model, which has been developed as the result of over 3 years of research, development and field testing, offers dealers the opportunity to sell a demonstrably superior product at a price that is, in some cases, hundreds of dollars less than competitors.

Some of the features include:

- Five port power — 5-speed gear box
- Tube frame
- Extremely lightweight
- Superior Yamaha front fork assembly
- Slim profile
- High ground clearance
- Spring loaded foot pegs

- Autolube oil injection
- Quick detachable lights
- Fully equipped for street or trail
- Plus GYT Kit availability

YAMAHA SINCE 1887

INTERNATIONAL CORPORATION · MONTEBELLO, CALIF.

375

Yamaha Enduro / Motocross / Trials Chart

Year	Model	Size	Color	Tank Trim	Front Wheel
1968	DT-1 / MX	246cc	Pearl White	Black Pinstripe	19-inch
1969	AT-1 / MX	123cc	Pearl White	Black Pinstripe	18-inch
1969	CT-1	171cc	Red	White Pinstripe	18-inch
1969	DT-1B / MX	246cc	Candy Gold	White Pinstripe	19-inch
1970	HT-1	89cc	Purple or Gold	White Pinstripe	18-inch
1970	AT-1B / MX	123cc	Competition Yellow	Black Pinstripe	18-inch
1970	CT-1B	171cc	Green	White Pinstripe	18-inch
1970	DT-1C / MX	246cc	Red	White Pinstripe	19-inch
1970	RT-1 / M	351cc	Purple	Gold Pinstripe	19-inch
1971	HT-1B	89cc	Dark Red	White Pinstripe	18-inch
1971	AT-1C / MX	123cc	Brilliant Red	White Pinstripe	18-inch
1971	CT-1C	171cc	Gold	White Pinstripe	18-inch
1971	DT-1E	246cc	Gold	White Pinstripe	19-inch
1971	DT-1C MX	246cc	Gold	White Pinstripe	19-inch
1971	RT-1B / MX	351cc	Black	Red Pinstripe	19-inch
1972	HT-1B	89cc	Gold	White Letters	18-inch
1972	AT-2 / MX	123cc	Bronze	White Letters	18-inch
1972	LT-2	97cc	Green	White Letters	18-inch
1972	CT-2	171cc	Red	White Letters	18-inch
1972	DT-2 / MX	246cc	Gold	White Letters	19-inch
1972	RT-2 / MX	351cc	Silver	Black Letters	19-inch
1972	SC-500 MX	496cc	NA	NA	NA
1973	LT-3	97cc	Grape	B&W Stripes	18-inch
1973	AT-3 / MX	123cc	Brigade Blue	B&W Stripes	18-inch
1973	CT-3	171cc	Gold Dust	B&W Stripes	18-inch
1973	DT-3	246cc	Competition Green	B&W Stripes	19-inch
1973	MX-250	246cc	Silver	Red Curved Stripe	21-inch

1973	RT-3	351cc	Baja Brown	B&W Stripes	19-inch
1973	MX-360	351cc	Orange	B&W Stripes	19-inch
1973	SC-500 MX	496cc	NA	NA	NA
1974	DT-100	97cc	NA	White Pinstripes	18-inch
1974	MX-100	97cc	Yellow	Black Stripes	18-inch
1974	DT-125	123cc	Red	White Pinstripes	21-inch
1974	MX-125	123cc	Yellow	Black Stripes	21-inch
1974	YZ-125	123cc	White	Curved Stripes	21-inch
1974	DT-175	171cc	Gold	White Pinstripes	21-inch
1974	MX-175	171cc	Yellow	Black Stripes	21-inch
1974	DT-250	246cc	Blue	Curved Stripes	21-inch
1974	MX-250	246cc	Yellow	Black Stripes	21-inch
1974	YZ-250	246cc	Yellow	Curved Stripes	21-inch
1974	TY-250	247cc	White	Yellow Trim	21-inch
1974	DT-360	351cc	Green	White Pinstripe	21-inch
1974	MX-360	351cc	Yellow	Black Stripes	21-inch
1974	SC-500	496cc	Yellow	Black Stripes	21-inch
1975	DT-100B	97cc	Orange	White Panels	18-inch
1975	MX-100B	97cc	White	Contrasting Panels	18-inch
1975	DT-125B	123cc	Red	White Panels	21-inch
1975	MX-125B	123cc	White	Contrasting Panels	21-inch
1975	YZ-C 125	123cc	Yellow	Black Racing Stripe	21-inch
1975	DT-175B	171cc	NA	White Panels	21-inch
1975	MX-175B	171cc	White	Blue Panels	21-inch
1975	TY-175B	171cc	Orange	White Panels	21-inch
1975	DT-250B	246cc	Orange	White Panels	21-inch
1975	MX-250B	246cc	White	Orange Panels	21-inch
1975	YZ-250B	246cc	Yellow	Dashed Stripe	21-inch
1975	YZ-250M	246cc	White	Red Racing Stripes	21-inch
1975	TY-250B	246cc	White	Dark Trim	21-inch
1975	YZ-360B	351cc	Yellow	Dashed Stripe	21-inch
1975	DT-400B	397cc	Yellow	White Panels	21-inch
1975	MX-400B	397cc	White	Contrasting Panels	21-inch
1975	TT-500C	499cc	White	Red Panels	21-inch

Yamaha Enduro/MX/Trials Notes: All models had tube frames, single-cylinder engines, return shifts, Ceriani-style front suspension, 3/4-length seats, upswept exhausts, drum brakes, and kick starters. All models except a couple of 500cc motocrossers were piston-port two-strokes. The 1975 YZ-125C had a six-speed gearbox; all others had five-speeds. All street legal Enduro models had full lighting, battery ignition, horn, and instruments. All motocross models had higher tuned engines, expansion chambers, magneto ignition, and no lighting equipment. No 1968-70 models had turn signals. All 1971-75 street legal Enduro models had turn signals. Torque Induction was introduced on all 1972 models. The tank letters of the 1972 models listed as trim spelled out Y-A-M-A-H-A. Whenever the same colors appear on the Enduro and Motocross models of a particular displacement within a given year, these models have been combined on one line.

    Yamaha 100 Notes: The LT series was replaced by the DT-100 in 1974.

    Yamaha 125 Notes: Unlike all the other Enduro models, the 125cc AT Enduros had electric starters. These electric starters with six-volt electrical systems were never particularly robust at starting a cold engine in adverse conditions, but kick starting was always easy with these models. The 1974 DT-125 had a high front fender. The 1975 YZ-125C had a monoshock and six-speed transmission.

    Yamaha 175 Notes: There were no 175 motocross models built during this period because the 175 racing class was as yet undeveloped. The 125 and 175 models were otherwise more or less identical other than displacement.

    Yamaha 250 Notes: Technically speaking, there was no separate motocross model in 1968. There was a GYT Kit performance option offered for the DT-1. Yamaha launched its famous Monocross monoshock rear suspension on the new for 1974 YZ-250. Both the 1975 MX-250B & YZ-250M had monoshock rear suspensions.

    Yamaha 360 Notes: The RT-2 MX had CDI. The YZ-360B had monoshock rear suspension.

    Yamaha 400 Notes: The 1975 MX-400B was a two-stroke monoshock model with dyno tested 38 horsepower at the rear wheel.

    Yamaha 500 Notes: The SC500 MX was a four-stroke, single-cylinder motocross model. The 1974 SC-500 was a two-stroke motocrosser. The 1975 TT-500C was an SOHC four-stroke motocrosser.

The Yamaha Enduro Series began with the 1968 DT-1 250 and continued long past the 1975 final year of these charts. The later two-strokes would be joined by TY trials models, SC four-stroke machines, and ever more sophisticated YZ motocross racers. Yamaha marketed a series of pint-sized Enduro and MX models for kids in 1971-75 that are not included in the chart. Like the full-size models, some of these designs have even continued well past 1975, the purview of this book. These machines were scaled-down direct copies of the larger models, although some, or possibly all, of the Motocross models did not have higher performance engines than the Enduro equivalents, as all their full-sized siblings did. As specifically derivatives designed for children below legal driving age, these minicycles have not been included in the chart.

    The 58cc JT-1 looked exactly like a tiny AT-1 or DT-1 of the same model year. It was upgraded to the JT-2 in 1972, correspondingly with its AT-2 and DT-2 big brothers. The GTI-80 and GT-80 MX models were introduced in 1972 as 73cc alternatives. These continued in production at least through 1975, while the Yamaha 60 models were discontinued after 1972. The TY80 trials model was introduced in 1974 and the more sophisticated YZ-80 motocrosser was added to the lineup in 1975. The little YZ has continued in production up through the present day. The 2013 YZ-85 makes a nice little $4000 toy for your kid. Buy him one. He will love you for it!

Figure H47 - Red 1971 Yamaha 125 AT-1C. ©Michael Kiernan, Classic Motorcycle Company, St. Louis, MO.

Figure H48 - Green 1970 Yamaha 175 CT-1B. The 125 and 175 Enduro models were practically identical except for engine displacement. The 125 Enduro had an electric starter and a motocross companion model in every production year. The 125 shown here has turn signals because all Yamaha Enduros got them beginning with the 1971 model year. ©1970 Yamaha Motor Corporation, U.S.A.

Figure H50 - Black 1971 Yamaha Enduro 360 RT-1B. ©Peter Abelmann, Germany

Figure H51 - Orange 1975 Yamaha DT-250B Enduro. ©1975 Yamaha Motor Corporation, U.S.A.

Yamaha YG-1 Rotary Jet 80

The original Yamaha 80 holds a very special place in my heart. It was my first real motorcycle, after a '57 Allstate Cruisaire. My Rotary Jet was a very early 1963 red and silver model, before the introduction of Autolube. There were many issues that were new to the Yamaha 80, and one of them was a selection of many colors, either in solids or with silver trim. One of the first-year brochures displayed a rich, deep purple with silver, and I have seen blue with silver, solid red, and I believe I vaguely remember seeing a white with silver and a yellow with silver. My YG-1 had turn signals, but some machines shown in the brochures of the period did not. I have seen versions of the 80 both with and without turn signals.

There were few competing 80-100cc Japanese tiddlers when the Rotary Jet was introduced in early '63, but several would appear over the next couple of years. The two biggest sellers, the plain putt-putt Honda 90 was launched six months after the Rotary Jet, and the Super 90, a legendary equal to the Rotary Jet, blasted onto the tarmac a year later. The Suzuki Trojan 80 was the only sporty street model in this class challenging the Rotary Jet until the Super 90. Yamaha really set a precedent with the introduction of the 80, quickly adding a trail model that would dominate the class in off-road racing for several years.

The Rotary Jet was a quick little sucker. Although the claimed top speed was 60 mph, the most a little shrimp like me could ever coax out of it was 53 mph, but it would get there in a hurry! Its big claim to fame was the new rotary valve engine. The carburetor is hidden away down in the crankcase; the canister above it is the air filter. You could remove the baffle in the exhaust pipe to try to intimidate the competition a bit, but you would not go any faster.

Yamaha did a hell of a job upstaging the big volume seller of the day, the Honda 50 Sport, at a price of only about $50 more. Let's run through the specs. As mentioned earlier, the color choices were more advanced and the metallic silver fenders and headlamp nacelle were metal instead of plastic. Both machines had four-speed footshifts, but the Yamaha was a rocker type. The Yamaha had real telescopic forks instead of the dinky leading link type on the Honda. The seat was of a softer foam and the handgrips were larger. The whole motorcycle had more of a big bike feel to it. As I said, mine had turn signals, but none of the Hondas did at that time. Both machines were kickstart and included rear footpegs, but the ones on the Yamaha folded up. The Yamaha's exhaust pipe was a clean, rounded, megaphone type, without an ugly seam like that on the Honda. The key was one of those strange little thingies with a fat plastic head that fit into the left side panel. The pressed steel frame was a smooth Y-shaped monocoque design. The enclosed chain guard, fender flaps, and chrome-paneled gas tank were similar features found on both models.

Although the Honda Super 90 eventually outsold the Rotary Jet, this is clearly the model that really launched Yamahas from American showrooms. The company's earlier models were certainly racy enough, easily blowing key Honda competitors into the weeds, but these never really sold in large numbers in the U.S. Any pre-1963 Yamaha has always been a pretty rare beastie in this country, unlike the very common Dreams and Honda 50's. It did not hurt Yamaha's fortunes a bit to become the company that popularized oil injection only about two years later, either!

382

James Rozee Speaks: "My first motorized two wheeler was a cut down Schwinn boys' bicycle frame with a big flat plate welded where the crank used to be. Bolted to that was a five-horsepower Briggs & Stratton! It was one of those homemade mini bikes you could build from plans bought out of the back pages of *Popular Mechanics*. It had a lawn mower stick shift throttle bolted to the cross bar, tiny go-kart wheels and a rear brake that rubbed on the rear diamond tread tire! I painted it red in the basement and got balled out for stinking up the whole house. First time out I pegged the throttle and the ungoverned engine took off like a rocket. The only problem was the rigid fork on the rough road made you not want to let go of the bars, so you could not shut it down without crashing! I finally hit the lever with my knee and slammed the rear brake, if you wanted to call it that, to slow down. After my Dad had a scare on it, we decided we needed a real motorcycle. My neighbor who had sold me the *Schwinn of Death*, took it back in trade plus cash on a 1963 Honda Sports C-110 50cc. This black beauty had no lights and had a custom aftermarket one into two straight pipe and it sounded great! Dad cut the end of the pipe off at an angle and it looked so cool. I learned how to ride on that little Honda. We would take it into the woods and trail ride, the very same place I ride today. The first time I went out, I got stuck in the snow. My chain fell off first, then my spark plug cap. We would also camp at the beach and ride in the sand. We would blast as fast as it could go along the beach, back when you could do that. I remember filling the gas tank up to the top, then after running the crap out of that Honda 50 all day long, I would check the gas tank fuel level and it had only gone down an inch! It was unreal. That four-speed never failed me. My next bike was a brand spanking new Sport 65 Honda. You will always love your first motorcycle most, just like your first true love or car. They are what you learned on...."

Figure H52 - Purple & Silver 1963 Yamaha YG-1. ©1963 Yamaha Motor Corporation, U.S.A.

Figure H53 - Blue & White 1962 Yamaha MF-1 50 Brochure Photo.

©1962 Yamaha Motor Corporation, U.S.A.

Figure H54 - Blue Yamaha 100 YL-1 Twin. ©Peter Abelmann, Germany

Figure H55 - Blue 1964 Yamaha 250 YD-3. ©Warren P. Warner

Figure H56 - Red Big Bear Scrambler at El Camino 2006. ©2006 Don Quayle, Costa Mesa, CA

Selected Yamaha Models Ratings Chart

Years	Model	Collectibility	Practicality	Desirability
1958 - 63	M-series Step-Thru 50's	B	D	D
1964 - 69	Riverside 55 / Campus 60	D	D	C
1963 - 69	YG 80 Series	C	C	B
1966 - 69	Twin Jet 100	B	C	B
1958 - 69	YA 125 Street Singles	A	D	B
1969 - 75	125/175 Enduro & MX	C	B	C
1958 - 65	YD-1/2/3 Street 250	C	D	C
1962 - 63	YDS-2 Sports	B	D	A
1962 - 68	Ascot & TD 250's	A	D	A
1964 - 70	YDS 250 Sport Series	B	D	B
1968 - 75	250 Enduro & MX	C	B	C
1966 - 69	305 Street Twins	C	C	C
1967 - 75	350 Street Twins	C	C	C
1970 - 75	360 Enduro & MX	C	B	B
1972 - 75	TX 500 Twin	C	C	D
1970 - 75	XS-1 650 Twin	A	B	B
1972 - 73	TX 750 Twin	B	C	C

Models Ratings Chart Definitions:

Years: These are the total production years for a particular model series. Some early model years within a series may be considerably more desirable than later years.

Models: In some cases many variations are included in this category and in others the models included are very homogeneous.

Collectibility: This is what most of you want to know, the bottom line on how likely the model or series is likely to climb in value over the coming years.

Practicality: This is an indicator of how adaptable the machine can be to ride for transportation or pleasure in the modern world, considering parts availability, fuel quality, comfort, performance and miscellaneous other obvious factors.

Desirability: This defines the nostalgic, emotional wow factor, without regard for collector values or everyday usage.

General: No machine is given a failing grade. If it made it into a rating chart, at least a few hobbyists find that model interesting.

Chapter 8: *You Meet the Nicest People on a Honda*

Queen of the Tiddlers

This is a story about the Honda 50 in all its forms and details, from the story of my own Cub to the Rally models produced in 1967. Models that should be mentioned are the C100, C102, C100T, C105T, CT90, CM91, C70, and all the Rally variations. According to Wikipedia, *60 million* Cubs have been produced worldwide as of 2008. Of course I realize that many of those millions are actually much later versions sold in various Asian and European countries, not the USA. The parameters of this book include only the specific models listed above. The first official importation of the C-100 model began August 1, 1959. The electric-start C-102 arrived eleven months later. The first Trail 50 came over in early '61 and it evolved into the C105T a year later. The now ubiquitous Trail 90 took over in 1964. Beginning in 1966, the CM91 coexisted with its 50cc Cub little brother and the C70 joined the classic Honda step-through family in 1972. The compact Trail 70 would explode onto the casual trail-riding scene in 1970, but that's another story. This is about what you might call the first two generations of step-through *scooters* with motorcycle-sized wheels.

I personally owned the original step-through, the kickstart C100 in 1967-70. The Cub was not my first choice of motorcycle, but it was the only way to slowly ease my parents back into acceptance of my being a motorcyclist. Although I was nineteen and a college student at the time, I respected my parents wishes. The deal I made with them is that the little Cub would never be licensed for the street. I would use it for trail riding only, and as underpowered and sissified as it was, it did an outstandingly reliable job of everything I asked of the little machine. I hauled it to trailing areas on a bumper rack, climbed hills carrying a passenger, hauled it across the lake in a boat to a special campground on numerous summer weekends, and dragged it through mud up to its axles more than once. I did not own the small size of spark plug wrench the little Honda used, so I never removed it. The only servicing it ever received were oil changes and occasional chain lubrication.

I paid $120 for the Honda 50 at my local Honda dealer when it was a year old with about 3500 miles on the odometer. The Kawasaki dealer allowed me $125 in a trade for a *new demonstrator* G3-TR 90 more than three years later. What a deal!! The Kaw was a superior trail bike in every way, but the total reliability of the little 50 was unparalleled. There is a part of the story yet to be told. From the time I bought the Cub until I traded it in, I continued to modify it, piece by piece. Then before sending it on its way to its next owner, I restored all the stock pieces. Here is its saga of metamorphosis.

As I am sure I have mentioned before, my parents were adamant in refusing to let me have another motorcycle, no matter how small, after I hit several things with my 1963 YG-1. After nearly three years had passed, I finally convinced my parents to let me buy a minibike for off-road riding only. I found this little jewel at my local Honda dealer instead, and my parents consented, as long as I stayed off the public streets where I could find more things to hit with it.

The machine was a '66 Cub in black with white leg shields and side covers. The seat, as you can see here, was black with a white perimeter. There were no turn signals, even though the empty lens were attached to the handlebars, and it was the kickstart-only model. The first thing I did was to remove the leg shields and change the countershaft sprocket to a twelve-tooth unit. The rear tire was changed to a full knobby and the front fender and exhaust pipe were removed. I replaced the quiet muffler with a primitive, single, short, straight pipe that made more noise, but how much racket can a Honda 50 make? It wasn't that loud, but it saved weight and looked more like a trail bike. Note the classic pudding-bowl helmet resting on the seat. If you could see the other side of this helmet, you would understand my parents' attitude. There are deep scratches down to the aluminum. It looks like a werewolf bit it!

Figure I1 (above)- Black 1966 Honda C-100 Cub Set Up for Trail Riding and Parked at the Edge of Pickwick Lake in far Northeast Mississippi. ©1968 Floyd M. Orr

Figure I2 (right) - The Trail Cub in its Muddy Element at the same location less than an hour later. ©1968 Floyd M. Orr

A very enterprising uncle of mine built me a bumper rack for the car, and I hauled the little tiddler all over the place. One of my favorite trail riding locations was at Pickwick Lake, right on the border of Mississippi, Tennessee, and Alabama. My aunt, the sister of the aforementioned Tim the Tool Man, had a lake house at Pickwick and we used to haul the little tiddler up there on the bumper rack for a bit of outdoor fun. All boys like to play in the mud and the edge of a receding lake provides plenty of mud! After putting my Kodak 126 Instamatic away, I just got a good grip on the handlebars and dragged the little beastie sideways out of the muck. A nearby stick came in handy to scrape the mud from underneath the rear fender, and away we went!

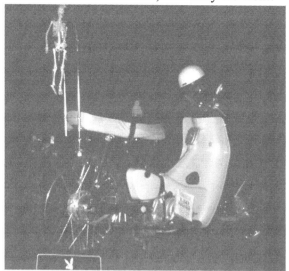

The photo above was taken in the winter, when boating adventures were not available. I generally did this trail riding at Pickwick in the off season. Another fun thing I used to do with the C-100 was to take it *in* the boat to Hugh White State Park at Grenada Lake. Back then at least, there was no boat ramp in HWSP. You had to launch the boat over at the main public ramp near the dam, and then drive it over to the small beach area in Hugh White State Park. My buddies and I would lift the Cub up into the boat and tie it down securely, and then head for the lake, a ninety-minute drive away. Upon arrival at the boat ramp, we would launch the boat with the bike still tied down in it, and drive the boat across the lake to the HWSP campground area. Upon arrival, we would lift the C-100 out of the boat, and onto the beach. Always with a fascinated crowd of envious onlookers, I would kickstart the C-100 and proceed up the very steep hillside path to the campground! Sometimes there would even be applause.

After I got bored with the Trail 50 concept, I took the Cub in a new direction. As a fan of Peter Fonda from *The Wild Angels* of 1966, with a little homage to his next movie, *The Trip*, I staged this little tiddler nightmare. Call it one of my artsy-fartsy days, in memory of Guido, The Killer Pimp, in *Risky Business*. I brought the front fender and leg shields back out of storage, but I left the straight exhaust pipe attached. I believe I even left the lower gearing intact, but I cannot remember for

Figure I3 (above) - The Chopper Cub in a Staged Night Pose Reflecting the Birth of the Psychedelic Era. ©1968 Floyd M. Orr

Figure I4 (right) - 1966 Chopper Cub. The fancy split exhaust system has been installed, but you can barely see it in this front view. ©1968 Floyd M. Orr

sure. You know what they say about The Sixties: if you can remember them, you probably were never there! I don't remember where I got the sissy bar, but I believe it was the banana seat support from a Schwinn Stingray or a similar copycat model. I installed it with a short-travel spring action so that a passenger could feel a bit of back and forth movement. Among the props featured in this staged Instamatic slide photo are a *Playboy* license plate, a plastic, glow-in-the-dark skeleton model, and a red Jade East Buddha-style container. A copy of *LSD: The Problem-Solving Psychedelic* (actually a very informative book I read back in about 1966 before The War on Drugs twisted any mention of the subject distinctly into an abnormally plastic-fantastic shape) rests against the leg shield. My ubiquitous pudding-bowl helmet hangs from one of the mirrors which have also been reinstalled, but are barely visible in this photo.

Judging from the leaves on the ground, I would say this photo of the Chopper Cub was taken in the autumn of 1968. Here you can get a good view of the sissy bar and white metalflake seat cover. The same talented uncle custom fabricated a straight, twin, bologna-sliced exhaust system that looked cool and decreased weight, but still did not make much racket. If you squint closely, you can see the fancy split exhaust pipe details.

Figure I5 - This view shows off the sissy bar and white metalflake seat cover. ©1968 Floyd M. Orr.

The pressed-steel handlebars were removed, along with the plastic headlight nacelle and speedometer housing. The chrome handlebars you see here are probably the later, higher version from the Sport 50. The handgrips are those soft, fat type made in Italy. Although the headlight was left in abstentia, the speedo was left secured in place with its bracket. Only the plastic housing surrounding it was removed. The remaining changes were that the front fender was removed and the same nice uncle who fabricated the exhaust system and bumper rack built a crushed black leather (not vinyl) pad for the sissy bar.

After more than three years of obedient Honda 50 abuse, I had acquired enough cash to move up market. I know this sounds positively insane now, and yes, it does make me wish I had bought a garage full of crated tiddlers in the '60's. I would like nothing more now than to have a fresh new Sport 50, a YG-1, a Scrambler 90, a blue '69 G3, and a Suzuki Maverick sitting in my garage waiting patiently for me to sigh contemplatively and wipe my drool off the gas tanks before I putted out of the garage for a quiet little ride.

Much of the general public probably remembers their first Honda impressions as *You meet the nicest people on* an electric start C-102. All the very earliest Honda models imported here had electric starters, a convenience unheard of on motorcycles of that era. We take those little pushbuttons for granted now, but back then, they were, "Wow!" Of course any of my ten cats, even the smallest one, could kickstart a Honda 50, but that was beside the marketing point. The little pushbuttons launched the entire phenomenon that became the subject matter of this book.

The Trail models became so popular and common on the backs of RV's and in campgrounds all across America that they hardly need any more press. Few people probably realize that Yamaha tried to compete with two-stroke versions from 1962 onward, but few were ever sold. Honda owned the step-through trail bike market then and they still do. Neither Trail 90's nor their Trail 70 little brothers are very rare, even today. You might label both the street and trail Honda step-throughs as the most successful motorcycles for non-motorcyclists in all of two-wheeler history. The Trail 90 would be imported through 1979 and the little fat-tired Trail 70 would continue through 1994! The street step-through

70 would finally end its run as the Honda Passport in 1983. As noted at the conclusion of this book, you can still buy a 110cc version, only now it is built in China as a copycat of the classic Honda design.

Figure 16 - This final photo of the Chopper Cub shows off its new chrome, high-rise handlebars and crushed leather backrest attached to the sissy bar. ©1968 Floyd M. Orr.

There was a footnote to the Cub story that is worth a brief mention. In 1967-8, in an attempt to sell a few more of the later production of the original Honda 50 Cub and CM91 Honda 90 step-through, the company released what it called the Honda Custom Group. This consisted of a series of four kits that dealers could install on the two step-through models to give them more of a *motorcycle look* with fiberglass gas tanks attached over the frames. They may have been referred to as Sport Kits back then, but my memory is a little fuzzy on that. All four Sport Kit designs included higher, chrome handlebars and a different seat and tank combo. I believe all the seat options were black and all the tanks were off-white fiberglass. I cannot recall the exact years the Sport Kit option was offered on Cub 50's and 90's, but I think it was 1967-8, and it could have been 1968 only.

Each kit was a little different in the particular styling accoutrements utilized. Two of these kits were more interesting than the second two. The Rally model had a long, skinny, off-white tank with a three-quarter, racing-style seat, and slightly raised chrome handlebars. A similar model called the Boss used a gas tank that dropped deeply downward with the underslung frame. With its black kneepads on the big tank and a deeply sculpted racing seat, it appeared even more motorcycle-like. Viewed from above, the "large" tank was actually very narrow. Both of these machines had a strange look about them and they are subsequently quite rare today. I doubt they offer much collectible value, though. You are still driving a Cub with an automatic clutch and a rocking three-speed foot shift.

Figure I7 - 1966-67 Black Honda CL-160 Scrambler. This is the machine I really wanted when I had to settle for the C-100 Cub out of economic and parental necessity. Little did I realize at the time how rare and special this machine would rapidly become. Within months of my purchase of the used C-100, the original, true CL-160 Scramblers were gone from the lineup forever. ©Troyce Walls, photographer

Honda Model Charts, 1959-75

Honda produced only four-cycle engines up through the 1972 model year. All but a few of the 50cc-90cc models throughout this period were SOHC type. Those few 50's and 90's were OHV engines. The 450 introduced in 1965 was the company's first street DOHC design and the Elsinore of 1973 was its first two-stroke. All Hondas had left side return shifts, with the exception of those few early dry-sump twins, as noted. Honda used Keihin brand carburetors from its own subsidiary. The company doesn't advertise the fact, but most of the Harley-Davidson big twins have been using Keihin carbs for decades because the old American-made Tillotsons were troublesome.

Figure I8 - White 1965 Honda CA-77 Dream with Red Seat and Chrome Crash Bars at the Barber Vintage Museum, Birmingham. This photo was mislabeled as a CB-92 Benly by the photographer, which it clearly is not, since this is a CA body style. According to the *Honda ID Guide,* the 124cc CA-92 was imported into the USA only during the second half of 1959 and that model did not have tank pads, round mufflers, or whitewall tires. The CA-92 was not even sold in white, at least not in the U.S. The combination of these features and others indicates this machine is a 1965 Dream 305. I am not sure the CA-77 was even sold in white with a red seat in significant numbers, so this fact alone makes this photo interesting.

Image by Chuck Schultz under Creative Commons license.

Honda 1959 Chart

Model	Name	Colors	Engine	HP	Wt.
C-100	Super Cub	Red - White - Black - Blue	49cc	4.5	140
CA-92	Benly Touring	Red - Black - Blue	124cc	NA	246
CB-92	Benly SS	Red/Silver - Blue/Silver	124cc	15	220
CA-95	Benly Touring	Red - Black - White - Blue	154cc	16.5	246
C-71	Dream Touring	Red - Black - White - Blue	247cc	23	372
CA-71	Dream Touring	Red - Black - White - Blue	247cc	23	372
CE-71	Dream Sport	Silver w/Black or Maroon	247cc	23	372
C-76	Dream Touring	Red - Black - White - Blue	305cc	25	372
CA-76	Dream Touring	Red - Black - White - Blue	305cc	25	372

Honda 1959 Notes: All 1959 models except the C-100 had dual seats, downswept exhausts and electric starters. The C-100 had kick start only and some had solo seats. All engines were SOHC twins except for the OHV C-100 single. No official 1959 prices are available, but there is unlikely to be a significant difference between the prices in 1959 and those in 1962. The blue CB-92 had a red seat and the red model had a black seat. All claimed dry weights are listed in pounds.

Figure I9 - A Very Rare Black Honda Dream ME. ©Troyce Walls

Honda 1960 Chart

Model	Name	Type	HP	Seat	Starter	Wt.
C-100	Super Cub	49cc Single	4.5	Dual	Kick	140
C-102	Super Cub	49cc Single	4.5	Dual	Electric	155
C-110	Super Sports	49cc Single	5	3/4	Kick	121
CB-92	Benly SS	124cc Twin	15	Dual	Electric	220
CA-95	Benly Touring	154cc Twin	16.5	Dual	Electric	246
C-71	Dream Touring	247cc Twin	23	Dual	Electric	372
CA-71	Dream Touring	247cc Twin	23	Dual	Electric	372
CE-71	Dream Sport	247cc Twin	23	Dual	Electric	372
CA-72	Dream Touring	247cc Twin	23	Dual	Electric	372
C-76	Dream Touring	305cc Twin	25	Dual	Electric	372
CA-76	Dream Touring	305cc Twin	25	Dual	Electric	372
CS-76	Dream Sport	305cc Twin	25	Dual	Electric	372
CSA-76	Dream Sport	305cc Twin	25	Dual	Electric	372
CS-77	Dream Touring	305cc Twin	25	Dual	Electric	372
CSA-77	Dream Touring	305cc Twin	25	Dual	Electric	372
CA-77	Dream Touring	305cc Twin	25	Dual	Electric	372

Honda 1960 Notes: All 1960 models except the Super Sports 50 and the two 305 Dream Sports had downswept exhausts. There were very few, if any, Super Sport 50's actually sold as 1960 models since it was introduced on December 1, 1960. No official 1960 prices are available, but it is unlikely to be a significant difference between the prices in 1960 and those in 1962. All claimed dry weights are listed in pounds. In essence, there really were only six different machines imported in 1960: 50, 50 Sport, 125 Sport, 150 Benly, 250 Dream and 305 Dream. All models had pressed steel frames and leading link front suspension. All the twins were OHC and the singles were OHV.

Honda 1961 Chart

Model	Name	Type	HP	Seat	Starter	Wt.
C-100	Super Cub	49cc Single	4.5	Dual	Kick	140
C-102	Super Cub	49cc Single	4.5	Dual	Electric	155
C-100T	Trail Cub	49cc Single	4.5	Solo	Kick	140
C-110	Super Sports	49cc Single	5	3/4	Kick	121
CB-92	Benly SS	124cc Twin	15	Dual	Electric	220
CB-92R	SS Racer	124cc Twin	16	Racing	Electric	220
CA-95	Benly Touring	154cc Twin	16.5	Dual	Electric	246
C-72	Dream Touring	247cc Twin	23	Dual	Electric	372
CA-72	Dream Touring	247cc Twin	23	Dual	Electric	372
CB-72	Hawk	247cc Twin	25	Dual	Electric	300
C-77	Dream Touring	305cc Twin	25	Dual	Electric	372
CS-77	Dream Touring	305cc Twin	25	Dual	Electric	372
CSA-77	Dream Touring	305cc Twin	25	Dual	Electric	372
CA-77	Dream Touring	305cc Twin	25	Dual	Electric	372
CB-77	Super Hawk	305cc Twin	27	Dual	Electric	300

Figure I10 - Red 1961-62 Honda 250 C-72 with Red Seat, Owned by Jens Joergensen of the Classic Honda Club of Norway ©Jon Arild Monsen, photographer

Honda 1961 Notes: No official 1961 prices are available, but it is unlikely to be significant differences between the prices in 1961 and those in 1962. All claimed dry weights are listed in pounds. The Hawk and Super Hawk were the first Hondas with either tube frames or telescopic front forks. The CB-92R would remain the jewel of Honda's entire history for its collectible status. There has never been another Honda quite like it: a race-inspired sporting machine with a pressed steel frame, leading link front suspension, and an electric starter combined with a hot cam, open megaphone exhaust, a racing-style seat and tank, and a tachometer (without a speedometer) mounted in the headlight nacelle.

Figures I11 & I12 - Two 1963 Hondas, a Red CB-92R and a Black Super Hawk. ©Michael Kiernan, Classic Motorcycle Company, St. Louis, MO.

Honda 1962 Chart

Model	Name	Engine	HP	Seat	Starter	Wt.	Price
CA-100	Cub	49cc	4.5	Dual	Kick	140	$245
CA-102	Cub	49cc	4.5	Dual	Electric	155	$275
CA-100T	Trail Cub	49cc	4.5	Solo	Kick	140	$275
C-110	Super Sports	49cc	5	3/4	Kick	121	$285
CA-110	Sports 50	49cc	5	Dual	Kick	140	$285
C-105T	Trail 55	54cc	5	Solo	Kick	140	$275
CB-92	Benly SS	124cc	15	Dual	Electric	220	$495
CB-92R	SS Racer	124cc	16	Racing	Electric	220	$520
CA-95	Benly Touring	154cc	16.5	Dual	Electric	246	$450
CA-72	Dream Touring	247cc	23	Dual	Electric	372	$560
CB-72	Hawk	247cc	25	Dual	Electric	300	$640
CL-72	Scrambler	247cc	25	Dual	Kick	315	$660
C-77	Dream Touring	305cc	25	Dual	Electric	372	$595
CS-77	Dream Touring	305cc	25	Dual	Electric	372	NA
CSA-77	Dream Touring	305cc	25	Dual	Electric	372	NA
CA-77	Dream Touring	305cc	25	Dual	Electric	372	$595
CB-77	Super Hawk	305cc	27	Dual	Electric	300	$645

Honda 1962 Notes: The 49cc and 54cc engines were OHV singles; all others were SOHC twins. All listed weights are in pounds. The CL-72 Scrambler offered several firsts for Honda. It was designed specifically for the American market, had a cradle tube frame, had twin upswept exhausts on the same side, and it was the first Honda twin without an electric starter. The out-the-door prices at Al's Cycle Shop in Memphis TN including setup charges were: 250 Dream $645, 305 Dream $695, Hawk $725, Super Hawk $765, and CL-72 $760. All claimed dry weights are listed in pounds.

Figure I13 - Black 1951 Dream E in a Museum (Where It Belongs). Image by Rikita under Creative Commons license.

Figure I14 - Red 1961 CB-92. Compare this model to the CB-82R shown previously. The most obvious visual distinctions are the dual seat and mufflers on the street version. Image by Khaosaming, photographer, under Creative Commons license.

Honda 1963 Chart

Model	Name	Type	HP	Starter	Wt.	Price
CA-100	Cub	49cc Single	4.5	Kick	140	$245
CA-102	Cub	49cc Single	4.5	Electric	155	$275
CA-110	Sports 50	49cc Single	5	Kick	145	$285
C-105T	Trail 55	54cc Single	5	Kick	140	$275
CA-105T	Trail 55	54cc Single	5	Kick	140	$275
C-200	Touring 90	87cc Single	6.5	Kick	188	$350
CA-95	Benly Touring	154cc Twin	16.5	Electric	246	$450
CA-72	Dream Touring	247cc Twin	23	Electric	372	$560
CB-72	Hawk	247cc Twin	25	Electric	350	$640
CL-72	Scrambler	247cc Twin	25	Kick	315	$660
C-77	Dream Touring	305cc Twin	25	Electric	372	$595
CS-77	Dream Touring	305cc Twin	25	Electric	372	NA
CSA-77	Dream Touring	305cc Twin	25	Electric	372	NA
CA-77	Dream Touring	305cc Twin	25	Electric	372	$595
CB-77	Super Hawk	305cc Twin	27.4	Electric	300	$645

Honda 1963 Notes: All 1963 models had dual seats except the Trail 55 had a solo seat. The Cub 50's and Trail 55's had three-speed transmissions. All other models had four-speeds. The Sports 50 acquired a four-speed during the production year. All claimed dry weights are listed in pounds. The stated weight for the CB-72 is wet.

Figure I15 - Red 1960 Honda C-71 250. Notice the oil tank on this rare early dry-sump Honda twin.
©Knut Hugo Hansen, President of the Classic Honda Club, Norway, owner and photographer

Figure I16 - Blue 1961 Honda CB-92 with Red Seat. This is apparently one of the red seat styles used on this model. The other one was a longer dual seat with strap and buckles, as shown in Figure I58. Image by Maysy, photographer, under Creative Commons license.

Honda 1964 Chart

Model	Name	Type	HP	Starter	Wt.	Price
CA-100	Cub	49cc Single	4.5	Kick	140	$245
CA-102	Cub	49cc Single	4.5	Electric	155	$275
CA-110	Sports 50	49cc Single	5	Kick	145	$285
CA-105T	Trail 55	54cc Single	5	Kick	140	$275
C-200	Touring 90	87cc Single	6.5	Kick	188	$350
CT-200	Trail 90	87cc Single	6.5	Kick	189	$330
CS-90	Super 90	89cc Single	8	Kick	176	$370
CA-95	Benly Touring	154cc Twin	16.5	Electric	246	$460
CB-160	Super Sport	161cc Twin	16.5	Electric	280	$530
CA-72	Dream Touring	247cc Twin	23	Electric	372	$560
CB-72	Hawk	247cc Twin	25	Electric	300	$640
CL-72	Scrambler	247cc Twin	25	Kick	315	$690
C-77	Dream Touring	305cc Twin	25	Electric	372	NA
CA-77	Dream Touring	305cc Twin	25	Electric	355	$595
CB-77	Super Hawk	305cc Twin	27.4	Electric	300	$665

Honda 1964 Notes: All 1964 models except the Trail 55 and Trail 90 had dual seats. All claimed dry weights are listed in pounds. The CB-160 was a late-year introduction and it is unknown if many were sold in the USA as 1964 models.

Figure I17 - Black Honda CB-160. Honda released the CB-160 in late 1964. I am not sure if some early models were imported with these low bars or not. ©Matt Hamilton, owner and photographer

Honda 1965 Chart

Model	Name	Type	HP	Starter	Wt.	Gears
CA-100	Cub	49cc Single	4.5	Kick	140	3
CA-102	Cub	49cc Single	4.5	Electric	155	3
CA-110	Sports 50	49cc Single	5	Kick	145	4
CA-105T	Trail 55	54cc Single	5	Kick	140	3
CS-65	Sport 65	63cc Single	6.2	Kick	171	4
CA-200	Touring 90	87cc Single	6.5	Kick	188	4
CT-200	Trail 90	87cc Single	6.5	Kick	189	4
CS-90	Super 90	89cc Single	8	Kick	176	4
CA-95	Benly Touring	154cc Twin	16.5	Electric	246	4
CB-160	Super Sport	161cc Twin	16.5	Electric	280	4
CA-72	Dream Touring	247cc Twin	23	Electric	372	4
CB-72	Hawk	247cc Twin	25	Electric	300	4
CL-72	Scrambler	247cc Twin	25	Kick	315	4
CA-77	Dream Touring	305cc Twin	23	Electric	372	4
CB-77	Super Hawk	305cc Twin	27.4	Electric	300	4
CL-77	Scrambler	305cc Twin	27.4	Kick	315	4
CB-450	Super Sport	444cc Twin	43	Electric	411	4

Honda 1965 Notes: All 1965 models except the Trail 55 and Trail 90 had dual seats. All claimed dry weights are listed in pounds. Only a few prices for 1965 models are available. The Cub with kick starting was $215, the new Sport 65 was $295, the Super 90 was $370, the new CB-160 was $530, and the Dream 305 was $560. This would be the only year both the CL-72 and CL-77 would be available side by side on the showroom floor. As detailed in the Scrambler chapter, there was a gradual transition from the 250 to the 305 concerning certain key components of the two models.

The big news was the mid-year introduction of the CB-450, the largest Honda yet. Before its official release, what we now call the *Black Bomber* was named the *Condor*. The 450 was a complex DOHC road burner with controversial styling and constant velocity carburetors that were yet to be fully tested. The company had not yet introduced a five-speed transmission and there was some buyer resistance to a Japanese company upping the ante in size and price, so not many CB-450's were sold in the beginning.

Figure I18 - 1966 Black CB-450. The first generation of the largest Honda ever at the time was nicknamed the Black Bomber by U.S. motorcyclists. The model had a four-speed transmission, a humpback tank, and came only in black. ©Michael Kiernan, Classic Motorcycle Company, St. Louis, MO.

Honda 1966 Chart

Model	Name	Type	HP	Starter	Wt.	Gears
CA-100	Cub	49cc Single	4.5	Kick	140	3
CA-102	Cub	49cc Single	4.5	Electric	155	3
CA-110	Sport 50	49cc Single	5	Kick	145	4
CS-65	Sport 65	63cc Single	6.2	Kick	171	4
CA-200	Touring 90	87cc Single	7.5	Kick	188	4
CT-200	Trail 90	87cc Single	7.5	Kick	NA	4
CT-90	Trail 90	89cc Single	7.5	Kick	180	4
CM-91	Honda 90	89cc Single	7.5	Kick	183	3
CS-90	Super 90	89cc Single	8	Kick	176	4
CA-95	Benly Touring	154cc Twin	16.5	Electric	246	4
CA-160	Touring	161cc Twin	16	Electric	286	4
CB-160	Super Sport	161cc Twin	16.5	Electric	282	4
CL-160	Scrambler	161cc Twin	16.5	Kick	282	4
CA-72	Dream Touring	247cc Twin	20	Electric	372	4
CB-72	Hawk	247cc Twin	25	Electric	300	4
CA-77	Dream Touring	305cc Twin	23	Electric	372	4
CB-77	Super Hawk	305cc Twin	28.5	Electric	350	4
CL-77	Scrambler	305cc Twin	28.5	Kick	338	4
CB-450	Super Sport	444cc Twin	43	Electric	412	4

Honda 1966 Notes: All 1966 models except the Trail 90 had dual seats. All claimed dry weights are listed in pounds. There probably is not forty pounds difference between the 150 and 160 Benlys, so the stated weights may be suspect. The 49cc and 87cc engines were OHV and the CB-450 was DOHC. All others were SOHC. The 1966 Sport 65 was $295 and the CL-160 was $580. No other prices are available for 1966 models.

Honda 1967 Chart

Model	Name	Type	HP	Starter	Wt.	Gears
P50	Little Honda	49cc Single	NA	Pedal	NA	1
CA-100	Cub	49cc Single	4.5	Kick	140	3
CA-102	Cub	49cc Single	4.5	Electric	155	3
CA-110	Sports 50	49cc Single	5	Kick	145	4
CS-65	Sport 65	63cc Single	6.2	Kick	171	4
CT-90	Trail 90	89cc Single	7.5	Kick	190	4
CM-91	Honda 90	89cc Single	7.5	Kick	183	4
CS-90	Super 90	89cc Single	8	Kick	176	4
CL-90	Scrambler	89cc Single	8	Kick	203	4
SS-125A	Super Sport	124cc Twin	13	Kick	234	4
CL-125A	Scrambler	124cc Twin	13	Kick	235	4
CA-160	Touring	161cc Twin	16	Electric	286	4
CB-160	Super Sport	161cc Twin	16.5	Electric	282	4
CL-160	Scrambler	161cc Twin	16.5	Kick	282	4
CL-160D	Scrambler	161cc Twin	16.5	Electric	282	4
CA-77	Dream Touring	305cc Twin	25	Electric	372	4
CB-77	Super Hawk	305cc Twin	28.5	Electric	350	4
CL-77	Scrambler	305cc Twin	28.5	Kick	338	4
CB-450	Super Sport	444cc Twin	43	Electric	412	4
CL-450	Scrambler	444cc Twin	43	Electric	420	4

Honda 1967 Notes: The P50 is a four-stroke moped. All 1967 models had dual seats except the P50 Little Honda and CT-90 Trail 90, which had solo seats. The '67 CL-450 is the only CL twin with an upswept exhaust pipe on each side. This model began as a kit for the humpback CB-450 and was technically called a CB-450D Super Sport when the kit was installed. All claimed dry weights are listed in pounds. The 1967 Sport 65 costs $295 and the top of the line CL-450 was only $995. No other 1967 prices are available.

Figure I19 - Red 1965 Honda Super 90 at the Barber Museum, Birmingham, AL.

Image by Redhawkrider under Creative Commons license.

Figure I20 - Black Honda Sport 65. Note the distinctive two-tone seat and slender tank.

©Don Quayle, Costa Mesa, CA

Honda 1968 Chart

Model	Name	Type	HP	Starter	Wt.	Price
Z-50A	Mini Trail	49cc Single	2	Kick	108	NA
P50	Little Honda	49cc Single	NA	Pedal	NA	NA
CA-100	Cub	49cc Single	4.5	Kick	140	NA
CA-102	Cub	49cc Single	4.5	Electric	143	NA
CA-110	Sports 50	49cc Single	4.8	Kick	145	NA
CS-65	Sport 65	63cc Single	5.0	Kick	171	$295
CT-90	Trail 90	89cc Single	7	Kick	190	$329
CM-91	Honda 90	89cc Single	7.5	Kick	183	$369
CS-90	Super 90	89cc Single	8	Kick	176	$394
CL-90L	5HP SCR	89cc Single	4.9	Kick	202	NA
CL-90	Scrambler	89cc Single	8	Kick	203	$342
SS-125A	Super Sport	124cc Twin	13	Kick	234	$450
CL-125A	Scrambler	124cc Twin	13	Kick	235	$470
CA-160	Touring	161cc Twin	16	Electric	286	$528
CB-160	Super Sport	161cc Twin	16.5	Electric	280	$574
CL-160D	Scrambler	161cc Twin	16.5	Electric	282	$593
CA-175	Touring	174cc Twin	17	Kick	267	$547
CL-175	Scrambler	174cc Twin	20	Electric	279	$643
CA-77	Dream Touring	305cc Twin	23	Electric	374	$597
CB-77	Super Hawk	305cc Twin	28.5	Electric	350	$695
CL-77	Scrambler	305cc Twin	28.5	Kick	338	$695
CB-350	Super Sport	325cc Twin	36	Electric	353	$747
CL-350	Scrambler	325cc Twin	33	Electric	346	$793
CB-450K1	Super Sport	444cc Twin	45	Electric	412	$964
CL-450K1	Scrambler	444cc Twin	43	Electric	402	$993

Honda 1968 Notes: The P50 is a four-stroke moped. The claimed horsepower for the Sport 65 changed from 6.2 at 10,000 rpm to 5.0 at 9000 rpm. All 1968 models had dual seats except the Z-50A Mini Trail, P50 Little Honda, and CT-90 Trail 90 which had solo seats. All claimed dry weights are listed in pounds. The CA-175 can be distinguished from its later brothers by its inclined cylinders. This model had six-volt electrics and it may have had an electric starter. *Cycle Guide* tested the CL-450 in September 1968. The price was listed as $995, the horsepower as 43, the weight as 415, and the quarter-mile as 14.94 seconds at 85 mph.

Figure I21 - Blue 1968 Honda SS-125 and 2012 Ferrari 458.

©Paul Davies, owner and photographer (of only the Honda, unfortunately)

Figure I22 - Close-up View of the Same Blue 1968 SS125A. ©Paul Davies, owner and photographer

Honda 1969 Chart

Model	Name	Type	HP	Starter	Wt.	Price
Z-50AK0-1	Mini Trail	49cc Single	2	Kick	110	NA
PC50	Little Honda	49cc Single	1.75	Pedal	106	NA
CA-100	Cub	49cc Single	4.5	Kick	140	NA
CA-102	Cub	49cc Single	4.5	Electric	143	NA
CA-110	Sports 50	49cc Single	5	Kick	145	NA
CS-65	Sport 65	63cc Single	5.0	Kick	171	NA
CT-70	Trail 70	72cc Single	5.0	Kick	143	NA
CL-70	Scrambler	72cc Single	4.9	Kick	174	$344
CS-90	Super 90	89cc Single	8	Kick	189	$362
CM-91	Honda 90	89cc Single	7.5	Kick	185	NA
CL-90L	5HP SCR	89cc Single	4.9	Kick	203	NA
CL-90	Scrambler	89cc Single	8	Kick	203	$376
CT-90K1	Trail 90	89cc Single	7	Kick	200	$399
SL-90	Motosport	89cc Single	8	Kick	216	$400
SS-125A	Super Sport	124cc Twin	13	Kick	231	$443
CL-125A	Scrambler	124cc Twin	13	Kick	235	$493
CA-160	Touring	161cc Twin	16	Electric	274	NA
CB-160	Super Sport	161cc Twin	16.5	Electric	280	NA
CA-175	Touring	174cc Twin	17	Kick	267	$427
CA-175K3	Touring	174cc Twin	17	Electric	270	NA
CB-175K3	Super Sport	174cc Twin	20	Electric	NA	NA
CL-175	Scrambler	174cc Twin	20	Electric	279	$642
CL-175K3	Scrambler	174cc Twin	20	Kick	274	$697
CA-77	Dream	305cc Twin	23	Electric	374	NA
CB-350K1	Super Sport	325cc Twin	36	Electric	353	$743
CL-350K1	Scrambler	325cc Twin	33	Electric	346	$797
SL-350	Motosport	325cc Twin	33	Electric	346	NA
CB-450K2	Super Sport	444cc Twin	45	Electric	412	$997
CL-450K1	Scrambler	444cc Twin	43	Electric	402	NA
CL-450K2	Scrambler	444cc Twin	43	Electric	402	$997
CB-750	750 Four	736cc Four	67	Electric	480	$1495

Honda 1969 Notes: The PC50 is a four-stroke moped. The Z-50, PC50, CT-70 and CT-90 had solo seats and the SL-350 had a 3/4 seat. All other 1969 models had dual seats. The Trail 90 got a metal front fender in 1969; previous models were plastic. The Trail 90 price listed includes setup charges. All claimed dry weights are listed in pounds. Two legendary Hondas debuted in 1969 that are only minimally detailed in this book because so much information is available elsewhere on these models. Both the Trail 70 and the 750 Four have had strong cult followings since their debut and they reside at opposite margins of the subject matter of *The Tiddler Invasion*.

Figure I23 - Blue 1969 Honda 750 Four at the Barber Museum, Birmingham, AL. So what is a 500-pound, 68-horsepower, highway screamer doing in a book about tiddlers? As far as the tiddlers were concerned, you might call the 750 Four the Wicked Witch of the East! More than any other single machine, for better or worse, this is the bike that truly wrote the epitaph of the tiddlers. The age of innocence was over and the age of astounding performance had begun.

Image by Chuck Schultz under Creative Commons license.

Honda 1970 Chart

Model	Name	Type	HP	Seat	Starter	Wt.	Price
QA-50	Minibike	49cc Single	1.8	Solo	Kick	86	NA
Z-50AK1	Mini Trail	49cc Single	2	Solo	Kick	110	NA
PC50	Little Honda	49cc Single	1.75	Solo	Pedal	106	NA
CA-100	Cub	49cc Single	4.5	Dual	Kick	140	NA
CT-70	Trail 70	72cc Single	5	3/4	Kick	137	$307
CT-70H	Trail 70H	72cc Single	5	3/4	Kick	137	$307
CM-70	Step-Thru	72cc Single	5	Dual	Electric	175	NA
CL-70K1	Scrambler	72cc Single	5	Dual	Kick	174	$317
CL-90L	5HP SCR	89cc Single	4.9	Dual	Kick	203	$325
CT-90K2	Trail 90	89cc Single	7	Solo	Kick	190	$340
CB-100	SS	99cc Single	11.5	Dual	Kick	190	$359
CL-100	Scrambler	99cc Single	11.5	Dual	Kick	190	$379
SL-100	Motosport	99cc Single	11.5	3/4	Kick	240	$425
CA-175K3	Touring	174cc Twin	17	Dual	Electric	270	NA
CB-175K4	SS	174cc Twin	20	Dual	Electric	297	$567
CL-175K3	Scrambler	174cc Twin	20	Dual	Kick	274	$595
CL-175K4	Scrambler	174cc Twin	20	Dual	Electric	305	$625
SL-175	Motosport	174cc Twin	19	3/4	Kick	247	$649
CB-350K2	SS	325cc Twin	36	Dual	Electric	370	$705
CL-350K2	Scrambler	325cc Twin	33	Dual	Electric	366	$737
SL-350	Motosport	325cc Twin	33	3/4	Electric	367	$795
SL-350K1	Motosport	325cc Twin	30	3/4	Kick	306	$819
CB-450K3	SS	444cc Twin	45	Dual	Electric	411	$1015
CL-450K3	Scrambler	444cc Twin	43	Dual	Electric	414	$1006
CB-750	750 Four	736cc Four	67	Dual	Electric	522	$1490
CB-750K1	750 Four	736cc Four	67	Dual	Electric	522	$1547

Honda 1970 Notes: The P50 is a four-stroke moped. The CT-70H had a four-speed transmission with a manual clutch. The far more common regular CT-70 used a three-speed with automatic clutch. The CL-175K3 was a CL that had the high, painted fenders, Ceriani-style front forks, and other styling cues of the SL series. The K4 looked like a smaller CL-350. All claimed dry weights are listed in pounds. SS = Super Sport.

Figure I24 - Black 1953 Honda Cub Motorbike at the Barber Museum, Birmingham, AL. Here we have the primitive origin of the Honda Cub.

Image by Chuck Schultz, photographer, under Creative Commons license.

Figure I25 - Red & Silver 1997 Honda Dream 50 at the Boxenstop Tubingen Museum, Germany. Here we have the ultimate Honda 50 nearly half a century later.

Image by Klaus Nahr, photographer, under Creative Commons license.

Honda 1971 Chart

Model	Name	Type	HP	Seat	Starter	Wt.	Price
QA-50	Minibike	49cc Single	1.8	Solo	Kick	86	$189
Z-50AK2	Mini Trail	49cc Single	1.9	Solo	Kick	118	$259
CT-70	Trail 70	72cc Single	5	3/4	Kick	137	$307
CT-70H	Trail 70H	72cc Single	4	3/4	Kick	136	$320
C-70K1	Step-Thru	72cc Single	5	Solo	Electric	165	NA
CL-70K2	Scrambler	72cc Single	5	Dual	Kick	174	$349
SL-70	Motosport	72cc Single	5	3/4	Kick	138	$359
CT-90K3	Trail 90	89cc Single	7	Solo	Kick	189	$365
CB-100K1	Super Sport	99cc Single	11.5	Dual	Kick	192	$385
CL-100K1	Scrambler	99cc Single	11.5	Dual	Kick	192	$399
CL-100S	5HP SCR	99cc Single	5	Dual	Kick	192	NA
SL-100K1	Motosport	99cc Single	11.5	3/4	Kick	198	$425
SL-125	Motosport	122cc Single	12	3/4	Kick	207	$519
CB-175K5	Super Sport	174cc Twin	20	Dual	Electric	275	$569
CL-175K5	Scrambler	174cc Twin	20	Dual	Electric	274	$599
SL-175K1	Motosport	174cc Twin	19	3/4	Kick	249	$649
CB-350K3	Super Sport	325cc Twin	36	Dual	Electric	345	$735
CL-350K3	Scrambler	325cc Twin	33	Dual	Electric	344	$735
SL-350K1	Motosport	325cc Twin	30	3/4	Kick	306	$819
CB-450K4	Super Sport	444cc Twin	45	Dual	Electric	405	$1050
CL-450K4	Scrambler	444cc Twin	43	Dual	Electric	397	$1015
CB-500	500 Four	498cc Four	50	Dual	Electric	427	$1345
CB-750K1	750 Four	736cc Four	67	Dual	Electric	522	$1595

Honda 1971 Notes: The CT-70H had a four-speed transmission with a manual clutch. The far more common regular CT-70 used a three-speed with automatic clutch. All claimed dry weights are listed in pounds. The stated weights for the CB-500 and CB-750 are wet.

Photos on the next page: What a difference a decade can make when you're having fun! The Super Hawk was Honda's top dog street machine in 1962. Its 27 horsepower was considered exciting news because it was almost as fast as traditional English machines twice its size. In 1972, the 500 Four was just a big old smoothie while the top banana was half again its displacement.

Figure I26 - Black 1962 CB-77 Super Hawk. ©1962 American Honda Motor Company

Figure I27 - 1972 Candy Jet Green Honda CB-500 Four. ©Douglas G. Sheldon, owner and photographer

Honda 1972 Chart

Model	Name	Type	Seat	Starter	Wt.	Price
QA-50	Minibike	49cc Single	Solo	Kick	84	$215
Z-50AK3	Mini Trail	49cc Single	Solo	Kick	117	$291
CT-70K1	Trail 70	72cc Single	3/4	Kick	154	$320
CT-70HK1	Trail 70H	72cc Single	3/4	Kick	154	$341
SL-70	Motosport	72cc Single	3/4	Kick	143	$383
C-70K1	Step-Thru	72cc Single	Solo	Electric	165	$334
CL-70K3	Scrambler	72cc Single	Dual	Kick	167	$356
CT-90K4	Trail 90	89cc Single	Solo	Kick	194	$407
CB-100K2	Super Sport	99cc Single	Dual	Kick	196	$444
CL-100K2	Scrambler	99cc Single	Dual	Kick	196	$464
CL-100S2	5HP SCR	99cc Single	Dual	Kick	196	$464
SL-100K2	Motosport	99cc Single	3/4	Kick	201	$508
SL-125K1	Motosport	122cc Single	3/4	Kick	209	$580
CB-175K6	Super Sport	174cc Twin	Dual	Electric	287	$671
CL-175K6	Scrambler	174cc Twin	Dual	Electric	284	$702
SL-175K1	Motosport	174cc Twin	3/4	Kick	249	NA
XL-250	Motosport	248cc Single	Dual	Kick	278	$870
CB-350K4	Super Sport	325cc Twin	Dual	Electric	344	$851
CL-350K4	Scrambler	325cc Twin	Dual	Electric	357	$855
CB-350F	350 Four	347cc Four	Dual	Electric	373	$1122
SL-350K2	Motosport	325cc Twin	3/4	Kick	309	$942
CB-450K5	Super Sport	444cc Twin	Dual	Electric	410	$1211
CL-450K5	Scrambler	444cc Twin	Dual	Electric	399	$1182
CB-500K1	500 Four	498cc Four	Dual	Electric	404	$1510
CB-750K2	750 Four	736cc Four	Dual	Electric	479	$1822

Honda 1972 Notes: The CT-70HK1 had a four-speed transmission with a manual clutch. The far more common regular CT-70 used a three-speed with automatic clutch. The CB-500K1 was road tested to have 50 horsepower. Honda did not officially publish horsepower figures in 1972. All claimed dry weights are listed in pounds. The new XL-series of single-cylinder Motosports debuted with even more emphasis on off-road use.

Figure I28 - Yellow 1973 Honda XL-250. Dirt bikes are rarely as collectible as street models of any equivalent period, so their emphasis is understandably minor in this book. The sole exceptions are the Yamaha T-Series and the Honda SL Series, both first generation off-road machines specifically designed for the American market. The Honda SL Motosports began to be replaced by the all-new, dirt-oriented XL Series beginning with the introduction of the XL-250 in 1972. These were a more serious foray into the off-road market for Honda, featuring frames and single-cylinder, four-stroke engines designed from the dirt up. The XL's would sell quite well to both casual and serious off-road riders who also needed at least acceptable street capability.

Image by Lorddiagram under Creative Commons license in the Public Domain.

Honda 1973 Chart

Model	Name	Type	Seat	Starter	Wt.	Price
QA-50K1	Minibike	49cc Single	Solo	Kick	84	$215
Z-50AK4	Mini Trail	49cc Single	Solo	Kick	117	$291
CT-70K1	Trail 70	72cc Single	3/4	Kick	154	$320
CT-70K2	Trail 70	72cc Single	3/4	Kick	154	$320
CT-70HK1	Trail 70H	72cc Single	3/4	Kick	154	$341
SL-70K1	Motosport	72cc Single	3/4	Kick	143	$383
C-70K1	Step-Thru	72cc Single	Solo	Electric	165	$334
CL-70K3	Scrambler	72cc Single	Dual	Kick	167	$356
XR-75	Motocross	72cc Single	3/4	Kick	141	$355
ST-90	Trailsport	89cc Single	Solo	Kick	190	$427
CT-90K4	Trail 90	89cc Single	Solo	Kick	194	$407
CL-100S3	5HP SCR	99cc Single	Dual	Kick	196	$464
SL-100K3	Motosport	99cc Single	3/4	Kick	201	$508
CB-125S	Super Sport	122cc Single	Dual	Kick	197	$503
CL-125S	Scrambler	122cc Single	Dual	Kick	196	$517
SL-125K2	Motosport	122cc Single	3/4	Kick	209	$642
TL-125	Trials	122cc Single	Solo	Kick	194	$594
CB-175K7	Super Sport	174cc Twin	Dual	Electric	287	$671
CL-175K7	Scrambler	174cc Twin	Dual	Electric	284	$702
XL-175	Enduro	173cc Single	3/4	Kick	243	NA
CR-250M	Elsinore	248cc Single	3/4	Kick	214	$1161
XL-250	Motosport	248cc Single	Dual	Kick	278	$870
CB-350K4	Super Sport	325cc Twin	Dual	Electric	344	$851
CB-350G	Super Sport	325cc Twin	Dual	Electric	359	$912
CL-350K5	Scrambler	325cc Twin	Dual	Electric	357	$855
CB-350F	350 Four	347cc Four	Dual	Electric	373	$1122
SL-350K2	Motosport	325cc Twin	3/4	Kick	309	$942
CB-450K6	Super Sport	444cc Twin	Dual	Electric	410	$1211
CL-450K5	Scrambler	444cc Twin	Dual	Electric	399	$1182
CB-500K2	500 Four	498cc Four	Dual	Electric	404	$1510
CB-750K3	750 Four	736cc Four	Dual	Electric	479	$1822

Honda 1973 Notes: The CB-750K3 was road tested to have 67 horsepower. Honda did not officially publish horsepower figures in 1973. All claimed dry weights are listed in pounds. The CB-350G had a front disc brake. The CL-450 of this and all years had a drum front brake, hence the lower retail prices than its CB equivalents. Honda releases its first two-stroke, the Elsinore 250 motocrosser.

Figure I29 - 1973 Honda CR-250M Elsinore 250. One year after the introduction of the XL-250 Enduro, Honda shocked the motorcycle world with the release of the company's first two-stroke. The Elsinore motocrosser cost about $300 more than the XL and weighed about sixty pounds less. Honda was out to show Yamaha where they could stuff their GYT Kits! Note the distinctive, polished aluminum gas tank and green number plates.

©Don Quayle, Costa Mesa, CA, owner and photographer

Honda 1974 Chart

Model	Name	Type	Seat	Starter	Wt.	Price
QA-50K2	Minibike	49cc Single	Solo	Kick	84	$272
Z-50AK5	Mini Trail	49cc Single	Solo	Kick	117	$352
MR-50	Elsinore	49cc Single	Solo	Kick	95	$386
CT-70K3	Trail 70	72cc Single	3/4	Kick	154	$432
XL-70	Enduro	72cc Single	3/4	Kick	143	$465
XR-75K1	Motocross	72cc Single	3/4	Kick	141	$437
ST-90K1	Trailsport	89cc Single	Solo	Kick	190	$466
CT-90K5	Trail 90	89cc Single	Solo	Kick	194	$513
XL-100	Enduro	89cc Single	3/4	Kick	201	$616
CB-125S1	Super Sport	122cc Single	Dual	Kick	197	$604
CL-125S1	Scrambler	122cc Single	Dual	Kick	196	$594
MT-125	Elsinore	123cc Single	3/4	Kick	207	$710
CR-125M	Elsinore	123cc Single	3/4	Kick	180	$813
TL-125K1	Trials	122cc Single	Solo	Kick	194	$688
XL-125	Enduro	122cc Single	3/4	Kick	209	NA
XL-175K1	Enduro	173cc Single	3/4	Kick	243	$795
CB-200	Super Sport	198cc Twin	Dual	Electric	287	$876
CL-200	Scrambler	198cc Twin	Dual	Electric	284	$865
MT-250	Elsinore	248cc Single	3/4	Kick	268	$937
CR-250M	Elsinore	248cc Single	3/4	Kick	214	$1267
XL-250K1	Motosport	248cc Single	Dual	Kick	278	$980
XL-350	Enduro	348cc Single	Dual	Kick	302	$1051
CB-350F1	350 Four	347cc Four	Dual	Electric	373	$1215
CB-360	Super Sport	356cc Twin	Dual	Electric	344	$1022
CB-360G	Super Sport	356cc Twin	Dual	Electric	359	$1085
CL-360	Scrambler	356cc Twin	Dual	Electric	357	$1022
CB-450K7	Super Sport	444cc Twin	Dual	Electric	410	$1399
CL-450K6	Scrambler	444cc Twin	Dual	Electric	399	$1371
CB-550	550 Four	544cc Four	Dual	Electric	423	$1671
CB-750K4	750 Four	736cc Four	Dual	Electric	479	$1944

Honda 1974 Notes: The MR-50 Elsinore is a two-stroke mini machine. The CB-125S1 received a front disc brake and tachometer in '74, reflecting its $100 price jump. The two-stroke lineup is expanded into the MT Enduro series. Horsepower ratings for the MT-125 and CR-125M were quoted as 10 and 17 from the dyno in August 1973 *Cycle* tests. Honda did not officially publish horsepower figures in 1974. All claimed dry weights are listed in pounds.

Figure I30 - 1974 Honda CH-350F1. This jewel-like small four-cylinder would remain a member of a rather exclusive club. It shall always be relatively rare because it was built for only two years and it was never a high-volume model. The four-cylinder engine was of course as smooth as silk, but it was only 22cc larger than the 350 twins, and only marginally faster, if any at all. With tons of class and cache, the CB-350 Four quietly whispered off into the sunset as its new cafe-styled 400 Four replacement burst onto the scene with the swoopiest header pipes in motorcycle history!

©Lars Eriksson of the Classic Honda Club, Norway, owner and photographer

Honda 1975 Chart

Model	Name	Type	Seat	Starter	Wt.	Price
QA-50K3	Minibike	49cc Single	Solo	Kick	84	$299
Z-50AK6	Mini Trail	49cc Single	Solo	Kick	117	$393
MR-50K1	Elsinore	49cc Single	Solo	Kick	95	$434
CT-70K4	Trail 70	72cc Single	3/4	Kick	158	$480
XL-70K1	Enduro	72cc Single	3/4	Kick	147	$513
XR-75K2	Motocross	72cc Single	3/4	Kick	142	$489
ST-90K2	Trailsport	89cc Single	Solo	Kick	190	$549
CT-90K6	Trail 90	89cc Single	Solo	Kick	198	$589
XL-100K1	Enduro	89cc Single	3/4	Kick	205	$669
CB-125S2	Super Sport	122cc Single	Dual	Kick	205	$656
MT-125K1	Elsinore	123cc Single	3/4	Kick	207	$768
CR-125M1	Elsinore MX	123cc Single	3/4	Kick	181	$892
TL-125K2	Trials	122cc Single	Solo	Kick	194	$749
XL-125K1	Enduro	122cc Single	3/4	Kick	214	$789
MR-175	Elsinore	171cc Single	3/4	Kick	204	$897
XL-175K2	Enduro	173cc Single	3/4	Kick	239	$886
CB-200T	Super Sport	198cc Twin	Dual	Electric	291	$949
MT-250K1	Elsinore	248cc Single	3/4	Kick	260	$999
CR-250M1	Elsinore MX	248cc Single	3/4	Kick	214	$1330
TL-250	Trials	248cc Single	Solo	Kick	218	$1060
XL-250K2	Motosport	248cc Single	Dual	Kick	278	$1090
XL-350K1	Enduro	348cc Single	Dual	Kick	302	$1166
CB-360T	Super Sport	356cc Twin	Dual	Electric	357	$1224
CL-360K1	Scrambler	356cc Twin	Dual	Electric	357	$1167
CB-400F	Super Sport	408cc Four	Dual	Electric	375	$1433
CB-500T	Street	498cc Twin	Dual	Electric	425	$1545
CB-550K1	550 Four	544cc Four	Dual	Electric	423	$1799
CB-550F	Super Sport	544cc Four	Dual	Electric	421	$1830
CB-750K5	750 Four	736cc Four	Dual	Electric	495	$2099
CB-750F	Super Sport	736cc Four	Dual	Electric	538	$2199
GL-1000	Gold Wing	999cc Four	Dual	Electric	610	$2899

Honda 1975 Notes: The MR-50K1 Elsinore is a two-stroke mini machine. The dyno chart in the April 1975 *Cycle* Road Test rated the horsepower of the XL-100K1 as eleven. The CR-250M1 had an as-tested 29 horsepower. The horsepower rating of 58 for the CB-750F is the dyno figure and the actual weight is as quoted in the May 1975 *Cycle* Road Test. Honda did not officially publish horsepower ratings in 1975. All claimed dry weights are listed in pounds.

Figure I31 - Red 1975 Honda CB-400F with Desmo. This spitting image of Mad Max's mutt is named Desmo, but he's no duck! ©Michael Kiernan, Classic Motorcycle Company, St. Louis, MO.

Figure I32 - Blue 1975 Honda CD-175. This photo was taken by the machine's owner on Clay Lane outside Norton Disney, Lincolnshire, England. This model was the antithesis of the CB-400F of the same year. The CD-175 was relatively rare in America, but this basic commuter model sold well in Europe for several years. Image by Clifford Feamley, owner and photographer, under Creative Commons license.

Honda Dream Charts

Honda Dream Timeline of Model Introduction Dates from *The ID Guide*

6/4/59 - CA-92 Benly Touring 125 / C-71 / CA-71 Dream Touring 250
8/1/59 - C100 Super Cub
9/1/59 - CA-95 Benly 150 (early) / CE-71 Dream Sport 250 / C-76 / CA-76 Dream 300
1/1/60 - CS-76 / CSA-76 Dream Sport 300 with upswept pipes and dry-sump
7/1/60 - C102 Super Cub
8/1/60 - CA102 Super Cub / CA-72 Dream 250 (early) / CA-77 Dream 305 (early)
9/1/60 - CS-77 / CSA-77 Dream Sport 305 with upswept pipes and wet-sump
3/1/61 - C-72 Dream Touring 250 / C-77 Dream Touring 305
8/1/62 - CA100 Honda 50 / CA102 Honda 50
4/1/63 - CA-95 Benly (late) / CA-72 Dream 250 (late) / CA-77 Dream 305 (late)
9/1/63 - CA200 Honda 90
4/1/65 - Sport 65
2/1/66 - CM-91 Honda 90
5/1/66 - CA-160 Touring 160
4/1/68 - CA-175 (CD-175) Touring 175
6/25/69 - CA-175 K3 Touring 175
7/1/70 - C70M Honda 70
4/01/72 - C70K1 Honda 70

All models had single carburetors. All except the 50cc and 90cc models and the very rare 1959 CE71 Dream Sport 250 had 16" wheels. The smaller models had 17" and the rare beastie had 18" wheels. All models had leading-link front suspension, except the 175's, which had telescopic forks. All the machines in this chart except the step-through 50's, 70's, and '90's had four-speed transmissions. Red seats may have been available on many blue 125cc, 150cc, 250cc, and 305cc models in the 1959-62 period. Red seats may have been available on red models and blue seats on blue models during the same period. The C77 305 may have had white seats available with some colors, too.

It seems that white became a Honda color choice sometime in 1960. Although many models have been offered in blue and/or white, Scarlet Red and Black were the most common Honda colors by far from 1959-67. A transition to candy colors of more varied shades began with the 1968 models, but this was happening as the base model Dream series was being phased out, so these models continued with the standard black-red-blue-white choices to the end of production.

423

Honda 50cc Singles Chart

Model	Years	Colors	Starter	Tail lamp	Emblems
C-100	1959-62	Red - Black - White - Blue	Kick	Small	Cub & Super Cub
C-102	1960-62	Red - Black - White - Blue	Electric	Small	Cub & Super Cub
CA-100	1962-70	Red - Black - White - Blue	Kick	Large	Honda 50
CA-102	1962-69	Red - Black - White - Blue	Electric	Large	Honda 50

Honda 50cc Singles Notes: All Honda 50 step-through models had OHV engines, 17-inch wheels, and three-speed transmissions with rocking foot shifter and automatic clutch. Blue models had blue seats and light blue leg shields and side covers. Some black Cubs had black seats with white side panels and black passenger straps. Some red Cubs had dark gray seats with white side panels and dark gray passenger straps. All others had white seats, leg shields, and side covers. A small number of C-100's, and maybe C-102's, were imported with solo seats and luggage racks.

Honda 70cc - 90cc Singles Chart

Model	Years	Colors	Details
C70M	1970 – 71	Bright Red – Pine Green Aquarius Blue	72cc OHC Kick & Electric Start
C70 K1	1972 – 73	Strato Blue – Poppy Yellow	Solo Seat & Luggage Rack Kick & Electric Start
CM91 90	1966 – 69	Red – White - Black All models had black seats.	White Shields & Side Covers 89cc OHC - 3-sp – Kick Start
CA200 90	1963 – 66	Red – White - Black	87cc OHV 4-speed – Kick Start Only

Honda 70cc-90cc Singles Notes: The CA200 Honda 90 had traditional styling and an OHV engine with a four-speed transmission and manual clutch. All the step-through models had OHC engines, three-speed rocking shifters and automatic clutches. The leg shields on these models were white. The side covers were body colored on the 70's and white on the 90's. All models had pressed steel frames and 17" wheels. Note that *Cycle* tested a white CA-200, as noted in the Bibliography.

Honda 125cc - 150cc - 160cc - 175cc Twins Chart

Model	Years	Colors	Details
C92 Benly 125	1959	Red – Blue – Black	Low, Pressed Steel Bars Turn Signals - No Tank Pads
CA92 Benly 125	1959	Red – Blue - Black	Chrome Handlebars - No Turn Signals - No Tank Pads
CA 95 Benly Touring 150	1959-63	Black – Red – Blue – White	Blackwall Tires – Flat Mufflers Small Knee Pads & Taillight
CA 95 Benly Touring 150	1963-66	Black – Red – Blue - White	Wide WSW – Round Mufflers Larger Knee Pads & Taillight
CA 160 Touring	1966-69	Black – Red – Blue – White	161cc OHC - Thin White Sidewalls
CA175 (CD 175)	1968-69	Black - Candy Red Candy Blue	Black Inclined Cylinders - Pressed Steel Frame – 6V
CA175 K3 (CD 175K3)	1969-70	Black - Candy Red Candy Blue	Vertical Cylinders - 6V - Single Downtube, Tubular Frame

Honda 125cc - 150cc - 160cc - 175cc Twins Notes: All models had OHC engines, single carburetors, electric starters and four-speed transmissions. All models had leading-link front suspension, except the 175's, which had telescopic forks. The CS92 Benly 125 is not listed because it was not officially available in the U. S. There may have been no blue offered on the 1968 and/or 1969 Touring 160.

Figure I33 - The Ubiquitous Honda Benly Touring 150/160. ©Troyce Walls

Honda Benly Touring 150 / CA-160

The Benly Touring 150 was introduced to American Honda dealers in September 1959, only one month after Honda had launched the legendary Honda 50 into our market. The Benly Touring was a high-volume, low-priced refrigerator of a motorcycle. If ever a motorcycle deserved to be called an appliance, the Benly is a shining example. This is one boring classic motorcycle. It is also deserving of a very special place in tiddler history as the machine that brought modern motorcycling to an eager herd of buyers ready for back to school excitement. Has there ever been a better reason to be excited about going back to high school or college in the fall than on a brand new Honda?

Of course the Honda 50 changed everything on two wheels in America. Without it there may never have been a sandcast 750 or a naked Gold Wing, much less the highly evolved two-wheeled cars that most motorcyclists ride today. You may have forgotten this, but the 80-100cc single-cylinder tiddlers that would become so ubiquitous everywhere from every brand were still a few years away at the beginning of The Sixties. Due basically to its OHC twin-cylinder, four-stroke engine, the Benly Touring became an instant success with the *step up to a real motorcycle* crowd in the early Sixties. The 150 was the lowest level machine that might not scare you on a road more traveled than a country lane. This trait, combined with its modern styling, refrigerator reliability, and its low price of about $500-550 out the door, depending on the dealer, put the Benly 150 in the motorcycle history books.

The 150 had a claimed 16.5 horsepower for a top speed of 84 mph with a tiny Japanese rider going down a very steep hill! The specs may have been fudged a bit, but the Benly was light years ahead of the American and European competition at the time of its introduction. The 165-175cc, ten-horsepower Harley-Davidson Super Ten, Pacer, and Scat had classic motorcycle styling along with classic piston-port two-stroke singles that drank manually mixed fuel and sputtered their unpleasant drivel out the exhaust. Harley-Davidson had not yet even discovered *real* suspension systems for their tiddlers, and anything interesting such as nice paint colors, a decent amount of chrome, a dual seat, and Buckhorn handlebars were optional at extra cost! They could (maybe) do an honest 60 mph downhill. So? Most Benlys could easily top 70-75 mph. The Triumph Road Sports Tiger Cub certainly had styling and charisma out its unreliable English wazoo, but its price was lofty and its dealers and servicing were few and far between. Did I mention how often it needed that servicing? What about the BSA tiddlers? They were about as exciting as a ratty old Ford Pinto. What else was available? Allstates, Cushman Eagles, Mustangs, and Vespas were the most common. The only thing resembling a real motorcycle among this bunch was the Allstate 250 Twingle, and its styling and performance was as inviting as a vacation to Austria in the winter. Of course Yamaha and Suzuki would very soon be challenging Honda's market share with zippy, sporty two-strokes in the 125-250cc size class, but the Benly Touring was the machine with the big head start in the race off the sales floor.

Out of the thousands of CA-95 150 and CA-160 models built, there were very few variations. All models were available in the ubiquitous black, red, white, and blue, and as with most of the early Hondas, the production numbers probably followed these four colors in descending order. The Benly Touring introduced Honda's *modern*, pressed-steel frame styling with square-shaped fenders and lines to the youth of America. The enclosed chain guard, twin seat with passenger strap, folding rear footpegs, squarely styled tank, sixteen-inch wheels, and low angelwing handlebars were a new look to American eyes. Everybody loved the quiet, but pleasant exhaust sound, electric starter, battery lighting, and decently comfortable suspension. Even a SOHC engine with a four-speed transmission was considered exotic for a small bike at that time, and with its horizontally split engine cases, it didn't even leak!

The original CA-95 was built with blackwall tires, slightly smaller knee pads on the tank, a 154cc engine, a smaller taillight, and a few other, very minor identifying elements. The mufflers were crudely welded with a seam left showing down the center of the top edge, and their sides were somewhat flat. In 1963 Honda changed the standard tires to wide whitewalls, altered the shapes of the tank pads slightly, enlarged the taillight for better visibility, and changed the mufflers to a more pleasantly rounded shape. The CA-160 was produced from '66 through '69. The 161cc, twin-carb CB-160 had already been introduced in late '64, so the Benly engine was changed to this displacement in 1966. The most distinguishing trait in 1966 became the narrower whitewall tires, the new model was renamed CA-160 and the Benly name was lost in the ozone forever.

James Rozee Speaks: "I have owned a few of the 150 and 160 Benly Touring models. I did find out the hard way that the 150 and 160 motors are different. and only a few body parts will switch over from the 150 to the 160. The 160 was the last of that Baby Dream look. The CD-175 was just not the same. The CD-175 was dropped here, but it sold well in Europe and Japan for years afterwards. One of the many quirks of the Dreams was that front fender crack. I have had many with it. and the bottom duck tail always gets munched. There was an aftermarket Honda wing you could buy to hide the crack. I had a few of them .They just clamped onto the front of the fender and looked really 'Pimp'. Back then you could buy all kinds of aftermarket chrome stuff to 'Pimp' your Honda with!"

Honda 250cc Dream Twins Chart

Model	Years	Sump	Tank Pads	Tires	Handlebars
C71 Touring	1959-60	Dry	None	Blackwall	Pressed Steel
CA71 Touring	1959-60	Dry	None	Blackwall	Chrome
CE71 Sport	1959-60	Dry	Black	Blackwall	Chrome
C72 Touring	1961	Wet	Black	Wide WSW	Pressed Steel
CA72 Touring	1960-66	Wet	Black	Wide WSW	Chrome

Honda 250cc Dream Notes: All models except the early CE71 had pressed steel frames, 16-inch wheels, leading-link front suspension, SOHC engines with single carburetors, downswept exhausts, electric starters, and four-speed transmissions. The early CE71's had 18-inch wheels. All dry-sump engines may or may not have had rotary (0-1-2-3-4-0-1-2-3-4) gearshifts. The CA-72 had a slightly larger tank from mid-63 through 1966. All models except the CE71 Dream Sport came in the traditional Honda colors of Scarlet Red, Black, Blue, or White. Some red or blue models may have had red or blue seats, in either the same or contrasting colors. All other seats, except that of the CE71, were black.

The CE71 250 was the only Dream Sport model that had downswept pipes. It had a solid silver painted tank without chrome side panels and came only in Black or Maroon. The CE 71 also had either a white seat or a black seat with white piping. One photo I have shows a red seat. There were only 390 CE 71 models produced.

Honda 305cc Dream Twins Chart

Model	Years	Sump	Tank Pads	Tires	Bars	Exhaust
C76	1959-60	Dry	None	Blackwall	Pressed	Down
CA76	1959-60	Dry	None	Blackwall	Chrome	Down
CS76	1960	Dry	Black	Blackwall	Pressed	Upswept
CSA76	1960	Dry	Black	Blackwall	Chrome	Upswept
CS77	1960-63	Wet	Black	Wide WSW	Pressed	Upswept
CSA77	1960-63	Wet	Black	Wide WSW	Chrome	Upswept
C77	1961-64	Wet	Black	Wide WSW	Pressed	Down
CA77	1960-63	Wet	Black	Wide WSW	Chrome	Down
CA77	1963-69	Wet	Black	Thin WSW	Chrome	Down

Honda 305cc Dream Notes: The 76 models were called 300's and the 77 models were called 305's, but they all had the same 305cc displacement. Models with upswept exhaust pipes, one on each side, were called *Sport*. Models with downswept exhaust systems were called *Touring*. Colors were black, red, white, or blue. All black or white models had black seats. Some blue or red models may have had blue or red seats, some in the same colors and some contrasting. All models had pressed steel frames, 16-inch wheels, leading-link front suspension, SOHC engines with single carburetors, electric starters, and four-speed transmissions. All dry-sump engines may or may not have had rotary (0-1-2-3-4-0-1-2-3-4) gearshifts. All wet-sump models had return shifts.

Figures I34 & I35 (next page) - Two Black 305 Dreams. The 1967 top example has the correct white sidewall tires. ©John, owner and photographer. **The lower 1968 machine has been restored, but with blackwalls and an optional windshield.** ©Steven Christmas, owner, restorer and photographer.

Honda Super Sports Charts

Honda Super Sport Timeline of Model Introduction Dates from *The ID Guide*

11/1/59 - CB-92 Benly Super Sport 125
12/1/60 - C110 Super Sports Cub with cream tank and long solo seat
2/1/61 - CB-72 Hawk 250
3/1/61 - CB-92R Benly Super Sport Racer 125
4/1/61 - CB-77 Super Hawk 305
11/1/62 - CA110 Sport 50 with chrome tank panels and dual seat with strap
7/1/64 - CB-160 Sport 160
10/1/64 - S-90 Super 90
4/1/65 - Sport 65
8/1/65 - CB-450 Super Sport 450
6/24/67 - CB-450D kitted CB-450
8/1/67 - SS-125A Super Sport 125
2/29/68 - CB-350 Super Sport 350
4/27/68 - CB-450 K1 Super Sport 450
4/1/69 - CB-450 K2 Super Sport 450
5/1/69 - CB-350 K1 Super Sport 350
6/6/69 - CB-750 Four
6/25/69 - CB-175 K3 Super Sport 175 (early & late)
2/10/70 - CB-350 K2 Super Sport 350
3/1/70 - CB-175 K4 Super Sport 175 / CB-450 K3 Super Sport 450
5/11/70 - CB-100 Super Sport 100
9/21/70 - CB-750 K1 Four
2/8/71 - CB-175 K5 Super Sport 175 / CB-350 K3 Super Sport 350 / CB-450 K4
2/10/71 - CB-100 K1 Super Sport 100
6/1/71 - CB-500 Four
1/01/72 - CB-100 K2 Super Sport 100
2/1/72 - CB-175 K6 Super Sport 175 / CB-350 K4 Super Sport 350
3/1/72 - CB-450 K5 Super Sport 450 / CB-750 K2 Four
4/1/72 - CB-500 K1 Four
5/1/72 - CB-350F 350 Four
9/1/72 - CB-125S
1/1/73 - CB-350G Super Sport 350 / CB-450 K6 Super Sport 450
2/1/73 - CB-750 K3 Four
4/10/73 - CB-500 K2 Four
5/1/73 - CB-175 K7 Super Sport 175
1974 - CB-125S1 / CB-200 / CB-350 F1 / CB-360 / CB-360G / CB-450 K7 / CB-550 Four
/ CB-750 K4 Four (specific release dates N.A.)
1975 - CB-125S2 / CB-200T / CB-360T / CB-400F / CB-500T / CB-550 K1 Four / CB-
550F Super Sport / CB-750 K5 Four / CB-750F Super Sport (specific release dates N. A.)

Honda entered the U.S. market in late 1959. The company sold less than 200 motorcycles in the U.S. in 1959, but of course that number would accelerate rapidly beginning in 1960, the first full year of Honda exportation to this country. Although Honda, both the man and the company, had been seriously involved with exotic, multi-cylinder engines in Grand Prix racing, with few exceptions the production models for the Japanese market were designed as strictly utilitarian transportation. As Honda got more involved with the American market of motorcycles as toys for sports enthusiasts instead of necessities for affordable transport, the company began to build more and more road sports models. This element of the company's production history can be clearly traced back to 1959.

Throughout the '60's, the Honda road sports models were designated with somewhat inconsistent nomenclature, and the particular characteristics inherent within the group were also variable. The bloodline officially begins with the 1959 125cc CB-92, even though it used a pressed steel frame and a single carburetor. By 1970 Honda had all of its designating ducks in order. The road sports models were all designated *CB-cc displacement class*. All the scramblers were designated *CL-cc displacement class*. Honda has continued to apply the *Sport, Super Sport, and Hawk* names to their sport models to the present day.

The Honda Super Sports nomenclature has been consistently inconsistent through the years. If the Honda model in question is the fastest street model of that displacement for that model year, then, for the purposes of this chart, it is considered a Super Sport. All of the Scramblers were a tiny bit slower and a little more versatile than their Super Sport model equivalents. There is at least one exception to all of the technical specifications as listed here. All of the twins had dual carbs except the CB-92. Most of the front and rear wheel diameters were the same at eighteen inches. Most had tube frames, but some had pressed steel frames and some had hybrid pressed steel/tube frames. Handlebars never had a cross brace, but the height and width varied considerably. Some models had rubber knee pads on the gas tanks and some did not. Some had fenders higher than others. Some had styling as lean as that of the scramblers, but others did not. Onward through the CB-fog....

Honda C110 Super Sports & Sport Cub Chart

Year	Color Choices	Tank	Side Covers	Seat Strap	Handlebars	Speeds
1960 - 62	Red - Black - White - Blue	Cream	Cream	No	Low	Three
1963 - 64	Red - Black - White - Blue	Chrome	Cream	Yes	Low	Four
1965	Red - Black - White - Blue	Chrome	Body Color	Yes	Low	Four
1966 - 67	Red - Black - White - Blue	Chrome	Body Color	Yes	High	Four
1968	Red - Black	Chrome	Body Color	Yes	High	Four

Honda C110 Notes: All C110's had 17" wheels, kickstarters, upswept exhausts, and pressed-steel frames. There may not have been any Super Sport 50's sold as 1960 models, since the C110 debuted so late in the year. The 1960-62 models with cream tank and three-quarter-length seat were called Super Sports. The models from November 1962 through 1968 were called Sport 50. The four-speed transmission was added at some point after the Sport 50 name, probably as a running change during 1963.

Honda Sport 50

I have to pay homage to the little tiddler that I have wished for the most often, and ridden a number of times, but never owned. This is the later version of the Super Sport Cub that I clobbered with my Rotary Jet 80 at wide-open throttle, right in the chain guard, wearing nothing more than a pudding-bowl helmet, a t-shirt, shorts, and sneakers without socks! Slap that horrific image right out of your head! Yes, it hurt, but we both were released from the emergency room within a few hours. There were miraculously no broken bones, but we used up the hospital's entire monthly allotment of Mercurochrome and bandages. Hiyo, Silver! Let's go back to those innocent days of yesteryear!

The first motorcycle I rode was a 1960 Harley-Davidson Super 10 and the second was a Benly Touring 150. The third was the very same red and cream, three-speed Super Sports 50 that I clobbered with my Yamaha 80. I lived to ride a few other Sport 50's in the mid-Sixties, too. What impressed me from the moment I saw that first Super Sports was that this was, indeed, a tiny motorcycle! There was nothing *scooter* about it. You swung your leg over the seat like a man should and you made sure it was in neutral and then kick-started the little jewel, just as if it was a Harley-Davidson Sportster that your cat could kickstart! The handgrips were of small diameter, a quality that did *not* say Sportster like the big fat ones on the Super 10 did. The engine was tiny and quiet. The Sport 50 felt a lot stronger than the step-through 50 with only one-half horsepower less. There was no substitute for cubic inches, but if you couldn't have those, Japanese technology, four gears, and a clutch went a long way toward making you feel like a real man. Just don't look too closely at the pressed steel frame and leading link front suspension. I remember like it was yesterday when my dad somewhat mysteriously asked me if I liked *the little Honda or the little Yamaha better*. My immediate reply had a lot to do with a steel front fender, a cubic inch, telescopic forks, and larger hand grips!

Figure I36 - Black Honda Sport 50. ©Troyce Walls

You can examine the detailed differences between the Sport 50's in the Super Sport Chart. The model was introduced in 1960 with a cream tank and side panels, low handlebars, a 3/4-length seat, and a three-speed transmission, albeit with a manual clutch, unlike its more numerous brothers. Through the years the model was available, the three-speeds increased to four, the seat got a little longer, the tank received body-color paint and chrome side panels, the side covers became body-colored, and the handlebars grew a little higher. The strangest anachronism was in the name. The later, four-speed models were call *Sport*, but the earlier, three-speed models were called *Super Sports*! One little tidbit you may not have surmised is that the only (regular motorcycle) Honda model aside from this one with an OHV engine was the short-lived Honda 90 (CA-200) of 1963-66, making the Super Sport and Sport 50 by far the longest running, highest production model, non-OHC Honda *motorcycle* ever!

This is exactly what has made me daydream about having one of these little beasties in my garage, or even in my living room, for decades. Although black was a very common color for this model, I personally prefer the other three colors a little more. Although these were produced in black, red, white, and blue up until 1968, the final year, when only red and black were built, red and black were far more common than blue or white. I think the reason I like the lighter colors is that they offer contrast to the standard black parts, showing off the fact that this is a tiny *motorcycle*. I like the look of the black tires, hand grips, and seat contrasting with the painted *motorcycle* parts. I want to say I am riding the real thing, baby! The Lone Ranger knew to approach Silver from the left side. Swing your leg over that saddle like a real man. We don't need no stinking electric starters! You aren't coordinated enough to start rolling smoothly with a clutch and manual transmission? What are you, a wuss?

James Rozee Speaks: "I love the small bikes. I once was going to collect every 50cc Japanese bike there was! I almost got all of them but was running out of room. I sold and traded most of them off. I still have a few left. I have owned many C-110's. I still have my bone-stock, last-year 1968 white one. The Sport 50's were such cool bikes. There were many small changes made through the years, some you can see, others you cannot. The presence of turn signals will indicate (pardon the pun) an early model. The signals were dropped in early 1963. The carb boot from the pressed frame to the carb was made in two sizes, depending on what carb manifold you had. Early ones had a rubber cover over the frame welds. There were rubber covers for the exhaust shields, too. The early white bikes had pure white side covers. Early blue models had a different shade of blue side covers than the later models. There were a handful of all-chrome models given to dealers as prizes. First-year Honda C-110 models had the heel-shaped tail light through early 1962. There was a cool racing seat and exhaust header megaphone that the factory offered, along with tuning tips."

Honda Sport 65 Chart

Year	Color Choices	Frame	Exhaust	Speeds	Starter
1965 - 69	Red - Black - White	Pressed Steel	Upswept	Four	Kick

Honda Sport 65 Notes: All S65's had OHC engines, cream side panels on dual seats, 17-inch wheels, distinctive tank shape with chrome side panels and black rubber pads, no turn signals, and mostly identical features.

Figure I37 - Black Honda Sport 65. ©Don Quayle, Costa Mesa, CA

Honda Super 90 Chart

Year	Colors	Intake	Fenders	Bars
1964 - 67	Black - Scarlet Red - Blue - White	Convoluted	Silver	Low
Early 1968	Black - Scarlet Red - Blue - White	Convoluted	Silver	Low
Late 1968	Black - Candy Red or Candy Blue	More Direct	Chrome	High
1969	Black - Candy Red or Candy Blue	More Direct	Chrome	High

Honda Super 90 Notes: All S90's had Y-shaped pressed-steel frames, 18-inch wheels, kick starters, OHC single-cylinder engines, four-speed transmissions, speedometer in the headlamp nacelle, body-colored rear shock covers, rubber gaiters over the front springs, and distinctively slender gas tanks with chrome side panels and rubber knee pads. The latest models had turn signals. Candy colors were offered beginning in April 1968. There may or may not have been black models with chrome fenders produced. There may have been white models with chrome fenders, too, but I seriously doubt it. As with many Honda models, restorers should watch carefully for running changes.

Figure I38 - Black 1966 Super 90. Image by Topsy1golf under Creative Commons license in the Public Domain.

Honda Super 90

The Honda Super 90, or S-90 if you prefer, should ring the Tiddlerosis nostalgia bell for many of you. I dare say that this model might be second only to the Honda 50 lineup in its ability to jerk tears of adolescent joy from more of you than any other true tiddler covered in this book.

The Honda 50 set America's youth afire with the step-through, quickly followed by the Super Sport 50, and the trail model soon grew into the ubiquitous Trail 90. The company's development of its 90cc class was not quite so quick or as smooth. Yamaha for once caught Honda with its pants down when it released the YG-1 Rotary Jet 80 in early 1963. Yamaha's two-stroke copycat 50cc step-through models never gained much sales success against the phenomenal Honda 50, but the release of the first big success in the new 80-90cc slot boosted Yamaha onto the American landscape. The YG-1 was only 73cc, but the little squirt combined a bigger bike feel with genuine acceleration spunk! Compared to its main competition on the sales floor at the time, the Honda Sport 50, the YG-1 offered larger handgrips, a softer seat, and a telescopic front fork. With its rotary valve and weighing hardly more than a Sport 50, the Yamaha 80 was a blast to ride.

Honda released its first model in this new size class in September '63, but the new C200 Honda 90 with its big fenders, OHV engine, and leading-link front suspension was something of a snooze. Its solid red, black, or white paint job was bland compared to the numerous solids or combinations with silver fenders offered on the much flashier YG-1, and of course the YG-1 was not called Rotary Jet for nothing. Even with 14cc less displacement, the YG-1 could run and hide from the heavier C200. Strangely enough, the step-through CM91 would not be released until 1966 and the sporty CL-90 would not appear until '67. Honda had to do something to stop this embarrassment by Yamaha!

Honda released the Super 90, or Sport 90 as it was sometimes called, in October 1964 to immediate sales success. Better late than never, the S-90 debuted with an OHC engine and telescopic front suspension to complement its much sportier styling. The distinctively pointy tank would remain the Super 90's trademark through its final model year of 1969. The only significant differences between the beginning and end of S-90 production would pertain to the finish. The '64-67 models were offered in the standard red, black, white, or blue, all with silver fenders. In keeping with the larger models in the Honda lineup, the '68-'69 S-90's were produced with chrome fenders and the new *candy* paint colors of red and blue. By that time, the proliferation of competing models within the S-90's displacement and price range had expanded exponentially. My guess is that far fewer S-90's were sold with the later trim, considering the many choices any young American punk enjoyed at that time, including the CL-90 and several Yamaha, Suzuki, Bridgestone, Kawasaki, and even Hodaka models.

In case you forgot, the YG-1 could still leave the Super 90 behind in a sprint up to about 50 mph, but the S-90 could reach 60-65, while the YG-1 ran out of steam at about 53-55. This meant the YG-1 was still the acceleration champ, and this model dominated racing during the period, but the long-term sales champ was undoubtedly the Super 90. There is probably only one 80-90cc classic tiddler that has outsold it, the ubiquitous Honda Trail 90. Slim tanks for the memories!

Honda CB-100 Super Sport Chart

Year	Colors	Tank	Side Covers	Rear Shocks
1970	Candy Ruby Red - Candy Blue Candy Gold	White Stripe	Body Color	Body Color
1971 - K1	Candy Ruby Red - Candy Gold Crystal Blue Metallic	White Lower Panel	Body Color	Body Color
1972 - K2	Light Scarlet Red - Aquarius Blue	Red or Blue Panel	White	Chrome

Honda CB-100 Notes: All models had SOHC engines with five-speed transmissions, single downtube frames, chrome fenders, 18-inch wheels, drum brakes, kick starters, turn signals, and separate speedometers.

Honda CB-92 & CB-92R Benly Super Sport 125 Chart

Year	Colors	Seat Colors	Seat	Exhaust
1959 - 62	Red or Blue	Black w/Red or Red w/Blue	Dual	Street Legal
1961 - 62 Racer	Red	Black	Racing	Megaphones

Honda CB-92 Notes: All the CB-92 Benly models had pressed-steel frames, leading link front suspension, uncovered chrome rear springs, SOHC twin engines with single carburetors, tiny windscreens attached to the headlamp nacelles, and silver painted front fenders, gas tanks, and side covers. The silver painted pieces were alloy on the early models and steel on the later ones. The black rubber knee pad was unusual in that it was one piece that wrapped around the rear edge of the tank. The 1962 CB-92 may have had a red seat without a center strap and with white piping on the sides. The CB-92R models had higher-tuned engines and a tachometer in place of the speedometer in the headlamp housing.

Figure I39 (next page) - Red 1963 Honda CB-92R Super Sports. Note the tiny windscreen, one-piece wraparound tank pad, racing seat, and megaphone exhaust pipes.
©Michael Kiernan, Classic Motorcycle Company, St. Louis, MO.

Honda Super Sport 125 Chart

Year	Colors	Tank	Frame	Fenders	Rear Shock Covers
1967 - 69	Black - Candy Red Candy Blue	Silver Painted	Body Color	Silver Painted	Body Color

Honda Super Sport 125 Notes: All models had SOHC twin engines with single constant-velocity carburetors, pressed-steel frames, instruments in the headlamp nacelle, rubber gaiters on the front springs, and four-speed transmissions. Note: At least one credible source has informed me that some SS-125's were painted yellow, a color that, according to the brochure chart, was reserved for the equivalent CL model, just as black was indigenous to the SS model. I cannot confirm the existence of yellow SS-125's, as I have never seen one, either in person or in a photo. I have never seen a black CL-125, either, but that does not prove they were never built and shipped to the USA. None of these additional color options are listed in the *Honda ID Guide*.

Honda CB-160 Super Sport Chart

Year	Colors	Tank	Fenders	Handlebars
1964 - 69	Scarlet Red - Black - Blue - White	Chrome Panels with Pad	Silver Painted	Western

Honda CB-160 Notes: All models had SOHC twin engines suspended from a tube frame painted the body color, four-speed transmissions, electric starters, speedometers in the headlamp nacelle, and drum brakes. None had tachometers or turn signals and all the headlights and front and rear shock covers were painted the body color. All fenders and side covers were silver. All gas tanks were painted the body color with chrome side panels and black rubber knee pads. All blue models had blue seats.

's Honda CB160 1967. Restored, and won a prize. 'Best 1960'

Figure I40 - Black 1967 Honda CB-160. ©Peter Horton, owner and photographer, U.K.

Honda CB-175 Super Sport Chart

Year	Colors	Tank	Side Covers	Rear Shock Covers
1969 - K3	Candy Blue - Candy Orange	Pad & White Lower Panel	White	Body Color
1970 - K4	Candy Ruby Red - C. Gold Candy Blue Green	White Lower Panel	Body Color	Chrome
1971 - K5	Crystal Blue Metallic C. R. Red - Candy Gold	Two Parallel Pinstripes	Body Color	Chrome
1972 - K6	Light Ruby Red - Candy Gold	Wide Black Stripe	Body Color	Chrome
1973 - K7	Hawaiian Blue Metallic - Candy Orange	B & W Stripe	Body Color	Chrome

Honda CB-175 Notes: All models had single downtube frames, 18-inch wheels, SOHC twin-cylinder engines, five-speed transmissions, separate instruments, drum brakes, electric starters, and turn signals.

Honda CB-200 Super Sport Chart

Year	Colors	Tank	Fenders	Side Covers
1974	Tahitian Red - Muscat Green Metallic	Black Side Panels	Chrome	Body Color
1975	Metallic Silver - Candy Gold	Pinstripes	Chrome	Body Color
1976	Parakeet Yellow - Shiny Orange	Solid Color	Chrome	Black

Honda CB-200 Notes: The CB-200 had a single downtube frame, 18-inch wheels, rubber gaiters on the front suspension and exposed, chrome rear springs, five-speed transmission, mechanical (non-hydraulic) front disc brake, separate instruments, electric starter, turn signals, and a distinctive, pleated, black vinyl strip down the center of the top of the gas tank.

Honda CB-72 Hawk Chart

Year	Colors	Handlebars	Fenders & Side Covers	Lower Fork Legs
1961 - 64	Scarlet Red - Black - Blue	Flat	Silver Painted	Body Color
1965 - 66	Scarlet Red - Black - Blue	Low-rise	Silver Painted	Body Color

Honda CB-72 Notes: All models had SOHC, twin-cylinder engines suspended from body-colored, tube frames, body-colored front and rear shock covers, speedo and tach in the headlamp nacelles, electric starters, and no turn signals. Blue models had blue seats. This color blue may or may not have been called Royal Blue. American Honda imported only 3479 Hawks, since most Americans were more than willing to pay $30-50 more for a Super Hawk.

Figure I41 - Red Honda CB-72 Hawk. Image by Rikita under Creative Commons license.

Honda CB-77 Super Hawk Chart

Year	Colors	Tach/Speedo Needles	Lower Fork Legs	Handlebars
1961 - 1964	Scarlet Red - Black - Blue - White	Opposite Directions	Body Color	Flat
1965	Scarlet Red - Black - Blue - White	Same Direction	Body Color	Low-rise
1966 - 1967	Scarlet Red - Black - Blue - White	Same Direction	Silver Painted Alloy	Low-rise
1968	Scarlet Red - Black	Same Direction	Silver Painted Alloy	Low-rise

Honda CB-77 Notes: All models had SOHC, twin-cylinder engines suspended from body-colored, tube frames, body-colored front and rear shock covers, speedo and tach in the headlamp nacelles, electric starters, and no turn signals. The engine was bored out to 305cc over the regular Hawk's 247cc. White models had white fenders and side covers. All others had silver ones, just like all the CB-72 models. Blue models had blue seats. The last 1000 1968 models can be identified by their chrome fenders and oval tail lamps. The early '68 models were replaced by the new 350's in the spring of 1968.

Figure I42 - 1967 Red Honda CB-77 Super Hawk.

©Michael Kiernan, Classic Motorcycle Company, St. Louis, MO.

Figure I43 - Black 1967 Honda Super Hawk. ©Michael Kiernan, Classic Motorcycle Company, St. Louis, MO.

Figure I44 - Blue 1964 Honda CB-77 Super Hawk at the Barber Museum, Birmingham, AL.

Image by Chuck Schultz under Creative Commons license.

Honda CB-350 Super Sport Chart

Year	Colors	Tank	Seat	Brake
1968 - K0	Candy Red - Candy Blue - Green	White Lower Panel with Black Pad	Plain	Drum
1969 - K1	Candy Red - Candy Blue - Green	White Panel w/Stripe & Pad	Plain	Drum
1970 - K2	Candy Ruby Red - Candy Blue - Candy Gold	Lower White Panel w/o Pad	Pleated	Drum
1971 - K3	Ruby Red - Green Metallic - Candy Gold	Black Curved Stripe	Square Pleats	Drum
1972 - K4	Red - Candy Gold - Candy Olive - Maroon Metallic	Black Stripe w/White Pinstripe	No Pleats	Drum
1973 - G	Candy Orange - Green Metallic - Purple Metallic	Black & White Stripes	NA	Disc

Honda CB-350 Notes: All models had hybrid, pressed-steel and single downtube frames, 18-inch wheels, chrome rear shock springs and covers, 325cc SOHC twin engines, dual seats, separate instruments, electric starters, and turn signals.

Figure I45 - Green & White 1968 Honda CB-350 Super Sport Outfitted for the Highway with Optional Fiberglass Saddlebags, Luggage Rack, Passenger Backrest, and Chrome Crash Bars. ©Michael Kiernan, Classic Motorcycle Company, St. Louis, MO.

Honda CB-350 Four Chart

Year	Colors	Tank	Fenders	Front Brake
1972 - 1973	Flake Matador Red - Candy Bacchus Olive	Orange & White Stripes	Chrome	Disc
1974	Glory Blue Black Metallic	Gold Stripes	Chrome	Disc

Honda CB-350 Four Notes: All models had single downtube frames, 18-inch wheels, SOHC four-cylinder engines with four carburetors and exhaust pipes, five-speed transmissions, chrome rear shocks and covers, separate instruments, electric starters, and turn signals.

Figure I46 - 1973 Red Honda CB-350F with Fiberglass Saddlebags. Image by Drahbany under Creative Commons license in the Public Domain.

Honda CB-360 Super Sport Chart

Year	Colors	Tank	Exhausts	Brake	Gears
1974	Hawaiian Blue Metallic Candy Orange	Black & White Stripes	Twin	Drum	6
1974 - G	Hex Green Metallic Candy Orange	Black & White Stripes	Twin	Disc	6
1975 - T	Light Ruby Red - Candy Riviera Blue Metallic	Black & White Stripes	Twin	Disc	6
1976 - T	Candy Ruby Red Candy Sapphire Blue	Black & White Pinstripes	Twin	Disc	6
1976 - CJ - T	Candy Antares Red	Solid Body Color	2-into-1	Drum	5
1977 - CJ - T	Candy Antares Red	Solid Body Color	2-into-1	Drum	5

Honda CB-360 Notes: All CB-360's had SOHC, 356cc, twin-cylinder, twin-carburetor engines in a milder state of tune than those of their CB-350, 325cc older brothers. All models had single-downtube frames, Ceriani-type front suspension, uncovered chrome rear springs, separate instruments, and turn signals. The *T* models had body-color, one-piece seat cowls and rear fenders and body-color front fenders.

Figure I47 - 1974 Red Honda CB-360. Image by Aaron Headly under Creative Commons license.

Figure I48 - 1976 Blue Honda CB-360T. Image by Annecananne under Creative Commons license in the Public Domain.

Honda CB-400F Super Sport Chart

Year	Colors	Tank	Side Covers	Bars	Gas Cap
1975	Light Ruby Red - Varnish Blue	Plain with Decal Only	Body Color	Low	Standard
1976	Light Ruby Red - Parakeet Yellow	Plain with Decal Only	Black	Low	Standard
1977	Candy Antares Red - Parakeet Yellow	Two-color Pinstripes	Body Color	High	Recessed

Honda CB-400F Notes: All CB-400 Super Sports had single-downtube frames, four-cylinder SOHC engines, four carbs, four-into-one exhausts, six-speed transmissions, Ceriani-type front suspension, uncovered chrome rear springs, separate instruments, front disc brakes, black headlamp nacelles, electric starters, and turn signals.

The CB-400F Super Sport introduced in 1975 has been considered a very special Honda since its inception. Built through the 1977 model year, this machine was a direct descendant of the CB-350F, a bike with legendary smoothness, jewel-like technology, and boring performance and styling. Honda released one of its most daring designs with the CB-400F, from its low bars to its swoopy four-into-one exhaust. *Now* we had all of the above, making this particular Honda like most Ferraris: an instant classic as soon as it rolled off the assembly line.

Figure I49 - 1975 Red Honda CB-400F. ©Michael Kiernan, Classic Motorcycle Company, St. Louis, MO.

Figure I50 (previous page, top) - 1975 Red Honda CB-400F with Later Bars. You can tell by the gas tank and side covers that this example originally had the low cafe handlebars. ©Michael Kiernan, Classic Motorcycle Company, St. Louis, MO.

Figure I51 (previous page, bottom) - A Museum Shot of a Red 1975 Honda CB-400F Super Sport with the Correct Cafe Bars. The low bars add to the racy look, no? Image by Rikita under Creative Commons license.

Honda CB-450 Super Sport Chart

Year	Colors	Tank	Brake	Headlamp	Gears
1965 - 1967	Black	Chrome Panels	Drum	Black	Four
1968 - K1	Black - Candy Red Candy Blue	Chrome Panels	Drum	Black	Five
1969 - K2	Candy Red - Candy Blue	Gold Stripe	Drum	Black	Five
1970 - K3	Candy Ruby Red Candy Blue - Candy Gold	White Stripe	Disc	Body Color	Five
1971 - K4	Candy Red - Candy Gold Blue Met. - Green Met.	Black Stripe	Disc	Body Color	Five
1972 - K5	Candy Brown - Candy Olive - Ruby Red	Gold Stripe	Disc	Black	Five
1973 - K6	Green Metallic Brown Metallic	Gold & Black Stripes	Disc	Black	Five
1974 - K7	Candy Orange Brown Metallic	Gold & Black Stripes	Disc	Black	Five

Honda CB-450 Notes: All CB-450's had single-downtube frames, 18-inch wheels, dual CV carburetors, and DOHC twin-cylinder engines. These last two attributes were introduced on the 450 for the first time on a street production Honda. The original 450, nicknamed the *Black Bomber*, had a speedo and tach housed in the headlight nacelle, humpback gas tank, silver painted fenders, and black plastic upper shock covers. The K1 had a trimmed down tank, separate instruments, and chrome fenders and rear springs. The K2-K7's all had sleek, painted gas tanks, chrome fenders, separate instruments, and sportier suspension styling with rubber gaiters on the front and chrome rear springs with chrome upper covers.

Figure I52 - 1966 Honda 450 Black Bomber. ©Michael Kiernan, Classic Motorcycle Company, St. Louis, MO.

Figure I53 - 1974 Honda CB-450 K7. You can see the difference eight years can make by comparing this seventh generation 450 to the first generation example pictured above.

Image by Guydraud, photographer, under Creative Commons license (GNU).

Honda CB-500 Four & Twin Chart

Year	Colors	Tank	Cylinders	Seat
1971	Candy Garnet Brown Star Light Gold / Candy Jet Green	Black Panels	Four	Flat
1972 - K1	Candy Garnet Brown Candy Jet Green / Candy Gold	Black Panels	Four	Flat
1973 - K2	Maxim Brown Metallic / Candy Bucchus Olive / Flake Sunrise Orange	Black Panels	Four	Flat
1975 - T	Glory Brown Metallic	Pinstripes	Two	Sloped

Honda CB-500 Notes: All CB-500's had chrome fenders, black headlamp nacelles, five-speed transmissions, and turn signals. All four-cylinder models had four carburetors and four exhaust pipes. The T model had a brown vinyl seat. The Fours had black rubber gaiters on the front springs and chrome upper rear shock covers. The Twin had Ceriani-type front forks and uncovered, chrome rear shock springs.

Honda CB-550 Four Chart

Year	Colors	Tank	Side Covers
1974 - K0	Flake Sunrise Orange / Boss Maroon Metallic / Freedom Green Metallic	Black Panels	Body Color
1975 - K1	Flake Sunrise Orange Candy Jade Green	Gold & Black Stripes	Black
1975 F	Flake Sunrise Orange Candy Sapphire Blue	White Honda Emblem	Body Color

Honda CB-550 Notes: All CB-550's had electric starters, five-speed transmissions, disc front brakes, chrome fenders, chrome rear shock covers, black rubber gaiters, turn signals, and black headlamps attached with chrome ears. The CB-550F Super Sport had four-into-one exhausts. All others had four pipes with distinctive tips.

Honda CB-750 Four Chart

Year	Colors	Tank	Side Panels	Headlamp
1969 - K0	Candy Blue Green / Candy Ruby Red / Candy Gold	Gold Stripe Black Stripe	Body Color Slotted	Body Color
1970 - K0	Candy Blue Green / Candy Ruby Red / Candy Gold	Gold Stripe Black Stripe	Body Color Slotted	Body Color
1971 - K1	Candy Ruby Red / Candy Garnet Brown / Valley Green Metallic / Candy Gold	Gold Stripe Black Stripe (w/Gold)	Body Color Solid	Body Color
1972 - K2	Flake Sunrise Orange / Brier Brown Metallic / Candy Gold	Gold Stripe Black Stripe (w/Gold)	Body Color Solid	Black w/Chrome Ears
1973 - K3	Flake Sunrise Orange Maxim Brown Metallic Candy Bucchus Olive	Black, White, & Gold Stripes	Body Color Solid	Black w/Chrome Ears
1974 - K4	Flake Sunrise Orange Boss Maroon Metallic Freedom Green Metallic	Black, White, & Gold Stripes	Body Color Solid	Black w/Chrome Ears
1975 - K5	Planet Blue Metallic Flake Apricot Red	Black, White, & Gold Stripes	Body Color Solid	Black w/Chrome Ears
1975 F	Flake Sunrise Orange Candy Sapphire Blue	Pinstripe	Black Solid	Black

Honda CB-750 Notes: All CB-750 K models had SOHC dry-sump engines, five-speed transmissions, four separate exhaust pipes, disc front brakes, electric starters, chrome fenders, chrome rear shock covers, black rubber gaiters, and turn signals. The 1969-70 K0 had larger, slotted side covers. The 750F Super Sport model had Ceriani-type front suspension, uncovered, chrome rear springs, four-into-one exhaust, and a body-colored cowl-type rear fender/seat base assembly.

Figure I54 - Blue Green 1969 Honda 750 Four. ©Michael Kiernan, Classic Motorcycle Company, St. Louis, MO.

Figure I55 - 1969 Honda CB-750 in Candy Blue Green. ©American Honda Motor Company, Inc.

Honda Motosport Charts

Honda Motosport Timeline of Model Introduction Dates from *The ID Guide*

3/1/69 - SL-90 Motosport 90
8/15/69 - SL-350 Motosport 350
2/1/70 - SL-100 Motosport 100
5/26/70 - SL-175 Motosport 175
9/1/70 - SL-350 K1 Motosport 350
3/22/71 - SL-125 Motosport 125
4/1/71 - SL-70 Motosport / SL-100 K1 Motosport 100
5/1/71 - SL-175 K1 Motosport 175
3/1/72 - SL-100 K2 Motosport 100 / SL-125 K1 Motosport 125
4/1/72 - SL-350 K2 Motosport 350
12/1/72 - SL-70K1 Motosport 70
2/1/73 - SL-100 K3 Motosport 100
4/1/73 - SL-125 K2 Motosport 125

Honda invented the street scrambler concept with its 1962 CL-72, a street motorcycle with dirt-bike styling and a little better off-road capability than the purely street models of the day. Americans had begun to discover the safer and more athletic joys of trail riding even before the CL-72 was introduced. Trail riding in America was a slowly growing sport until Yamaha put everybody and his hound dog on knobby tires with its 250cc DT-1 in 1968. The Enduro came with trials universal tires, of course, but many riders changed to real knobbies as soon as the original tires wore out. The Enduro proceeded to have babies the following year and soon trails everywhere were being torn up by Enduros of all sizes, as well as their motocross brothers. Honda's first response to the ring-ding onslaught was the Motosport SL series, a line of bikes that were too heavy to really stomp the Yamahas into the dirt. However, they certainly had long-lasting, sweet-sounding engines and the legendary Honda bullet-proof reliability. The first Motosport released was the SL-90, followed by the heaviest of the Motosport bunch, the SL-350, introduced in late 1969 with a heavy frame and electric starter. The big 350 would begin to improve its *dirtability* with the K1 model of 1971.

Honda SL-70 Motosport Chart

Year	Color Choices	Tank	Taillight Bracket	Speedometer
1971-72 K0	Light Ruby Red - Aquarius Blue - Summer Yellow	White Stripe	Chrome	Optional
1973 K1	Fire Red - Candy Yellow Candy Riviera Blue	Yellow Panel	Painted	Standard

Honda SL-70 Notes: All SL-70's had black exhausts with chrome shields, silver double-downtube frames, four-speed transmissions, and body-colored fenders.

Figure I56 - 1971-72 Aquarius Blue Honda SL-70 Motosport with Optional Speedometer.

Image by Ltpreston, photographer, under Creative Commons license in the Public Domain.

Honda SL-90 Motosport Chart

Year	Color Choices	Tank	Frame	Exhaust
1969	Candy Ruby Red - Candy Blue	Silver Stripe	Silver	Chrome

Honda SL-90 Notes: All SL-90's had upswept exhausts, 19" front wheels, kickstarters, horizontal cylinders, four-speed transmissions, and body-colored fenders. Note: Some SL-90's may have had black frames, as shown in the '69 Honda brochure. According to my own personal recollection, I rode a friend's SL-90 in 1969, and I think it had a black frame. The first silver-framed SL I remember encountering was another friend's SL-350 of several months later. The SL-90 was the first SL model released, and it is the only one showing a black frame in the brochure. Since we are discussing my memory of more than thirty-five years ago, it is quite possible that I am just plain wrong on this issue. The April 1969 *Cycle World* contained a full-color, two-page ad of the SL-90 clearly displaying an 11" x 12" photo of a Motosport 90 with a black frame.

Honda SL-100 Motosport Chart

Year	Color Choices	Tank	Frame	Nacelle	Handlebars
1970 - K0	Ruby Red - Sapphire Blue Emerald Green	White Stripe	Silver	Body Color	No Crossbrace
1971 - K1	Ruby Red - Emerald Green Mars Orange	White Stripe	Silver	Body Color	No Crossbrace
1972 - K2	Candy Ruby Red Tortoise Green Metallic	Yellow Panel	Silver	Body Color	Crossbrace
1973 - K3	Fire Red - Candy Riviera Blue	White Decal	Black	Black	Crossbrace

Honda SL-100 Notes: All SL-100's had flat-black exhausts with chrome shields, kickstarters, five-speed transmissions, Ceriani-style front forks, uncovered rear springs, and body-colored, steel fenders. The exhaust consisted of a downswept pipe that turned upward from underneath the engine to a few inches above the rear axle at the end.

Honda SL-125 Motosport Chart

Year	Color Choices	Tank	Frame	Side Covers
1971 - K0	Strato Blue Metallic Poppy Yellow Metallic Candy Emerald Green	Black Stripe	Silver	Body Color
1972 - K1	Special Silver Metallic	Red Stripe	Black	Body Color
1973 - K2	Special Silver Metallic	Red Stripe	Black	Matte Black

Honda SL-125 Notes: All SL-125's had tube frames, tachometers, kickstarters, five-speed transmissions, 18-inch rear wheels, 21-inch front wheels, painted steel fenders, uncovered chrome rear springs, Ceriani-type front forks, high fenders, and flat-black exhaust pipes with chrome shields. The pipes were of the downswept header pipe, and then upswept at the end, variety.

Honda SL-175 Motosport Chart

Year	Color Choices	Tank Pinstripe	Seat	Exhaust Shield
1970 - K0	Candy Ruby Red - Candy Sapphire Blue Candy Topaz Orange	Below Stripe	Short	Slots
1971-72 K1	Light Ruby Red - Candy Sapphire Blue Poppy Yellow Metallic	Above Stripe	Long	Holes

Honda SL-175 Notes: All SL-175's had tachometers, two-into-one exhausts with downswept headers and upswept mufflers, silver frames, body-color fenders, five-speed transmissions, kickstarters, and Ceriani-style front forks. The exhaust pipes were black and the heat shields were chrome. The K1 model had a slightly longer seat and a different gas tank. All models had a wide white stripe on the side of the tank with a pinstripe either above or below the wide stripe, as shown in the chart. Yellow models had black stripes.

Honda SL-350 Motosport Chart

Year	Color Choices	Frame	Tank	Starter	Front Wheel
1969-70 K0	Ruby Red - Sapphire Blue - Candy Gold	Single Downtube	White Stripe	Electric	19"
1970-71 K1	Ruby Red - Sapphire Blue - Topaz Orange	Double Downtube	White Stripe	Kick	19"
1972-73 K2	Marina Blue Metallic Candy Panther Gold	Double Downtube	Yellow Trim	Kick	21"

Honda SL-350 Notes: All SL-350's had candy paint, silver tube frames, flat-black downswept exhausts that curved upward at the end, five-speed transmissions, Ceriani-style front forks, and exposed rear springs.

Figure I57 - Candy Gold 1969-70 Honda SL-350 Motosport.

Image by Redhawkrider under Creative Commons license.

Selected Honda Models Ratings Chart

Years	Models	Collectibility	Practicality	Desirability
1959 - 69	C-100 & C-102 Cubs	C	A	C
1961 - 69	Super Sport & Sport 50	C	B	B
1961 - 65	Trail 50 & 55	C	D	C
1965 - 69	Sport 65	B	C	C
1963 - 66	C-200 Touring 90	C	C	C
1964 - 75	Trail 90	D	B	C
1966 - 69	CM91 Step-Through 90	D	C	D
1964 - 69	Super 90	A	C	B
1967 - 69	Scrambler 90	B	C	B
1969	Motosport 90	B	C	C
1970 - 75	CB/CL/SL/XL 100	D	C	C
1959 - 62	125 Benly Sport & SS	A	D	A
1967 - 69	SS/CL 125 Twins	B	C	B
1971 - 75	All 125 Singles	D	B	C
1974 - 75	MT & Elsinore 125	D	C	C
1959 - 68	Benly Touring	C	A	C
1965 - 69	Super Sport 160	B	C	B
1966 - 67	Scrambler 160	B	C	A
1968 - 75	CB/CL/SL/MR/XL 175	C	C	C
1974 - 75	CB & CL 200	C	B	D
1959 - 69	250 & 305 Dreams	B	B	C
1961 - 68	Hawk & Super Hawk	B	B	B
1962 - 68	CL-72 & CL-77	B	C	A
1972 - 75	XL 250 & 350	C	B	C
1968 - 73	CB & CL 350	C	A	B
1969 - 73	Motosport 90, 175, & 350	C	B	B
1972 - 74	CB-350 Four	A	C	C
1974 - 75	CB/CL/CBG 360	C	B	C
1975	CB-400F Super Sport	A	A	A
1965 - 75	CB & CL 450 & 500T	B	C	B
1971 - 75	CB-500/550 Four	B	C	C
1975	550 Super Sport	C	B	C
1969-75	CB-750 Four	A	B	A
1975	750 Super Sport	B	B	B

1975	Gold Wing	B	B	A

Models Ratings Chart Definitions:

Years: These are the total production years for a particular model series. Some early model years within a series may be considerably more desirable than later years.

Models: In some cases many variations are included in this category and in others the models included are very homogeneous.

Collectibility: This is what most of you want to know, the bottom line on how likely the model or series is likely to climb in value over the coming years.

Practicality: This is an indicator of how adaptable the machine can be to ride for transportation or pleasure in the modern world, considering parts availability, fuel quality, comfort, performance and miscellaneous other obvious factors.

Desirability: This defines the nostalgic, emotional wow factor, without regard for collector values or everyday usage.

General: No machine is given a failing grade. If it made it into a rating chart, at least a few hobbyists find that model interesting.

Figure I58 - Blue Honda 125 CB-92 with Red Seat. ©American Honda Motor Company, Inc.

Figure I59 - 1958 Honda 50 Cub. This machine is an unusual color. The metal bodywork is dark blue, the front fender and side covers are light blue, the leg shields are off-white, and the solo seat is red. If this exact color combination was ever imported into the USA, the numbers were surely quite small. ©1958 American Honda Motor Company, Inc.

Figure I60 - White 1966 Honda 90. By this time, the color choices for the step-through models had settled down considerably. All versions of this model had black seats with white leg shields and side covers.
©Michael Kiernan, Classic Motorcycle Company, St. Louis, MO.

Figure 161 - Black 1966 Honda CB-160 with Stock Western Bars. Contrast this photo with the CB-160 with low European bars shown earlier in this book. You can really see the many details of the changes in Honda styling cues between this 1966 CB and the 1972 CB-350 shown below. ©Michael Kiernan, Classic Motorcycle Company, St. Louis, MO.

Figure 162 - Candy Gold 1972 Honda CB-350 K4 Super Sport. Image by Nicolas Will in Brooklyn, owner and photographer, under Creative Commons license.

Figures 163 & 164 (next page) - The introduction of the Gold Wing in 1975 definitively ended the era of the tiddlers. Honda had already conquered most of the motorcycle market for small, affordable machines. Now they were going after the big touring market shares held mainly by Harley-Davidson and BMW. As we soon learned, ordinary box-stock, "stripper" Gold Wings like the two examples pictured here would almost never be seen on the streets of America. Honda would conquer the touring market with Gold Wings loaded with accessories, and these original 1000cc models would grow and grow and....

462

Figure I63 - Blue 1975 Honda Gold Wing at the Barber Museum. Image by Silosarg under Creative Commons license.

Figure I64 - Another 1975 Blue Gold Wing. Image by Tommi Nummelin under Creative Commons license.

Figure I65 - The Classic 1963 Advertising Slogan That Launched Honda's Success in the U.S. Market.
©1963 American Honda Motor Company, Inc.

Chapter 9: *The Howl of a Honda Scrambler*

This chapter differentiates the many variations of Honda street scramblers built in The Sixties. A few models continued into The Seventies, but these types of motorcycles were mostly a Sixties phenomenon. Honda began producing Scramblers for the American market in 1962, and these models quickly became some of the most cherished Hondas, both then and now. Honda may not have invented the concept of the street scrambler, but the specific development of the 250cc CL-72 for the American market started a trend that raged throughout the U.S. marketplace. The slim tank and upswept exhaust concept actually debuted in 1960 on the tiny little C110, also known as the Super Sport Cub. The Scramblers continued up through the last CL-450 of 1974, and the emasculated CL-360 continued alone in its swan song year of 1975.

The information has been gathered from books, magazines, brochures, and websites. I realize that Honda made running changes throughout the production periods and that model years are not as important in some cases as the *K* designations. The point is to disseminate as accurate information as possible. I am not the world's expert on Honda details, but I am certainly one of the world's biggest fans of Sixties Japanese tiddlers in general and Honda Scramblers in particular.

Figure J1 - 1963 Red Honda 250 CL-72 with Alloy Tank and Other Racing Parts. ©Michael Kiernan, Classic Motorcycle Company, St. Louis, MO.

Honda Scrambler Specification Chart

Model	Years	Size	HP	Wheels	Wt.	Price
CL-70	1969-73	72cc	4.9 hp	17" - 17"	174	$344
CL-90	1967-69	89cc	8 hp	18" - 18"	203	$380
CL-90L	1968-70	89cc	4.9 hp	18" - 18"	203	$380
CL-100	1970-72	99cc	11.5 hp	18" - 18"	196	$464
CL-100S	1971-73	99cc	5 hp	18" - 18"	196	$464
CL-125A	1967-69	124cc	13-hp twin	17" - 17"	235	$470
CL-125S	1973-74	122cc	Single	18" - 18"	196	$517
CL-160	1966-67	161cc	16.5 hp	18" - 18"	282	$580
CL-160D	1967-68	161cc	16.5 hp	18" - 18"	282	$593
CL-175	1968-73	174cc	20 hp	18" - 18"	279	$645
CL-175K3	1969	174cc	20 hp	19" - 18"	274	$697
CL-200	1974	198cc	NA	18" - 18"	291	$865
CL-72	1962-65	247cc	25 hp	19" - 19"	315	$660
CL-77	1965-68	305cc	28.5	19" - 19"	338	$695
CL-350	1968-73	325cc	33 hp	19" - 18"	346	$793
CL-360	1974-75	356cc	NA	18" - 18"	357	$1170
CB-450D	1967	444cc	43 hp	18" - 18"	NA	NA
CL-450	1968-74	444cc	43 hp	19" - 18"	402	$1049

Figure J2 - 1962 Red Honda 250 CL-72 Scrambler.

©Michael Kiernan, Classic Motorcycle Company, St. Louis, MO.

Honda Scrambler Specification Chart Notes: The pre-release '62 Honda lineup brochure with the CL-72 with the unreleased small tank shows an introductory price of $660. The 1964 brochure shows $690 for the CL-72. All claimed dry weights are listed in pounds.

Honda Scrambler Timeline of Model Introduction Dates from *The ID Guide*

3/1/62 - CL-72 Scrambler 250
7/1/65 - CL-77 Scrambler 305
3/1/66 - CL-160 Scrambler 160
3/1/67 - CL-90 Scrambler 90
5/1/67 - CL-160D Scrambler Kitted CB-160
6/24/67 - CB-450D kitted CB-450 & CL-450
7/1/67 - CL-125A Scrambler 125
1/1/68 - CL-175 with CL-160 styling
2/1/68 - CL-350 / CL-450K1
8/1/68 - CL-90L 5-hp Scrambler
3/1/69 - CL-70 Scrambler 70
5/1/69 - CL-175K3 with Motosport styling / CL-350K1 / CL-450K2
2/10/70 - CL-350K2 Scrambler 350
3/1/70 - CL-70K1 / CL-175K4 CL-450K3
5/26/70 - CL-100 Scrambler 100
2/10/71 - CL-70K2 / CL-100 K1 / CL-100S 5-hp model
2/24/71 - CL-175K5 / CL-350K3 / CL-450K4
1/01/72 - CL-100K2 / CL-100S2 5-hp model
2/1/72 - CL-175K6 / CL-350K4
3/1/72 - CL-450K5 Scrambler 450
4/1/72 - CL-70K3 Scrambler 70
1/1/73 - CL-125S single-cylinder model
3/1/73 - CL-350K5 Scrambler 350
5/1/73 - CL100S3 5-hp model / CL-175K7
1974 - CL-125S1 / CL-200 / CL-360 / CL-450K6 (specific release dates N.A.)
1975 - CL-360K1 Scrambler 360 (specific release date not available)

The Honda Scrambler Charts

Honda CL-70 Scrambler Chart

Year	Color Choices	Tank	Exhaust Shield
1969 - K0	Candy Red - Candy Blue	Silver	Chrome
1970 - K1	Candy Sapphire Blue - Candy Topaz Orange	Silver	Chrome
1971 - K2	Candy Red - Candy Sapphire Blue Candy Topaz Orange	Stripes	Chrome
1972 - 1973 - K3	Candy Ruby Red - Candy Sapphire Blue	Pinstripes	Black

Honda CL-70 Notes: All CL-70's had Y-shaped, pressed-steel frames, SOHC engines. four-speed transmissions, chrome fenders, upswept exhausts on the right side, and turn signals. The tank and seat patterns were distinctive on each K series. The 1969 model had a slim tank with the speedo mounted in the headlight shell. All other models had a rounder gas tank with the speedometer in its own housing.

Honda CL-90 Scrambler Chart

Year	Color Choices	Tank	HP	Fenders	Speeds
1967	Candy Red - Black - Candy Blue	Silver	8	Chrome	Four
1968	Candy Red - Black - Candy Blue	Silver	8	Chrome	Four
1968 - L	Candy Red - Candy Blue	Silver	5	Chrome	Four
1969	Candy Red - Black - Candy Blue	Silver	8	Chrome	Four
1969 - L	Candy Red - Candy Blue	Silver	5	Chrome	Four
1970 - L	Candy Red - Candy Blue	Silver	5	Chrome	Four

Honda CL-90 Notes: All CL-90's had Y-shaped, pressed-steel frames, SOHC engines, speedometers in the headlight shell, kick starters, upswept exhausts on the right side, canister-shaped air filters, and no turn signals. *Cycle Guide* tested the CL-90 in August 1967. The article stated that the CL-90 had alloy fenders, cost $380, had 8 hp at 9500 rpm, and weighed 203 pounds.

Figure J3 (next page) - 1973 Honda CL-100. Image by Steve Henderson under Creative Commons license (GNU).

Honda CL-100 Scrambler Chart

Year	Color Choices	Muffler	Exhaust Shield	Tank	Engine
1970 - K0	Red - Blue - Orange	Chrome	Chrome	White Stripe	Standard
1971 - K1	Blue - Yellow - Orange	Chrome	Chrome	White Stripe	Standard
1971 - S	Blue - Yellow - Orange	Chrome	Chrome	White Stripe	Detuned
1972 - K2	Blue Metallic - Yellow	Chrome	Chrome	Pinstripes	Standard
1972 - S2	Blue Metallic - Yellow	Chrome	Chrome	Pinstripes	Detuned
1973 - S3	Ruby Red - Blue Metallic	Black	Chrome	White Stripe	Detuned

Honda CL-100 Notes: All CL-100's had SOHC engines, five-speed transmissions, kickstarters, single-downtube frames, separate speedometers, turn signals, chrome fenders, and upswept exhausts on the right side.

Honda CL-125 Scrambler Chart

Year	Color Choices	Frame	Cylinders	Tank	Speeds
1967	Blue - Yellow	Y-type	Twin	Silver	Four
1968	Candy Red - Candy Blue - Yellow	Y-type	Twin	Silver	Four
1969	Candy Red - Candy Blue - Yellow	Y-type	Twin	Silver	Four
1973	Ruby Red - Blue	Downtube	Single	White Stripe	Five
1974	Candy Ruby Red	Downtube	Single	White Stripe	Five

Honda CL-125 Notes: All CL-125's had chrome fenders. The early twin-cylinder models had little in common with the later single-cylinder models other than displacement. The twins are far more interesting, unusual in the history of Honda marketing strategy, and collectible. The Twins were similar in design to the CL-90 and the later Singles were similar to the CL-100. The unique design of the Twins included a SOHC twin-cylinder engine with a single carburetor suspended from a pressed steel Y-type frame. This design was similar only to the single-cylinder CL-90. The later 125 Singles, although of an excellent overall design, were hardly unique, as they were straightforward big brothers of the CL-100 in every facet of their design.

Figure J4 - 1966-67 Honda CL-160 in Black (of course). ©Troyce Walls, photographer

Honda CL-160 Scrambler Chart

Year	Color Choices	Skid Plate	Tank	Starter	Special Notes
1966	Black & Silver	Yes	Silver	Kickstarter	Factory-built CL
1967	Black & Silver	Yes	Silver	Kickstarter	Factory-built CL
1967	Black - Red - Blue - White	No	Silver	Electric & Kick	Dealer-installed CL kit on CB-160
1967-68 D	Silver - Candy Blue - Candy Orange	No	Body Color	Electric & Kick	Black Frame

Honda CL-160 Notes: All CL-160's had tubular backbone frames, 18" wheels, four-speed transmissions, inclined cylinders, no turn signals, and silver fenders. The early models had silver tanks and side covers, and body-colored frames, headlamps, chain guards, and front forks. These included the true, black models, as well as the blue, white, and red CB-160's dealer-converted into CL's. I have in my collection a Honda brochure with a 1968 copyright on it that includes the CL-160D with color availability listed as black, red, blue, and white. This same brochure includes the CL-175 available only in Silver, Candy Blue, or Candy Red, all with a black frame. The final version of the CL-160 featured tanks and side covers in candy colors with black frames and other components. This final batch of CL-160's were very similar to the last CL-77's and the earliest CL-175's with black frames and trim with Silver, Candy Blue, or Candy Orange tanks and side covers.

All these changes took place between March 1966 and January 1968, so the number of each type or *look* of CL-160 produced was minimal. If you stand back and look at the whole picture, it seems that the company launched its first *smaller* Scrambler less than two years before an overall styling upgrade was scheduled for most of the Honda motorcycle lineup. As parts supplies were depleted for the older style components, the machines were upgraded to the newer style. The process began at the beginning of 1968 and was fully complete by early 1970. The models driving this operation were the CB and CL 350's, a pair of totally new designs that would replace the aging Dream/Hawk/Scrambler paradigm that had been in place since 1960-1962. If you squint at the picture just right, you will see that the 160/175 models were likely considered the stepchildren. They were placed in a state of flux, constantly evolving throughout 1967 as the old parts ran out and the designers could fully incorporate the new look. This consisted of candy paint, turn signals with D.O.T. mandated specs, chrome or body-colored fenders, instruments in housings separate from the headlamps, five-speed transmissions, and K-Series model designations.

Cycle World tested the CL-160 in December 1966. The price was listed as $610, weight 270, 0-60 in 11.0 and the quarter at 17.9 at 71 mph. *CW* noted the inherently smoother 360-degree crankshaft of the 160's, as opposed to the vibrating 250's and 305's with a 180-degree crank.

Cycle tested the CL-160 in July 1966. The machine did an 18-second quarter with a 67-mph ending speed. The maximum claimed speed was 76 mph, claimed weight was 282, and the price was $580. They mentioned that the transmission gearing was shorter than that of the CB-160. *Cycle* in May 1967 did a more complete test of the CB & CL-160. The testers changed their tune a bit. The transmission ratios were identical, but the CL had a two-tooth larger rear sprocket, a sidestand (and centerstand), and rubber gaiters instead of painted metal fork spring covers. The CB rear sprocket has 38 teeth, and the CL outran the CB at the dragstrip, posting 18.9 vs. 19.3 with a 175-pound rider. The fully tested CL-160 did 0-60 in 17.1, the quarter in 18.6, and had a top speed of 73.

Honda CL-160: A Sixties Icon

Figure J5 - Black 1966-67 Honda CL-160 Scrambler. You can get a good look at the special items that distinguish a true CL-160 Scrambler from the later kitted CL-160D in this photo. Note the unpainted, polished metal skid plate and rubber gaiters on the front forks. Although it is not distinguishable from this viewpoint, you can clearly see the shorter CL front fender in the previous photo, Figure J4. Unlike some of its larger brothers, the CL-160 had an eighteen-inch front wheel. I assume that the gearing of the CL was slightly lower than that of the CB, as with the other CB/CL pairs, but I am not certain of this point. ©Troyce Walls, photographer

Honda created a model for the American market in 1962 simply named the Scrambler, a 250cc SOHC twin with a single-downtube frame, cross-brace handlebars, a sleek gas tank, and the sweetest-howling upswept, crossover exhaust pipes in motorcycle history. The CL-72 continued through its 305cc iteration as the CL-77, beginning in '65, but a little brother was obviously needed for the exploding marketplace. The CL-160 was introduced to America in 1966, and in its official form at least, was built for only two model years.

All the original CL-160's had black frames with silver gas tanks, fenders, and side covers. There was a skid plate underneath the engine that blocked the access for an electric starter, so all models had kick starters only. Unlike any other American-model Hondas, the CL-160 evolved into the CL-175 in an unusual manner. At the end of 1967, Honda dealers were shipped only CB-160's in the normal black, white, red, and blue colors for all Hondas. Dealers could order CL Kits to convert CB's into CL models prior to placing them on the showroom floor. This meant that in late 1967 and throughout '68, you could buy a new CL-160 that looked mostly like the original with the exception of the presence of an electric starter, the absence of a skidplate, and the availability of four colors. These kitted CB's retained the longer front fenders and body-colored front spring covers of the original Super Sport machines. Some or most of these models also had body colored gas tanks instead of silver ones. (Maybe all of them did, but I cannot be sure about this.) This model evolved into the CL-175 with the color choices replaced by black, candy blue, and candy orange in 1968, and the CL-175 continued to evolve until it became the K4 model in 1970, at which time its styling finally became mostly identical to all the other Honda Scramblers of that year.

The original, black, kickstart CL-160 with its skidplate has become a legend in its own time, a model sought by collectors as a very special Honda. Its 282 pounds offered a compact alternative to its larger 305cc, 350cc and 450cc brothers, while its sixteen horsepower OHC twin offered considerably more adult hauling power than its little tiddler siblings. The CL-160 filled a very entertaining niche in the on and off road motorcycle market. I wish I had one now!

Some of you regular Tiddlerosis readers may have already figured out by now that I have always been a sucker for two particular types of Honda tiddlers: specific CL models and rare blue versions of certain models. In a few cases these two parameters overlap, such as in the CL-90, but for the most part, they remain separate. Although red is not my favorite color, when you combine bright red with a sufficient amount of silver or chrome trim, I get pretty overheated for those little sweethearts, too. You won't find me driving a red car. I even prefer Corvettes and Ferraris in some other color, but motorcycles, that's a horse of a different color.

The particularly gorgeous type of CL-160 I lust for is a blue, red, or white CL-kitted CB-160, the model briefly sandwiched between the original, *pure*, black CL-160 and the later CL-160D. The D models all had black frames with different colored tanks. The ones I like have red, blue, or white *frames*. The CL-kitted CB-160's were assembled by dealers on CB-160's from what were referred to as *CL kits*. I understand that these were offered in the same four colors as the CB of the time: red, blue, black, and white, although I don't think I have ever seen a blue or white one. I am certain that I saw a number of red and black ones in my local dealership in 1967, and possibly 1968. Yes, we all know the CL-160 was continued as the CL-160D with black frames and body-colored gas tanks, and those were created from components added to the standard CB frame, too.

I know these were built and sold in 1967 because that was a special transition time for me. I had already crashed the daylights out of my '63 red and silver YG-1, leading my parents to wisely take it away from me and replace it with a pool table in our basement. If you're a fan of *That '70's Show*, you know what I'm talking about! Add a pool table and subtract the weed and you have my parents' basement in 1965-67. After a few years of pool hall maturity, I had finally talked my parents into letting me buy a mini-bike in the summer of '67. Yeah, I know all the hip kids were in San Francisco with the big sickles *and* the weed in 1967, but I was in Mississippi hoping just to swing my leg over something without pedals. I managed to upgrade my parents to a sweet little '66 C-100 Cub if I promised to ride it mostly off-road. I found that innocent little black Cub at the Honda shop while drooling over the CL-160's. Even though I knew the *real* CL-160's didn't have no stinking electric foo-foo starters, I was still drawn like a hippie to Woodstock by the red and silver beauties that looked just like Scramblers when they were actually Super Sports in Scrambler suits. I'm not sure what I would have done if I had actually seen a blue one on the showroom floor. If I could have rustled up $630, I could have just let my parents throw me out of the house, keeping the pool table for themselves. I guess it all was a moot point because $630 was a lot of cash loot for a college kid in Mississippi in the Sixties.

As soon as I saw the original Honda Scrambler, the CL-72, in my 1962 Honda brochure, I knew I was hooked. As if the beautiful red and silver paint combination wasn't enough, this thing created the best howl of any twin-cylinder engine in all of motorized history! If you have never heard one with its baffles removed, as most were back in those good old days, you've missed a true aural treat. A couple of years after I calmed my parents down, I rode a CL-77 and a CL-160 and these have always reserved a special place in my motorhead brain. A close friend of mine even had a red CL-160 with a pair of open, upswept megaphones that produced a similar scream, although a little higher pitched, and was a treat to ride! The bike I eventually sold is the one I most wish I hadn't, the blue 1970 CL-350 I drove to San Francisco from Mississippi twice.

If you study this series of machines carefully, you will see that the progression ran as follows. The CB-160 arrived in late 1964. The CL-160 followed in early 1966 and production continues into 1967. Production of the true CL stops and the shipment of CL kits begins in May 1967. The CL kits drift even further from the original look of silver tanks with varied frame colors as 1968 approaches. Production of the CL-160D was phased into the CL-175 at the beginning of 1968. The earliest CL-175 model looked almost identical to the 160, except it had chrome fenders, a five-speed gearbox, and turn signals.

Here is what I think actually happened in America in 1962-68. The CL-72 was introduced as a model created especially for the American market in 1962, and it was an immediate success here. These models were sold in red, black, and blue (in that order of production numbers). The blue ones are extremely rare. The CL-77 picked up production in higher numbers with the same colors in about the same production ratios. The CB-160 was introduced as the little brother of the CB-77 in 1964. It was produced in black, red, white, and blue (probably in that order). Although I have an early-release brochure showing the CB-160 with the CB-125, the 125 was never imported here. The CL-160 was released in 1966 in black only. Beginning in late '67, Honda had been selling CL-160's like hotcakes, leaving the CB's holding down the showroom floors, so they ceased production of the CL and had the dealers convert whatever CB's they wished to CL's with the CL kits.

When you examine the models closely, you will see specific components. Of course the CB had an electric starter and the CL had a skid plate. The CL had black rubber gaiters covering the front springs and the CB had painted plastic covers. The front fender was obviously much longer than the one on the CL. The tank, bars, and pipes are the three items everyone's eyes notice, so this makes even my memories of forty years ago a little hazy! I think I remember the earliest kitted CL's as looking exactly like the true CL's in every way except for the electric starter / skid plate swap. Now as a much more mature adult, I am not so sure the dealers ever disassembled the front forks to change to the rubber gaiters. Did they change to a shorter CL front fender? This certainly seems more likely than the fork cover change, so I think there is a possibility that the front fenders were changed. Did these kitted CL's come in white, blue, red, and black? Absolutely. Was white the rarest color, with blue close behind? Yes. Did they continue to build a lot of black ones that looked very much like the true originals? Yes, but I actually remember seeing more red ones, both on the showroom floor and on the street. Remember, I said that the original CL-72 and CL-77 numbers were higher in red than black, although I can never be certain that it's true. I also think the CB numbers for all three displacements were higher for black than red. Every one of all these models used what I call body colored frames. In other words, what we call a black or red CB or CL had a black or red frame. This also included the chain guard, rear shock covers, headlight shell, and upper fork tubes. Some later models had silver lower fork legs, no matter what the frame color. The lower fork legs were either body color or silver, depending on the model and year. The front spring covers were either body colored plastic on the CB's or black rubber gaiters on the true CL's.

Now comes the hard part. In '67 and '68, Honda was in the process of phasing out the 160, the 305, and the old way of styling their machines. As we all know, by 1970, Hondas had an all-new look that coordinated the 175, 350, and 450, and even the smaller models to a somewhat lesser extent. This new look included painted tanks on all models, chrome rear springs and upper shock covers, chrome fenders, and matching candy paint colors on the tanks, side covers, and miscellaneous other items. All frames were now black, with no exceptions but the silver ones on the SL's. I think the 160/175 sizes were never as big sellers in the U. S. as the 305/350 sizes. This encouraged the company to phase in the smaller category more gradually as it sold out of the older components. The generation break between the older and newer larger models seemed to be more consistent and abrupt.

The sole exception to this is the last version of the CL-77. This machine was built in small numbers in the short space of time when the company had switched to chrome fenders, black frames, and candy paint on everything, but the CL-350 was not yet fully up to production speed. This machine came in the same styling of the last of the CL-160D's: candy painted tanks and matching side covers with black frames. A different seat and a few other details also distinguished it stylistically from its earlier, more common CL-77's.

Let's finally cut to the chase. I cannot swear in court that I have ever actually seen a CL-160, either in the metal or in a photo, of this mysterious type. I may or may not have seen a CL-160 as it is pictured in the 1968 brochure and the *ID Guide* with CB front fender and side covers in silver and tank, headlamp shell, ears, and front spring covers in red. The frame and chain guard on this bike are also red, and I don't ever recall seeing any Honda frame in any candy color. The brochure does not claim this to be a candy color, but the *Honda ID Guide* does. My biggest complaint with the *ID Guide* by far is that it leaves out a lot of model year detail changes in its descriptions. If I did not know for a swear-in-court fact that several of these detailed changes have been left out of the Honda Sport and Super Sports 50 category, then I would not be so certain that similar details have been omitted from the CL-160 description.

Did Honda paint a few CL-160 gas tanks in the old red color and have their dealers install them on CB-160's in the same old colors, as both the brochure and the *ID Guide* show? Were any of these in candy colors? Were any of them blue? Did Honda build a few very late CL-160's made with Candy Blue or Candy Orange tanks and side covers on black frames? Probably; however, I have personally never seen one, but one of my corresponding Tiddlerosis fans swears that he used to work in a Honda shop where these candy colored models were sold. The obvious inconsistency is that if no CB-160's were ever built with candy colored frames, how could they possibly convert them to CL-160's in as stated candy colors? The secret word is black. The stated color of the bikes has always been the color of the frame, up until the time of these last CL-160's with candy tanks and side covers. All of these had to have been built from black CB's. The ones with silver tanks have always hidden in the forest of the earlier CL's, but the orange and blue ones were all actually black CB's! Although I have been informed by a fellow enthusiast that dealers did convert a few white CB's with the new candy tanks, I doubt that any red or blue CB's were converted in this manner without suffering a serious barf attack as a result of the color clash!

When you are trying rebuild your machines, I suggest that you examine the following components: the serial number to determine the production sequence, the frame and chain guard color, the front spring covers, and the side covers. I personally don't think any were built with candy colors and silver side covers. I don't think there were ever any candy frames or chain guards, either. How could there be? There were never any Candy Blue or Candy Orange CB-160's!

The 1968 brochure photos of the CB-160, CL-160, and CL-175 delineate the history of these models. Note that the red tank on the CL-160D looks just a bit off-color, but I would not make too much of this. I am quite sure I have seen CL-160's painted just like this one. Note, however, that the Candy Orange of the CL-175 is an altogether different shade, and the side covers match the tank. Since the candy colors are not listed in this brochure for the CL-160, I assume this is an early '68 brochure. Although not pictured here, according to the *ID Guide*, the obvious conclusion is that the CL-160 was apparently sold in CL-175 colors for a brief period in late 1967, or even early 1968. This refers to the tank and side covers being in silver, Candy Blue, or Candy Orange, with everything else in black. Other than the colors, all 175's had chrome fenders, five-speed transmissions, and turn signals, and no 160's had these things.

As a Tiddlerosis fan who worked for a Honda dealership in the '60's pointed out long ago, the CL Kits were installed on CB's in many color combinations. These included a blue tank on a white frame, silver tank on a white frame, red tank on a white frame, and the same tank colors on a black frame. One of the things that has always confused me is that in the 1968 Honda brochure picturing a kitted CB, the bike shown has a red tank on a red frame, and the two shades of red do not exactly match! This stupid photo has been confusing me for decades! What dealer would do that? Keep in mind that Honda was changing to candy colors in 1968 and the tank was a candy red, whereas the CB frame and other components were in the old red/blue/black/white non-candy paint types.

Here is my true confession. My first real, official *date* was with a shy, brainy type with long, straight, dark hair and large, bewitching eyes. Even my mom always knew that I was ga-ga over my First-Fifth Grade sweetheart who had long, straight dark hair and big brown eyes. She probably graduated Valedictorian from high school long after I lost contact with her. The point of this story is that I am still a sucker for big brains, long, dark straight hair, and big brown eyes. My first Honda brochure happened to be a little black and white thing from Al's Cycle Shop in Memphis. Yes, Gladys, the same shop where Elvis bought his Hondas. I can swear on a can of Castrol that Elvis did indeed own at least one Honda, and so did Priscilla. I was cruising down Highway 51 South in Whitehaven (Memphis) one day in 1968 or '69, when I saw The King on his black Dream. He was sitting at the forward edge of the Graceland driveway, waiting to pull out into the traffic stream. Priscilla was next to him on an obviously custom painted *pink* Dream or Benly Touring. She was wearing a little foo-foo helmet styled for girls but his identity was not at all disguised with a helmet. This was Elvis riding bareheaded on a Honda Dream and there wasn't a single photographer, fan, or screaming girl in sight. Now *those* were the good old days! This 1962 brochure was the first year of the CL-72, and the first time I saw that machine. That experience was just like seeing an attractive girl of the particular type described for the first time. I am a sucker for skinny motorcycles with crossbrace bars and upswept pipes on the same side, just as I am a sucker for smart women with long, straight, dark hair and big brown eyes!

As I have repeatedly described in earlier passages of this book, I have been a big fan of trail riding since the beginning of my motorcycle experience. The first really exciting, fast trail ride I experienced was on the back of a very special CL-160 in 1969. One of my pals and fellow Psychology Majors in college who was a lot more mechanically inclined than I was rebuilding old Hondas for a hobby, and he was particularly fond of the CL-160. When I first met him, he was riding the trails, believe it or not, on a Super Hawk with tall, apehanger bars, of all things! (This guy had a real knack for high speed riding. He would later graduate from what we now call Top Gun school and fly fighter jets for the U.S.A.F.) My favorite of all the old Hondas he rebuilt was a red, kitted CB-160. This bike had a red frame with silver tank and side covers. the most common, and probably the most attractive, CL-kitted combination of the era. He had replaced the klunky single muffler with a pair of big chrome megaphones, re-jetted the carbs respectively, and removed the electric starter. Did this howler outdo the sound of the original CL-72 with the baffles removed? No, but it was the second-best sound I have ever heard from a twin. Did it go like stink, even off-road? Absolutely. When I got him down to as low as $250 for this screamer and still did not buy it from him, did this turn out to be the motorcycle mistake of my personal lifetime? Absolutely. Are you still reading about this obsession forty years later? Absolutely.

Honda CL-175 Scrambler Chart

Year	Color Choices	Tank	Frame	Starter	Fenders
1968 - K0	Silver - Candy Blue Candy Orange	Solid Color	Backbone	Kick	Chrome
1969 - K1	Silver - Candy Blue Candy Orange	Solid Color	Backbone	Electric	Chrome
1969 - K3	Candy Blue Candy Orange	White Stripe on Top	Downtube	Kick	Body Color
1970 - K4	Candy Ruby Red Candy Sapphire Blue Candy Topaz Orange	White Stripe	Downtube	Electric	Chrome
1971 - K5	Strato Blue Metallic Candy Topaz Orange Poppy Yellow Metallic	Black Stripe	Downtube	Electric	Body Color
1972 - K6	Magna Red Varnish Blue Metallic	Pinstripes	Downtube	Electric	Chrome
1973 - K7	Light Ruby Red Turquoise Green Metallic	White Stripe	Downtube	Electric	Chrome

Photo J6 - 1972 Honda CL-175. Like all the 1972 Hondas, the base color and stripe patterns were somewhat muted. This K6 example was dark blue, called Varnish Blue Metallic by Honda. ©Michael Kiernan, Classic Motorcycle Company, St. Louis, MO.

Honda CL-175 Notes: All CL-175's had black frames, five-speed transmissions and turn signals. The 1970 K4 had a black exhaust heat shield. All other models had chrome heat shields. The K0-K1 models were mostly identical to the CL-160D, except the 175's had black frames, headlamps, and forks with rubber gaiters. The fenders were chrome and the front one was abbreviated from that of the 160. The side covers were body-color and the seat had gold piping. The 1969 K3 had several SL Motosport components, including Ceriani-type front suspension, high, painted fenders, and a similar gas tank design.

Cycle Guide tested the CL-175 in June 1968. Although all photos were in B&W, the magazine stated that the machine had a blue tank and side covers. The seat had longitudinal pleats. The weight was listed as 284. *Cycle World* tested the CL-175 that looks like a CL-160 with turn signals in October 1968, claiming that few parts on the 175 are interchangeable with the 160. The data included $645, 20 hp at 10,000 rpm, 269 pounds with a half tank of fuel, a top speed of 77, 0-60 in 11.5, 18.5 at 70 mph in the quarter. *Motorcyclist* tested the CL-175 in September 1968, recording 16.52 in the quarter, an 80-mph top speed, and a weight of 284 pounds. The price listed was $586 in the LA area.

Honda CL-200 Scrambler Chart

Year	Color Choices	Tank	Muffler	Exhaust Shield	Speeds
1974	Candy Riviera Blue	White Stripe	Black	Chrome	Five

CL-200 Notes: All CL-200's had single mufflers, chrome fenders, turn signals and electric starters.

Photo J7 - 1974 CL-200. Note the unusual optional black luggage rack that matches the black muffler. Contrast the paint pattern of this bright blue CL-200 with the darker, muted style of the 1972 CL-175 K6. Image by Thadanator under Creative Commons license (GNU).

Honda CL-72 Scrambler 250 Chart

Figure J8 - Red 1962 Honda CL-72 at the Barber Museum.

Image by Chuck Schultz, photographer, under Creative Commons license.

Year	Color Choices	Muffler	Fenders	Seat Strap	Tank Emblem
1962	Red - Black - Blue	Baffles	Polished Alloy	Side Buckles	Dream 250
1963	Red - Black - Blue	Baffles	Polished Alloy	Side Buckles	Dream 250
1964	Red - Black - Blue	Slip-on	Painted Alloy	Side Buckles	250
1965	Red - Black - Blue	Slip-on	Silver Painted Steel	Fastened Underneath	250

Honda CL-72 Notes: All CL-72's had 19" wheels, single-downtube frames, kickstarters, hydraulic cylinder steering dampers, steel lower fork legs painted body color, 7-inch single leading shoe brakes, and silver-painted, seamless gas tanks and side covers. All other body parts were painted body color. A few rare models had alloy gas tanks with racing-style, pop-up gas caps and a few other special racing accoutrements. None had electric starters, tachometers, or turn signals. The passenger strap was attached to the sides of the seat with chrome buckles above the chrome trim strip. The 1965 updates listed with the same features as the CL-77 of that year may be incorrect. Some or all of these changes may never have appeared on the CL-72, but they probably did. The Honda brochure of 1962 shows a first-year CL-72 with a slimmer tank with a pointed pad that is not shown anywhere else, even in the *ID Guide*. All other photos of even the earliest CL-72's show a slightly bulkier tank with more oval tank pads. The photo in the brochure was of a pre-production model with numerous detailed differences.

The Complete Book of Motorcycling in 1964, clearly shows a CL-72 with SLS front brake, body-color lower fork legs, and a slip-on muffler, indicating that the slip-on muffler instead of internal baffles actually began with the 1964 250 model. The seat in this photo is of the CL-72 type with the strap buckles. The book correctly lists 1964 Honda models with the Hawk and Super Hawk shown, but only the CL-72 available that year, and not the as-yet-unreleased CL-77.

Figure J9 - Rare 1963 CL-72. Note the optional alloy tank with quick-release gas cap and uncovered chrome rear springs. ©Michael Kiernan, Classic Motorcycle Company, St. Louis, MO.

Figure J10 - Red 1962 Honda 250 CL-72 Scrambler. This is a fully restored machine that was recently listed for sale for $7495. ©Michael Kiernan, Classic Motorcycle Company, St. Louis, MO.

Figure J11 - 1963 CL-72 Special. ©Michael Kiernan, Classic Motorcycle Company, St. Louis, MO.

Figure J12 - Close-up View of the Rare Slotted and Vented Chainguard. ©Michael Kiernan, Classic Motorcycle Company, St. Louis, MO.

Figure J13 - 1965 Red CL-72. This is the same machine that is in color on the cover. Compare the details of this machine with those of the CL-77 photos on the next few pages.

©Knut Hugo Hansen, President of the Classic Honda Club of Norway.

Honda CL-77 Scrambler 305 Chart

Year	Color Choices	Frame	Tank	Muffler	Fenders	Brakes	Forks
1965	Red - Black - Blue	Body Color	Silver	Slip-on	Silver Painted	7" SLS	Steel
1966	Red - Black - Blue	Body Color	Silver	Slip-on	Silver Painted	8" DLS	Alloy
1967	Red - Black - Blue	Body Color	Silver	Welded	Chrome	8" DLS	Alloy
1968	Silver - Candy Blue Candy Orange	Black	Body Color	Welded	Chrome	8" DLS	Alloy

Honda CL-77 Notes: All CL-77's had 19" wheels, single-downtube frames, hydraulic cylinder steering dampers, and kickstarters. The gas tanks and side covers were painted silver and the frame and several smaller parts were the body color. The lower front fork legs were painted silver on the later models with double leading shoe front brakes. Early model lower fork legs were painted body color. None had electric starters, tachometers, or turn signals. The earliest models had bolt-on mufflers. These were first supplanted by mufflers welded to the top exhaust pipe only; then both pipes were welded on the later models, including all with the later styling changes, as next described.

Some small number of the final production had a different look, featuring tanks and side covers in the body color with frames and all trim pieces painted black. The seat had gold piping around the upper seam. There is some question as to the time period in which these were built. The CL-350 was introduced in the Spring of '68, so these were probably late '67 and early '68 models. The look was very similar to that of the CL-160D and CL-175 of the same time frame. Only the CL-175 had both turn signals and electric starter. The CL-160D had an electric starter.

Cycle World tested the CL-77 in December 1965. The price was listed as $720 and the weight at 337. That figure may or may not be with gas and oil. The carbs are 26mm and the horsepower is 27.4 at 9000 rpm. The data recorded included 0-60 in 9.0, 16.7 at 79 mph quarter mile, and a 90-mph top speed.

Total U.S. sales included 10,071 CL-72's and 66,757 CL-77's. (Bud Ekins has stated a higher figure of 89,000 for the total without specifying a 250/350 breakdown.) About 650 1962 CL-72's were shipped to the U.S. The first 15,000 CL-77's had the painted steel forks and 7" SLS front brakes.

Figure J14 - Black 1967 CL-77. Note the round tail lamp and muffler welded to the top exhaust pipe.
©Michael Kiernan, Classic Motorcycle Company, St. Louis, MO.

Figure J15 - A Different Black CL-77. Note that the muffler is welded to the top pipe and the heat shield ends in front of the rear shocks. ©Michael Kiernan, Classic Motorcycle Company, St. Louis, MO.

Figure J16 - Red Late 1967 CL-77. ©Michael Kiernan, Classic Motorcycle Company, St. Louis, MO.

Figure J17 - Right Side of the Same machine. ©Michael Kiernan, Classic Motorcycle Company, St. Louis, MO.

Figure J18 - This close-up clearly shows the longer heat shield and the muffler welded to both pipes.
©Michael Kiernan, Classic Motorcycle Company, St. Louis, MO.

Evolution of the Original Honda Scrambler

This may be the most controversial article in *The Tiddler Invasion*. At the very least, it can be considered the heart and soul of the nostalgic power of this book. There are experts, namely Bill Silver of California and Ed Moore of Texas, whom I consulted while researching the subject, who have probably taken apart and reassembled more CL-72's and CL-77's than I have ever seen. Although I have spent countless hours studying the subject, I still have many more questions than answers. Honda introduced its first model designed specifically for the American market with brochures in 1962. The Honda 250 Scrambler arrived at dealers officially on March 1st. The first physical machines to arrive on our shores already had differences from the bikes shown in those earliest brochures. The constant changes continually evolved the CL-72 and CL-77 from 1962 until a point after which their replacement CL-350 had arrived on February 1, 1968. As we all know, Honda did not make calendar year changes on their machines until The Seventies, but few Hondas continually changed so much while visually remaining much the same as these first two CL models did. I think I have a somewhat tenuous grasp of what these changes were, but the actual order, timing, and other details are beyond the scope of this book. Bill Silver's more detailed explanations can be found in his books listed in the Bibliography. These machines, along with their Hawk and Dream brothers, are his specialty. Mine is scatterbrained all over the place!

The following is a summation of the components you can examine when viewing a Honda 250 or 305 Scrambler. You will have to consult Bill Silver's specialty materials to learn the exact serial numbers that denoted these changes. Understand that I cannot be absolutely certain that I have stated any of these details correctly. The order of the changes listed here or the concept of overlap from one model to another may be incorrect. These are the two parameters that have proven the most difficult for me to analyze correctly. Just keep in mind that I may not be approaching a particular issue in the correct order, but at least I can steer you in the right direction of what to look for on a CL-72 or CL-77. These issues will be discussed in roughly the order in which I believe they occurred.

Gas Tanks: The earliest brochure photo I have shows a gas tank that apparently was never produced or imported. It appears to be of a smaller capacity and the knee pads have a different shape. All the production tanks, including the alloy racing kitted model mentioned below, have the same tank pads. They look like a half-moon turned ninety degrees with the flat side parallel with the bottom edge of the tank. The second tank issue was that of an alloy gas tank. As far as I know, there were some CL-72's produced with alloy tanks. The third issue is that some sources have mentioned a special alloy tank with a racing-type, pop-open gas cap. Although I have photos of at least one such machine, I cannot verify how many of these were produced. These were part of a dealer-installed racing kit. The 1962 and '63 CL-72, sometimes referred to as Series I, had tank emblems that stated *Dream 250*. All later ones said *Honda 250* or *Honda 300*. All the tanks were seamless up through 1965, which of course included all 250 models. The 305 tanks from some point in the 1966 production year until the end had seams down the center. All tanks from 1962 through 1966 were either polished aluminum or silver-painted steel. The great majority of course were steel. During the 1967 model year, and continuing to be sold well into 1968, the last batch of CL-77's had tanks painted in candy colors other than silver.

Fenders: The evolution of the Scrambler fenders followed a pattern similar to that of the gas tanks. The earliest ones, with production ending prior to 1964, were polished alloy. The 1964 and '65 CL-72 fenders were still alloy, but they were painted silver. All the 305's had steel fenders. The 1965-66 models appeared just like those on the 250's in painted silver. Some of the last 305's with the "traditional" paint style may have had chrome fenders and some of the final batch may have had silver painted fenders. Whether this point is verifiable or not, most of the early CL-77's had silver fenders and most of the late ones had chrome fenders, with the early/late change occurring during the 1967 model year. The front lower fork legs will be discussed next. Since the forks support the fenders, there were two different mounting hole patterns in the fenders. The early ones had eight holes and the later ones only six. Since both CL-72 alloy fenders and CL-77 steel fenders were utilized during the 1965 model year, as were the two types of lower fork legs, several different combinations of fender and front forks were manufactured in 1965. You can distinguish the 72/77 fenders by their length. The trailing edges of both the front and rear steel fenders of the CL-77 were an inch or two longer than those of the alloy fenders of the CL-72.

Lower Fork Legs & Front Brakes: The single-leading-shoe front drum brake of the early Scrambler provided barely adequate stopping power for the prodigious weight of the machine. Honda fixed this problem during the 1966 production year. Parts were sourced from the Super Hawk and CB-450 to adapt the eight-inch, double-leading-shoe brake from the 450 to the Scrambler 305. This assembly included silver-painted aluminum lower fork legs and a six-hole fender bracket. This means the 7" SLS brake, eight-hole fender, and frame-colored steel fork legs go together and the 8" DLS brake, six-hole fender, and silver fork legs comprise the later package. All CL-72's had the first assembly, and so did all the 1965 and early '66 CL-77's. Just remember that all 250's had alloy fenders and all 305's had steel fenders.

Chain Guards: The earliest 250's had slotted chain guards with little "scoops" cut into the upper trailing edge. First the scoops were deleted and later the slots were, too. These delicate, lightweight chain guards tended to crack from vibration, so many of the early type were lost to the junkyard. Most likely the chain guards with scoops are the 1962-63 Series I models. The slots continued from the 1964 Series II 250's well into CL-77 production, possibly as far as early '67. At some point, these disappeared, too, and the remaining 305 Scramblers all had solid chain guards.

Seats: There were three seats used, with the third being the very rare seat provided as part of the dealer-installed racing kit. The early seats had the center strap fastened on the sides with "buckles". The later ones had a longer passenger strap that went over the chrome trim strip on the seat and attached to the seat base underneath. The last batch of 250's (built alongside the 305's) had the longer seat strap. All the 305 Scramblers had the longer seat strap and the 1962-64 250's had the buckles. In addition to these three seat types, the last CL-77's had the gold piping around the upper perimeter of the seat.

Miscellaneous Bits: The early CL-72's had hollow axles and sandcast front hubs. The wheel rims were copies of the European Akront type and the spokes were larger. The rear wheel could be easily removed from the fixed final drive, leaving the sprocket in place, supposedly to simplify rear wheel or tire changes in racing conditions. Some early CL-72's also had different handgrips with *Honda* molded into them.

Last & Noisiest: The basic exhaust system remained the same throughout the production of the CL-72 and CL-77 series, but the muffling and heat shield changed. The heat shield ended before the pipes jutted outward around the rear shock on the original series. When viewed from the side, the two-piece shield runs from the rear edge of the cylinder to approximately the rear frame rail. On the final batch of CL-77's with the muffler welded onto both exhaust pipes, the shield continues all the way to the leading edge of the muffler. The Series I CL-72's were all produced without that wretchedly ugly muffler and (I think) spark arrestor attached to the ends of the beautiful crossover pipe design. This would include all 1962 and 1963 models, and maybe some of the earliest '64's. Most of the 1964 models were the first with the bolt-on mufflers, although you rarely saw one with the muffler because most owners removed them as soon as they could locate a wrench! There were baffles inside the ends of the sleek pipes of the early CL-72's, but these were usually also removed by the owners. The baffles were changed to a different model when the factory added the external muffler. I believe the original baffles may have been a little longer. The factory's sound barrier battle with its customers escalated as the models continued. The first mufflers were bolted on. You can spot them by the little black rubber seal rings around each pipe. The next models had the muffler welded to the top pipe and slipped onto the lower pipe, showing the same black rubber seal, except only on the lower pipe. The final version had the muffler welded to both pipes. Many riders bought Snuff-or-Nots from the aftermarket and mounted these in the ends of the open exhaust pipes. These consisted of a large flat-washer shape inside the exhaust tip and attached to a knob adjuster mounted to the outside edge of each exhaust pipe. The rider could simply reach back and flip each washer to the "closed" position whenever a reasonable level of muffling was necessary; otherwise let the howling begin!

Here is a final recap of the subject and then I shall shut up. There were basically three series of CL-72's and three series of CL-77's, with a lot of overlap between models, model years and series. The S1 CL-72's had all the classic, special bits. S2 began in early 1964 with the altering of many parts and the addition of the dreaded muffler. S3 was the transition into the production of 305's-only when the last CL-72's were practically identical to the earliest 305's. The S1 CL-77's had the same small brakes, ugly (but easily removable) muffler and other pieces as the late 250's, except all had steel fenders. The S2 models kicked in during the 1966 model year with partially or wholly welded mufflers, larger brakes, and different fenders and fork legs. The final series brought the candy paint jobs, black frames, and longer heat shields. There is just one more thing you need to do. Go back to the last paragraph in the CL-77 notes (just before the beginning of this article) and notice how many *more* of the later 250 and 305 Scramblers were built than the rare early models just described. Now let's move on to the 350's... finally!

Honda CL-350 Scrambler Chart

Year	Color Choices	Muffler	Exhaust Shield	Tank & Trim	Seat
1968 - K0	Candy Red - Candy Blue Daytona Orange	Single	Black	Body Color & White	Plain
1969 - K1	Candy Red - Candy Blue Daytona Orange	Single	Black	Body Color & White	Pleated
1970 - K2	Candy Ruby Red Candy Topaz Orange Candy Sapphire Blue	Twin	Chrome	White Stripe	Soft Pleats
1971 - K3	Strato Blue Metallic Candy Topaz Orange Poppy Yellow Metallic	Twin	Chrome	Black Stripe	Squares
1972 - K4	Magna Red Candy Panther Gold	Twin	Chrome	Pinstripes	NA
1973 - K5	Light Ruby Red Hawaiian Blue Metallic	Twin	Chrome	White Stripe	Pleated

Honda CL-350 Notes: All CL-350's had hybrid, pressed-steel with single-downtube frames, electric starters, 19" front wheels, and five-speed transmissions. The 1969 models can be distinguished from the '68's by their front fender reflectors, pleated seats, and a body-colored stripe added to the lower tank panel. The 1972 and later models were a little slower with milder cams and different carburetors. The sharp high-rpm performance of the early models would never return, even through the later, 356cc CL-360 models.

Cycle World tested the CL-350 in April 1969. Strangely enough, this is a test of the 1968 model just prior to the release of the '69. This test mentions the double-walled exhaust system that weighs 23 pounds and the suspension that is a little too taut for the dirt. The data includes: 363 pounds with half a tank, 15.38-second quarter-mile at 81 mph, top speed 102, 0-60 in 6.8, and a speedometer error of a registered 70 being an actual 65. The price was listed as N/A. *Cycle Guide* tested the CL-350 in November 1969. It is not clear why they are calling this a *new* model when it was introduced back on 2/1/68. The K1 had been introduced on 5/1/69, but the model pictured is definitely a '68. The data listed is: 33 hp at 9500 rpm, 345 pounds, 96 mph top speed, 0-60 in 10.8, $750. The story mentioned the lagging mechanical tachometer of which I am familiar.

Honda CL-360 Scrambler Chart

Year	Color Choices	Mufflers	Exhaust Shields	Tank
1974 - K0	Muscat Green Metallic	Black	Chrome	Black Stripe
1975 - K1	Candy Orange	Black	Chrome	Black Stripe

Honda CL-360 Notes: All CL-360's had electric starters, separate mufflers, Ceriani-style forks, and six-speed transmissions.

Figure J19 - 1975 Candy Orange CL-360 K1. You can easily distinguish the CL-360 from its CL-350 predecessor by its sleek, Ceriani-style front forks.

Image by Mick, photographer, Northamptonshire, England, under Creative Commons license.

Honda CL-450 Scrambler Chart

Year	Color Choices	Exhaust	Mufflers	Tank	Speeds
1967 - K0	Metallic Silver Candy Red - Candy Blue	Left & Right Side	Dual Chrome	Silver	Four
1968 - K1	Metallic Silver Candy Red - Candy Blue	Left Side	Single Chrome	Body Color	Five
1969 - K2	Metallic Silver Candy Red - Candy Blue	Left Side	Single Chrome	Gold Stripe	Five
1970 - K3	Candy Ruby Red - Candy Sapphire Blue Candy Topaz Orange	Left Side	Single Chrome	White Stripe	Five
1971 - K4	Strato Blue Metallic Candy Topaz Orange Poppy Yellow Metallic	Left Side	Single Chrome	Black Stripe	Five
1972 - K5	Magna Red Planet Blue Metallic	Left Side	Separate Chrome	Pinstripes	Five
1973 - K5	Magna Red Planet Blue Metallic	Left Side	Separate Chrome	Pinstripes	Five
1974 - K6	Candy Sapphire Blue Flake	Left Side	Separate Black	Black & White Stripes	Five

Honda CL-450 Notes: All CL-450's had single-downtube frames, DOHC engines, CV carburetors, chrome fenders, and electric starters. All except the 1967 K0 had turn signals. The K0 had upswept pipes on each side. The K1-K4 had left-side pipes ending in a single muffler. The K5-K6 had separate bullet-type mufflers on the left side. The K4 had a unique one-piece heat shield. Note that the 1967 K0 was officially designated the CB-450D because it was originally a CL kit, similar to the one for the CB-160 of the same time period, for the four-speed *Black Bomber*. The model was called a Super Sport, not a Scrambler, in Honda advertising. This model was produced for only eight months until the *real* CL could be released with its signature pipes on the left side. There may have been some of this rare model shipped from the factory in Japan. In its May '68 test of the CL-450, *Cycle World* reported the following data: $1035, 45 hp at 9000 rpm, 399 pounds with a half-tank, 106 mph top speed, 0-60 in 4.3, quarter-mile in 14.88 at 86 mph.

Figures J20 & J21 (next page) - These two Honda CL-450 models may be more than one model year or K number apart. The second machine is clearly a 1971 Candy Topaz Orange K4, but the upper photo displays characteristics of both the K2 and K3. This is a prime example of a machine that may have been either produced as is by the factory or modified in the restorative process. The tank and Candy Blue color are the same as the late 1968 or early '69 model, but the headlamp nacelle and ears are blue like the K3. The pleated seat and round holes in the muffler shield are K3 items, but the gold side cover emblems are K2 issue.

Figure J20 - Blue 1970 CL-450 Scrambler. ©Michael Kiernan, Classic Motorcycle Company, St. Louis, MO.

Figure J21 - Orange 1971 CL-450 K4. Image by Jayt1980 under Creative Commons license in the Public Domain.

CL-350 K2 Scrambler

Some of us have always drooled over the prospect of owning a Triumph Trophy 500 or 650, one from about 1967 when the styling seemed to have reached perfection. The pipes were still one on each side in '66 and by '69 the mufflers were way too big and the exhaust tips extended all the way to the end of the bike. The bulbous mufflers distorted the parallel lines of the over-and-under exhaust system. The '67 model had the crossover pipes on the left side with small mufflers. The exhaust pipe from the right cylinder ended a few inches ahead of its sister pipe below, showing off the sexy curves of both. You loved the bullet-shaped mufflers and the trim, painted gas tank and fenders. The headlamp was not too large and the speedometer was in its own pod behind the headlamp. The black rubber gaiters on the front forks screamed *sport*. The wide, flat seat and handlebars spelled comfortable control. The right-side kick starter swung through a full, smooth arc and brought a masculine burble to life. The gears shifted firmly. The vibration from the big twin was present but tolerable. The sound was a sweet howl as the revs ramped up onto the cam. The suspension produced that legendary Triumph handling. When you rode a Triumph, you felt as if you commanded respect...

...At least when it ran. The electrical system was designed by the infamous Lucas, Prince of Darkness, and that sweet burble did not always begin just because you kicked the starter a few times. You may have felt that you could live with the vibration, but the electrical components of the machine could not. Things shook loose and off... a lot. Limeys may have liked their shifters on the right, but you never really got used to it. You felt your baby was safe parked in your basement or warm, locked garage, but the relentless oily mess it made on your garage floor was not so endearing. You gave up a little top-end performance by choosing a model with a single carburetor. It added its own mess to the floor whenever you tickled the carb to start the engine, but if you had chosen a bike with two of these cantankerous Amals, keeping them in proper synch would have been a real annoyance. Vibration has side effects, you dig? Yes, but the handling of the Triumph Tigers and Trophies was superb and they had that styling thing *down*!

Somebody had a better idea. Why not take that big 650 twin and cut the displacement in half? Add an overheard cam, high compression, a second carburetor designed in Japan where they don't leak, and a fifth gear for a 9500-rpm horsepower peak. Add an electric starter, tachometer, chrome fenders, bright lights, turn signals, and reliable electrics, too. Give it a side stand for convenience and a centerstand for servicing. Add a soft seat and make the suspension a little too taut, although not as bone-jarringly stiff as that of its predecessor. Last of all, rubber-mount everything so the high-frequency vibration from the relatively small, high-strung twin does not wreak a havoc load of side effects. What have you got? A 1970 Honda CL-350 K2 Scrambler that is softer, faster, better handling, more reliable, more convenient and more comfortable than its 305cc predecessor.

We chose the K2 model because several trim and color issues made this model a distinct improvement over its K0 and K1 brothers. Most of all, for the first time in Honda history, the K2 had a direct copy of those gorgeous bullet mufflers from the '67 Trophy and Tiger! Honda had certainly started off with the right stuff in the design of its CL-72 exhaust system. However, far too many enterprising owners unscrewed the baffles and found out exactly how far they could throw them. That brought on the abominable bolt on, and then welded-on, muffler until the 1968 CL-350 received its one-piece muffler *box*. Honda tried to draw your attention away from the box by covering it with a black heat shield, but they were not fooling anyone. Underneath it all was still a *box*. The CL-175 had a box, too. Even the CL-450 had a box! The company finally came to its senses and gave the CL-350 K2 a proper set of mufflers. They were not obtrusive, but just loud enough to produce a very sweet howl whenever you revved it up on the cam and then gently backed off the throttle. The perfect marbly burble scream of the CL-72 or CL-77 sans baffles or ugly muffler was not quite regained, but a sound level that both the rider and the nearby citizens could live with had been attained.

Unfortunately this K2 perfection lasted only through the next year's K3 model. Honda uglied up the color and trim choices and changed the gas tank shape for the K4. Worst of all, they mellowed out the cam grind just a bit. The CL-350 would never again produce such a sweet top end rush to the redline. The audible howl might be the same, but the adrenaline injectors were stifled a bit. The whole concept pointed to the direction Honda and most of the other manufacturers were going. They all slowly but surely dribbled themselves into a boring oblivion of blandness as the decade wore on. This is a key reason why this book is what it is: 1955-75 was a very special time in America. The peak time, the best of the best in motorcycle years was in 1969-71. Styling and performance were reaching new heights and prices were incredibly low. Best of all, at that time little else mattered.

Easy Rider launched a phenomenon in June 1969 that has never been duplicated. The movie inspired thousands of young men to saddle up their motorcycles and head across country to see the USA, from their Hondas, not Harley-Davidsons. In spite of this movie being Peter Fonda's second foray into the glorification of Harley-Davidson choppers, Harley was actually at a low point in its popularity in 1969. The Japanese onslaught on their large road machines was only just beginning. Harley-Davidson had just gotten its first glimpse of its future nemesis when the Honda 750 Four was released on 6/6/69. *Easy Rider* was released only twenty days later. Was that a seminal month, or what!? Six years later Honda would totally take control of the big touring market with the launch of the Gold Wing, but in June 1969, things were happening, baby! Bob Dylan might have been singing "Ballad of a Thin Man" to Harley-Davidson in 1969 because the company just could not seem to figure out that their financial future, no matter how much they desperately tried to deny it, lay in the extended forks, apehanger handlebars, and bad-boy image of the choppers. The company would have an epiphany and come to its senses more than a decade later, but in 1966, an elegant blue chopper followed by one stretched out to cartoon dimensions in '69, were ignored by the very company that built them. Honda owned the market in 1969 like it had never been owned before.

This brings me to what is probably the most interesting personal motorcycle story I have to tell. I met a guy in college in September 1969 who I would still consider one of my closest friends more than forty years later. Now retired like me, he owns a gold BMW sport touring machine on which he has seen the USA a few times. My current machine is the opposite, a noisy little forty-year-old dirt bike built the exact same year as the focal point of this nostalgic story. At the time we met, I rode a Honda 50 Cub set up for trail riding and I cannot even remember what machine he rode in the dirt with me. What is important is that within a few months I would ride a Kawasaki G3-TR and he a CL-100 on the dirt trails near campus. When we weren't out getting muddy, we entertained ourselves by endlessly planning the trip across country to the West Coast we were going to take in June 1971. He and I are both long-range planners and we wallowed in the excitement of our future trip endlessly over the eighteen-month preparation period.

The first subject of our ruminations was of course precisely what machines we were going to ride on this journey not exactly favorable to a CL-100 or G3-TR. Being somewhat more staid and sensible than me, my future traveling companion made his selection rather easily. He would probably settle on a CB-350 and it would probably be gold, and with little further trepidation, yes it was. On the other hand, my imagination was filled with prospective concepts.

My first choice was a Mach III. Shut up! I hear your snickering from here! Try to remember how primitive touring machines still were in 1970. When the magazines tested the Mach III, they were impressed with its tolerable level of high-frequency vibration. Of course it slurped fuel, but it had all the passing power in the world. Yes, it sounded like a two-stroke, but that triple-plated burble was quite distinctive for its day. I loved the way the Mach III fit my lanky body and my obsession with skinny motorcycles. Yes, the crankcase is wide, but the styling of the tank and fenders is skinny, so there! When I officially began my search for my future long-distance steed, the Mach III was the metallic charcoal one with barely discernible black racing stripes on the sculpted gas tank. Although no one could complain that the color combination was even the least bit tacky, that one has always been a bit too subdued for my tastes. Before I was ready to finalize my choice, Kawasaki changed the color scheme to bright red with white stripes, a combination I liked much better. Although I would have preferred a bright blue hue, I had decided that I would be quite happy going *bub-dub-drubble-bub* on a bright red machine.

Stand back because here comes the monkey wrench! The trails we rode were not made by the two of us. They were made by another friend I use to ride with, a guy I first met out on the pipeline when I was still riding my Cub. He was on a... stop snickering before you even start! He was howling down the muddy, hilly pipeline on a black Super Hawk *with apehanger bars*! A lasting friendship soon ensued and before long I had graduated up to a *real* trail bike, the G3-TR, and so had he with an early SL-350. Where I had easy handling and maneuverability, he had torque and tonnage. Over the months to come, he and I would continually expand the local trail riding arena to include a delicious pair of trail loops, each connecting with the pipeline. For every steep hill or deep gully he slogged that big dog through, I made a little shortcut *cheater trail*, as I called them, with my little Kawasaki 90. Altogether we produced two extensive loops that could be ridden in a challenging manner in either direction. Riders from all over campus loved it and I was still riding those same trails on my AT-1CMX years later. By the way, guess who bought the exact same trail machine a few months before I did? His was geared down a little and had a 21-inch front wheel. Mine was (and is) a 1971 model, exactly the same as his, and I still own it. My machine has been geared even lower for a top speed of about 45 mph and has a high, plastic, Preston Petty front fender, a Skyway silencer, and a key switch so I would not be afraid to park it somewhere. We both replaced the AT-1's biggest weakness, the factory rear shocks. To this day, I still love the 1971 Yamaha AT-1 motocrosser more than any other trail bike!

Figure J22 - Red 1971 Yamaha AT-1CMX (foreground) with the Blue 1971 CL-350 K2. Note the K3 tank with the black stripe replacing the stolen K2 tank. ©1975 Floyd M. Orr

My trail riding buddy with the electric-start 350 Motosport was also one of those guys who liked to rebuild somewhat worn motorcycles and resell them for a profit. His specialties at the time were the Honda 160's and 305's. Between the Super Hawk and SL-350 he took me for a ride on a machine that affected my motorcycle outlook for life! He had rebuilt a red CL-kitted CB-160 into an unusual trail machine. The tires and suspension were stock for that bike, but he had breathed on the powerplant just a bit, letting it exhale through a pair of chrome, upswept, crossover megaphones that howled like a banshee. He offered to sell me that machine several times. Once I got the price down to something like $250, and yet I still did not hand over the cash. What a total fool I was! If there is one bike I should never have sold, it is the one this story is about and if there is one bike I should have bought, it was that one!

When it came time to suggest to my associates that I wanted to buy a Mach III to go to California on, most people tried to talk me out of it. The SL-350 owner was the one who was successful. I had always kept in mind three Hondas that I would consider for my trip: the CL-350, CL-450, and CL-175. Yes, I said 175. That was my fall back choice in case my poverty kept me from affording one of the other three. Okay, so I would have to cruise a little slower. I was hell-bent on going and a slow motorcycle wasn't going to stop me! Now I know you want to ask why a CL instead of a CB? If you have read much of this book, you already know by now that I am addicted to the Scramblers for their style, feel, and trail compatibility. There was no question that if I did not choose the Kawasaki Triple, my selection would be a Honda CL. Of course the 450 offered the most highway power and stability, but the Honda 450's are top-heavy. The scale may not show that much weight difference between the 350 and 450, but the feel at the handlebars certainly does, particularly at slow speeds. Besides that, there was the matter of $300 more in initial cost, which now seems small until you do the math and see that the 450 cost forty-percent more than the 350. Once I saw the new 350 K2 with its softly pleated seat and separate bullet mufflers, the choice was on the way. Speaking of on the way, not only did my friend and I travel long distance that year on our Honda 350's, several other local associates did, too. One went from Mississippi to Maine and back on a '69 CB-350 and another joined us on a CB-450. By the way, two other guys I knew took my advice and went out and bought a matched pair of gorgeous blue 1971 Mach III's! They went to Las Vegas and other long distance destinations and returned to tell me how much they both loved the machines they had selected for their trip! If you have read the rest of this book, you already know why I finally sold my CL-350 in 1978... to buy one of those.

We had been planning our trip for several months when I met the guy who would eventually purchase a CB-450 and join us on our journey. I went over to visit the SL-350 owner one day and there was a first-year BSA Rocket III parked in the front yard. It turns out it was owned by the roommate who would soon enough join our entourage. The Rocket was a dog that always had some problem or another. Never mind that it was only a few months old when I first saw it. Its owner unceremoniously dumped it on a chump so he could move on to a machine that ran more often than it didn't. Now there were three. The part of the Super Hawk / CL-160 / SL-350 / AT-1 owner is over for the remainder of this story, but his influence on my cycling history has continued. He would later become the first rider I knew to buy a first-year Z-1, and guess what he did to it? He replaced the four bulky but quiet exhaust pipes for a pair of flat-black megaphones that howled like a... you know. After one drive on that beast, I searched for years to find a four-cylinder from one of The Big Four that looked, and particularly *felt*, like an early Kawasaki Z-1, only smaller and lighter. Thus began my love affair with a Honda 550 Nighthawk that would endure for more than twenty years.

All of us were basically mature nerds who had sense enough to know that it would be preferable if we purchased our new long-distance steeds enough ahead of time to break them in well and learn whatever foibles they might have possessed. Some of us had not entirely given up running the pipeline or trail loops, either. One of the reasons 1971 had been selected for our big getaway was that the SL-350 owner and I were both graduating. He would depart his Air Force ROTC program to become a jet pilot as planned. That's why there was a gap between his AT-1 trailing days and his disturb the neighbors Z-1 days. Between October 1970 and June '71 the Candy Sapphire Blue CL-350 would be my trail bike. I had sold the G3-TR to buy the Honda and I had no idea I would be returning to Mississippi State University and continue riding the same trails my friend and I had so carefully made. As fate would have it, my two touring pals were returning to old girlfriends and further studies at MSU. One had not yet graduated and the other was still in graduate school. What does this have to do with this story? I would depart their company two days into the journey.

Before we depart for the trip, let me describe what my CL-350 was like as a trail bike. I rode the trail loops and screamed down the pipeline many times, both before and after my two trips to California. Like my friend's overweight SL-350, the CL had gobs of torque and low-speed grunt power, even if the gearing was a bit tall for trials work. Just notch the lever back and forth through the first three gears and steer. The standing position was not bad, certainly an improvement over any CB. The front fender was small enough to avoid all but the worst of mud clogs. The tires were not even as knobby as Trials Universals but they gripped decently enough. Running the pipeline was like running a fast, hilly, muddy fire road in a straight line, something the CL-350 took to with aplomb. After returning from San Jose the second time, I met a new rider with a CL-350 K3 and we blasted the pipeline numerous times, usually at night with a couple of fun-loving young women on the rear seats! Although the CL-350's were excellent pipeline haulers, considering the darkness, weight of passengers, and most of all the mud, it was a minor miracle there were never any unpleasant mishaps.

As for mishaps with the CL-350, there were precisely five, including every possible description of mishap. (Actually there were six, but you will find it funnier if I describe the missing event later within its context.) The first happened in the opening months of ownership when I was mostly trail riding the bike. The owner of the gold CB and I were out cruising dirt roads one day when my back wheel slid gently into a small ditch when I tried to suddenly dodge a mud puddle. Before I even had time to think about it, I was tossed off onto my hands and knees in the ditch. The 350 plowed its way a little further along, held nicely upright by the walls of the three-foot ditch! My knees were sore for a couple of days; end of story. The next mishap was that the screws holding on the exhaust heat shield vibrated out. I caught the falling shield with my left leg and found a couple of replacement screws; end of story. The third event is amusing now, but not so much then. Early in my first trip across country, I camped out for a week in Rocky Mountain National Park at Estes Park. This was my first of many times to visit one of my favorite places in America. I was loading up the CL-350 to go somewhere one morning when all of a sudden, the blacktop of the camping spot heated up and the bike fell off its centerstand, right onto a rock! That would not have been so bad if a big boulder had not smashed into the left side of the gas tank! No leaks, no problems other than the obvious cosmetic one; end of story. The fourth event hurt the 350 a lot more than it hurt me. After the two trips across country, the SOHC Twin developed a common malady for the model, a leaking head gasket. By that time my mechanic had to replace the worn cam with the later generic model. As mentioned earlier, this would turn out to be the leading reason I sold the Scrambler when I bought the 1971 Mach III. The high-rpm peak was diminished forever and the only thing that could have been done about it would have been to ask the mechanic if he could round up a top-notch cam from an early, wrecked CL-350. The fifth and final mishap hurt me a lot more than it hurt the CL-350. After riding across country twice and running the pipeline at night with abandon and putt-putting up and down what was essentially a trials course numerous times, I finally crashed the CL-350. I t-boned a small dog who ran right into my path one night on a deserted county road in Mississippi, only a few miles from my house. The people who scraped me off the coarse pavement told me that I had slid some sixty feet, backwards, feet first, on my stomach, wearing only a T-shirt. What I remember most was seeing sparks flying from the CL-350 sliding alongside me. My first thought, like any truly addicted motorcyclist, was that the lovely and wonderful CL-350 was finally destroyed. As it turns out, I didn't suffer any broken bones or maladies other than a serious case of road rash. That road ground my ankle right down to the bone. Of course it was no coincidence that that was the last time I rode a motorcycle in sneakers! As luck would have it, all the sparks were coming from the corner of the luggage rack. The slide tore up one footpeg rubber, bent the clutch lever and left a minor scar on the luggage rack. The CL-350 escaped going to the hospital. The emergency room released me to the care of my parents a few hours later; end of story.

How did the CL-350 do as a long-distance touring machine? Just fine, thank you. The bike had the dealer-installed Hondaline luggage rack and I added a pair of cheap leather saddlebags that draped over the frame underneath the seat. The most unusual items I carried on my journeys were a Sears two-man umbrella tent. It was the old bulky canvas type with an external aluminum frame. The second bulky item was a cot with an aluminum frame that could be disassembled. The plan was to camp out in state and national parks for most of the trip. The tent was easy to set up and roomy for one person, and the cot made sleeping on damp or uneven surfaces more comfortable. The amazing part is that I managed to haul these two bulky items, a sleeping bag, and my clothes and toiletries on a CL-350!

There were only three modifications to the stock machine and they all proved their worth over time. As was trendy then, I cut off the hard Honda handgrips and replaced them with the soft, bulbous type that are larger diameter in the center than at the ends. Although the Honda's vibration level was not severe, these softer grips certainly helped, particularly on the long distances I had planned to cover. Two other alterations were far less common. One was an idea I had to increase the bike's security and the other was something I am to this day amazed needed changing in the first place. The gas tank was not bolted onto a Honda 350 and it could be removed without tools. There was no lock on the seat latch or helmet holder, either. Before I left home the first time, I purchased a small length of chain of just the right gauge, enclosed it in a piece of bicycle inner tube, and added a padlock. This could be attached to the seat and swing arm to lock the seat, tank, and my helmet to the machine when parked in a questionable area. I never understood why the 350's needed such an elaborate shift linkage system of rods and adjustments that seemed mostly to just add slack and notchiness to the shifting process. I rode the 350 to California and back the first time before I figured out that the linkage could be removed completely from the shifting process. I bought a short shift lever from my local Honda dealer and bolted it directly onto the shifter shaft. The shifts were quick, neat, and clean, with lots of solid feel. Why in the world did Honda think they needed that sloppy, complicated shift linkage? I have no idea.

The three of us left Monkey State MS and drove up through Arkansas into southern Missouri the first two days of the trip. The route avoided any interstates available, involving lots of cruising through small towns and gawking at the scenery. Two days is how long it took me to realize that these other guys had a different viewpoint of the trip than I did. They were motorcycle touring; I wanted to get somewhere. At that time in my life I had never been west of Dallas, east of Atlanta, or north of Nashville. My Southern experience had reached all the way to Key West. I wanted to see what the non-South was like, and I wanted to see it ASAP. On the third morning of our journey, I woke up and announced that I was going it alone from that point onward. The other two were welcome to come find me later once I got someplace. Although they did manage to find me in Estes Park a week or so later, and again in San Francisco a few weeks after that, the rest of the time it was just me and my trusty steed.

Once on my own, I searched out freeways like a heat-sinking missile. If there was an interstate for going wherever I was going, me and the CL-350 were on it, baby, cruising at 70 mph and above all the way. Since I had previously learned to Loc-tite the screws in the exhaust heat shield, nothing fell off and there were no mechanical failures whatsoever, not even a flat tire. There was at least one incident of running out of gas. The 2.4 gallon tank of the CL is one of the few things the CB is actually better at, especially out in the deserted Western *no man's land*. The worst situation was one when the sign said "next gasoline 105 miles". That was just about the extent of the CL's range. I had to walk the last five miles to a grimy little no-name station with its walls literally lined with five-gallon gas cans to be sold at rip-off prices. I might have hitched a ride back for some of that five miles. I cannot seem to recall actually carrying the can that far and I don't remember just throwing the empty can off the side of the road, either.

The itinerary took me directly from Missouri to Estes Park. A fellow student back at MSU had told me that two places I would like were Estes Park CO and Santa Barbara CA. He was right on both counts. Although I had passed many a fellow traveler on a Honda 350, 450, or 750, Estes Park was truly full of them! There was a little pizza joint where many tourists my age gathered every night and many of them were there on not so large motorcycles, just like me. Bob & Tony's Pizza was still there on Elkhorn Avenue when my wife and I vacationed in Estes Park in 2000. I stayed a week in that heaven before I finally got bored. The only incident was the boulder-gas tank confrontation. When my previous companions arrived, they thought it was a funny story. As the kids on *That 70s Show* often say, *Burn!*

Figure J23 - The quaint little pizza hangout was still in business when my wife and I vacationed in Estes Park in June 1999. For this economy, that's some staying power! ©1999 Floyd M. Orr

I left Estes Park, drove directly up to Interstate 80 and headed to California, entering the state the first time at Lake Tahoe. After sleeping in a tent for days, I was ready for a real bed. The best deal around was a high-rise dormitory room at San Francisco State. Dorm rooms were rented out very cheaply to vagabond students like me that summer. My touring friends found me at that dorm easily enough and we stayed there a few days until they became antsy to continue touring. I would not see them again until we were all back at MSU about a month later. My total journey lasted six weeks. I do not remember if they or I returned home to Mississippi first. They spent the rest of their time just as they had the earlier portion, riding all over the countryside and visiting national parks and monuments. We all went to see Moby Grape at the Fillmore West. I locked down my gas tank and seat and we took our helmets inside. There was only one thing left for the street gangs to steal and they took it: a 49-cent bungee cord from my luggage rack. This was the last week of June and the Fillmore West would be closed before I got back home less than a month later.

All I really cared about at that time was spending time in the Bay Area, far from the brain strangling Bible Belt of the South. One interesting experience I had was meeting a local guy who was familiar with the route of the legendary Mustang/Charger chase in the movie *Bullitt*. I took him for a ride on the CL-350 one afternoon as he directed me along the actual path of the famous chase. Were those hills as steep as they appeared in the movie? Yes. Was the ride fun? Yes.

After that point in the story, I honestly cannot remember the exact order of events as they unfolded. You know what they always say about the Sixties, although the effects had not yet worn off from the early Seventies, either. The first thing I discovered was that I did not care much for San Francisco weather. There is still a green San Francisco State sweatshirt hanging in my closet along with a warm, quilted jacket with a hood I could tie down underneath my helmet. I quickly discovered that the suburbs of San Jose were more my speed weather wise. I remember a ride down to Stanford, where I dismounted and walked around campus for a while before continuing southward. I rode down Highway 101 to Los Angeles at some point because I remember being there. Can you believe I had little interest in cruising Highway 1? I clearly remember visiting the UCLA campus, but I have little recollection of the ride down from the Bay Area. I don't think I spent even one night in the LA area, but forty years have fogged in my airport on the issue.

Onward through the fog.... You are not going to believe the rest of this story, but I shall be glad to swear on a stack of Bibles or a case of Castrol 20/50, whichever you think is more appropriate, that to the best of my knowledge, this story is absolutely as stated. I had departed Mississippi with a smidgen over $200 cash, a decent amount of money back then, but certainly not enough to stash inside a fuel line in a gas tank. As I have said, 98% of my goal for the trip was to freely experience a place where minds were socially larger than a thimble, the weather was drier than a swamp, and there were things to do on a Saturday night other than circle the Sonic drive-in in your pickup truck. All I really cared about seeing were a few college campuses other than Monkey State, the Rocky Mountains, Santa Barbara, and most of all San Francisco. I did not realize until I had arrived that Frisco's weather was as wet as Mississippi's and a whole lot colder. The most surprising thing about LA was that it was cold, too, at least at night. When my cash had dribbled down to less than $3, I knew it was time to head for the barn.

This was the first week of July and I knew that out in the desert at least, it would be hotter than a lit firecracker, so I crossed the desert at night in one long endurance run. before I crashed at a motel somewhere in New Mexico. I remember being up for about twenty-four hours. How long was I on that CL-350 with the sound of The Stones' "Gimme Shelter" ringing in my head? I cannot say for certain. I do know that I took I-10 out of LA and rode until I-10 met I-20 east of El Paso. I stayed in another cheap motel near Fort Worth and reached Mississippi State MS after one last day's ride. I believe I must have had Dad's BankAmericard *for emergency use only* and that's how I paid for those few nights in motels. The cash I carried was mostly just for food. Some of that was spent at several visits with my fellow companions to the best IHOP in the world, a particular one located in San Francisco. There are only two things I remember clearly from that fast journey from LA to home. I drove nearly 24 hours and then slept nearly 24 hours on that section from LA to Nowhere New Mexico and the sun was so hot on that ride from Nowhere NM to Foat Wuth that the glue on my throttle handgrip melted. I had to squeeze the grip tightly to hold the throttle open on much of that long section of I-10 and I-20. This may not have happened if I had left the stock Honda grips installed, but the softer rubber offered a nice cushion from the high-speed vibration. I don't know why that particular song stuck in my head, but it did. "It's just a shot away... It's just a kiss away".

Before the end of that summer, the CL-350 was loaded up again. As soon as I could replenish my cash supply, I was back on I-20 West, heading for San Jose. The only difference from the first trip was that this time I knew exactly where I wanted to go. I took I-20 to I-10 to LA, just as I had on my earlier return trip, only this time the weather was somewhat milder. I rode up Highway 101 on one long afternoon trip to my final destination in San Jose. I cannot remember a single moment from that end-of-summer journey other than pondering how the cityscape between the two major metropolitan areas never seemed to dissolve into wilderness, as do so many interstate areas in Mississippi. The CL-350 was just as it always was, totally trouble free. I stayed in the Bay Area for nearly three months, generally in the Sunnyvale, Campbell, and Mountain View suburbs. My only transportation was the same Candy Sapphire Blue motorcycle.

The CL-350 and I were at a party in a house in a seemingly nice upper-middle-class neighborhood in Mountain View one night in December 1971. The Scrambler was parked out front at the curb. If memory serves, I was skinny-dipping out back in the heated swimming pool. The area seemed so benevolent that I had not bothered to utilize my homemade seat lock. Some petty criminal stole the CL-350's gas tank and sliced up the seat with a knife. What a stinking jerk, whoever he was. I bummed a ride home from the party and bummed another ride to the nearest Honda dealer the next day to buy a new seat and tank. The jackass who had earlier stolen my 49-cent bungee cord may have had an axe to grind with our three Mississippi license plates, but by the time of the incident in December my Honda had California plates. I did not have plans at that time to ever ride it back to Mississippi. Remember, the petty thief stole a Sapphire Blue gas tank with a big dent in its left side. With the bike as my only transportation, I had few options at the Honda dealership. I purchased a new seat, but the only tank he had in stock was a K3 model in Strato Blue Metallic with a black stripe instead of a white one.

Within a couple of weeks, my life would change forever and I had no clue what was coming. I had never missed spending Christmas with my parents until that time, and as it turned out, I would spend every Christmas with them until they were gone. They sent me a plane ticket home for Christmas. To make a long story short, my dad needed me to join the family business because he was slowly losing his sight due to glaucoma. After Christmas we made an arrangement with someone I knew back in California who knew an interstate trucker who could haul the CL-350 back to Mississippi for me. The Sapphire Blue 350 with the Strato Blue gas tank would spend the next five years back in Mississippi running the pipeline and the trail loops, at least until I bought the Yamaha AT-1 motocrosser to take over that duty in 1973.

I moved to Dallas in 1976 and the CL-350 went with me. Actually it went further than that. The same guy that I met because he owned a BSA 750, the same guy that toured the West on his CB-450 with our friend on the CB-350, moved to Austin soon thereafter and I rode the CL-350 down there and left it in his garage. Austin and the Texas Hill Country were wonderful places to ride a bike back in the less crowded Seventies, so I left the CL-350 in Austin for a couple of years for just that purpose. By 1978 I could no longer keep ownership of an early Mach III stuffed into the back of my imagination. I found a blue '71 model just like the ones my other friends had ridden throughout the Western U.S. and sold the CL-350 to a local kid in Austin for $500, only $230 less than what it had cost new eight years earlier.

The Honda Scrambler had indeed done its share of "scrambling". It had struggled up the heights of Trail Ridge near Estes Park, sputtering to a top speed of about 40 mph, never mind the *constant velocity carburetors*. It had slid sixty feet on its side on pavement. It had pitched me into a ditch. It had hauled ass down the pipeline by moonlight putting wide grins on all our faces. It had puttered over the tight trails through the Mississippi woods countless times. It had provided me with reliable transportation in temperatures from just above freezing to over a hundred. It had cruised America's freeways for endless hours at over 70 mph, not that far from its top speed of about 95, loaded down like a pack mule. It had been vandalized. It had ridden the rain grooves of California freeways. I had taken my mom for a fast ride and she finally understood my motorcycle obsession when she couldn't wipe the smile off her face. The bike had been pickup trucked, eighteen wheelered, and U-Hauled. The Honda CL-350 Scrambler was the bike I never should have sold. Show me the magic.

Figure J24 - Blue 1971 Honda CL-350. This pathetic shot taken from the steps of a water tower is the only photo I have of the glorious machine that served me so well, as described in this story. ©Floyd M. Orr

Figure J25 - *Easy Rider* Replica - Captain America Harley Davidson Chopper featured in *Easy Rider* by courtesy of Deutsches Zweirad und NSU Museum, Germany.

Image by Joachim Kohler, photographer, under Creative Commons license (GNU).

Chapter 10: *Back to the Future*

Aprilia

Aprilia RS 50 & RS 125

Figure K1 - Black & Yellow Aprilia RS-50. Machine owned by Tyler Matthews, Flagstaff, AZ. Image by Tybersk8er under Creative Commons license in the Public Domain.

The Aprilia RS 50 is the raciest 50cc bike ever offered to the public for legal street use in the USA. The Italian company introduced the Mark I model in 1995 as a little brother to the RS 125, introduced in '93 and still in production. The RS 50 Mark II was built from 1999 through 2005 and the Mark III was launched in 2006. Although most of the RS 50's produced have been painted red and/or black, the latest version is marketed in a shade of white the company calls Blanco Glam. The little pseudo-racer also looks good in Fluo Red with white trim. As with most of the prior year models, the '09 also came in black. The RS 50 has been offered in a variety of colors and graphics patterns over the years, most of some combination of black, red, white, and silver in flashy patterns. No technical component of the RS 50 has been left in the past. Although the wheels are still seventeen inches, just like those on the original Honda 50, the tire compound and tread have been strongly influenced by the racetrack and the brakes are discs. The engine is a 50cc liquid-cooled two-stroke making six horsepower through a six-speed transmission. The top speed claimed is between 50 mph and 70 mph, and I'm sure that is a function of gearing and rider weight. Two nonracetrack-inspired items are the oil injection and electric starter, but the aluminum, perimeter box frame, full fairing, fat gas tank, thin seat pads, upside down fork and monoshock all scream racer!

Of course the price for this exotic little hotrod minisquirt is a lot bigger than its displacement, and that's the leading reason the little Italian is rare on American streets. I have never seen a new RS 50 listed at less than $3595, the official 2004 base price, making it somewhat higher than the cost of a Kawasaki Ninja 250!

In 2013 Piaggio, the company famous for its pioneering Vespa scooters, owns Aprilia as well as Gilera, Moto Guzzi, and the RS 50's legendary competitor on the streets of Europe, the Derbi.

Figure K2 - Dark Blue & Red Aprilia RS-125. Image by JDM under Creative Commons license in the Public Domain.

Aprilia Scarabeo

The Scarabeo is the Porsche of motor scooters, an unparalleled classic beauty. The first Scarabeo was released in Europe in 1993. I am not sure if it came to the USA that same year or not. Aprilia has always been famous for its road racing machinery, including scooters. The company extensively raced its RS 125 and RS 50 motorcycles and the SR 50 scooter, molded in the conventional style of a large body on small wheels. The SR 50 used top-shelf technical components and so have all the Scarabeos the company has produced. The original Scarabeo was a 50cc two-stroke like the SR 50, but there have also been four-strokes in the 100, 125, 200, 300, and 500 classes. Even the big 500 monster is a 460cc *single*! The 200 has a DOHC engine with four valves.

The Scarabeo is a style of scooter that was first sold back in the early Sixties by several manufacturers, most notably the Rabbit 90 and the Motobi Scooterino. The Rabbit 90 two-stroke was a slender, stylish scooter with 15-inch wheels, electric starter, and three-speed transmission with automatic clutch. It was distinguished from the Honda Cub of its day by its hand shift and floorboards instead of footpegs. The Scooterino was a 75cc OHV model with a three-speed hand shift, manual clutch, slender floorboards and 16-inch wheels. The Scooterino had a claimed dry weight of 152 pounds and a top speed of 44 mph. The Rabbit 90 had a claimed dry weight of 184 pounds and a top speed of 52 mph. The Scarabeo Ditech 50 weighed 190 pounds and I believe the claimed top speed was 50, but it may have been more than that. As you may have surmised, the Ditech 50 has not been sold in the USA at least since the end of 2005, when two-stroke street machines were finally outlawed by the EPA for emissions reasons.

Big-wheel scooters have been marketed in the U.S. in recent years under three price strata. The flood of no-name brand models from China and sold on the Internet for $1500-$2000 are the bottom level. Most of these are powered by the 110cc OHC Honda copycat engine. The Kymco People series is built in Taiwan and priced in the middle, such as the $1999 MSRP for the People 50 in 2011. The Scarabeo models have held the top position with their beautiful bodywork, high-tech mechanicals and matching price levels. Aprilia has been owned by Piaggio, the parent company of Vespa, since 2004. The 100 OHV and 200 OHC models debuted in 2008. Prices for the 2009 models were $2699 and $3499. No more recent prices are available: these are the last ones shown on the Aprilia website. A four-valve 50 model was apparently added to the line in 2009, but I am not sure if it has ever been sold in the USA. The 2008-09 models came in only two colors each. The multiple color choices of elegant shades such as Lemon Acid, Ocean Blue, and Orange Tropical from the earlier Ditech models are history. Some sources say that the 2006 models were the last Scarabeos built in Italy. The 2007 and later models are built in China, a fact dealt with quite discreetly by the company.

Figure K3 - Beige Aprilia Scarabeo 50 in Italy, 2007.

Image by James & Winnie Maeng under Creative Commons license.

Honda

1990 Honda NS50F

This racy little two-stroke Honda 50 was exported to the USA for only one model year. The NSF mated a liquid-cooled 49cc reed-valve engine to a six-speed transmission. This little 180-pound tiddler came only in a punk rock suit with wild pink and turquoise graphics on a white base. The all-black engine, exhaust, and tube frame were shipped uncovered, but a fairing, lower cowl, and radiator shroud were optional. A tach and engine guard were also on the option list. The machine rolled on seventeen-inch wheels with a tube frame and a solo racing seat nestled in a plastic housing. A small storage area was underneath the lift-up seat panel behind the rider. Has the NS50F become a desirable collectible? It probably has to at least some degree since it was the fastest 50 in the USA in its only production year. However, with its two-stroke engine and unusual styling, the NS50F has always been an incongruent coda to the Honda tiddler legend.

Honda Dream 50: Jewel of the Orient

Figure K4 - 1998 Red & Silver Honda Dream 50. ©Terje Saethre, owner and photographer

This little jewel is probably the ultimate tiddler. I often think about this rare little beauty and feel like a bloomin' idiot for not buying one of these rarities when it was available, even at the ridiculous $5495 price! If I had coughed up twice the sticker price of my '83 Nighthawk 550 for a machine that practically has to scream up to 10,000 rpm before it really begins to get out of its own way, it would have been identical to this one. If I were to pay my money, it would have to be red and silver and it would have to have lights and a speedo and tach, just like this one. Many were sold in solid red or black and silver, and most, if not all, were sold without lights. I am not even sure if this particular model with lights and a speedo was ever sold in the U. S., but I have collected numerous photos of Dream 50's. Some look like this one and some look like pure racers. They all are as attractive as Brigitte Bardot in 1962, which is when the original racer of which this is a replica, was built. I have a fever dream that has two flavors. One looks just like the a 1997 Dream 50, and the other looks like a red and silver CL-72 or a blue CL-350 K2 or K3 or a CL-90. Uh-oh, I'm having an orgasm all over myself. Anyone out there got a towel?

Figure K5 - Silver 2004 Honda Dream 50. This Honda Media photo shows the later iteration of the Dream 50 ready for the racetrack with velocity stacks, dual black megaphones, and no lighting equipment. ©2004 American Honda Motor Company, Inc.

The photos I have of the Dream 50 are mostly of similar 1997 models and black and silver 2004 models. I also have at least one photo of a solid red one. It has a DOHC 50cc single cylinder engine, six-speed gearbox, and other such technical stuff. I know it was built in small numbers as a tribute to the CR110 of 1962. Since neither the 1997 model or the 2004 one is in the *Honda ID Guide*, I assume neither was ever officially imported here. However, it is quite obvious that a number arrived through the gray market. There are even photos of the 2004 model on Honda's Media Pages. Maybe this indicates that some quantity of the later model were sent to the USA. Nevertheless, it is the original 1997 model in red and silver that really starts my motor!

Honda Rebel Chart

Year	Model	Color	Side Covers	Price
1985	250 Rebel	Pearl Stellar Black / Candy Supreme Red	Chrome	NA
1986	250 Rebel	Candy Eiger Blue & Pearl Stellar Black	Chrome	NA
1986	250 Limited	Pearl Stellar Black w/Gold Trim	Chrome	NA
1986	450 Rebel	Pearl Stellar Black Monte Rosa Silver Metallic	Chrome	NA
1987	250 Rebel	Candy Wineberry Red / Black	Chrome	NA
1987	450 Rebel	Black / Candy Glory Red	Chrome	NA
1996	250 Rebel	Magna Red	Red	NA
1997	250 Rebel	Black / Enamel Cream Pearl Shinning Yellow / White	Body Color	NA
1999	250 Rebel	Black	Black	$2999
	Rebel 2-Tone	Candy Glory Red & Black	Red	$3199
2000	250 Rebel	Black	Black	$2999
	Rebel 2-Tone	Pearl Halcyon Silver & Black	Silver	$3199
2006	250 Rebel	Black / White	Body Color	$3099
2007	250 Rebel	Black / Red	Body Color	$3199
2008	250 Rebel	Black / Silver	Body Color	$3199
2009	250 Rebel	Black / Ultra Blue Metallic	Body Color	$3999
2012	250 Rebel	Candy Red / Matte Silver	Body Color	$4190
2013	250 Rebel	Candy Red / Black	Body Color	$4190

Honda Rebel Notes: All 250 models were 234cc SOHC twins with five-speed transmissions. All 450 models were 447cc SOHC twins with six-speed transmissions. All Rebels had front disc brakes. The 1999 model weighed 306 pounds dry. As shown in the chart, the company took the Rebel in and out of production several times. One online source states the horsepower as 17 for the 250 and 38 for the 450. The rating for the 2012 model may be higher.

The Rebel was preceded by the 250 Custom in 1982 and 1983. Both had thick, two-tiered seats, conventional frames, standard-rake suspension, and drum brakes. Both models used the same engine as the later Rebels, but the 1983 model had belt drive. The 450 Rebel was preceded in 1982-83 by three cruiser variations utilizing the same engine as the later Rebel. These included the Hondamatic with a two-speed transmission with a torque converter, the E model with drum brakes and other similarities with the 250 Custom, and the 450 Custom model with Comstar cast wheels and disc front brake.

Figure K6 - White 2006 Honda Rebel 250. ©2006 American Honda Motor Company, Inc.

Honda VTR-250 Interceptor Chart

Year	Colors	Trim	Seat	Wheels	Decal
1988	Ross White or Black	Brad Blue	Blue	Blue	Interceptor
1989	Ross White	Florida Blue & Holiday Blue	Black	White	Honda
1990	Ross White & Nordic Blue	Nordic Blue	Black	White	Honda

Honda VTR-250 Notes: All VTR-250's had liquid-cooled, DOHC, four-valve, 249cc V-twin engines with six-speed transmissions, single, black exhaust pipes, black engines, Pro-Link rear suspension, and full fairings. The '88 and '89 models had an unusual internal disc front brake within the wheel hub. The 1990 model had a conventional external front disc brake. The claimed dry weight was 331 pounds. Some sources put the VTR's horsepower at about 29 and the wet weight at approximately 355 pounds.

Figure K7 - Blue & White 1990 Honda VTR 250. Image by Mike Schinkel under Creative Commons license.

Figure K8 - Red Honda VTR 250 Trellis. ©Troyce Walls

Honda CBR250R Chart

Year	Model	Colors	Wt.	Price
2011	CBR250R	Black / Red & Silver	357	$3999
2012	CBR250R	Black / Red & Silver Red, White, & Blue	357	$4099
2013	CBR250R	Black / Red / Pearl White with Red & Blue Trim Blue-Orange-White-Red	357	$4199

Honda CBR250R Notes: All models are powered by a 249cc, fuel-injected, DOHC, liquid-cooled, four-valve 24-hp single. All models have six-speed transmissions, single-shock rear suspension, 17-inch wheels, and front and rear disc brakes. All weights listed are in pounds and wet. Optional ABS adds nine pounds and $500 to the price.

Figure K9 - 2012 Red, White & Blue Honda CBR250R ABS. ©2012 American Honda Motor Company, Inc.

Kawasaki

Kawasaki 125 Eliminator

Kawasaki has marketed an unusual 125cc single in recent years called the Eliminator. This machine was obviously a descendant of Kaw's earlier, dragster-styled road machines and a little brother of the much larger Eliminator line. This modern little bike was distinguished by its long wheelbase and very low seating position. Obviously it was a cruiser with a specific flavor. The powerplant was a straightforward, air-cooled, 124cc SOHC Single with twelve horsepower and a five-speed transmission. The front wheel was a 17-incher with a disc brake and the rear was fifteen inches with a drum brake. The machine used conventional dual-shock rear suspension and had a claimed dry weight of 320 pounds. Total production lasted from 2006 through 2009 with a final sticker price of $2799. The prices of the earlier EL 125 models are unavailable. The first year machines came in Black and the final year models in Metallic Phantom Silver. I have also seen a bright metallic blue example, but I do not know its model year.

Figure K10 - Silver 2009 Kawasaki 125 Eliminator. ©2009 Kawasaki Motors Corporation, U.S.A.

Kawasaki 250 Ninja

Kawasaki's smallest Ninja has been produced for decades under numerous model names. Z250 Ninja, 250R, GPX250R, EX250R, EX250F4, EX250-F8, and Ninja 300 are basically all the same machine. No motorcycle has been produced so long under so many names this side of a Harley-Davidson! Obviously this little Super Squirt has been very successful in the marketplace or this phenomenon would never have happened. By comparison you can see that although Honda's 250 Rebel cruiser and Kawasaki's mini-bullet began life at almost the same time, the little Kaw has been in *continuous* production, but the Rebel has not. Where the Rebel carries the soul of the Harley-Davidson Super 10, the Ninja carries the soul of the Ducati Diana and Bultaco Metralla, meshing its history with the 1967 Kawasaki Samurai.

All 250 Ninjas have water-cooled, DOHC, 248-9cc twin-cylinder engines with eight valves, counterbalancer, electronic ignition, electric starter, six-speed gearbox, Uni-Trak single-shock rear suspension, Ceriani-type front forks, cast alloy wheels, and front and rear disc brakes. The 1986-87 models had 16-inch wheels, 37 hp at 14,000 rpm, and a top speed of 95 mph. The 1988-2007 models had more enclosed bodywork and produced the same thirty-seven horsepower at 12,500 rpm. Surprisingly, the updated model benefited from slightly lower gearing that actually increased both acceleration and top speed. These models could top 100 mph. The 2008-13 models have catalytic converters on a two-into-one exhaust and weigh 22 additional pounds. The Ninja got a wheel size update to seventeen inches in 2008. The displacement was increased to 296cc in 2013. All claimed dry weights are in pounds. These range from the 304 pounds of the 1986 model, which remained unchanged until 2008, when it increased to 333. The weight increased again to 375 in 2010.

Figure K11 - Silver Kawasaki EX250F7F Ninja. ©Kawasaki Motors Corporation, U.S.A.

The displacement was increased to 300cc for the 2013 model year. Several other changes brought the weight up to 379 for the base model or 384 pounds with the optional ABS. The original 1986 model had launched for under $3000, but the price has now crept up to $4799 for the 2013 base 300 or $5499 with ABS. The 2013 models have Digital Fuel Injection and run on regular unleaded. Most of the price gains came after the 2007 model year, when the base price was still only $2999. The base price of the 2012 model still held at $4199. Some of the later price increases reflect Special Edition paint and graphics packages that were typically a $200-$250 option.

The 250 Ninja has been offered in one or two standard colors each model year. As you would guess, Lime Green, Blue, Ebony, White, and Bright Red have been the most common color choices. There was a small half-fairing that would be found only on the first two model years. Otherwise most of the 250 Ninjas are very similar in appearance. You can also spot the later models that have the SE Graphics. The 300 without ABS comes in a choice of Pearl Stardust White, Lime Green and Ebony, or Ebony. The ABS model includes an SE Graphics Package of Lime Green and Ebony. Color selections from recent model years have included Metallic Island Blue, Passion Red, Candy Lime Green, Pearl White, and Metallic Spark Black.

Figure K12 - Blue 2010 Kawasaki Ninja 250. ©2010 Kawasaki Motors Corporation, U.S.A.

Suzuki

Suzuki GZ250, TU250X, & GW250

Figure K13 - Black 2010 Suzuki GZ250. ©2010 Suzuki Motor of America, Inc.

Suzuki has produced a trio of 250cc bikes over the past fifteen years, representing three levels of performance and rider appeal. The GZ250 Marauder was marketed from 1998 through the 2010 model year. The Marauder was the continuation of Suzuki's EN Series of beginner machines. With its low, stretched-out style and seating position, the Marauder was Suzuki's single-cylinder competition to the inline twin Honda Rebel and Yamaha 250 V-twins. You can see from the look of its fat front tire and moderate handlebar height that the Marauder was more like a tiny Harley-Davidson Fat Boy than a skinny chopper. With its simple, low-stress engine design, the Marauder was basically a pussycat intended to intimidate no one.

Suzuki added a new 250cc Single model to the lineup in 2009. The TU250 offered a totally nostalgic romp back to The Sixties! The TU shared many of the basic design components of the Marauder, such as the single-cylinder, SOHC powerplant, five-speed transmission, forward-sloping dual rear shocks, and single downtube frame with the engine as a supporting member. The TU offers styling similar to a traditional '60's machine with upright seating, rounded tank with kneepads, and standard-sized laced wheels. Its nostalgic look is only skin deep over its fuel injection, catalytic converter, and front disc brake. In modern fashion, there is no kick starter.

Figure K14 - 2013 Gray Suzuki TU250X. ©2013 Suzuki Motor of America, Inc.

Figure K15 - Black 2013 Suzuki GW250. ©2013 Suzuki Motor of America, Inc.

The new GW250 is being released just this year. This is a new hotrod Suzuki styled in the modern idiom begun by Honda's Hawk GT decades back. The translation is a machine that in most respects is a very sporty bullet bike without a fairing. Of course the engine must be *styled* for its part in the visual attack of this type and there are generally less expensive fiberglass pieces to repair or replace in case of a minor mishap. Unlike the GZ and TU machines, this 250 Suzi is ready to do business! The twin-cylinder GW Inazuma (where oh where did they get *that* name?) will surely go after some of the market share held by the venerable Ninja 250 and the recently introduced CBR250R. Now the rider who seeks a certain excitement level from a new tiddler has several choices!

Modern Suzuki 250 Chart

Model	Years	Engine	Gears	Brakes	Wheels	Wt.	Price
GZ250	1998-2010	Single	5	Disc / Drum	16 / 15	331	$2999
TU250X	2009-2013	Single	5	Disc / Drum	18 / 18	326	$4399
GW250	2013	Twin	6	Disc / Disc	17 / 17	403	$5999

Modern Suzuki 250 Notes: All claimed dry weights are listed in pounds. All models are SOHC. The GZ and TU models have traditional laced wire wheels and twin rear shocks with exposed rear springs. The GW has three-spoke mag wheels and monoshock rear suspension. The GZ models all had carburetors; the TU and GW models are fuel injected. The 2013 TU model is not legal in California even though it has a catalyst exhaust. The GW is liquid-cooled and all other models are air-cooled. The price listed for the GZ was in 2010, its last year of production. The TX250X was priced at $3499 in 2009, its first year. The price of the GW is unconfirmed at the time of publication, listed by an outside source, not on the Suzuki website.

Yamaha

Yamaha YSR 50

Figure K16 - Red & White Yamaha YSR 50 Brochure Cover. ©Yamaha Motor Corporation, U.S.A.

The YSR 50 was produced from 1987 through 1992. Although the model was street legal, its most popular use was as a pit bike and as a racer in its own class on small, go-kart-type tracks. The YSR was a miniature bullet bike with a 50cc two-stroke engine and a top speed of about 55 mph, although some models were limited to 37 mph at the factory. The YSR weighed 165 pounds soaking wet. It rolled on fat, high-performance rubber mounted on twelve-inch wheels. The frame and chassis were as sophisticated as those of its bigger brothers. An aluminum perimeter frame enclosed a Monocross rear suspension. The YSR had a full race fairing and front disc brake, too. It was a serious little racer!

The largest current pocketbikes built in China are just now catching up to the sophistication and performance level of the YSR models from twenty-five years ago. These latest models are about 58 inches long, and 35 inches high. They weigh 140-150 pounds and produce up to 15.5 (probably exaggerated) horsepower with 110cc, Honda-derived, four-stroke, single-cylinder engines. Although the power and technology of the powerplant of these most recent models may be beyond that of the 50cc reed valve in the YSR, few if any of these machines from China are street legal. Like its big brother the Yamaha 650 twin, the YSR 50 well deserves its cult status.

Like its role model, Eddie Lawson's factory YSR500 racer, our YSR50 comes with a full fairing, tail cowl and square frame top rails.

The YSR50 has good lighting equipment. There's also a centrally-mounted speedometer that's back-lighted for easy nighttime reading.

A 49.3cc reed-valve two-stroke engine uses Yamaha's exclusive Energy Induction System for better low- and mid-range torque. Ignition is by maintenance-free Capacitor Discharge.

Front suspension is handled by a set of telescopic forks. Pressed-steel "disc" wheels are painted to match the body color.

Up front the YSR50 uses a single hydraulic disc brake. At the rear is a mechanical drum.

The frame on our smallest high-performance street bike looks a lot like that of our largest high-performance street bike. Being of a rugged, yet lightweight rectangular steel design.

An aircraft-type fuel cap is used, along with a 2.11 gallon tank.

The new YSR50 utilizes a close-ratio 5-speed transmission.

Our YSR50 delivers a smooth stable ride. Thanks to a Monocross suspension utilizing a box-section swingarm.

Even though the engine is relatively simple in design, the exhaust system isn't. Our "multi-expansion tuned exhaust with silencer" is both efficient and very quiet.

The tires on the YSR50 are like the rest of the bike: small yet very efficient. The front tire is a 3.50×12 and the rear measures 4.00×12.

YAMAHA
We make the difference.

LIT # 15119-64-0
Printed in Japan

Figure K17 - Excerpt from the Yamaha YSR 50 Brochure. The title of this page was *Look What We Have Been Reduced To.* ©Yamaha Motor Corporation, U.S.A.

Figure K18 - 1989 Blue & White Yamaha YSR 50.

©Michael Kiernan, Classic Motorcycle Company, St. Louis, MO.

1984-86 Yamaha RZ 350

Figure K19 - Red & White Yamaha RZ350 Brochure Page. ©Yamaha Motor Corporation, U.S.A.

After the big *gas crisis* of 1973-74, America became a different nation, at least for a while. Motorized high performance was slowly strangled and squashed almost completely out of existence in the U.S. by The Big Trifecta. Cars would face off with Corporate Average Fuel Economy ratings, emissions limitations demanded by the Environmental Protection Agency, and of course the auto safety movement that had been initially launched by Ralph Nader's 1965 book, *Unsafe at Any Speed*. Motorcycles dodged the bullet that splattered into the grilles on most cars, but there were still a number of changes that would eventually be mandated for bikes, especially the street models. All headlights would be permanently locked into the ON position and the battery would be required to power parking lights for a minimum length of time in case of a breakdown. Kill switches would arrive on handlebars. Exhaust and intake systems would be muffled, and oh, yeah, get those noisy, stinky, smoky, oily, gas-hog two-strokes off the streets of America!

By 1977, Yamaha, Suzuki, and Kawasaki had completely joined Honda in the production of overhead cam street models for the U.S. market. Honda expanded its four-stroke engines into lawnmowers and outboard motors. Kawasaki launched the Jet Ski revolution and Suzuki eased into America's small car market. You may not be aware that a relatively short-lived personal watercraft brand named Tiger Shark utilized Suzuki two-stroke engines. Yamaha changed the course of the Jet Ski Revolution in 1987 when it introduced the lazy man's small boat with handlebars, the WaveRunner. Honda finally entered the personal watercraft market in 2002 with four-stroke sit-down jet skis. In an almost identical pattern to what they had done to two-stroke street bikes in the Seventies, the EPA Nazis turned their political power upon jet skis in the 2000's. As any motorcycle nut knows, the companies should not have been surprised by this action or unprepared for it, either. Instead of putting their large motocross and enduro two-stroke powerplants into their watercraft, all they had to do was begin installing their large OHC engines instead. The weight, price, and complication would increase. but we would all survive.

Figure K20 - 1985 Yamaha RZ3550 Kenny Roberts Special.

Image by Mark Romanoff, owner and photographer, under Creative Commons license (GNU).

As we all know, the core of Yamaha's motorized reputation began with the YDS-1. The company has truly mastered the world of high-performance two-stroke technology and development. Kawasaki may have added a center cylinder and Suzuki added water cooling, but the genuine innovators worked at Yamaha. The company has probably done more to advance the development of rotary valves, oil injection, reed valves, and monshocks than any other. Hondas were as reliable as hair dryers, Suzukis were stylish, and Kawasakis were fast in a straight line. Yamaha produced the best handling Japanese motorcycles. During certain periods, Yamaha absolutely dominated racing with their rapid two-strokes. A new name became synonymous with winning on a yellow and black two-stroke racing machine, whether on tarmac or dirt. Kenny Roberts was the Tiger Woods or Lance Armstrong of his racing era, but without the scandals or disgrace.

The EPA had not actually *banned* two-stroke street machines. They had just made it harder to qualify the emissions restrictions of a company's entire product line. Yamaha could not resist having one last fling. They took everything their engineers had developed over the decades and stuffed it into a YDS finale. The RZ350 was of course the final development, at least for the U.S. market, of the company's highly successful RD 350. It was the first street Yamaha to utilize a perimeter frame and the only one of the entire long-running YDS/RD lineage to have a fairing. The 347cc twin had Yamaha's YPVS (Yamaha Power Valve System), Monoshock rear suspension, Autolube oil injection, CDI ignition, liquid cooling, six-speed transmission, and three disc brakes. The claimed dry weight of 331 pounds rolled on eighteen-inch wheels with seriously selected rubber. Never mind the gas mileage: the tank held 5.3 gallons. The front brake discs were slotted and the front suspension was air assisted. The turn signals made it legal, but you had to kick it yourself. The RZ350 was the first motorcycle with catalytic converters. California models had three of the things!

The RZ350 is of course a cult survivor like its ancestors the XS-1 and RD 350. It is one of those magical machines that will always have a fan base. That makes it collectible and possibly pricey, but it also ensures that parts, service, and a fan club will always be there for support. The RZ350 has always been a big hit on the amateur racing circuits. You just cannot coax this much power and handling out of a heavier, more ponderous DOHC engine. There were two color choices in each of its three production years, with minor changes differentiating the models. A red and white or red, white and blue color scheme was offered in each year, but the RZ350 will probably remain most memorable in its Kenny Roberts Special Competition colors of yellow with black trim. Call it a *Road Zinger of 350 Bumblebees.*

Figure K21 - Yamaha RZ350 Kenny Roberts Special Brochure Page. ©Yamaha Motor Corporation, U.S.A.

Yamaha XV-250 Cruisers

Figure K22 - Beige 1988 Yamaha Route 66. ©1988 Yamaha Motor Corporation, U.S.A.

Yamaha introduced a competitor to Honda's Rebel in 1988, going one better with an actual V-twin engine of modest dimensions. Styled and positioned in the marketplace as a direct complement to the Rebel 250, Yamaha's Route 66 was an especially clever machine. Only Honda knows why the company kept jerking its Rebel off the market for some years and then returning it little changed a few years later. Coincidentally or not, you can see from the chart above that the Rebel was removed from the U.S. marketplace from 1988 through 1995 and Yamaha slipped the Route 66 right into the Rebel's previous parking space.

Weighing in at 302 pounds dry, with the unmistakable look of a little Sportster chopper, the first-year Route 66 was offered in Melting Black or Splendid Beige. The beige was replaced by Luminous Red in 1989 and Ivory was added to the choices in 1990, the last year of the Route 66. In typical fashion, the Route 66 was priced a few hundred above that of the far more common Rebel. All models used a 249cc SOHC V-twin, five-speed transmission, disc front brake, Ceriani-type front forks, solo seat with passenger pillion, and spoke wheels, 18-inch front and 15-inch rear. The XV-250 would continue in production for other markets in 1991-93, but there were only three model years produced of the Route 66 for the American market.

In 1994 Yamaha brought the Route 66 back with a new name, 250 Virago. The XV-250 picked up right where it had left off in 1990, only with a new name. The little V-twin would continue in production with its larger Virago brothers through 2007, commonly in colors such as red, maroon, and black. Yamaha would rename the little machine again in 2008 as part of the Royal Star family of Yamaha cruisers. The 250 V-Star continues in 2013 in Deep Blue for $4290. Its measured wet weight of 326 pounds has changed negligibly since 1988. It still features laced wheels of the same sizes, dual rear shocks, five speeds, and an air-cooled SOHC V-twin. It still uses transistor ignition and a single 26mm Mikuni carb. The sticker price has inched upward from approximately $3000 twenty-five years ago, but the kids of today can still experience the thrill of riding a real motorcycle that is essentially a 1988 Route 66.

There is a particular poignancy to the Honda Rebel 250 and the Yamaha XV-250 models in that the two Japanese giants finally began to market modern soul mates of the Harley-Davidson ST 165, Super 10, and Pacer from decades earlier. Of course technically these old and new series of machines have absolutely nothing in common, but stylistically from a marketing viewpoint they are the same. In typical fashion for Harley-Davidson, everything was optional at extra cost on the little Harley two-strokes. This gambit guaranteed that few identical examples would be produced. It also means that most examples were plain-Jane Hummer replicas with low handlebars and solo seats. However, some of these primitive two-stroke putts-putts were turned into little factory choppers with Buckhorn handlebars and Buddy Seats or passenger pillions. You could also add chrome doodads and leather saddlebags to complete the look. Harley tried to compete with the Japanese tiddlers with its Aermacchi Italian models in the '60's and '70's. Now The Tiddler Invasion has come full circle yet again with the Japanese brands building tiddlers that look like little Harley choppers.

Figure K23 - Purple 2009 Yamaha 250 Star. ©2009 Yamaha Motor Corporation, U.S.A.

Selected Post-1975 Models Ratings Chart

Years	Models	Collectibility	Practicality	Desirability
1995-2004	Aprilia RS 50	A	D	A
1992-2012	Aprilia RS 125	A	D	A
1993	Aprilia Scarabeo	C	C	B
1990	Honda NS50F	B	C	C
1997-1998	Honda Dream 50	A	D	A
2004	Honda Dream 50R	A	D	A
1985-2013	Honda Rebel 250	D	A	D
1988-1990	Honda VTR-250	C	B	C
2011-2013	Honda CBR250R	C	A	C
2006-2009	Kawasaki 125 Eliminator	D	B	C
1986-2013	Kawasaki 250 Ninja	D	A	C
1987-1992	Yamaha YSR 50	B	C	A
1984-1986	Yamaha RZ 350	A	C	A
1988-1990	Yamaha Route 66	B	B	B
1994-2013	Yamaha XV-250	C	A	C

Models Ratings Chart Definitions:

Years: These are the total production years for a particular model series. Some early model years within a series may be considerably more desirable than later years.

Models: In some cases many variations are included in this category and in others the models included are very homogeneous.

Collectibility: This is what most of you want to know, the bottom line on how likely the model or series is likely to climb in value over the coming years.

Practicality: This is an indicator of how adaptable the machine can be to ride for transportation or pleasure in the modern world, considering parts availability, fuel quality, comfort, performance and miscellaneous other obvious factors.

Desirability: This defines the nostalgic, emotional wow factor, without regard for collector values or everyday usage.

General: No machine is given a failing grade. If it made it into a rating chart, at least a few hobbyists find that model interesting.

Chinese Brands

The Cheap Chinese Scooter Phenomenon

Quite a bit has changed since I first published this article on *Blogger News Network* in August 2008. Nearly all the links included in that original article are now invalid, mostly because so many of the online Chinese scooter dealers have since gone out of business. Can you say *fly by night*? The proliferation of $4 gasoline had brought renewed interest in economical two-wheeled transportation, particularly the latest styles of motor scooters from Japan and China. The Internet and the manufacturing boom in China were, and are, playing key roles in this new market, offering a wide variety of machines in the $1000-$1700 price bracket. In 2013, let's up that to the $1500-$2500 bracket. Decreasing competition among the retailers combined with the move to higher levels of product has moved even these bottom-feeders *up market*. All the two-stroke engines are long gone. Even the pitiful little 50cc scooters now have OHV engines, and of course they are pokey. At the other end of the scale, the Chinese brands have moved ever further into the motorcycle market and developed 250cc and even 300cc scooters. Just a few years ago, the Chinese motorcycles were mostly 50's with a smattering of 150-200cc models. Now nearly all of their motorcycles are 250cc and above.

Small motorcycles and scooters have fascinated me since the 1950's. I followed the evolution of the Cushman Eagle, the Whizzer, the Simplex, and the Mustang (yes, Maybelle, there was a line of small motorcycles built in the U.S. under the Mustang brand name in the '50's and early '60's). Many Americans ordered their small two-wheelers from the Sears & Roebuck catalog back then. Although these models were all marketed under the Allstate or Sears brands, most motorcyclists from the era know these were manufactured by Cushman, Puch, Vespa, and Gilera. Scooter fans of the time generally rode Vespas and Lambrettas, both built in Italy. Even my cat Powduh Puff knows that once we met the nicest people on a Honda at the end of 1959, everything about the motorcycle world changed forever.

You can still buy a Vespa motor scooter that will cost you as much as a Honda Rebel, go a lot slower and provide less driving entertainment, as well as less safety. Would you prefer to hit a pothole with a twelve-inch front wheel or an eighteen-inch one? Would you rather have the bulk of your transportation's weight distribution directly underneath you or hanging out back with your caboose? Yes, Maybelle, that $329 Allstate Cruisaire from Sears is now pretty much the same as that $3500 Vespa 125 from the snooty-environmentalist scooter dealership next to the Starbuck's down on the campus drag. You can still meet the nicest people on a Honda. Now it's a $3000, 250cc Rebel twin instead of a $300, 50cc Cub with 4.5 horsepower and the cutest little legshields you've ever seen.

There is another alternative, folks, and its source is a company called Lifan, and it has a lot more in common with Honda than just an Asian heritage with five letters in the name. If you saw Ted Koppel's four-part story on China recently, you learned about Lifan. The company builds several small engines, one of which has been used in so many different scooters and go-karts from China that you will swear it's the second coming of the Honda 50, which in a bizarre way, it is. One of the Lifan designs is a direct copy of the legendary, small Honda single. The Chinese version is 110cc and you can find it powering vehicles all over the Internet. The second common Lifan design is a 150cc single that is even more common than the 110cc model. The plot thickens immeasurably when you discover that not only do the Chinese copy everyone else, but they copy their own Chinese competitors' designs like crazy! There are countless affordable scooters built in China and sold on the American Internet. I hope to untangle some of the confusion and educate you exactly as to what sort of gas-sipping transportation is available to any American with a credit card and an online connection right now. Although Lifan is the market leader in more ways than one, there are numerous other brands.

Before we get to the actual models available, you need to understand a few basic marketing concepts. When Honda first approached its future dealers in 1959, it shocked the handlebars off them with the future sales figures the company was proposing and predicting. Spreading eastward from the ubiquitous loading docks of L.A., Honda developed an enormous dealer network. Yamaha and Suzuki were left standing on the docks saying, "Me too, me too." Lifan and the other Chinese brands seem to have little interest in developing dealer networks. The World Wide Web is the leading Lifan dealership. This means little customer service, of course. I'm sure many of you will immediately think anyone who buys a cheap Chinese scooter online gets what he deserves. There is more than a grain of truth to this concept, of course. The more experienced you are with motorcycles and marketing, the more likely you are to have a good experience with this manner of doing business. Then there's that $3000+ Italian scooter. The Vespa is only the most legendary. The Aprilia Scarabeo is one gorgeous hunk of scooter with brilliant engineering and a Ducati price! Kymco is a Taiwanese brand that sells through both established dealers and online, and even their prices will choke a small moped. There is no doubt at all that the online marketing is a key element in the price competitiveness of Lifan and other Chinese brands.

Although there may seem to be literally hundreds of different brands, models, and model names of Chinese scooters, they actually boil down to only about six different types. The lowest and slowest are the 50cc models. In previous years, most of these used two-stroke engines; now they are mostly four-stroke. At the opposite end of the price and power scale are the 250cc models. These mostly compete with the Honda Rebel in price and the ability to drive legally on freeways; whereas the 50cc models might need to be duck-walked up a steep hill. In between these two extremes lie the most commonly usable scooters for transportation, the 150's using either the Lifan engine or a direct copy of it. I have seen horsepower ratings ranging from 7 to 9.8 hp for these models, and some websites even claim that many of these are actually 125cc engines masquerading as 150's. Whatever the case, these scooters are plenty strong enough to climb hills, carry two people, and scramble out of the way of marauding Honda Cubs. For the sake of simplicity here, I am lumping all 50's and 250's into one group each, but I am separating out the 150's into four types. The reason for this is that you can imagine that most of the 50cc models are just slower, cheaper versions of many of the same 125/150cc versions. Most of the 250cc types are outfitted to look like giant turtles with huge seats, windshields, and storage capacity bordering on excessive. For many practical reasons, only the 150's come in a large variety of styling types, although the usages of all types are more determined by their engine displacements than by their styling cues.

Before I proceed any further, I want to insert a disclaimer. Although I have been having a kitten for one of these 150cc jewels for years, I don't want to give up any more garage space or one of my classic Japanese motorcycles, either. Take this story however you want. Not only have I never ridden one of these Chinese scooters, I haven't been on any scooter since I replaced my 1957 Allstate Cruisaire with a 1963 Yamaha Rotary Jet 80! If you want to throw out this whole story with the saltshaker, I ask only that you think before you close your mind to the idea. I do know a few things about pooter-scooters.

Beginning right smack in the middle, we have the 150cc Chinese scooter with modern styling. It is distinguished by its 13-inch wheels, sleek and stylish lines and graphics, speedometer/tachometer/fuel gauge instrument panel, up-front glove box, under-seat helmet storage, and a luggage rack of some sort that may or may not include a matching storage box in the price. If not, the matching box is usually an option. Some of the more deluxe models have a rear disc brake, but most have a drum brake in the rear with a disc only in the front. At a price of $1400-$1700 to your driveway, this is the ringleader of the pack for your cost-effective transportation needs. If you study the websites closely, you will see that there is a virtual multitude of these critters scattered all over the net. Although they are sold with many different brand and model names, and enough color and graphics choices to boggle the mind of an Internet neophyte, they are all basically the same scooter with the exact same engine.

The second type of 150cc scooter is styled to look pretty much like a 1957 Cruisaire, but its features and attributes are much the same as the model with more modern styling. For about the same price as the modern variant, this model usually trades the tach and storage capacities for the retro styling, and its wheels are usually 12″ in diameter. Most of these have drum rear brakes, although there could be a few models with discs in the rear.

The third variety of the 150cc models is a fully adult sized and equipped model with a gigantic seat and a windshield. As you may have already guessed, this is one of those models commonly sold as a 250cc version, too, for a $1000 (more or less) premium added to the price of the 150cc variant. Of course you get the privilege of buzzing down I-95 with the eighteen-wheelers for that price premium. I'm sure having one of those monsters buffet your big windshield as it passes is a barrel of monkeys. The 150cc, all-but-the-freeway legal models lack the 13″ wheels, tachometer, and wild graphics of the sportier 150cc variant described above, but otherwise are the steal of the bunch for two-wheeled transportation comfort. I can only guess that their 12-inch wheels and drum rear brakes are the result of strict cost-cutting. These models are generally priced only about $200 more than the sporty, thirteen-inch-wheeled versions with exactly the same 150cc engine. Not only does Powduh Puff know which version is obviously faster, he also knows which type is more comfortable. You whips out your credit card and you makes your choice.

The last scooter type is the one that makes my Tiddlerosis heart go pitty-pat, pitty-pat. It is a somewhat skinnier model with 16-inch wheels, legshields that are not as wide as a circus fat lady, and that sweet little 110cc copycat engine. The only catch is that the online retailers charge as much for this one as they do for the big cruiser described above. I guess they know the beauty of selling a Honda clone. This design is currently far less available than all the other scooter types described in this article, but access to it is slowly increasing. The bigger wheels are the key. You don't have to fear potholes with quite the same level of trepidation and the overall handling is better balanced. These models usually include a tachometer, but the design of the whole instrument cluster is a bit less perfect than that of either the large cruiser or the modern sporty type. The graphics packages and color choices leave a little to be desired, too. Blatantly inspired by the Honda Cub, the Aprilia Scarabeo, and the Kymco People, with the first extinct and the latter two overpriced, this little sweetheart is somewhat irresistible. I hope this model proliferates and improves in the future.

I should give an honorable mention to yet another variant that tries to split the difference between the sporty type and the cruiser type. This model is usually referred to as having *European styling*. It has a windshield a little smaller than that of the standard cruiser and the 13-inch wheels of the sportster. The seat is between the sizes of these two types, and it usually has more downward slope toward the front edge. I am not a fan of this type simply because the windshield and instrument panel do not turn with the handlebars. To a decades-old fan of the sort of two-wheelers that would not embarrass Peter Fonda or Steve McQueen, this effect is quite disconcerting to me. The eerie feeling of sliding off the front end of the seat and not being sure exactly which way my front wheel is pointing gives me the cooties. If this design happens to start your motor, you will find it somewhat less common, like the Honda 50 clone, and priced about the same as that model, as well as the even larger cruiser. Other than the disconcerting elements, the reason I give this model only an honorable mention is that if I wanted a sporty model, I would go completely in that direction, but if I wanted a cruiser, I would go in the opposite direction. This European type seems to be a somewhat silly compromise, being neither the fastest nor the most practical.

You may have noticed that I have not included any actual, specific model names or brands in this article. Nor have I included any plugs for the horde of online retailers of cheap Chinese scooters. Like the Chinese operations in other fields of marketing, the brand names, rules, and reputations seem to change daily with their underwear. There is no substitute for thoughtful research before you decide to make a purchase. I do want to mention Northern Tool, a respected American catalog company that carries at least a few of these low-priced scooters. The main operation and warehouse of Lifan is located in Dallas, Texas. A typical competitor of Lifan is Tank, and the crazy part is that I cannot even tell you if Tank is in any way related to Lifan or not. Such is the mysterious world of cheap Chinese scooters. The Kymco USA site will show you their whole lineup, if you don't mind whipping your credit card a little harder. Feast your eyes on the Aprilia Scarabeo, made in the same country that produces Ferraris. Scooter Depot displays many of the models discussed in this article, but I cannot speak for their reputation. I could list many more dealers with nearly identical models, similar prices, and unknown reputations, but this article is long enough already. Go out there and save some gas!

Cheap Chinese 150cc Scooter Chart

Model	Size	Wheels	Tach	Wind-screen	Wt.	Rear Brake	Price
Economy	Small	13-inch	Yes	No	265	Drum	$907
Economy	Small	13-inch	Yes	No	235	Drum	$907
Economy +	Medium	13-inch	No	No	255	Drum	$1007
Ruckus	Small	10-inch	No	No	224	Drum	$1007
Eagle GY6	Medium	13-inch	Yes	No	265	Drum	$1007
Classic	Medium	10-inch	No	No	214	Drum	$1107
Sunny	Medium	10-inch	No	No	256	Drum	$1107
Sports 9.6	Medium	13-inch	Yes	No	305	Drum	$1207
Big Ruckus	Large	13-inch	No	No	295	Disc	$1894
Big Wheel	Medium	16-inch	Yes	No	265	Disc	$1407
Phoenix 9.6	Medium	16-inch	Yes	No	282	Disc	$1777
BMS 200	Medium	16-inch	Yes	No	271	Disc	$1449
Sports Touring	Large	13-inch	Yes	Yes	305	Disc	$1627
Touring	Large	12-inch	No	Yes	298	Disc	$1417

Cheap Chinese Scooter Notes: All models have the same 150cc OHV engine and CVT automatic transmission with eight horsepower and electric starter. The basic model categories in the chart apply to scooters sold by many different U.S. dealers under a variety of brand names, but they all boil down to these same models. There are many paint, trim, and decal variations and the brand names mean very little. The prices listed are for general comparison purposes only, since some online dealers advertise a low price and then tack on a hefty shipping charge. All prices quoted include shipping and are currently from Scooter Depot. The Touring model has an ammeter and fuel gauge. The claimed top speed for nearly all the models is 55 or 60 mph. One disappointing issue with some models is that the speedometer numbers in kilometers are large with smaller mph markings. The Sports & Phoenix 9.6 models claim to have 9.6 hp and a top speed of 65 mph. All models have steel tube frames, front disc brakes, and standard front and rear suspension. The BMS 200 is a 200cc scooter with 11 hp. The price of this model is from GoKartsUSA. Rokeeta and Lifan seem to be the closest thing to a reliable *brand*. All claimed dry weights are listed in pounds.

Cheap Chinese Motorcycle Chart

Model	Size	HP	Gears	Wheels	Wt.	Rear S.	Price
Ninja	250	18.8	5	17-inch	304	Mono	$2247
Naked	250	18.8	5	17-inch	304	Mono	$2497
Bobber	250	17	5	21/18	329	None	$2397
Katana	250	15.8	5	16/15	243	Mono	$1849
Cruiser	250	13	5	18/15	295	Dual	$2397
Enduro	250	11.5	5	21/18	266	Mono	$2098
Lifan	200	NA	5	18-inch	284	Mono	$1574
Ninja	150	9.4	CVT	17-inch	231	Dual	$1897
Metro	110	6	4	17-inch	180	Dual	$1595

Cheap Chinese Motorcycle Notes: All models have OHV Single engines, disc front brakes, telescopic front suspension, and electric starters. All claimed dry weights are listed in pounds. The Enduro has a drum rear brake; all the remaining models have disc rear brakes. The Katana (called Khaos by Extreme Scooters) is a 250 Twin with a drum rear brake. The ES price for the Ninja 150 is $1699. The Metro is a copy of what was essentially the last Honda step-through sold in the USA. Other than the brand name and country of origin, there are few significant differences from the last Honda 110. The automatic clutch, legshields, drum brakes, and leading link front suspension will take you back to the C-102. Close your eyes and dream....

Motorsickle Movie Monkeybusiness

The Wild One (1953) – Brando rode his own T-bird and the rest of his gang rode Triumphs. Lee Marvin's gang all rode Harleys. Although Marvin had to learn to ride for the part, he later got involved in desert racing with a Triumph Cub.

Bye Bye Birdie (1963) - Rock star Birdie sure does like to ride his big English bike through stuff!

The Great Escape (1963) – A large German bike that is actually a disguised Triumph TR6 Trophy turns into a motocrosser or enduro for the big jump. IMDB says a '62 T-bird actually made the jump, but that cannot be right! A Thunderbird is even klunkier than a Trophy!

Viva Las Vegas (1964) - Watch Elvis and Ann-Margret stand up on the seats of a Honda Sport 50 and a Honda Cub!

Roustabout (1964) - Elvis rides a Super Hawk with Scrambler handlebars and his guitar strapped to an unusual luggage rack. A bonus is that you get to watch a stunt rider and Elvis (another stunt rider?) circle the "Wall of Death" on a Harley-Davidson Scat.

How to Stuff a Wild Bikini (1965) - If you want to see more Yamaha Big Bear Scramblers than you have ever seen in your life, buy or rent the 1965 beach movie, *How to Stuff a Wild Bikini*. The grand finale of the movie is a cross-country motorcycle race featuring the entire herd of surfer bums and their beach bunnies. The funny part is that every last one of them is riding a 1965 Yamaha Big Bear Scrambler! What a case of Tiddlerosis!

The Wild Angels (1966) - Yes, I know on the surface it looks like just another youth market exploitation flick, but read the credits. This movie was so obviously the progenitor to both *The Trip* and *Easy Rider*. Directed by Roger Corman and starring Peter Fonda, Bruce Dern, Diane Ladd, Nancy Sinatra, and Michael J. Pollard, the movie was low-budget, but at least a little thought had gone into the development of its plot and style. Unlike the raked out Captain America machine of 1969, Fonda's mount in *The Wild Angels* is both stylish and rideable. The $360,000 budget brought in $6.5 million, a hefty sum in 1966. Thirty million posters were eventually sold worldwide, mostly black-and-white blowups of Fonda sitting on his elegant springer chopper.

Coogan's Bluff (1968) - This cop show has a good motorcycle chase with Clint Eastwood on a Triumph Bonneville pursuing a nameless villain on a Triumph Trophy. You can tell Clint has the faster machine because his has a tachometer.

Easy Rider (1969) - We have all certainly memorized the movie by now, so here are a few tidbits as described by Captain America himself in his autobiography, *Don't Tell Dad*. Hold onto your chain guard because some of these shocked even me! Most of the traveling was actually done on those radical choppers. They were not hauled from location to location on a trailer. Dennis Hopper was a tyrannical director and later voted for Dan Quayle as a Republican! Peter has always been as far out on the left wing as his famous father and sister. They really were smoking weed in the movie, particularly the scene by the campfire that made Jack Nicholson very famous. They did not shoot the movie in chronological or geographical order. The movie crew had to hightail it to New Orleans to catch Mardi Gras in February 1968, so that was shot first. They were supposed to shoot in a real commune in Taos NM, but the locals attacked and destroyed it before the shoot, so they built a fake one outside Los Angeles. There were numerous scenes actually shot in Taos and other parts of Arizona and New Mexico, though. Not a bit of the movie was shot in Texas because Fonda and Hopper were paranoid about the state after the JFK assassination. Although the riders were supposedly traveling east of New Orleans after the scenes there, they were actually "shot" near Krotz Springs LA *west* of Baton Rouge. Krotz Springs is very close to Morganza, where the boys had supposedly been harassed by the locals, who also murdered Nicholson's character, *before* they went to New Orleans. The most fascinating part of the entire background story is that the guys who harassed them at the restaurant *and* the guys who murder them in the climax were not actors, but actual local residents of Morganza and Krotz Springs. Some of the disparaging lines spoken by the locals in the restaurant did not originate from a script. These were things actually said by the local restaurant customers when Fonda, Hopper, and Nicholson first walked into the place, in costume but ahead of the film crew!

Little Fauss and Big Halsey (1970) - This is easily the best movie featuring Yamaha motocrossers and the type of amateur racing circuit that was prevalent during the period. Robert Redford rides a red 1970 DT-1C MX 250 and Michael J. Pollard tries to keep up on a white 1969 AT-1 MX 125 throughout the movie. Added bonuses are that the plot and characters are well scripted and Revlon cosmetics model Lauren Hutton makes her debut in the buff.

On Any Sunday (1971) - Malcolm Smith steals the show in this Bruce Brown documentary about motorcycle racing of many varieties. Classic Hondas, Yamahas, Suzukis, and Hodakas are featured, along with a few European brands.

Freebie and the Bean (1974) - This little-known classic buddy comedy was the progenitor of more modern flicks such as *Lethal Weapon*, *Beverly Hills Cop*, and *Bad Boys*. There are many classic cop-car stunts in the movie, but it is James Caan's commandeering of a hapless rider's Montesa Cota trials bike and subsequent chase through San Francisco that motorsickle fans will enjoy.

Rollerball (1975) - Few seem to know exactly what type or brand of motorcycles are hidden underneath the space-cadet armor on the machines shown in this movie, but few seem to really care, either. The bikes travel around on a circular board track designed for roller derby. From the sounds, they are apparently four-strokes, but who knows if the sound was not dubbed over a bunch of yipping two strokes to make them sound sexier?

Figure K24 (previous page) - Red 1964 Honda Super Hawk from *Roustabout*. Image by Midnight Bird, photographer, under Creative Commons license.

Figure K25 (next page) - Captain America Harley-Davidson Chopper Replica, as Featured in *Easy Rider*, by Courtesy of Deutsches Zweirad and NSU Museum. Image by Joachim Kohler, photographer under Creative Commons license (GNU).

The Tiddler Trivia Test

1. This brand was originally imported into the U.S. under the Omega moniker.
(a) Tohatsu (b) Yamaguchi (c) Yamaha (d) Honda (e) Suzuki (f) Kawasaki

2. What did the early Honda 350's have that the later models did not?
(a) Racier cam grind (b) Electric starter (c) Pleated seat (d) Constant velocity carbs

3. What was the model at the top of the Mustang lineup?
(a) Thoroughbred (b) Palomino (c) Stallion (d) Black Lightning

4. The Runpet Sport was made by:
(a) Pointer (b) Yamaguchi (c) Yamaha (d) Tohatsu (e) Rabbit (f) Suzuki

5. Which brand could be identified by its flat-bottomed headlamps back in The Sixties?
(a) Yamaguchi (b) Tohatsu (c) Rabbit (d) Yamaha (e) Marusho (f) Suzuki

6. What Japanese brand produced the first transverse, horizontally-opposed twin-cylinder?
(a) Honda (b) Yamaha (c) Suzuki (d) Tohatsu (e) Marusho (f) Kawasaki

7. Which model was influenced by the products of a U.S. boat builder?
(a) Cushman Jetsweep (b) Mustang Pony (c) H-D Topper (d) Cushman Eagle

8. Which brand had electric starters on all models except the bottom of the lineup?
(a) Pointer (b) Yamaguchi (c) Honda (d) Tohatsu (e) Hodaka (f) Suzuki

9. What was the first brand name to drop out of the U.S. market?
(a) Hodaka (b) Yamaguchi (c) Omega (d) Marusho (e) Rabbit (f) Tohatsu

10. When did Ducati first market its Desmo models in the USA?
(a) 1965 (b) 1966 (c) 1967 (d) 1968 (e) 1969 (f) 1970

11. Which brand has never sold outboard motors in the U.S.?
(a) Yamaha (b) Honda (c) Tohatsu (d) Yamaguchi (e) Suzuki

12. Which brand built the engines for the Tiger Shark personal watercraft?
(a) Honda (b) Yamaha (c) Kawasaki (d) Suzuki (e) Tohatsu

13. Which company owns the name Jet Ski?
(a) Yamaha (b) Kawasaki (c) Suzuki (d) Honda (e) Bridgestone

14. Which company built only dirt bikes to be imported into the U.S.?
(a) Hodaka (b) Yamaguchi (c) Tohatsu (d) Bridgestone (e) Pointer

15. Which brand sells golf carts in the U.S.?
(a) Honda (b) Suzuki (c) Yamaha (d) Kawasaki (e) Marusho

16. What is probably the rarest of the Allstate models sold by Sears?
(a) Scrambler (b) 125 (c) 175 (d) Sport 60 (e) Sabre (f) SR 125

17. Which company marketed a 600cc convertible in the U.S. in 1965?
(a) Yamaha (b) Suzuki (c) Kawasaki (d) Bridgestone (e) Honda

18. Which brand used the foot shift lever as the kick starter?
(a) Mustang (b) Rex (c) Jawa (d) Montesa (e) Ossa (f) NSU (g) Zundapp

19. Which brand first sold a model in the U.S. with an automatic transmission?
(a) Yamaguchi (b) Honda (c) Rabbit (d) Yamaha (e) Marusho

20. The Simplex brand was built in what city?
(a) Cincinnati (b) Detroit (c) Houston (d) Los Angeles (e) New Orleans

21. Which company painted practically all of its early models red, black, white, or blue?
(a) Honda (b) Yamaha (c) Bultaco (d) Pointer (e) Tohatsu (f) Montesa

22. Which of these was never a European scooter built in the Sixties?
(a) Bultaco El Toreador (b) Triumph Tina (c) Motobi Scooterino (d) Zundapp Bella

23. Which brand first offered a water-cooled street model in the U.S.?
(a) Yamaha (b) Kawasaki (c) Marusho (d) Rabbit (e) Suzuki

24. What was the first Japanese street scrambler?
(a) Big Bear (b) CL-72 (c) Trail Breaker (d) Trailmaster (e) YDS-3C

25. Which of these does not describe the NSU Max and Maxi models?
(a) single downtube frame (b) standard solo seat (c) four-stroke single (d) four-speed foot shift

26. What did the Bridgestone GTR have that was unusual for the time?
(a) tachometer (b) halogen headlamp (c) chrome bores (d) oil pressure gauge

27. What was special about the Sport 65 as a new Honda tiddler?
(a) OHC engine (b) tachometer (c) upswept exhaust (d) no electric starter

28. The Hodaka brand was created from what early Japanese import brand?
(a) Tohatsu (b) Pointer (c) Yamaha (d) Yamaguchi (e) Suzuki (f) Rabbit

29. What was special about the new 1963 Yamaha 80cc YG-1?
(a) turn signals (b) monocoque frame (c) rotary induction (d) top speed

30. What brand has always been designed and sized for Americans?
(a) Honda (b) Yamaha (c) Suzuki (d) Kawasaki (e) Montesa

31. Which extinct brand can claim the same thing?
(a) Yamaguchi (b) Hodaka (c) Tohatsu (d) Pointer (e) Rabbit

32. What was the final year of the Triumph Tiger Cub?
(a) 1966 (b) 1967 (c) 1968 (d) 1969 (e) 1970 (f) 1971

33. Which Honda model had a black frame in early ads and brochures, but the production
version used a silver frame?
(a) SL-90 (b) XL-175 (c) SL-350 (d) XL-250

34. What is the earliest machine in this book with oil injection?
(a) Allstate 175 (b) Suzuki X-6 (c) Bridgestone 7 (d) Yamaha YG-1

35. Which company has never sold anything in the U.S. except motorcycles?
(a) Rabbit (b) Pointer (c) Tohatsu (d) Bridgestone (e) Suzuki

36. Which of these was not a Harley-Davidson model?
(a) Ranger (b) Sprite (c) Pacer (d) Scat

37. Which brand was also marketed as the Lilac?
(a) Marusho (b) Yamaguchi (c) Bridgestone (d) Tohatsu (e) Omega (f) Hodaka

38. The Harley-Davidson Topper used what type engine?
(a) 125cc two-stroke (b) 125cc four-stroke (c) 175cc two-stroke (d) 165cc two-stroke

39. How many gears (speeds) did the Cushman Eagle have?
(a) One (b) Two (c) Three (d) Four

40. What model sported a storage trunk?
(a) Marusho 500 (b) Pointer Lassie (c) Bridgestone 90 (d) Rabbit Superflow

41. The Harley-Davidson Hummer was based on a design by what brand?
(a) Triumph (b) Simplex (c) Ducati (d) DKW (e) BSA (f) BMW

42. What company built the Servi-Cycle?
(a) Simplex (b) Mustang (c) Harley-Davidson (d) Cushman

43. What company built the Highlander?
(a) Mustang (b) Cushman (c) Simplex (d) Harley-Davidson

44. What did the 1964 Yamaha YG-1 have that would change the world of motorcycling?
(a) self-canceling turn signals (b) oil injection (c) monocoque frame (d) rotary shift

45. The Harley-Davidson Super 10 was built only in what years?
(a) 1960-61 (b) 1962-64 (c) 1958-61 (d) 1959-63

46. Which brand was once sold at Monkey Ward?
(a) Benelli (b) Yamaguchi (c) Tohatsu (d) Montesa (e) NSU

47. What was new on the 1963 Harley-Davidson Pacer and Scat?
(a) Rear Suspension (b) Tele-Glide Fork (c) Buckhorn Bars (d) Buddy Seat

48. Which one of these can be purchased new in this century?
(a) Whizzer (b) Mustang Stallion (c) Simplex Senior (d) Simplex Moped

49. Which brand utilized rotary valves, but not rotary shifts?
(a) Honda (b) Kawasaki (c) Yamaha (d) Bridgestone

50. What size engine did the line of Triumph Tiger Cubs have?
(a) 250cc (b) 200cc (c) 175cc (d) 150cc

51. What was the 250cc Bultaco street model called?
(a) Metralla (b) Lobito (c) Scorpion (d) Impala

52. What was the name of the smallest BSA?
(a) Bullet (b) Commuter (c) Bantam (d) Cheetah

53. Which brand was also marketed as the Riverside brand name?
(a) Yamaha (b) Benelli (c) Tohatsu (d) Yamaguchi (e) Suzuki (f) Hodaka

54. What company built a 50cc, single-cylinder, street model with twin carbs and twin exhausts?
(a) Rex (b) Mobylette (c) NSU (d) Motebecane (e) Jawa (f) Suzuki

55. Which brand produced the Hillbilly model?
(a) Yamaha (b) Suzuki (c) Kawasaki (d) Yamaguchi (e) Tohatsu (f) Bridgestone

56. What company built the Pioneer?
(a) Bultaco (b) BSA (c) Ducati (d) Ossa (e) Suzuki (f) Tohatsu (g) Allstate

57. What was the name of the last 250cc street-sport Ducati sold in the U.S.?
(a) Catalina (b) Diana (c) Monza (d) Riverside

58. What was the name of the smallest Ducati?
(a) Cadet (b) Sprite (c) Little Duck (d) Banzai

59. What company built the 50cc Fireball Scrambler?
(a) BSA (b) Motobi (c) Puch (d) Benelli (e) Suzuki (f) Jawa

60. What four companies built the Allstate models for Sears?
(a) BSA-Puch-Mustang-Gilera (b) Cushman-Puch-Vespa-Gilera (c) Puch-DKW-Benelli-Bridgestone (d) MotoMorini-Cushman-Lambretta-Puch

61. There was a Mr. _____ who founded the company.
(a) Yamaguchi (b) Yamaha (c) Honda (d) Suzuki (e) Hodaka

62. Which of the following does not describe the BSA Starfire Scrambler of 1963?
(a) Roadster & Trials versions available (b) 250cc 4-stroke (c) Not street Legal (d) Single cylinder

63. Which of these machines had a foot shift?
(a) Allstate 125 (b) Rex Como (c) Ducati Falcon 50 (d) Allstate Cheyenne

64. Which of these describes the Ducati Super Falcon?
(a) 80cc two-stroke (b) 200cc four-stroke (c) upswept exhaust (d) four-speed transmission

65. Which of these was not a Montesa?
(a) Cappra (b) Cota (c) Gazelle (d) Impala

66. Which of the following was true of the 1962 Ducati 250 Scrambler?
(a) double downtube frame (b) offroad version of the Diana (c) Desmo OHC (d) five-speed transmission

67. The Como, Monaco, Piccolo, and KL-35 were models built by what brand?
(a) Bianchi (b) Motobi (c) Benelli (d) Rex (e) Zundapp (f) NSU

68. Which of these does not describe the Motobi Catria Sport and Imperial Sport models?
(a) OHV single (b) pressed steel frame (c) uncovered rear springs (d) vertical cylinder

69. How did the Jawa 250cc and 175cc models differ from the very similar Allstate Puch equivalents?
(a) 16-inch wheels (b) single pistons only (c) four-speed foot shift (d) piston-port

70. Which model is generally considered the most collectible Honda?

(a) GB-500 (b) CB-92R (c) 750 Four Sandcast (d) CL-kitted CB-450

71. How many different 125-class models were sold by Sears?
(a) One (b) Two (c) Three (d) Four

72. What was the last single-cylinder BMW street model sold in the U.S.?
(a) R-25 (b) R-69S (c) R-27 (d) R-100

73. What distinguished the Pointer Super Lassie above all else?
(a) Electric-start only (b) Gas tank integral with the frame (c) No side covers (d) All of these

74. Which of these was not an oil injection system trademark brand?
(a) Injectolube (b) PowerLube (c) Autolube (d) Posi-Force (e) Superlube

75. Which brand aside from BMW also used an Earles front fork?
(a) Rex (b) DKW (c) NSU (d) Zundapp (e) BSA (f) CZ

76. Which Japanese two-stroke brand built its street scrambler models with twin exhaust pipes on one side like Honda?
(a) Yamaha (b) Suzuki (c) Kawasaki (d) Bridgestone

77. Where were Mustang Motorcycles built?
(a) Baton Rouge LA (b) Glendale CA (c) Lancaster PA (d) Mobile AL

78. Who built the two most expensive 50cc motorcycles by a significant margin?
(a) Bridgestone & H-D (b) DKW & Ducati (c) Motobi & NSU (d) Aprilia & Honda

79. Which brand was last to market a street two-stroke in the USA?
(a) Bridgestone (b) Suzuki (c) Kawasaki (d) Yamaha

80. Which brand offered more road racers for sale to the public than any other?
(a) Montesa (b) BSA (c) Yamaha (d) Honda (e) NSU (f) Kawasaki

81. Cushman was allied with what foreign brand of scooters?
(a) Mobylette (b) Lambretta (c) Vespa (d) Rabbit

82. Which brand was never marketed through catalog sales in the USA?
(a) Miyata (b) Silver Pigeon (c) Benelli (d) Cushman (e) Vespa (f) Gilera

83. Which of the following describes the only 250cc model in the BSA lineup of 1968?
(a) Wet-sump engine (b) OHC (c) Starfire (d) Upswept exhaust

84. Which brand was not distributed from some point in the middle of the USA?
(a) Hodaka (b) Pointer (c) Bridgestone (d) Allstate

544

85. Which machines failed in the USA principally due to reliability issues?
(a) Pointer (b) Rex (c) Lambretta (d) Marusho (e) Miyata (f) Motobi

86. What is probably the strangest thing about the BMW R-27 250 single?
(a) Earles front fork (b) Kickstarter (c) Cylinder (d) Headlamp nacelle

87. Which of these was belt-driven?
(a) Simplex Servi-cycle (b) H-D Hummer (c) Lambretta 175 TV (d) Aprilia 50

88. How did Lambretta distinguish itself from Vespa?
(a) Twin-cylinder engine (b) Four-stroke (c) Rotary valve (d) Steel tube frame

89. Where should a motorcyclist put Snuff-or-Nots?
(a) Air filter box (b) Exhaust pipe (c) Under the seat (d) Handlebar ends

90. Which brand marketed a ratchet-type kick starter without a spring return?
(a) Jawa (b) NSU (c) Zundapp (d) Cushman (e) Mustang (f) Simplex

91. Which brand marketed the Banty Rooster model in the U.S.?
(a) Yamaguchi (b) Miyata (c) BSA (d) Hodaka (e) Benelli (f) None of these

92. What kind of motorcycle did Elvis ride in the "Wall of Death" in *Roustabout*?
(a) Honda 305 (b) H-D Scat (c) BSA Catalina (d) Yamaha 250 (e) Triumph Tiger Cub

93. What were all the competitors riding in the race in *How to Stuff a Wild Bikini*?
(a) Big Bears (b) CL-77's (c) Hurricane Scramblers (d) Hodaka Road Toads

94. What was the name of Ossa's street model?
(a) El Bandido (b) Scorpion (c) Wildfire (d) Cappra (e) Plonker (f) Del Playa

95. Which of these Aermacchi H-D models was marketed in the USA the longest?
(a) Leggero (b) Baja 100 (c) Rapido (d) SX-250

96. What feature was not on the new Honda 450 of 1965?
(a) Constant velocity carbs (b) DOHC (c) Five-speed (d) Electric starter

97. What motorcycle did Elvis ride in *Viva Las Vegas*?
(a) Super Hawk (b) Big Bear (c) H-D Pacer (d) Honda Sport 50 (e) Honda Dream

98. What did Yamaha dare to briefly name its MF-1 50 in advertising?
(a) Maestro (b) Thunderclap (c) Lightning (d) Flash (e) Blue Streak (f) Thunderbolt

99. Who had a front disc brake on the street first?
(a) Honda (b) Yamaha (c) Lambretta (d) Aprilia (e) NSU (f) Zundapp

100. What year was the last over-50cc street two-stroke marketed in the U.S.?
(a) 1976 (b) 1977 (c) 1978 (d) 1986

Whiffs of Magical Memories...

...I Remember Them Like It Was Yesterday

I could not wait for each new Sears catalog to arrive. There was that Allstate Moped that maybe one day I could afford for only $179.95 in 36 easy payments. No more pedaling uphill! The hardtail 125 would prepare me visually for the Super 10 I would meet in 1960, but I choked on the thought of its hand shift. It had only a single seat so I could not carry a passenger. What I really wanted was that Allstate 175 in black with a dual saddle!

A couple of young punks I knew in high school, identical twins actually, rode these strange, gangly, antique-looking Simplex machines. They were identical, just like their pilots. Those belt drives looked weird, man.

Some of us had a scooter, usually an Allstate Cruisaire. The kick starter had no cache. The bulbous body had no style, at least not any we wanted to be seen with, and the ponderous hand shift was klunky, but at least it had a clutch. The innocent *putt-putting* exhaust and small wheels rolled us to school without pedaling, but it just wasn't quite a *motorcycle*!

That Harley-Davidson Super 10 was *so* American, so stylish with its big wheels, Buckhorn handlebars, swoopy Buddy Seat, and hardtail non-rear suspension. I remember the way the oversized footpegs flopped down loosely, not spring-loaded. The handgrips were large, fit for a real man. The kick starter was on the left side where you had to stand beside the machine, holding it off the stand with those tall bars, and kick it vigorously several times to start it.

There was one guy in town who had a Sportster. He was a real guy, a man's man. Of course I don't really remember him, his name or what he looked like. I don't even remember his girlfriend. But I remember the swoopy style of that rolling thunder he rode.

The first time I saw a Honda, I wondered if the name was meant to look and sound American. Some of the local rednecks mispronounced it as Hondo, like the old John Wayne western. This was a Benly Touring 150 with bodywork that seemed so *modern* at the time. The kick starter *folded*, but you did not even have to use it.

The first time I saw a Honda Super Sports Cub, I marveled at its tiny jewel-like presence. Its handgrips seemed too small, like its quiet sound, yet it was a *real* motorcycle nonetheless. The footshift was only a three-speed, but you had to learn the process of starting and shifting with a clutch.

546

Just as some of the local yahoos thought a Honda was a Hondo and a Yamaha was a Yammahaw, I the super nerd, thought it was a YaMAha.

There was a Honda dealership in the small town, but one bigger than the town I resided in, that was famous for having a virtual motorcycle junkyard out back, behind its little building. There were the remains of Honda 50's and Hawks, Dreams, and Benlys. Deceased Yamahas and even the occasional Suzi lounged in that graveyard of adolescent dreams. The man and his wife who owned the shop were legendary as Mr. & Mrs. Grouch, two selfish old critters who could be so nice, if only they would allow a punk like me to make a meager bid on a few of those wretched, disassembled bodies. I wanted so desperately to put together a tiddler I could afford and ride! Years later, when I was almost an adult, they gave me the best deal on a new Honda that would travel far and wide below my Captain America helmet.

My mom would drive me over there on a Sunday afternoon when the little dealership was closed, just so I could cup my hands around my eyes and stare through the glass into the dimness, ogling the machines therein. When the shop was open, I could smell that special whiff of the two-stroke oil in the dingy little Yamaha shop on a back street in a small town. I think the flavor was DA Speed Sport.

One lazy summer afternoon, a fellow tiddler buddy and I went over to see Dub Terry. That was his real nickname and he was the official Fonzie of our little town. He owned a beautiful red Honda Hawk that had been developed into what I would later come to know as a flat-tracker. It had a Super Sports 50 gas tank painted red, semi-knobby tires and open exhausts. The legend was that he would challenge some kid to a race. After the kid had zipped off down the road, Dub would come howling by on that fierce machine on one wheel. We later called it a wheelie.

You can never forget the first time you heard a Honda 250 or 305 Scrambler unmuffled in the distance. There was a special *underwater warble* to it that has never been duplicated to this day. When you rode one of these beasts in the dirt, the seat and suspension were misunderstandably stiff. That is the best way I can describe it.

The first time you sat down on a Hodaka and the soft seat and suspension went *squish!* you knew that dirt bikes had matured into what they were supposed to be.

The CL-350 was much softer and sweeter than its immediate predecessor. It had an electric starter, but I didn't use it much. I liked the feel of kicking it alive like a real man. The stroke of the kick starter seemed a bit short as the engine went *thump-thump* only once whenever it failed to fire on the first kick when cold. It always seemed to fire on one cylinder first for a few seconds before the second cylinder kicked in.

No one ever forgets his first Mach III experience. Two pipes on one side and only one on the other? Cool! And then there was the alien sound of *dub-dub-drubble-bub*. And then the carbs sucked so much air so fast that you completely forgot about the exhaust noise.

We all knew what a Ferrari was and that it had this *sound of ripping silk* shriek, but we had never heard a *motorcycle* that made that sound. The first CB-750 we encountered impressed us with its four pipes, front disc brake, and oversized instruments properly tilted back to stare us in the face. We knew it was a new kind of speed when we heard it scream down the street.

Answers to the Tiddler Trivia Test

1. F	11. D	21. A	31. B	41. D	51. A	61. C	71. D	81. C	91. F
2. A	12. D	22. A	32. B	42. A	52. C	62. C	72. C	82. A	92. B
3. A	13. B	23. E	33. A	43. B	53. B	63. D	73. D	83. C	93. A
4. D	14. A	24. B	34. A	44. B	54. A	64. A	74. B	84. A	94. C
5. F	15. C	25. A	35. B	45. A	55. B	65. C	75. A	85. D	95. C
6. E	16. A	26. C	36. B	46. A	56. D	66. B	76. C	86. B	96. C
7. C	17. E	27. A	37. A	47. A	57. B	67. D	77. B	87. A	97. D
8. A	18. C	28. D	38. D	48. A	58. A	68. D	78. D	88. D	98. C
9. B	19. C	29. C	39. B	49. C	59. D	69. B	79. B	89. B	99. C
10. E	20. E	30. D	40. D	50. B	60. B	70. B	80. C	90. D	100. D

Appendix

Glossary

Black Bomber - Nickname given to the original Honda 450 that was available only in black.

Buckhorn - A handlebar in the shape of two upside down U's offered as an option on many Harley-Davidson models, from the little tiddlers covered in this book to the Sportster. H-D even owns a copyright on the Buckhorn name.

Buddy Seat - A soft dual seat design that slopes downward in the middle with a passenger grab rail at the rear. Like the Buckhorn bars, the Buddy Seat is an option on all the same Harley-Davidson models and the name is copyrighted.

Carburetor - There were five common motorcycle carburetor brands and types from the Sixties that deserve mention. The British Amal brand generally required flooding before a cold start. The American Tillotson carb design was not particularly reliable. The German Bings held a generally consistent reputation. Honda used its own subsidiary brand, Keihin, later also adopted by Harley-Davidson. Most of the other Japanese brands, particularly the two-strokes, used Mikunis that always enjoyed an impeccable reputation.

CDI - Capacitor Discharge Ignition was introduced to the motorcycle world with the 1969 Kawasaki Mach III. This system uses a *black box* circuit board to replace the conventional points and condenser in a motorcycle ignition system.

Ceriani - An Italian brand of polished front forks and suspension that was widely copied as the sleek, clean styling became popular in the late Sixties.

Claimed Dry Weight - Motorcycle manufacturers tended to weigh each new model completely dry of any fluids to advertise the lowest weights possible. In the early days, the motorcycle press usually reprinted these weights in road tests. As the Sixties progressed, more and more of the media, led by *Cycle World*, weighed each tested machine and reported the wet weight.

CV - Constant Velocity carburetor design as created by Honda's carb subsidiary Keihin. The CV carbs debuted on the Honda 450 of 1965. They were designed to aid everyday carburetor response and to automatically adjust to air density changes; however, it took several years for the company to fully debug the design.

Desmo - Slang for Desmodromic Valve System. Ducati built and imported OHC singles into the USA from the earliest era covered in this book. As of the mid-Seventies, no Ducati has utilized valve springs.

DOHC - Double Overhead Cam. The Honda 450 was the first mass-produced twin with this feature and the Kawasaki Z-1 carried it to a four-cylinder design.

Ears - A slang term for the two metal pieces, usually triangular in shape, that attach a headlight to a motorcycle.

Gaiters - The black rubber covers over the front suspension springs of many sporting motorcycles. Gaiters were commonly used on machines from England initially and then the style was adopted for many Japanese models, as well as some American ones.

GYT - Genuine Yamaha Tuning was introduced to refer to the dealer sold or installed packages of high performance engine parts that turned a Yamaha Enduro into a motocrosser. The GYT Kits, as they were referred to, usually included a higher compression head, larger carburetor or carb internals, expansion chamber exhaust pipe, and miscellaneous small components.

Hardtail - A motorcycle with no rear suspension.

HP - Gross horsepower, measured at the crankshaft, as commonly reported in the U.S. during the period. All cars sold in the USA beginning with the 1972 model year reported net horsepower, as measured at the drive wheels. A few of the later horsepower figures quoted in this book may have been net values. Reading between the lines in the model charts, you can see where Honda and other brands retreated from reporting official horsepower claims in the early Seventies as the public came to expect the more realistic net ratings.

Hummer - Officially this was the name of a special economy version of the Harley-Davidson S-125 introduced in 1955 as a cheaper alternative to the 165cc ST model introduced in 1953. In common motorcycle slang, the term Hummer has been applied as a generic reference to all the American-built, small Harley two-stroke models except the Topper scooter. (No, Melvin, this is not the reward you get for correctly pronouncing Jawa, Puch, or Yamaguchi.)

Humpback - The nickname given to the original Honda 450, along with Black Bomber, because of the model's bulbous, humpbacked gas tank shape.

Kaw - Nickname for a Kawasaki.

Leading Link - This type of front suspension has several variations, most of which aid the front wheel with sensitivity to small road irregularities at the expense of stability over harsher bumps or terrain. The most common examples of this difference can be observed when comparing the Honda Cubs and Dreams to the Super 90 and Hawks. Telescopic front forks are nearly always employed on sporty road machines and dirt bikes.

Monocoque - A type of frame design that was touted by the Yamaha YG-1 and other small machines in the early Sixties. The monocoque was essentially a smoother, one-piece, pressed steel frame that extended from the steering head to and including the rear fender. In contrast, the pressed steel frames of the early small Hondas and Dreams consisted of several pieces welded together.

Monoshock - A single long-travel rear shock absorber that controls the swing arm movement, as introduced by Yamaha initially for its off-road models. Practically all high-performance modern machines have monoshock rear suspensions today.

NA - Not Available is noted in the charts whenever verifiable information was unavailable at the time of publication.

Nacelle - Japanese motorcycle builders, particularly in the early years, tended to design artistic headlamp holder (nacelle) shapes to accommodate speedometers, tachometers, and warning lamps behind the light fixture with most of the electrical wiring for the whole machine contained within the headlamp nacelle.

OHC - Overhead Cam.- All the Honda twins have had OHC engines since the beginning of the U.S. imports in 1959. With the exception of a handful of expensive, low-production models such as the 1961 Jaguar E-type, few cars sold in the USA had OHC engines during the same time period.

OHV - Overhead Valve was the type of four-stroke engine design that was more sophisticated than the flathead type, but more primitive and limited in high-rpm capability than the overhead cam type. Practically all the four-stroke European machines of the day except the Ducatis had OHV engines. Honda essentially launched its attack on the British OHV twins with its OHC twins.

Oil Injection - A method of storing a supply of two-stroke oil on a machine so that no premixing of gas and oil is necessary for a two-cycle engine. The Allstate/Puch Twingles had oil injection years before any other brand, but little was made of this feature in a marketing sense. The oil was stored in a small tank of about one quart inside the main gas tank of the Allstate 175 and 250. Yamaha grabbed all the marketing credit when the company launched its new Autolube system on the 1964 YG-1. Most other two-stroke brands were forced to either develop a patented system of their own with a fancy name or face a slow death in the marketplace. Bultaco offered a primitive version on its Metralla in which the rider pushed a little plunger on the oil tank a certain number of times to complement whatever volume of gasoline he had just pumped into the main fuel tank.

Ricegrinder - A nickname for a Japanese motorcycle, usually applied in a derogatory manner by riders of the more expensive BMW's, Ducatis, Harley-Davidsons, etc.

Return Shift - This is the standard type of foot shift pattern that most motorcycles have had for decades. You begin in Neutral, shift through the forward gears and return. Designers have employed several different patterns through the years, one or more of which was usually favored by each manufacturer, although standardization has eliminated most of the variations. The most common pattern has always had First on the bottom with Neutral above it and the higher gears above Neutral, however, some builders often placed Neutral at the bottom or top of the pattern and shifted either all-up or all-down for the forward gears.

Rocking Shift - Most Italian brands had a foot shift lever with a toe piece on the front end and a heel tab in the rear. The shifter was connected in the center so that a rider could use either end tab to up or down shift, whatever his preference. This left the tops of shoes unscuffed from the upward lifting of a toe shifter. Many early, particularly small, Japanese models, such as the Honda Cub 50, employed a rocking shift, too.

Rotary Shift - A foot shift that places Neutral in the shift pattern between the top gear and First Gear so that the rider can go directly from the top gear into Neutral, then into First, with a single movement of the shift lever in the same direction. The pattern is described in the book as 0-1-2-3-4-0-1-2-3-4. Rotary shifts were popular in Japan when early models began to be exported, particularly on smaller, lower-powered, or more pedestrian machines. Several early Japanese models from Bridgestone, Pointer, Suzuki, and Kawasaki used rotary shifts, but they fell rapidly out of favor with the sporting riders of the USA.

Rotary Valve - An induction method for two-stroke engines that is more advanced and efficient than the standard piston-port type. Rotary valves were popular with most of the Japanese brands. You can spot a rotary valve model by its *invisible* carburetor hidden inside the engine case.

SOHC - The Single Overhead Cam engine design was best exemplified in the Sixties by the Honda twins and Ducati singles.

Suzi - Nickname for a Suzuki.

Tiddler - In conventional motorcycle slang, the word refers to the many 50cc-175cc, single-cylinder, Japanese motorcycles imported into the USA in the '60's and '70's. Most users of the term apply twin-cylinders, 250cc, or highway performance as the upper cutoff point for the application. For the purposes of this book, *The Tiddler Invasion* loosely applies more broadly to the boom in small machines from all origins that occurred generally between 1955 and 1975.

Trials Universal - A tire tread pattern that was extremely common on off-road and dual purpose machines built in Japan for the U.S. market. This was a densely packed block pattern arranged evenly and symmetrically around the tire. It was not a particularly good design for mud or slick pavement, but a distinct compromise.

Twingle - The slang term for the Allstate 175 and 250 models that have two pistons housed within a single combustion chamber. This engine design is not exactly a single or a twin, but a hybrid between the two.

Water Buffalo - A nickname given to the first mass-produced water-cooled two-stroke street model, the Suzuki GT-750 LeMans.

Bibliography

This Bibliography is a listing of sources for the material contained in this book as well as a list of sources of further research for the readers. Note that *Cycle* Magazine operated under three different titles during this period. All but a few of these books and periodicals have been out of print for years.

Big Book of Harley-Davidson, The, Thomas C. Bolfert, Harley-Davidson, Inc., 1989.

Bike Journal International, June 1993, article on the Kawasaki 650 Commander.

Classic Honda Motorcycles: Identification Guide to the Collectible Models 1958-90, Bill Silver, edited by Lee Klancher, Second Edition (of next entry), Octane Press, August 1, 2012.

Classic Honda Motorcycles Illustrated Buyer's Guide, Bill Silver, MBI Publishing Company, 2000.

Classic Japanese Motorcycles Illustrated Buyer's Guide, Ron Burton, MBI Publishing Company, 2000.

Complete Book of Motorcycling, The, by Lynn Wineland and the editors of *Hot Rod Magazine*, Petersen Publishing Company, 1964.

Complete Illustrated Encyclopedia of The World's Motorcycles, The, Erwin Tragatsch, Quarto Limited, an imprint of Holt, Rinehart and Winston, 1977.

Cycle, October 1966, road test of the Bultaco 175 Campera.

Cycle, December 1966, comparison test of the Honda 305 Dream, Super Hawk & Scrambler.

Cycle, January 1967, test of the Bridgestone 175 Hurricane Scrambler. The test described the unusual shifter mechanism of this model. You could push or pull a lever on top of the transmission that would switch it from a rotary four-speed to a standard five-speed return shift.

Cycle, February 1967, test of the Bultaco Metralla.

Cycle, March 1967, test of the Yamaha YDS Electra 250 and a movie review of *The Wild Angels*.

Cycle, April 1967, test of the Kawasaki F-21M 238 Scrambler and a full-color, two-page ad for the new Samurai; Benelli full-line ad from Cosmopolitan Motors.

Cycle, May 1967, tests of the Montesa 250 Scorpion and Honda CB & CL 160's.

Cycle, June 1967, test of the Samurai, Samurai SS, and 250 Road Racer; a Snuff-or-Not ad.

Cycle, July 1967, test of the Bridgestone 100 and 175 Racers, ad for three Montesa 250's: Scorpion, Impala Sport, and La Cross.

Cycle, August 1967, tests of the Benelli 250 Barracuda and Bridgestone 350 GTR.

Cycle, September 1967, tests of the Suzuki X-5 Sting Ray and Honda CB-450.

Cycle, December 1967, tests of the Kawasaki C2SS Road Runner 120 and the Ossa 230 Pioneer & 230 Stiletto.

Cycle, January 1968, Road Tests of the Ducati 160 Monza Junior and the Yamaha YDS-5 Catalina.

Cycle, February 1968, Road Test of the Harley-Davidson Rapido.

Cycle, March 1968, Road Test of the Kawasaki 350SS Avenger.

Cycle, April 1968, Road Tests of the BSA 441 Shooting Star & Victor Special and the Hodaka Ace 100.

Cycle, May 1968, Road Tests of the Honda CB & CL 350, Zundapp KS 100 ISDT Replica and the Yamaha DT-1 and two-page ad spreads of new models from Yamaha and Suzuki; an ad for the Benelli Mojave 360 says to *test ride it at Montgomery Ward.*

Cycle, July 1968, Road Tests of the Yamaha 350 Grand Prix YR-2, Benelli 125 Sprite, and Bultaco Lobito K100 Scrambler.

Cycle, August 1968, Road Tests of the Benelli Riverside Mojave 360 and Bridgestone 100 Trail.

Cycle, September 1968, Road Tests of the Bultaco Matador and Kawasaki 175 Bushwhacker.

Cycle, November 1968, Road Tests of the Honda CB-450K1 and the Ossa 230 Wildfire Street Scrambler.

Cycle, December 1968, Road Tests of the Honda 90 Trail and Suzuki TC-305 Laredo Street Scrambler.

Cycle, January 1969, tests of the Kawasaki 238 Green Streak Scrambler and Sears SR-125.

Cycle, February 1969, Road Tests of the Benelli 650 and Ducati 350 SSS (Street Scrambler Sport).

Cycle, April 1969, Mach III road test (still called Blue Streak), foldout Kawasaki lineup brochure, and 10,000 mile test of a CB-160. A Honda two-page color spread advertises the Motosport 90 clearly with a black frame.

Cycle, May 1969, test of the Yamaha AT-1 Enduro & AT-1MX.

Cycle, June 1969, Road Tests of the Bridgestone Mach II 200 RS & SS and Suzuki T-500 Titan Mark II.

Cycle, July 1969, Road Tests of the Honda SL-90 and Yamaha Big Bear.

Cycle, August 1969, Road Test of the Honda 750 Four.

Cycle, September 1969, BSA 250 Starfire test, Bridgestone 100 TMX ad and Suzuki Stinger ad and road test.

Cycle, October 1969, Road Test of the Yamaha CT-1 Enduro 175.

Cycle, December 1969, tests of the Honda SL-350 and Kawasaki G31M Centurion 100.

Cycle, February 1970, Road Tests of the Ducati 250, 350, & 450 Desmos and the Bultaco 100 & 125 Lobitos.

Cycle, April 1970, Road Test of the Yamaha RT-1 360 Enduro and an obituary for Floyd Clymer.

Cycle, May 1970, Road Tests of the Bridgestone GTO, Kawasaki Trail Boss, and Yamaha 650 XS-1.

Cycle, June 1970, Road Test of the Kawasaki Bighorn.

Cycle, July 1970, Road Tests of the Honda CB-450 and Suzuki T-350 Rebel.

Cycle, September 1970, Road Test of the Honda SL-100.

Cycle, December 1970, Comparison Test of the Bridgestone GTR, Harley-Davidson Sprint SS, Honda CB-350, Kawasaki A-7 Avenger, Suzuki T-350 Rebel and Yamaha R-5.

Cycle, January 1971, Road Test of the Honda SL-350K1.

Cycle, February 1971, Road Tests of the Benelli 650 Tornado, Ossa Pioneer, and Yamaha 90 HT-1 Enduro.

Cycle, April 1971, Road Tests of the Bultaco Matador, Honda CB-175 K5, Kawasaki 250 Enduro, and Suzuki TS-125R Duster.

Cycle, July 1971, tests of the Hodaka 100/B & Super Rat and Yamaha RT-1B & RT-1BMX.

Cycle, November 1971, tests of the Mach II & III and the DT-2 MX & RT-2 MX, a shiny silver foldout ad with full specifications for the 1972 Kawasaki lineup, and a multi-page Yamaha ad with many photos and specs of the 1972 lineup.

Cycle, December 1971, Road Test of the Kawasaki Mach IV and full-color, two-page ad for the 1972 Yamaha Enduro line.

Cycle, March 1972, Road Tests of the Suzuki 380 Sebring, Honda CB-100, and Yamaha LS-2.

Cycle, April 1972, Road Test of the Honda XL-250 Motosport.

Cycle, August 1972, Road Tests of the Honda CB-350 Four and Kawasaki 90 G3-SS.

Cycle, October 1972, Road Test of the Suzuki TS-400J Apache.

Cycle, November 1972, Road Tests of the Kawasaki Z-1 and Suzuki GT550J Indy.

Cycle, February 1973, Introduction of the Benelli Sei: "Benelli Drops the Bomb: 750 Six".

Cycle, March 1973, Road Test of the Yamaha TX-750.

Cycle, April 1973, Road Test of the Kawasaki Mach I 250 & Mach II 350.

Cycle, May 1973, Road Tests of the Suzuki GT-750 K and Yamaha RD-350.

Cycle, July 1973, Road Test of the Yamaha TX-500 Twin.

Cycle, August 1973, tests of the Honda CR-125M, MT-125, & CB-500K2 and the Kawasaki H-1D & F-7 175 Enduro and a three-page color ad for the Kawasaki Z-1.

Cycle, November 1973, Road Tests of the Honda CB-750K3 and Benelli 250 Phantom.

Cycle, May 1974, Comparison Test of the Honda 125, Kawasaki 90, Suzuki 50, and Yamaha 60.

Cycle, June 1974, Road Tests of the Bultaco 250 Alpina and Kawasaki KZ400.

Cycle, September 1974, Road Test of the Suzuki TS-185L Sierra & TC-185L Ranger.

Cycle, January 1975, Road Tests of the Kawasaki Z-1A and Suzuki RE-5 Rotary.

Cycle, February 1975, Road Tests of the Honda CB-500T and Kawasaki 125 Enduro.

Cycle, March 1975, tests of the Honda CB-400F Super Sport, Montesa V75 Enduro 250, and Yamaha Monoshock YZC-125.

Cycle, April 1975, Road Tests of the Honda XL-125 K1 and Gold Wing and the Yamaha RD-125B.

Cycle, May 1975, Road Tests of the Honda CB-750F and the Suzuki GT-750M.

Cycle, June 1975, Road Tests of the Yamaha RD-200B and MX-400B.

Cycle, October 1975, test of the Honda CR-250M Elsinore.

Cycle, November 1975, Road Test of Yamaha RS-100C, an upcoming 1976 model.

Cycle 1975 Buyer's Guide, by the editors of *Cycle Magazine*, 1975 (1974 models).

Cycle 1976 Buyer's Guide, by the editors of *Cycle Magazine*, 1976 (1975 models).

Cycle Guide, March 1967, Road Tests of the Benelli 250 Barracuda, Bridgestone 175 Scrambler, and Yamaha 100 Trailmaster.

Cycle Guide, April 1967, Comparison Test of the Honda CA, CB, & CL-160's. This was actually more of an article than a road test. No figures were compiled or published, not even in a *claimed* format.

Cycle Guide, May 1967, Road Tests of the Suzuki X-5 and Yamaha 180.

Cycle Guide, June 1967, Comparison Test of the Bridgestone 90, Bultaco Lobito, Honda Trail 90, Suzuki 80 & 120, and the Yamaha Trailmaster 100.

Cycle Guide, August 1967, test of the Honda CL-90. The article states that the CL-90 has alloy fenders. The data: $380, 8 hp at 9500 rpm, and 203 pounds.

Cycle Guide, September 1967, Road Test of the Bultaco Metralla, Harley-Davidson Rapido, and Suzuki AS-100, the new rotary valve model.

Cycle Guide, October 1967, Comparison Test of the Harley-Davidson M-50, Honda Sport 50 and Rally 50, and Yamaha U-5.

Cycle Guide, November 1967, Road Tests of the Honda Super Hawk, Kawasaki Avenger, and Yamaha Big Bear 305.

Cycle Guide, December 1967, Road Tests of the Kawasaki W2-SS and 238 Scrambler.

Cycle Guide, January 1968, Road Tests of the Bridgestone 350 GTR, BSA Starfire 250, Bultaco Campera, and Suzuki 500 Five.

Cycle Guide, March 1968, Road Tests of the Honda 125 SS, Jawa Californian 250, and Yamaha 180 Scrambler.

Cycle Guide, April 1968, Road Tests of the Kawasaki 120 Road Runner and Yamaha 125 street scrambler.

Cycle Guide, May 1968, Road Test of the Bultaco Matador, a 1968 Cycle Preview (of new models) and a Zundapp 100cc ad. A Honda CL-77 is shown with silver fork legs, DLS brake, and a slip on muffler.

Cycle Guide, June 1968, Road Tests of the Honda CL-175 and Yamaha DT-1.

Cycle Guide, July 1968, Road Tests of the Suzuki Raider, Honda 125 Scrambler, and Triumph Trophy 250.

Cycle Guide, September 1968, road test of the CL-450. The price was listed as $995, the hp as 43, the weight as 415, and the quarter-mile as 14.94 at 85 mph.

Cycle Guide, November 1968, Road Test of the Honda CL-350.

Cycle Guide, December 1968, Road Test of the Hodaka Ace 100.

Cycle Guide, January 1969, Road Test of the Bridgestone 100 Trail and Yamaha YDS-5 Electra.

Cycle Guide, February 1969, Road Test of the Kawasaki Sidewinder 250.

Cycle Guide, June 1969, Road Test of the Kawasaki G3-TR.

Cycle Guide, July 1969, Road Test of the Yamaha CT-1 Enduro, Mach III, and a Honda Motosport 90 with a silver frame.

Cycle Guide, August 1969, Road Tests of the Suzuki T120 and the Yamaha R3.

Cycle Guide, December 1969, Road Tests of the Bultaco 125 Lobito and Suzuki Savage.

Cycle Guide, January 1970, Road Test of the Ossa Pioneer 175 and a back page ad of the Honda CL-175K3 (with no mention of an electric starter).

Cycle Guide, February 1970, Road Tests of the Kawasaki Trail Boss and Honda SL-350.

Cycle Guide, March 1970, multi-page foldout ad of the 1970 Yamahas and a test of the DT-1C; test of the Harley-Davidson Baja and a two-page, color ad of the Baja/Rapido; OSSA 175 trail test.

Cycle Guide, May 1970, tests of the Hodaka Super Rat and Kawasaki A7 350, A7SS 350, and Big Horn 350.

Cycle Guide, September 1970, tests of the RT-1 MX, Honda 175 Motosport, and Mach III (red) and an ad for the Yamaha HS-1 90 street model.

Cycle Guide, February 1971, 5000-mile owner's report on the Mach III (red); Ossa Pioneer ad, multi-page color ads for the new Triumph and BSA street/trail 250's that may have never been imported, with a pictorial story on some of the same models.

Cycle Guide, March 1971, Road Tests of the Honda 750 Four, Yamaha XS-1, and the Triumph Bandit DOHC 350 that never came to the U.S.

Cycle Guide, April 1971, Road Tests of the Harley-Davidson XS-350 Sprint and Suzuki Hustler 250.

Cycle Guide, August 1971, Road Tests of the Honda CB-500 Four & SL-125, Kawasaki Avenger, and Suzuki Titan.

Cycle Guide, September 1971, Road Tests of the Kawasaki 350 S2 Triple and the BSA Rocket III 750 Triple.

Cycle Guide, November 1971, Road Tests of the Yamaha AT-2 & DT-2 Enduros and DS-7 Twin.

Cycle Guide, December 1971, Road Tests of the Kawasaki H2 Mach IV, Hodaka B+, and the BSA 500 SS that may not have made it to the U.S.

Cycle Guide, April 1972, ad for the Suzuki TM-250, TS-90, TC-90, and 185 Enduro, and tests of the Kawasaki Mach III, Honda XL-250, CZ 175 Trail, and the BSA 500 MX that may not have come to the USA; multi-page, color, full-line Harley-Davison ad.

Cycle Guide, June 1972, tests of the SL-350K2, Yamaha XS-2, and Ossa Plonker, and an ad for the Kawasaki Big Horn.

Cycle Guide, July 1972, tests of the Honda CB-175 and Yamaha DT-2MX.

Cycle Guide, October 1972, tests of the Harley-Davidson Sprint SS-350, 1973 Z-1, Honda 500 Four, and Yamaha 200 CS-5; ad for Jawa CZ 350 Californian.

Cycle Guide, December 1972, Road Test of the Honda CB-100.

Cycle Guide, November 1973, Road Tests of the Honda CB-200 and 1974 Yamaha RD-350.

Cycle Guide, December 1973, Road Tests of the Honda CB-350 Four and Yamaha DT-125A.

Cycle Guide, March 1974, Road Test of the Kawasaki 400 S3 Triple.

Cycle Guide, May 1974, ads for the Yamaha TY250 Trials, TY80 Trials, and the Hodaka Wombat, and a road test of the Suzuki T-500L Titan.

Cycle Guide, June 1974, tests of the Yamaha TY-250 Trials and the Triumph TR5T 500 Trail that never made it to America.

Cycle Guide, September 1974, Road Tests of the Kawasaki H2B Mach IV, Ossa 250 Phantom, Suzuki RL-250 Exacta Trials, and Yamaha TX650A.

Cycle Guide, October 1974, Road Test of the Kawasaki KZ 400.

Cycle Guide, January 1975, Road Tests of the Honda CB-400F Super Sport and Kawasaki 175 F7 Enduro.

Cycle Guide, February 1975, Road Test of the Suzuki RE-5 Rotary.

Cycle Guide, April 1975, Road Tests of the Honda Gold Wing and Suzuki GT-380M Sebring.

Cycle Guide, July 1975, Road Tests of the Honda CB-750F and Kawasaki H1F 500 and an ad for the CB-750F & CB-400F; Harley-Davidson SX-175 & SX-250 ad.

Cycle Guide, September 1975, test of the Kawasaki KX-250A.

Cycle Guide, October 1975, Road Tests of the Kawasaki KH-400A3 and the Suzuki TS-185M Sierra; Harley-Davidson ad for the SX-175 that may be for the 1976 model.

Cycle Guide, December 1975, Road Tests of the Honda CB550F Super Sport and the Yamaha DT-175C Enduro.

Cycle Guide Road Test Annual, 1970 (1969 models).

Cycle Guide Road Test Annual, 1973 (1972 models).

Cycle Prices: The Complete Motorcycle Buyer's Bible, RPM Sales Corp., 1975.

Cycle World, January 1962, Scooter Test of the Vespa 150 Grand Sport.

Cycle World, February 1962, Road Tests of the Harley-Davidson Sprint and BSA Catalina Scrambler; article introducing the Pointer 125 Senior & Super Lassie 90.

Cycle World, March 1962, Road Test of the Motobi Catria.

Cycle World, April 1962, Road Test of the Yamaha 250 YD-3.

Cycle World, May 1962, tests of the Honda Super Hawk and Lambretta 150/LI.

Cycle World, July 1962, Road Test of the Jawa 250.

Cycle World, August 1962, tests of the Rabbit Superflow, Ducati Scrambler, and Cushman Trailster, Road Impression of the Rex KL-35, and brand advertising, including the Suzuki El Camino, Rabbit Minor and Superflow, and the Pointer Comet, Senior, Super Lassie, and Lassie.

Cycle World, October 1962, Road Tests of the Suzuki El Camino 250 and Lambretta 175/TV.

Cycle World, December 1962, Road Test of the Honda CL-72 250 Scrambler.

Cycle World, January 1963, Test of the Yamaha YDS-2 & TD-1 and the Tohatsu Runpet Sport, plus Ducati and Yamaguchi SPB ads.

Cycle World, February 1963, first Miyapet ad, Allstate 250 SG Twingle Road Test, Triumph ad.

Cycle World, March 1963, Test of Omaha Trail 50.

Cycle World, April 1963, Pointer Comet & Super Lassie Road Impression.

Cycle World, May 1963, Cushman Eagle Scooter Test, Ducati 250 Monza test and Ducati ad.

Cycle World, June 1963, Honda Hawk Road Test.

Cycle World, July 1963, Tohatsu Trailmaster Test and BSA SS-90 350 Test.

Cycle World, August 1963, Bridgestone 7 Road Impression, tests of the Harley-Davidson Sprint racer, Montesa 175, and Triumph Trials Cub.

Cycle World, September 1963, Road Impression of the Mustang Thoroughbred.

Cycle World, November 1963, test of the Yamaha Ascot Scrambler and Suzuki Trojan 80 Road Impression.

Cycle World, December 1963, full-line Rabbit ad and Ducati Diana test.

Cycle World, January 1964, Road Test of the Bultaco Metralla and a Road Impression of the Honda 90.

Cycle World, April 1964, Road Impression of the Yamaha 80 YG-1. It did not yet have oil injection.

Cycle World, May 1964, Road Impression of the Simplex Senior, Hodaka Ace 90 ad, Ducati ad, and closeout prices first advertised for the Pointer Super Lassie. This issue includes a story on the Harley-Davidson Brezza scooter that was never approved by the company for sale in the U.S., but five were imported from Aermacchi for market testing.

Cycle World, July 1964, tests of the Yamaha YDS-3 and Triumph Mountain Cub.

Cycle World, August 1964, Scooter Test of the Vespa 90, Trial Test of the Bultaco 200 Matador, first ad appears for Omega 125cc with electric start from Ken Kay for $435, Rabbit 90 ad, Bridgestone 90 ad. An ad for the CL-72 was shown with a *Dream* tank badge. Early models had the word *Dream* included on the tank badges.

Cycle World, September 1964, tests of the Honda Super Hawk and Lambretta 200/TV.

Cycle World, November 1965, Road Test of the Ducati Diana 5-speed.

Cycle World, December 1964, YG-1 ad touting Autolube. At this early date, it is referred to as Yamaha Injection System instead of Autolube. First ad of the 1965 Marusho 500 ST is also in this issue. A full road test of the Marusho is in this same issue, and so are brief impressions of the Suzuki Hillbilly and Bridgestone 90; Ducati ad.

Cycle World, January 1965, Suzuki full-line ad, Triumph Mountain Cub ad; the Omega was advertised for $454. James T. Crow's fascinating story of drome rider Louis "Speedy" Babs is also in this issue.

Cycle World, February 1965, Road Impression of the Honda Super 90.

Cycle World, March 1965, Road Impression of the Ducati Cadet 90.

Cycle World, April 1965, tests of the Montesa Impala Super Sport and Garelli Rex 90cc KL-100.

Cycle World, May 1965, Road Tests of the Honda CB-160 and Benelli Sprite 200, Road Impression of the Allstate Sport 60, first story on the Honda 450, Bridgestone full-line, three-page, color ad.

Cycle World, June 1965, Road Test of the Yamaha 305 & Big Bear.

Cycle World, July 1965, Road Test of the Ducati 160.

Cycle World, August 1965, Road Test of the Ducati Diana 250 Mark III and a Road Impression of the Rabbit S-402 BT scooter.

Cycle World, September 1965, Road Tests of the Honda 450 and Omega 125.

Cycle World, October 1965, Road Tests of the Suzuki X-6 and Ossa 175 SE; movie review of *How to Stuff a Wild Bikini*.

Cycle World, December 1965, tests of the Honda 450, CL-77 305 Scrambler, & Trail 90, and Benelli 250 Sprite.

Cycle World, January 1966, Road Test of the Harley-Davidson Sprint CRS.

Cycle World, February 1966, tests of the Bridgestone 175 Dual Twin & 90 Mountaineer.

Cycle World, March 1966, tests of the Kawasaki 175 F1TR, Yamaha 100, and Bridgestone 90.

Cycle World, April 1966, Road Test of the BSA 441 Victor Special and a Road Impression of the Harley-Davidson M-50 Step-Through.

Cycle World, May 1966, Road Impression of the Suzuki 80.

Cycle World, July 1966, Road Test of the Yamaha YM-1 305 and a Road Impression of the Honda CM-91 Step-Through 90.

Cycle World, August 1966, Road Test of the Kawasaki 650 W1.

Cycle World, September 1966, Road Impression of the Hodaka Ace 90.

Cycle World, October 1966, Road Test of the Montesa Impala Sport 250.

Cycle World, December 1966, tests of the Honda CL-160 Scrambler and Kawasaki 250.

Cycle World, January 1967, Road Test of the Bridgestone 175 Street Scrambler.

Cycle World, February 1967, Road Test of the Benelli 250 Barracuda and Jawa 350 Californian.

Cycle World, March 1967, tests of the Yamaha Grand Prix 350 and Trailmaster 100.

Cycle World, May 1967, tests of the Suzuki X-5 Invader 200, Zundapp 125 ISDT Replica, and the Marusho 500 Magnum Electra.

Cycle World, June 1967, tests of the Kawasaki 350 Avenger and Honda CT-90 Trail 8-speed.

Cycle World, July 1967, Road Test of the BSA Starfire and a Road Impression of the Kawasaki CTSS 120.

Cycle World, August 1967, road test and two-page ad of the Bridgestone GTR, Ducati ad, and a Honda ad showing the Rally 90 and the CL-77 with a slip-on muffler.

Cycle World, November 1967, The History of Japanese Motorcycles by W. B. Swim and the introduction of the new CB-450D called Super Sport under New Models and Products; Ducati Cadet ad; Bultaco Metralla Road Test.

Cycle World, December 1967, Road Tests of the Suzuki 500/Five and the Ossa 230 Wildfire.

Cycle World, February 1968, test of the Yamaha DT-1, Ducati and Triumph ads.

Cycle World, May 1968, Road Test of the Honda CB & CL-450 and an Impression of the Hodaka 100.

Cycle World, June 1968, Road Test of the Yamaha YR-2 & YR2-C and an Impression of the Montesa Scorpion.

Cycle World, July 1968, Road Impression of the Kawasaki 120 Road Runner.

Cycle World, August 1968, Road Test of the Benelli Riverside Mojave 360 and an Impression of the Bridgestone 100 Trail.

Cycle World, September 1968, Road Test of the Benelli Barracuda 250 and Impressions of the Jawa 90 Cross and the Vespa 150 Sprint.

Cycle World, October 1968, Road Tests of the Honda CL-175 Scrambler and Suzuki T-305 Raider.

Cycle World, November 1968, Road Tests of the Harley-Davidson Sprint SS-350 and Sears SR-250; Road Impression of the Suzuki KT-120.

Cycle World, January 1969, complete introduction to the Honda 750 Four.

Cycle World, February 1969, Road Test of the Suzuki T-350 Rebel and a Road Impression of the Suzuki TS-125 Stinger.

Cycle World, March 1969, Road Test of the Suzuki Savage.

Cycle World, April 1969, Road Tests of the Kawasaki Mach III and G3-SS, and the Honda CL-350, and a full-color, two-page ad for the new SL-90 Motosport (with a black frame).

Cycle World, May 1969, Impression of the Honda SL-90.

Cycle World, June 1969, Road Test of the Yamaha 250 YDS-6C and an Impression of the Yamaha Trailmaster 100 six-speed.

Cycle World, August 1969, Road Test of the Honda 750 Four and Jawa 402 Gelandesport.

Cycle World, September 1969, Road Test of the Bultaco Campera 175.

Cycle World, October 1969, Road Test of the Ossa Pioneer 250.

Cycle World, December 1969, Road Tests of the Bridgestone 100 TMX and Honda SL-350.

Cycle World, January 1970, Road Tests of the Kawasaki Big Horn and Bultaco Lobito Mk. II 100.

Cycle World, March 1970, Road Test of the Yamaha 650 XS-1.

Cycle World, April 1970, Road Test of the Suzuki TS-90 Honcho.

Cycle World, May 1970, Road Test of the Harley-Davidson Baja 100.

Cycle World, June 1970, Road Test of the Yamaha RS-350.

Cycle World, July 1970, Road Tests of the Honda CB-450 and Kawasaki Samurai SS.

Cycle World, August 1970, Road Test of the Triumph Trophy 250 and Impressions of the Hodaka 100/B & Super Rat and Yamaha AT-1 & AT-1 Motocross.

Cycle World, September 1970, tests of the Honda CL-100 & SL-100 and the Montesa King Scorpion.

Cycle World, October 1970, Road Tests of the Bridgestone 350 GTO and Suzuki T-500 III Titan.

Cycle World, November 1970, Road Tests of the Honda CB & SL-175's and a Road Impression of the restyled CL-175.

Cycle World, December 1970, Road Tests of the Honda SL-350 and Ossa 250 Stiletto.

Cycle World, January 1971, Road Test of the Kawasaki Mach III and an Impression of the Bultaco Lobito 175.

Cycle World, February 1971, tests of the Yamaha RT-1B & JT-1 Mini Enduro; Harley-Davidson Sprint SX-350 ad, Ducati R/T 450 ad; article on the new BSA/Triumph 350 twin that never made it to the U.S.

Cycle World, April 1971, tests of the Honda SL-125 Motosport and Kawasaki 125 Enduro.

Cycle World, July 1971, tests of the CB-350K3, Yamaha CT-1C Enduro, and the Ossa Pioneer.

Cycle World, September 1971, Road Tests of the Kawasaki 350 S2 and Ducati R/T 450 Desmo; ads for the Vespa lineup and a color back cover for Ducati R/T 450.

Cycle World, October 1971, Road Test of the Honda CB-500 Four.

Cycle World, December 1971, tests of the Suzuki GT-750, Yamaha LT-2MX, and Zundapp 125 Enduro.

Cycle World, March 1972, Road Tests of the Kawasaki Mach IV 750 and Suzuki 185 Sierra.

Cycle World, June 1972, Road Test of the Suzuki GT-380 Sebring.

Cycle World, October 1972, Road Test of the Hodaka 125 Wombat and a preview of the Kawasaki Z-1.

Cycle World, November 1972, Road Test of the Benelli Tornado 650-S.

Cycle World, December 1972, Road Test of the Yamaha TX-750.

Cycle World, January 1973, Road Test of the Suzuki GT-550 Indy.

Cycle World, February 1973, Road Tests of the Suzuki TS-125J Duster and the Yamaha LT-3MX & RD-350.

Cycle World, March 1973, Road Test of the Kawasaki Z-1.

Cycle World, April 1973, tests of the Bultaco 175 & 350 Alpinas and the Yamaha 360 MX.

Cycle World, June 1973, Roads Tests of the Harley-Davidson TX-125 and the Kawasaki 250, 350, 500, and 750 Triples.

Cycle World, November 1973, tests of the Honda XL-350 and Montesa King Scorpion 250 Automix.

Cycle World, April 1974, Enduro 175 Comparison Test of the Honda XL-175, Kawasaki F-7, Suzuki TS-185L, and Yamaha DT-175.

Cycle World, May 1974, Road Test of the Kawasaki KS-125 Enduro and the Triumph Trophy Trail TR5T (that never made it to the USA).

Cycle World, August 1974, Road Test of the Benelli Sei.

Cycle World, September 1974, tests of the Honda CB-200 and 1975 Yamaha YZ-250M Monoshock.

Cycle World, April 1975, Road Test of the Honda GL-1000 Gold Wing.

Cycle World, July 1975, test of the Kawasaki KX-250A and Bultaco Alpina 350.

Cycle World, August 1975, tests of the CB-500 Super Sport & the Yamaha YZC-125 MX and an ad for the full Hodaka line, including the new 250 Thunderdog to be released in mid-1975.

Cycle World, September 1975, Tour Test of the Suzuki RE-5 Rotary.

Cycle World, October 1975, tests of the Ossa Super Pioneer 250, Suzuki GT-185M Adventurer and the Yamaha TT500C (1976 model).

Cycle World Motorcycle Road Test Annual, 1969 (1968 models).

Cycle World Motorcycle Road Test Annual, 1971 (1970 models).

Cycle World Motorcycle Road Test Annual, 1976 (1975 models).

Don't Tell Dad, Peter Fonda, Hyperion, 1998.

Encyclopedia of the Harley-Davidson, The: Celebrating 100 Years, Peter Henshaw & Ian Kerr, Chartwell Books, Inc., 2003.

(*Floyd Clymer's*) *Cycle*, December 1958, Test of the Honda Dream and the debut of a Yamaha in the USA.

(*Floyd Clymer's*) *Cycle*, June 1960, Test of the Cushman Super Eagle.

(*Floyd Clymer's*) *Cycle*, July 1960, Test of the BSA Starfire Scrambler 250.

(*Floyd Clymer's*) *Cycle*, October 1960, Test of the Honda 150 Benly Touring.

(*Floyd Clymer's*) *Cycle*, December 1960, Test of the Mustang Thoroughbred.

(*Floyd Clymer's*) *Cycle*, January 1961, Test of the NSU Super Max.

(Floyd Clymer's) Cycle, July 1961, Introduction of Ducati Monza & Diana.

(Floyd Clymer's) Cycle, November 1961, Test of the Jawa 350.

(Floyd Clymer's) Cycle, December 1961, Test of the Harley-Davidson Sprint.

Floyd Clymer's Cycle, February 1962, Test of the Yamaguchi SPB Scrambler.

Floyd Clymer's Cycle, June 1962, Test of the BMW R-27 250.

Floyd Clymer's Cycle, August 1962, Test of the Yamaha 250 YDS-2.

Floyd Clymer's Motor Cycle, March 1963, Test of the Tohatsu Runpet 50.

Floyd Clymer's Motor Cycle, August 1963, Tohatsu Sport LE 125 ad.

Floyd Clymer's Motor Cycle, October 1963, Ducati Bronco Tour Test.

Floyd Clymer's Motor Cycle, January 1964, Tests of the Yamaha 80 and Ducati Mountaineer.

Floyd Clymer's Motor Cycle, March 1964, ad for the Yamaha YG-1 ($340), ad for the B7 and B50 Bridgestones, and a two-page B&W ad for the new U. S. Suzuki Motor Corporation administrative offices and warehouse under construction in Anaheim CA.

Floyd Clymer's Motor Cycle, June 1964, Road Test of the Honda 90 (white) and ad for the 18-hp Rabbit Superflow; Triumph Tiger Cub ad; introductory article for the new Simplex Senior.

Floyd Clymer's Motor Cycle, July 1964, Bridgestone 90 ad, two-page B&W ad for the new 27-hp YDS-3 for $630 and the new YA-6 for $454, both with oil injection.

Floyd Clymer's Motor Cycle, August 1964, Riverside 55 for $285 ad, new 1965 Yamaha announcement with details of the YA-6, YDS-3, and Riverside 55, all with oil injection; Ducati 5-speed ad.

Floyd Clymer's Motor Cycle, October 1964, ad for the Yamaha YG-1 with oil injection for $350 and Ducati Bronco and 5-speed ad in two parts; ad for Mustang trail model.

Floyd Clymer's Motor Cycle, July 1965, road test of the Yamaha Big Bear Scrambler.

Floyd Clymer's Motor Cycle, December 1965, road test of the Ossa 175 street model.

Floyd Clymer's Motor Cycle, January 1966, road test of the Bridgestone 90 Sport.

Floyd Clymer's Motor Cycle, February 1966, road tests of the Benelli Barracuda 250, Suzuki X-6 Hustler, Yamaha 50cc step-through, and Yamaha YL-1 twin.

Floyd Clymer's Motor Cycle, March 1966, road test of the Bridgestone 175 Dual Twin.

Floyd Clymer's Motor Cycle, April 1966, road tests of the Honda CB-160 Super Sport and Triumph Mountain Cub.

Floyd Clymer's Motor Cycle, May 1966, road test of the Yamaha 305 Cross Country.

Floyd Clymer's Motor Cycle, July 1966, road test of the Honda CL-160 Scrambler.

Floyd Clymer's Motor Cycle, August 1966, road test of the Rex KL-100 & KL-55.

Floyd Clymer's Motor Cycle, September 1966, road test of the Jawa Californian 350 Twin.

Great Bikes of the 70s, Petersen Publishing Company, 1981.

Hamlyn Guide to Japanese Motor Cycles, The, C. J. Ayton, The Hamlyn Publishing Group Limited, 1982.

Harley-Davidson: The Complete History, Patrick Hook & Garry Stuart, PRC Publishing, Ltd., 2002.

History of the Honda Scrambler, Bill Silver, edited by Mike Fitterling, Kindle E-book, Vintage Honda Publications, October 25, 2012.

Hodaka Story, The, a pamphlet printed and distributed to dealers by Pabatco

Honda Motorcycle Identification Guide 1959-2000, American Honda Motor Company, Inc., 2000. There were no 1966 CL-72's, although the Hawk continued into 1966; includes a page of all the tank badges applied to U.S. models.

Hot Rod Magazine, January 1964, full road test and detailed article on the Yamaha YDS-2.

Illustrated Buyer's Guide Harley-Davidson Classics 1903-1965, Jerry Hatfield, Motorbooks International, 1997.

Illustrated Harley-Davidson Buyer's Guide, Allan Girdler, Motorbooks International, 1986.

Kawasaki ID Guide (no publication details available).

Modern Cycle, November 1966, test of the Honda CL-160. The testers also noted the smoother 360-degree crankshaft. The data listed was $588, 279 pounds and a top speed of 83!

Motorcycle Buyer's Guide, Bob Greene, Petersen Publishing Company, 1970

Motorcycle Classics, Doug Mitchel and the Auto Editors of *Consumer Guide*, Publications International, Ltd., 1995 (hardcover).

Motorcycle Sport Book, 3rd Annual Edition, Bob Greene, Petersen Publishing Company, 1968. The Honda CL-77 Scrambler weighs 360 pounds, has red fork legs and no slip-on or welded-on muffler, and is priced at $695.

Motorcycle Sport Book, 4th Annual Edition, Bob Greene, Petersen Publishing Company, 1969

Motorcycle Sport Quarterly, Edited by Bob Greene, Petersen Publishing Company, Summer 1970

Motorcycle Sport Quarterly, Edited by Bob Greene, Petersen Publishing Company, Fall 1970

Motorcycle Sport Quarterly, Edited by Bob Greene, Petersen Publishing Company, Winter 1971.

Motorcycle Sport Quarterly, Edited by Bob Greene, Petersen Publishing Company, Spring 1971

Motorcycle Sport Quarterly, Edited by Bob Greene, Petersen Publishing Company, Summer 1971

Motorcyclist, September 1968, test of the Honda CL-175, recorded 16.52 in the quarter, an 80-mph top speed, and a weight of 284 pounds. The price listed was $586 in the Los Angeles area.

Old Bike Journal, December 1994, cover story on a restored 1962 Honda CL-250 Scrambler.

Petersen's Motorcycle Buyer's Guide, By the Editors of *Motorcyclist Magazine*, Petersen Publishing Company, 1973

Petersen's Motorcycle Buyer's Guide, By the Editors of *Motorcyclist Magazine*, Petersen Publishing Company, 1974

Petersen's Motorcycle Buyer's Guide, By the Editors of *Motorcyclist Magazine*, Petersen Publishing Company, 1975

Popular Science, May 1969, "Kawasaki Mach III: The Hottest Thing on Two Wheels".

Road Test's Sport Cycle featuring HONDA, Road Test Publications, Autumn 1966.

Standard Catalog of Japanese Motorcycles 1959-2007, The, Doug Mitchel, Kraus Publications, 2007.

Internet Bibliography

Allstate Cruisaire - scooterlounge.com/vespa/buyers-guide/vespa-sears.shtml
Allstate Model Numbers - allstateguy.tripod.com/id9.html
Allstate Retro Specialists - Motor West, Inc. - motorwestmotorcycles.com
Allstate Scooter Photos - mopedarmy.com/photos/brand/139/
Aprilia RS 50 Specifications - whitedogbikes.com
Aprilia RS 125 - bikez.com/motorcycles/aprilia_rs_125_2013.php
Aprilia Scarabeo - scootersales.com.au
Aprilia Scarabeo 50, 100, & 200 Reviews - scootersales.com.au
Aprilia Scarabeo History - scootercommunity.com.au/blogs
Aprilia USA - apriliausa.com
Barber Vintage Motorsports Museum - barbermuseum.org
Barber Museum Photos by Scott A. Craig - craigcentral.com/bikes/barber.asp
Benelli Mojave 360 - mybenellis.com/mojave.html
BMS 110 Honda Copycat - motobuys.com/bms-bi-metro-xlt-110.html
BMS Scooter Dealer - gokartsusa.com/moped-scooters.aspx
Bridgestone Capsule History - motorbike-search-engine.co.uk
Bridgestone Hurricane Scrambler - classicjapcycles.com
Bridgestone Motorcycles - bridgestone.skew.org
Bridgestone Motorcycles (Scott's) - bridgestonemotorcycle.com
Bultaco Brochures - storm.oldcarmanualproject.com/mpbultacometralla.htm
Bultaco Metralla Photos - seitz.us/metralla
Bultaco Metralla on YouTube - youtube.com/watch?v=XfjL1Ngvplk
Bultaco Model Reference Guide - cemoto.tripod.com/bultaco.htm
Classic Motorcycle Company - michaelsmotorcycles.com
Cushman Club of America - cushmanclubofamerica.com
Cushman Scooters - hobbytech.com
DomiRacer - domiracer.com
Ducati: Bevel Heaven - bevelheaven.com/brochure-index-range.htm
Ducati History - ducati.com/history/60s/mark_3/index.do
Extreme Scooters - Chinese Scooter Dealer - extreme-scooters.com
Fillmore West Shows - chickenonaunicycle.com/Fill%20West%20Shows.htm
Fuji Rabbit Scooters - fujirabbit.com
Happy Scooters - Chinese Scooter Dealer - happyscooters.com
Harley-Davidson Aermacchi Model Specs - aermacchi-world.de/thebikes.html
Harley-Davidson Aermacchi Racers - msolisvintagemotorcycle.com/home
Harley-Davidson CR Sprints - vft.org/Sprint/SprintCRPage.html
Harley-Davidson History - harleydhistory.freehostia.com/1960.htm
Harley-Davidson Hummer - harleyhummer.com
Harley-Davidson Hummer Club - harleyhummerclub.org
Harley-Davidson Restoration Photos - harleyrestoration.com
Harley-Davidson Sprint & Aermacchi Two-Stroke Parts - motomacchi.com
Harley-Davidson Topper Club - harleytopperclub.com
Hodaka - Strictly Hodaka - http://www.strictlyhodaka.com

Honda 50 - http://www.honda50.net
Honda - Classic Honda Club Norway - classichonda.no
Honda - Classic Honda Club Norway (Lars Eriksson's site) - hondahobby.no
Honda - Classic Honda Club Sweden - classichonda.se
Honda - Early Motorcycle Ads - vf750fd.com/vf750f/vin_1.html
Honda History - smokeriders.com/History
Honda Media Pages - hondanews.com
Honda Models - motorera.com/honda/index.htm
Honda Motorcycle Ads for Sale - vintageadsandstuff.com
Honda Motorcycle History - motorcycle.com/manufacturer
Honda Motorcycle Photos - classichondabikes.com
Honda Motorcycles - powersports.honda.com
Honda Rebel Review - fromthehandlebars.com/news/2009/sep/22
Honda Street Twins - motorcycleclassics.com/classic-japanese-motorcycles
Honda - Vintage Honda Benlys - theworldofmotorcycles.com
Jawa/CZ Registry - jawaczregister.org/links.php
Kawasaki History - motorshopdemammoet.com/kawasaki_history.htm
Kawasaki Motorcycle Identification Guide - classicjapcycles.com/articles
Kawasaki Motorcycles - kawasaki.com
Kawasaki Ninja 250 - 250ninja.net/
Kawasaki Triples Paint Chart - 3cyl.com
Kawasaki Triples Resources - kawtriple.com/mraxl/
Lambretta Model Specifications - lambretta.co.uk/models.html
Marusho / Lilac Motorcycle Register - marusholilac.com
Michael's Motorcycles - michaelsmotorcycles.com
Miscellaneous Early Motorcycle & Scooter Histories from Thailand - gt-rider.com
Motobi Motorcycle History - wheelsofitaly.com/wiki/index.php?title=Motobi
Motorcycle Specifications - motorcycle-specs.com
Motor West (BMW/Puch Restorations) - motorwestmotorcycles.com
Mustang Motorcycle Club of America - mmcoa.org
Ossa Brochures - lamaneta.net/motoguapa/historia8.html
Savoy Vintage Motorcycles for Sale - savoyvintagecycles.com/sales.html
Sheldon's European Motorcycle Universe - cybermotorcycle.com/index.html
Suzuki GZ250 Marauder - popularmechanics.com/cars/motorcycles
Suzuki GZ250 Marauder History - topspeed.com/motorcycles
Suzuki Media Pages - suzukicycles.com/Press.aspx
Suzuki Model History - suzukicycles.org
Suzuki Motorcycles - suzuki.com
Suzuki Vintage Advertising - pinterest.com/dadsvintageads
Suzuki 1966 X-6 Hustler at Jay Leno's Garage - jaylenosgarage.com
Tomahawk Boat Manufacturing Company - fiberglassics.com/library/Tomahawk
Triumph Motorcycle Brochures - motobrit.com/motc2/mpages/bro/bro-tri.php
Triumph 1964 Tiger Crashed by Bob Dylan - theselvedgeyard.wordpress.com
Triumph Tiger Cub Club - tigercubclub.co.uk
Vintage Honda (Bill Silver's site) - http://www.vintagehonda.com/

Vintage MX Bikes in the Movies - vintagemx.us/movies.htm
Walneck's Classic Cycle Trader - walnecks.com
Whizzer Motorbikes - whizzermotorbike.com
Wikipedia - en.wikipedia.org/wiki/Main_Page
Yamaha Model Identification - merrittmotorcyclesalvage.com
Yamaha Motorcycles - yamaha-motor.com
Yamaha Vintage Dirt Bike I.D. Guide - off-road.com
Yamaha YD-Series Brochures - classicyams.com
Yamaha YSR50 - ysr50.com
Yamaha YSR50 Parts - ysr50.org
Zundapp Bella - zbic.org/Discussion/message_list.asp?ForumID=3
Zundapp Fool - zundappfool.com/index.html

Photo Credits

Introduction

A1. 1965 Red Honda CL-72 Scrambler (cover) - Knut Hugo Hansen, photographer
A2. 1965 Red Bultaco Metralla 200 (back cover) - Michael's Motorcycles - (MK)
A3. 1964 Red Yamaha YG-1T (back cover) - Yamaha Motor Corporation, U.S.A.
A4. 1958 Blue Honda Super Cub - Mj-bird, photographer - (CC)
A5. 1963 Yamaha MF-2 Brochure - Yamaha Motor Corporation, U.S.A.
A6. 1948 Black Harley-Davidson 125 S - Charles "Mutt" Hallam, photographer
A7. Chrome Honda C-100 - Troyce Walls, photographer
A8. 1967 Black Honda CA-160 - Michael's Motorcycles - (MK)
A9. 1961 Red Harley-Davidson Sprint - Michael's Motorcycles - (MK)
A10. 1959 Ducati 200 SS - Michael's Motorcycles - (MK)
A11. 1966 Black BMW R-27 - Michael's Motorcycles - (MK)
A12. 1972 Kawasaki H2 750 Triple - Michael's Motorcycles - (MK)
A13. 1973 Kawasaki Z-1 900 - Michael's Motorcycles - (MK)
A14. 1975 Yamaha MX-250B - Yamaha Motor Corporation, U.S.A.
A15. 1987 Red Honda Rebel - Michael's Motorcycles - (MK)
A16. 1962 Red Harley-Davidson Pacer with Buckhorn Bars - Charles "Mutt" Hallam

Chapter 1 - Happy Days

B1. (1962) Red C-102 Cub with Gray & White Seat, D. Bellwood, photographer - (GNU)
B2. 1959-65 White Cushman Eagle - Chuck Schultz, photographer - (CC)
B3. 1963 Bridgestone 7 Ad - Bridgestone Corporation
B4. 1964 Black Suzuki T10 - Michael's Motorcycles - (MK)
B5. 1963 Honda CB-92R - Michael's Motorcycles - (MK)
B6. 1969 Kawasaki Full Line Brochure Front Page - Kawasaki Motors Corp., U.S.A.
B7. 1969 Kawasaki Tricycle Ad - Kawasaki Motors Corporation, U.S.A.
B8. 1967 Red Ducati Diana Mk. III - Michael's Motorcycles - (MK)
B9. 1964 Red Allstate Cruisaire - Michael's Motorcycles - (MK)
B10. 1968 Suzuki AS-50 Colt Brochure - Suzuki Motor of America, Inc.
B11. 1964 Yamaha YG-1T Brochure - Yamaha Motor Corporation, U.S.A.
B12. Black Honda CA-160 - Troyce Walls, photographer
B13. 1970 Green Yamaha XS-1 650 - Michael's Motorcycles - (MK)
B14. 1973 Kawasaki Z-1 900 Brochure - Kawasaki Motors Corporation, U.S.A.
B15. Black Bultaco Metralla Close-up - Jordi Carrasco, photographer - (CC)
B16. Black Honda CA-160 - Troyce Walls, photographer
B17. 1969 Kawasaki Mach III - Kawasaki Motors Corporation, U.S.A.
B18. 1983 Candy Presto Red Honda Nighthawk 550 - Floyd M. Orr Collection
B19. Purple 1963 Yamaha YG-1, Hamamatsu, Japan - PekePON, photographer - (CC)
B20. Red & Silver 1963 Yamaha YG-1 with Saddlebags - Floyd M. Orr Collection
B21. 1968 Yellow Honda CT-90 - Zul32, photographer - (CC)
B22. 1962 Red Yamaha Omaha Trail Brochure - Yamaha Motor Corporation, U.S.A.

B23. 1970 Gold Bridgestone TMX 100 - Michael's Motorcycles - (MK)
B24. 1969 Kawasaki 90 G3-TR Brochure - Kawasaki Motors Corporation, U.S.A.
B25. 1969 Suzuki Cat Brochure - Suzuki Motor of America, Inc.
B26. 1970 Yellow Yamaha AT-1B Enduro - Yamaha Motor Corporation, U.S.A.
B27. 1971 Yamaha AT-1CMX Muddy - Floyd M. Orr Collection
B28. 1965 Super Hawk - Mick from Northamptonshire, England, photographer - (CC)
B29. 1966 Black BMW R-27- Michael's Motorcycles - (MK)
B30. !966 Yamaha Twin Jet 100 Brochure Cover - Yamaha Motor Corporation, U.S.A.
B31. 1962 Yamaha MF-1 50 Brochure Cover - Yamaha Motor Corporation, U.S.A.

Chapter 2 - Americans

C1. 1947 Whizzer 150 - Yesterdays Antique Motorcycles, photographer - (GNU)
C2. 1952 Whizzer Pacemaker 700 Series - Russ Davis, photographer - (GNU)
C3. Red Simplex Servi-Cycle at the Barber Museum - Chuck Schultz, photographer - (CC)
C4. 1960 Black Mustang Stallion - Michael's Motorcycles - (MK)
C5. 1962-65 Red Cushman Super Silver Eagle - Chuck Schultz, photographer - (CC)
C6. Blue Cushman Eagle - Chuck Schultz, photographer - (CC)
C7. 1962 White Cushman Super Silver Eagle - Michael's Motorcycles - (MK)
C8. 1962 White Cushman Super Silver Eagle Close - Michael's Motorcycles - (MK)
C9. 1965 Allstate Compact - Ken Ashbrook, owner and photographer
C10. 1952 Red Allstate 1-hp Scooter - Michael's Motorcycles - (MK)
C11. 1956 Red Cushman Allstate, Barber Museum - Chuck Schultz, photographer (CC)
C12. 1964 Red Allstate Cruisaire - Michael's Motorcycles - (MK)
C13. 1964 Red Allstate Cruisaire with Spare Tire Option - Ken Ashbrook, photographer
C14. 1965 Allstate Sport 60 - David Struble, owner and photographer
C15. Allstate ISDT Scrambler Close - Troyce Walls, owner and photographer
C16. (1954) Maroon Allstate 250 SGS - Troyce Walls, owner and photographer
C17. (1954) Maroon Allstate 250 SGS - Troyce Walls, owner and photographer
C18. Allstate ISDT Scrambler - Troyce Walls, owner and photographer
C19. Smiths Speedometer Showing 1554 Miles on ISDT - Troyce Walls, photographer
C20. Allstate ISDT Scrambler - Troyce Walls, owner and photographer
C21. Allstate ISDT Scrambler Close - Troyce Walls, owner and photographer
C22. (1954) Maroon Allstate 250 SGS - Troyce Walls, owner and photographer
C23. 1967 Black Sears SR 250 - Dan Spanncraft, owner and photographer
C24. Allstate ISDT Scrambler - Troyce Walls, owner and photographer
C25. 1965 Allstate 250 - Dennis Bratland, photographer - (CC)
C26. 1968 Sears 124 Left Side - Michael's Motorcycles - (MK)
C27. 1968 Sears 124 Right Side - Michael's Motorcycles - (MK)
C28. (1954) Maroon Allstate 250 SGS - Troyce Walls, owner and photographer
C29. Allstate Scrambler ISDT - Troyce Walls, owner and photographer
C30. 1960 Red Harley-Davidson Super 10 - Charles "Mutt" Hallam, photographer
C31. 1948 Black Harley-Davidson 125 S - Charles "Mutt" Hallam, photographer
C32. 1951 Red Harley-Davidson 125 S Tele-Glide - Charles "Mutt" Hallam, photographer
C33. Black Hummer in Austin TX - Floyd M. Orr Collection

C34. 1959 Red Harley-Davidson STU 165 with Accessories - Charles "Mutt" Hallam
C35. 1961 Red Harley-Davidson Super 10 - Charles "Mutt" Hallam, photographer
C36. 1964 Black Harley-Davidson Pacer - Charles "Mutt" Hallam, photographer
C37. 1962 Red Harley-Davidson Scat - Charles "Mutt" Hallam, photographer
C38. 1961 Harley-Davidson Sprint Right Side - Michael's Motorcycles - (MK)
C39. 1961 Harley-Davidson Sprint Left Side - Michael's Motorcycles - (MK)
C40. Red Harley-Davidson SS-350 Sprint - Troyce Walls, photographer
C41. Red 1968 Harley-Davidson Sprint CRS - Warren P. Warnes, photographer
C42. 1966 Red Harley-Davidson M50 - Chuck Schultz, photographer - (CC)
C43. 1962 Red Harley-Davidson Pacer with Buckhorn Bars - Charles "Mutt" Hallam
C44. White Cushman Super Eagle at the Barber Museum - Chuck Schultz - (CC)

Chapter 3 - Europeans

D1. 1950 DKW RT 125 at the Audi Museum - Lothar Spurzem, photographer - (CC)
D2. 1955 NSU Superlux - Lothar Spurzem, photographer - (CC)
D3. 1957 Supermax - Huhu Uet, photographer - (GNU)
D4. 1964 Black BMW R-27 - User R69S Jeff Dean, photographer - (PD)
D5. 1957 White BMW R-26 - Michael's Motorcycles - (MK)
D6. 1961-64 Zundapp Bella 200 - ChiemseeMan, photographer - (PD)
D7. 1962 Zundapp 250 S - Piero, photographer - (GNU)
D8. Sea Green Zundapp Bella R-154 - Lothar Spurzem, photographer - (CC)
D9. Black NSU Super Max - Rikita, photographer - (CC)
D10. Maroon Jawa 250 Type 353 - Lukfa, photographer - (GNU)
D11. 1968 Red Jawa Cross 90 - Michael's Motorcycles - (MK)
D12. 1963 Jawa Price List - Floyd M. Orr Collection
D13. 1967 Triumph Mountain Cub Right Side - Michael's Motorcycles - (MK)
D14. 1964 Triumph Tiger Cub - Alan, photographer - (CC)
D15. 1967 Triumph Mountain Cub Left Side- Michael's Motorcycles - (MK)
D16. 1967 Triumph Mountain Cub Close - Michael's Motorcycles - (MK)
D17. BSA Shooting Star - TR001, photographer - (CC)
D18. 1970 BSA 441 Victor Special - Michael's Motorcycles - (MK)
D19. 1962 Vespa GL 150 - Christian Scheja, photographer - (CC)
D20. 1963 Vespa 150 - Paulgoo, photographer - (PD)
D21. 1977 Vespa P200E - Jay Cross, photographer - (CC)
D22. Lambretta 150 - Piero Tasso, photographer - (GNU)
D23. 1967 Lambretta SX200 - Mick in Northamptonshire, England, photographer (CC)
D24. Ducati Sport 48 - Alf van Beem, photographer - (PD)
D25. 1964 Ducati Bronco 125 - Dennis Bratland, photographer - (CC)
D26. 1965 Ducati Monza - David Cassady, owner and photographer
D27. 1969 Silver Ducati 350 Desmo Cafe Racer - Michael's Motorcycles - (MK)
D28. 1972 Ducati 350 Scrambler - The Javelina, photographer - (CC)
D29. Red & Gold Ducati 200 SS - Ronald Saunders, Warrington, UK, photographer - (CC)
D30. 1970 Ducati Mach 1 - Spath Chr., photographer - (PD)
D31. 1966 Red Ducati Monza Jr. 160 - Michael's Motorcycles - (MK)

D32. 1962 Blue Ducati Diana Mark III 250 - Michael's Motorcycles - (MK)

D33. 1964 Ducati Mach 1 - El Caganer, photographer - (CC)

D34. 1983 Honda Nighthawk 550 - Floyd M. Orr Collection

D35. 1967 Ducati Diana Mk. III Front - Michael's Motorcycles - (MK)

D36. 1967 Ducati Diana Mk. III Rear - Michael's Motorcycles - (MK)

D37. 1965 Red Benelli 125 Cobra - K. Ivoulin, photographer - (CC)

D38. 1968 Benelli Riverside Nuovo Luincino 125 - Michael's Motorcycles - (MK)

D39. 1968 Benelli Riverside Nuovo Luincino 125 - Michael's Motorcycles - (MK)

D40. Benelli Riverside 250 - El Caganer, photographer - (CC)

D41. 1972 Benelli 650S Tornado - El Caganer, photographer - (CC)

D42. Red Motobi at the Barber Museum- Chuck Schultz, photographer - (CC)

D43. 1960 Motobi 125 Right Side - Michael's Motorcycles - (MK)

D44. 1960 Motobi 125 Left Side - Michael's Motorcycles - (MK)

D45. 1960 Motobi 125 Rear View - Michael's Motorcycles - (MK)

D46. 1970 Motobi 125 Sport Special - Huhu, photographer - (PD)

D47. 1963 Montesa Impala 175 - Peprovira, photographer - (GNU)

D48. 1965 Black Montesa Impala Sport 250 - Michael's Motorcycles - (MK)

D49. 1965 Black Montesa Impala Sport 250 - Michael's Motorcycles - (MK)

D50. 1962 Impala C Front View - Peprovira, photographer - (CC)

D51. 1958 Blue Ossa 150 in Zamora, Spain - Antramir, photographer - (CC)

D52. 1972 Ossa Plonker 250 - Michael's Motorcycles - (MK)

D53. 1967 Bultaco Price List - Floyd M. Orr Collection

D54. 1969 Bultaco Lobito Mk. III 125 - Peprovira, photographer - (GNU)

D55. 1967 Silver Bultaco Metralla - Michael's Motorcycles - (MK)

D56. 1970 Bultaco Price List - Floyd M. Orr Collection

D57. 1970 Bultaco Specifications Sheet - Floyd M. Orr Collection

D58. 1966 Bultaco Metralla Mk. II 250 - Peprovira, photographer - (GNU)

D59. 1965 Red Bultaco Metralla 200 - Michael's Motorcycles - (MK)

D60. 1965 Red Bultaco Metralla 200 Close - Michael's Motorcycles - (MK)

D61. 1967 Silver Bultaco Metralla 250 Mk. II - Michael's Motorcycles - (MK)

D62. 1962 Blue & White Ducati 125 TS - Michael's Motorcycles - (MK)

D63. 1965 Tiger Cub - Mick from Northamptonshire, England, photographer - (CC)

Chapter 4 - Early Asians

E1. Early Mitsubishi Silver Pigeon - Mitsucarman, photographer - (GNU)

E2. 1963 Pointer Specifications Sheet - Floyd M. Orr Collection

E3. 1963 Pointer Super Lassie Brochure - Floyd M. Orr Collection

E4. Letter from Pointer - Floyd M. Orr Collection

E5. Rabbit 150 Touring - Eric, photographer - (CC)

E6. Black Marusho 500 at the Barber Museum - Chuck Schultz, photographer - (CC)

E7. Red Marusho ST500 - Troyce Walls

E8. Hodakas at the AMA Vintage Motorcycle Days - Jamie Aaron, photographer - (PD)

E9. Hodaka Combat Wombat, Barber Museum - Chuck Schultz, photographer - (CC)

E10. 1963 Bridgestone B-50 Ad - Bridgestone Corporation

E11. 1963 Bridgestone 7 Ad - Bridgestone Corporation
E12. 1964 Bridgestone 7 Ad - Bridgestone Corporation
E13. 1964 Bridgestone 50 & 90 Ad - Bridgestone Corporation
E14. 1965 Black Bridgestone 50 Sport - Neil Geldof, Connecticut, USA
E15. 1965 Bridgestone Price List - Bridgestone Corporation
E16. 1965 Bridgestone People & Personalities Ad - Bridgestone Corporation
E17. 1967 Tiny Bridgestone Brochure - Bridgestone Corporation
E18. 1967 Sexy Dual Twin Ad from *Cycle* 5/68 - Bridgestone Corporation
E19. Four 1967 Bridgestone 90's Brochure - Bridgestone Corporation
E20. 1967 Bridgestone 350 GTR Ad from *Cycle World* 8/67 - Bridgestone Corporation
E21. 1970 Bridgestone GTO from Full Line Brochure - Bridgestone Corporation
E22. 1968 Red Bridgestone GTR - Michael's Motorcycles - (MK)
E23. 1967 Red Dual Twin Brochure Photo - Bridgestone Corporation
E24. 1969 Front Page of Bridgestone Full Line Brochure - Bridgestone Corporation

Chapter 5 - Suzuki

F1. Black Suzuki 250 T-20 & White Honda 90 with Classic Cars - Floyd M. Orr Collection
F2. 1968 Red Suzuki TC-250 Scrambler - Suzuki Motor of America, Inc.
F3. 1964 B&W Suzuki Hill-Billy Ad - Suzuki Motor of America, Inc.
F4. 1964 Black Suzuki T-10 250 Right Side - Michael's Motorcycles - (MK)
F5. 1963 Suzuki Classic 50 & El Camino 250 Ad - Suzuki Motor of America, Inc.
F6. 1964 Black Suzuki T-10 250 Left Side - Michael's Motorcycles - (MK)
F7. 1964 White Suzuki M31 - Dick Feightner, owner and photographer
F8. 1964 Suzuki Singles Price List - Suzuki Motor of America, Inc.
F9. 1964 Suzuki Twins Price List - Suzuki Motor of America, Inc.
F10. 1964 Suzuki Cavalier M12-2 Brochure - Suzuki Motor of America, Inc.
F11. 1966 Red X-6 Scrambler Indoors - Michael's Motorcycles - (MK)
F12. 1966 Red X-6 Scrambler Close - Michael's Motorcycles - (MK)
F13. 1966 Red X-6 Scrambler Right Side - Michael's Motorcycles - (MK)
F14. 1966 Red Suzuki X-6, Salon de la Moto, Paris - The Supermat, photographer - (CC)
F15. 1967 Black Suzuki B-105P Bearcat 120 - Don Quayle, photographer
F16. 1969 Suzuki AS-50 Colt Brochure - Suzuki Motor of America, Inc.
F17. 1969 Suzuki 50 Maverick Brochure - Suzuki Motor of America, Inc.
F18. 1970 Lime Green Suzuki AC-50 Maverick - Dick Feightner, photographer
F19. 1975 Aspen Yellow Suzuki TM-100 Contender - Suzuki Motor of America, Inc.
F20. 1967 B&W Stingray 200 Ad from *Cycle* 7/67 - Suzuki Motor of America, Inc.
F21. 1969 Suzuki 125 Stinger Brochure - Suzuki Motor of America, Inc.
F22. 1971 Lime Green Suzuki 125 Stinger - Michael's Motorcycles - (MK)
F23. 1972 Blue Suzuki Titan 500 - Michael's Motorcycles - (MK)
F24. 1972 Suzuki 90 Rover J Brochure - Suzuki Motor of America, Inc.
F25. 1967 Dark Blue Suzuki B-120 - Suzuki Motor of America, Inc.
F26. 1969 Suzuki Savage 250 Brochure - Suzuki Motor of America, Inc.
F27. 1973 Suzuki Pine Green 125 Prospector K Brochure - Suzuki photo
F28. 1974 Suzuki RL-250 Exacta - Don Quayle, owner and photographer

F29. 1975 Red Suzuki GT-380 - Reg McKenna, photographer - (CC)

F30. 1975 Suzuki RE-5M - Gtregs75, photographer - (CC)

F31. 1975 Suzuki RE-5 Rotary Instrument Panel - Michael's Motorcycles - (MK)

F32. 1968 Red Suzuki T-500 - Suzuki Motor of America, Inc.

F33. 1972 Suzuki GT-380 Sebring - Reg McKenna, photographer - (CC)

F34. 1973 Suzuki GT-750 in Pearl Red & Tan - Edward A. Zunz III, photographer - (CC)

F35. 1975 Suzuki GT-550 Indy Brochure - Suzuki Motor of America, Inc.

F36. 1975 Suzuki GT-750 LeMans - Suzuki Motor of America, Inc.

F37. Black Suzuki T10, Salon de la Moto, Paris 2011 - The Supermat, photographer - (CC)

Chapter 6 - Kawasaki

G1. 1964 Omega 125 Ad - Kawasaki Motors Corporation, U.S.A.

G2. 1970 Kawasaki G3-SS Bushmaster Brochure - Kawasaki Motors Corporation, U.S.A.

G3. 1964 Kawasaki SG - Kawasaki Motors Corporation, U.S.A.

G4. 1965 Kawasaki B8S - Kawasaki Motors Corporation, U.S.A.

G5. Kawasaki G31M Centurion 100 - Kawasaki Motors Corporation, U.S.A.

G6. 1966 Kawasaki 650 W1 Brochure - Kawasaki Motors Corporation, U.S.A.

G7. 1966 Kawasaki 100 D1 Brochure - Kawasaki Motors Corporation, U.S.A.

G8. 1966 Kawasaki F2TR 175 Trail Brochure - Kawasaki Motors Corporation, U.S.A.

G9. 1968 Red Kawasaki W2SS Left Side - Michael's Motorcycles - (MK)

G10. 1968 Red Kawasaki W2SS Right Side - Michael's Motorcycles - (MK)

G11. 1967 Samurai, Avenger, & Commander Ad - Kawasaki Motors Corporation, U.S.A.

G12. 1967 Samurai Brochure: *Fun People Go Kawasaki* - Kawasaki Motors Corp., U.S.A.

G13. 1967 Kawasaki Avenger - Kawasaki Motors Corporation, U.S.A.

G14. Kawasaki 650 SS at the Barber Museum - Chuck Schultz, photographer - (CC)

G15. 1968 Kawasaki C2 SS Brochure - Kawasaki Motors Corporation, U.S.A.

G16. 1969 Kawasaki 90 G3-TR Brochure - Kawasaki Motors Corporation, U.S.A.

G17. 1968 Kawasaki C2 TR brochure - Kawasaki Motors Corporation, U.S.A.

G18. 1967 Kawasaki Commander W1 650 Brochure - Kawasaki Motors Corp., U.S.A.

G19. Early 1967 Kawasaki Samurai 250 Brochure - Kawasaki Motors Corporation, U.S.A.

G20. 1971 Kawasaki F81M 250 Brochure - Kawasaki Motors Corporation, U.S.A.

G21. 1971 Kawasaki Avenger SS 350 Brochure - Kawasaki Motors Corporation, U.S.A.

G22. 1971 Kawasaki 100 Trail Boss Brochure - Kawasaki Motors Corporation, U.S.A.

G23. 1974 Kawasaki 175 Enduro Brochure - Kawasaki Motors Corporation, U.S.A.

G24. 1973 Kawasaki 900 Z1 Brochure - Kawasaki Motors Corporation, U.S.A.

G25. 1972 Kawasaki 175 F7 Enduro Brochure - Kawasaki Motors Corporation, U.S.A.

G26. 1975 Kawasaki Z1 900 Brochure - Kawasaki Motors Corporation, U.S.A.

G27. 1971 Kawasaki 500 Mach III Brochure - Kawasaki Motors Corporation, U.S.A.

G28. 1973 Kawasaki S-1 250 Brochure - Kawasaki Motors Corporation, U.S.A.

G29. 1973 Kawasaki S-2 350 Brochure - Kawasaki Motors Corporation, U.S.A.

G30. 1974 Kawasaki S-3 400 Triple Brochure - Kawasaki Motors Corporation, U.S.A.

G31. Late 1970 Candy Red Kawasaki H1 Brochure - Kawasaki Motors Corp., U.S.A.

G32. Early 1970 Peacock Gray Kawasaki H1 Brochure - Kawasaki Motors Corp., U.S.A.

G33. Late 1970 Kawasaki Mach III in European trim - Kawasaki Motors Corp., U.S.A.

G34. 1972 Pearl Candy Orange Kawasaki H1 Brochure - Kawasaki Motors Corp., U.S.A.
G35. 1972 Kawasaki H2 750 Triple Brochure - Kawasaki Motors Corporation, U.S.A.
G36. 1972 Kawasaki H2 Left Side - Michael's Motorcycles (MK)
G37. 1972 Kawasaki H2 Engine Close-up - Michael's Motorcycles (MK)
G37. 1973 Kawasaki S-2 350 Brochure - Kawasaki Motors Corporation, U.S.A.
G38. 1971 Candy Blue Kawasaki Mach III - Floyd M. Orr Collection
G39. Yvon Duhamel's Racing Triple - Chuck Schultz, photographer - (CC)
G40. 1974 Kawasaki KX-125 Brochure - Kawasaki Motors Corporation, U.S.A.
G41. 1970 Kawasaki F5 Big Horn Brochure - Kawasaki Motors Corporation, U.S.A.
G42. 1969 Yellow Kawasaki A7 SS Brochure - Kawasaki Motors Corporation, U.S.A.
G43. Kawasaki H1-R Road Racer - Andrew Basterfield, photographer - (CC)
G44. 1969 Kawasaki 90 G3-SS Brochure - Kawasaki Motors Corporation, U.S.A.

Chapter 7 - Yamaha

H1. 1957-58 Yamaha 250 YD-1 - Rikita, photographer - (CC)
H2. 1959 Gold YDS-1 - Peter Abelmann, Germany, owner and photographer
H3. 1959 Gold & White Yamaha YDS-1 - Rikita, photographer - (CC)
H4. 1962 Yamaha YDS-2 Brochure - Yamaha Motor Corporation, U.S.A.
H5. 1962 Black Yamaha YA-5 Brochure Crop - Yamaha Motor Corporation, U.S.A.
H6. 1963 Yamaha Red MJ-2 Brochure - Yamaha Motor Corporation, U.S.A.
H7. 1964 Blue Yamaha YD-3A 250 - Warren P. Warner, owner and photographer
H8. 1963 All Red YG-1 Brochure - Yamaha Motor Corporation, U.S.A.
H9. 1964-65 Yamaha Full Line Brochure - Yamaha Motor Corporation, U.S.A.
H10. 1963 Purple Yamaha YG-1 Brochure - Yamaha Motor Corporation, U.S.A.
H11. 1966 Yamaha Twin Jet 100 on Red - Yamaha Motor Corporation, U.S.A.
H12. 1966 Yamaha Big Bear Scrambler Brochure - Yamaha Motor Corporation, U.S.A.
H13. 1967 Yamaha 60 with Rotary Valve & Oil Injection - Yamaha Motor Corp., U.S.A.
H14. 1967 Yellow Yamaha Trailmaster 100 Brochure - Yamaha Motor Corp., U.S.A.
H15. 1967 Red Yamaha Santa Barbara 125 Brochure - Yamaha Motor Corp., U.S.A.
H16. 1968 Yamaha Grand Prix 350 & GP Scrambler - Yamaha Motor Corp., U.S.A.
H17. 1966 Red Yamaha Big Bear 250 Scrambler Brochure - Yamaha Motor Corp., U.S.A.
H18. 1964 Black Yamaha YDT-1 Sparkle - Warren P. Warner, owner and photographer
H19. 1965 Blue YDS-3 - Chris A. Harris, Australia, owner and photographer
H20. 1968 Yamaha Grand Prix & GP Scrambler Brochure - Yamaha Motor Corp., U.S.A.
H21. 1968 Red YAS1-C - Peter Abelman, Germany, owner and photographer
H22. 1969 Blue Yamaha AS2-C 125 Scrambler - Yamaha Motor Corporation, U.S.A.
H23. 1967 Black YM2-C Big Bear 305 Scrambler - Peter Abelmann, Germany
H24. 1969 Candy Gold Yamaha DT-1B Brochure - Yamaha Motor Corporation, U.S.A.
H25. 1955 Maroon Yamaha YA-1 in a Museum - Rikita, photographer - (GNU)
H26. 1962 Black Yamaha 125 YA-5 Brochure - Yamaha Motor Corporation, U.S.A.
H27. 1963 Red Yamaha 125 YA-5 Brochure - Yamaha Motor Corporation, U.S.A.
H28. 1965 Yamaha Ascot & Daytona Brochure - Yamaha Motor Corporation, U.S.A.
H29. 1966 Yamaha Ascot & Daytona Brochure - Yamaha Motor Corporation, U.S.A.
H30. 1964 Red Yamaha TD-1B with Fairing - Warren P. Warner, photographer

H31. 1967 Yamaha TD-1C Right Side - Warren P. Warner, photographer

H32. 1967 Yamaha TD-1C Left Side - Warren P. Warner, photographer

H33. 1969 White & Red Yamaha TD2 - Ytak171, photographer - (GNU)

H34. 1970 Blue & White Yamaha G6S 80 - Yamaha Motor Corporation, U.S.A.

H35. 1970 Purple & 1972 Gold DS-7 250's - Peter Abelmann, Germany, photographer

H36. 1972 Red Yamaha XS-650B - Michael's Motorcycles - (MK)

H37. 1972 Purple & White Yamaha RD-200 - Yamaha Motor Corporation, U.S.A.

H38. 1973 Blue & Gold Yamaha TX-650 - Michael's Motorcycles - (MK)

H39. 1973 Blue Yamaha RD-60 - Jimmy Singer, owner and photographer

H40. 1970 California Orange Yamaha HS-1 90 Twin - Don Quayle, Costa Mesa, CA

H41. 1971 Competition Yellow Yamaha HS-1B 90 Twin - Peter Abelmann, Germany

H42. Red & White Yamaha RD-350 - John Goetzinger, photographer - (CC)

H43. 1968 Yamaha DT-1 Museum Photo - Rikita, photographer - (GNU)

H44. 1968 Yamaha DT-1 - Don Quayle, Costa Mesa, CA, owner and photographer

H45. 1968 Yamaha DT-1 Enduro Brochure, Page 1 - Yamaha Motor Corporation, U.S.A.

H46. 1968 Yamaha DT-1 Enduro Brochure, Page 2 - Yamaha Motor Corporation, U.S.A.

H47. 1971 Brilliant Red Yamaha 125 AT-1C Enduro - Michael's Motorcycles - (MK)

H48. 1970 Green CT-1B 175 Enduro Brochure - Yamaha Motor Corporation, U.S.A.

H49. 1972 Silver Yamaha RT-2 Enduro Brochure - Yamaha Motor Corporation, U.S.A.

H50. 1971 Black RT-1B - Peter Abelmann, Germany, owner and photographer

H51. 1975 Orange Yamaha DT-250B Enduro Brochure - Yamaha Motor Corp., U.S.A.

H52. 1963 Purple & Silver YG-1 Brochure Photo - Yamaha Motor Corporation, U.S.A.

H53. 1972 Yamaha MF-1 Brochure Photo - Yamaha Motor Corporation, U.S.A.

H54. Blue Yamaha YL-1 - Peter Abelmann, Germany, owner and photographer

H55. 1964 Blue Yamaha YD3-A - Warren P. Warner, owner and photographer

H56. Red Yamaha Big Bear Scrambler Close at El Camino 2006 - Don Quayle

Chapter 8 - Honda

I1. 1966 Black Honda C-100 Cub at Pickwick Lake - Floyd M. Orr Collection

I2. 1966 Black Honda C-100 Cub in the Mud - Floyd M. Orr Collection

I3. 1966 Black Honda C-100 Cub Night Cub - Floyd M. Orr Collection

I4. 1966 Black Honda C-100 Chopper Cub - Floyd M. Orr Collection

I5. 1966 Black Honda C-100 Sissy Bar - Floyd M. Orr Collection

I6. 1966 Black Honda C-100 Chrome Bars - Floyd M. Orr Collection

I7. 1966-67 Black Honda CL-160 - Troyce Walls, photographer

I8. 1965 White CA-77 Dream at the Barber Museum - Chuck Schultz, photographer (CC)

I9. (1957) Black Dream ME - Troyce Walls, photographer

I10. 1961-62 Red C-72 Dream with Red Seat - Jon Arild Monsen, photographer

I11. 1963 Red CB-92R Right Side- Michael's Motorcycles - (MK)

I12. 1963 Black Super Hawk Right Side - Michael's Motorcycles - (MK)

I13. 1951 Black Honda Dream E in a Museum- Rikita, photographer - (CC)

I14. 1961 Red Honda CB-92 Left Side - Khaosaming, photographer - (CC)

I15. 1960 Red C71 Dream with Red Seat - Knut Hugo Hansen, owner and photographer

I16. 1961 Blue CB-92 with Red Seat Left Side - Maysy, photographer - (CC)

I17. Black CB-160 Right Side - Matt Hamilton, owner and photographer
I18. 1966 Honda CB-450 Black Bomber - Michael's Motorcycles - (MK)
I19. 1965 Red S-90, Barber Motorsports Museum - Redhawkrider, photographer - (CC)
I20. Black Sport 65 - Don Quayle, Costa Mesa, CA, owner and photographer
I21. 1968 Blue SS125A with White Ferrari - Paul Davies, owner and photographer
I22. 1968 Blue SS125A - Paul Davies, owner and photographer
I23. 1969 Honda CB-750 Four, Barber Museum - Chuck Schultz, photographer - (CC)
I24. Honda Cub Motorbike at the Barber Museum - Chuck Schultz, photographer - (CC)
I25. 1997 Honda Dream 50 at Boxenstop Tubingen - Klaus Nahr, photographer - (CC)
I26. 1962 Black Honda CB-77 Left Side - American Honda Motor Company, Inc.
I27. 1972 Candy Jet Green CB-500 - Douglas G. Sheldon, owner and photographer
I28. 1973 Yellow Honda XL-250 - Lorddiagram, photographer - (PD)
I29. 1973 Honda Elsinore 250 Front - Don Quayle, owner and photographer
I30. 1974 CB-350F1 - Lars Eriksson, Norway, owner and photographer
I31. 1975 Red CB-400F with Desmo - Michael's Motorcycles - (MK)
I32. 1975 CD-175 - Clifford Feamley, Lincolnshire, owner and photographer - (CC)
I33. Black Honda CA-160 Left Side - Troyce Walls, photographer
I34. 1967 Black Dream 305 Left Side - John, owner and photographer
I35. 1968 Black CA-77 Dream - Steven Christmas, owner and photographer
I36. Black Honda C-115 Sport Cub Right Side - Troyce Walls, photographer
I37. Black Sport 65 Front - Don Quayle, Costa Mesa, CA, owner and photographer
I38. 1966 Black Honda S-90 Top View - Topsy1golf, photographer - (PD)
I39. 1963 Red Honda CB-92R Left Side - Michael's Motorcycles - (MK)
I40. 1967 Black CB-160 (UK) - Peter Horton, owner and photographer
I41. Red Honda CB-72 Hawk Indoors - Rikita, photographer - (CC)
I42. 1967 Red Honda CB-77 Super Hawk - Michael's Motorcycles - (MK)
I43. 1967 Black Honda CB-77 Super Hawk - Michael's Motorcycles - (MK)
I44. 1966 Blue Super Hawk, Barber Museum - Chuck Schultz, photographer - (CC)
I45. 1968 Green Honda CB-350 with Saddlebags - Michael's Motorcycles - (MK)
I46. 1973 Red Honda CB-350F with Saddlebags - Drahbany, photographer - (PD)
I47. 1974 Red Honda CB-360 with Luggage Rack- Aaron Headly, photographer - (CC)
I48. 1976 Blue Honda CB-360T Left Side - Annecananne, photographer - (PD)
I49. 1975 Red Honda CB-400F Super Sport Low Bars- Michael's Motorcycles - (MK)
I50. 1975 Red Honda CB-400F Super Sport High Bars - Michael's Motorcycles - (MK)
I51. 1975 Red Honda CB-400F Museum Photo - Rikita, photographer - (CC)
I52. 1966 Honda Black Bomber Right Side - Michael's Motorcycles - (MK)
I53. 1974 Honda CB-450K7 Right Side - Guydraud, photographer - (GNU)
I54. 1969 Blue Green Honda CB-750 Four Sandcast - Michael's Motorcycles - (MK)
I55. 1969 Blue Green Honda CB-750 Four - American Honda Motor Company, Inc.
I56. Blue Honda SL-70 Left Side - Ltpreston, photographer - (PD)
I57. 1969-70 Gold SL-350 at the Barber Museum - Redhawkrider, photographer - (CC)
I58. Blue Honda CB-92 with Red Seat - American Honda Motor Company, Inc.
I59. 1958 Blue Honda 50 Cub with Red Seat - American Honda Motor Company, Inc.
I60. 1966 White Honda 90 CM91 - Michael's Motorcycles - (MK)
I61. 1966 Black Honda CB-160 with Western Bars - Michael's Motorcycles - (MK)

I62. 1972 Candy Gold CB-350 K4 - Nicolas Will, Brooklyn, photographer - (CC)

I63. 1975 Blue Gold Wing at the Barber Museum - Silosarg, photographer - (CC)

I64. 1975 Blue Gold Wing - Tommi Nummelin, photographer - (CC)

I65. 1963 *You Meet the Nicest People* Ad - American Honda Motor Company, Inc.

Chapter 9 - Honda Scramblers

J1. 1963 Red CL-72 Alloy Tank Exhaust Close - Michael's Motorcycles - (MK)

J2. 1962 Red Restored CL-72 Left Side - Michael's Motorcycles - (MK)

J3. Honda CL-100 Right Side - Steve Henderson, photographer - (GNU)

J4. Honda Black CL-160 Scrambler Left Side - Troyce Walls, photographer

J5. Honda Black CL-160 Scrambler Right Side - Troyce Walls, photographer

J6. 1972 Blue CL-175 K6 Left Side - Michael's Motorcycles - (MK)

J7. 1974 Blue CL-200 Left Side - Thadanator, photographer - (GNU)

J8. 1962 Honda CL-72. Barber Vintage Museum - Chuck Schultz, photographer - (CC)

J9. 1963 Red CL-72 Alloy Left Side - Michael's Motorcycles - (MK)

J10. 1962 Red $7495 CL-72 Left Side - Michael's Motorcycles - (MK)

J11. 1963 Red CL-72 Alloy Right Side - Michael's Motorcycles - (MK)

J12. 1963 Red CL-72 Alloy Right Side Close - Michael's Motorcycles - (MK)

J13. 1965 Red CL-72 Cover Photo - Knut Hugo Hansen, owner and photographer

J14. 1967 Early Black CL-77 Left Side Round Taillight - Michael's Motorcycles - (MK)

J15. 1967 Early Black CL-77 Left Side - Michael's Motorcycles - (MK)

J16. 1967 Late Red CL-77 Left Side - Michael's Motorcycles - (MK)

J17. 1967 Late Red CL-77 Right Side - Michael's Motorcycles - (MK)

J18. 1967 Late Red CL-77 Left Side Close - Michael's Motorcycles - (MK)

J19. 1975 Orange CL-360 - Mick from Northamptonshire, England, photographer - (CC)

J20. 1970 Blue Honda CL-450 Left Side - Michael's Motorcycles - (MK)

J21. 1971 Orange CL-450 Left Side - Jayt1980, photographer - (PD)

J22. 1971 Yamaha AT-1CMX & Blue 1971 Honda CL-350 K2 - Floyd M. Orr Collection

J23. Bob & Tony's Pizza, Estes Park, CO - Floyd M. Orr Collection

J24. 1971 Blue Honda CL-350 K2 from the Water Tower - Floyd M. Orr Collection

J25. *Easy Rider* Replica Side View- Joachim Kohler, photographer - (GNU)

Chapter 10 - Moderns

K1. Aprilia RS-50 Front View - Tybersk8er, Flagstaff, AZ, photographer - (PD)

K2. Dark Blue & Red Aprilia RS-125 Right Side - JDM, photographer - (PD)

K3. Beige Aprilia Scarabeo 50 in Italy - James & Winnie Maeng, photographer - (CC)

K4. 1998 Honda Dream 50 Left Side - Terje Saethre, owner and photographer

K5. 2004 Honda Dream 50 Right Side - American Honda Motor Company, Inc.

K6. 2006 White Honda Rebel 250 Right Side - American Honda Motor Company, Inc.

K7. 1990 Blue & White Honda VTR 250 - Mike Schinkel, photographer - (CC)

K8. Honda VTR 250 Trellis Right Side - Troyce Walls, photographer

K9. 2012 Honda CBR250R ABS Right Side - American Honda Motor Company, Inc.

K10. 2009 Kawasaki Eliminator 125 - Kawasaki Motors Corporation, U.S.A.

K11. Silver Kawasaki EX250F7F Ninja - Kawasaki Motors Corporation, U.S.A.

K12. 2010 Blue Kawasaki Ninja 250 - Kawasaki Motors Corporation, U.S.A.
K13. 2010 Black Suzuki GZ250 Right Side - Suzuki Motor of America, Inc.
K14. 2013 Suzuki TU250X Right Side - Suzuki Motor of America, Inc.
K15. 2013 Black Suzuki GW250 Right Side - Suzuki Motor of America, Inc.
K16. Red & White Yamaha YSR50 Brochure Cover - Yamaha Motor Corp., U.S.A.
K17. Yamaha YSR 50 Brochure Details Page - Yamaha Motor Corporation, U.S.A.
K18. 1989 Blue Yamaha YSR50 Front View - Michael's Motorcycles - (MK)
K19. Red Yamaha RZ350 Brochure - Yamaha Motor Corporation, U.S.A.
K20. 1985 Yamaha RZ350 Kenny Roberts - Mark Romanoff, photographer - (GNU)
K21. 1985 Yamaha RZ350 Kenny Roberts Brochure - Yamaha Motor Corp., U.S.A.
K22. 1988 Beige Yamaha Route 66 Brochure - Yamaha Motor Corporation, U.S.A.
K23. 2009 Purple Yamaha Star 250 - Yamaha Motor Corporation, U.S.A.
K24. 1964 CB-77 from *Roustabout* - Midnight Bird, photographer - (CC)
K25. *Easy Rider* Replica Front View - Joachim Kohler, photographer - (GNU)
K26. 1963 Red Honda CB-92R - Michael's Motorcycles - (MK)

Source Codes

American Honda Motor Company, Inc., P. O. Box 2200, Torrance, CA 90509-2200 - powersports.honda.com

Bridgestone Corporation, Bridgestone Americas, Inc., 535 Marriott Drive, P. O. Box 140990, Nashville, TN 37214, (615) 937-1000 - bridgestone.com

CC - Creative Commons License

GNU - GNU's Not Unix License

Kawasaki Motors Corporation, U.S.A., P. O. Box 25252, Santa Ana, CA 92799-5252, (800) 661-7433 - kawasaki.com

MK - Michael Kiernan of Classic Motorcycle Company aka Michael's Motorcycles, 3537 Chouteau Avenue, St. Louis, MO 63103, (314) 772-5758 - michaelsmotorcycles.com

Model years in parentheses are unconfirmed approximations.

PD - Public Domain Photo

Suzuki Motor of America, Inc., P. O. Box 1100, Brea, CA 94822 - suzukicycles.com

Yamaha Motor Corporation, U.S.A., 6555 Katella Avenue, Cypress, CA 90630, (800) 962-7926 - yamaha-motor.com

Motorcycle Photo Index

Motorcycle Chart Index

About the Author

The Tiddler Invasion is Floyd M. Orr's seventh book in his self-titled Nonfiction in a Fictional Style Series (NIAFS). Each book in this series may seem at first glance to be completely unlike the others, but that is true only in the surface subject matter. All the author's books are somewhat autobiographical and generally wallow in the nostalgia of The Sixties. Each one just approaches Sixties nostalgia from a different standpoint, whether that origin is the subject of politics, economics, sports cars, boats, sociology, or small motorcycles.

Floyd M. Orr got in on the ground floor of The Sixties Tiddler Revolution. He had friends with many Honda, Yamaha, Cushman, Vespa, and other brands from 1960 onward. He learned to ride on a 1960 H-D Super 10, his first scooter was a 1957 Allstate Cruisaire and his first real motorcycle was a 1963 Yamaha YG-1. He lived in Mississippi until the mid-'70's, so all his experiences and dealer availabilities came from that region. This meant that his exposure to Suzukis was limited in the early days, but he had considerably more direct contact with the other Big Three.

The author has lived most of his adult life in Texas, in the Austin metro area since 1980. He is now retired with his wife and ten cats.

Figure K26 - A Final Farewell Close-up Look at This Elegant Red Honda CB-92R, the Holy Grail of Collectible Tiddlers. ©Michael Kiernan, Classic Motorcycle Company, St. Louis, MO.